Masterpieces
of
War Reporting

By the same author

HITLERISM (1932)

FROM BISMARCK TO HITLER (1935)

RACE: A HISTORY OF MODERN ETHNIC THEORIES (1939)

A SURVEY OF EUROPEAN CIVILIZATION, 2 vols. (1941-1942)

A TREASURY OF GREAT REPORTING (with R. B. Morris) (1949)

A TREASURY OF BIOGRAPHIES (1950)

GERMAN NATIONALISM: THE TRAGEDY OF A PEOPLE (1952)

Hier Hielt Die Welt Den Atem An (1953)

THE MEANING OF NATIONALISM (1954)

THE AGE OF REASON (1955)

THE WORLD IN THE TWENTIETH CENTURY (1955)

BASIC HISTORY OF MODERN GERMANY (1957)

DOCUMENTS OF GERMAN HISTORY (1958)

HISTORIC DOCUMENTS OF WORLD WAR I (1959)

THE WAR: A CONCISE HISTORY 1939-1945 (1960)

THE IMPERIALISM READER: Documents and Readings on
    Modern Expansionism (1962)

Masterpieces
of
War Reporting

The Great Moments of World War II

Edited by

LOUIS L. SNYDER

Julian Messner, Inc.   New York

Published by Julian Messner, Inc.
8 West 40th Street, New York 18

Published simultaneously in Canada
by The Copp Clark Publishing Co. Limited

Library of Congress Catalog Card No. 62-16675

Printed in the United States of America

FOR IDA MAE

*Co-editor and Co-worker
and
expert stylist*

TABLE OF CONTENTS

Introduction *xv*

The War Begins: German Assault on Poland as Seen by British and German Reporters *1*

***Athenia* Torpedoed:** Sinking of a British Liner with 1,450 Persons Aboard in the First Atrocity of the War *5*

Britain Goes to War: Oswald Garrison Villard on the Opening Days in London *14*

War Lord to the Front: The *Hamburger Anzeiger* Tells How the *Fuehrer* Goes to His Troops *18*

***Blitzkrieg* in Poland:** Otto Tolischus Recounts the Swift and Overwhelming Conquest in a Lightning Dash by Hitler's Legions *19*

Warsaw Surrenders: A German Report on the Capitulation of the Polish Capital City *23*

Scapa Flow: How Lieutenant Günther Prien in the U-47 Penetrated the Naval Base and Sank the Battleship *Royal Oak* *26*

The *Admiral Graf Spee:* On-the-Spot Account of the Scuttling of Nazi Germany's Phantom Pocket Battleship in Montevideo Harbor *30*

Nazi Juggernaut Crushes Norway: Leland Stowe Tells the Story of Treason Behind Hitler's Paralyzing Conquest *35*

Storming of Eben-Emael: Combat Reporter Dr. Mansfield Tells How Germans Captured Giant Belgian Fortress in a Little Over 24 Hours *45*

Bombing of Rotterdam: *Times*man C. Brooks Peters Relates Destruction by the *Luftwaffe* After the City Had Capitulated *49*

Conquest of Belgium: M. W. Fodor Retreats Along With a 200-Mile Belgian Refugee Line in "The Greatest Mass Exodus in History" *53*

Dunkirk: Douglas Williams of the *Daily Telegraph* Witnesses the Survival of an Allied Army in a Miracle of Deliverance *57*

Fall of Paris: Capitulation of the French Capital as Witnessed by French, German and American Reporters *62*

Exodus From Paris: Quentin Reynolds Shares the Retreat of Refugees as Nazi Armor Crushes France *71*

Sieg Teutonia: William L. Shirer Broadcasts the Story of How Hitler Humiliated France at Compiègne   *75*

Battle of Britain: Four American Correspondents Describe the Ordeal of London Under Attack by the *Luftwaffe*   *81*

The *Jervis Bay:* Tania Long Tells How a British Liner Sails Gloriously into Hopeless Battle Against a German Pocket Battleship and Thereby Saves Convoy HX 84   *91*

Coventry: Massive *Luftwaffe* Attack on the Midlands Manufacturing City as Seen From German and Allied Sides   *94*

Dateline London: Rebecca West Describes a Day in Town During Hitler's Attempt to Smash Britain From the Air   *98*

Rats of Tobruk: Jan H. Yindrich, United Press, Tells How the Australians Used Bayonets Against Unwilling Nazis   *104*

Nazi Icarus: Rudolf Hess Parachutes to Field in Scotland After 800-Mile Flight to Warn British   *106*

Conquest of Crete: A German Report on the First Airborne Invasion in History   *109*

***Wehrmacht* Attacks Russia:** Combat Reporter Karl Heinz Seiss on the Opening Hours   *113*

Bombing of Moscow: Erskine Caldwell Sees the *Luftwaffe's* Attempt to Smash the Russian Capital   *115*

Sinking of the *Barham:* Veteran A. P. Newsman Larry Allen Witnesses the Swift Death of a Great British Warship   *119*

Pearl Harbor: Tragedy at Honolulu as Japan Makes Surprise Attack on American Outpost in the Pacific   *123*

Sinking of the *Prince of Wales* and *Repulse:* Cecil Brown Cables Eyewitness Story of the Destruction of Two Great British Warships   *127*

Death at the Volga: A German Report on a Battalion's Suicide Stand Against the Onslaught of Four Siberian Divisions   *133*

Corregidor: Philippine Journalist Carlos P. Romulo Retreats with MacArthur's Forces   *137*

Battle of Moscow: Star Red Reporters Ilya Ehrenburg and Konstantin Simonov Record the Story of the Beginning of Retribution for Hitler   *143*

Singapore: Japanese and American Reports on the Fall of Mighty British Bastion in Southeast Asia   *149*

MacArthur's Dash! H. R. Knickerbocker Narrates the Drama of General's Escape from the Philippines by Sea and Air and Its Aftermath   *156*

Bataan: Japanese Treatment Of U.S. Prisoners Revealed in Eyewitness Report of Death March   *160*

Burma: Jack Belden Accompanies General "Vinegar Joe" Stilwell on One of the Most Bitter Retreats of Modern Times — *164*

Battle of the Coral Sea: Stanley Johnston Describes the Sinking of U. S. Aircraft Carrier *Lexington* — *169*

Bombing of Cologne: Robert E. Bunnelle Gets the Story of the First Great Air Armada Over Germany's Big Industrial Center — *174*

Midway: Ensign G. H. Gay, Wounded and Afloat in the Sea, Watches the Battle as Japanese Ships Pass by in Flames — *179*

Fall of Sevastopol: Soviet War Correspondents Recall the Defense of the Mighty Crimean Naval Base — *183*

Guadalcanal: American Newsmen Describe the First of a Long Series of Offensives That Finally Paralyzed Japanese Power in the Pacific — *190*

Dieppe Raid: A. B. Austin of the London *Daily Herald* Accompanies British Commandos on One of the Costliest and Most Tragic Exploits of the War — *198*

British Cruiser *Curacao* Lost: Crash With the Giant Liner *Queen Mary* Is Revealed by United Press Eyewitness — *203*

General Clark's Pre-Invasion Mission to North Africa: Godfrey B. Courtney Tells How a Daring American General Loses Pants But Saves Face — *205*

El Alamein: The Defeat of Marshal Rommel in One of the Decisive Battles of the War as Recorded by American and German Correspondents — *211*

Operation Torch: Leo Disher, United Press, Receives Twenty-six Assorted Wounds While Covering the Battle of Oran — *219*

Leningrad, 1943: Soviet Journalist Nikolai Tikhonov Reports the Breaking of the Blockade of Russia's Second City — *223*

Epic of Stalingrad From Both Sides: Soviet Correspondent Roman Karmen Witnesses the Death Throes of Paulus's Sixth Army, and Heinz Schröter, War Correspondents' Staff of the Sixth Army, Sees Horror in the Cellars — *226*

Hell 26,000 Feet Up: Walter Cronkite, United Press, Representing "The Writing Sixty-ninth," Accompanies American Raid on Wilhelmshaven — *239*

Ghosts of War: Ernie Pyle Reports From the Battlefields of North Africa — *241*

Conquest of Tunisia: British and American War Correspondents Report a Brilliant Allied Victory in North Africa — *245*

One-Man War Survey: Irwin Shaw Discovers That the Favorite Subject of G.I. Conversation Is Women, Women, Women — *259*

x • Contents

Death of a Pilot: Hugh Baillie, United Press, Reveals the Story of Pete Peterson, the Man Who Didn't Come Back   *261*

Invasion of Sicily: John Mason Brown Narrates the Landings in the Next Step in Liberation of Europe   *264*

Rescue Off Kolombangara: John F. Kennedy, Harvard '40, Is Hero in the Pacific as Destroyer Splits His PT Boat   *270*

The Patton Slapping Affair: American and British Versions of an Incident in the Sicilian Campaign   *274*

Chungking: Brooks Atkinson Finds That After Six Years of War Free China Is Still Undefeated   *281*

Saved by Jungle Headhunters: Eric Sevareid, CBS Correspondent, Parachutes into Mountains of Burma From Crippled Transport Plane   *284*

Naples: Herbert L. Matthews Observes How the Germans Left the University in Smoldering Ruins   *287*

Role Reversal: James Reston, of *The New York Times*, Reports How British and Germans Change Positions in the War   *289*

Patriot at War: Arthur Krock Reports on the Role of Bernard Baruch, the Nation's Elder Statesman, on the Home Front   *292*

Women at War: Margaret Bourke-White, *Life* Photographer, Survives Sinking of Transport Off West Coast of Africa   *295*

Tribute to Shorty: Pvt. William Saroyan on the Sweetheart of Company D—a Pooch of Undetermined Origin   *302*

Square-Cut Diamond: Allen Churchill, a Navy Reporter, Tells the Story of a Raucous Marine   *306*

Tarawa: Richard W. Johnston on the Toughest 60 Hours in Marine Corps History   *310*

Poker for Keeps: John Steinbeck Tells How a Yank Paratrooper Talks Eighty-seven Germans into Surrender   *314*

Bombing of Monte Cassino: German and Italian Reports on the Destruction of Benedictine Monastery   *319*

Anzio: Homer Bigart Reports How U.S. Observer, Circled by Nazis, Orders Barrage on His Own Post   *325*

A Dog's Life: Love at First Sight Wins a Battle on the Italian Front for a Shrewd Canadian   *328*

Cassino: Christopher Buckley, London *Daily Telegraph*, Watches an Operation in Destruction   *329*

"Lili Marlene": Edgar Clark on the Bitter-Sweet Song That Became Top Favorite of Both Axis and Allied Troops   *332*

Sevastopol: Harrison Salisbury Relates How Death, Not Ships, Arrived
for 25,000 Germans Trapped on Russian Shelf — 335

D-Day: Five Combat Reporters Describe the Greatest Invasion in History as Hitler's Fortress Europa Is Smashed From Air, Sea and
Ground — 337

Courage Under Fire: Richard D. Macmillan Reports No Purple Heart
for Tilly — 352

Liberation of Russia: Vassili Grossman with the Red Army in Poland
and Byelorussia — 355

Second Battle of Britain: Ernest Hemingway Tells How London
Fought Hitler's Vengeance Weapon #1 — 360

"To Be Forgiving": Virgil Pinkley, Reporting German Robot Attack
on London, Contrasts a Dead Child and a Sermon — 368

Sensation at Notre Dame: Robert Reid, BBC Correspondent, Makes
a Remarkable Running Commentary — 370

Return of the Native-by-Adoption: Gertrude Stein Describes Her
Return Describes Her Return to the City to the City of Light — 373

Florence: Bernard Berenson Narrates Sadistic Destruction by Retreating Germans — 378

International Crash Force: Martha Gellhorn Watches the Eighth
Army Smash into Powerful Gothic Line Before Onset of Winter — 382

V-2 Rocket Attack: Henry B. Jameson on Bombardment of England by
Hitler's New Vengeance-Weapon — 386

Hurtgen Forest: Henry T. Gorrell, United Press, Tells How a War
Correspondent Covers the Start of a Major Offensive in Germany — 389

Cossack Exploits: Maurice Hindus Interviews Soviet Leader General
Nikolai Kirichenko — 392

Battle of the Bulge: John Wilhelm and James Cannon Tell How Yanks
Fought Their Way Out of German Trap — 396

Battle for Budapest: S.S. Combat Reporter Kalweit Recounts the
German Defense of the Hungarian Capital — 400

Iwo Jima: William F. Tyree, United Press, sees U.S. Marines Storm
Ashore on a Tiny Island 600 Miles From Tokyo — 402

Remagen Bridge: Americans Seize a Vital Link Across the Rhine
with Ten Minutes to Spare — 405

Jump into Germany: Richard C. Hottelet Obtains One of the Last
Big Stories of the European War — 409

Road to Berlin: Hal Boyle Rides Along at Full Speed with Rampaging
American Military Machine — 414

xii • Contents

In Desert Germany: British Journalist V. S. Pritchett Surveys the Scene Gone Beyond Argument 416

Death of F.D.R.: Walter Lippmann and Tom Reedy Record a Nation's Tribute and Farewell to its Commander-in-Chief 422

Hitler's Inferno: Eyewitnesses Edward R. Murrow, Gene Currivan and Robert Reid Describe Nazi Death Factory at Buchenwald 426

Fall of Leipzig: Edward R. Murrow Broadcasts an Eyewitness Story of the Taking of a City 437

Torgau: U.S. Newsmen Witness the Meeting of American and Russian Troops at the Elbe River 442

Mussolini Killed! American and Italian Reports of the Ignominious End of Italy's Sawdust Caesar 446

End in Italy: Hubert D. Harrison Reports the Italian Surrender for the Combined British Press 452

Götterdämmerung: Pierre J. Huss of International News Service, on the Last Days of Adolf Hitler 455

Preliminary Surrender: Chester Wilmot, Speaking for BBC, Records the Ceremony of Surrender to Montgomery at Lüneburg Heath 460

Berlin Falls: American Newsmen Describe the Devastated Capital of the Third Reich 465

End of the War in Europe: Edward Kennedy of the Associated Press Beats the World Press on German Surrender and Is Promptly Accused of Unethical Journalistic Double Cross 471

Final German Capitulation at Reims: Charles Collingwood of CBS Broadcasts "Perhaps the Best News the World Has Ever Had" 474

V-E Day: In the Midst of Global Celebration Gordon Cobbledick of the Cleveland *Plain Dealer* Points to Japanese Steel on Okinawa 480

Aftermath: CBS Correspondents Describe the Last Few Days Following Germany's Surrender 483

Kamikazes: Phelps Adams's Eyewitness Account of Attack on Admiral Mitscher's Flagship by Japanese Suicide Pilots off Okinawa 487

Hara-Kiri: Alva N. Dopking Tells How Two Okinawa Generals Died Under the Nipponese *Samurai* Code 495

Hiroshima: American and Japanese Accounts of the First Atomic Bomb Dropped on Japan 498

Nagasaki: William L. Laurence of *The New York Times* Sees the Dropping of Second Atomic Bomb 506

Victory: *Yank* Reporters Record the Pattern of Celebration as World War II Comes to an End 514

Contents • xiii

Tokyo Bay: Robert B. Cochrane, Baltimore Sunpapers War Correspondent, Covers the Surrender Ceremony Aboard the Battleship *Missouri*
520

Execution of Laval: Leon Pearson Reports the Death of a Hated Vichyite
527

Nuremberg: Kingsbury Smith, International News Service, Sees Ten Nazi Leaders Pay on the End of a Rope for Their Crimes
529

Index
539

Introduction

World War II was the best reported war in history. No conflict was ever as thoroughly, as graphically, as brilliantly reported. From a corps of determined and dedicated men, millions of words poured into the presses and over the air. Hugh Baillie, president of the United Press, paid tribute to them (*Editor and Publisher,* August 28, 1943):

> My hat is off to all war correspondents. The steady flow of news from all battlefronts is the result of untiring efforts of a small army of correspondents who endure the same hardships and face many of the same perils as the actual combat troops whose activities they are reporting. And when I say untiring I mean it literally. You must be tough to last as a war correspondent. Often exposed to enemy strafing or shell fire, subsisting on army grub, bathing and shaving out of a pint canteen cup or tin hat, wriggling up precipitous landslides to observe the enemy from behind boulders, bivouacking on the ground under the stars, your sleep (when you try for some) interrupted by explosions and flares, breathing hot dust—all these combine to create a type of life which army slang terms "rugged."

Thirty-four American correspondents were killed in line of duty. Byron Darnton of *The New York Times* gave his life on a landing in New Guinea, October 18, 1942. On April 18, 1945, Ernie Pyle, modest, soft-voiced, a man small in stature but a giant in courage, a reporter who had covered the war from North Africa to the doorstep of Japan, was struck by a Japanese machine-gun bullet through the left temple. He died just as battle-hardened Americans conquered the ten-mile-square island of Ie.

World War II reporters were a serious, hard working lot. Vanished into newspaper morgues was the old-time flamboyant, swashbuckling correspondent, with his trench coat and epaulets, brim-down hat and blackthorn cane. Virtually all the new breed hated the bloody business of war, its loneliness, mud, filth, graves, eternal specter of death. But they had a job to do, and they performed it well.

During the great conflict people everywhere were hungry for honest, dispassionate, objective news reports from the front lines. To meet that specific need these masterpieces of reporting were written by topflight journalists on the spot. Their stories were composed in foxholes and dugouts, inside or on the decks of ships in combat, in the cramped quarters of fighting planes, on battlefields and hedgerows, in the open countryside and in battered cities. They reveal the trivial and the bizarre as well as the significant. Distilled from millions of words, they capture the drama and pathos of twentieth-century war.

Who will ever forget the reporting masterpieces that came out of World War II? There was William L. Shirer with his magnificent ad lib portrait of a triumphant Hitler at Compiègne in 1940. There was Cecil Brown going down with the *Repulse* on December 11, 1941 ("All hands on deck, prepare to abandon ship. May God be with you!"). There was George Hicks speaking from the American flagship *Ancon* on D-Day, June 6, 1944 ("The whole side of the battlewagon lights up in a yellow flare."). Or Edward R. Murrow, sickened by what he saw in the liberated concentration camp of Buchenwald, April 15, 1945 ("I pray you to believe what I have said about Buchenwald. . . . For most of it I have no words."). These and many others find an honored place in any collection of great war reporting.

Plan of this Book

It is the purpose of this book to present the outstanding reporting of World War II. The accent is on combat reporting. There are many from American sources, although pieces from British, French, Russian, German, Italian and Japanese newspapers are included specifically to demonstrate how both sides viewed special stories.

Gathering this material proved to be a formidable task. Much of the vast wordage about the war was merely rewriting of official dispatches. Some of it was elaborate guesswork based on rumor or misinformation. Only a small portion of news stories could be selected. It was a voyage of literary discovery with no guarantee that months of work with musty files and yellowed clippings would result in usable pieces. Three weeks in newspaper morgues in Madrid yielded no selections at all; four weeks in Rome and Florence on a similar search brought just one story. On the other hand, the newspaper division of the New York Public Library and the Imperial War Museum in London proved to be treasure troves of journalistic game.

The work represented here is by professional reporters who were there. When terrorized refugees retreated from Paris in June 1940, Quentin Reynolds was trapped with them. When Wilhelmshaven was bombed on February 26, 1943, Walter Cronkite, representing the United Press, went along in one of the attacking planes to get the story firsthand. Included also are stories by such well-known authors as André Maurois, Ernest Hemingway, Irwin Shaw, William Saroyan and Gertrude Stein. Drama critics Brooks Atkinson and John Mason Brown wheedled combat assignments at front stage center and turned out the superb stories included in this book.

The selections are arranged chronologically. An attempt has been made to present the over-all story in a reasonably continuous narrative, although not every important or decisive event is included. Conversely, some of the less significant aspects are given because a gifted reporter was there to describe it. To maintain the pattern of continuity, each report is introduced with a note giving the background of the event and placing it in its historical setting.

The choices are highly personal. No claim is made for omniscience or infallibility of judgment. The standards are those employed in editing, with Richard B. Morris, *A Treasury of Great Reporting* (Simon & Schuster, 1949, revised paperback edition, 1962).

The Raw Material of History

In a very real sense the reportage collected in this book constitutes the raw material of history. This is the work of eyewitnesses, the trained reporters who wrote it down as soon as they saw it. Admittedly, errors crept into their dispatches. But by and large most of these reports are accurate, as exact as possible considering the circumstances under which the news was gathered. They furnish important source material for the historian.

Some professional historians are reluctant to recognize the news report as equivalent in authority to governmental communiqués or reports by combat commanders. To such historians the report seems to gather accuracy if it is entwined in red tape or stamped with a seal of secrecy as part of the "archives." There is weakness in this point of view. Official governmental communiqués were regarded by all the belligerent governments as weapons of war and as such they served a purpose. Much too often they juggled the facts. And combat commanders were human enough to regard their own reports as the last word in accuracy.

Most war correspondents sought for the plain truth of what happened. They were trained to note the significant and avoid the inconsequential. They tell a fascinating and at the same time a dreadful story—of heroism, cowardice, comradeship, starvation, of tears, blood and sweat. They deserve a salute.

And Cordial Thanks

My special thanks go to Miss R. E. B. Coombs of the Imperial War Museum in London for her friendly and painstaking cooperation. I am grateful to C. Edmonds Allen, director of special services of United Press International for his assistance. My warmest thanks go to Signorina Alba Rosa Bettazzi of Florence, Italy. Lora Orrmont nurtured this project from beginning to end; without her the tasks would have multiplied indefinitely. Once again I express my gratefulness to Ida Mae Snyder, without whom this book would have remained an unattainable dream.

Louis L. Snyder

New York City
August 1962

Masterpieces
of
War Reporting

The War Begins: German Assault on Poland as Seen by British and German Reporters

[September 1, 1939]

At dawn on September 1, 1939, Adolf Hitler, without a declaration of war, sent his legions hurtling across the borders of Poland. The time was past for the bungling of diplomats, the threats and counter-charges, the loud polemics, the appeals to reason and justice. The Nazi Fuehrer now had the war he had willed and wanted. This infinitely squalid mind finally had its way.

The first British dispatch of World War II is reprinted below.

A sense of foreboding comes through the second story by an anonymous German combat reporter who describes the last hours and minutes before the attack. In 1914 the Germans had gone to war in an excess of exuberance, with parades and songs and kisses and flowing beer. But this time it was a bit different. The war spirit was absent. There was something wrong. With the exception of die-hard Nazi fanatics and the wilfully blind, both the German public and army sensed a time of trouble.

INVASION OF POLAND
GERMAN ATTACK ACROSS ALL FRONTIERS
WARSAW AND OTHER CITIES BOMBED
WAR WITHOUT A DECLARATION

(The Times, London, September 2. 1939. Reprinted, by permission, from The Times.)

From Our Own Correspondent

WARSAW, Sept. 1—Hostilities began at 5:30 this morning on German–Polish frontiers with a heavy and apparently unannounced bombardment of Katowice from the air. The city was attacked with high explosive bombs. As far as is known there had been no declara-

1

tion of war. Krakow, Tczew (near the Danzig border) and Tunel (between Krakow and Czenstochkowa) were attacked with incendiary bombs.

At 6:15 the air raid sirens sounded for the first time in Warsaw, but no bombs fell until 9 A.M., when the capital was attacked from the air with incendiary and explosive bombs. Many Polish fighters went up to intercept raiders and there were thrilling aerial combats. The casualties resulting from this raid are unknown.

Subsequently during the day the capital was raided five or six times. On one occasion, between 4:30 and 5:30, the bombers attacked the centre of the city and flew down the Vistula bombing the bridges. Several of them crashed. For the most part the bombers were chased away by the Polish fighters and anti-aircraft fire, and the damage was almost entirely done outside the city in the suburbs. Seven people were killed at a place 40 miles form Warsaw. One flight of bombers in being chased unloaded their bombs on the country resort of Otwock, 15 miles from the capital. Of these 6 bombers, 4 escaped and 2 were brought down either by fighters or the anti-aircraft guns. In the afternoon excited crowds watched the flight of German bombers above Warsaw, swooping and twirling as light quick-firing guns peppered the sky with puffs of smoke.

The outbreak of war was received most calmly by the inhabitants of Warsaw. When the sirens sounded, the people ran into the streets and looked up at the sky until A.R.P. squads drove them indoors.

Reports from Katowice state that the German aeroplanes have been coming over in squadrons of 50 every half hour, and that there have been many casualties. The anti-aircraft guns went into action only after the second wave. Since mid-day telephonic communication has been cut off. At that time a correspondent in Katowice reported that the population was beginning to be shaken by the terrific bombing, but that there, as elsewhere, they were behaving with extraordinary stoicism. . . .

The German invasion was launched from Slovakia, East Prussia, and the main body of the Reich. Attack was made against Zrkopane from Slovakia. . . .

The news of the German invasion amazed the officials of the Polish Foreign Office, who had been up all night studying the latest dispatches. Until late yesterday, when Herr Hitler's "minimum demands" were published by the official German news agency, it was thought that the exchange between London and Berlin was going on satisfactorily. . . .

The German excuse for invasion—namely, "the invasion by Polish diversionist bands near Gleiwitz"—is described as a tissue of lies.

THE MARCH INTO POLAND

(Kampferlebnisse aus dem Feldzüge in Polen, 1939, herausgegeben von Generalstab des Heeres [Berlin, 1940], pp. 1–2. Courtesy of E. S. Mittler & Sohn. Translated by the editor.)

"No hurrah–patriotism! No superficial sentimentalism!"

Evening of August 31! Darkness! Light rain!

The tents are broken down. All around everything is quiet. But through the ether flashes message after message.

There—light clacking of gear—the brief glow of a flashlight—the dull gleam of helmets. The tramping off of the decamping 2nd Company is swallowed by the mugginess of this night.

Now it has gone so far! Quietly the gray column shoves forward. The men are calm and serious. Here and there one hears a joke spoken half aloud. Vehicles whirr by and disappear within seconds. We are marching. . . .

The men don't feel the weight of their full munitions cases. No grenade thrower gripes about his full pack. Again and again their hands feel for their hand grenades.

What are these men thinking about as they march?—home, parents' house, friends, a beloved girl—all in the past. . . . Before them lies the night, lies uncertainty, battle! Before them lies the war! And perhaps death.

A caterpillar–tractor clanks by us. The heavy weapons show us that we are not alone. No hurrah–patriotism! No superficial sentimentalism! All of us see the hard necessity of this night. In Garnsee people still remain on the streets. The tramp of boots bounces off the houses, and at the end of the town we come to our assigned ready spot. The company commander comes back from the battalion commander. Everything is ready. Fences are cut down so that they won't hold up the assault in the early morning.

Now we lie down in the wet grass of the fields. After the rain there is a heavy fog which gets deeper and deeper. The hours fly by. In the east gray daylight. We carefully exercise our legs stiffened by the cold, and we lie and wait. . . .

Minutes pass by! The hands on our watches get close to 4:30. We know that at that time the batteries will break out in thunder, the heavy shells will carve out a road for us, the attack will be made easier.

Three minutes more . . . two minutes . . . only one minute . . . seconds. . . .

Four-thirty!

There is no sound. Feverish waiting! Quiet. . . . All contours disappear in the fog. But time marches inexorably on. The large minute hand approaches to nine. There! Suddenly a boom. Another one. . . . Still another. . . . Again and again. Seconds later the shells come whirring over our heads. In uninterrupted rows. Now into the land of the enemy. . . .

We, however, looked with staring eyes and tensed nerves into the fog. Over there, somewhere in the fog is that invisible wall, the border!

The war has begun!

Athenia Torpedoed: Sinking of a British Liner with 1,450 Persons Aboard in the First Atrocity of the War

[September 3, 1939]

Three days before the outbreak of war, Hitler, wearing his grey uniform, addressed the Reichstag: *"I do not want to fight women and children. . . . He who departs from the rules of humane warfare can expect the same from us."*

Within a few days, on September 3, 1939, a German submarine torpedoed the British passenger liner Athenia *250 miles west of the northern Irish coast. Aboard the ship were 1,450 persons, including 314 Americans. If the German warriors were anxious to increase their unpopularity in the United States, they could scarcely have chosen a better method than this sinking.*

At once the British Admiralty issued a statement charging that the sinking was in deliberate violation of the 1930 treaty by which Germany had renounced the right ever to use unrestricted submarine warfare. The German Ministry of Information at first announced that the Athenia *must have struck a floating mine. When London countered that no British mines had been laid in the area of the sinking, Dr. Joseph Goebbels, the little mouse-doctor propaganda minister, charged that Winston Churchill himself had arranged the sinking to draw the United States into the war as quickly as possible.*

It was the Lusitania *case of World War I all over again. Clearly, World War II was not going to be a chivalrous, gentlemanly business.*

The first four reports below give the story of the sinking of the Athenia *as seen by American and British reporters from London, Greenock, Glasgow and Halifax. The fifth story, from the* Hamburger Anzeiger, *is reproduced exactly as it appeared in the* news columns of that newspaper. Note *the editorial slant. German journalists found it most difficult to distinguish between straight reporting and editorializing.*

5

ATHENIA SUNK WITHOUT WARNING

(United Press, September 4, 1939. By permission of United Press International.)

"Germany had struck its first blow."

LONDON, Sept. 4—The British government today announced the rescue of approximately 1,400 persons aboard the torpedoed liner *Athenia*, including 314 Americans, except those killed by the explosion, and denounced the attack as a violation of Hitler's pledged word.

Although a radio broadcast in Berlin denied that a German submarine had torpedoed the British liner 250 miles off the Irish coast, Winston Churchill, First Lord of the Admiralty, told the House of Commons that the ship "was certainly torpedoed without the slightest warning."

The *Athenia* sinking was denounced as "an act of piracy," and both houses of Parliament echoed the "disgust and indignation" of the British people.

The *Athenia* was torpedoed during the first 24 hours of the Second World War, was left to sink while rescue ships started for Scottish and Irish ports with the survivors.

Capt. James Cook, master of the 13,581-ton British liner bound for Montreal, wirelessed that his ship had been torpedoed by a German submarine 250 miles west of Inishtrahull Island, off the northern Irish coast.

Nearly all the passengers were believed to be Americans and Canadians, fleeing home from the war zone.

Most of them were tourists. As many as 100, according to line officials, were American college girls returning from a two-month tour of the Continent.

They had gone to Glasgow, Liverpool or Belfast, most of them, to take other ships and had been accommodated aboard the *Athenia* when their own ships proved loaded to capacity or were held in British ports.

The liner had left Glasgow at noon Friday, Liverpool at 4 P.M. Saturday and Belfast during Saturday night for Montreal, its passengers happy in the thought that they were racing for home, safe from the war.

Newly reconditioned, its passenger quarters rebuilt, the *Athenia* carried lifeboats for 1,830 passengers in addition to the crew.

The sinking brought home to Britons for the first time the fact that they really were at war and that Germany had struck its first blow.

EYEWITNESS STORIES FROM GREENOCK, SCOTLAND

(Associated Press, September 5, 1939. By permission of Associated Press.)

"I don't like the German war tactics."

GREENOCK, SCOTLAND, Sept. 5—Victims of the war's first sea tragedy, 600 shaken and weeping survivors of the British liner *Athenia* arrived on rescue ships today.

Two hundred of those arriving were injured.

One survivor, John McEwan, of Glasgow, said a submarine torpedoed the *Athenia* and then twice shelled the vessel as her lifeboats were being lowered.

A member of one of the rescue crews said the first SOS from the *Athenia* was received at 10 P.M. (G.M.T.) Sunday.

"I saw the *Athenia* take her final plunge, stern first, the next morning," he declared. "I saw a group of five boats and in the water a number of young children who had been drowned. The boats were full, some of them badly flooded and some had people clinging to their sides."

Glasgow mobilized hospitals and nursing homes to accommodate the injured, while other agencies planned to care for other refugees, many of them thinly clad and weak from exposure to the winds of the North Atlantic.

Perhaps the saddest sight of all was 9-year-old Roy Barrington, of Toronto. His mother went down with the *Athenia*.

Pathetic scenes were enacted as the first of the rescued arrived at Glasgow's Adelphia Hotel.

Women and children limped weakly from motor busses, wearing navy boiler suits and pajamas, some with curtains around their heads and most of them without shoes.

Almost all of them were bandaged.

Children who had lost their parents were carried weeping into the hotel. Some had lost their voices. There were wives without husbands, husbands without wives. All were desperate for news of survivors from other rescue areas.

Mr. and Mrs. W. H. Cox, of Neepawa, Manitoba, said they just had got into a lifeboat when the rope broke, throwing them into the water.

Mrs. Cox said: "We were soon taken back into the boat, but we had to bail with our shoes. While we rowed during the night we were almost submerged by the swell from the submarine as it passed under us."

A Mrs. Brown, from New Orleans, and her 11-month-old baby were rescued. She said the torpedo struck close to her cabin, carrying away the companionway to the deck above.

"I handed the baby to someone on the deck above me and scrambled up myself later. When I found the baby in the same lifeboat with me I was crazy with joy."

"We had a terrible time," said McEwan, "and we knew at once what it was.

"There was a great deal of smoke when the torpedo struck our vessel. But through the smoke I could see the submarine break the surface and, before we knew where we were, it had opened up with its gun and fired two shots at us.

"Every lifeboat was away an hour after we were struck. The liner first of all listed and then righted herself and began to go slowly down by the head.

"We learned afterward that a woman on whom an operation had just been performed had been left on the *Athenia*. One of the lifeboats went back and took her off."

A Mrs. Turner, of Toronto, World War widow, said: "I am the luckiest woman on earth. I was looking over the rail when the torpedo smashed us. The ship lurched violently and I was thrown to the deck.

"When I came to I saw several people lying dead on the deck. And then I heard the two shells.

"Later I found myself in a lifeboat—the water was up to my waist."

Prof. Damon Boynton, of Cornell University, alighting from one of the destroyers, said:

"I was in a boat twelve hours before I was picked up. I don't want to say anything more except this—I don't like the German war tactics."

AT GLASGOW

(*The London* Daily Telegraph, *September 6, 1939. Courtesy of* The Daily Telegraph.)

From Our Special Correspondent

"The swine has hit us."

GLASGOW, Tuesday—I learn from Galway that Capt. James Cook of the *Athenia*, when he landed there today, stated definitely that the liner was shelled by a submarine after she had been torpedoed.

The captain says that the torpedo went right through the ship to the engine room. After this the submarine broke surface and fired a shell which was aimed at the wireless equipment.

As far as can be ascertained tonight, the number of those who perished was about 380, out of 1,102 passengers and 320 crew. One member of the crew estimates that 25% of the American travelers were killed by the explosion of the torpedo and the liner's boilers. . . .

The majority of the fatal casualties were due to the explosion, when the torpedo struck the *Athenia* just aft of the bridge and below the waterline. Some, however, were drowned when boats capsized by being driven into the screw of the Norwegian [rescue] vessel by a heavy swell. Others were drowned when a lifeboat, overfull, capsized.

All accounts of the torpedoing confirm that the "U"-boat commander shelled the *Athenia* after he had torpedoed her. John McEwan, a deck storeman, said to me:

"We heard a terrific bang. We knew at once what it was, and put on our lifebelts and went to our boat stations. There was a great deal of smoke, but through the smoke we could see the submarine break surface, and then, before we knew where we were, the commander had turned a gun on us."

Claud Barrie, a bedroom steward, of King's Park, Glasgow, gave me a dramatic account of the torpedoing:

"It was exactly 7:30, and dinner time. I was in the pantry, helping the waiters, when there was a violent explosion. The lights went out, and the ship gave a lurch.

"I am an old soldier, and at once smelt cordite. 'It can't be,' I thought to myself. But my mate said, 'The swine has hit us.' The ship suddenly took a list.

"We ran to the alleyways to warn our passengers, and then up on deck, in time to see the periscope of the submarine disappear.

"I got my passengers away in our boat, the third to get away on the starboard side. We had no sailors. They were all killed. Six stewards, under the third class steward, acted as crew. We were jammed tight and for eight and one half hours were rowing about in a heavy swell and squall.

"It was about 1:30 A.M. when the Norwegian steamer came in sight. She took off the first survivors about 4 A.M. We were taken aboard the Swedish yacht. Altogether there must have been more than 400 in the yacht, but she only had stores for 100, and 309 of us were transferred to the two destroyers which came up later.

"It was 11:45 A.M., just 24 hours after war had been declared, that the *Athenia* gave a sudden lurch and went down stern first. Up to the last her radio was working, and I am wondering if any of the operators were drowned. . . .

"I saw some sad sights. One poor little girl of about 11, in a pretty pink frock, somehow in the crush fell overboard from a boat. A man dived in for her, but he could not get to her and the swell carried our boat away. . . .

"I shall never forget the look on the face of one young fellow as he clambered aboard from a lifeboat and saw a body being committed to the sea. The name of the woman was mentioned. It was his mother. . . .

"There was a brighter side. One wealthy woman, who was helping to bale out our boat, used her shoe, forgetting that she had hidden in it several hundred dollars when she took to the boat.

"As she bailed out, the notes were scattered to the wind, but she only laughed, and, despite their condition and anxiety, many others in the boat laughed, too.". . .

It is heart-rending to be in the lounge of one of Glasgow's hotels to-night. Wandering backwards and forwards is a young Pole who saw his wife and four children drown. He dived to their rescue, but struck an object, was knocked unconscious and dragged on board a boat.

He is nearly demented, and is begging everybody to speak to him, as he says it will save his reason.

In another corner is a boy whose home is in Washington and who believes that his father and mother have been taken in the Swedish yacht to America. No one dares to tell him that their bodies were seen before the destroyers left the scene. . . .

At least four boys in this hotel are orphans, although they do not know it, and everything is being done to keep the news from them and keep them amused. . . .

One old lady died in a lifeboat during the night, and while the other passengers were snatching sleep, her body was gently lowered overboard. More than one lifeboat was swamped when being lowered into the water and the sea came in up to the gunwales. The occupants were bailing with their boots and shoes half the night.

AT HALIFAX

(*James F. King, Associated Press, September 13, 1939. By permission of Associated Press.*)

"Hang on a little longer."

HALIFAX, N.S., Sept. 13—More than 200 ill-clad and shaken survivors of the liner *Athenia* were moved swiftly toward their homes tonight after telling of a nightmare at sea—of a "torpedo" streaking toward their ship, of a periscope slipping past a crowded lifeboat, of survivors screaming in fear of another "explosion."

Some still clutched their life preservers as they came ashore from the rusty American freighter *City of Flint* where for ten days they had lived in accommodations built only for a small crew.

The tales told here today revealed both courage and hysteria, hardship and lighthearted ingenuity as counterparts of the war's worst sea tragedy.

Tall, pretty Mary Lee Humlong, San Angelo (Texas) college student, who had sailed from Glasgow aboard the *City of Flint*, told reporters:

"When the sea became rough, especially the first night after the survivors came on board, some of those in the holds began screaming and became hysterical at every noise. Some shouted, 'We're being torpedoed.' "

Franklin Dexter, of Boston, kissed his bride of a month good-by and placed her in a lifeboat, remaining aboard the *Athenia* to see that there were enough boats for the women and children. He was picked up later.

Mrs. Dexter said: "Oh, it was terrible. I can't describe it."

"We almost hit the submarine," said Mary Katherine Underwood, of Athens, Texas. "We were in a boat with thirty-eight women and only three men. A while after we left the *Athenia*'s side we saw the periscope of the submarine and nearly hit it. I didn't see her come to the surface."

Miss Caroline Stuart, of Plainfield, N.J., said:

"I rowed for eight continuous hours. Look at these hands."

They still were covered with blisters.

Wearing a borrowed chef's hat, Mrs. McMillan Wallace, of Hamilton, Ont., told of seeing a periscope just before the *Athenia* was struck.

"The boy in the crow's nest was the first to sight it," she said. "He shouted down, and I could see a periscope sticking out of the water about an eighth of a mile away. I didn't see the torpedo but I saw a white streak of foam running out from the submarine. Then I heard the crash."

The lifeboat of Elizabeth Brown, of Houston, Texas, capsized just after she removed her life preserver. Tersely, she said, "I saw one man gasp for breath and die. It was horrible."

G. W. Dow, of Lone Pine, Cal., almost strangled by oil scum as he clung to the side of a lifeboat, gave credit for his life to an elderly lady "who kept reaching over the side and patting me on the head saying, 'Hang on a little longer.' "

Youngest of the survivors was 10-month-old Nicola Lubitsch, daughter of the Hollywood motion picture director, Ernst Lubitsch.

The child, with a smear of candy around her face, "cooed" at onlookers as she was taken off the rescue ship.

"CHURCHILL LIES"—*HAMBURGER ANZEIGER*

(Hamburger Anzeiger, *September 15, 1939. Translated by the editor.*)

"We repeat the questions. Answer them, Mr. Churchill!"

BERLIN, September 14—The British campaign of lies against Germany is distinguished by a remarkable poverty of ideas. The atrocity propaganda in connection with the sinking of the *Athenia* continues.

Mr. Churchill makes a serious error if he believes he can turn aside these questions which German public opinion has demanded that he answer.

We repeat the questions. Answer them, Mr. Churchill!

1. *Why was the* Athenia *torpedoed near the English and not the German coastline?*

2. *How do you explain that the* Athenia *was surrounded by a swarm of ships just when she was sunk?*

3. *If the* Athenia *were really struck amidships by a torpedo, how was it that all her passengers were rescued?*

4. *Why was it that the* Athenia *was the only passenger ship sunk and why were there so many American passengers on it at the time?*

We can ask more questions, Mr. Churchill. But these four are enough to make clear to whose advantage was this sinking! The peculiar circumstances leave no doubt as to the identity of the real culprit.

Do you really believe, Mr. Churchill, that Germans would seek out a passenger ship with Americans on board in order to further her already good relations with America?

No, Mr. Churchill! The only one who was interested in the sinking of this ship was you, yourself. You worked it all out with great care. You believed that a new *"Lusitania* case" would bring America into the war against Germany.

The *Athenia* was not torpedoed by a U-boat, but was sunk by sabotage. Even before the ship left England, there was talk of sabotage.

All indications are that the sinking of the *Athenia* was carefully staged in order to embarrass Germany. You, yourself, Mr. Churchill, have said in London that in war anything goes. You have said that a real Englishman will not turn back from any infamy in order to strike at the enemy. You have said openly that in case of a war of England against Germany, Americans would soon be on England's side. The British Admiralty would find the way quickly.

Mr. Churchill, anyone who has had anything to do with you knows exactly what you think. We repeat—this ship was sunk by your orders alone. But this time, Mr. Churchill, Americans are wise to you. They know that you have fallen into the grave you have dug for others. Public opinion knows it. And if you decide on another Athenia *case, you will be answered by the laughter of the world.*

Britain Goes to War: Oswald Garrison Villard on the Opening Days in London

[September 3, 1939]

"We shall win. We are certain that we shall win in the end."

Oswald Garrison Villard, liberal American journalist, was in London during the initial hours and days of the war. He believed that the new World War had been brought about by "criminal lunacy on the one hand and almost incredible ineptness and weakness and diplomatic folly on the other." But, nevertheless, he was filled with admiration when he watched what was going on in London. "I should unqualifiedly say that this is humanity at its best did not one thought force itself upon me: if these indomitable people would only bring their great qualities to bear upon their government and foreign policy and demand greater and wiser statesmanship, such calamities would not befall them."

("*London Blackout,*" The Nation, *September 16, 1939. By permission of* The Nation.)

. . . As I sat in Parliament on Friday, September 1, to hear Chamberlain announce that war was at hand unless the Germans accepted his ultimatum—and he was sure, he said, that they would not—I could not help recalling how many such fateful scenes had taken place in that historic chamber, how many times English leaders had ordained there the deaths of multitudes of their fellow-citizens because of their own stupidities and blunders or in order to carry on imperialistic policies of their own, long since pilloried by history.

It was a scene to remember as long as I live. Yet I believe I have seen in that very House of Commons moments of greater excitement, of more profound emotion. Mr. Chamberlain spoke earnestly, sincerely, at times passionately in his justified indignation. Munich was far behind him. Yet neither his address nor those of Arthur Greenwood for Labor and Sir Archibald Sinclair for the Liberals sounded emotional depths, nor did the last two stir their parliamen-

14

tary hearers to more than perfunctory applause. It was all over in twenty-five minutes. And it left me far from feeling that I had witnessed one of the most fateful scenes in all history; I have surely, at other times, seen a larger attendance of members—perhaps a number are already in service—and the London *Times* was incorrect in saying the galleries were crowded, for the side galleries were in the main empty.

As for the public at large, whether it is stunned, or numbed by the months of expectancy of the worst, or lacks imagination, or is trained to accept what its political leaders hand down to it, or whether it is inspired by a glorious courage and traditional faith, its attitude moves you to tears. I was near tears when I visited two stations to watch the evacuation of the children, and saw the quiet, unobtrusive sorrow of the mothers saying good-by. For the children it was a grand excitement—no more school and an adventure in the country. I wondered once more whether we should honor the Wright brothers for teaching us to fly or bewail their fatal invention of a machine which brings death to whole populations.

Fifteen minutes after I heard Neville Chamberlain announce over the radio that a state of war existed, the sirens screamed and people ran for the air-raid shelters. At the first one I came to, it was "women and children first"; the second, near my hotel, was full, so I sat outside, convinced that it was a trial alarm. Soon after the "all's well" we had another alarm. Last night I was waked at 2:45 A.M. with the insistent demand that I descend to the cellar at once, and when I refused to hurry a porter came for me: "It's orders, sir." So there we sat in a cellar hallway, in all kinds of costumes, with gas masks on laps (except a few of us), but everybody calm and cheerful and no one showing any trepidation. Indeed, in the daytime the only persons to show concern are the mothers whose children are still here—far too many remain in the city. The spirit of co-operation is really wonderful; everyone wants to do his or her share, and everyone is so courteous that it seems quite unnecessary to post signs telling what constitutes good manners in an air-raid shelter!

The streets are full of new constables; all, old and new, wearing "tin hats," the new men still in "cits" but with armbands. There are innumerable new auxiliary firemen, fine-looking fellows in dark blue uniforms, and a thousand taxicabs have been supplied with trailers and transformed into quite powerful fire-engines equipped with axes, hose, rope ladders, and the like. There are air-raid protection wardens galore. Every other car has a sticker to show that it belongs to the fire service, or A.R.P., or the transport or evacuation branches. Signs everywhere call for volunteers to fill the sandbags—millions must have been filled already. The sky is full of beautiful silver-gray balloons, the "balloon barrage" that is counted on to entangle any invading aircraft in the steel cables which hold them in place. At least fifty can be seen from my window as I write. Nothing else is overhead; not an airplane ever passes.

If there is much to cheer and hearten, if the thoroughness of the organization is astounding, if there is every evidence that England begins this war as far along as it was, say, in 1915, and even later as to conscription, ominous signs of what is to come are on every hand. You cannot help starting when you read the placards telling you where to get gas masks for "children under two." You get a shock when you unexpectedly pass a first-aid station and read the notice, "Walking casualties this way." And you cannot get used to seeing store windows blocked out by sandbags or completely boarded over. But what moved me most was a visit to a great 700-bed hospital from which every patient who could be moved has been moved. All its scientific work has stopped; its whole life has been made over; and here it stands, empty but in such complete readiness that it gives you a sinking at the pit of your stomach: in the front hall are thirty tables for the first to come, with a huge morgue not far away. It was night when I visited it, and the building of course was dark. The chief nurse radiated joy over the completeness of everything—even over the rubber boots the staff will wear when the gas cases come in.

Two kindly surgeons took me up on the roof. There was London in the dark—incredibly more majestic, more thrilling than by day or with its usual lights; more mysterious, more questioning of the why and wherefore. A hundred feet above the street, we could see only a few light spots and the faint, will-o'-the-wisp lights of buses and motors. "I wonder," I said to myself, "whether London has been as dark as this since Will Shakespeare walked the Strand." My astonishment never ends that I walk the streets of London with a shaded flashlight to find my way as if I were on a Berkshire hill. I wonder if I too should be able to pilot a car through the dark with only parking lights and those well wrapped, while the "Stop" and "Go" greens and reds and ambers have shrunk to little shaded crosses. Every night not London alone but all England down to the smallest village is blacked out. Just now every place of amusement is closed. Piccadilly Circus is as quiet as a hamlet in Kent. And in these black and murky streets everybody is eager to help everyone else, to put the stranger in the right bus, on the right road.

"We shall win," said my doctor friends on that hospital roof. To the west tremendous flashes of lightning, the rumbling of thunder gave just the atmosphere the moment called for. "We shall win," said the doctors, "because every man and woman in this hospital is at his or her post in the dark—quiet, determined, efficient, prepared for the worst, uncomplaining, certain that we shall win in the end. And as they are, so is England."

War Lord to the Front: The *Hamburger Anzeiger* Tells How the *Fuehrer* Goes to His Troops

[September 4, 1939]

"Fuehrer, command! We follow you, if necessary, to the death!"

It was front-page news for the entire German press when the Fuehrer *put on his tunic and went forth to war. The following dispatch, which appeared on the front page of the* Hamburger Anzeiger *on September 4, 1939, three days after the beginning of the war, was obviously designed to stiffen the backbone of a shocked and disappointed people.*

(Hamburger Anzeiger, *September 4, 1939. Translated by the editor.*)

BERLIN, September 4—The *Fuehrer* last Saturday moved to join his soldiers on the Eastern Front.

All the streets and squares of Berlin, including the Wilhelmsplatz, are in deep darkness. The standard of the *Fuehrer* waves from the top of the Chancellery. The people are gathered in thick crowds. They press against the police lines.

Finally, the gates of the Reich Chancellery open. A second of expectant silence. An automobile with dimmed headlights proceeds slowly into the Wilhelmstrasse. Now the people cannot contain themselves any more. They break through the ranks of the security police and push forward. A single cry of joy fills the air. And then come the "*Heils!*" They reverberate along the whole length of the Wilhelmstrasse. It sounds like an oath: *Fuehrer*, command, we follow in blind obedience, in unconditional readiness for sacrifice, in steel-hard will and belief in the victory of our just cause.

Fuehrer, command! We follow you, if necessary, to the death.

18

Blitzkrieg in Poland: Otto Tolischus Recounts the Swift and Overwhelming Conquest in a Lightning Dash by Hitler's Legions

[September 11, 1939]

"Again God has been with the bigger battalions. . . ."

The Blitzkrieg *formula was devilishly effective. First, destroy the enemy air force while it was still on the ground. Then immobilize communications and transportation by effective bombing from the air. Next, dive-bomb and machine-gun troop concentrations. Now the light forces— motorcycle infantry, armored cars and trucks dash behind the enemy lines. Then medium-size tanks surge forward followed by motorized infantry. Finally, the regular infantry advances forward together with heavy artillery units.*

Hitler pushed this strategy in Poland with speed and precision. Weather conditions were excellent—the plains were baked in sunshine and the rains on which the Poles had counted to halt the invader just did not come. And there were no natural barriers to hold up the Germans.

More than 4,000 German planes converged on the hapless Poles, and these were followed by thousands of motorized vehicles and tanks. Seventy divisions of highly trained troops, at least fourteen of them Panzer *(armored) divisions, pushed across the borders. On the first day Warsaw was bombed three times as three great German armies headed toward the Polish capital from East Prussia, from Pomerania and from the south.*

The Poles resisted bravely, but they were thrown into confusion by Hitler's tactics. They had no time either to resist effectively or to retreat. It was hopeless. Within a week Warsaw was reduced to a mass of ruins and the entire industrial and mining region of the country, concentrated in the south, was in Nazi hands.

Ten days after the beginning of the invasion, Otto Tolischus, foreign correspondent for The New York Times, *sent in this dispatch. History seemed to be repeating itself. At the beginning of World War I, on August 23, 1914, Richard Harding Davis had reported in similar vein:*

19

The German army moved as smoothly and compactly as an Empire State Express. There were no halts, no open places, no stragglers. . . . For 26 hours the gray army rumbled by with the mystery of fog and the pertinacity of a steam roller. . . . Like a river of steel it flowed, gray and ghostlike.

Tolischus's report revealed that not only had the Polish defenses cracked wide open but a new era in warfare had begun. He guessed that the Poles might be able to offer further resistance by withdrawing into the eastern swamps. But six days later the Soviet army invaded Poland from the east. That was the end. Poland, a country of 50,000 square miles and 35,000,000 people, perished in just one month.

Tolischus followed up this dispatch with a series of brilliant reports to his newspaper. In 1940 he was awarded the Pulitzer prize for distinguished foreign correspondence.

(The New York Times, *September 11, 1939. By permission of* The New York Times.)

WITH THE GERMAN ARMIES IN POLAND, September 11—Having hurled against Poland their mighty military machine, the Germans are today crushing Poland like a soft-boiled egg.

After having broken through the shell of Polish border defenses, the Germans found inside, in comparison with their own forces, little more than a soft yolk, and they have penetrated that in many directions without really determined general resistance by the Polish Army.

That is the explanation of the apparent Polish military collapse in so short a time as it was gathered on a tour of the Polish battlefields made by this correspondent in the wake of the German army, and, sometimes, in the backwash of a day's battle while scattered Polish troops and snipers were still taking potshots at motor vehicles on the theory that they must be German. But such is the firm confidence of the Germans that a cocked pistol in front of the army driver is held to be sufficient protection for the foreign correspondents in their charge.

Even a casual glance at the battlefields, snarled by trenches, barbed-wire entanglements, shell holes, blown-up roads and bridges and shelled and gutted towns, indicates that the Poles made determined resistance at the border. But even these border defenses seem weak, and beyond them there is nothing.

It is a mystery to both Germans and neutral military experts on the tour with the writer that the Poles made no provisions for second or third lines and that in retreat they did not make any attempt to throw up earthworks or dig trenches such as helped the Germans stop the Allies after the Marne retreat in 1914.

In fact, the only tactics the Poles seemed to have pursued in the retreat were to fall back on towns from which, later, they were either easily driven out by artillery fire or just as easily flanked. But presumably neither their number nor their equipment, which, judging from the remnants thrown along the road of retreat, was pitifully light as compared with the Germans', permitted them to do anything else in view of the enormous length of the border they had to defend.

Again God has been with the bigger battalions, for the beautiful, dry weather, while converting Polish roads into choking dust clouds on the passage of motor vehicles, has kept them from turning into mud as would be normal at this time of year; this has permitted the German motorized divisions to display the speed they have.

But the Germans have proceeded not only with might and speed, but with method, and this bids fair to be the first war to be decided not by infantry, "the queen of all arms," but by fast motorized divisions and, especially, by the air force.

The first effort of the Germans was concentrated on defeating the hostile air fleet, which they did not so much by air battle but by consistent bombing of airfields and destruction of the enemy's ground organization. Having accomplished this, they had obtained domination of the air, which in turn enabled them, first to move their own vast transports ahead without danger from the air and, second, to bomb the Poles' communications to smithereens, thereby reducing their mobility to a minimum.

Today the German rule of the air is so complete that, although individual Polish planes may still be seen flying at a high altitude, the German army has actually abandoned the blackout in Poland. It is a strange sensation to come from a Germany thrown into Stygian darkness at night to a battlefront town like Lodz, as this correspondent did the night after the Germans announced its occupation, and find it illuminated although the enemy is only a few miles from the city.

With control of the air, the Germans moved forward not infantry but their tanks, armored cars and motorized artillery, which smashed any Polish resistance in the back. This is easy to understand when one has seen the methods of open warfare attempted by the Poles and an almost amateurish attempt at digging earthworks for machine-gun nests.

To German and neutral experts the Poles seem to have clung to eighteenth-century war methods, which, in view of modern firing volume and weight, are not only odd but also futile. This does not mean that the Poles have not put up a brave fight. They have, and the Germans themselves freely admit it.

As a purely military matter, the German army is the height of efficiency. It moves like clockwork, without hurry and apparently almost in a leisurely manner. Yet that army moves with inexorable exactitude. The roads into Poland are jammed but not choked with heavy vans and motor trucks carrying food and munitions, while the Poles have to depend mainly on their smashed railroads or on horse carts. Bombed bridges are soon passable for the Germans and they move forward quickly. Communications lines follow them almost automatically.

Poland may not be lost yet and may be even able to offer further resistance by withdrawing into the eastern swamp. But as long as the present disparity between the military resources and her will to fight exists she faces terrible odds.

Warsaw Surrenders: A German Report on the Capitulation of the Polish Capital City

[September 29, 1939]

"Mother, I am alive! Those are German soldiers."

Warsaw, a dead city, covered with ruined and burnt-out buildings, surrendered on September 29, 1939. A pall of smoke hung over the streets. Here and there a few isolated Polish units held out, but to no avail. The defeat was bitter, overwhelming, total.

Here is a dispatch by a German combat reporter on the last days of Warsaw. Much of German World War II reporting, as this piece indicates, was designed as propaganda to convince both public and military forces that Hitler's arms were invincible.

(Der Sieg in Polen, herausgegeben vom Oberkommando der Wehrmacht [Berlin, 1939], pp. 151–153. Courtesy of Zeitgeschichte Verlag. Translated by the editor.)

On Tuesday, September 26, after our artillery and planes had bombarded the fortress of Warsaw before assaulting it, and as the German infantry went to the attack, two Polish emissaries came to the German sector west of Wesola. Both officers, a captain of cavalry and a first lieutenant, wanted to carry on special negotiations.

The German general answered that there could be only unconditional surrender.

On Wednesday at eight o'clock there appeared under a flag of truce a Polish general, an army leader, a first lieutenant, and a captain, who were led to the German headquarters over that road to Marki that hitherto had been used by all emissaries. After nearly an hour of discussion the talks were broken off, but an armistice was agreed upon as well as the principles of surrender. Since the Polish emissaries had no access to telephones and openly admitted that there was no order in Warsaw, the cessation of hostilities was set at the end of two hours.

Meanwhile, Polish armed guerrillas, a wild crowd, who were not subject to the orders of the Polish commander of Warsaw, attacked at Grochow despite the armistice. Then three representatives of the city of Warsaw under the leadership of the City President appeared for further negotiations. All three of them proved to be fanatics, and their entire conduct indicated that the suffering people of Warsaw were influenced not by the Polish military but by the hate-filled City President of Warsaw.

The German conditions recognized the soldierly defense of Poland. The Poles would relinquish their weapons at certain places inside the boundaries of the city. They were given until Friday, the 29th, after 8 P.M., to leave the city in closed ranks. Then they will be led to camps and from there allowed to go home. The Germans will enter Warsaw on Monday, October 2.

The Poles admitted the generosity of the German negotiations and of the German conditions of surrender.

The Polish officers, all of whom spoke excellent German, admitted candidly the destructive results of the final German attack from the air and on land. The lack of water in the final stages finished it all off.

The German army immediately placed sufficient medical supplies and sanitation personnel at the disposal of the wounded.

Along the Vistula dam up to the great bridges of Praga toward Warsaw there is an asphalt road, which at one time was illuminated by a series of bright vaulted lamps. To the right were country houses and summer cabins and very elegant villas, to the left on the shores of the Vistula stood boat houses, garden houses and similar small buildings. On the river, bobbing up and down, were sailboats, rowboats and small sports boats.

Close behind the German position, embedded in a second dam, in a pointed corner at the upper Vistula dam, begins No Man's Land. Just a few hours ago German scouts had passed through this area. From the villas and the boat houses, in the darkness, had come a steadily increasing fire. Now the weapons were quiet. Along the road there are the usual war scenes: shattered masonry, dead horses, deserted tombs. Polish street barricades have already been cleaned away.

The city suburb is called Sachsenwinkel. From a side street a young woman runs toward us. "Mother, mother!" she cries. "Mother, I am alive! Those are German soldiers."

It is a young German woman, who comes from Darmstadt. She had been trapped here. She strokes the uniform of one of our men.

She laughs and cries at the same time. She wants to know our names.

"I shall never forget those names as long as I live," she said. "The first three Germans that I met."

She had cowered in a cellar with Poles, and the Polish police had wanted to take her, a German, out. Always fleeing from the Poles, always new persecutions, always changing her clothes. Her mother is in Darmstadt. The young woman talks to her mother as if she were there standing on that road from Praga to Warsaw.

"Mother, I have been rescued," she says. "German soldiers...." She puts a sisterly arm around a soldier.

Weaponless Polish soldiers come up to us. Many of German origin among them are as happy as children, because the battle is over and because they can now talk with Germans. But Polish soldiers, too, curse the war, which, they say, they never understood, anyhow. Now they greet us warmly, and they smile at us in trusting fashion.

All they want to do is to get behind the plow that awaits them at home.

There is much to say about their attitude, but one must be silent about a defeated enemy.

Many new groups of civilians appear. Now we can recognize some from the wealthy classes. Despite the seriousness of the times, the women use powder and make-up, and many of them wear expensive furs.

There are scenes that are indescribable. Amidst the ruins one sees these Polish people who must bear the blame before history for the misfortunes of their country.

At night we rest in a little summer cabin in a good district. We find a Polish comic paper which is scarcely four weeks old. In it the *Fuehrer* is shown riding a galloping horse straight into a sea of Polish bayonets.

The cannons are silent all over Poland. The war is over. Before us lie the open bridges over the Vistula to Warsaw. We forget all, we thank the soldiers, we thank fate for being allowed to march singing on this campaign in great comradeship with the fighting battalions.

Scapa Flow: How Lieutenant Günther Prien in the U-47 Penetrated the Naval Base and Sank the Battleship *Royal Oak*

[October 13–14, 1939]

"We have sunk a battleship. We have heavily damaged another battleship. And we are out!"

"Do you think that a determined C.O. could take his boat into Scapa Flow and attack the ships there?"

Admiral Karl Doenitz, commander of the German U-boat fleet, was talking to one of his young officers, Lieutenant Günther Prien. "Let me have your reply by Tuesday."

On the appointed day Prien gave his reply to his commanding officer: "Yes, sir."

It would take some doing. Two U-boat commanders, Emsmann and Henning, had tried the same feat toward the end of World War I. They had not come back. At Kirk Sound, one of the several entrances to Scapa Flow, the main anchorage of the British fleet, there were blockships sunk athwart the channel at its narrowest points. Prien believed that he could take his U-47 and penetrate this passage. During the period of the new moon there would be suitable tides for his submarine to enter and leave the channel. It was a hazardous undertaking, but Prien was confident that it could be done.

The story of how Lieutenant Prien pushed into the enemy mousetrap on the night of October 13–14, 1939, and sank the Royal Oak *was told by a German journalist in the following report subsequently broadcast through Germany by the German High Command. The dangerous feat, which took place only a few weeks after the beginning of the war, sent a thrill of pride through Germany. The British, though distressed by the loss of the* Royal Oak *and the damaging of the obsolescent aircraft carrier, H.M.S.* Pegasus *(Prien thought he had damaged the battle-cruiser* Repulse*), paid tribute to the daring and skill of the U-boat commander. His accomplishment was, indeed, unique in the history of naval warfare.*

26

The report given here may be contrasted with this entry from Prien's "Log of the U-47":

Cruisers not visible, therefore attack on the big fellows. Distance apart, three thousand meters. Estimated depth, seven and a half meters. Impact firing. One torpedo fired on northern ship, two on southern. After a good three and a half minutes, a torpedo detonates on the northern ship; of the other two nothing is to be seen.

About! Torpedo fired from stern; in the bow two tubes are loaded; three torpedoes from the bow. After three tense minutes comes the detonation on the nearer ship. There is a loud explosion, roar, and rumbling. Then come columns of water, followed by columns of fire, and splinters fly through the air. The harbor springs to life. Destroyers are lit up, signalling starts on every side, and on land, two hundred meters away from me, cars roar along the roads. A battleship has been sunk, a second damaged, and the other three torpedoes have gone to blazes. All the tubes are empty. I decide to withdraw.

("Die Tat von Scapa Flow," *in* Fahrten und Flüge gegen England, Berichte und Bilder, herausgegeben vom Oberkommando der Wehrmacht [*Berlin*, *1941*], *pp. 30–32. Courtesy of Zeitgeschichte Verlag. Translated by the editor.*)

They ran through the last of the narrows. The barricade is behind them, the damned barricade, and before them is the wide bight of Scapa Flow surrounded by barren hills.

Captain-Lieutenant Prien and his crew of the "U——."

Unbelievable that they could possibly have done it! First the frightfully heavy current up there at the rocky island, the intricate entrance—the barricade. Lieutenant Emsmann and his brave crew were lost in an English mine field, on October 18, 1918, in an attempt to enter the same Scapa Flow with U-boat 116.

Scapa Flow! Here in this very bight Admiral von Reuter sank the interned warships of the Skaggerak fleet. There is a smell of history at this spot. The commander must have thought of it when he took his first look through the periscope.

In the north he sees remarkable serrated shadows at high tide, shadows with three masts, with topmasts and mainyards. English warships? There they are—sitting ducks in the haven of the British Home Fleet. Only what ships were they?

The Captain-Lieutenant strains his eyes. The one lying farthest north has two funnels. That must be the *Repulse*, the battle-cruiser, rebuilt to protect her against torpedo attack, as the English boldly claim. The other, anchored a bit farther south, was the *Royal Oak*, one funnel, a little more compact in form, but not quite as slender as the other warship. This old valiant seawagon had been rebuilt twice after the war. The Captain-Lieutenant goes to the attack, releases his torpedoes and turns to get out of the bight the way he had come in.

Did the torpedoes hit? Suppose all of them went astray. Suppose they orbited back to the sub? Or went aground? Who knows what else could happen? Don't think about it! Impossible, considering the painstaking care taken by the torpedo mate and the torpedo officer to see that the tin fish ran true. Don't think about it, only don't think about it!

They must get out! As quickly and as carefully as possible they must get out! They did not want to become prisoners of the English. There was much yet to be done by that U-boat. A good boat she was and she had a magnificent crew, all of whom had that air of comradeship so vital in the submariner's life.

Noisily the U-boat pushed along its escape course. Thunder rolled across the water. The commander looked around. An immense pillar of smoke rose suddenly like a white standard sprung from the sea foam near the farthest north battlewagon. Then fireworks broke from the pillar.

A few seconds later and again a crash. Now there arises high from the most southerly warship a pillar of fire, four, always more, terrible but beautiful fireworks crackling and rolling. Blue, violet, orange colors, green, yellow, blood red, like the Northern Lights they flashed in flaming rays. Then the water pillars disappear, and there remains only consuming, greedily licking, blazing fire. Ship parts whirl into the air, machinery, yard tackle, deck gear.

Just like the *Queen Mary*, thought the Captain-Lieutenant. It just didn't seem possible what power an ordinary torpedo has. It makes steel scrap, it tosses turrets like balloons into the air, it pushes pipes and masts through each other and bends deck planks as if they were griddle cakes being smashed by a blacksmith's fists.

Once again the U-boat commander looks around. What he sees now almost takes his breath away—the ship with the two stacks, the *Repulse*, lying with its bow deep in the water, is heavily damaged. Since the ship which lay closer by had partly concealed it, the torpedo could be shot only at the part which could be seen.

Of the one-masted ship up there nothing more can be seen other than a great cloud of smoke which towers over the spot where the unfortunate ship went down. The cloud shimmers like a broad black flag and gradually begins to draw away leeward.

More signals begin to appear all over the bight, signal lanterns blink on all sides, searchlights point their fingers and vanish over seemingly ghostlike shadows of the anchored ships, graze the stone cliffs and the rocky shore, remain fixed on the heavily damaged warships, always searching for the enemy, that enemy who with reckless courage had penetrated into these waters. Now he will be sought out by destroyers and motorboats which will hurl their depth bombs.

The Captain-Lieutenant pushes further into the night. The bight, major repository of English warships, is now a boiling witches' cauldron. Detonations roar in the distance.

"Depth charges," says the commander. "They believe that we're still inside. Well, let them!"

They roll at top speed out of the narrows, steering carefully alongside the razor-sharp reefs, which already had brought disaster to a German U-boat in World War I. They do not speak. Everyone does his job, everyone has his mind on his assigned tasks. Perspiration streams from hot brows. Here and there an oil-stained hand quickly wipes a beady forehead, a fist suddenly pulls up a pair of sailor's trousers, a pair of eyes steal a glance at the commander, who calmly but surely guides his boat through all the dangers and terrors of enemy waters filled with obstructions and mines. . . .

The Captain-Lieutenant looks at his watch and talks to his crew over the loud-speaker system: "We have sunk a battleship. We have heavily damaged another battleship. And we are out!"

The *Admiral Graf Spee:* On-the-Spot Account of the Scuttling of Nazi Germany's Phantom Pocket Battleship in Montevideo Harbor

[December 17, 1939]

The Admiral Graf Spee, *launched at Wilhelmshaven in 1934, was the pride of Nazi Germany and the symbol of her rising naval power. The most modern of three armored ships which Germany had been allowed to build under the Treaty of Versailles, she was a miracle of naval construction—a fast, light, heavily armored battleship unmatched for her size in power and speed. She could do 28 knots. Her six 11-inch guns could cause trouble for any enemy warship on the high seas. "She was a sight to stir a seaman's heart," commented one impressed observer.*

On August 21, 1939, the Graf Spee, *with Captain Hans Langsdorff in command of a crew of 1,107 men, steamed unobserved out of the "wet triangle" of the North Sea. When war broke out, the German Naval High Command flashed these orders to Captain Langsdorff:*

> Your mission is to disrupt and strangle enemy shipping by every available means. You are as far as possible to avoid contact with enemy naval forces. Even inferior warships should be engaged only if such action is conducive to your main task of interference with the enemy's supply lines.

The sleek warship headed for the southern seas to prey on Allied commerce. Soon British freighters began to disappear in the South Atlantic. The British Admiralty decided to form special squadrons to hunt down the "phantom ship" that was menacing the safety of the seas.

The British finally caught up with the Graf Spee *on December 13, 1939. In a spirited battle off the Brazilian–Uruguayan coast, the German warship was damaged by the British heavy cruiser* Exeter *and the light cruisers* Ajax *and* Achilles. *Below deck, imprisoned in the* Graf Spee's *brig, sixty British seamen, who had been transferred from nine merchant ships sunk by the raider, cheered wildly and counted as the German warship shuddered from the blows of seventeen British shells.*

Captain Langsdorff finally decided to put into a neutral port and rush through urgently needed repairs. He was motivated by the plight of many wounded seamen aboard (there were thirty-six dead in the encounter). Moving into the waters of Montevideo harbor, he requested fifteen days to repair the damage to his ship. But the Uruguayan authorities ordered him to leave by the afternoon of December 17, or be interned with his crew.

It was a world-wide sensation. Would the Graf Spee *move into the open seas to resume the battle? Global attention was riveted on the naval drama being played out at Montevideo.*

Meanwhile, a cold war of nerves was fought over the air waves. The British Admiralty filled the ether with reports of a gigantic naval concentration outside the harbor. These inspired reports, rumors and speculations undoubtedly had an effect on the outcome of the drama.

On Sunday afternoon, December 17, the Graf Spee, *watched by a great crowd on shore, moved seaward. What happened then was described in the following on-the-spot report by Ricardo Diaz Herrera who gave the dramatic details for United Press.*

Several days later Captain Langsdorff was found dead, a suicide, in his room. He left a last letter addressed to the German ambassador in Buenos Aires:

> Your Excellency, after a long struggle I have decided to destroy the battleship *Admiral Graf Spee* in order to prevent her falling into enemy hands. I am firmly convinced that this was the only possible decision once my ship had been led into the trap of Montevideo. . . . I have made up my mind to stand the consequences of this decision. . . . I can only prove by my death that the members of the armed forces of the Third Reich are ready to die for the honor of the flag. . . .

POCKETSHIP FORCED TO LEAVE URUGUAY, IS SUNK IN FLAMES

(Ricardo Diaz Herrera, December 17, 1939. By permission of United Press.)

"The four-steel sides of the *Graf Spee* were torn outward like wrapping paper."

MONTEVIDEO, Dec. 17 (U.P.)—The German pocket battleship *Admiral Graf Spee,* $19,000,000 worth of sleek fighting steel, was blown up and sunk by her Nazi crew tonight at the entrance to Montevideo harbor while Allied warships waited just over the horizon to pounce upon the trapped and crippled sea raider.

The *Graf Spee* was destroyed at 7:50 P.M. on the personal orders of Fuehrer Adolf Hitler, seated in his Reichs Chancellery more than 6,000 miles away.

Barely 10 minutes before the deadline of the Uruguayan government's order to the *Graf Spee* to leave port or be interned for the rest of the war, terrific explosions of the warship's ammunition stores began tearing the ship to pieces.

The searchlights of the British cruiser *Cumberland,* whose guns she had cheated, played about the shattered war vessel as she sank beneath an enormous pall of smoke and leaping flames.

The *Graf Spee,* one of Germany's three sea-raiding pocket battleships, was scuttled approximately eight miles off the port of Montevideo in the Plata River because her 46-year-old captain, Hans Langsdorff, realized the hopelessness of the odds.

The sinking took place at latitude 34 degrees 56 minutes south and longitude 56 degrees 14 minutes west.

German officials said none of the *Graf Spee*'s officers or crew of nearly 900 perished in the sinking.

All of them were put aboard the nearby German tanker *Tacoma* or removed at the last minute aboard launches.

"If I cannot run the British blockade I'll sink the ship," said Captain Langsdorff, a veteran of the Battle of Jutland where he fought the British aboard the old *Grosser Kurfuerst.*

Just as 21 years ago the German imperial fleet was scuttled at Scapa Flow before the eyes of astonished British Admiralty heads, lined up in all their gold braid to receive it in surrender, the *Graf Spee* was sent to the bottom by her crew, who chose to destroy it rather than suffer the humiliation of defeat or capture.

Before he touched off the ammunition stores at 5:50 P.M. (EST) and wrecked the streamlined greyhound, Captain Langsdorff left a letter with German Minister Otto Langamann.

He protested bitterly against the Uruguayan government's refusal to give the *Graf Spee* more than 72 hours to repair her wounds, and said:

"Under the circumstances there remains nothing for me to do but sink my ship, blowing it up near the coast and disembarking as many as possible of the crew.

In Wednesday's 18-hour battle against the British cruisers *Ajax, Achilles,* and *Exeter,* the *Graf Spee* finally ran for port, with her 11-inch guns out of commission, and 36 dead and 60 wounded aboard her, but not until she had cut the 9,390-ton *Exeter* apart, killed 61 British officers and seamen, and wounded 23 others.

Then began a diplomatic tussle in which the Allies tried to drive the pocket battleship out of port, while the Germans tried to obtain a promise of shelter.

On Friday came Uruguay's decision. The *Graf Spee,* despite the gaping holes in her sides and her crippled guns, was ordered to leave by 6 P.M. (E.S.T.) today.

Outside the estuary of the Plata River, just beyond the three-mile limit of territorial waters, hovered the British cruisers *Ajax* and *Achilles,* ready to fight the battle begun Wednesday, and nearby was the 10,000-ton Cumberland. It was believed that the big French battleship *Dunkerque,* one of the world's most formidable men-o'-war built especially because of the Nazi pocket battleships, was somewhere near, ready to pitch into the fray.

At 3:25 P.M. the anchor chains of the *Graf Spee* began groaning and squeaking.

It was a bright, sunlit afternoon, one of the longest days of the year in the South American summer.

Then at 4:19, the *Graf Spee* moved slowly out of her berth, after 300 of her crew had been transferred to the *Tacoma.*

A rapidly swelling throng on shore watched anxiously to see whether the battleship would head for the open sea toward the waiting enemy warships or southwest up the Plata River toward Buenos Aires.

Uncertainly and slowly, the 10,000-ton ship nosed toward the Argentine coast, halted as though balking at death and then moved on again.

At 5:50 o'clock the *Graf Spee* was eight miles outside the harbor, a mile outside the limit of Uruguayan territorial waters.

Suddenly a thunderous blast rocked the ship from stem to stern. The first powder magazine had gone up.

Only a few minutes earlier the German legation had been indignant at questions as to whether the *Graf Spee* might be scuttled.

A crowd of 50,000 persons, drawn by the possibility of witnessing a great naval battle should the *Graf Spee* elect to run the Allied gantlet, saw the explosion from shore.

So great was the first explosion that the four-steel sides of the *Graf Spee* were torn outward like wrapping paper.

Great bubbles of black smoke poured from inside the ship and from her gun turrets. She listed to one side and began settling rapidly. Sirens of other ships in the harbor added to the din of the explosions.

Explosion followed explosion, each one sending the *Graf Spee* deeper into the water.

Flames continued to shoot into the air as the vessel settled slowly stern first.

The central control tower was ripped off by the first explosion and the entire warship was sprayed with fuel oil which ignited all portions of the vessel.

Some of the flames shot 60 feet into the air.

As the hulk settled in the water the *Cumberland* and an unidentified British destroyer approached at full speed.

The semi-official newspaper *El Pueblo* had announced simultaneous with the *Graf Spee*'s departure from Montevideo that Captain Langsdorff had said:

"If I can not run the British blockade I'll sink the ship at 8 P.M." (6 P.M. EST)

Flames continued to envelop the *Graf Spee*'s superstructure for some time after the rest of the ship was submerged.

Two Montevideo port administration tugs and two small steamers, the *La Valleja* and *Jaguari*, approached the *Graf Spee*. Two Argentine tugs also were nearby. One tug returned to port here and reported it could not approach the warship because the blasts caused the ship's great steel plates to buckle outward.

At 8 P.M. (E.S.T.) the *Tacoma*, with the bulk of the *Spee*'s crew, was moving into the inner harbor of Montevideo. It was not certain what would happen to her, but Uruguayans took it for granted all the *Spee*'s crew would be interned for the duration of the war. The *Tacoma* was escorted by the Uruguayan cruiser *Uruguay*.

Germans emphasized that no officer nor member of the crew went down with the doomed pocket battleship.

Captain Langsdorff rode away across the River Plata toward Buenos Aires in a motor launch with a group of his men, looking back on his burning ship with which he had terrorized merchant shipping in the South Atlantic for three months.

The Uruguayan tug *Huracan* met the launch carrying Captain Langsdorff toward Buenos Aires and wirelessed marine headquarters here asking whether the German Commander should be allowed to proceed. The reply was that Captain Langsdorff was free to go wherever he desired.

Nazi Juggernaut Crushes Norway: Leland Stowe Tells the Story of Treason Behind Hitler's Paralyzing Conquest

[April 9, 1940]

"I believe this to be the most important newspaper dispatch I have ever had occasion to write."

It was called the "Phoney War" during the winter of 1939–1940. It came to a sudden end on April 9, 1940. For on that day Hitler sent his legions into Denmark and Norway and within a few days he was master of both countries.

The Fuehrer regarded Scandinavia as vital for his cause. Sweden had already announced her neutrality, which Hitler grudgingly accepted as long as he had access to Swedish ore. Control of Denmark and Norway was equally important, for they would give Germany bases for air assault on Britain, harbors for German naval units to operate in the North Atlantic, and additional sources for food. At the same time, by holding Denmark and Norway, Hitler could deny their food products to a hungry Britain.

Hitler worked out to the smallest detail his plans for occupying the two Scandinavian countries. He did everything possible to confuse the Western Allies. Marshal Hermann Goering proclaimed loudly for the press that "a decisive blow must be struck in the West." The Fuehrer sent a heavy concentration of troops to the western front and the Swiss border to divert the enemy's attention. Then, early on the morning of April 9, 1940, he struck at both Denmark and Norway. Denmark fell within a few hours, Norway within twelve hours.

A week later, on April 16, 1940, the story behind the conquest of Norway was revealed to the world in an extraordinary dispatch, reprinted here. Leland Stowe had a brilliant record. In 1930, while working with the New York Herald Tribune, he was awarded a Pulitzer prize for international reporting for his coverage of the sessions of the Reparations Commission at Paris. When World War II began, Stowe was told that at thirty-nine he was too old for a combat reporter. He moved at once to the

35

Chicago Daily News. *Throughout the war, from seven countries and a dozen battle fronts, the "old man" of war journalism flashed to his home office a superb series of reports.*

(*Baltimore* Evening Sun, *April 16, 1940. By permission of the Chicago* Daily News.)

STOCKHOLM, April 16—For the first time the story behind Germany's paralyzing twelve-hour conquest of vital Norwegian ports on Tuesday, April 9, can be told. Between midnight and noon on the bewildering day, Norway's capital, all her principal seaports and her most strategic coastal defenses fell into German hands like an overripe plum.

Norwegian people were stunned as the Belgian people must have been stunned in 1914, and most of them still have not the slightest conception of how this incomprehensible tragedy could have happened.

I spent these hours in Oslo, together with the only other American newspapermen who were on the spot—Warren Irvin, of National Broadcasting Company, and Edmund Stevens, of the *Christian Science Monitor*—and we ourselves could scarcely believe the evidence of our own eyes.

But I had to remain in Oslo through four days of German occupation to learn how this miracle of lightning naval and military occupation was made possible. Then I could scarcely believe my ears. After that, with the last train connections to Sweden severed, Irvin and myself decided to try somehow to get across the border. It was the only possible way to give a detailed account of the most astonishing thing that has happened since the second World War began.

Norway's capital and great seaports were not captured by armed force. They were seized with unparalleled speed by means of a gigantic conspiracy which must undoubtedly rank among the most audacious, most perfectly oiled political plots of the past century.

By bribery and extraordinary infiltration on the part of Nazi agents and by treason on the part of a few highly placed Norwegian civilian and defense officials, the German dictatorship built a Trojan horse inside of Norway. Then, when the hour struck, the German plotters spiked the guns of most of the Norwegian Navy and reduced its formidable fortresses to impotence.

Absolute control of only a handful of key men in administrative positions and the navy was necessary to turn the trick and everything had been faultlessly prepared. The conspiracy was about ninety per cent according to schedule. Only in two or three places was it marred by unexpected hitches, but Norway's sea gates were already wide open.

For the success of the German plan, the capture of three key cities was essential, these being Oslo, Bergen and Narvik. It is known that Narvik was betrayed to the Germans by its commanding officer. How Bergen's harbor defenses were taken remains a mystery, as far as I can learn. But most important of all to the Nazi plot was the immediate domination of Oslo fjord with its mighty fortresses and the forcing of its virtually impregnable narrows at Drobak, together with the seizure of the great Norwegian naval base at Horten.

Only in this manner could the Germans penetrate to Oslo and deliver an almost irreparable blow to Norway's parliamentary government. To seize all of Oslo fjord and force its narrows would have appeared impossible to any foreign government except the Nazi dictatorship, but by methods even more astonishingly efficient than those which it used against Austria and Czechoslovakia the inconceivable was accomplished. Until now, I believe, the outside world has had to guess how it was done.

To understand the conspiracy's scope one must go back somewhere near the climax of the plot. In Oslo I learned, on the most reliable authority, that Germany's sea forces and troop ships sailed from German ports for their Norwegian adventure during the night of Thursday, April 4—three full days before the British mined the upper Norwegian coast between Bergen and Narvik.

I also was informed with impressive assurance that the German Army chiefs strongly opposed Führer Adolf Hitler on the plan to invade Norway because they insisted that communication lines for an army of occupation in Norway would be most dangerously limited and exposed. Nazi radical leaders supported der Führer and the decision was taken against the regular army chief's counsels.

On Friday night, April 5, while the German fleet and transports already were streaming toward Norway, an event of enormous historical importance occurred in Oslo and, until now, has probably never been reported. The German Legation held a soiree to which it invited 200 persons representing Norway's influential personalities. All the members of the Government were invited, as well as many officers of the defensive forces, leading bankers, shipping executives and industrialists. The invitation emphasized the importance of the soiree by reading, "White ties, uniforms and decorations."

Despite the great formality imposed, it was no official dinner. Norway's elite had been invited to see an "unusually interesting film." It proved to be the motion picture, "Baptism of Fire," depicting in the most graphic details Germany's aerial destruction in Poland. For more than an hour the distinguished Norwegian audience sat in icy silence, gripped by the horror of many of the scenes. Afterward the German Minister explained that the film was not a war, but a peace, film, since it showed what nations which elected peace would save their people from suffering. The Norwegians left the German Legation that night filled with gloomy, ominous thoughts.

In Oslo I learned that Major Vidkun Quisling, leader of the pro-Nazi Norwegian party, called the Camling, and now Premier of the so-called National Government set up after the German occupation, was in Berlin at the time the film was shown in Oslo and while the expedition was being organized. He returned to Oslo on Saturday, April 6. On Sunday night the British sowed mine fields below Narvik. On Monday Berlin's press flamed against this provocation. In the first hours of Tuesday, April 9, Norway's naval defenses were betrayed to the German fleet and the first German troops landed at Fornebo, Oslo's airport, a few hours after daybreak.

This brings us to the methods by which Oslo fjord and Oslo itself were captured from the sea early in the morning hours of April 9. The Germans could not enter without controlling the vital Norse naval base at Horten. At 1:30 o'clock that morning—three and a half hours before Berlin's ultimatum was handed to Foreign Minister Dr. Halvdan Koht—the commander of three Norwegian warships at Horten received an urgent message. It was supposedly signed by Dr. Koht himself and accepted as coming direct from the Government via the Ministry of Foreign Affairs. It ordered Norwegian ships which were about to come up the fjord and to put all their men ashore immediately—without their arms.

Without questioning the origin of the order, the commander ordered all his men ashore except stokers and messmen.

From here on a slight hitch which was costly for the Germans occurred. The Norse minelayer *Olaf Trygvason* had unexpectedly put in for repairs the previous evening. Its presence apparently was unknown to the leaders of the conspiracy in Oslo. This was the only Norwegian war vessel which did not receive the order and so remained in condition to fight. Afterward the Norwegian sailor who verified these developments declared, "It was only through treason that the Germans got in."

Meanwhile, an even greater coup had been scored by the plotters. The narrows of Oslo fjord were mainland controlled from Drobak. About 11:30 o'clock in the morning of April 9 these mines were all rendered harmless by being electrically disconnected from the Drobak central. The mystery of who ordered this done remained unsolved when I left Oslo, but this move enabled the German cruiser to penetrate the narrows before dawn.

At 4:30, still half an hour before the German Minister handed the ultimatum to Dr. Koht, a German cruiser believed to have been the *Emden*, accompanied by two submarines, reached Horten. The three Norse war vessels were completely helpless but the little mine layer, *Olaf Trygvason*, blocked the entrance to the narrows. It immediately discharged torpedoes and sank the cruiser and a submarine. It was reported, though I was unable to confirm this, that the cruiser *Blücher* also was sunk by the narrows fort, called Oskarsborg.

In any case, all other crews were ashore without arms at Horten, and by daybreak the Germans landed marines and seized Horten. The way through the narrows was open and Oslo defenseless from the sea.

I talked to another Norwegian who was a member of the Horten naval base that night. He confirmed all the main details of the above events, including the fact that two German cruisers were sunk.

"Later the Germans got about one hundred men ashore," he related. "There was some fighting. We had four men killed; the Germans two. But there was nothing we could do. The officers on our ships ran up white flags. We didn't know why and I still don't know why. We thought they had orders from the Government."

In this fashion Norway's capital was betrayed from within and the German occupation of Oslo assured before its Government knew what had happened or Parliament had courageously refused to capitulate.

Before the Germans' capture of Horten the Oslo Government had already ordered mobilization as a precaution. Accordingly, before daybreak on April 9 scores of young Norwegians reported at the Horten railroad station. They were immediately surrounded by the German marines landing party and placed aboard other German ships which came up.

When German warships approached the formidable Oskarsborg fortress, at the narrows above Horten, so it was stated there afterward, they radioed the fortress commander not to shoot. According to report, the Nazis said, "We've got your own men aboard." The fortress guns remained silent and the German warships passed into Oslo's inner harbor. The occupation of Oslo was then inevitable.

Meanwhile, we had spent an eerie night in Oslo's Grand Hotel with a succession of air alarms, the first of which sounded at 12:35 o'clock in the morning, about the time mobilization was ordered.

At first I could not believe my ears, as the sirens were so different from those in Helsinki. They sounded like motor cars honking in a traffic jam. Later Stevens and I decided that the Norwegians were only air-alarming as a precaution. So I refused to get up until 7 o'clock, when a Finnish diplomat informed me of the ultimatum and the Government's decision to leave.

At 7:45 o'clock, while we still had not the slightest idea what had happened in Oslo fjord and at Horten, five Nazi bombers suddenly came roaring over the rooftops, so low they almost touched them. We watched them some, expecting bombs momentarily. For two and a half hours German planes dived over the city, always only three or five in number. They were intended to terrorize the population into surrender and the authorities into inaction while the first troops landed by air at Fornebo outside the city.

Thousands of Osloans gazed curiously and fearfully, but no panic occurred. None of us dreamed that German warships were in the inner harbor and that Oslo was already doomed. We still thought that British ships and planes might come at any moment. It seemed utterly incredible that the narrows of Oslo fjord could have been forced by the Germans, and its powerful forts silenced.

The same madness of incomprehensible events continued all day long. First was mystification over the complete lack of defense of the city by its naval forces and coastal forts. Then it was the immunity of the low-flying Nazi planes to thousands of machine-gun bullets which pattered almost incessantly until after 10 o'clock. Then it was the further fact that only one anti-aircraft battery seemed to be firing against the German planes, and this became silent after firing only a few shells, all of which were inexplicably wide of the mark.

Finally, at 10:30 o'clock, came an equally fantastic lull in which German planes only circled occasionally and absolutely nothing seemed to happen. Tens of thousands of people clustered in the streets and on the sidewalks, looked and waited, utterly baffled. We all asked where were the British, but also where were the Germans.

Meanwhile, I had a great battle to get the telegraph office to accept a dispatch without a special Government press card.

At 9 o'clock in the morning Stevens and myself could find no responsible chief at his post in the telegraph building, only groups of perplexed employes standing in the corridors—those few who had reported for work. It was only through the personal intervention of Raymond Cox, first secretary, who remained in charge of the American Legation, that our first dispatches were finally accepted, and the only ones which were allowed to pass for more than twenty-four hours.

But Norway's capital in every quarter was the scene of dazed disorganization, completely without leadership. Apparently even the men who had been called to the colors did not know where to go or simply forgot about it. The streets were filled with men of fighting age, all standing watching the German planes, waiting and speculating, but doing nothing and going nowhere.

It was like this until 2:30 o'clock in the afternoon. Then, as I rushed up to the hotel desk, a porter asked me, "Aren't you going out to see the Germans come in?"

"What do you mean, the Germans?"

"Yes, they are marching up Carl Johan Boulevard any minute now."

I called Irvin and Stevens and we rushed outside into the strangest conceivable scene. Oslo's beautiful main boulevard was jammed with people all flocking to see the Germans come in. Strangest of all, Norwegian policemen were calmly forming lines along the sidewalks and clearing the streets for the Germans' triumphal entry. One of the policemen told me that the Germans would be there within ten minutes.

All this and what followed I told in a dispatch which was filed that afternoon—but the Germans had just taken over the telegraph building and I learned two days later that not a line of my dispatch was ever sent. Meanwhile, we supposed that the world knew most of the story.

We waited half an hour on the hotel balcony with an excellent view all the way up the boulevard to its beginning, at the foot of the hill on which the royal palace stands. Shortly before 3 o'clock, two trucks filled with a dozen German soldiers rolled up the street. The soldiers lolled in them, with their guns dangling, as if they had been assured that they had not the slightest resistance to fear. From the rear of the second truck two machine guns poked their noses meaningfully straight down the boulevard. Their operators lay prone with intent, hard faces, ready to fire. This was the only show of force, and all that was needed.

At 3 o'clock there was a murmur through the crowd. We could see two mounted men swinging into the boulevard in front of the palace, then six more, then the head of a marching column in field gray. The mounted men were Norwegian policemen actually escorting the German troops which were occupying the capital. We looked uncomprehendingly. Later I was told that Norwegian policemen never carry any kinds of arms. This was also why they failed to fulfill the Government's order to arrest Major Quisling.

The German column marched steadily nearer through a lane of

20,000 or 30,000 Osloans, fully half of which were men of military age. A tall, broad-shouldered officer, Gen. Nikolaus von Falkenhorst, and two other officers marched directly behind the mounted police. Then came the German regulars in columns of threes, as if to make the line look as long as possible. One of nine carried light machine guns; all toted compact aluminum kits and bulky shoulder packs.

They were hard-muscled, stony-faced men. They marched with guns on their shoulders, with beautiful precision. Mostly, they stared straight ahead, but some could not restrain triumphant smiles toward the onlookers. Several times General von Falkenhorst and the other two officers returned Nazi salutes from persons in the crowd who must have been German advance agents who had been busy in Oslo for weeks before the crowning moment. From our hotel balcony two Nazis gave the salute. I noticed in particular the beaming face of a chic, slim, blond German woman whose husband had been very active in our hotel since we arrived on the previous Thursday.

It was a thin, unbelievably short column. It required only six or seven minutes to march past. It was composed of only two incomplete battalions—less than 1,500 men in all. Norway's capital of nearly 300,000 inhabitants was being occupied by a German force of approximately 1,500 men!

The last of the German troops went by without a single jeer or hiss, without a single tear noticeable on any Norwegian face. Like children, the people stared. Thousands of young men stood watching this occupation parade. Not one hand or voice was raised. We could discern no sign of resentment upon any face about us. This was the most incomprehensible thing among all the incomprehensible things of the fantastic twenty-four hours.

Somehow it seemed as if curiosity was the strongest sentiment in the throng of Osloans who watched the Germans come in. No other emotion was betrayed in the countless faces we scanned anxiously. The only indignant people we met or saw that day were foreigners. The Norwegians of Oslo seemed stunned beyond recovery. Every one acted curiously like children suddenly given a chance to see a parade of strange creatures out of prehistoric times—something which had no connection with real life.

But within two hours real life was making itself felt in Oslo. The Germans had occupied the capital without dropping a bomb, without firing a shot within the city limits. They simply had paraded in and taken it over much as Frenchmen or Italians might parade into a colonial interior village somewhere in Africa. Now they went to work. It was the urgent task of the tiny force of 1,500 men to seize key places in the nation's capital. They did it swiftly, without any fear of interruption.

When I hurried into the telegraph building I had hopes. There were still no German troops guarding the door. But immediately I knew it was too late. The tip-off came when a woman employe, who had always addressed me in perfect English, spoke to me in German and tried to refuse my message on the grounds that I had no special telegraph card. But her chief had already accepted my dispatch at 1 o'clock.

Finally, she accepted it reluctantly, together with $64 worth of Norwegian crowns, which had to be paid in advance. Then she told me in German that I must see Fraulein Hauge tomorrow morning or no more messages would be accepted. Of course, my own and all other dispatches for the next twenty-four hours were never sent. The Germans had closed all the wires, as well as telephone lines, to the outside world.

The next day, Wednesday, was as unbelievable as the events of April 9 had been. German troops now stood guard in the Parliament, the university, the city hall and other public buildings. My first shock came early in the morning as I passed the Storting (Parliament). Two score German soldiers filled the open windows on the third floor of the building, all singing lustily, while one pumped joyfully at his accordion. Osloans stood watching and listening on the sidewalks below. I looked closely, but as far as I could see they were simply curious and somewhat entertained.

As on the previous night after the occupation, the city's cafes were filled in almost normal fashion and a large number of young men were lolling in them as if there were no such thing as a regular Norwegian army, ready to offer resistance to an invader, only fifty miles north of the capital. Wherever we went we saw groups of young people clustered around German soldiers on guard. Some of them chatted pleasantly with the soldiers, some stared at their rifles and machine guns and asked questions about them. Many young girls gazed admiringly at the men in field-gray uniforms.

Outside the telegraph building I encountered an open car with half a dozen hardened German regulars who had a machine gun mounted for action. The crowd laughed and joked with the soldiers; one man, apparently half-intoxicated, shouted "*Deutschland über Alles!*" several times. The soldiers laughed. The chief of the machine-gun crew looked down upon his admirers with an indescribable smile. He stood up proudly like a member of a conquering Roman legion who realized that he had the right to do so.

Such scenes, far from infrequent, had not ended when I left Oslo on Friday. By that time, however, many young Norwegians had disappeared from the capital with packs on their backs. A great many more went when the Germans landed 20,000 troops on Oslo's quays on Thursday afternoon. This sight at last awakened many men from the daze which they had been in. Many others, however, still remained in the capital on Friday—seemingly a large part of the men.

On Wednesday evening we discovered that the Quisling Government had been formed in room 430 of the Continental Hotel. I went there about a matter which was said to require the new Premier's personal decision. Three Germans in civilian clothes, and one Norwegian, were in room 430. After waiting, I saw Major Quisling very briefly, but he turned for advice to a sharp-faced German who introduced himself as Reichsamtsleiter Schoedt.

The Reichsamtsleiter decided the matter while another German assisted in giving further directions. From there, we were referred to the German Legation, where we were received courteously. It appeared that the German military censorship was not yet completely organized and nothing could be arranged about the transmission of dispatches until the next day.

Nevertheless, we made another call at the telegraph building. The public hall was deserted when we entered after passing German guards. Inside, two German privates were standing. While we wrote our cablegrams they began an exercise in mass psychology. They marched fifteen or twenty steps, slowly and calculatedly pounding the heels of their boots down on the cement floor at every step. Each step echoed loudly and menacingly against the ceiling. After a few second's pause, the two soldiers pounded their heels again.

They continued this exercise as long as we were in the hall. The echo of their hobnailed heels was amazingly eloquent.

This is how Norway's capital was captured without a bomb being dropped and without a shot being fired within several miles of the city.

I believe this to be the first story of any completeness to reach the outside world. I also believe it to be the most important newspaper dispatch I have ever had the occasion to write. It is my conviction, for the sake of history and also for the sake of the ultimate restoration of security and freedom in all three Scandinavian countries, that it is crying to be told now. I am closing it with the earnest hope that it will reach America and the outside world quickly.

Storming of Eben-Emael: Combat Reporter Dr. Mansfield Tells How Germans Captured Giant Belgian Fortress in a Little Over 24 Hours

[May 11, 1940]

"Our army marches to the decision."

Commanding the Albert Canal was the pivot of the Belgian defense— Eben-Emael, probably the most strongly fortified single stronghold in the world. For months the Germans had painstakingly prepared the assault. They constructed a full-scale model of the target based on accurate reports by espionage agents. Engineers and parachutists were made familiar with every square inch of the structure.

On May 10, 1940, paratroopers from twelve Luftwaffe *planes, each carrying a dozen men armed with explosives, guns and ammunition, landed on the flat roof of the fortress. Protected by smoke screens, they pushed detonating charges into the barrels of the big guns, dynamited ventilator shafts and destroyed ammunition elevators. Troopers crawled over the great structure, rendering its defense impossible. Meanwhile, a commando unit approached from the land side and joined the paratroopers in the final attack. At 12:30* A.M., *on May 11, 1940, the garrison surrendered.*

It was an uncannily fantastic operation. Here is the story told by Dr. Mansfield, a German combat reporter.

(*Kriegsberichter Dr. Mansfield, "Der Sturm auf Eben–Emael," in Dr. Kurt Hesse*, Ueber Schlachtfelde Vorwaerts [*Berlin, 1940*], *pp. 23–27. Courtesy of Wilhelm Limpert Verlag, Berlin. Translated by the editor.*)

Scarcely 20 kilometers north of Lüttich and about 30 kilometers as the crow flies west of Aachen lies the Belgian fort of Eben–Emael. As the corner prop of Lüttich it was assigned the important task of barring any crossing of the Albert Canal and the Meuse River at the entrance into Belgian territory.

The entire defense girdle of Lüttich is one of the most modern

45

installations of its kind anywhere. Among the individual defense units of Lüttich, Eben–Emael occupies a commanding position. The many individual works comprising the fortress are built on a plain of some 200 acres. The fortress arises steeply over the Albert Canal up to a height of 80 to 90 meters. Its summit is a mighty platform with an area of over a thousand square meters. Two 12-centimeter guns, more than 30 guns of 7.5 and 6 centimeters calibre, 20 double machine guns, and 15 searchlights of 400 millimeters make up the armament. To service it a crew of 1,200 men was brought to Eben–Emael. In the casemates are power controls, weapon forges, workshops, munitions dumps, hospitals—in short, everything necessary for resistance to attack.

The first thrust of the German army had to be made against Eben–Emael in order to blast a path over the Meuse toward Lüttich. This attack was made with a dash and spirit unique in the storming of fortified positions. During the early hours of May 10 parachute troops under command of Captain Koch and First Lieutenant Witzig, in an incredibly bold action, landed on the superstructure of Eben–Emael. At the same time a commando unit under First Lieutenant Mikosch attacked at Maastricht over the Meuse, fought up as far as Canne, in order to cross the Albert Canal, the last obstacle before Eben–Emael, and then, by storming the fortress from the land side, join up with the paratroopers.

Before Mikosch's commandos reached Canne, they found that the Belgians had blown up the bridge over the Albert Canal. Simultaneously, from the fort of Eben–Emael came a wild artillery fire designed to frustrate the crossing of the Albert Canal. In spite of it the commando unit fought on through the defensive nests of the tenaciously battling Belgians, through street barricades, and around mine fields, against ever increasing enemy fire.

In the early afternoon the spearhead of the ground troops reached the area of Canne. Over there, beyond the enemy positions, they could see their paratrooper comrades. The two groups of German troops were in radio communication. Between them were the aforementioned Belgian machine-gun emplacements, the bunkers and outer works of the fortifications. The Belgian fire did not lessen. The enemy sent up star shells in the darkness, while the searchlights of the fort were riveted on the Albert Canal. It was necessary despite the heavy fire and the meter-high steel walls that the Canal be crossed in the darkness.

The leader of the commando unit gave his orders. One after another the shock troops laden with battle packs went down the scaling ladders into boats and in drill order rowed to the other shore and there climbed up ladders placed on the steep walls there.

Thus, during the night not only companies but also their ammunition and supplies were brought over the canal despite the rough terrain and unbroken enemy fire. Suddenly, another obstacle emerges over there in the vicinity of the village of Eben–Emael. The only entrance into the armored works is through flooded sluice locks. Sergeant Major Portsteffen with a selected group of storm troopers risks it over the flooded areas in rubber boats. In the face of a scorching enemy fire and with some casualties he makes it to the other side and begins to move on to the 20-meter high platform on which the paratroopers await him.

Just before 6 o'clock in the morning, almost exactly 24 hours after the landing of the paratroopers on the armored platform, the junction with the commandos is made. Now the storm troopers move against the defense works. Position after position is blown up. Again and again the detonations of disintegrating bunkers and gun emplacements thunder through the morning.

The well-aimed fire of German guns rattles from both sides of the Albert Canal. The defensive fire becomes weaker and weaker. Shortly after 12 o'clock the fire from the fortress ceases altogether.

On May 11 at 12:30 P.M. the white flag goes up to announce the sending of a flag of truce officer and the surrender of the fortifications. About a hundred dead and wounded of the enemy lie among the ruins of the armored works. A thousand men are taken prisoner.

Thus it was that a relatively weak German paratroop unit, inferior in numbers and weapons, a small body of death-defying men, hurtled from the air into the midst of iron and fire, and through their boldness and cold-bloodedness captured this strong bastion of the Belgian defensive girdle. One can see in the villages of Canne and Emael how furious the fighting has been in those 24 hours. Over there, at the outskirts of Canne bordering on the Albert Canal, are hastily discarded Belgian uniforms and weapons, steel helmets, guns, cartridge cases. Among them are dead Belgian soldiers, lying where they were struck by bullets or grenade splinters.

The houses on both sides of the streets are smashed beyond recognition. Animals wander freely among the ruins. That is the village of Emael. On an assembly area just in front of the fort are gathered the Belgian prisoners, who glance at the German soldiers with a combination of resignation and respect. These were the Germans who with irresistible energy broke down all resistance.

Through the dark casemates and works of the fortress we climb to the platform. Over us flies a German combat squadron of planes against the enemy. From a few kilometers to the south comes the thunder of the big guns.

Our army marches to the decision. We are certain after this heroic deed at Eben–Emael that it will win, no matter what the odds.

Bombing of Rotterdam: *Times*man C. Brooks Peters Relates Destruction by the *Luftwaffe* After the City Had Capitulated

[May 14, 1940]

"Modern warfare," said the German officer, "demands that whenever there is resistance it must be broken by all means possible."

The news was slow in coming out of the Netherlands. The German bombing of the center of Rotterdam took place on May 14, 1940. Not until six days later, on May 20, did word come to the world from the Netherlands Legation in Paris about the attack on an open city.

It was an almost incredible story. On Tuesday afternoon, May 14, two squadrons of German bombers flew over Rotterdam in close formation, and from a height of 4,500 feet dropped a cargo of delayed-action bombs on the heart of the great seaport. The city had already capitulated, but the raid, nevertheless, was carried on with savage fury. The communiqué from Paris reported:

> Scenes reminiscent of Dante's 'Inferno' ensued, with fires and explosions everywhere. Buildings over an area of more than five square miles were destroyed. A moderate estimate is that in this monstrous work of destruction, horrifying as a nightmare and absolutely without precedent, at least 100,000 people must have perished.

In Berlin, on May 22, foreign correspondents were called in to see German newsreels of the appalling destruction. Parachute cameramen, who had jumped with the parachute troops landing in Rotterdam, took an astounding series of pictures. The movies showed the city burning fiercely. This raid, the correspondents were told, exceeded in power and intensity even that on Warsaw. The spoken commentary: "The responsibility for this rests on a government that criminally did England's bidding and afterward cowardly left the people to their fate."

The aim was obvious. The world was to be warned by Nazi Schrecklichkeit, by "frightfulness" that would ensure the surrender of both France and England.

The full story of Rotterdam was not revealed until May 23, 1940, when C. Brooks Peters, foreign correspondent for The New York Times, *who was accompanying the German Army of Occupation in the Netherlands, wired the details to New York. The hand of German censorship shows clearly in this dispatch, especially in Peters' attention to distorted German figures on the Dutch dead and wounded and to the German explanation of the raid. Nevertheless, the report indicated that the bombing of an already capitulated city was unnecessary. German cities were destined to pay tenfold for this attack.*

(The New York Times, *May 23, 1940. By permission of* The New York Times.)

WITH THE GERMAN ARMY OF OCCUPATION, ROTTERDAM, May 23—This beautiful Netherland city, principal shipping center for a far-flung Colonial empire, is today a sad skeleton of its former self. For on Tuesday, May 14, dive bombers of the German Air Force rained high explosives on approximately one square mile in the center of the city. The area bombed is a shambles with almost every single building so thoroughly razed that words cannot adequately describe the appearance of the wreckage.

Amazingly enough, the bombing occurred after the commanding Netherland general had capitulated. Negotiations had been in progress between the two commanders on surrender or evacuation of the city by Netherland troops. The defending general, it is said, after having broken off negotiations, reopened them but failed to inform the Germans in time, specifically the latters' commander.

Meantime, the Germans say, they instructed their air force to attack that part of the city allegedly occupied by troops immediately after expiration of the time limit. When they learned of the decision to surrender, the Germans declare, it was too late to recall "all the dive bombers that had set out to eject the enemy."

How many German planes were "recalled" and how many attacked is not definitely known. It is suggested by German military officials that the havoc had been worked by 27 planes in nine and one half minutes. The dive bombers did a thorough, accurate job. For they devastated and reduced to ashes the wide area they attacked without damage at all points in most places outside.

The entire central section of the city situated on the north bank of the Maas was affected. All the buildings flanking the river on the north bank were destroyed. Today they are still smoldering in some places.

It is not known how many civilians lost their lives in the holocaust

—perhaps it will never be known. A German officer estimated the number at probably "several thousand" while Netherland sources placed the figure between 10,000 and 15,000. Later German figures given to us declared that 300 persons were killed and 365 wounded while 6,000 had been evacuated into the country before the attack began.

In modern warfare, a German officer explained, there are no longer "open" and "fortified" cities but merely "defended" and "undefended" cities. Rotterdam, he insisted, was "defended" and, he added, "modern warfare demands that whenever there is resistance it must be broken by all means possible."

By taking up posts within the city, Germans declare, the defenders exposed themselves and their city to this fate.

We drove through ruins patrolled by armed Netherland police. The faces of pedestrians were sober, pensive, somber. Coolsingle Street, whose tall buildings mostly had housed banks and business concerns, was reduced to street level. The telegraph building, although damaged, and a new modern 12-story apartment house unscathed except for broken windows, were almost the only upright buildings in the vicinity. The clock in the telegraph building had stopped at 4:30.

Small canals in this sector were filled with debris, broken bits of furniture and household furnishings. In the sectors adjoining the immediate center of attack, weary civilians were salvaging what remained of their belongings.

Germans who had taken up posts on the south bank of the Maas say Netherlanders destroyed whole blocks of buildings on the north side of the river to be able to cover the main bridge. Neutrals in Rotterdam believe the Germans were correct in this assertion. Netherland artillery, the Germans declare, stationed behind defensive positions fired at the Germans over the central part of the city and the river.

Tied to a wharf and camouflaged, the liner *Statendam* was still burning. Germans allege she was set afire by British and Netherland shells. Fighting within Rotterdam, Germans say, began at 8 A.M. on May 14. The Netherland commander procrastinated about evacuation or surrender, they declare, because he hoped reinforcements from the Utrecht sector would arrive in time to assist him.

We drove to Rotterdam in German Army cars from Dusseldorf, after a night almost three hours of which were spent in air-raid shelters, crossing the frontier near Gennep. Soon we came to the first line of defense, the Peel Line. All the way to Rotterdam, however, we saw few traces of heavy fighting, although almost every bridge had been blown up in a futile endeavor to hold up the German advance.

Barbed wire was everywhere, but heavy steel and concrete and wooden obstacles placed across the streets to impede the German advance had been pushed aside by German sappers. Bunkers that we saw along the road leading from Gennep via Hertogenbusch, Tilburg, Breda and Dordrecht to Rotterdam appeared to have been taken for the most part without a struggle. . . .

Germans say the very speed of their invasion rendered it merciful to the human pawns who sought to obstruct their passage. For, they say, only 100 Netherland soldiers were killed and 850 wounded in the entire campaign.

Neutral observers of the invasion allege that the Fifth Column played an important role in the occupation, diverting the attention of the troops in The Hague and Rotterdam for some time. Ensconced in roof tops and windows, Netherland National Socialists fired on the Netherland defenders, who were obliged to divide their forces all over the interior towns in an effort to clean up this unlooked for enemy within. . . .

Through the entire campaign, it is said, only 700 British soldiers were on Netherland soil, and 80 of them were sappers who blew up the huge oil tanks at Rotterdam.

Conquest of Belgium: M. W. Fodor Retreats Along With a 200-Mile Belgian Refugee Line in "The Greatest Mass Exodus in History"

[May 17, 1940]

"A huge serpent of automobiles wound its way out of the capital."

On May 10, 1940, apparently as the result of the fiasco in Norway, Neville Chamberlain handed in his resignation as Prime Minister. He was succeeded by Winston Churchill, England's man of destiny. "As I went to bed about 3:00 A.M.," Churchill later wrote, "I was conscious of a profound sense of relief. . . . I was sure that I should not fail. Therefore, although impatient for the morning, I slept soundly."

At the dawn of that very day, Hitler, glowing with a sense of power, struck at Belgium, Holland and Luxembourg. The German assault was much the same as that attempted in 1914—a surge through Belgium and across northern France. But this time the immediate goal was not Paris but, instead, the Channel ports. Hitler's purpose was to drive a wedge between the Allied armies in the north and south. The strategy included the conquest of Holland.

German Blitz tactics had been used before in Poland, but once again there was an element of surprise. Bridges, railway stations and forts were quickly immobilized by the Luftwaffe and Hitler's zealous parachutists. German tanks, followed by the slower moving infantry, smashed through the thin border defenses. Skirting the northern end of the "impregnable" Maginot Line, the mechanized German armies headed toward the Ardennes forest.

All the British forces on the Continent, together with a French army, pushed rapidly northward to the Meuse River to help the Belgians. But the German armored columns moved irresistibly onward. Even Hitler was surprised by the staggering success of his Blitzkrieg.

Meanwhile, Belgian refugees took to the roads, blocking them and adding immeasurably to the military confusion. Hitler sent his warbirds to create panic on the roads as the Belgian defenses crumbled.

M. W. Fodor, foreign correspondent for the Chicago Daily News, found

53

himself caught for thirty hours in this interminable caravan of Belgian refugees headed for France. After reaching safety behind the Allied lines in northeast France, he sent in a report describing the ordeal of what he believed to be "the greatest mass exodus in history." That may have been a bit exaggerated, but the story did convey the idea of the total dislocation caused by Hitler's lightning war.

(*Chicago* Daily News, *May 17, 1940. By permission of the Chicago* Daily News.)

BEHIND ALLIED LINES, NORTHEAST FRANCE, May 17—For six days I watched the cavalry of a gallant small nation which twenty-six years ago had suffered under the aggressor's heel. Gallant little Belgium did her best but the pressure of the totalitarian war machine exerted upon her by the Nazis was too much.

A week ago the totalitarian war commenced and Brussels, unwarned, though not surprised, was subjected to wave after wave of German Heinkels—as many as 100 at a time—while forty miles away, in the region of the Albert Canal, 2,000 German bombers pounded Belgium's army.

Belgium's army was determined to withstand the worst shocks of motorized troops, but the aerial bombardment was so fierce that at last, without sufficient aerial support, the Belgians had to yield. Likewise, five days later, in the Namur-Givet sector, though fighting fiercely against overwhelming odds and in face of ceaseless aerial pounding which only the most superior troops might withstand, the Belgians were again forced to give way.

But the Germans were not satisfied to employ the most frightful of methods against the army. Following their well-known intimidation tactics, they employed aerial bombardment against Belgium's major cities. Every day Brussels was bombarded.

Those of us living in the capital got used to these bombardments, which came at regular intervals: at 2:30 A.M.; from 4:45 to 6 A.M., and from 3 to 7 P.M. But there were two days when air-raid alarms followed each other without intervals.

But as bad as the Brussels bombardment was, it was only child's play compared with the fate suffered by cities in the fortified areas, such as Antwerp, Louvain, Namur, Liege and Gembloux. Beautiful Louvain met, for the second time, the fate it suffered in the first World War. Again the town was hit by German incendiary bombs and its famous library, reconstructed by American funds, was once more a target. Namur was bombed to smoldering ruins and Antwerp badly damaged.

This continuous pounding by heavy bombs had terrified the population of eastern Belgium and ever since the beginning of the war, refugees continued in an unending procession through Brussels. The first wave of refugees was reminiscent of another evacuation— they were poor people, frightened by bombs and shells, leaving their homes with only a few portable bits of belongings.

All had blankets swung over their shoulders, bundles on their backs. Most of them walked, or if their luggage was too heavy, packed it on bicycles which they pushed along. Others, more fortunate, rode in motor trucks or carts. Many carried favorite pets and one woman refused a seat in a truck because she was not allowed to take her old wire-haired terrier with her.

As the days passed and the bombardment of cities became more intense, the number of exiles rapidly increased. Belgium and Holland harbored some of the richest upper and middle classes in any country outside of the United States. The diamond merchants of Antwerp, the clothiers of Verviers and Louvain, the industrialists of Liege, in turn, began to leave their homes, and for the last four days, a huge serpent of automobiles wound its way out of the capital.

This trail of cars still moving into France must be at least 200 miles long and the greater part of Belgian's population is included in it.

Can you blame these Belgians? They learned the meaning of German occupation in 1914, and they had a taste of totalitarian methods in the recent bombardments.

There were brand-new Packards and La Salles, as well as the oldest types of cars in this moving chain. But whether luxurious or ramshackle, they all looked alike; their tops were heavily overloaded. The rich carried rugs, the poor, mattresses. When the endless chain stopped for examination, the people stepped from their cars and rich and poor mingled to exchange experiences.

There was the efficient lady from Antwerp, a member of a respectable merchant family, married to a former colonel of the Belgian Lancers. Her diamonds were as large as monacles and she complained to me:

"You know, we left our lovely house in Antwerp because my husband was an officer of the Lancers and the Germans would shoot him. But now we are afraid that he may have trouble in France, because he did not join the army lately. But his sight is so poor, he just could not do it."

Refugees in automobiles keep on the right side of the road, while from the opposite direction, troops, endless troops with perfect equipment, pour toward the Antwerp front.

Among the taxis, automobiles and huge lorries of this moving serpent, one occasionally meets other queer vehicles. The inhabitants of a small city on the Albert Canal used the cars of a local undertaker for their evacuation. It was a gruesome sight to see young women and children seated inside the hearse, the glass walls of which had been made more resistant by planks fixed over the glass. Many women fainted in the intolerable heat of the closed vehicles.

A poor woman stood near the roadside with an abandoned trailer containing her remaining possessions. Will her husband return with their broken-down car to pick her up?

It must take three days for such a refugee automobile to reach France in this chain. With all the facilities granted him, your correspondent managed to make it in thirty hours.

We were repeatedly bombed by high-flying German planes but I suppose their bombs were aimed at the road rather than at us.

Before joining the caravan I left Brussels on Wednesday afternoon for Louvain. From 10 o'clock in the morning we heard the booming of big German guns against the mighty second line of Belgium's defense. Bombers were raiding Louvain and more than once I saw a huge aerial battle between the Germans and the opposing forces.

There was no doubt that these German raiders were receiving a tremendously hot reception. Slender fighters circled around the Heinkels giving them a rough handling.

Dunkirk: Douglas Williams of the *Daily Telegraph* Witnesses the Survival of an Allied Army in a Miracle of Deliverance

[May 28–June 4, 1940]

"None showed the slightest sign of demoralization or discouragement."

Operation Dynamo was its code name. John Masefield called it the "Nine Days' Wonder." Others described it as a "Pyrrhic victory" or as a "glorious defeat." It was in truth one of the most thrilling rescues in history.

On May 12, 1940, Hitler's Germans, paced by fast-moving Panzers, smashed their way into France. On May 21 they reached Abbéville near the English Channel. One military observer called it the "Battle of the Pockets" because of the manner in which the invaders were cutting up great sections of the defending forces. An army of 400,000 British Expeditionary Forces, Frenchmen and Poles was gradually being pushed back toward the Channel. It was almost completely encircled and separated from the main French forces in the south.

Hitler threw more and more troops into the ever constricting appendix inside which the Allies seemed to be trapped. The endangered troops pushed back to Dunkirk, the only possible means of escape. What happened there was high drama. More than 335,000 Allied soldiers snatched from the Nazi inferno lived to fight another day.

The British Admiralty quickly grasped the situation as the trap closed. It arranged for a rescue fleet of 665 civilian craft and 222 naval units. Never before had such a motley fleet put to sea. There were ships and boats of every size and every vintage—Belgian drifters, Thames River steamers, Dutch fishing smacks, coasters, mine sweepers, colliers, motor boats, paddle steamers, lifeboats, rescue launches, picket boats, sloops, shrimp catchers, tugs, yachts, fire floats. Anything that could float made its way to Dunkirk. The port, smashed by German shellfire, was covered with billowing smoke.

Manning the fleet was an extraordinary conglomeration of week-end

57

sailors, yachtsmen, fishermen, pub crawlers, brokers from the City in bowler hats—Englishmen of every type and description. White-haired oldsters mingled with pink-cheeked sea scouts on this amazing rescue mission.

The evacuation lasted for nine days from May 28 to June 4, 1940. On June 1, in the middle of the operation, Douglas Williams of the London Daily Telegraph, *meeting the rescued troops at a Channel port, sent in a dispatch which caught the spirit of those stirring days.*

Most of the world was deeply moved by this heroic achievement. Robert L. Duffus, of the staff of The New York Times, *commented in an editorial:*

> So long as the English tongue survives, the word Dunkirk will be spoken with reverence. For in that harbor, in such a hell as never blazed on earth before, at the end of a lost battle, the rags and blemishes that have hidden the soul of democracy fell away. There, beaten but unconquered, in shining splendor, she faced the enemy. . . .
>
> This shining thing in the souls of free men Hitler cannot command, or attain, or conquer. He has crushed it, where he could, from German hearts.
>
> It is the great tradition of democracy. It is the future. It is victory.

(Douglas Williams, in the London Daily Telegraph, *June 1, 1940. By permission of the London* Daily Telegraph.)

AT A SOUTH-EAST COAST PORT, Friday—Undeterred by heavy German gunfire and constant bombing, which increased as the day wore on, the Navy today continued the stupendous task of ferrying the B.E.F. home to England across the Channel under the very noses of the encircling German army.

As the German forces thrust impatiently against the British rearguard a number of boats of all sizes and descriptions shuttled to and fro across the 45 miles of water in an intensive effort to evacuate the large body of soldiers still remaining on the beaches around Dunkirk.

From dawn this morning I stood for hours on the dock and watched a succession of vessels, British, French, Dutch, and Belgian, unloading endless columns of tired, hungry, dirty but cheerful British and French soldiers, rescued as by a miracle at the eleventh hour from what had a couple of days ago appeared to them inevitable elimination.

To-day I saw one tiny craft measuring less than 25 feet long arriving loaded to the gunwales with 25 men having taken 12 hours to make the crossing.

The men so fortunately snatched from enemy hands had most of them been lying for hours—some for days—on beaches around Dunkirk, hungry and thirsty, constantly bombed and machine-gunned by low-flying aircraft, yet maintaining perfect discipline, raising no murmur of complaint and patiently awaiting the orders of their officers to embark.

The vessels waiting to transport them to safety were compelled owing to the shallowness of the water to lie at least half a mile off the beach, and to reach the small boats in which to cross this gap many of the men had to wade waist or even neck deep through water covered with a thick scum of oil from the petrol tanks destroyed by the Royal Air Force at Dunkirk.

Five chief reasons made possible the success of an evacuation which many had believed impossible and which in many ways was immensely more difficult than the withdrawal of our forces from Gallipoli in the last war:

1. The magnificent and sustained defense put up by the army against the advancing Germans. The behavior of the troops during their last days of intensive trial has been more amazing than words can express.

2. Brilliantly carried out demolitions designed to block the enemy's progress.

3. Incessant R.A.F. attacks on the enemy's rear positions.

4. The continued fine weather, for had wind created a swell on the beaches embarkation would have been rendered immensely more difficult.

5. The great gallantry of the French army, whose brilliantly fought rear-guard action has enabled the British force to withdraw to the coast with the minimum of loss.

All day long and during the night evacuation continued. Rescue vessels raced across the Channel loaded with men to the fullest capacity as fast as conditions would permit, steamed back at full speed across the narrow strip of water to return again with undiminished enthusiasm for fresh batches.

Officers and men aboard destroyers evinced a touching solicitude for the comfort of their charges. Cabins were opened indiscriminately for the use of army officers, their wet clothes dried, and hot tea and rum served out to all ranks.

Many vessels showed the greatest gallantry under heavy fire from German batteries and from dive-bombing aeroplanes.

Their position at Dunkirk becomes hourly more dangerous as German batteries begin to receive a full allotment of ammunition from their supply columns. Shelling of the town directed at the moles to destroy the landing jetties becomes more and more intense.

Parts of the town are in flames, and entire quarters in ruins. Outside, the main roads present scenes of confusion and destruction. Innumerable abandoned motor-cars and lorries lie ditched in every field, while others set alight blaze fiercely.

Bodies of refugees killed by German machine-gun bullets are seen at frequent intervals, and everywhere long lines of soldiers hurry down to the sea and safety.

Yet the work of evacuation continues uninterruptedly with calm efficiency, while a powerful rear-guard fights magnificently to delay the constantly increasing masses of German troops that are being thrown into the fight in one last desperate attempt to capture the remainder of our force before it can be embarked.

The rear-guard, containing some of our finest regiments, has a dangerous and heroic rôle and its position of honour involves its safety far more than of the troops it is so gallantly protecting.

Every possible precaution has been taken for its final withdrawal, which will have the additional protection of heavy fire from warships which have already heavily shelled German positions from where they lie anchored outside the harbour.

The enemy is not making headway as fast as he expected, not only because of the unyielding resistance he is meeting but also because the roads have either been destroyed by land mines or are blocked with hundreds of abandoned or wrecked vehicles.

As an additional impediment the countryside has been turned into a vast lake by flooding.

Arrangements for receiving the thousands of men as they land are excellent. From the quayside, where each receives an apple and a piece of chocolate to stay their hunger, they are marshaled into waiting trains and proceed to a point where they find ready for them a hot meal and plenty of cigarettes.

They are then reloaded into their trains and taken to a certain depot where they are routed to barracks in various Commands to be reclothed and relaxed by a bath and rest.

I was enormously impressed by their wonderful condition and good spirits. Many sang "Roll out the Barrel" as they waited to disembark or gave three cheers for the ships' companies.

All showed the strain of the past few days of hunger, sleeplessness and constant attack printed on their faces in heavy lines of fatigue.

Most of them had their equipment and rifles, and while their uniforms were soiled, few showed any hint of untidiness or neglect. None showed the slightest sign of demoralization or discouragement.

Some of them who apparently had to swim from the beaches had lost part of their clothing and wore a blanket wrapped around them tied with a piece of string.

For these fresh uniforms were available at the quayside, and several hundred were quickly refitted with warm clothing.

With them came staff and regimental officers in sodden boots and muddy uniforms, all of whom had lost all their personal kit except what they stood up in.

One general told me that he had been under the painful necessity of personally burning his kit with petrol lest his uniform might fall into the hands of the enemy to be used by spies.

Leaflets scattered by German planes over Dunkirk urging "British and French soldiers to lay down your arms. You are surrounded." were regarded as jokes and tossed away.

Some of the soldiers told me they had rowed in small boats several miles from shore before being picked up.

An officer related how seventy parachutists dressed as refugees had been dropped behind one division and had started to shoot them from the rear, until they were rounded up and disposed of.

In the confusion of the fighting, tanks appeared and disappeared in all directions and one guards officer told me how on one occasion six heavy 36-ton enemy tanks drove in a circle around regimental headquarters. Bullets fired by the besieged garrison bounced off the thick armour like peas, and the situation was only saved when the tanks suddenly moved off to a fresh objective apparently as a result of orders received by wireless.

Another of the many stories reported to me as I stood on the quayside had a touch of humour rare in German military mentality. A British unit using wireless to communicate with its divisional commander found that the Germans were intercepting signals. One night a German operator broke in on the circuit and with great impertinence asked, "Are you moving headquarters again tonight?"

As I left the dock two young RMAC doctors rushed up to me. "Which destroyer," they asked, "is the next to go back to Dunkirk? We have urgent orders to proceed there to reinforce the medical staff."

I stared at them in amazed admiration of their courage.

That the town was in flames, that every hour German occupation became more and more inevitable had apparently not entered their minds. They had their orders, they would carry them out.

Fall of Paris: Capitulation of the French Capital as Witnessed by French, German and American Reporters

[June 10–14, 1940]

June 4, 1940. Winston Churchill speaks to the House of Commons: "What has happened in France and Belgium is a colossal military disaster. The French Army is weakened. Belgium is lost. The whole of the Channel ports are in Hitler's hands. We must expect another blow struck almost immediately at us or the French."

It came the next day, June 5, and it was directed at the French. Several weeks earlier, General Maurice Gamelin had been replaced by General Maxime Weygand, who at once began to fashion a defense-in-depth south of the Somme and Aisne rivers. But it was far too late. French troops were falling back before the methodical, concentrated onslaughts of Hitler's mechanized forces along more than a hundred miles of the hastily constructed Weygand Line. The trouble was that the French lacked not only the manpower but also adequate airpower.

On June 10 the French Government left Paris for Tours, where it remained only four days and then fled to Bordeaux. That same day, as strong German forces were crossing the Seine west of Paris, Mussolini entered the war. President Roosevelt commented: "The hand that held the dagger has struck it into the back of its neighbor." French troops at the Italian border were now tied down and unable to come to the aid of their comrades in the north.

The situation deteriorated hourly. On June 12, a German spearhead crossed the Marne at Château-Thierry, scene of a notable American victory in World War I.

What to do about the City of Light? Clearly, Hitler would not hesitate to subject it to the same hideous bombardment from the air that he had visited upon Warsaw and Rotterdam. The Allied command decided to surrender Paris without a fight. On June 14, Nazi legions pushed into the capital. They found the streets deserted and the city ghostly still.

How did sensitive Frenchmen feel when they saw Paris for the last time? André Maurois, exponent of "the new biography" and famed for his life of Shelley titled Ariel, *was advised by friends to leave Paris as soon as possible. In his report on those distressing last days, reprinted in the first selection below, he paid glowing tribute to the courage of his countrymen.*

In the second selection German combat reporter Leutnant Kiekheben-Schmidt tells of the capitulation from the German point of view. Note his attention to the "generosity" of the German Fuehrer *in not subjecting Paris to the fate of Warsaw. In the third report Louis P. Lochner, who had been head of the Associated Press Bureau in Berlin for twelve years, describes his reactions on entering Paris with the vanguard of German troops.*

PARIS, A CITY HALF-DEAD

(*André Maurois,* The Battle of France [*London, 1940*], *pp. 199–202. By permission of André Maurois.*)

"Heaven knows when I shall see it again, free and happy."

For a long time we couldn't believe it, Paris was so quiet and beautiful. Every morning when I opened my window I could see the loveliest of pale blue skies, the trees of the Bois de Boulogne, the Arc de Triomphe, and the Fort of Mount Valérien looking in the mist like a Florentine convent. In the garden below, the *concierge* was watering the begonias of which she was so justly proud. In the flat underneath a workman whistled a military tune as he mended a tap. Nothing had changed. It could not be true that the Germans were getting perilously near Paris.

Then we were bombed for the first time. At first no one could see the planes. One of my children said: "Look, a swarm of bees!" He had just discovered the two hundred German bombers shining in the sunlight. We did not realize that bombs had been dropped. We thought it was just a demonstration. But after they had gone a friend telephoned: "It's been very serious. Over a thousand bombs." We went to see the craters, the ruined houses, the factories that were burning still. So it had been a big raid after all. It was extraordinary to see how little it had impressed the Parisians.

On Sunday the 9th we began to read in the papers and to hear. on the radio quite unexpected names of places. Nantes. . . . Pontoise. . . . Was it possible the Germans were only half an hour from us by car, while we went on living and working just as usual? In the

Champs Elysées, the terraces of the cafés were full. We had lunch in the open courtyard of one of the big hotels in the Place Vendôme. There were lots of people at the tables. The only sign of imminent departure was a large number of lorries outside the *Ministère de la Marine*. Sailors were carrying out boxes and papers. We met the editor of a Paris newspaper and asked him whether this meant evacuation. He said the government was divided on the subject. We went to the cinema: it was nearly full. We saw the attack on Narvik and the Paris raid. The tragedy of last week had already become entertainment.

Monday the 10th was the crucial day. Early in the morning we had three telephone calls from political friends. They all said that the government had decided to leave Paris and advised my wife to go as soon as possible. A little later I received orders to fly to London in the afternoon on a short mission. My wife said: "Before we start packing I want to take a last look at Paris." We went out at eight o'clock in the morning. We saw the Dôme des Invalides, with its soft golden trophies, walked along the Seine, swathed in a blue mist, said good-bye to the Louvre and then to Notre Dame. We noticed that many Parisians were making the same pilgrimage. Most of the women and many of the men had tears in their eyes, but I heard not a single word of despair. Everyone was alive to the unbelievable charm of the city we loved and were now to leave. We felt certain, too, that a civilization that had produced beauty such as this could not die.

We went back home and, as millions of Parisians must have been doing at that moment, began to ask ourselves what we could save and take with us. I cannot think of anything more distressing than to look around one's familiar surroundings, at the books one has collected with so much care, at the cupboard full of friendly letters, and to think: "I've only one car, I must choose and I can choose very little." We chose what we thought was absolutely essential or so dear to us that we could not part with it; and when we had chosen, it was ten times too much. In any case we had not bags enough for all the books and letters, so we went out again to buy them.

I cannot find words to express how much I admired the courage of the Parisians on that tragic Monday. They knew their impending doom. Many of them could not leave. They all carried on with their jobs as well as they were able, as if it had been any ordinary working day. The girls in the shops did all they could to help these unforeseen customers. In the streets the police conscientiously regulated the flow of cars. Some bricklayers were at work on a house. There was no hurry, no disorder, and the gentle behaviour of all made it more heartbreaking than ever to leave the city at such a time.

In the afternoon I drove to the aerodrome. The town was now very empty and the roads leading out of Paris shockingly congested. The weather was hot and thundery. Three weeks before I had witnessed the evacuation of Belgium. But this was the evacuation of a city and not of an agricultural countryside, and I was struck by the absence of men and the fewness of the cyclists. Most of the cars were driven by women and full of children and old people. It was from the plane, piloted by an R.A.F. officer, that I saw Paris for the last time. Heaven knows when I shall see it again, free and happy. I am told by friends who arrived later that evacuation had left it a city half-dead, looking very empty and curtained by the German barrages on the Seine, but that it remained calm, courageous, orderly, and incredibly beautiful.

GERMAN SOLDIERS IN FRANCE'S CAPITAL

(*Kriegsberichter Leutnant Kiekheben-Schmidt,* "Die Deutschen Soldaten in Frankreich's Haupstadt," *in Dr. Kurt Hesse,* Ueber Schlachtefelde Vorwaerts [*Berlin, 1940*], *pp. 221–227. Courtesy of Wilhelm Limpert Verlag. Translated by the editor.*)

"We just did not know that the Germans would reach Paris so quickly!"

For the fourth time in 125 years German troops have entered the capital of France. In 1814 and 1815 Field Marshal Blücher led the victorious Prussians into the city. In 1871 the united Prussian–South German army forced the capital to capitulate. Now in 1940 the soldiers of Greater Germany have conquered Paris.

"Whoever has Paris has France," an old saying has it. The French themselves have lifted Paris to so great a position of importance that the loss of their capital city is very much like a man losing his head.

The capital of France was taken in battle. The moment the situation became grave the French quickly set up a defensive semicircular line around the city running roughly through Pontoise-Dammartin-Meaux. The Germans were already exerting pressure on Compiègne, Crépy-en-Valois, Thelle, etc., and were meeting ever-stiffening resistance. The numerous barricades, mine fields, field fortifications, and defensive bunker nests had to be taken by storm before the commandant of Paris surrendered the city itself without a struggle.

Just as Frenchmen had taken every possible means to defend the city, so did the German troops prepare themselves for the attack. Only the generosity of German leadership—and that means the *Fuehrer,* the Commander-in-Chief himself—protected Paris from the fate of Warsaw. Frenchmen, especially those in Paris, owe a vote of thanks to the commandant of Paris, General Dentz, for his intelligent handling of the situation.

On June 11 and 12 the German army, after heavy sacrifices, broke enemy resistance in the field and conquered the aforementioned defensive positions. On June 13 it stood at the gates of Paris. About 7 o'clock on that day the German High Command issued a radio proclamation saying that it was ready to begin negotiations for the surrender of Paris. Simultaneously, it announced that it was sending an officer with a flag of truce and invested with full powers for negotiation. The automobile bearing this officer was clearly marked, but in the vicinity of St. Brice—about 10 kilometers from Paris—it was fired upon from behind a heavily defended barricade. The fairness of the Germans is attested by the fact that even after this outrage they issued a second radio proclamation about 11:30 in which it was pointed out that any further defense just did not make sense.

This reasonable demand for the capitulation of Paris must have convinced General Dentz. On the morning of June 14, about 6 A.M., he himself sent out an officer with a flag of truce. This led to negotiations, after which the French commander accepted the German conditions for the surrender. Indicating the unsuspecting nature of the enemy command was this remark: "We just did not know that the Germans would reach Paris so quickly!"

The triumphal entry of German troops into Paris from three sides began at 9 A.M. on June 14. It is worthy of note that for the first time the capital of France was taken from the north, since in both the occupations of 1814 and 1871 the entry came from the west. The city was like any other great metropolis on a hot Sunday afternoon. There were but few people in the streets and the shops were closed.

Gradually, some evidence of life appeared in the northern suburbs. Here lived—and this must be emphasized—the working population of the great city. The great majority of these people preferred to stay in their homes rather than flee the city. In contrast to these people, those with a bad conscience, such as plutocrats, Jews, and other warmongers, as well as the timid, honest burghers of the inner city and the western sectors, had speedily deserted the city.

With traditional discipline the German troops marched into Paris. They made a fine impression. The German flag flew over the Arc de

Triomphe, the tomb of the Unknown Soldier, the Quai d'Orsay, the buildings at the Place de la Concorde, the Hotel de Ville, and other public buildings, including the Eiffel Tower. In the early afternoon there was a formal review of German troops on the Champs-Elysées.

An extraordinary impression was made on the ever-increasing crowds of curious people when two planes of the German *Luftwaffe* landed on the Place de la Concorde, while other squadrons of aircraft circled the city. One man, who had lived through the bombardment of the Polish capital, exclaimed: "Thank God that it turned out this way!"

On the evening of June 14 several oil tanks and some supply dumps went up in flames on the outskirts of the city. This sabotage was apparently the work of irresponsible elements. The German military commander of Paris made it clear to the French officials that such provocations must be stopped at once.

With police cooperation the sabotage ceased. The first night in Paris under German control went by more quietly than any night in this war. The next morning many stores opened their doors. The field-gray of the German uniform was to be seen everywhere. German columns rolled on without interruption. The echoes of German boots reverberated endlessly through the streets.

The Parisians are happy, heartily happy, to have avoided a worse fate. They can get an idea of what might have happened as they listen to the roar of battle to the south. For in that direction the German army goes to the attack.

PARIS A DEAD CITY

(Louis P. Lochner, "Germans Marched into a Dead Paris," Life Magazine, July 8, 1940. By permission of Associated Press.)

"We have no quarrel with bravely fighting French soldiers."

BERLIN (by cable)—I have passed through many ghost towns in Belgium and northern France since the western offensive began on May 10 but no experience has become more indelibly fixed in my mind than that of entering the French nation's incomparable capital, Paris, on June 14, immediately after the first German vanguard. It seemed inconceivable, even though I stood on the spot, that this teeming, gay, noisy metropolis should be dead. Yet dead it was. It seemed inconceivable that it was in German hands. Yet occupied by German arms it was.

Except for Parisian police standing at street corners there was hardly a soul in this city of over four million. Everybody had fled before Germany's irresistible advance—70% to nearby towns and villages, 30% into the privacy of their homes.

You who have been to Paris, just imagine this picture: at the Place de la Concorde no such merry-go-round of honking autos, screaming news vendors, gesticulating cops, gaily chatting pedestrians as usually characterizes this magnificent square. Instead, depressing silence broken only now and then by the purr of some German officer's motor as it made its way to the Hotel Crillon, headquarters of the hastily set up local German commandery. On the hotel's flagstaff, the swastika fluttered in the breeze where once the Stars and Stripes had been in the days of 1919 when Wilson received the cheers of French crowds from the balcony.

What was true of the Place de la Concorde was true everywhere. Boulevards normally teeming with life, lined with cafes before which sit apéritif-sipping Parisians, were ghost streets. We saw only one cafe on the Champs-Elysées open. Paris' famed galaxy of luxurious hotels had vanished behind shutters. We saw the swastika instead of the tricolor flying atop the Eiffel Tower, from the flagstaff of the Quai d'Orsay, from the City Hall and, most grotesque of all, from the Arc de Triomphe.

Finally, around 10 P.M. we saw a German officer crossing the boulevard at the Place de l'Opera and asked him whether he knew of any hotel where we might stay at least one night. "Hotel Scribe has been requisitioned by our army," he said. "Maybe you'll have luck." To the Scribe we went, tired, dirty and bedraggled, in unpressed clothes intended for life at the battle front. The hotel's elegant manager received a mild shock as he saw our uncouth party. "Sorry," he first begged off, "but 160 rooms have been requisitioned by the commandery for higher German officers."

Up spoke the lieutenant colonel in charge of our party of nine foreign correspondents (among whom were three Americans) and representatives of the Army, Propaganda Ministry and Foreign Office —30 all told: "I command you to make rooms available for our party," he said firmly.

We were voraciously hungry but the hotel manager insisted he didn't have anything eatable in the establishment. He suggested that we might get something at the Hotel Ritz where he knew several German officers had eaten earlier in the evening. So our unpresentable war correspondents' squad invaded the sacred precincts of this swanky hostelry. A vain manager almost had an apoplectic stroke, then mumbled something about his kitchen being already closed and the cook and waiters gone home. Our doughty lieutenant colonel wasn't to be bluffed. "Chauffeurs, attention," he called to our drivers. They snapped into line, clicked their heels. "Anyone of you know anything about cooking?" To this the rotundest and portliest of the lot said: "*Zu Befehl* [at your service], *Herr Oberstleutnant,* I can cook." Our guardian officer answered: "All of you chauffeurs go down into the kitchen and make yourselves useful."

Five minutes later the clatter of high boots of two of our uniformed army chauffeurs made us turn our heads in the direction of the basement steps. They breathed heavily as they carried in a case of champagne. There was no fancy service. Bottles were given us right out of wooden cases. Nobody cared.

At the same time four waiters in immaculate evening dress hove into sight. Where the manager picked them up we don't know but apparently it seemed like sacrilege to him to have army privates attempt to serve a meal in an exclusive hotel as though they were ladling food in an army soup kitchen. As if by magic, delicious ham, mellow cheese, tastily prepared scalloped eggs appeared. Such was our sumptuous repast that first night.

Our touching experience of that first eerie night in Paris will ever cling to my memory. Entering Paris just before twilight, we made a slow trip through the heart of the city. The first historic site was the Arc de Triomphe, with the monument to the Unknown Soldier and the Eternal Flame. Here alone of all Paris there was a formidable gathering of humans. They were an indescribably pitiful lot— mothers and wives in mourning, children sobbing softly, white-haired men with tears trickling down their cheeks.

"We have no quarrel with bravely fighting French soldiers," the officers whispered to us. "Our quarrel is with the French politicians who misled them." Others confessed to me that they fully grasped the tragedy of the situation when they tried to imagine French officers standing at the Tomb of the Unknown Soldier near the Imperial Palace on Unter den Linden in Berlin. Whenever German officers or soldiers approached the monument they saluted. They also left untouched one bouquet of red, white and blue flowers with black ribbon, placed there on the second day of the occupation.

Another scene at this tomb profoundly impressed me with its tragedy for France and satisfaction for Germany: the Sunday, June 16, parade of General Kurt von Briesen's famed division up the Champs-Elysées past the Arc de Triomphe and into the Avenue Foch. To the French, it meant humiliation; to the Germans, the realization of the dream which every nationalist had dreamed since the Treaty of Versailles. Hitler was choosy in picking the division accorded this honor. Briesen's forces had covered themselves with military glory during the Battle of Kutno in Poland. In the general's own words to me: "They have fought on fifty battlefields. They're sculpted of the best German oak. Their eyes shine as they go forth to battle just as they shine now parading here."

Exodus From Paris: Quentin Reynolds Shares the Retreat of Refugees as Nazi Armor Crushes France

[June 15, 1940]

"This silent symphony of despair never stopped."

Quentin Reynolds, a gregarious, good-humored, talented American war correspondent, made a habit of appearing at hot combat areas throughout the war. Here is his dispatch telling how he shared the retreat of the refugees from Paris to Tours. It is a classic description of the impact of war on a panic-stricken people.

(The Wounded Don't Cry [*New York, 1941*], *pp. 64–69. Copyright 1941 by Quentin Reynolds. By permission of E. P. Dutton and Company, Inc.*)

. . . The Government had left. The cable office and the wireless had moved south. With the exception of a few newspapermen who had been assigned to the deathwatch the entire press had left. They had to leave. They had to follow their communications. Hotels were closed. There were no telephones, and not a taxicab on the streets. Today Paris was a lonely old lady completely exhausted. The last of the refugees were leaving, some on bicycles, some on foot, pushing overladen handcarts.

I had stayed behind to write the story of the siege of Paris, confident that the army would hold out in the north. Now it developed that there would be no siege of Paris. A lonely old lady was not a military necessity. She was to be reluctantly abandoned. The problem of how to leave Paris was solved by one of those incredible bits of luck that come only to fools who have waited too long. The Grand Boulevard was almost deserted this morning. One middle-aged woman was sitting at a table at a sidewalk café, one of the very few where one could still get coffee and bread. She was telling a few bystanders of her plight. She had driven into the city that morning in her small one-seated car. She had the car and two hundred francs, that was all. She would stay in Paris but she needed money. With

71

money one could buy food even from Germans. She wanted to sell her car. Sell her car? For weeks people had been combing Paris, looking for cars. Offering fantastic prices, offering anything for means of leaving when the time came. I bought the car on the spot. She gave me the key, I gave her five hundred dollars, which left me with five. No signing of papers, no transferring of ownership. I don't know her name, yet, but I had the car.

Now I was mobile. Now I, too, could follow the Government, follow the wireless and the cable offices. My car was a Baby Austin, no bigger than a minute. Its tank was full of gasoline, enough to carry me a few hundred miles. There was room in it for a knapsack, a mattress, a typewriter and a steel helmet. And so the tiny car and I said farewell to Paris and headed south.

We didn't catch up with the great army of refugees until we passed the city limits. From then on we were a member of this army. It is one thing to see thousands of weary refugees in the newsreels; it is something quite different to be one of them. We moved slowly, sometimes we would be held up for as long as three hours without moving. The road stretched from Paris to Bordeaux four hundred miles away and it was packed solid that entire distance. Thousands of these people had come from the north, many had been on the road for two weeks. They had only one thought: move south. Move away from terror that swooped down from the skies. Move away from the serfdom that would be theirs under German rule. Few had any money. Few knew where they were going.

Some rode in open trucks and large, open wagons drawn by horses. Inevitably the sides of these would be buttressed by mattresses. These were not for sleeping. These were protection against machine-gun bullets. Refugees coming from Belgium and from Holland and refugees who had come from the north had been machine-gunned by Messerschmitts not once or twice but repeatedly. This is not rumor; it is fact.

Thousands in our army of refugees rode bicycles and they made the best time. Often a military convoy came down the road against our tide of traffic. Then we would stop and wait interminably until it passed. Those on bicycles managed to keep going, winding in and out of the massed traffic.

Thousands were walking, many carrying huge packs on their shoulders. This was a quiet, patient army. There was little talk. The hours passed slowly. My uniform and military pass gave me priority. And yet in eight hours I had only covered fifty miles.

It started to rain as night fell. Now we began to be held up by trucks and automobiles that had run out of gasoline. There was no gasoline to be had. Women stood on the roadside crying to us for gasoline as we passed. We could only look ahead and drive on. The rain continued to fall softly and the night grew very dark, which made us all breathe easier. Even German bombers can't see through a pall of blackness.

Individuals would emerge from the mass when we stopped. Here on the roadside was a woman lying asleep. Her head pillowed on her bicycle. Here was a farm wagon that had broken down. A man and woman with their three children, the youngest in the mother's arms, looked at the wreck. The rear axle had broken and when the wagon collapsed its weight had completely smashed one wheel. They stood there looking at it, their faces empty of everything but despair. The road was completely jammed now. A man went from car to car asking: "Is my wife there? She has lost her mind. She has lost her mind."

He asked me and I said: "No, she isn't here." And he looked his amazement at hearing his mother tongue. He was English, had owned a bookstore in Paris. We heard a strange laugh and he ran toward it quickly. I followed. He had found his wife. She had left their car and now she had returned to it. She kept laughing.

Their car had run out of gasoline. They had no food. The woman laughed and then cried a little and said, "Help us."

I took the man back to my tiny car. I showed him my gasoline meter. I had less than three gallons left. There was no room in my car for anything. I had no food, I couldn't help. People around us looked on, saying nothing. There was nothing to be said. Thousands were in the same predicament. But this woman had cried. That was breaking the rule a little bit. No one else was crying.

Our army went on through the night. Hours later a whisper ran back: *"Alerte . . . alerte."* It had started perhaps miles ahead and had come back to us. The very few cars that had been showing lights snapped them off. Boche bombers were somewhere overhead in that black, unknown world above us. We were very quiet, thousands of us. I stepped out of my car. I flashed my light once to see where we were. I was in the middle of a bridge. Not a good place to be with German bombers overhead. But there was no place to go.

We stood on the bridge, kept from going either backward or forward by the press of cars and trucks and wagons and bicycles and people and by the blackness of the night. Far to the right we could see occasional flashes and now and then hear the sound of the guns. Faintly now we heard the hum of a plane. It may have been the drone of fifty planes, flying high. It's hard to tell at night. Then it stopped. It may have been a French plane or fifty French planes.

Our army resumed its weary, tragic march. Now some turned off the road. We were in a beautiful part of France. It was raining too hard to sleep in the fields that bordered the road. I drove as long as I could but the intense blackness of night strains your eyes as effectively as strong light does and when I had gone off the road twice I gave up.

Occasionally a car crawled by or a silent bicyclist or a few on foot passed. From the thousands and thousands ahead and behind came an overwhelming silence that somehow had the effect of terrific, overpowering noise. This silent symphony of despair never stopped It was impossible to sleep. We sat in our cars and our wagons and waited for the dawn. It took hours for it to come and when it arrived it was a murky dawn. Without food or drink, we set forth south, always south.

We passed through small towns. Streams of cars half a mile long would be lined up at a gasoline pump that had run dry days before. Now we passed stranded cars every few minutes. Sometimes people pushed their cars, hoping that there would be fuel in the next town. There was no fuel in the next town. There was no fuel and there was no food. We were the stragglers in this army. For more than a week it had been passing this road.

At one town we passed a railroad station. A long freight train was just pulling in from Paris. The doors of the freight cars were open and humanity poured out, spilled, overflowed. These were the cars on which the famous sign, "Forty men, eight horses," was scrawled during the past war. Forty men. There were at least one hundred men and women and children in each of these freight cars. At each station the doors were opened for five minutes. This train had been on the road nearly three days from Paris. Once the train had been machine-gunned. Not one, but everyone I spoke to, told me the same story. It had been machine-gunned by eight German planes. French fighters had come and driven them off. Had anyone been hit? No one knew.

The congestion increased the farther south we went. People looked even wearier. Thousands of them had walked from Paris. We were a hundred and fifty miles from there now. Finally I arrived at Tours. . . .

Sieg Teutonia: William L. Shirer Broadcasts the Story of How Hitler Humiliated France at Compiègne

[June 21, 1940]

"We look for the expression on Hitler's face, but it does not change."

There was not an ounce of magnanimity in Adolf Hitler. When he heard the news of the French collapse, he went almost instinctively into the first step of the Schuhplattler, *a happy Bavarian clog dance. It was a study in devilish joy, an awkward, automatic war dance, duly recorded for posterity by a German photographer.*

The Fuehrer *resolved to humiliate the French at the very spot in the Forest of Compiègne where the Germans, on November 11, 1918, had been forced to sign the World War I armistice. He called the French plenipotentiaries to Marshal Foch's private railway car—the very one in which the French military leader had laid down his terms. For Hitler this was the sweet fruit of revenge.*

Present to report the proceedings for the Columbia Broadcasting System was William L. Shirer, former foreign correspondent for the Chicago Tribune. *Shirer, one of the truly great reporters of World War II, broadcast a remarkable, on-the-spot, improvised report of the proceedings. From a few notes he told the entire story from beginning to end.*

(*CBS, June 21, 1940. By permission of William L. Shirer.*)

ANNOUNCER—At this time, as the French government considers Germany's terms for an armistice, Columbia takes you to Berlin for a special broadcast by William Shirer in Germany. We take you now to Berlin. Go ahead, Berlin.

SHIRER—Hello, America! CBS! William L. Shirer calling CBS in New York.

William L. Shirer calling CBS in New York, calling CBS from Compiègne, France. This is William L. Shirer of CBS. We've got a microphone at the edge of a little clearing in the Forest of Compiègne, four miles to the north of the town of Compiègne and about forty-five miles north of Paris. Here, a few feet from where we're standing, in the very same old railroad coach where the Armistice was signed on that chilly morning of November 11, 1918, negotiations for another armistice—the one to end the present war between France and Germany—began at three-thirty P.M., German summer time, this afternoon. What a turning back of the clock, what a reversing of history we've been watching here in this beautiful Compiègne Forest this afternoon! What a contrast to that day twenty-two years ago! Yes, even the weather, for we have one of those lovely warm June days which you get in this part of France close to Paris about this time of year.

As we stood here, watching Adolf Hitler and Field Marshal Göring and the other German leaders laying down the terms of the armistice to the French plenipotentiaries here this afternoon, it was difficult to comprehend that in this rustic little clearing in the midst of the Forest of Compiègne, from where we're talking to you now, that an armistice was signed here on the cold, cold morning at five A.M. on November 11, 1918. The railroad coach—it was Marshal Foch's private car—stands a few feet away from us here in exactly the same spot where it stood on that gray morning twenty-two years ago, only— and what an "only" it is, too—Adolf Hitler sat in the seat occupied that day by Marshal Foch. Hitler at that time was only an unknown corporal in the German army, and in that quaint old wartime car another armistice is being drawn up as I speak to you now, an armistice designed like the other that was signed on this spot to bring armed hostilities to halt between those ancient enemies—Germany and France. Only everything that we've been seeing here this afternoon in Compiègne Forest has been so reversed. The last time the representatives of France sat in that car dictating the terms of the armistice. This afternoon we peered through the windows of the car and saw Adolf Hitler laying down the terms. That's how history reversed itself, but seldom has it done so as today on the very same spot. The German leader in the preamble of the conditions which were read to the French delegates by Colonel General von Keitel, Chief of the German Supreme Command, told the French that he had not chosen this spot at Compiègne out of revenge but merely to right a wrong.

The armistice negotiations here on the same spot where the last armistice was signed in 1918, here in Compiègne Forest, began at three-fifteen P.M., our time, a warm June sun beat down on the great elm and pine trees and cast purple shadows on the hooded avenues as Herr Hitler with the German plenipotentiaries at his side appeared. He alighted from his car in front of the French monument to Alsace-Lorraine which stands at the end of an avenue about two hundred yards from the clearing here in front of us where the armistice car stands. That famous Alsace-Lorraine statue was covered with German war flags, so that you cannot see its sculptured works or read its inscriptions. I had seen it many times in the postwar years, and doubtless many of you have seen it—the large sword representing the sword of the Allies, with its point sticking into a large, limp eagle, representing the old empire of the Kaiser, and the inscription underneath in front saying, "To the heroic soldiers of France, defenders of the country and of the right, glorious liberators of Alsace-Lorraine."

Through our glasses, we saw the Führer stop, glance at the statue, observe the Reich war flags with their big swastikas in the center. Then he strolled slowly toward us, toward the little clearing where the famous armistice car stood. I thought he looked very solemn; his face was grave. But there was a certain spring in his step, as he walked for the first time toward the spot where Germany's fate was sealed on that November day of 1918, a fate which, by reason of his own being, is now being radically changed here on this spot.

And now, if I may sort of go over my notes—I made from moment to moment this afternoon—now Hitler reaches a little opening in the Compiègne woods where the Armistice was signed and where another is about to be drawn up. He pauses and slowly looks around. The opening here is in the form of a circle about two hundred yards in diameter and laid out like a park. Cypress trees line it all around, and behind them the great elms and oaks of the forest. This has been one of France's national shrines for twenty-two years. Hitler pauses and gazes slowly around. In the group just behind him are the other German plenipotentiaries—Field Marshal Göring, grasping his Field Marshal baton in one hand. He wears the blue uniform of the air force. All the Germans are in uniform. Hitler in a double-breasted gray uniform with the Iron Cross hanging from his left breast pocket. Next to Göring are the two German army chiefs, Colonel General von Keitel, Chief of the Supreme Command, and Colonel General von Brauchitsch, Commander-in-Chief of the German Army. Both are just approaching sixty, but look younger, especially General von Keitel, who has a dapper appearance, with his cap lightly cocked on one side. Then we see there Dr. Raeder, Grand Admiral of the German Fleet. He has on a blue naval uniform and the invariable upturned stiff collar which German naval officers usually wear. We see two nonmilitary men in Hitler's suite—his Foreign Minister, Joachim von Ribbentrop, in the field-gray uniform of the Foreign Office, and Rudolph Hess, Hitler's deputy, in a gray party uniform.

The time's now, I see by my notes, three-eighteen P.M. in the Forest of Compiègne. Hitler's personal standard is run up on a small post in the center of the circular opening in the woods. Also in the center, is a great granite block which stands some three feet above the ground. Hitler, followed by the others, walks slowly over to it, steps up, and reads the inscription engraved in great high letters on that block. Many of you will remember the words of the inscription. The Führer slowly reads them, and the inscription says, "Here on the eleventh of November, 1918, succumbed the criminal pride of the German Empire, vanquished by the free peoples which it tried to enslave." Hitler reads it, standing there in the June sun and the silence. We look for the expression on Hitler's face, but it does not change. Finally he leads his party over to another granite stone, a small one some fifty yards to one side. Here it was that the railroad car in which the German plenipotentiary stayed during the 1918 armistice negotiations stood from November 8 to 11. Hitler looks down and reads the inscription, which merely says: "The German plenipotentiary." The stone itself, I notice, is set between a pair of rusty old railroad tracks, the very ones that were there twenty-two years ago.

It is now three twenty-three P.M., and the German leaders stride over to the armistice car. This car, of course, was not standing on this spot yesterday. It was standing seventy-five yards down the rusty track in the shelter of a tiny museum built to house it by an American citizen, Mr. Arthur Henry Fleming of Pasadena, California. Yesterday the car was removed from the museum by the German army engineers and rolled back those seventy-five yards to the spot where it stood on the morning of November 11, 1918. The Germans stand outside the car, chatting in the sunlight. This goes on for two minutes. Then Hitler steps up into the car, followed by Göring and the others. We watch them entering the drawing room of Marshal Foch's car. We can see nicely now through the car windows.

Hitler enters first and takes the place occupied by Marshal Foch the morning the first armistice was signed. At his sides are Göring and General Keitel. To his right and left at the ends of the table we see General von Brauchitsch and Herr Hess at the one end, at the other end Grand Admiral Raeder and Herr von Ribbentrop. The opposite side of the table is still empty, and we see there four vacant chairs. The French have not yet appeared, but we do not wait long.

Exactly at three-thirty P.M. the French alight from a car. They have flown up from Bordeaux to a nearby landing field and then have driven here in an auto.

They glance at the Alsace-Lorraine memorial, now draped with swastikas, but it's a swift glance. Then they walk down the avenue flanked by three German army officers. We see them now as they come into the sunlight of the clearing—General Huntziger, wearing a brief khaki uniform; General Bergeret and Vice-Admiral Le Luc, both in their respective dark-blue uniforms; and then, almost buried in the uniforms, the one single civilian of the day, Mr. Noël, French Ambassador to Poland when the present war broke out there. The French plenipotentiaries passed the guard of honor drawn up at the entrance of the clearing. The Frenchmen keep their eyes straight ahead. It's a grave hour in the life of France, and their faces today show what a burden they feel on their shoulders. Their faces are solemn, drawn, but bear the expression of tragic dignity. They walked quickly to the car and were met by two German officers, Lieutenant Colonel Tippelskirch, Quartermaster General, and Colonel Thomas, Chief of the Paris Headquarters. The Germans salute; the French salute; the atmosphere is what Europeans call "correct"; but you'll get the picture when I say that we see no handshakes—not on occasions like this. The historic moment is now approaching. It is three thirty-two by my watch. The Frenchmen enter Marshal Foch's Pullman car, standing there a few feet from us in Compiègne Forest. Now we get our picture through the dusty windows of the historic old *wagonlit* car. Hitler and the other German leaders rise from their seats as the French enter the drawing room. Hitler, we see, gives the Nazi salute, the arm raised. The German officers give a military salute; the French do the same. I cannot see Mr. Noël to see whether he salutes or how. Hitler, so far as we can see through the windows just in front of here, does not say anything. He nods to General Keitel adjusting his papers, and then he starts to read. He is reading the preamble of the German armistice terms. The French sit there with marblelike faces and listen intently. Hitler and Göring glance at the green table top. This part of the historic act lasts but a few moments. I note in my notebook here this—three forty-three P.M.—that is, twelve minutes after the French arrived—three forty-three—we see Hitler stand up, salute the three with hand upraised. Then he strides out of the room, followed by Göring, General von Brauchitsch, Grand Admiral Raeder is there, Herr Hess, and, at the end, von Ribbentrop. The French remain at the green-topped table in the old Pullman car, and we see General Keitel remains with them. He is going to read them the detailed conditions of the armistice. Hitler goes, and the others do not wait for this. They walk down the avenue back towards the Alsace-Lorraine monument. As they pass the guard of honor, a German band strikes up the two national anthems *Deutschland über Alles* and the *Horst Wessel Song.*

The whole thing has taken but a quarter of an hour—this great reversal of a historical armistice of only a few years ago.

ANNOUNCER—You have just heard a special broadcast from the Compiègne Forest in France, where on the historic morning of November 11, 1918, representatives of the German army received from the Allies the terms of the armistice which ended the First World War, and where today, June 21, 1940, representatives of the French government received from Führer Adolf Hitler the terms under which a cessation of hostilities between Germany and France may be reached. As you know, the actual terms presented to the French plenipotentiaries have not yet been made public.

MUSIC—*Organ*

ANNOUNCER—This is the Columbia Broadcasting System.

Battle of Britain: Four American Correspondents Describe the Ordeal of London Under Attack by the *Luftwaffe*

[August 27–September 17, 1940]

We shall defend our island and, with the British Empire around us, we shall fight on unconquerable until the curse of Hitler is lifted from the brows of men. We are sure that in the end all will be well.

Thus spoke Winston Churchill on June 17, 1940, on the day when France sued for peace. The next day the Battle of Britain began.

Hitler's aim was to make himself supreme in the air before the invasion of England. He would sweep the Royal Air Force from the skies, destroy its airfields, and smash all plane factories to bits. But, unfortunately for him, the R.A.F. struck back on German air bases in northern France. By August 20 Churchill was telling the House of Commons: "Never in the field of human conduct was so much owed by so many to so few."

Infuriated by this opposition, Hitler turned on London. He sent his bombers across from Calais up the Thames valley against the British capital. The Luftwaffe *came in squadrons of 50 or 100, first by day and then by night. These great air armadas closed in over London. For weeks at a time they came, at first aiming at docks, the water supply system, power plants, railroad stations and gasworks, but later dropping their bombs indiscriminately. Many historic landmarks of London disappeared in the holocaust.*

Despite this exercise in frightfulness, Londoners refused to knuckle under to Hitler. If anything, their morale—from Cockneys to dowagers —heightened under the ordeal. Several thousand were killed or wounded each week during the worst of the air Blitz, *but the Londoners carried on. They crowded into the underground and into bombproof shelters, while civilian spotters and fire fighters fought the flames left by the* Luftwaffe. *It was "thumbs up" and "carry on" in an almost unique display of mass heroism.*

Newsmen marveled at the fighting spirit of Londoners under fire. Following are four stories by topflight American correspondents, each attesting to the superb behavior of the British public under air attack.

LONDONERS DANCE AND SING DURING GERMAN AIR RAID

(Dwight L. Pitkin, Associated Press, August 27, 1940. By permission of Associated Press.)

"Jerry seems to have buzzed off."

LONDON, Aug. 27—Robbed of their sleep by Adolf Hitler's nocturnal bombers, thousands of Londoners danced and sang until almost dawn today, ignoring intermittent sounds of gunfire and the drone of airplane motors overhead.

The air-raid alarm came as homebodies were retiring and as West End theaters were thronged with amusement seekers. When the German bombers kept sweeping over in relays and the all-clear signal failed to sound, many decided to make a night of it.

In most theaters the audiences stayed on when the shows were over and responded with zest to stage managers' suggestions for impromptu concerts.

At the Hippodrome, Prime Minister Winston Churchill's son-in-law, the comedian, Vic Oliver, organized an informal "songfest."

At Prince's Theater Arthur Riscoe called for "partners for the girls," and generals, Royal Air Force officers and naval men stormed the stage. Riscoe said it "was more like a New Year's party than an air raid."

Aircraftsman H. Kapinsky, of the Royal Canadian Air Force, who was selling shoes in Cleveland, Ohio, six months ago to earn money for a musical education, was the life of the party at the Hippodrome, where he got a chance to display his tenor voice by singing "Irish Eyes are Smiling."

Family groups had singing parties or played cards in air-raid shelters.

Many persons caught away from home when the sirens shrilled their warnings went without supper because the large restaurants closed their doors during the raid. Regulations compelled saloons to close also, but cafes and milk bars remained open and did a rushing business.

Hundreds, defying possible danger, remained on street corners to watch the spectacle as searchlights and bursts from anti-aircraft guns lighted the skies. Many walked leisurely home when they were unable to get transportation.

Busses and taxis reappeared as if by magic when the all-clear signal finally was sounded at 3:40 A.M.

These London taxicabs, incidentally, may look old-fashioned to Americans, but they can go places in a hurry in an air raid.

I had a half-hour's ride in one from a hotel in the western residential district to Fleet Street while the raid was at its height. Whenever we came to anything that looked like a military objective, the driver, who seemed to know his way by instinct in the blackout, pushed the accelerator down to the floor and took the corner on two wheels.

When we reached my destination he seemed to lose all interest in speed and sauntered off to the nearest shop for a cup of tea—although the sky was bright with pyrotechnics.

Henry Jackson, an Associated Press employee, was in a bus en route to the office when the air-raid warning sounded. Escorted by the bus conductor, playing a harmonica, the passengers marched off to an air-raid shelter singing "Tipperary" and "Pack Up Your Troubles in Your Old Kit Bag."

They continued the journey when the conductor announced "Jerry seems to have buzzed off," but it took Jackson five hours and twenty minutes to complete a ten-mile journey that normally takes an hour.

CORRESPONDENT DRIVES THROUGH TEN MILES OF WRECKAGE

(*Raymond Daniell,* The New York Times, *September 8, 1940. By permission of* The New York Times.)

"Demolished homes gaped like space between teeth pulled out by a dentist. . . ."

LONDON, Sept. 8—For at least ten miles this correspondent drove through London's East End—the area which the Germans had selected for their principal attack. Up one side of the Thames and down another were the grim, sometimes grizzly marks of war.

For miles there was hardly a window intact. Block after block where delayed-action bombs lay buried beneath the pavement was roped off and patrolled by police who shooed off sightseers. Children darted in and out of tenement-house doorways on the edge of these abandoned residential sections, while cats and dogs foraged among garbage pails left unemptied.

Human suffering was great in this whole area which fell victim to its proximity to military objectives and the inaccuracy of German bombers who, even after dark, showed their respect for searchlight crews and anti-aircraft batteries by maintaining an altitude from which accurate aim is well-nigh impossible.

Still, whether by the law of averages or by luck, the raiders did inflict serious but not crippling damage in their mass daylight and night attacks.

They damaged locks, lighting services, factories, warehouses, railroad tracks, even trains. Tonight bombs dropped near a station. But the tragedy was that for every military objective hit, grief and tragedy struck a score of humble homes.

Churches, hospitals and old people's homes, it seemed to this correspondent, appeared to have a fatal attraction for German bombs —and this was a completely unescorted trip, guided only by the senses of smell and sound without guidance from official sources.

At the edges of sections which felt the fullest fury of the German attack, broken windows indicated that somewhere near a bomb had fallen. Demolished homes gaped like space between teeth pulled out by a dentist here and there.

At other places there were great craters in the streets and buildings with their fronts torn off, exposing to gaping crowds of sightseers the bedrooms and living rooms of these humble homes.

Nothing is more tragic than an "open house" which stands like a stage set after the curtain is lifted, opened up by bombs, with cherished household belongings and pictures hurled into topsy-turvy disarray, unless it be the sight of those helpless and homeless ones who poured into central London tonight carrying babies and pillows, clutching prized belongings and unconsciously casting their eyes skyward each time a bomb went off as they went to the cellars of hotels and other buildings to try to sleep on boards and concrete with the nightmare of what had undergone still before their waking eyes.

Thousands of them now are being sheltered under Government auspices in hotels, schools and other public buildings. Central London, which only a year ago was being evacuated, was tonight the reception area for refugees from one of its poorest and most congested areas.

Through the bar of one of this great city's big hotels there passed a melancholy procession of old women and children carrying pillows and bound for underground ballrooms to pass the night. Upon their faces were written tragedy, suffering and fear.

They were exactly like people this correspondent has seen fleeing from those inexorable floods which sometimes devastated the valleys of the Ohio and Mississippi rivers in the United States. And that is what this *Blitzkrieg* of the air is like—some hideous upheaval of nature in which man is helpless to resist or protect himself from lightning or high water. Perhaps that accounts for the calm fatalism which seems to pervade among the people.

They are living through hell and behaving like angels.

EDWARD R. MURROW SEES A GREAT SURGE OF DETERMINATION SWEEP THE ENGLISH ISLAND

(*CBS, September 15, 1940. By permission of Edward R. Murrow.*)

"Minds have become hardened and callused."

September 15, 1940

During the last week you have heard much of the bombing of Buckingham Palace and probably seen pictures of the damage. You have been told by certain editors and commentators who sit in New York that the bombing of the palace, which has one of the best air-raid shelters in England, caused a great surge of determination—a feeling of unity—to sweep this island. The bombing was called a great psychological blunder. I do not find much support for that point of view amongst Londoners with whom I've talked. They don't like the idea of their King and Queen being bombed, but, remember, this is not the last war—people's reactions are different. Minds have become hardened and callused. It didn't require a bombing of Buckingham Palace to convince these people that they are all in this thing together. There is nothing exclusive about being bombed these days. When there are houses down in your street, when friends and relatives have been killed, when you've seen that red glow in the sky night after night, when you're tired and sleepy—there just isn't enough energy left to be outraged about the bombing of a palace.

The King and Queen have earned the respect and admiration of the nation, but so have tens of thousands of humble folk who are much less well protected. If the palace had been the only place bombed the reaction might have been different. Maybe some of those German bomb aimers are working for Goebbels instead of Göring, but if the purpose of the bombings was to strike terror to the hearts of the Britishers, then the bombs have been wasted. That fire bomb on the House of Lords passed almost unnoticed. I heard a parcel of people laughing about it when one man said: "That particular bomb wouldn't seriously have damaged the nation's war effort."

I'm talking about those things not because the bombing of the palace appears to have affected America more than Britain, but in order that you may understand that this war has no relation with the last one, so far as symbols and civilians are concerned. You must understand that a world is dying, that old values, the old prejudices, and the old bases of power and prestige are going. In an army, if the morale is to be good, there must be equality in the ranks. The private with money must not be allowed to buy himself a shelter of steel and concrete in the front-line trench. One company can't be equipped with pitchforks and another with machine guns. London's civilian army doesn't have that essential equality—I mean equality of shelter. One borough before the war defied the authorities and built deep shelters. Now people arrive at those shelters from all over town and the people who paid for them are in danger of being crowded out. Some of those outsiders arrive in taxis, others by foot. Since it's a public shelter they can't be barred by the people whose money went into the digging. This is just one of the problems in equality that London is now facing.

There are the homeless from the bombed and fire-blackened East End area. They must be cared for, they must be moved, they must be fed and they must be sheltered. The Lord Mayor's fund, contributions from America, from unofficial agencies, are in the best tradition of Anglo-Saxon generosity and philanthropy, but no general would desire to rely upon such measures for the care and maintenance of injured troops. The people have been told that this is a people's war, that they are in the front lines, and they are. If morale is to be maintained at its present high level, there must be no distinction between the troops living in the various sections of London.

Even for those of us who live on the crest of London, life is dangerous. Some of the old buildings have gone, but the ghosts, sometimes a whole company of ghosts, remain. There is the thunder of gunfire at night. As these lines were written, as the window shook, there were a candle and matches beside the typewriter just in case the light went out. Richard Llewellyn, the man who wrote *How Green Was My Valley,* sat in the corner and talked about the dignity of silence while the guns jarred the apartment house. We went out to dinner, and the headwaiter carefully placed us at a table away from the window. "There might be," he said, "one of those blasts." In the West End of London, life follows some kind of pattern. The shops are still full of food; the milk arrives on the doorstep each morning; the papers, too, but sometimes they're a little late. Much of the talk, as you would expect, is about invasion. On that score there is considerable confidence. Everyone is convinced that it will be beaten back if it comes. There are some who fear that it will not come.

October 1, 1940

There is occurring in this country a revolution by consent. Millions of people ask only, "What can we do to help? Why must there be eight hundred thousand unemployed when we need these shelters? Why can't the unemployed miners dig? Why are new buildings being constructed when the need is that the wreckage of bombed buildings be removed from the streets? What are the war aims of this country? What shall we do with victory when it's won? What sort of Europe will be built when and if this stress has passed?" These questions are being asked by thoughtful people in this country. Mark it down that in the three weeks of the air *Blitz* against this country more books and pamphlets have been published on these subjects than in any similar period of the war. Remember also that I am permitted to record this plan of political and social salvation at a time when this country fights for its life. Mark it down that these people are both brave and patient, that all are equal under the bomb, that this is a war of speed and organization, and that the political system which best provides for the defense and decency of the little man will win. You are witnessing the beginning of a revolution, maybe the death of an age. All these moves, Dakar, the pact with Japan, diplomats flying hither and yon, mean only that a large section of the world is waiting to be told what to do, as the Germans were waiting seven years ago.

Today, in one of the most famous streets in London, I saw soldiers at work clearing away the wreckage of nearly an entire block. The men were covered with white dust. Some of them wore goggles to protect their eyes. They thought maybe people were still buried in the basement. The sirens sounded, and still they tore at the beams and bricks covering the place where the basements used to be. They are still working tonight. I saw them after tonight's raid started. They paid no attention to the bursts of antiaircraft fire overhead as they bent their backs and carried away basketfuls of mortar and brick. A few small steam shovels would help them considerably in digging through those ruins. But all the modern instruments seem to be overhead. Down here on the ground people must work with their hands.

THE LAST STAND OF JOCK EVANS

(*Robert J. Casey, Chicago* Daily News, *September 17, 1940. By permission of the Chicago* Daily News.)

"He was the psychological equivalent of the medieval leper, ringing his bell and shouting 'Unclean, unclean.'"

HOTSPOT, SOUTHEAST ENGLAND, Sept. 17—In the large matters of threatened invasion by aerial bombs and artillery fire people have given little thought to Jock Evans, upon whose thin breast nobody will ever pin any medals, even posthumously.

He will never have a public funeral with muffled drums, muted trumpets and suchlike tokens of civic gratitude; it is most unlikely that he will ever have any funeral at all.

In the years before the war he had done nothing to distinguish himself. He had some sort of dock job where the dust hadn't been too good for his lungs. Because of bad eyes and other deficiencies, he had been rejected for military service even at the end of the last war, when medical examiners hadn't been so particular.

In other words, though nobody noticed it at the time, he was made of the stuff heroes are made of.

So far as concerns the elements that have made England to date, he was an architect's model for the spirit of the British Empire.

Jock Evans, to get on with it, was in his most recent career, an air-raid precautions warden. In a year's drill in how to put on the gas mask, how to revive fainting women, how to direct people to the nearest shelter, he had never shown more than ordinary aptitude.

Jock Evans was on duty last night. He had been on duty most nights in the past month, as he would be now with warnings on all the time and never an all-clear. He had phoned to the central control at 11 P.M. that he had seen a bright light somewhere—his superiors, remembering Jock, suspected it might be somebody with a too-bright cigar.

He had stationed himself near the telephone kiosk on the edge of an outlying suburb where the artillery shells still land each day when the town is shelled. He had had no occasion to move from his post at night when the big crump fell.

The big crump was a dud. For a moment Jock felt glad of that. The shriek of it had been pretty nerve-racking. But after awhile when he remembered he had better go run over and look at it he wasn't reassured. It wasn't a dud. He had looked at enough diagrams and sketches to know. It was a time bomb—and a big one.

He told all this to his chief in his report a minute later.

"Where is it?" inquired his chief.

"In the garden," said Jock.

Then the same order:

"Get people out, empty nearby houses and keep people away!"

"Yes, sir," said Jock Evans.

Maybe it might be as well to mention here something of the nature of a time bomb, especially for Americans, who so far haven't had much experience with such things.

In the first place, it is not like the old-type torpedo with nose fuse which could be unscrewed by a handy man with a monkey wrench. This is more complicated. The timing device is a simple interior arrangement of acid working on metal.

By varying the thickness of the metal density, the acid rate of corrosion may be set for anything between one minute and one month. Eventually the acid reaches the fulminating charge and the neighborhood goes to pieces.

There have been some hints that in what followed after his report to control Jock didn't show any great judgment, but the same might have been said of Dewey if he had run into a mine in Manila Bay. He followed out his orders. In less than an hour he had evacuated the few homes in the immediate vicinity. Then he stationed himself to warn off traffic.

There wasn't much to do until about 7 o'clock in the morning, when workers and sight-seers began to pass afoot, on bicycles, and in automobiles.

The odd feature of a community which is being continuously bombed is the inquisitive interest in lethal hazards. Jock Evans suddenly found himself alone in a two-man job. The bomb lay almost at the junction of two lanes, giving access to it from four directions.

Mr. Evans solved this problem as best he could. He roped off the street a hundred yards behind the bomb then took up his post at the middle of the crossing.

Dozens of persons heard and heeded his call during the next two hours: "Time bomb here. Keep away, keep away."

One of those who passed was the priest of the neighborhood Anglican church, to whom is owing the best description of Jock Evans' last stand.

"He hardly needed to point out the bomb," said the padre. "It was lying there in a grass plot right behind him, and it was evident he knew all about it. His face was white and drawn, but there wasn't any tremor in his voice. I couldn't get it out of my head, as he sang out the warning and blew his whistle, that he was the psychological equivalent of the medieval leper, ringing his bell and shouting 'Unclean, unclean.'

"I had told him to get away from the corner, block off the streets with ropes. But he said, 'My duty is to stay here. Please go on, sir; don't set a bad example.' I went to telephone for help."—

The bomb went off at 9:10 blew a crater forty feet wide. No trace has been found of Evans.

The *Jervis Bay*: Tania Long Tells How a British Liner Sails Gloriously into Hopeless Battle Against a German Pocket Battleship and Thereby Saves Convoy HX 84

[November 5, 1940]

"Still her last remaining gun could be heard barking defiantly between the thunderous explosions of the raider's heavy guns."

On that early November evening Convoy HX 84 was steaming slowly and silently over the Atlantic. There were thirty-eight ships in the convoy, including eleven tankers, all zigzagging in nine parallel lines to Britain. Aboard were priceless cargoes of food, machinery and oil, the lifeblood of war.

Suddenly, into the midst of this great convoy sailed the powerful Admiral Scheer, *a 10,000-ton, thirty-knot pocket battleship, pride of Hitler's navy. For the German raider the three dozen freighters were sitting ducks. It would all be over very soon.*

Sole guardian and escort for the convoy was the Jervis Bay. *Neither in-appearance nor in fact could she inspire confidence in the seamen she was supposed to protect. An old passenger and cargo vessel of Australian ancestry, she was called an "armed cruiser." But she was a poor excuse for a man-of-war.*

But the Jervis Bay *sailed into hopeless battle against the powerful German battleship, thereby enabling the convoy to flee to safety. The story was told a few days later by Tania Long of the New York* Herald Tribune. *Miss Long missed one important angle—the gallantry of Captain Fogarty Fegen of the* Jervis Bay. *A big, tough, forty-seven-year-old Irish bachelor, son of an admiral, Captain Fegen went down with his ship. In a brief hour he won for himself a posthumous Victoria Cross as well as a reputation that will long be remembered in Britain for courage and defiance.*

91

(*New York* Herald Tribune, *November 13, 1940. By permission of the New* York Herald Tribune.)

LONDON, November 12—Sinking and afire from stem to stern but with her guns blazing to the last, the 14,164-ton armed British merchant cruiser *Jervis Bay* fought a German warship at dusk last Tuesday and enabled a convoy of thirty-eight merchantmen to scatter.

Twenty-nine of the freighters escaped and twenty-four reached a British port today. The fate of the nine others is uncertain. All may have been sent to the bottom after the destruction of the *Jervis Bay*.

The battle took place in the North Atlantic, 1,000 miles from America. The Nazi raider is believed to have been one of the 10,000-ton pocket battleships, the *Admiral Scheer*, or the *Lützow*, formerly the *Deutschland*.

Among the surviving vessels were the 16,698-ton motor liner *Rangitiki* and the 4,951-ton *Cornish City*, whose distress signals last week were the first indications that a raider was active in the shipping lanes of the North Atlantic.

The German high command said the entire convoy had been destroyed, but the *Jervis Bay*, fighting as gallantly as the armed merchant cruiser *Rawalpindi* had done against the *Deutschland* last winter, sacrificed herself to allow nearly three-fourths of the vessels to escape in the gathering gloom.

Details of the action were told by some of the men, who, aboard the freighters in convoy, watched the *Jervis Bay* steaming out from the line to meet the powerful raider. In peace time the *Jervis Bay* sailed between England and Australia carrying freight and the poorest classes of immigrants.

British and foreign vessels in the convoy, eyewitnesses recounted, followed one another across the calm sea. It had been a perfect day. Just as darkness was gathering the silence was shattered by a distant explosion. Then came the scream of a shell from below the horizon. It fell a few yards from a ship.

The shell was followed by another. Soon the silhouette of a warship emerged and the firing grew more intense. Immediately the order to scatter was given and, as the ships obeyed, the raider began to concentrate on the *Rangitiki*, the largest vessel in the convoy.

The raider stood off about seven or eight miles as she poured shell after shell in the direction of the *Rangitiki*. Suddenly, when it seemed that the merchantman could no longer escape the devastating fire, the *Jervis Bay* steamed straight out in front of her, turned slightly and raced toward the attacking warship.

The crew of the *Jervis Bay* must have known that she stood little chance against the raider's superior armament, but they manned their guns and blazed away furiously, drawing away fire from the *Rangitiki*.

As the convoy ships disappeared one by one into the safety of the night, the *Jervis Bay* fought grimly on. The battle did not last long. The *Jervis Bay*, battered from stem to stern, began to burn. Soon she was blazing. Still her last remaining gun could be heard barking defiantly between the thunderous explosions of the raider's heavy guns.

Full details on what happened then are not available. The Admiralty said that nearly two hours after the beginning of the engagement an explosion was seen aboard the *Jervis Bay*.

A British captain of one of the convoy ships, interviewed on landing today, said he thought the raider was a pocket battleship and believed the shells were fired from eleven-inch guns.

Coventry: Massive *Luftwaffe* Attack on the Midlands Manufacturing City as Seen From German and Allied Sides

[November 15, 1940]

The unstable Fuehrer *was infuriated by the reaction of Londoners to the attacks of his* Luftwaffe. *Why wouldn't those* verdammte *Englishmen give up like the people of Warsaw or Rotterdam? What was holding them up? Frustrated, he turned to the ports of Dover, Bournemouth, Portsmouth, Southampton. Then, in November 1940, he shifted his attention to the industrial Midlands.*

On the night of November 15, 1940, Hitler ordered a devastating attack on Coventry. Some ninety-four miles northwest of London, Coventry stood on a small hill at the confluence of several tributaries of the Avon. The home of a beautiful cathedral, this city of 200,000 people was also a manufacturing center where munitions and war materials took precedence over such industries as making motor cars, art-metal work, iron-founding and woolens. As such it became a top priority target for the Luftwaffe, *to which it became a fair target in war.*

Coventry suffered heavily from Hitler's attack from the air. Many lost their lives; houses as well as factories were wrecked; essential services were paralyzed. The men of the Royal Air Force who later struck back at German cities never forgot Coventry.

The assault on Coventry was witnessed from a Luftwaffe *plane by an anonymous German war correspondent whose report is reprinted here. The second selection records the attack as witnessed by Alfred Wall, Associated Press foreign correspondent.*

THE ATTACK ON COVENTRY

("Der Angriff an Coventry," in Fahrten und Flüge gegen England, Berichte und Bilder, *herausgegeben vom Oberkommando der Wehrmacht [Berlin, 1941], pp. 138–139. Courtesy of Zeitgeschichte Verlag. Translated by the editor.)*

"A little more to the right, just a bit more."

On the night of November 15, 1940, in good weather and in clear moonlight, squadrons of German aircraft made a massive attack on the English armaments center of Coventry in the Midlands. In the late evening hours the devastating effects of countless bombs could be seen in the industrially important installations of the city. The roaring attacks continued without pause until early in the morning.

Coventry—how often has this city in the heart of England been the target of individual attacks by our flyers! In good and in bad weather. In the area of this city and its sister cities of Birmingham and Wolverhampton important factories of the English armaments industry have been hit. Here tools and motors were made for British aircraft.

The night was in full moon as we came to the ready room. We had an idea that our job this time was something special. The group commander began by giving us in the beginning in brief but precise words all necessary navigational and technical weather details. This attack, he says, must be an extraordinary success for our air force. Painfully accurate flying by our own pilots and careful bombing are of the greatest importance on this mission.

Our "Caesar," heavily loaded with bombs, is the first plane of its group to get away. It takes course for England. We all know that a long, difficult flight is before us. Fortunately, the storms that had bothered us in the last few nights had disappeared. Through clear skies, some clouds, and light haze we fly toward the English coast. In this favorable weather, cities, rivers, and canals are good signposts.

We are greeted by flak on the coast. Searchlights poke excitedly through the darkness. But we hold true to our course. Our first test through the enemy flak is soon behind us. From a fair distance we recognize the London area. Other planes must have already made their visits there. There are clouds of smoke over the city and we can see the flash of exploding bombs on the ground. From a great height we can see the curve of the Thames. A cupola of lights rises up to meet us, and the first shells burst near us. But we hold our bombs— they are destined for another target that evening.

It has become very quiet in the plane. In the enclosed stall and in the canopy men study the maps by the dull lights of their little pocket flashlights. We are surrounded by deep black night. When the Midlands come into view, the game begins again with the searchlights and the antiaircraft guns.

A cry of surprise. Far to the north of us there is a tremendous fire. Is that Coventry already? That is our target—the great fire before us must be the work of our comrades who had flown in before us. Over the burning city many trace-bombers hang in their parachutes for minutes.

The picture is becoming clearer. German bombs must have caused tremendous damage in these hours before midnight. Conversation in the plane stops. We go to the attack. Calmly the commander gives the pilot his flight directions: "A little more to the right, just a bit more. So, now we are just right."

We come closer and closer. The terrible picture comes into focus. Thick smoke hovers over the city far out into the country. We can clearly see the flames crackling. An especially large burst of flame near countless others shows that a great industrial area must have been heavily hit.

We remain over the target. Flak is shot desperately at us. Around us the lightning of exploding shells.

We look directly into the destruction and see the great craters of fire and the greater part of the industrial city in flames. At this moment we release our bombs. A shudder goes through the plane. Down below there is a brilliant flash in a new explosion. We are the first plane in our group of German fighter planes; others were there before us. Others will follow until the dawn of the new day, which will reveal the extent of the attack on Coventry.

COVENTRY SHATTERED

(Alfred Wall, Associated Press, November 15, 1940. By permission of Associated Press.)

"In Coventry tonight frenzied men tore at piles of brickwork and concrete covering the bodies of their women and children."

COVENTRY, ENGLAND, November 15—German bombers have blasted the heart out of this once peaceful city in the English midlands with a dusk-to-dawn raid which turned parts of the city into an inferno and left at least 1,000 dead and injured.

Coventry's beautiful and famous brownstone cathedral is a smoking wreck. Only its big main spire, 303 feet high, remains standing. All the rest of the medieval structure, started in 1373 and completed in 1450, lies in a tangle of broken stone and crumpled debris.

In a quick dash tonight into the still burning sector of the stricken town, a vital industrial center, I scrambled over great piles of brick and stone.

The town was like a scene out of Hades between dusk and dawn while German raiders dumped their bombs in ceaseless relays.

A full moon shone last night, but its brilliance was dimmed by a pall of smoke and the glare of fire from burning buildings.

Scarcely a street escaped the pounding of the raiders. It was the worst continuous attack experienced by any city—including London —since the siege of Britain began.

All night long, the narrow streets where Lady Godiva rode on her horse nearly 1,000 years ago trembled and crumbled with the thunder of diving planes, the screams of bombs and their explosions and the roar of anti-aircraft cannonade.

Searchlights stabbed vainly through the shroud of smoke in an attempt to spot the invaders. Rifles and machine guns crackled as the city's defenders tried to shoot scores of flares out of the sky.

At least two hospitals were hit. There were casualties in one; in another all glass was blown from the operating theatre.

Store after store was damaged, but authorities said that supplies were not affected materially and that there would be no food shortage.

The aeronautical expert of the press association also said the Germans "failed lamentably" to hit military targets.

Several other midlands towns were raided, and in one, 24 houses were demolished, 150 damaged extensively and a bomb dropped on a school shelter full of people.

In Coventry tonight frenzied men tore at piles of brickwork and concrete covering the bodies of their women and children.

Herbert Morrison, Minister of Home Security, came from London to direct the first relief efforts. With him came his wife.

The first thing they did was to halt a frightened caravan of refugees seeking safety in the country.

The awful experience of the night before was written in the pinched faces that peered at the Minister's limousine from trucks, wagons and automobiles.

Royal Air Force pilots took fire hoses from the hands of firemen reeling with fatigue, and played streams of water on the smoldering heaps of rubble which are all that remain of some of Britain's finest examples of Tudor architecture.

Dateline London: Rebecca West Describes a Day in Town During Hitler's Attempt to Smash Britain From the Air

[January, 1941]

"My God, you move fast for your age."

The behavior of Britons under German air assault was one of the wonders of the war. Newsmen from all over the globe who were there testify to the extraordinary courage of the civil population under assault, and especially to the great good humor of all classes as "old Hitler" sought to crush them.

The following piece written by Rebecca West is revealing. Traditional British traits—courage, modesty, humility—shine through the sentences of this report. This is British journalism at its best. Rebecca West is one of the all-time greats in the history of reporting. Here is the consistently superb reportorial artist.

("A Day in Town," The New Yorker, *January 25, 1941. Copyright © 1941* The New Yorker Magazine, Inc.)

Before I could leave with Mrs. Raven, who was going to drive me to the High Dashwood station, I had to chase our ginger cat, Pounce, and lock him into the pantry. This war has revealed cats as the pitiful things they are—intellectuals who cannot understand the written or spoken word. They suffer in air raids and the consequent migrations exactly as clever and sensitive people would suffer if they knew no history, had no previous warning of the nature of modern warfare, and could not be sure that those in whose houses they lived, on whose generosity they were dependent, were not responsible for their miseries. Had Pounce found himself alone in the house and free, he would probably have run out into the woods and not returned to the dangerous company of humans.

"Well, you've lost the eight-forty-seven," said Mrs. Raven, looking at her watch and chuckling. All the world over, the most good-natured find enjoyment in those who miss trains or sit down on frozen pavements.

"Yes, we've lost the eight-forty-seven," I said, with the proper

98

answering chuckle, and we loaded in the basket of vegetables I was taking up to my sister. We set off through the shining morning, with the sky an innocent blue over the thin gold plating of the stubble fields. But for the nests of sandbags and barbed wire at the turns in the lanes, it could have been pretended that England had not a trouble in the world. The Georgian red brick of High Dashwood was glowing rosily in the sunshine, the very color of contentment. And luck was with us, for a London train was waiting in the station.

"What train is this?" I asked a porter, looking at my watch. It was twenty to ten.

"The eight-forty-seven," he answered.

There were two men in the compartment I took, London office workers who had come down to stay the night with relatives in High Dashwood because their homes were in the heavily bombed areas of south London and they had felt the need of a night's unbroken sleep. "One night in five I must have my rest," said the one, "so my old auntie looks for me Monday, and then Saturday again, and so on." "I can't get that many," said the other, "what with being in the Home Guard and all." They compared notes on the easiest way of getting from point to point in the City, avoiding the damaged tube stations and the roped-off areas. "Ah, but you hadn't thought of Porkpie Passage. Never even heard of it, I shouldn't wonder," the one said triumphantly, but broke off because, while the train was standing at a station, we heard the wail of an air-raid warning. "They're late this morning," he said, and shook his pipe at the window. "There's a pretty sight for you," he said. From an airdrome behind some houses, a squadron of fighters was rising in battle formation, as precisely aligned and synchronized as an ideal *corps de ballet*.

Nothing worried these two very much, I gathered, except the delay in the mails, which, they said, showed faulty organization, not to be excused by the present circumstances. "Ought to be able to do better than that," one of them said, "considering things haven't been so bad, really." They were still grumbling about it when we reached our terminus, which was looking more cheerful than I had ever known it. This was because all the smoke-dimmed glass had gone and the sunshine was pouring in through the iron ribs. There were no taxis in the station, as it had been impossible to sweep up all the finer splinters of glass, so I carried the vegetable basket till I got clear of the building, and then set it down at a street corner and looked round for a taxi. The streets about seemed oddly empty. I assumed that there had been a bad raid the night before and that people were not yet about again.

Across an otherwise trafficless patch of street, I saw a taxi, which had just deposited its fares at a house in a side street and was driving off. I ran to catch it, and while I was running the all-clear sounded. That is why I did not hear the shouts of a young policeman who was running after me and presently caught me by the arm. "You're running straight toward a time bomb," he said. "Can't you see that notice?" "No," I said, and then I mentioned a fact that had always before seemed to be not a disadvantage but, rather, a shield from unnecessary distractions. "I'm so short-sighted that I can't read notices," I said. "Get yourself some spectacles then," he said, and wiped his brow. "My God," he breathed, "you move fast for your age."

I carried the vegetables for another block, and found myself in a crowded street. Everyone wore the expression characteristic of people in a raided town. It is not unlike the look on the faces of pregnant women. It is as if they were drained of their strength by a condition against which there can be no rebellion and of which they are not ashamed. I found a taxi, which took me by roundabout ways to the square where my husband and I live. Down one of the streets I saw a house where I have often dined, its whole front laid open and its familiar wallpapers brightly lining its nothingness.

Before our apartment house the janitors stood pale and heavy-eyed. The one who took the basket out of the taxi said, "A bomb fell in the square gardens last night, but only on the soft earth. Nobody was hurt and the glass hasn't gone." The old man who took us up in the elevator said, "Did you know that John Lewis's has gone? It's gutted, gutted to the ground floor, and I nearly died of it. Just listen what happened to me. You know, me and my wife live at 8 Harley Street—we're caretakers there now all the doctors there have gone into the Army. Well, what would my wife do but every night put on her hat and go out to the shelter under John Lewis's. I often reasoned with her about it. 'What's the good of doing that?' I said. 'What's the good of going to a great store like that, which sticks its head up and asks to be bombed? Why not stay here, in a house that's just a house, among a thousand just the same as itself?' But she would have her way, and away she'd go every evening as soon as the sirens went. And last night she'd gone off as usual, and I was sitting in our basement snug as could be, and all of a sudden I heard one of those awful bombs, and I said, 'Sure as knife's knife, that's over by John Lewis's and I ran out into the street, and there I saw it blazing, and I hared along to the shelter, the way

I haven't since I was a boy, and I said to the chap at the door of the shelter, 'Look here,' I said, 'look here, my wife's down there,' and he said, 'What if she is? They're all coming out now,' and, believe me or not, she was the very last to come out, and when she comes along, I said to her, 'Well, where's your new rug and your new cushion what I bought you for the shelter yesterday?,' and she said, 'Oh, I was so upset I couldn't think of anything like that,' and of course I couldn't be angry with her, being so glad she was all right, but of course we'll never see them again, though I've asked. But this morning, after breakfast, I said to her, 'Now you've got to go down to your sister at Chipping Norton as quick as we can put you on a train,' and I sent her off at half past eight, for there's some people that can't cope with emergencies, and though she's been as good a wife as I could wish, I don't feel she's been sensible, not over these air raids."

Inside my apartment, I looked at my shopping list with distaste. I had meant to buy some more blackout lampshades, some extra parts of a dinner service, and some electric-light fittings, all from John Lewis's, and I did not know where else I would get them. I would have to find somebody who could tell me which stores had been bombed and which hadn't. But first I had to hurry off to deliver the vegetables at my sister's apartment. She is a lawyer, and she lives in one of those old Inns, as they are still called, which are inhabited chiefly by lawyers. She lives on the top two floors of the tall Regency house where Charles Dickens once worked as an office boy. I carried the basket of vegetables up the four flights, and the door was opened by the Austrian Jewish refugee, a friend of my sister's, who does the housework, a colored handkerchief about her head, a broom in her hand. She was a doctor of philology and had been a happy and patient scholar in the field of medieval poetry. Now the opportunity to handle a broom represented an unhoped-for run of good luck. She murmured, "*Ach, die gute Gemüse!* We are so glad of them, for it is so hard to do shopping now. Whenever I take the basket and go out, the warning goes and all the shops shut, and when the all-clear goes I am sure to be making jam or seeing one of the refugees from your sister's committee."

At that moment, the warning went, and I fled. All over London, when sirens go, people spring apart. If the warning finds one too far from home, one may be forced to take refuge in a public shelter and waste precious hours, and when the all-clear sounds, one runs out to take advantage of the fact that the shops and post offices are open. My taxi whirled me homeward through poorer quarters than I had yet seen that day, where the damage had an unchivalrous air. At a corner, a rag-and-bone shop and three stories of frowsty lodgings over it were still recognizable for what they had been, but were twisted like barley sugar. It seemed unnecessarily presumptuous of the Germans to spoil what had, in its essence, never been unspoiled. During the latter part of the journey, I made myself dizzy by swivelling round to look out of the back window to see, against the blue sky, the trails of exhaust fumes which marked a fight between a German and an English plane.

At home, the butler gave me a lunch of coffee, tinned tongue, and bread and jam, which I ate off a tray in the lounge, with machine guns tapping at each other somewhere overhead. I wondered how, with so much going on, I was to get up to Hampstead, where I was to have a conference with a friend who owns a paper of which I am one of the editors. But the telephone rang, and it was my friend. She had left Hampstead and gone to her house in the country for the excellent reason that there was a time bomb in her Hampstead garden. We settled a matter about book-reviewing. Then the all-clear sounded and I ran out to find lampshades otherwhere than John Lewis's, to change my books at the Times Book Club, and to buy a chest of drawers I had seen in a shop window and needed for the country house.

Back in my apartment, I found my husband sitting in the lounge. He had three days' holiday before him and was to drive me back to the country. I thought he was looking rather pale, and I asked him if anything was the matter. He said, "Yes, it has all been very unfortunate. When I got to the Ministry this morning, I found that the whole front porch had been blown up and that you had to go in at the back entrance. And I was not unhappy about this till, in the middle of the day, I suddenly learned what everybody had supposed I knew: that Black, one of my colleagues whom I got on with best, an older man whom I liked and respected, with whom I had had a lot of pleasant talk, had been killed by the blast."

The butler brought us tea and said, "I was wondering if I might keep this as a souvenir, seeing that it fell in the kitchen." He held out to us a piece of shrapnel the size of a man's hand. "But did it not smash the windows to smithereens?" I asked. "It made a hole exactly its own size," he replied, "but the splintered glass held. That varnish we painted the windows with seems very serviceable."

While we were drinking our tea, my husband said, "Are those two women ready?" For we were taking down not only the housemaid but the cook. "I can hear them packing up things in the kitchen," I said. "What things?" he asked. "Oh, china, cruets, boot-polishing kits—all sorts of oddments we had forgotten in the hurried move to the country," I said. "Well, we had better take down something of the things we really value," he said. "What would you like to take?"

We looked round the lounge without much interest. "Let us go through the whole flat and look at what we have," I said, and we pushed back the tea table and walked through our rooms. Everything we saw seemed a victim of a sudden, irreparable depreciation of value. It was no longer worth its price, because of the people who lay dead under the whorled laths and plaster of a hundred rag-and-bone shops. It was sometimes distressing, because of other, less corporeal deaths. We have a Rembrandt drawing, a minute, cunning, loving piece of magic, a few strokes of a pencil which show, receding into an immense distance, mile upon mile upon mile of Holland. We have a Dufy that shows Burgundy as it is after the vines have been sprayed with copper sulphate, a blue land, deep bright blue, delphinium blue. They had become portraits of enslaved countries, unvisitable, dangerous.

Nothing in the apartment was now as dear to me as the few fields we owned in the country, as our haystacks, as our Jersey cows, or the bullocks we are fattening for the market. Yet, when we opened the drawing-room door and saw the long, narrow Empire table which throughout my married life has stood in front of the window, I felt all my muscles go tense. "What has happened to it?" I asked. "What has happened to it?" Each of the three panels that made up its top bulged unevenly, as if forced apart by some inner strain. Its two wide legs were thrusting clumsily outward, and the bar that joined them was ready to drop out of its sockets. I went up and touched it, and saw that every joint was gaping. Nothing had hit it, but it stood there like something dead and unspeakably mangled. Under the gentlest blow, this honestly and beautifully made article of furniture would have fallen to pieces on the floor. I felt a sick yet distant anger that was extreme and not quite my own, an anger that might have been felt by the long-dead cabinetmaker who had made this table. Behind me, the butler said, "It was like that when I came in this morning. I understand several people have noticed that the furniture under their windows has been affected like this. It has something to do with the vibrations from the blasts." Beyond the table, through the obscuring varnish on the windowpanes, I could see London, veiled by the smoke that was still rising from the ruins of John Lewis's store.

Rats of Tobruk: Jan H. Yindrich, United Press, Tells How the Australians Used Bayonets Against Unwilling Nazis

[April 17, 1941]

"He was the only bloke who showed any fight."

In late March 1941 the powerful Afrika Korps *under a competent leader, Field Marshal Erwin Rommel, launched an attack against the Allies in North Africa, and soon pushed them back into Egypt. Behind them at Tobruk the British left a lone Australian division. The Australians turned out to be a thorn in the German flank. Rommel lost precious time and strength in his effort to dislodge the self-styled "rats of Tobruk." The reluctance of German troops to fight against cold bayonets was depicted in this dispatch by Jan H. Yindrich for United Press.*

(New York *World-Telegram, April 17, 1941. By permission of United Press International.*)

WITH THE BRITISH EMPIRE GARRISON BESIEGED AT TOBRUK, April 14 (Via Cairo and London, Delayed)—Australian infantrymen, British artillerymen and machine gunners and Royal Air Force pilots are beating back attack after attack by German tank, armored car and infantry forces on this outpost more than 80 miles behind the Axis lines in the Libyo-Egyptian frontier.

Every weapon, from dive bombers to bayonets, is being used. The Germans are attacking persistently and in great force.

They have attacked under cover of darkness and under cover of blinding, searing sand and dust storms.

Their tanks have been stopped and their infantrymen have been routed by the bayonets of the Australians. . . .

"My opinion of the Germans now is that in hand-to-hand fighting they are on a par with the Italians," an Australian told me after he had led a bayonet charge against them. "In a scrap where it is every

104

man for himself they go to pieces, perhaps because they are trained so well. . . ."

A 23-year-old Australian, who took part in two days' fighting, a former traveling salesman from Sydney, was one of a patrol of seven who routed 40 Germans and brought back one prisoner.

"About 300 German infantrymen, supported by tanks, had made five attacks on our part of the line," he said. "Then about 40 Germans got inside our wire. I took six men with me, in order not to weaken our post too much.

"We were under German machine-gun fire and we went out at the double. We lay down about 100 yards from the Germans. Our people were blazing away over our heads. Then we tore into them with the bayonet. I got the shock of my life, because not one of them wanted to fight. They had machine guns and automatic rifles, but none of them stood by his gun.

"I bayoneted four of them myself and my bayonet stuck in the fifth. He was the only bloke who showed any fight. He grabbed my rifle and pulled me down on him. Another Jerry was coming up behind me but my corporal saved my life. He finished the German off.

"I bashed several other Germans over the head with the butt of my rifle till it broke. Then I picked up a stone. Thinking it was a hand grenade, the remainder of them groveled. One of them shouted: 'Peace, it is peace,' and then in French, 'S'il vous plaît'—'if you please.'

"I must have killed about twelve of them altogether."

Nazi Icarus: Rudolf Hess Parachutes to Field in Scotland After 800-Mile Flight to Warn British

[May 10, 1941]

"The most extraordinary flight of this or any other war."

Rudolf Hess, No. 3 Nazi, was a stiff, dark-haired, beetle-browed man with deep-set, staring eyes. His star rose with Hitler's. Eventually, he became Deputy Fuehrer, *Leader of the Nazi Party, Member of the Secret Cabinet Council for Germany, Reich Minister without Portfolio, and Member of the Ministerial Council for the Defense of the Reich. As deputy to Hitler he could make decisions in the name of the Leader. He was at Hitler's side as aggression was plotted against Austria, Czechoslovakia and Poland.*

After the war broke out, the puppylike Hess, who had been deliriously happy in the shadow of his Fuehrer, *was gradually pushed into the background. He fretted and fumed about his bad luck. Would it not be wonderful if he, the devoted servant, could win back his beloved Leader by a magnificent act of sacrifice? It was a terrible tragedy, he thought, for Germans and British, blood brothers, Aryans all, to fight one another. He would fly alone to England, make peace with the British cousins, and get them to join in the war which Hitler intended to wage soon on the Russians.*

Hess's flight was an overnight sensation, but it was a complete failure. The British, instead of being overwhelmed by his act of generosity, merely put him in prison. Winston Churchill later said:

> Whatever may be the moral guilt of a German who stood near to Hitler, Hess has, in my view, atoned for this by his devoted and frantic deed of lunatic benevolence. He came to us of his own free will, and, though without authority, has something of the quality of an envoy. He was a medical and not a criminal case, and should be so regarded.

Hess's behavior at the Nuremberg trial after the war proved that Churchill was correct in his appraisal. The No. 3 Nazi had undergone a mental collapse.

106

(*Associated Press, May 13, 1941. By permission of Associated Press.*)

LONDON, Tuesday, May 13—Rudolf Hess, No. 3 Nazi and high in German war councils, has parachuted to safety in Scotland after a fantastic, forbidden warplane flight from the Reich, where his disappearance has been reported with the official comment that he suffered from "hallucinations."

Circumstances surrounding the 800-mile flight by Adolf Hitler's closest confidante suggested that Hess deliberately had deserted the Nazi camp.

Unarmed and unresisting, he floated down last Saturday to a Scottish farm field where a farmer armed with a pitchfork awaited him. Suffering a broken ankle, but appearing in good humor, Hess was removed to a Glasgow hospital.

An official from the British Foreign Office sped to Glasgow from London to interview Hess, who, in coming to England, defied Hitler's long-standing rule barring Hess from flying.

Hess was quoted as saying that he had intended to land his Messerschmitt plane but was unable to find a suitable spot, and then stalled it for a crash as he bailed out.

Hours after Britain's official announcement of his parachute landing the German wireless ignored the London report, merely broadcasting the original official German announcement that Hess was missing and had left a confusing letter which suggested he was suffering mentally.

While the British statement did not specifically say that he had deserted, it made three observations of seeming inescapable significance:

That Hess had brought along photographs taken at varying years in his life to establish his identity if it were questioned.

That he had arrived in a plane which could not possibly have had enough gasoline for a return to Germany—and thus, inferentially, that his trip was clearly not a one-man offensive but a one-way flight.

That the Messerschmitt's guns were empty.

This most extraordinary flight of this or any other war was disclosed in London a few hours after the Germans in Berlin had announced that Hess—Hitler's political heir but once removed—was missing, that he presumably had taken a forbidden plane flight and had cracked up, that he appeared to have been suffering "hallucinations" and had "left behind a confused letter."

The magnitude of his determination to escape was indicated in another way, for he left behind his wife Ilse, whom he married in

1927, and their 3-year-old son. What their fate will be depends on Adolf Hitler.

The story of Hess' 800-mile strange and lonely flight to England, as told in the Government's announcement from Downing street, showed that he first crossed the Scottish coast last Saturday night.

He flew on in the direction of Glasgow and later—just when was not disclosed—he bailed out. His Messerschmitt crashed. Taken to the Glasgow hospital he first identified himself as "Horn," but later by his correct name.

The announcement issued here said:

"Rudolf Hess, the deputy Führer of Germany and party leader of the National Socialist party, has landed in Scotland in the following circumstances:

"On the night of Saturday, the tenth, a Messerschmitt 110 was reported by our patrol to have crossed the coast of Scotland and to be flying in the direction of Glasgow.

"Since the Messerschmitt 110 would not have fuel to return to Germany this report was at first disbelieved.

"Later on a Messerschmitt 110 crashed near Glasgow. Shortly afterward a German officer, who had bailed out, was found with his parachute in the neighborhood suffering from a broken ankle.

"He was taken to a hospital in Glasgow where he at first gave his name as Horn but later on he declared that he was Rudolf Hess.

"He brought with him various photographs of himself at different ages apparently in order to establish his identity.

"These photographs were deemed to be photographs of Hess by several people who knew him personally. Accordingly, an officer of the Foreign Office who was closely acquainted with him before the war has been sent up by airplane to see him in the hospital."

So fantastic was his solo flight out of the Reich that the British themselves, after thorough identification of their hostage, announced it only late tonight, two days after he landed in Scotland, and they were still openly at a loss over what to make of it.

If Hess should talk he could lay bare to the British the entire framework of their Nazi enemy—information of inestimable value.

The announcement made the identification positive by referring to him as "Rudolf Hess, the deputy Führer of Germany and party leader of the National Socialist party."

Subsequently, the Ministry of Information declared that he had been identified as Rudolf Hess beyond "all possible doubt."

Conquest of Crete: A German Report on the First Airborne Invasion in History

[May 20, 1941]

"It was a raging hell."

As soon as they had all Greece, the Germans prepared to invade Crete. That island, like Malta, seemed safe for the Allies, protected as it was by the Royal Navy centered at Alexandria and by a substantial garrison. In addition, many of the troops who had been evacuated from Greece were added to the island's defending force. Major General Bernard C. Freyberg, a competent New Zealander, was assigned to command the island garrison.

Hitler was determined to take the island. He ordered the Luftwaffe *to bomb the harbor of Suda and the three Cretan airfields. On May 20, 1941, German paratroopers swarmed over the island in the first great airborne invasion in history. They quickly seized Maleme airfield. On the third and fourth days the Royal Navy frustrated German seaborne landings. But parachuting Germans, including the former heavyweight boxing champion of the world, Max Schmeling, dropped onto Crete in such numbers that the British position became hopeless. It was all over in ten days. The Royal Navy succeeded in evacuating 17,000 Empire troops.*

In the following report the Frankfurter Zeitung *described the fighting during the first two days.*

(Frankfurter Zeitung, *June 21, 1941. Courtesy of the* Frankfurter Zeitung. *Translated by the editor.*)

CNOSSUS ON CRETE—In the early hours of May 20 the motors of the Junkers transport planes are heard for the first time directly over the central and western portions of the island. The doors open. Many thousands of dead-tired troopers hurtle into the air, their chutes open, and like inflated sails they glide with their living freight down toward the ground.

The assault from the air on this island fortress was made at four separate places—at Erakleion (Candia), at Rethymno, at the main city of Canea, and to the west at Maleme airfield. Few Germans, few even among the paratroopers, have ever heard of these places. But those names were to burn themselves during the last two weeks into the hearts of the soldiers. They were the spots of heaviest combat. Those names will glow for centuries.

People talk about the "mathematical precision" of German victories. How foolish! But nowhere is it more silly than in connection with Crete. Missions can be planned with extreme care, but at the critical moment what counts most are the courage and ability of the combat troops and the fixity of purpose of the leadership. Many German paratroopers were caught while in the air in a hail of British defensive fire. Others, even after a gentle glide through the air or after a hard fall on foreign soil, and then after freeing themselves from the shrouds of their chutes, had to face the fire of the enemy.

It was a raging hell. Worst of all was the terror of the unknown into which the troops had jumped after the doors of their craft opened. But not a single one hesitated. Not one made the next man wait. Head over heels they tumbled into space down to the gray sand and into the glowing lightning of enemy fire.

Out of the sky into mortal danger they storm—the general as well as the junior officer and trooper, the staff physician as well as the mechanic. They cling to the good earth they have won and with their tommy guns they strike back at the enemy. They rush to the weapons that have come down by parachute and then defend themselves against the fire of the numerically superior enemy. Thus, it went on all that long Tuesday morning, the long afternoon, all through the night, and again the following morning.

Many things happened all at once. Reinforcements came out of the air, and to them the dead-tired comrades made their way. But they were outmanned and the pressure of the enemy became stronger and stronger. The sun shone pitilessly on the bare stones. There was little water. Many had no water at all. Their tongues stuck to the roofs of their mouths, their throats were parched. They lay on the open slopes or on the shore of Maleme. Enemy shells exploded among them. Their own artillery was far away in Greece.

The dead lay silent on the ground. Others who were wounded called for medical orderlies and for water.

Then came the night, the long, lonely night. Here and there groups of ten or twelve huddled together. The burning heat of the day gave way to a cutting cold. All knew that the next morning would be as hot as the preceding one. They would be thirsty again. Tired and exhausted, they would have to face a fresh and rested enemy. Yet—and all knew it—they could not give in. They would starve and thirst and fight until they won the victory.

The individual fighters knew little about the general situation. Each one had his own enemy in front of him, with whom he had to settle accounts—whether it was an Australian or a New Zealander or whether it was thirst and heat or cold and hunger. That German soldier knew only that he had to hold out and that he had to have continuing faith in his leadership.

On the morning of the second day this was the situation: the para-troopers held the edges of the airfields at Candia and Rethymno. Both airfields, as well as both cities, were in British hands. Other paratroopers were in front of the main city of Canea. But to the west most of the airfield of Maleme was in German possession. The taking of this airfield was the happiest event of that first day. The outcome of the entire battle depended on this coup.

But thus far it was all inconclusive. Even now no German plane could land in Maleme without danger, for the strip was covered with enemy fire. More—the big guns of the British in the south were plastering Maleme with their shells. German aircraft accomplished wonders, destroying many British emplacements and scattering marching columns. Without the *Luftwaffe* the troops who had landed could not possibly have halted their foes on the ground. But the planes could not remain for long over Crete, and those British bat-teries were so strongly shielded that they could not be reached by bombs from the air.

As Wednesday morning dawned over Crete it became clear that the crisis was at hand. Germans had landed at more spots. The enemy was no longer surprised but he was at least put into disorder. The Germans had demonstrated their superiority in hand-to-hand fight-ing and above all they had won a precious airfield. But in this excit-ing moment that airfield could not be used for the landing of transport planes. British fire still covered the area.

On the second day more thousands of paratroopers jumped to reinforce the troops on the ground. They made the situation better by helping to counteract the pressure of the enemy. But the decision could not come from them. Everything depended on whether it would be possible to bring bigger army units to Crete. But any-one who that afternoon saw the shell-pocked and bomb-crippled airfield and the shores of Maleme could well doubt that it was pos-sible to bring in such reinforcements.

On the morning of May 21 Junkers planes circled over Maleme, the airfield below them covered with holes and piles of sand and stones. Even if they managed to land in that mess, they would not be able to take off again. The pilots had no other choice than to fly back. With heavy hearts they turned their planes north and headed back to Greece. The Germans below, who had been fighting furiously, were now alone. With burning eyes they watched the planes disappear.

How long would it be before help came? They did not know. They knew only that they had to hold on.

Then came bad news about the fate of the sea squadrons. Mountain troops were to be brought in by motor boats. But the day went by and they did not appear. Only later was it learned that a British cruiser had come across the boats and had scattered them. Some 200 of these mountain troops and seamen lost their lives, but most of them were rescued.

Perhaps in few engagements has the steadfastness of the German soldier been demonstrated as well as in this one. Among those saved was a group of 64 men who had taken to rubber boats. All these men stayed together as a unit under the blistering sun during the third day of the attack. Their boats were so overcrowded that they had to throw their clothes overboard. By accident they came across a Greek cutter, which they hailed and boarded. They reached Maleme, anyhow. But they brought more than only themselves and their will-power to the battle. They were "almost naked, but they had their weapons." They had never separated themselves from their guns and machine guns, even though shipwrecked. After a few hours they were ready and able to add their strength to that of their comrades.

In the history of war there are few examples as proud as this accurate account of the division's report . . . "almost naked, but with their weapons."

Meanwhile, the fate of Maleme and with it the outcome of the battle of Crete was being decided. On the afternoon of the second day the pilots of the transport planes were able to land a battalion of mountain troops on the airfield and the shores of Maleme. The big guns of the British still roared from the south, the field itself was still full of holes and rubble. But the pilots, threatened by instant death, nevertheless landed their precious cargo right in the middle of the airstrip with all its holes and stones. They had to make zigzag landings. Some, losing their momentum could not make it. That tiny spot was a veritable hell on earth.

But success came by that evening. At long last the first battalion of mountain troops was on Cretan soil.

Wehrmacht Attacks Russia: Combat Reporter Karl Heinz Seiss on the Opening Hours

[June 22, 1941]

"The German attack cannot be stopped."

June 22, 1941 was a fatal day in Adolf Hitler's life. It was too bad for him that his court astrologers did not point out the significance of that day on which he turned on Soviet Russia. He had not conquered the Near East and hence was not obtaining the oil he needed so badly for his tanks, planes and transports. He would get this vital life-blood for his war machine by conquering the Bolshevik rats. It would be pleasant to complete his crusade against Bolshevism.

Within a few hours Hitler's arch enemy, Winston Churchill, was broadcasting his reaction to the news. Terming the event "the fourth climacteric of the war," Britain's indomitable Prime Minister went on to say: "Any man or state who fights against Nazidom will have our aid. Any man or state who marches with Hitler is our foe."

Both Hitler and the German public expected a quick, knockout blow within a matter of weeks. In the following dispatch, Karl Heinz Seiss of the Frankfurter Zeitung *described the opening hours as he saw the action from a* Luftwaffe *plane.*

(Frankfurter Zeitung, *June 23, 1941. Courtesy of the* Frankfurter Zeitung. *Translated by the editor.*)

This combat unit, which since the liberation of the Rhineland, occupation of the protectorate, Austria and Poland, and the campaign in the West has taken part in every important military action, is now doing its share in the decisive struggle in the East.

Slowly the first rays of the dawn appear. On the airstrips the motors of the planes warm up. Then machine after machine make their way into the air and point their noses toward the east. Gradually, the German border gets closer. We can recognize troop movements, and star-shells—signals of our own troops—burst high into the air.

The attack against the enemy begins. There is the spot just below. A marvelous sight to see. On one side of the river is a great city, on the other side the harbor. Below us are many large hangars and at the edge of the airstrip, lined up as on parade, there is a mass of Soviet Russian fighter planes.

The bombs from our plane fall accurately with excellent results. Right on the nose! The enemy craft on the ground burst into flames, and the fires spring from one to the other. The other crews roar incessantly to the attack. Bomb after bomb falls.

Now defense activity becomes more active. Flak fire rises up. It begins to buzz like a hornet's nest. Russian fighter planes. But it is a desultory defense. The German attack cannot be stopped. The crews can see that under us another munitions depot has blown up. Thick smoke swirls and rises—a hit on a benzine or oil depot.

The sun is a blood-red ball on the horizon as the squadron makes its way home. Only two planes fail us. From the first comes word that because of motor failure it must make an emergency landing behind our lines, and the second makes a similar report. All the others are all right. One of our crew has been hit but, fortunately, it is only a light flesh wound.

Bombing of Moscow: Erskine Caldwell Sees the *Luftwaffe*'s Attempt to Smash the Russian Capital

[July 22, 1941]

"The chimes on the Kremlin clock struck a quarter-hour. It sounded as if it were coming from another world."

On July 22, 1941, just a month after German armies attacked Russia, the Luftwaffe *appeared in force over Moscow, the Russian capital. Hitler's fliers had been amazingly successful over Warsaw and Rotterdam, where they not only had caused tremendous material damage but had succeeded in striking terror into the hearts of the civilian population. They expected the same reaction at Moscow.*

They were badly mistaken. Present to record the story of the bombing of Moscow was an American novelist and short-story writer, Erskine Preston Caldwell, born in 1903. Caldwell was noted for his earthy stories of life among Southern sharecroppers and of Negro-white conflicts. An eye-witness of the Russian resistance to invasion by Germany, he wrote this striking report on the Luftwaffe *striking at Moscow.*

The bombing of Moscow began exactly one month after war started. The four million citizens of the city had been prepared for its coming by a series of practice air-raid alarms, and half an hour before the first explosive, a one-thousand-pounder, dropped in front of the Kremlin gates, practically everyone in the city was sitting in a shelter.

Everyone who was not in some way connected with air-raid defense was compelled to go to a shelter. The penalty for violating the order was fine and imprisonment. Few attempted to evade the law, thousands stood in line on the streets nightly waiting for shelters to open.

I went down into one of the subway shelters that first night and, along with several thousand others, was herded along the tracks deep into the tubes. Militiamen paced up and down along the catwalks ordering the people to sit down. No one was allowed to stand up or to move to another position once he had sat down. After an hour I decided to go up to see what was happening. I walked up the tracks to the station platform. A militiaman ordered me back. I protested, and said that I wanted to leave. He was as firm as a Soviet militiaman can be until I took out my night pass and showed it to him, saying something about being an American and having duties to perform even during air raids. The night pass was of no value during raids, a special raid pass being necessary for such times, but by talking fast and waving the night pass as though it were something that could not be ignored, I succeeded in getting past him. The next day I secured a raid pass, and I was never held in a shelter as long as I remained in Moscow.

The Germans dropped everything they could unload from two hundred planes that night, coming over the city in waves at half-hour intervals for five and a half hours. Thousands of fire bombs about the size and shape of prizewinning cucumbers were showered on buildings and streets. Weeks of training in fire-fighting had its results when city fire-fighting brigades and citizens posted on every roof of the city prevented Moscow from burning to the ground. As fast as the incendiaries fell they were snuffed out with sand or by dunking them into barrels of water which had been placed on top floors and rooftops. Occasionally a fire would get started, and its fiery red glow would flare up for a short time and then die down as it was brought under control.

During all this time explosive bombs were whistling downward, blasting into buildings and tearing craters in streets. The raid was directed at the entire city, the Kremlin not excepted, and for miles in all directions the sound of exploding bombs rocked and jarred the night. The hailstorm of fire bombs came down without letup for three hours, and the only times bombs were not falling were when the raiders, their racks empty, streaked back towards the west. There was only a short interval of time before a new wave of fully loaded planes came in from the northwest to dump their loads.

The air defense was in action continuously for those five and a half hours. Searchlights by the hundreds stabbed their beams into the sky, most of them being concentrated in a ring around the city. Anti-aircraft guns cracked and boomed all night long from another circle, filling the night with dazzling star-bursts. This city defense formed a complete circle around Moscow. The ring was about three miles deep, with alternating sections of searchlights and anti-aircraft artillery. The defense was concentrated five miles from the center of the city, and had a circumference of about fifty miles.

Inside the ring, which meant the greater portion of Moscow, machine-guns and lighter artillery were mounted on rooftops. These shot a continuous stream of fire at the low-flying Luftwaffe during its first raid. Tracer bullets that left streaks of red, yellow, or green in their wake crisscrossed the sky. A rapid-firing cannon that shot five shells in five seconds was used for close-range action. These big cannon rattled windows and made an ear-splitting noise that sounded as if the world were being blown to smithereens. The most dazzling sight of all was the shower of flaming onions, tracer shells that were fired from artillery. These flaming onions went up in strings of six, each one being a different color. The object of using this type of ground-fire was to enable gunners to trace the course of the large caliber shell aimed at the low-flying craft. It had twice the range of machine-gun tracer fire. In addition, the shells burst upon contact, whereas machine-gun bullets could merely penetrate.

For the first and only time, the Luftwaffe flew low over Moscow. The planes, when caught in searchlight beams, were usually at heights of about 1,000 feet, although I saw one plane, which looked like a huge silver moth, at five hundred feet. At the peak of the raid I saw a plane, caught in the web of five searchlight beams, suddenly nose-up and apparently come to a dead stop in the air. It had been hit by fire from one of the quick-shooting rooftop cannon. There was an explosion, the plane shook like a leaf in a storm, and a moment later it nosed down and plummeted to earth like a dead duck. Halfway down it burst, into flame. A moment later a parachute fluttered open and drifted slowly downward with a figure of a man dangling like a puppet from its harness. Just after the first parachute, a second one streaked downward, unopened. It fell like a stone in the street.

After the first two hours, the Germans apparently changed their tactics. Later waves of planes began dropping flares over the city, long strings of brilliant glows that lighted up the streets until newspaper print could be read on the bulletin boards on the sides of buildings. As the flares drifted slowly downward like feathers in still air, demolition bombs rained on the city. Not far from where I stood an oil bomb plowed into an apartment house, its liquid spraying the entire block. A yellowish glow sprang up instantly, and while the smoke and flame shot upward a cloud of debris peppered buildings several hundred feet away. The Germans overhead concentrated on the glow, releasing tons of explosives at the target they had made.

In the midst of all this there were no human sounds, except for the clatter of feet on tin roofs as fire brigades scampered over the buildings to get at incendiary fires. There were killed and wounded, but there was no sound of their voices. There were no shouts and yells, no excited cries. The people who were at work went about their duties with silent determination. Down in the streets only the militia and civilian fire defense workers were about. Red Army soldiers sat in shelters alongside civilians. The people in the shelters could hear the thuds and earth-rumbling explosions of five-hundred-, thousand-, and two-thousand-pound bombs, but they knew nothing of the fiery display above that turned Moscow's night as light as day.

Several times there were intervals of absolute calm when not a single sound could be heard anywhere. Once during one of these moments, the chimes on the Kremlin clock struck a quarter-hour. It sounded as if it were coming from another world.

But there were few such momentary lulls. The crashing of demolition bombs into buildings, the whine of machine-gun bullets, and the deafening bang-bang of rapid-fire cannon on the rooftops went on and on hour after hour. More parachute flares were dropped, most of them in the vicinity of the Kremlin, which evidently was one of the major targets of the Luftwaffe. Once in a while a plane dived down to within a few hundred feet of the rooftops as though seeking an objective. But they climbed back or ducked into clouds as soon as possible when ground-fire began ripping into them.

Most of the time the raiders were invisible. The slick oily drone of their motors never ceased. Even during momentary lulls of bombing, there were always several planes overhead, and after a while it was easy to gauge their height and direction accurately. The sound of their motors was an unending chorus against the crash of bombs.

Sinking of the *Barham*: Veteran A.P. Newsman Larry Allen Witnesses the Swift Death of a Great British Warship

[November 25, 1941]

"She wobbled over heavily, like some punch-drunk fighter."

The British battleship Barham, *built in 1915, had taken part in the Battle of Jutland in 1916. In the years of peace she sailed the Mediterranean much of the time on business for the British Empire. On November 25, 1941, came her rendezvous with death. Steaming grandly in a line of British warships in the Mediterranean off the Libyan coast, she was struck by four torpedoes. She sank within a few minutes.*

Aboard another battleship on that day was Larry Allen, a veteran Associated Press seagoing war correspondent attached to the British Mediterranean fleet. Allen wrote his eyewitness story on board the Queen Elizabeth *for transmission when the censor would permit it. The British Admiralty, for strategic reasons, withheld announcement of the* Barham's *loss until January 30, 1942.*

Meanwhile, Allen, on December 1, 1941, nearly lost his life when the cruiser Galatea *was torpedoed. He was hitch-hiking home by air to recuperate from injuries and the shock of a near drowning when his story of the* Barham *appeared in the world's press.*

(*Associated Press, November 25, 1941. By permission of Associated Press.*)

ABOARD THE BRITISH MEDITERRANEAN FLAGSHIP *Queen Elizabeth,* Nov. 25, 1941 (Delayed by Censor)—The British battleship *Barham,* struck by four torpedoes from an enemy submarine, exploded and sank within five minutes today off the Libyan coast.

I saw the *Barham* go down in a huge cloud of flame and smoke in one of the most spectacular scenes of the war.

The blast was so great that it was believed the attacking submarine may well have been destroyed by concussion.

The fleet was making a wide westward sweep in search of Axis

119

convoys when a single submarine made a daring daylight penetration of the destroyers screening the battleships.

At a range of 700 yards, the submarine fired its salvos, apparently at the *Queen Elizabeth.*

Just at that moment, this battleship made a quick zigzag, and the torpedoes sped on to strike the *Barham,* which was following closely in battle formation.

In the commander's cabin I heard the successive clanging crash of the torpedoes and raced to the upper deck.

The *Barham,* a 31,000-ton giant, already was listing heavily to port.

As I watched, she wobbled over more heavily, like some punch-drunk boxer.

From quarterdeck to forecastle, all along her starboard side, hundreds of men began leaping into the calm blue water that contrasted with the ruddy rays of the setting sun.

As the bodies struck the sea, they forced up little fountains which shone like diamonds.

Score after score of sailors plunged from the battleship. Soon I could see hundreds of heads bobbing above the surface. Some sailors managed to throw rubber floats down from the ship, upon which clambered dozens of men soon after they hit the water.

That all happened between 4:25 and 4:30 P.M., November 25. Executive officers of the *Barham* ordered: "Abandon ship!" Immediately afterward a heavy list developed and the *Barham* blew up at 4:30.

As the battleship *Valiant* veered away from the *Barham,* this flagship continued moving slowly eastward. The *Barham* was violently shaken by a series of blasts and burst into a great mass of flame and then was enveloped by a huge cloud of black smoke.

The air reeked with cordite fumes. Immediately with the explosions I saw huge sheets of armor plating, whole sections of the battleship, and the *Barham*'s big motor launch flung hundreds of feet into the air, falling with a loud smack into the sea dangerously near this battleship and the *Valiant.*

The tremendous compression of the air seemed to muffle the explosion.

All I felt aboard this battleship, which had pulled away about 1,000 yards distance was a brisk gust of air.

Then black smoke spread over so wide an expanse of sea that I no longer could see the men or rafts in the water.

From both sides of the *Queen Elizabeth* destroyers steamed full speed into the smoke that was the funeral pyre of one of Britain's greatest fighting ships.

They started picking up survivors and hunting the submarine simultaneously.

As the smoke drifted away, there was nothing to be seen of the *Barham*.

Within a few seconds of the explosion of her magazines, she had vanished. It had happened so quickly that it was difficult to believe what my own eyes had seen.

Five minutes previously, the *Barham* had been steaming majestically behind this flagship. Now she didn't exist.

Scores of officers and seamen of the *Queen Elizabeth* who had rushed on deck from a tea-time snack stood helplessly as they watched the *Barham* die in a matter of moments.

The busy destroyers picked up about 500 of the *Barham*'s 1,400 men, including Vice-Admiral Pridham Wippell, his secretary and twelve other officers.

The submarine apparently passed almost directly between the *Barham* and the battleship *Valiant* just after firing the torpedoes.

It was so close inboard that the explosion of the torpedoes forced it momentarily to the surface. Some of the officers aboard this battleship said they saw the conning tower bob above the water.

Then came the tremendous explosion of the *Barham*'s magazines, and several officers expressed belief that the submarine being so near, must have been crushed by the underwater concussion.

I was the only correspondent to witness the *Barham*'s finale. I shall never forget how bravely it seemed to fight to stay afloat with four gaping holes in her port side, but the great torrents of water pouring into her soon drew her over on her side.

Then she blew to bits amid billows of smoke.

It is also amazing, considering the explosion, that 500 men escaped death.

Awed by this spectacle, many officers of this battleship like myself found it hard to believe the *Barham* was gone. When nothing but black smoke could be seen on the horizon, many of them remarked, "Well, we cannot win all the time."

"But it was tough to see the old *Barham* go that way," they added. "She would rather have fought it out."

Two hours after the *Barham* was gone, Captain C. B. Barry of this battleship told the ship's company over the loud-speaker, "You will all be glad to know that approximately 500 were saved from the *Barham*, including the vice-admiral and his secretary."

Then, as every man aboard stood silently at his action station, an emotion-choked voice came over the speaker:

"This is the padre speaking. While we are thankful for those who are saved, let us not forget those who lost their lives, or, rather, have gone to a better life. . . . Let us pray.

"Oh, Lord, grant those who have died Thy peace; let Thy protection shine upon them—these men who have given their lives for freedom."

This was the simple, moving requiem for the men of the *Barham*.

Pearl Harbor: Tragedy at Honolulu as Japan Makes Surprise Attack on American Outpost in the Pacific

[December 7, 1941]

"People who heard the radio warnings were skeptical until explosions wrenched the guts of Honolulu."

Japanese militarists, with scant regard for the Japanese people, had long since decided on expansion into Asia. As far back as 1931 the war party arranged for the invasion of Manchuria and later of China proper. Remembering that Japan had found opportunities for expansion during World War I, the militarists, at the outbreak of the European war in 1939, called for a "Greater East Asia Co-Prosperity Sphere." China was no longer enough. Why pursue Chiang Kai-shek into the vast, barren interior of China? How about the Dutch, French and British possessions in the South Pacific? Oil, tin, rice—these were the magic magnets.

On September 27, 1940, Japan signed the Tripartite Pact with Germany and Italy. On April 13, 1941, she obtained Stalin's promise of neutrality. When Germany invaded Russia, only the United States stood between Japan and her dreams of expansion.

It came in the summer of 1941 when Tokyo, taking advantage of the helpless Vichy government, moved into northern Indo-China. The United States, Britain and the Netherlands East Indies countered by freezing Japanese assets in their respective countries. Resentment was strong against the United States, again in the way.

On October 16, General Hideki Tojo, the bellicose Razor Brain, succeeded the moderate Prince Konoye as Premier. The army leaders, now holding power, began to push for war against the American colossus.

Events moved quickly. In early November Tojo sent Saburo Kurusu to Washington. Japan was annoyed because the Roosevelt administration was seeking to halt her expansion by shutting off supplies of scrap iron and steel and at the same time supporting Chiang Kai-shek. On November 25 a Japanese task force set out with secret orders to attack Pearl Harbor. On December 7, 1941, while "peace talks" were going on in Washington, the Japanese struck at a series of targets across the Pacific.

123

What happened at Pearl Harbor was described in this account. The gravity of the blow can be sensed through the heavy veil of censorship. The damage was much more extensive than this report revealed: at Pearl Harbor eight battleships, three cruisers, three destroyers and many other ships were sunk or put out of action. All this was published later.

Isolationism in the United States vanished overnight. Senator Burton Wheeler, arch-isolationist, commented: "The only thing to do now is to lick hell out of them."

(Time, *December 15, 1941. Reprinted by permission of* Time, The Weekly Newsmagazine; *copyright* Time Inc., *1941.*)

The U.S. Navy was caught with its pants down. Within one tragic hour—before the war had really begun—the U.S. appeared to have suffered greater naval losses than in the whole of World War I.*

Days may pass before the full facts become known, but in the scanty news that came through from Hawaii in the first 36 hours of the war was every indication that the Navy had been taken completely by surprise in the early part of a lazy Sunday morning. Although the Japanese attackers had certainly been approaching for several days, the Navy apparently had no news of either airplane carriers sneaking up or of submarines fanning out around Hawaii. Not till the first bombs began to fall was an alarm given. And when the blow fell the air force at Pearl Harbor was apparently not ready to offer effective opposition to the attackers.

In fine homes on the heights above the city, in beach shacks near Waikiki, in the congested district around the Punchbowl, assorted Japanese, Chinese, Portuguese, Filipinos, Hawaiians and *kamaainas* (long-settled whites) were taking their ease. In the shallow waters lapping Fort de Russy, where sentries walked post along a retaining wall, a few Japanese and Hawaiians waded about, looking for fish to spear. In Army posts all over Oahu, soldiers were dawdling into a typical idle Sunday. Aboard the ships of the Fleet at Pearl Harbor, life was going along at a saunter. Downtown nothing stirred save an occasional bus. The clock on the Aloha Tower read 7:55.

The Japs came in from the southeast over Diamond Head. They could have been U.S. planes shuttling westward from San Diego. Civilian estimates of their numbers ranged from 50 to 150. They whined over Waikiki, over the candy-pink bulk of the Royal Hawaiian Hotel. Some were (it was reported) big four-motored jobs,

* Between April 6, 1917, and Nov. 11, 1918, the U.S., according to *Jane's Fighting Ships* for 1918, lost 1 armored cruiser, 2 destroyers, 1 submarine, 3 armed yachts, 1 coast guard cutter and 2 revenue cutters—but not a single capital ship.

some dive-bombers, some pursuits. All that they met as they came in was a tiny private plane in which Lawyer Ray Buduick was out for a Sunday morning ride. They riddled the lawyer's plane with machine-gun bullets, but the lawyer succeeded in making a safe landing. By the time he did, bombs were thudding all around the city. The first reported casualty was Robert Tyce, operator of a civilian airport near Honolulu, who was machine-gunned as he started to spin the propeller of a plane.

Torpedoes launched from bombers tore at the dreadnaughts in Pearl Harbor. Dive-bombers swooped down on the Army's Hickam and Wheeler Fields. Shortly after the attack began, radio warnings were broadcast. But people who heard them were skeptical until explosions wrenched the guts of Honolulu. All the way from Pacific Heights down to the center of town the planes soared, leaving a wake of destruction.

With anti-aircraft guns popping and U.S. pursuits headed aloft, pajama-clad citizens piled out of bed to dash downtown or head for the hills where they could get a good view. Few of them were panicky, many were nonchalant. Shouted one man as he dashed past a CBS observer: "The mainland papers will exaggerate this."

After the first attack Governor Poindexter declared an emergency, cleared the streets, ordered out the police and fire departments. Farrington High School, the city's biggest, was converted into a hospital. But the Japanese attackers returned.

Obvious to onlookers on the Honolulu hills was the fact that Pearl Harbor was being hit hard. From the Navy's plane base on Ford Island (also known as Luke Field), in the middle of the harbor, clouds of smoke ascended. One citizen who was driving past the naval base saw the first bomb fall on Ford Island. Said he: "It must have been a big one. I saw two planes dive over the mountain and down to the water and let loose torpedoes at a naval ship. This warship was attacked again and again. I also saw what looked like dive-bombers coming over in single file."

When the first ghastly day was over, Honolulu began to reckon up the score. It was one to make the U.S. Navy and Army shudder. Of the 200,000 inhabitants of Oahu, 1,500 were dead, 1,500 others injured. Not all the civilian casualties occurred in Honolulu. The raiders plunged upon the town of Wahiawa, where there is a large island reservoir, sprayed bullets on people in the streets. Behind the Wahiawa courthouse a Japanese plane crashed in flames.

Washington called the naval damage "serious," admitted at least one "old" battleship and a destroyer had been sunk, other ships of war damaged at base. Meanwhile Japan took to the radio to boast that the U.S. Navy had suffered an "annihilating blow." Crowed the Japs: "With the two battleships [sunk], and two other capital ships and four large cruisers heavily damaged by Japanese bombing attacks on Hawaii, the U.S. Pacific Fleet has now only two battleships, six 10,000 ton cruisers, and only one aircraft carrier."

Perhaps more important than the loss of ships was damage to the naval base, some of whose oil depots may have gone up in flames. Heaviest military toll was at Hickam Field, where hundreds were killed and injured when bombs hit the great barracks and bombs were reported to have destroyed several hangars full of planes.

These reports may have been inaccurate—most of them came through in the first excitement of the attack and could not be confirmed. Thereafter virtually the only news about Hawaii came through a few bare communiqués from the White House. It was all too likely that there was serious damage which was not reported.

But the curtain of censorship settled down. The Fleet units which were fit for action put to sea. The White House said that several Jap airplanes and submarines were downed, but what happened in the next grim stage of the deadly serious battle was hidden for the time being by the curtain.

The first crashing blows were so widespread that it looked as if the Japanese were trying to realize their "Heaven-sent," Hell-patented ambition of dominating the Pacific all at one fell shock. Actually there was no such crazy plan. They had, instead, a pattern of attack which was brilliant, thorough, audacious, and apparently in its first two days, successfully carried through.

Japan's gambit had two essentials: 1) strike at the heart of the main U.S. force and split it from the Allied forces to the East; 2) lay the groundwork for the destruction of the latter.

Sinking of the *Prince of Wales* and *Repulse*: Cecil Brown Cables Eyewitness Story of the Destruction of Two Great British Warships

[December 11, 1941]

"I never saw such happiness on men's faces."

At 5 A.M. *on the morning of December 11, 1941, four days after Pearl Harbor, a Tokyo broadcast claimed that Japanese torpedo bombers had sunk the giant 35,000-ton British battleship* Prince of Wales *and the heavy cruiser* Repulse. *The news sped around the world. Many people refused to believe it. The report was dismissed as an example of Japanese arrogance, as propaganda designed to confuse and frighten the people of the Allied nations.*

The report was true. Admiral Tom Phillips, Commander-in-Chief of the Royal Far East Fleet, an officer whose discretion did not match his personal courage, had taken the two great battlewagons 150 miles north of Singapore without an adequate air cover. The move was suicidal, the result catastrophic.

Exactly twenty-four hours after the Tokyo broadcast there came into the New York offices of the Columbia Broadcasting Corporation a cable from Cecil Brown, Columbia's correspondent in Singapore. Brown had been on the Repulse *and he had escaped. His story was rushed on the air and repeated four times that day.*

It was one of the great news stories of World War II. Paul White, director of news broadcasts for CBS, was not quite sure of British income tax regulations when he cabled Brown: "HAVE NOTIFIED YOUR BANK YOU DID ONE GRAND JOB." In Singapore, recovering from his ordeal, Brown remarked: "My God! A thousand-dollar bonus!" Other newsmen were not slow in expressing their envy of Brown's feat.

From this point on it became clear that for the rest of the war it would be not only dangerous but foolhardy to commit heavy naval ships to action without adequate air screens. Pearl Harbor revealed the strength of Japanese airpower. The sinkings off Singapore gave further evidence of Japan's power.

Here is the eyewitness story of how the Prince of Wales *and the* Repulse *ended their careers in the South China Sea, fifty miles from the Malaya coast and a hundred and fifty miles north of Singapore.*

(*CBS, December 11, 1941. By permission of Cecil Brown.*)

I was aboard the *Repulse* and with hundreds of others escaped. Then, swimming in thick oil, I saw the *Prince of Wales* lay over on her side like a tired war horse and slide beneath the waters. I kept a diary from the time the first Japanese high level bombing started at 11:15 until 12:31 when Captain William Tennant, skipper of the *Repulse* and Senior British Captain afloat, shouted through the ship's communications system, "All hands on deck, prepare to abandon ship. May God be with you."

I jumped twenty feet to the water from the up end of the side of the *Repulse* and smashed my stop watch at thirty-five and a half minutes after twelve. The sinking of the *Repulse* and the *Prince of Wales* was carried out by a combination of high level bombing and torpedo attacks with consummate skill and the greatest daring. I was standing on the flag deck slightly forward amidships when nine Jap bombers approached at ten thousand feet strung in a line, clearly visible in the brilliant sunlit sky. They flew directly over our ship and our anti-aircraft guns were screaming constantly.

Just when the planes were passing over, one bomb hit the water beside where I was standing, so close to the ship that we were drenched from the water spout. Simultaneously another struck the *Repulse* on the catapult deck, penetrating the ship and exploding below in a marine's mess and hangar. Our planes were subsequently unable to take off. At 11:27 fire is raging below, and most strenuous efforts are under way to control it. All gun crews are replenishing their ammunition and are very cool and cracking jokes. There are a couple of jagged holes in the funnel near where I am standing.

It's obvious the Japs flew over the length of the ship, each dropping three bombs so that twenty-seven bombs fell around us at first in their attack. Brilliant red flashes are spouting from our guns' wells. The *Prince of Wales* is half a mile away. Destroyers are at various distances throwing everything they have into the air. A splash about two miles off our port beam may be anti-aircraft but we are uncertain. At 11:40 the *Prince of Wales* seems to be hit. She's reduced her speed. Now they're coming to attack us. The communications system shouts "stand by for barrage." All our guns are going. We are twisting and snaking violently to avoid torpedoes. The Japs are coming in low, one by one in single waves. They're easy to spot. Amid the roar of the guns aboard the *Repulse* and the pompoms of anti-aircraft fire, we are signalled, "We've a man overboard."

Two Jap aircraft are approaching us. I see more of them coming with the naked eye. I again count nine. They're torpedo bombers and are circling us about a mile and a half or two miles away. 11:45 —now there seems to me more bombers but they are circling like vultures at about one thousand feet altitude. The guns are deafening. The smell of cordite is almost suffocating and explosions are ear shattering and the flashes blinding. The officer beside me yells, "Here comes a tin fish."

A Jap torpedo bomber is heading directly for us, two hundred yards above the water. At 11:48 he's less than five hundred feet distant, plowing onward. A torpedo drops and he banks sharply and his whole side is exposed to our guns but instead of driving away he's making a graceful dive toward the water. He hits and immediately bursts into flame in a gigantic splash of orange against the deep blue sky and the robins-egg blue water. Other planes are coming, sweeping low in an amazing suicide effort to sink the *Repulse*.

Their daring is astonishing, coming so close you can make out the pilot's outline. One coming in at 11:48 to our starboard just dropped a torpedo. A moment later I hear shouts of joy indicating that he was brought down but I didn't see that. We also claim we brought down two high level bombers previously but I didn't see these crash. At least at the moment I have no recollection of seeing them.

At 12:01 another wave of torpedo bombers is approaching. They are being met with everything we've got except our fourteen inchers. Beside me the signal officer flashes word from Captain Tennant to the *Prince of Wales*. "We've eluded all torpedos this second attack." It's fascinating to watch our tracer bullets speeding toward the Jap bombers. 12:03—we've just shot down another torpedo bomber who is about four hundred yards away and we shot it out. All of its motors are afire and disintegrating pieces of the fuselage are flying about. Now it disappears over the surface of the water into scrap. The brilliant orange from the fire against this blue sky is so close it's startling. All the men are cheering at the sight. It's so close it seems you could almost reach out and touch the remains of this Jap bomber.

At 12:15 the *Wales* seems to be stopped definitely. I've been too busy to watch the attacks against her but she seems in utmost difficulty. Her guns are firing constantly and we are both twisting. One moment the *Wales* is at our starboard, the next it's at our port. I'm not watching the destroyers but they have not been subjected to air attacks. The Japs are throwing everything recklessly against the two capital ships.

There's fire aboard us, it's not out. I just saw some firemen and fire control parties. The calmness of the crews is amazing. I have constantly roved from one side of the flag deck to the other during the heavy firing and attacks and the cool precision of all hands has seemed unreal and unnatural. Even when they are handing up shells for the service guns, each shell is handed over with a joke. I never saw such happiness on men's faces. This is the first time these gun crews have been in action in this war and they are having the time of their lives. 12:20—I see ten bombers approaching us from a distance. It's impossible to determine whether this will be a high level attack or another torpedo bomber attack. "Stand by for barrage" comes over the ship's communication system.

One plane is circling around, it's now at three or four hundred yards approaching us from the port side. It's coming closer, head on, and I see a torpedo drop. It's streaking for us. A watcher shouts, "Stand by for torpedo" and the tin fish is streaking directly for us. Some one says: "This one got us." The torpedo struck on the side on which I was standing about twenty yards astern of my position. It felt like the ship had crashed into a well-rooted dock. It threw me four feet across the deck but I did not fall and I did not feel any explosion. Just a very great jar. Almost immediately it seemed we began to list and less than a minute later there was another jar of the same kind and the same force, except that it was almost precisely the same spot on the starboard side.

After the first torpedo, the communication system coolly announced: "Blow up your life belts." I was in this process when the second torpedo struck and the settling ship and the crazy angle were so apparent I didn't continue blowing my belt.

That the *Repulse* was doomed was immediately apparent. The communication system announced, "Prepare to abandon ship. May God be with you." Without undue rush we all started streaming down ladders, hurrying but not pushing. It was most difficult to realize I must leave the ship. It seemed so incredible that the *Repulse* could or should go down. But the *Repulse* was fast heeling over to port and walking ceased to become a mode of locomotion. I was forced to clamber and scramble in order to reach the side. Men were lying dead around the guns. Some were half hidden by empty shell cases. There was considerable damage all around the ship. Some of the men had been machine gunned. That had been unquestioned fact.

All around me men were stripping off their clothes and their shoes and tossing aside their steel helmets. Some are running alongside the three quarters exposed hull of the ship to reach a spot where they can slide down the side without injuring themselves in the jagged hole in the ship's side. Others are running to reach a point where they have a shorter dive to the water. I am reluctant to leave my new portable typewriter down in my cabin and unwilling to discard my shoes which I had bought just a week before. As I go over the side the *Prince of Wales* half a mile away seems to be afire but her guns are still firing the heaviest. It's most obvious she's stopped dead and out of control due to her previous damage.

The air attack against the *Prince of Wales* carried out the same scheme directed against the *Repulse*. The Japs were able to send two British capital ships to the bottom because of first, a determined air torpedo attack and, second, the skill and the efficiency of the Japanese operations. It's apparent that the best guns and crews in the world will be unable to stem a torpedo bombing attack if the attackers are sufficiently determined.

According to the best estimate obtainable, the Japs used in their operations against both the *Wales* and the *Repulse* eighty-six bombers; eighteen high level bombers and approximately twenty-five torpedo bombers against the *Repulse* and probably another equal number against the *Prince of Wales*. In the case of the *Wales*, however, the Japs started the torpedo bombing instead of initial high level bombing. In the first attack, one torpedo hit the *Wales* in the after-part. Some survivors believe the *Wales* was hit twice in the initial attack, then followed two more torpedo attacks, both successful. The final attack on the *Wales* was made by high level bombers around ten thousand feet. When that attack came, the *Wales* was sinking fast and everyone threw himself down on deck.

Most of the guns were unmanageable as a result of the list and the damage. I jumped into the water from the *Repulse* at 12:35. While I was in the water, the *Wales* continued firing for some time. The *Wales* suffered two direct hits by bombs on the deck. Like the attack on the *Repulse*, the Japs flew across the length of the *Wales* in a single line, each bomber dropping a stick. One officer said a child of six could see some of them were going to hit us. During the entire action Admiral Tom Phillips, Commander in Chief of the Far East Fleet, and Captain Leech, Skipper of the *Prince of Wales*, were on the bridge.

While the torpedo bombers were rushing in toward the *Wales*, dropping tin fish and machine gunning the decks, Phillips clambered up on the roof of the bridge and also atop the gun turrets to see better and to direct all phases of the action. When it was apparent that the *Wales* was badly hit, the Admiral issued an order to the flag officer for the destroyer then lying alongside close by. "Signal to Singapore to send tugs to tow us." Evidently up to that moment, Phillips was not convinced that the *Wales* was sinking. The last order issued by Phillips came at approximately 1:15. It said, "Blow up your life belts."

Later the ship was under water. Phillips and Leech were the last from the *Wales* to go over the side and they slid into the water together. It's probable that their reluctance to leave the ship until all possible men had left meant their death, since it's most likely they were drawn down by the suction when the *Wales* was on her side and then settled at her stern with her bow rising into the air.

Swimming about a mile away, lying on top of a small stool, I saw the bow of the *Wales*. When Phillips signalled to ask Singapore to send tugs, the *Wales* already had four torpedoes in her. Like the *Repulse*, the *Wales'* gun crews were very cool and although many guns were no longer effective the crew stood beside them. When the final high level bombing attack came, only three guns were capable of firing, except the fourteen-inchers which naturally did not go into action. I did not meet Phillips but last week when I visited the *Wales* at the naval base, I had a long talk with Captain Leech. He's a jovial, convivial, smiling officer who gave me the impression of the greatest kindliness and ability. The *Wales* carried a complement of seventeen hundred; the *Repulse* twelve hundred and fifty officers and ratings. When the *Wales* sank, the suction was so great it ripped off the life belt of one officer more than fifty feet away. A fortunate feature of the sinking of both the *Repulse* and the *Wales* was that neither blew up.

Since the tide was strong and there was an extremely powerful suction from both ships, it was extremely difficult to make any progress away from the ship in the thick oil. The gentle, quiet manner in which these shell-belching dreadnaughts went to their last resting place without exploding was a tribute of gratitude from two fine ships for their fine sailors.

Death at the Volga: A German Report on a Battalion's Suicide Stand Against the Onslaught of Four Siberian Divisions

[December 14, 1941]

"Come and help me. I can't see. They've gouged out my eyes."

With lighthearted abandon the Germans surged on to the soil of Russia. Surely these sub-human Reds could not withstand the mighty German Wehrmacht! The invaders were shocked to learn quickly that they had been wrong. Hitler complained that the Russians did not seem to know when they were beaten. For some strange reason they continued to fight. A quiver of fear went through the German ranks. The enemy was ferocious; he was vicious; he fought like a cornered animal; he actually enjoyed the use of cold steel.

In the following report Dr. Heinrich Haape describes the German advance up to December 1941 when Hitler's forces reached a point beyond Kalinin northwest of Moscow. The reporter's aim was to describe the feat of a German suicide battalion in withstanding the attack of four Siberian divisions, but at the same time he gave a terrifying picture of the revenge taken by Russians on isolated German troopers.

(Dr. Heinrich Haape, in association with Dennis Henshaw, Moscow Tram Stop [London, 1957], pp. 226–229. By permission of Wm. Collins Sons & Co. Ltd.)

The casualty register made depressing reading that night. There had never been so many names to enter. 14th December was a black day for the 3rd Battalion. 182 casualties, dead, wounded or frost-bitten; in one afternoon we had lost more men than in the whole of the Russian campaign up to that point. But the "suicide battalion" had held out for many valuable hours against the Siberian hordes.

It was nearly midnight before I finished and was able to get back to the battle-post. At last I had time to have a chat with Neuhoff about his health. He told me he was feeling very run down and

133

depressed. He had lost his appetite and his resistance was rapidly being weakened by the repeated attacks of dysentery, which seemed to be getting worse. Neuhoff was obviously a very sick man, who was fending off a complete collapse only by a supreme effort of will power. He would not take the sleeping pills I offered him, saying that he had no time to sleep with things in their present serious condition, but he took a supply of Tanalbin as a palliative against his bowel trouble. There was no more I could do for him at the present.

The old *Oberstabsarzt* was still seated on the box when I returned to the sick bay. I suggested that he should take a rest at the battle-post and with an effort he got up and went.

By 3 A.M. all seriously wounded men had been evacuated to the rear areas. The panje wagons had kept up a constant shuttle service and the drivers, particularly the Russian volunteers, Kunzle and Hans, had worked heroically through the unbearably cold night. Towards dawn I was awakened from a light sleep by Müller, who said: "There are cries from the wood in front of us. They sound like cries for help."

With an effort I roused myself and went outside with Müller. True enough, about 400 yards away someone was shouting for help. They were unearthly, agonised cries. I awoke Tulpin and Heinrich, sent Müller to Battalion H.Q. to alert a few soldiers and, accompanied by Heinrich and Tulpin, walked towards the shouts.

Cautiously, with guns at the ready, we crunched through the snow towards the wood. It might be a trap. The cries became louder and more pleading: "For God's sake help me, someone! Where is everyone? For God's sake come and help me."

At the fringe of the wood we saw a figure staggering towards us, his arms outstretched. He did not seem to see us. We called out to him: "What's the matter?"

"Aaah!" he screamed. "Come and help me. I can't see. They've gouged out my eyes."

In a few strides we were at his side and shone a torch on his face. Where his eyes had been were only two bloody holes; bits of flesh hung on his cheekbones and the blood had streamed down his face and frozen there.

Tulpin grabbed his arm and quickly led him out of the wood, while Heinrich and I walked slowly backwards after them, keeping the muzzles of our guns pointed towards the trees. The man spilled out his story. He was an artilleryman—one of four men who had gone out to lay telephone wires to an observation point beyond our positions.

"We weren't expecting to see any Russians," he said, ". . . then suddenly several shots and the other three dropped in the snow. I ran back the way we had come—straight into the arms of the Russians. They grabbed hold of me and dragged me along . . . I shouted for help and one of them told me to keep quiet . . . he spoke broken German . . . but I kept on calling for help. Then they said something to each other and threw me to the ground. One of them came at me with a knife . . . there was a terrific flash of light, a sharp pain and then the same with my other eye . . . then total darkness. The man who had hissed at me in broken German grabbed my arm and whispered into my ear: 'There. Go straight forward, to your brothers, the other German dogs, and tell them we'll destroy them all. We'll cut out their eyes and send what's left to Siberia— that will be Stalin's revenge. Now get going.' And he gave me a push and I heard them run away through the snow." The man finished and broke into deep sobs.

At the sick bay we did our best for him, but it was a poor best. There was nothing anyone could really do for him. He would live, but in darkness for the rest of his life.

Then the Russians, determined to seize that vital escape road from Kalinin, attacked again just as dawn broke. Our soldiers grabbed their machine-guns from the warm ovens and fired into the waves of Red troops that poured out of the wood. The attack petered out in the snow in front of our hastily-prepared positions. And as they retreated, our artillery and mortars let them have it.

No sooner had they disappeared than our men were out among the dead Russians, stripping them of their fur caps, fleece-lined jackets and those magnificent felt boots. There were about sixty pairs of boots for distribution and preference was given to men with light frost-bite. In that way they could be kept battle-worthy. We could count on no replacements, and even if any did arrive their fighting value would not amount to much. Every single man counted in the bitter struggle to preserve the front, for only by keeping our front line intact could we save the trapped divisions in Kalinin, and with luck perhaps save our own lives. The only soldiers sent back were those who were half-dead and totally unable to fire a rifle.

And as we managed to hang on to our small section of the front, so were the trapped units of the Ninth Army streaming out of Kalinin along the road to Staritsa. Men who would fight again. If the entire 3rd Battalion of Infantry Regiment 18 was wiped out it would be worth while in the overall strategy, provided the beleaguered army in Kalinin made good its escape. Even we could see that. We recognized the military necessity for what we were doing but it was heartbreaking to see the battalion being slowly hacked to death.

Nevertheless, there had been a tremendous upsurge of self-confidence in the battalion following the dawn attack. In addition to the sixty Red soldiers whom we had stripped of their warm clothing, fully twice as many again—not so warmly clad—were lying dead on the battlefield. Close on 200 frozen corpses lay in front of our positions, grim mementoes of the action.

But what pleased the sick-bay staff more than the pile of Russian corpses was that the sightless artilleryman had been avenged. Stolze had heard shooting in front of his sector and had sent Schnittger out with nine men to investigate. They had come across the patrol of fifteen Russians, who had just shot down the three artillerymen and blinded the fourth. Schnittger and his men had lain in ambush in the wood, and at close range had riddled the Red patrol with their bullets. Not a single Russian escaped.

Neuhoff called a conference to discuss the situation and while we were talking, Regimental H.Q. phoned to say that the main defensive line had been formed that afternoon to the rear of Gorki. Kalinin had been held long enough to enable the withdrawal of the Ninth Army to the new positions.

The Ninth Army had got out of the trap! We had managed to hold the road to Staritsa long enough for 100,000 men to get away to the south.

Neuhoff put down the field telephone and for the first time relaxed a little. He turned to us and said: "It seems our job is over. Thank you, gentlemen."

We left Krasnova and toiled back across the frozen Volga leaving the bodies of one hundred and twenty of our comrades on the battlefield. Close on a hundred and fifty others had been wiped from the battalion's strength by wounds or frost-bite.

Sixty-four Iron Crosses had been won in the battalion's suicide stand and the German radio devoted a special programme to the little battalion that had withstood the onslaught of four Siberian divisions so that half an army could escape.

We did not hear the broadcast. Retreating armies jettison their radio sets.

Corregidor: Philippine Journalist Carlos P. Romulo Retreats with MacArthur's Forces

[January 1, 1942]

"The smell of the place hit me like a blow in the face."

During the period between December 8 and December 31, 1941, operating under continuous bombardment, these units (of which Colonel Carlos P. Romulo was an officer) planned and directed the delaying actions that made possible the withdrawal of the North and South Luzon forces into the Bataan Peninsula; they planned and executed the evacuation of Manila and through prodigies of labor, working to complete exhaustion of personnel, brought about the movement of supplies and equipment which ·made possible the prolonged defense of Bataan.

This citation by the U.S. War Department told the story. After the abandonment of the naval base at Cavite on December 11, 1941, and the air attack on Manila on December 27, General Douglas MacArthur's Filipino-American defense forces retreated to the rock fortress of Corregidor Island and the wilderness peninsula of Bataan. It was the only possible solution for a grave military problem. Here the Americans and Filipinos held out for several months under most trying circumstances.

Romulo had been editor and publisher of DMHM Newspapers, a chain of newspapers in the Philippines. Before Pearl Harbor he had written a series of forty-five articles for newspapers throughout the United States. In these articles he gave ample warning of Japanese pretensions in the Far East. A fervent admirer of American culture and way of life, Romulo enraged Tokyo. The Japanese militarists placed a blood price on his head. For his articles Romulo was awarded the 1942 Pulitzer prize for distinguished correspondence.

Romulo arrived at Corregidor early on New Year's day at the very moment when Japanese troops were goose-stepping into Manila. To the east Cavite was in flames. To the west was the jungle peninsula of Bataan, where the Filipino-Americans were to make a last stand.

Corregidor finally fell on May 6, 1942. From Australia, General Mac-Arthur, who had escaped from Corregidor, paid this tribute to the de-

fenders: "Corregidor has sounded its own story at the mouth of its guns. It has scrolled its own epitaph on enemy tablets. But through the bloody haze on its last reverberating shot I shall always seem to see a vision of grim, gaunt, ghostly men, still unafraid."

Romulo, too, escaped from the Philippines. When MacArthur returned to Leyte on October 19, 1944, the remarkable Philippine warrior was with him.

(From I Saw the Fall of the Philippines *by Carlos P. Romulo. Copyright 1942 by Carlos P. Romulo. Reprinted by permission of Doubleday & Company, Inc.)*

At six-thirty in the morning that New Year's Day I walked into the Malinta Tunnel on Corregidor.

The smell of the place hit me like a blow in the face. There was the stench of sweat and dirty clothes, the coppery smell of blood and disinfectant coming from the lateral where the hospital was situated, and over all the heavy stink of creosote, hanging like a blanket in the air that moved sluggishly when it moved at all.

▪▪ ▪▪ ▪▪ ▪▪▪ ▪▪▪ ▪▪ ▪▪ ▪▪ ▪▪ ▪▪▪ ▪▪ ▪▪▪ ▪▪ ▪▪▪ ▪▪ ▪▪▪ ▪▪ ▪▪ ▪▪ ▪▪ ▪▪▪ ▪▪ ▪▪▪ ▪▪ ▪▪▪ ▪▪ ▪▪▪ ▪▪ ▪▪▪* It had been taken for granted that in the event of war all the inhabitants of Corregidor would take shelter in the tunnel and its cluster of branching laterals sunk into the solid stone of "the Rock."

As many as five thousand people gathered there during raids. Those who could not get in were unprotected. I think the population of Corregidor at this time was around nine thousand—a number that would shrink rapidly in the death-dealing months to come.

I stood there gaping, bewildered and alarmed by the bedlam going on about me. This was the final refuge of a fortress we had all assumed had been prepared and impregnable for years.

Now that disaster was upon us, soldiers were rushing about belatedly installing beds and desks and sewage drains and electric lights. ▪▪ ▪▪ ▪▪ ▪▪▪ ▪▪ ▪▪▪ ▪▪ ▪▪▪ ▪▪ ▪▪ ▪▪ ▪▪ ▪▪▪ ▪▪ ▪▪▪ ▪▪ ▪▪

The tunnel was wide enough to permit two ambulances to drive side by side down its city-block-long length. Its stone arch was damp. Everywhere was the graveyard smell of wet rock, where it wasn't overwhelmed by sharper and even less pleasant odors.

* The sections blacked out indicate lines expunged by U.S. censors because the information might have been valuable to the enemy at the time.

Soldiers were sleeping along the sides of the tunnel, on cots and ammunition cases, or curled up on the cement floor. Their boots were in one another's faces. Ambulances rolled within a few inches of their heads. The bombs that fell night and day shook the further-most stone laterals of the tunnel.

They slept on, drugged by sheer exhaustion.

Above their heads on the stone walls of the tunnel were pasted colored pictures clipped from magazines of American planes. Where soldiers under happier circumstances pinned up the pictures of their sweethearts or of movie stars, these men put pictures of bombers and pursuit ships. They were the sweethearts these fellows wanted to see!

Nobody paid any attention to me. I wandered in and out of the laterals carrying my luggage. These cavelike places were the offices for Ordnance, Quartermaster, Anti-Aircraft, Harbor Defense, Finance, Signal Corps, and USAFFE headquarters. The hospital was the largest and the best-organized lateral in the tunnel. From it jutted perhaps a dozen smaller laterals. These were for the women, the president and high commissioner, the doctors and officer patients, the operating ward, the medical ward, the dental ward and other wards, the laboratory, X ray, and the hospital mess. In this mess President Quezon, his family and Cabinet, Commissioner Sayre and his staff took their meals.

I got out of the hospital lateral as fast as I could. The sight of the wounded men and the desperately working doctors and nurses depressed me and I thought a tunnel was a crude place for a hospital.

I had yet to see the field hospitals at Bataan!

I lugged my equipment through the entrance to the USAFFE lateral. I had some trouble getting it through because the baggage of our Advance Echelon that had arrived a week before was still strewn about in masterly confusion. I had thought the smell of the tunnel bad and the hospital lateral worse. The stench of this branch lateral can't be talked about. My stomach began to do nip-ups.

But the Advance Echelon members who were working in the lateral didn't seem to be objecting to the atmosphere. There they were—all of them except General MacArthur—the men who had been my fellow workers until our separation that historic Christmas Eve.

Could that have been only the week before? I felt as if I hadn't seen these men for years. There was General Sutherland, serious and distinguished over his desk, exactly as he had been in headquarters on the Old Wall. And the vacant desk next to his, at the farthest end of the lateral, I knew instinctively was MacArthur's. There were Adjutant General Carl D. Seals, Major Kenneth F. Sauer, Colonel Savage, Major George Britt of the Southern drawl—it was a reunion. These were the men I had started out with under MacArthur. I expected some sort of a welcome—I didn't know just what kind.

They didn't even look up. They were working at their desks like the bewitched men toiling underground that you read about in European fairy tales. Their desks, I learned later, had been salvaged from headquarters at Topside, where the staff had been quartered until it had been blasted off the Rock by seventy-four Japanese planes several days before. Electric bulbs, hung in makeshift fashion from the stone ceiling, lent a queer light to the stone cave and made the whole scene macabre and unreal.

Colonel Diller was the first to notice me. He came up and shook hands. "You just arrived? Hungry?"

Then the others welcomed me. I realized they were glad to have me there. Only the tension was great and life was not quite real in the tunnel on Corregidor. One moved, worked, tried to eat, tried to breathe, in a dream.

I admitted to Colonel Diller that I was very hungry. I had not eaten, I told him in a feeble attempt to joke, since the year before. That had been yesterday—that had been in the year 1941, in Manila. Both seemed a long time ago.

Colonel Diller led me through the laterals and outside the tunnel entrance to the tent that was the officers' mess. As we left the tunnel I saw him look up at the sky. It was a habit one learned: to watch the sky over Corregidor and Bataan. A treacherous place, the sky.

I asked if I might wash before breakfast. The colonel pointed to the hillside. I saw nothing, but I followed the direction of his finger and found a faucet jutting from the rock that yielded a thin trickle of water. When I rinsed my mouth I found it was from the sea. The water mains had been knocked out by Japanese bombs. The bath I had taken in my home the night before would be my last authentic bath in three months.

Even salt water was rationed on the Rock. I learned to bathe and shave on a cupful a day. Only you don't really bathe with salt water —the salt simply cakes on top of the grime and becomes another layer of your skin.

The breakfast coffee was made with salt water. I had to leave the tent after drinking mine. One can't drink salt-water coffee every day and not get sick. Once in a while it isn't so bad.

When I came back to the table I smelled fried bacon and eggs and cheered up. But the bacon was stiff with salt, and my second attempt at the salt-water coffee wouldn't wash it down. The once piece of toast I got was thick and heavy. I thought the breakfast was horrible. Later I was to look back on it and remember it as a feast. But that was after I got used to the swarms of flies that were everywhere. Every person on Corregidor moved in his own personal aura of flies.

Later I was to call myself a fool for having lost that New Year's morning breakfast. The egg I had that morning of my arrival was the last I saw on Corregidor. Very soon our meals would be cut to two a day.

On Bataan they would eat but once a day.

After breakfast I set out to pay my respects to President Quezon in the hospital lateral. I missed directions and tried to enter the adjoining lateral. An officer on duty at the door barred my way.

"No admittance, Major," he told me good-naturedly. "This is No Man's Land!"

I had tried to enter the women's lateral. About fifty or sixty of the nurses lived there; there were perhaps another fifty on Bataan. Mrs. Quezon and her two daughters had their beds in this long stone dormitory, as did Mrs. Sayre, Mrs. Luther B. Bewley and her daughter Virginia. Mrs. MacArthur remained with her husband in the general's white cottage not far from the tunnel.

When I first entered the lateral occupied by the president and the high commissioner I could not perceive anything because of the gloom. Then I saw it was about as wide as an average bedroom and lined with about forty beds. Members of Commissioner Sayre's staff had the beds nearest the entrance.

I could not see the president at all. Then I heard him coughing and his weak voice called out to me:

"Hello, Romulo!"

At the farthest end of that damp and gloomy hole I saw the President of the Philippines. He was propped up by pillows on a white iron hospital bed. Under the sheet his emaciated body looked like a skeleton. His gray hair was long and tangled.

But Quezon's eyes held their old fire, their burning intensity.

As I walked toward him between the beds I was caught up sharply by a memory of only a few weeks before. I had introduced the President to America on a radio broadcast from his beautiful bedroom in Malacanan Palace that overlooked the Pasig River. The bedroom was mirrored, air-conditioned, decorated with brocades, heavy rugs, and antique Spanish furniture. Then, gold-braided aides had tiptoed about at the beck and call of the magnificent Quezon, the adored leader of seventeen million souls.

Despite his look of illness and the surrounding squalor, Quezon's spirits were high. He sat up and crossed his legs under the sheet. He looked exactly like Mahatma Gandhi.

"Romulo," he began eagerly, "have you read President Roosevelt's statement that help is on the way? And that our independence will be established and protected?"

There was hope and confidence in his every word.

Two days before, under the strangest of circumstances, he had renewed his oath of office as President of the Philippines.

"I wish you had been here for the ceremonies," he told me.

I said I was sorry to have missed them. But I have a program, pasted in the diary that I started writing this day and kept every day I spent on Corregidor, announcing the "inauguration of His Excellency Manuel L. Quezon, President of the Philippines, and of the Honorable Sergio Osmena, Vice-President of the Philippines, on December 30, 1941. Somewhere in Luzon, Philippines." The oaths were administered by Honorable José Abad Santos, Chief Justice of the Supreme Court of the Philippines. MacArthur and Sayre made speeches. Miss Virginia Bewley played "Hail to the Chief" and the national anthems of the United States and the Philippines on a hand organ.

Sounds impressive! But the ceremony took place in the mess tent outside the tunnel, where I had just struggled through the horrible breakfast.

"And do you know," President Quezon said indignantly, "that when the time came to broadcast my inauguration ceremonies, I found there was no radio on Corregidor! I told General MacArthur we must have a radio here. How can we communicate with the outside world? With the occupied areas?"

████████ ████ ██ ██ ██ ████ ████████ ████
███ █ ████████ ████████ ███ ████████ MacArthur had immediately ordered General Marshall in Manila to bring equipment for a radio-broadcasting station. The order came as Major Teague and Lieutenant Ince were demolishing all radio stations in the city, in the split second before they blasted the last.

As we talked we were constantly interrupted by a parade of men carrying towels and shaving kits past the president's bed.

Battle of Moscow: Star Red Reporters Ilya Ehrenburg and Konstantin Simonov Record the Story of the Beginning of Retribution for Hitler

[January 29, 1942]

Hitler started his first general offensive against Moscow on October 2, 1941. Exactly two months later, on December 2, he ordered Berlin editors to reserve space on their front pages for an important announcement. "The Soviet Union is finished!" he shouted.

That official announcement of the fall of Moscow never came. The Germans reached the outskirts of the little Moscow–Volga canal port of Khimki, five miles north of Moscow. From this point there was a commuters' bus line into the city, but the Germans never got to use it.

Hitler's position was still strong. His armies had advanced 600 miles into the Soviet Union since the June invasion. In the north his troops were before Leningrad; in the south they were before Sevastopol; in the center they were within sight of Moscow. However, added to the strength of the enemy was one of the worst winters within memory. Hitler had been so confident that his men would take Moscow quickly that he had not even outfitted them with winter clothing. Russian guerrillas, operating in the German rear, broke German lines of communication and isolated units. Even as Napoleon before him, Hitler was caught in a trap.

The Russian counterattacks carried them into Mozhaisk near Moscow and Rostov, the latter an important German strong point. The liberation of Mozhaisk was a portent for the future. While the Nazi press hysterically announced the imminent end of the Red Army, the Russians prepared further gigantic blows at the invader.

The story of Mozhaisk was told briefly by Ilya Ehrenburg, star Red reporter, most famous and popular of Soviet journalists. Born in 1891, Ehrenburg left Tsarist Russia at the age of seventeen, but returned home after the Bolshevik Revolution. Four years later he left to work in France, but shortly before Hitler's invasion of the Soviet Union, he returned again to his homeland. The second report is by another journalist popular in the Soviet Union, Konstantin Simonov.

By American standards both these reports are lush and old-fashioned.

143

Consciously or unconsciously, Soviet newsmen mingled straight reporting with opinion and propaganda. The Russians, of course, were invariably heroes, the Germans "rats." On occasion, Ehrenburg lapsed into stream-of-consciousness narration. This was highly subjective, tendentious reporting. Nevertheless, Russians were delighted by such staccato recitals and omniscient pronunciamentoes.

THE MOZHAISK FRONT NEAR MOSCOW

(*Ilya Ehrenburg, in* Soviet War News Weekly, *London, January 29, 1942.*)

"We have to wipe them out."

I have before me a German map found in an abandoned car. Two arrows on the map point to the heart of Russia—Moscow. One pierces Odintsovo, the second Golitsyno. This is a November map of the so-called "Mozhaisk sector."

To Russia, the name of this ancient town has become a symbol. "They are still at Mozhaisk," Moscow people used to say to each other. The Germans regard Mozhaisk as their last stop before the Red Square. Instead, it became their journey's end. We have entered Mozhaisk.

When I met Lieutenant General Govorov he was scanning his map of the campaign. Red arrows point west, their spearheads stretching far beyond Mozhaisk. Yet the campaign has just begun. Ahead lie Vyazma and Smolensk. Mozhaisk was the scene of the final act in the great battle for Moscow. Every detail of this battle was watched by Stalin.

I spoke to the general whose troops have taken Mozhaisk. Govorov is a veteran artilleryman, having been in the service for 25 years. He fought the Germans in 1916, participated in the Civil War, and breached the Mannerheim Line in 1940. Artillery has always been the pride of Russian arms. It sustained the Red Army during its most difficult days.

The general told me about the artillerymen who defended Moscow in October. At times they had to cope with the situation unaided. But they didn't let the Germans pass. Now our artillery has changed to the offensive.

"We are going for the enemy's fortifications," said Govorov. "Artillery is doing its share in every phase of the battle. Automatic weapons are so extensively used to-day that we cannot possibly limit our operation to silencing enemy gun emplacements. Drive them underground? No, we have to wipe them out! The artillerymen can no longer be guided merely by orders for the infantry. It is waging battle in its own right."

Thus a new art of warfare is being created in the flames of war. All night long the telephone has been ringing at headquarters. The general gets no sleep. Heavy-eyed, he pores over his maps. "No, to the right," he directs a unit through the receiver. He is present at every stage of the battle.

Red Army men march forward, trampling down the snow. Telephone wires are being repaired. Guns are booming. A straight road runs west from Mozhaisk. So far we have covered only the first lap. The road is still long. From here to the extreme capes of Europe, to Finisterre, "the end of the earth," stretches the Kingdom of Death.

It is a difficult road. But the Red Army continues its relentless march across the snow. The road will be traversed.

BATTLE FOR MOSCOW

(Konstantin Simonov, Moscow *[Moscow 1943], pp. 19–23. Foreign Languages Publishing House, Moscow.)*

"Moscow was calm and stern in those days."

All through October, November and the beginning of December, the Germans kept coming closer to Moscow with every day. Their rout near Moscow began on December 5, when our troops launched their counter-offensive. The question of future victory had been decided when the country learned that the State Defence Committee, with Stalin at its head, was remaining in Moscow; and particularly, on November 6 and 7, when, in accordance with the great Soviet traditions, the meeting of the Moscow Soviet was held and the Parade passed through the Red Square, at both of which occasions Stalin spoke.

On these days, the Germans were at the very gates of Moscow. In places they were no more than sixty to seventy kilometres away. The danger was great and menacing. But just because the danger was so tremendous—in this Parade, in the words of Stalin there was such great force, such confidence in victory, such lofty, calm courage, that every Soviet citizen, whether at the front or in the rear, no matter where he was on that day, felt with all his heart that Moscow would never be surrendered, and that in the end victory would be ours.

The Germans continued to advance on November 8, 9, 10, and 15, approaching ever closer to Moscow. And our troops continued to retreat with heavy fighting. But actually this could no longer be called a retreat. There was a feeling that near Moscow an enormous steel spring was slowly contracting, acquiring tremendous force in the process. It was contracting to strike in release.

Air raids on the city continued day and night. The Germans captured new villages daily. Their tanks would break through now in one place, now in another. Tens of thousands of Moscow women erected fortifications, dug trenches and anti-tank pits at the approaches to Moscow. They worked tirelessly, in mud and sleet and cold. They worked in the very same clothes they had on when they came, for there were no special work clothes for them. And Moscow itself was cold and uninviting, there was no fuel for heating purposes—every car that came from the East brought arms and arms alone. There were fewer people in Moscow. Some had gone to the front, others to build fortifications. But every one of those who remained did the work of three, and sometimes of four. The whole city seemed to have turned into a military camp. People spent their nights in the factories, sleeping two or three hours a day. The front was so close that newspaper correspondents managed to visit the forward positions and return to the city with fresh news for their papers twice a day.

All the principal war plants had been evacuated to the rear. But the Muscovites were faced with the task of continuing to forge arms for Moscow within the city itself. And all the small workshops, all the remaining plants began to produce arms for the troops fighting near Moscow. Places that used to put out primus stoves were now producing grenades; where household utensils used to be manufactured fuses and detonators were being turned out. A factory that used to manufacture adding machines began, for the first time in Moscow, to manufacture automatic rifles, turning out its first consignment of rifles for the twenty-fourth anniversary of the October Revolution. Thousands of skilled workers had been evacuated to the rear, comparatively few remaining in Moscow. But to their assistance came housewives, wives of men who had left for the front, juveniles and schoolchildren.

Moscow youngsters in the winter of 1941–42! Some day a good children's author will write a wonderful book about them. They were everywhere. They replaced their fathers in the factories. They turned out automatic rifles, grenades, shells and mines. They replaced nurses in hospitals. They went on duty during air raids at the local A.R.P. posts. In their school workshops they made bags for presents and parcels for the front, made tin mugs and knitted mittens and gloves. Like their grown-up brothers, sisters and fathers they too took part in the defence of Moscow. And if ever a monument to Moscow's defenders is erected on one of the Moscow squares, among the bronze figures, next to that of his father with an automatic rifle in his hands, there should be the fifteen-year-old son who in the autumn of 1941 forged this rifle for him.

Moscow was calm and stern in those days. The closer the Germans came, the closer it was to the beginning of December. the more alarmed, as it seemed, the Muscovites should have become at the constantly decreasing distance between the Germans and Moscow, the calmer and more confident they became, the more furiously they fought at the front, the more intensely they worked in Moscow itself. The capital of a great people showed great examples of heroism.

The thinned divisions of the Moscow defenders fought with the fury of men whose backs are to the wall—thus far and no further. And they went no further. If the Germans succeeded in capturing a village or gained another bit of territory in those days it meant that there was no longer a single defender left alive there.

And while the few remaining barriers of Soviet defenders near Zvenigorod, Dedovsk, Chernaya Gryaz, Skhodnya, near Kashira and in the suburbs of Tula were harassing and bleeding with Hitler's divisions, which were already beginning to doubt their ultimate success and growing more savage as a result, echelons carrying tanks, cannon of various calibre, and regiments and battalions of eager young Red Armymen, well clad in warm winter uniforms and equipped in full with the finest of armaments, were speeding regularly, a new echelon every ten to fifteen minutes, over the few trunk lines connecting the capital with the rear.

None knew where these echelons were unloaded, whither this tremendous number of people, tanks, and guns disappeared. They had been moving through the whole of November and the beginning of December. But none of them appeared at the front. Only with their hearts and their soldier's intuition did the men at the front guess their presence. And this increased the force of their resistance tenfold.

Scores of divisions and tank brigades were swallowed up in the great forest around Moscow, somewhere quite near the front. These divisions and brigades were like a heavy, executioner's sword which

Stalin had raised over the heads of the Germans, who were already appointing quartermasters for billeting troops in the warm houses of Moscow.

By December 4, the steel spring had contracted to its limit, and on December 5 all the reserves concentrated near Moscow, all that had been made ready for the blow with such painstaking care and iron self-restraint, all the troops and artillery, all the tanks, in a word, all that had been concentrated around and beyond Moscow in accordance with Stalin's strategic plan to form a huge fist of crushing power, struck out at the Germans. The spring had contracted as far as it would go and now it was released with incredible force. The word which the whole country was waiting to hear with bated breath—"Offensive"—became a reality. Our army near Moscow had gone over to the offensive. The names of villages and towns near Moscow again began to appear in the war communiques, but in reverse order now. Through snow and over ice, in the bitter frosts and blinding snowstorms, our army advanced steadily. That tremendous and great advance, which people later began to call the winter destruction of the Germans near Moscow had begun.

Moscow! Winter is again approaching. The first snowflakes glitter in the deflected white rays of automobile headlights. With a clattering of hoofs, a mounted patrol rides through a deserted square. The slender spires of the Kremlin towers pierce and vanish in the late November skies.

Moscow! Millions of Soviet fighters, from the snow-covered peaks of the Caucasus to the leaden waves of the Barents Sea, dream of you today. They see you before them—proud and invincible, having thrown back from your ancient walls the alien, iron-clad hordes.

Moscow—to the Russian people you have ever been a symbol of their Native Land, the symbol of life. And henceforward you have also become for them the symbol of victory, a victory which does not come of itself, but which must be won, as you won it under your ancient walls.

Singapore: Japanese and American Reports on the Fall of Mighty British Bastion in Southeast Asia

[February 15–20, 1942]

For 123 years the British had held on tenaciously to Singapore, their island stronghold in Southeast Asia. This was their most important naval base in the Far East, another Gibraltar. Who would dare attack it? And how?

Pearl Harbor was the signal for Japanese attack not only on Manila, Midway, Wake, and Guam, but also on Malaya and Singapore. Showing respect for the Royal Navy, the Japanese struck overland in January 1942 through the jungles of the Malayan Peninsula. They would storm the great naval base from the land side. They would catch the British with guns pointing in the wrong direction.

A well-trained Japanese army of more than 200,000 men pressed through jungles, swamps, rice fields and rubber forests toward Singapore. Meanwhile the great naval base was subjected to daily poundings from the air. The rampaging Japanese headed for the reservoirs on the mainland, without which Singapore was useless.

British and Australian reinforcements arrived just in time to share the defeat. For Winston Churchill it was "the greatest disaster to British arms which history records."

In the first story reprinted here the fall of Singapore was announced by Radio Tokyo and recorded by an Associated Press listening post. The second story was by the first American correspondent to arrive in Singapore as well as the only one left to witness its fall—C. Yates McDaniel of the Associated Press. Born in 1906 to missionary parents in Soochow, China, McDaniel was educated in the United States, worked on various Southern newspapers, and in 1935 became a foreign correspondent. He escaped from Singapore on February 13, 1942, two days before the formal surrender. He turned up in Batavia on February 20 to describe a week of wild adventure.

149

FALL OF SINGAPORE

(Broadcast by Radio Tokyo, February 15, 1942, as recorded by Associated Press. By permission of Associated Press.)

"This absolute strategic superiority of Japan cannot be overcome by England and the United States."

The mighty British bastion of Singapore fell to Japanese forces today and military leaders here immediately hailed conquest of this Gibraltar of the Pacific as placing Japan in position "to control the fate of India and Australia."

Army headquarters in Malaya announced the resistance of Singapore's defenders ended in unconditional surrender at 7 P.M. (6 A.M., Eastern War Time), thus capping a ten-week drive down the Malay Peninsula.

The immediate strategic value of the island fortress was stressed tonight by Col. Hideo Ohira, chief of the army press section at imperial headquarters here, in a radio address to the nation commemorating the victory. He warned the people, however, this was "only one phase of a war which has a long way to go."

He said that in addition to Japanese military might the "smugness and overconfidence of the Anglo-American front" were responsible for their successive setbacks.

"The passing of the British stronghold into Japanese hands," he added, "not only is a striking blow to the Allies but seriously impedes communications between their territories in the Indian and Pacific oceans. Japan is in position to control the fate of India and Australia.

"This absolutely strategic superiority of Japan cannot be overcome by England and the United States. Moreover, Singapore's fall constitutes a double blow to Chungking, which has been cut off from Anglo-American aid completely."

Headquarters of the Japanese army in Malaya announced that Lieut. Gen. A. E. Percival, commander of the British army, and Lieut. Gen. Tomoyuki Yamashita, the Japanese commander in chief, had signed the surrender terms which called for cessation of hostilities. The battlefield ceremony took place at the Ford Motor plant at the foot of Bukit Timah, a hill northwest of the city, where the bitterest and bloodiest fighting of the entire seven-day battle on Singapore island took place.

Dispatches from Singapore island said the British imperials resisted fiercely throughout the last hours of their back-to-the-sea struggle, fighting from strongly defended nests in the suburbs while flames which appeared to have merged into a solid block of fire swept Singapore.

But the dispatches said three converging columns of Japanese troops had virtually encircled the city and cut the defenders' lines into pieces, seized the reservoirs upon which they depended for water supply, captured three of their four airdromes, stormed the fortified island of Blakang Mati south of the harbor and silenced the big coastal guns which had thrown a protective bombardment over the city.

Imperial headquarters said all hope of a British evacuation had been destroyed by the Japanese navy, which had sunk, damaged or beached thirty-two ships, including many warships, to the south of Singapore.

Four British officers, headed by Major Wilde, a member of the British army staff, approached Japanese headquarters with a white flag and informed the Japanese of Singapore's willingness to surrender.

Lieut. Gen. Yamashita gave them the conditions for surrender and the British departed, announcing they would return to discuss the conditions.

The British emissaries later returned and signed the articles calling for unconditional surrender.

The scene was one of scorched desolation. Dive bombers carried on their attacks and the array of artillery continued to thunder up to the very hour of surrender.

Singapore's tropical foliage was black from the showers of soot which had steadily sifted through the sky for seven days.

Huge shell and bomb craters were everywhere, and in many places only shattered and dwarfed stumps remained where orchards and plantations had flourished.

The decisive blows were delivered Saturday when the Japanese completed occupation of the area around the vital MacRitchie and Peirce water reservoirs northwest of the city.

The Pya Lebar radio station also was captured, although fiercely fighting nests of British held out desperately.

Then one Japanese column advanced southward on a six-mile front and reached the northern suburbs of Singapore itself.

A second column skirted the reservoirs to the east and reached the

Kalang river, where it is crossed by the road from Singapore to Seletar airdrome in the north of the island.

Then this column struck southward toward the coast east of Singapore.

This maneuver had the effect of splitting the defending forces which by then were streaming eastward, along with refugees, toward the Changi forts at the extreme northeastern end of the island.

A third Japanese column, which had taken Bukit Timah, completed the encirclement of the city by attacking southward and reaching Alexander road in the western section of the city.

From this position harbor installations were set flaming by dive bombing and artillery. Coastal batteries and machine-gun nests were knocked out, and Blakang Mati seized.

Sembawang, Seletar and Tengah airdromes were in Japanese hands by then, leaving only the Kalang airdrome under British control.

ESCAPE FROM SINGAPORE

(*C. Yates McDaniel, Associated Press, February 20, 1942. By permission of Associated Press.*)

"The most beautiful sight I ever expect to see—
a British destroyer."

Seven and a half days after we left Singapore's flaming waterfront, we—fifty-five men and a plucky Chinese girl—reached safety at Batavia.

I escaped from doomed Singapore, February 13, aboard the last vessel to leave the battered and burning fortress, and reached Batavia during an air raid alarm this morning. In my seven-and-one-half day journey I abandoned a bombed ship, was cast up on an uninhabited island, made my way through a storm in a small launch to Sumatra, crossed that island's mountain wilds by truck, rail, pony cart, and completed 1,200 roundabout miles safely through the Indian Ocean aboard a destroyer.

From the salt-water-soaked pulp that is left of my journal, I shall attempt to piece together my story, which, in a larger sense, is the story of the last days of Singapore—of the few who succeeded in escaping and the many who failed.

Early on the morning we left, we were looking at the peaceful scene of little islands when two Japanese light bombers circled and glided toward us. The old ship shuddered when the bombs exploded, just astern. A few minutes later two more planes came over, at not more than 500 feet. This time they didn't miss. The decks seemed to bounce up to meet us as we flopped on our faces. I found a gaping hole through the forward hold. Ten minutes later there was another ear-splitting crash, followed by the hiss of escaping steam. The ship listed and began settling. The engineer emerged from the boiler room and assured us that the boilers wouldn't explode, because he had opened the valves.

The officers gave no order to abandon ship, but within ten minutes a lifeboat was lowered. Before it hit the water fifteen sailors tumbled in and pulled away, too terrified to heed the officers' shouts to come back.

After having looked over the damage, the captain ordered the other two lifeboats overside. Miss Lim, the only woman passenger, got into one. Some of us remained on board, hoping that at least one of the leaky boats would reach the nearest islands, five miles away, and return before we had to swim for it. The captain said he believed that we might have another two hours, but the fire in the coal bunker was spreading and the list was getting worse.

Propped against a coil of rope, I tried to continue my journal, but I was forced to drop the job twice to answer the call of "All hands to fight fire."

We got the fire under control, but Japanese planes came over again and again. One was so low that I saw a bomb swinging on the wing rack; but the pilot didn't drop it. I helped to hoist the life rafts overboard, but the rotten bamboo lashings broke and the rusty tanks sank.

We were about ready to swim for it when one of our lifeboats returned. Thirty-six of us, including the captain and all but one officer, climbed in. Six men volunteered to remain aboard to wait for the next trip, as our boat was leaking badly and we were crammed in like sardines. After an hour of bailing, rowing and sailing, we touched on a coral reef. We waded ashore on the little island of Bangka. Japanese planes knew exactly where we were, and we knew there was little hope of our being rescued. Wet sand, mosquitoes and ants didn't help our situation.

Early February 14, as we were breakfasting on a cigarette, a tin of muddy water—which neither tasted nor smelled like tea—and one small biscuit, the lookout reported launches approaching our ship, which was barely afloat. Some were sure that it was a rescue party, but Captain Henry Steele, formerly attached to the public relations office at Singapore, and I, feared that it was a Japanese patrol. Our skipper said he would surrender if it was the enemy. Steele and I, in a quick huddle, decided that we'd make a break for the jungle in the center of the island. We weren't going to get caught by the Japanese after all we'd been through. But the launches belonged to a rubber planter on a nearby island, who said he would try to rescue us at nightfall. Our hopes were dimmed soon afterward as Japanese planes appeared and flew up and down the beach. They circled away; then we heard bombs exploding. They then circled over us again, and there were more bombs. This process continued for two hours. We were not the targets, but two ships that were sheltering at an island near us were. Toward noon a formation of seven bombers circled over our stricken ship. We saw two bursts forward. The old pride of the Yangtze reared by the stern. Our captain turned away and took off his cap. It was the first and only emotion he displayed.

Our first officer and the doctor put out in a launch to see whether the other ships needed help. We waited, knowing that if we didn't get away that night we probably never would, for we could hear planes over the area. After sundown, the first officer reported that he had taken six badly wounded women from the ships, on which casualties were heavy. All hands were ordered to the beach. We waited an hour, knee-deep in water, while the officers decided on how to get us out to the launches, for the tide was out and even our lifeboats could not approach within a half-mile. Finally we were ordered to make our way as best we could, and the next forty-five minutes were the worst I ever experienced. I clambered over coral rocks and slipped into holes. All around, men were pushing ahead through the darkness, swearing each time they fell and shouting in an effort to keep together. Then I plunged off a rock into the water.

I carried on, swimming, until I was hoisted into a lifeboat full of exhausted men. Somehow, with one oar and with everyone shouting orders, we managed to reach the launch.

Fifty-five men and the one Chinese girl, exhausted and soaked, their legs bleeding from coral cuts, boarded a launch that should have carried only fifteen. Others gave up and turned back to the island to wait until we could send help.

If the night on the island had been miserable, the one aboard the launch was indescribable. Waves rolled over the deck where we were sprawled, wet and shivering; but we were still hoping to make Sumatra before dawn brought Japanese bombers. Behind us chugged a smaller launch, on which our skipper and doctor were working over the wounded men. Daybreak found us approaching the mouth of a river, up which we worked until late afternoon. No one was quite certain where we were, except somewhere in Sumatra.

Late that afternoon we got a big thrill when, rounding a bend, we saw the White Ensign (the British naval flag) flying over warships anchored at a wharf. Ashore, we found members of the Malayan command staff. We had seen them last in Singapore three days before. They had left ahead of us and had got through unscathed.

Early the morning of February 16 we resumed our slow journey upriver. By noon we had reached the motor roadhead, hungry and cramped. But we soon were cheered by the warm hospitality of the Netherlands military and civilians, who fed us and provided a truck for the 400-mile drive across Sumatra.

I sat all night beside the driver, talking and giving him cigarettes to keep him awake, while the rest of our party slept. Every few miles local guards halted us, but courteously waved us on. They were taking no chances on a surprise approach by an enemy patrol. Dawn found us on top a volcanic range that forms the backbone of Sumatra. Monkeys in nearby trees howled their morning hymn to the sun. One official en route had tried to halt us for fear our truck would break down and we would fall prey to tigers; but only one black panther and one civet cat crossed the road, and the truck didn't break down.

At midafternoon we reached the northwest of Sumatra. The hotels were full of refugees from Malaya and the south of Sumatra, but a good Netherlands lady took us in and gave us food. Officials held little hope of our getting out, but the next morning came news that there was a slim chance of leaving by warship if we pushed immediately on. No taxi was available, so we hired pony carts and drove to the railway station during a beating of tom-toms used to sound air raid alarms. Half an hour later we arrived at the port. Effects of a bombing were visible everywhere. Later in the afternoon we saw the most beautiful sight I ever expect to see—a British destroyer, hull down on the horizon steaming full speed toward the harbor.

MacArthur's Dash! H. R. Knickerbocker Narrates the Drama of General's Escape From the Philippines by Sea and Air and Its Aftermath

[March 18, 1942]

"MacArthur's appointment? It's dinkum. It's excellent."

In early March 1942 it was clear that, despite their heroism, American and Filipino troops could not hope to hold off the Japanese forces in the Philippines.

What to do about General Douglas MacArthur? For months the brilliant commander had stood firm against every operation the Japanese could devise. Should he remain in the islands and surrender with his battered troops or should he be removed from the scene to be used later for the certain grand counterattack against the Japanese?

President Roosevelt made the decision. On March 17, 1942, on F.D.R.'s orders, MacArthur relinquished his command in Bataan. Lieutenant General Jonathan Wainwright was placed at the head of the American-Filipino force to conduct the closing phases of a gallant but hopeless defense. MacArthur was ordered to proceed to Australia to assume supreme command of the Allied forces in the southwest Pacific. He swore that he would one day return to the Philippines. He kept his word.

The story of MacArthur's dash of seven days through enemy-infested jungles and waters and its immediate repercussions was told by H. R. Knickerbocker, chief of the Chicago Sun *Foreign Service. In 1931, Knickerbocker, at that time with the Philadelphia* Public Ledger *and the New York* Evening Post, *was awarded a Pulitzer prize for distinguished foreign correspondence.*

(Chicago Sun, *March 19, 1942. By permission of the Chicago* Sun.)

MELBOURNE, AUSTRALIA, March 18.—Speeding through enemy-infested waters by night and hiding in jungles by day, Gen. Douglas A. MacArthur, his wife, his four-year-old son and members of his staff reached Australia after a harrowing seven-day trip by sea and air.

The story of their dash from the Philippines begins at night in the heart of a faraway theater of war which the Japanese apparently had dominated so thoroughly that it became a miracle that any American should still be holding out anywhere there.

One can vizualize the blacked-out beach and the secrecy with which this little party set out to run the gauntlet of the Japanese. They chose to do it in speedboats. Once loaded and with everybody battened down in their seats, the boats crept out and suddenly opened up with full speed.

They roared out, but roaring was preferable to crawling at a pace which the enemy submarines could detect anyway. By night they depended chiefly on their swiftness to avoid torpedoes and shell-fire. But that speed is extremely painful in small boats which skip over the waves like outboard motor boats racing in a choppy sea.

Everybody was shaken badly and bruised, but at dawn came a respite.

They pulled into a jungle cove and hid all day.

All the next night they sped and felt the slam of boats leaping from wave to wave, but by the next day they had reached their first objective.

This was the rendezvous for the airplanes which were coming to fetch them.

For three days they waited for the airplanes.

The day before yesterday they embarked and yesterday they were in a tiny town of 700 persons in Australia's "never never land."

That is the briefest kind of story of their trip, but far more interesting are a few items of information they brought out with them.

The most surprising fact is that three-fourths of the Philippine Islands are still in the hands of American and Filipino troops. The Japanese hold only the ports and portions of the periphery of the principal islands, and there are some islands where there are no Japanese at all.

Most of the land fighting has been done by the Filipino Scouts and the Filipino constabulary, those long established elite native troops for whom the American regular Army officers have the greatest respect. They are officered by Americans.

There is no lack of water either on Corregidor or Bataan peninsula. On Corregidor recently, new wells were developed which have proved highly satisfactory and on both places during the wet season there is far too much water.

If you ask why the Filipino troops fought so well, the one answer is "because they suffered some casualties, because the Japs killed and wounded them and they didn't like it and got mad and decided to make killing Japs their principal business, and they have done it in a highly scientific, butcher-like manner.

"Food is not bad but the worst deprivation is doing without fresh vegetables and salad. There is no scurvy, although we used neither medically-prepared vitamin tablets nor lime juice. Our health may have been helped by the fact that we had some canned tomatoes, beans and peas."

In answer to the query as to how the Japanese were treating the people in the occupied Philippines such as Manila, the answer was:

"The natives are being treated pretty well, for the Japs want to drive a wedge between them and the Americans. But for the most part they remain loyal to us. The Japs have killed too many Filipinos to arouse much enthusiasm for them."

The question as to how the besieged people in Bataan peninsula could find out what was going on in Manila was answered as follows:

"We get the Manila papers three days after publication. We have our people everywhere."

Finally, in answer to the question whether it was true that the Japanese general, Masaharu Homma, commanding the enemy forces before Bataan, had committed suicide out of chagrin over his failure and defeat by numerically inferior forces, the answer was:

"We think it is true. It made Tokyo very angry. The name of a new Japanese general appeared too soon in the place of the old one. It must be true."

A summing up question was asked:

"Will the fortress of Corregidor and the American lines on Bataan peninsula hold?"

The answer was, "Yes."

MacArthur's appointment as United Nations commander for the South Pacific and the knowledge that American troops are here in considerable strength have brought the first sure hope of victory in an area where the Japanese have plunged so far forward with such uninterrupted success that many persons despaired of stopping them with the resources here available.

Recent events have informed the world that the United States is in the Pacific War with all its power and under the leadership of the best general that the United Nations possess. Australians have experienced more joy in these two facts than they have had since the war began.

They now feel confident that Australia will not fall, and that from this fortress eventually the Japanese will be hurled back to an ultimate and crushing defeat.

It also has been a day of great relief to the correspondents who, like myself, have flown across most of this enormous continent and have visited many of its great cities. While the outside world and the United States did not know what was going on in Australia, the correspondents knew that the Americans were here in swarms and throngs and that it was a strain to have to refrain from any mention of them whatever.

I had the opportunity in Adelaide and while flying here to test the reaction of the ordinary people as distinguished from the sometimes more diplomatic expressions of the press.

I asked several Royal Australian Air Force officers what they thought of MacArthur's appointment. One said:

"It's dinkum. It's excellent. It's the best thing that's happened since the war began."

Another said:

"It will be the saving of the Pacific situation. MacArthur is so great a leader that he will inspire not only ourselves, but also the American people to fight far better than we would have fought before."

All through the Australian comment ran the interesting thought that MacArthur, being the most popular military leader, if not the most popular man in the United States, would never be let down by the American people. This meant that as long as he commanded this area Americans would insist that every possible help in men and arms be sent here.

Among the Australian armed forces there is not the faintest trace of jealousy that an American should be made their commander in chief, although only a little while ago there had been some criticism of the British high command.

Maj. Gen. Henry Gordon Bennett, an Australian, whom many had considered a candidate for the supreme Pacific command, came out immediately with high praise for MacArthur and made it plain that he considered it a high honor to work under him.

As a consequence it is considered possible that Gen. Bennett may be placed in charge of the Australian troops under MacArthur, whose domain, it is understood, comprises everything from Singapore to New Zealand.

We rode in a Dutch airplane from Perth to Adelaide and met many Dutch refugees rescued by their daring air force after the Japanese invaded Java. These people know better than we what it means to fall before an invader.

When they heard of Gen. MacArthur's appointment several women wept for joy and cried: "This is the happiest day of our lives since the war began." And Dutchmen nodded gravely, emitting deep "Jas!"

Bataan: Japanese Treatment of U.S. Prisoners Revealed in Eyewitness Report of Death March

[April 10–15, 1942]

"We all wondered if we would get out of the box car alive."

For the Japanese, conquest of the Philippines was absolutely essential. The islands were strategically important and they possessed a wealth of natural resources. Shortly after Pearl Harbor, the Japanese made landings at various points in the Philippines and by Christmas 1941 they succeeded in taking most of the main island of Luzon with the exception of the area around Manila Bay. American and Filipino troops backed up on the Bataan Peninsula and the island of Corregidor.

About twenty-five miles long and twenty miles wide across its base, Bataan juts out from Luzon like a great finger pointed at Cavite twelve miles away. With its two extinct volcanoes, its ravines and mountain streams, its hills and jungles, Bataan was ideal terrain for defense. It had only two roads adequate for a mobile army and these were covered with tank traps and barbed-wire entanglements.

Lieutenant General Masaharu Homma expected to take Bataan in short order. He tried everything—frontal assaults, flank actions, concentrated artillery bombardment, sea-borne infiltrations. For ten weeks he was held off by General Douglas MacArthur's stubborn defense.

The defenders had little ammunition, little food, few medical supplies. They ate the meat of dogs, iguanas, monkeys, mules, carabao and snakes, and whatever berries and vegetables they could find in the jungles. Thousands came down with malaria, scurvy, dysentery and beri beri. The troops sang desperately:

> *We're the battling Bastards of Bataan;*
> *No mama, no papa, no Uncle Sam;*
> *No aunts, no uncles, no cousins, no nieces;*
> *No pills, no planes, no artillery pieces.*
> *. . . And nobody gives a damn!*

The Japanese took Bataan. It was a slow and costly process. Tokyo had to commit more than 200,000 troops before MacArthur's American-Filipino force capitulated.

*It was not long before rumors about an infamous "death march" on
Bataan penetrated to the mainland. The full story was not revealed until
almost two years later when the U.S. Army and Navy jointly released an
official account of Japanese mistreatment of prisoners after the fall of
Bataan. In the following section of the report, Captain (later Colonel)
Willam E. Dyess, Air Corps, of Albany, Texas, who escaped from the
Philippines after almost a year as a Japanese prisoner, gave a first-hand
account of the horrors endured by the prisoners. After he made his statement to the War Department, Dyess was killed in a crash of his fighter
plane at Burbank, California, while he was preparing to go back and
fight the Japanese who had tortured him.*

*(Joint release by the U.S. Army and Navy, Washington, January 27, 1944.
Courtesy of the U.S. Department of Defense.)*

"The march of death" began when thousands of prisoners were
herded together at Mariveles airfield on Bataan at daylight on April
10, 1942, after their surrender. Though some had food, neither Americans nor Filipinos were permitted by their guards to eat any of it.
They were searched and their personal belongings taken from them.
Those who had Japanese tokens or money in their possession were
beheaded.

In groups of 500 to 1,000 men, the prisoners were marched along
the national road of Bataan toward San Fernando, in Pampanga
province. Those marchers who still had personal belongings were
stripped of them; the Japanese slapped and beat them with sticks, as
they marched along without food or water on a scorchingly hot day.

Colonel Dyess, in a middle group, gave this description of "the
march of death":

"A Japanese soldier took my canteen, gave the water to a horse,
and threw the canteen away. We passed a Filipino prisoner of war
who had been bayoneted. Men recently killed were lying along the
roadside, many had been run over and flattened by Japanese trucks.

"Many American prisoners were forced to act as porters for military equipment. Such treatment caused the death of a sergeant in my
squadron, the 31st Pursuit. Patients bombed out of a near-by hospital, half dazed and wandering about in pajamas and slippers, were
thrown into our marching column of prisoners. What their fate was
I do not know. At 10 o'clock that night we were forced to retrace
our march of two hours, for no apparent reason.

"At midnight we were crowded into an enclosure too narrow to
lie down. An officer asked permission to get water and a Japanese

guard beat him with a rifle butt. Finally a Japanese officer permitted us to drink water from a near-by carabao wallow.

"Before daylight the next morning, the 11th, we were awakened and marched down the road. Japanese trucks speeded by. A Japanese soldier swung his rifle from one of them in passing, and knocked an American prisoner unconscious beside the road.

"Through the dust clouds and blistering heat, we marched that entire day without food. We were allowed to drink dirty water from a roadside stream at noon. Some time later three officers were taken from our marching column, thrown into an automobile and driven off. I never learned what became of them. They never arrived at any of the prison camps.

"Our guards repeatedly promised us food, but never produced it. The night of the 11th, we again were searched and then the march resumed. Totally done in, American and Filipino prisoners fell out frequently, and threw themselves moaning beside the roadside. The stronger were not permitted to help the weaker. We then would hear shots behind us.

"At 3 o'clock on the morning of April 12 they shoved us into a barbed-wire bull pen big enough to accommodate 200. We were 1,200 inside the pen—no room to lie down; human filth and maggots were everywhere.

"Throughout the 12th, we were introduced to a form of torture which came to be known as the sun treatment. We were made to sit in the boiling sun all day long without cover. We had very little water; our thirst was intense. Many of us went crazy and several died. The Japanese dragged out the sick and delirious. Three Filipino and three American soldiers were buried while still alive.

"On the 13th, each of those who survived was given a mess kit of rice. We were given another full day of the sun treatment. At nightfall we were forced to resume our march. We marched without water until dawn of April 14, with one two-hour interval, when we were permitted to sit beside the roadside.

"The very pace of our march itself was a torture. Sometimes we had to go very fast, with the Japanese pacing us on bicycles. At other times, we were forced to shuffle along very slowly. The muscles of my legs began to draw and each step was an agony.

"Filipino civilians tried to help both Filipino and American soldiers by tossing us food and cigarettes from windows or from behind houses. Those who were caught were beaten. The Japanese had food stores along the roadside.

"A United States Army colonel pointed to some of the cans of salmon and asked for food for his men. A Japanese officer picked up a can and hit the colonel in the face with it, cutting his cheek wide open. Another colonel and a brave Filipino picked up three American soldiers before the Japs could get to them. They placed them on a cart and started down the road toward San Fernando. The Japanese seized them as well as the soldiers, who were in a coma, and horse-whipped them fiercely.

"Along the road in the province of Pampanga there are many wells. Half-crazed with thirst, six Filipino soldiers made a dash for one of the wells. All six were killed. As we passed Lubao we marched by a Flipino soldier gutted and hanging over a barbed-wire fence. Late that night of the 14th we were jammed into another bull pen at San Fernando with again no room to lie down. During the night Japanese soldiers with fixed bayonets charged into the compound to terrorize the prisoners.

"Before daylight on April 15 we were marched out and 115 of us were packed into a small narrow-gauge box car. The doors were closed and locked. Movement was impossible. Many of the prisoners were suffering from diarrhea and dysentery. The heat and stench were unbearable. We all wondered if we would get out of the box car alive.

"At Capiz Tarlac we were taken out and given the sun treatment for three hours. Then we were marched to Camp O'Donnell, a prison camp under construction, surrounded with barbed wire and high towers, with separate inner compounds of wire. On this last leg of the journey the Japanese permitted the stronger to carry the weaker.

"I made that march of about 85 miles in six days on one mess kit of rice. Other Americans made 'the march of death' in 12 days, without any food whatever. Much of the time, of course, they were given the sun treatment along the way."

Burma: Jack Belden Accompanies General "Vinegar Joe" Stilwell on One of the Most Bitter Retreats of Modern Times

[May 4, 1942]

"This is probably my last message."

For Tokyo, Burma was a prime target, its conquest to be synchronized with that of Malaya and Singapore. On December 9, 1941, only two days after the assault on Pearl Harbor, Japanese units were already pushing across the Isthmus of Kra into Burma. Full-scale invasion came in mid-January 1942. The objective was Rangoon at the mouth of the Irrawaddy. The scheme was to cut off the Burma Road and throttle the Chinese.

Inside Burma two lonely divisions of British and Indian troops prepared to meet the invader. It was no contest. Within several weeks one Japanese force had cut through the jungles to capture Moulmein opposite Rangoon, after which it spread out and crossed the Salween with the aim of circling around the north to Rangoon. Another force pushed into Northern Burma in the direction of Lashio, terminus of the Burma Road.

On the news of the Japanese invasion, Lieutenant-General Joseph W. Stilwell led a Chinese force into Burma. Stilwell, a tough, scrappy fifty-nine-year-old American who had won the name "Vinegar Joe" and had been newly appointed chief-of-staff to Chiang Kai-shek, soon found himself trapped. The British, unable to use their mechanized equipment, headed toward India. Stilwell and the Chinese stayed on too long. Now that they were cut off from the Burma Road they had to get out before the Japanese could outflank them.

It turned out to be one of the wildest retreats in modern times. To get to Assam, Stilwell and his group had to cut through a great triangle of jungle bounded on the east by the Irrawaddy River, on the south by a dry belt, and on the northwest by the Himalaya Mountains. The obstacles included deep forests, wet jungle, mountain streams, elephants, poisonous snakes. The retreating force sloshed through rivers, struggled through jungles, streamed up and down mountain sides.

164

General Stilwell's reaction was clear-cut and honest: "I claim we got a hell of a beating. We got run out of Burma, and it is humiliating as hell. I think we should find out what caused it and go back and retake it."

War correspondent Jack Belden accompanied Stilwell on that amazing forced march and rearguard action. His semi-garbled reports poured in to the London bureau of Time *and were then cabled to New York. Here is his story of the final debacle as pieced together in* Time's *editorial offices.*

("The Fever of Retreat," by Jack Belden, from History in the Writing, *by the Correspondents of* Time, Life *and* Fortune, *ed. by Gordon Carroll; copyright Time Inc. 1945.)*

STILWELL'S HDQ, NORTH BURMA—This is probably my last message. The roads are crowded with thousands of refugees who are under constant aerial strafing, suffering from food and water shortage, and wearied from the pace that on the Shan States front carried the Japanese forward 25 miles a day.

The railway leading to a deadend at Myitkyina has been smashed by Jap bombers, interrupted by Burmese saboteurs. Jeeps, which may be able to negotiate oxcart tracks, are being commandeered to carry out the wounded, but the majority must walk. Whether they escape depends upon whether Alexander and Stilwell can block off roads to stem the Jap advance, and whether the rains come to bog down Jap motor columns.

(MORE)

First Add, EVACUATION—In the midst of writing I heard a sudden roar, looked overhead, and a transport plane was coming in low. I heard "Hurray, hurray!" from American enlisted men as the plane landed. "Don't that plane look good! Go kiss it." Someone sang, *God Bless America.*

The list is now being made out of those who will evacuate. At any rate I won't go, and "Uncle Joe" will stay to the last to direct his troops. I must write fast now and can only set down jumbled impressions of the last days of Burma before they come to take this message.

Last night I stood on Ava Bridge beside two Scotch soldiers who were ready to plunge a stick that would set off 2,000 pounds of explosives and wreck the second largest bridge in the Far East across the Irrawaddy, in the hope of holding off the Japanese on the other side. As I watched, British 25-pounders, manned by Indians, were hurling shells at Mandalay, which has been burning since April 4th and is overrun with *dacoits* and traitors who are shooting at the Chinese garrison in the darkness through the flattened ruins of a city of one-time 120,000 population. This ends a definite stage of the war as now all the rice, salt, oil and tin are in Jap hands, and what remains of Burma will make it difficult to support large armies. Hordes of helpless refugees are streaming northward now.

(MORE)

Second Add, EVACUATION—I continue to write this from Stilwell's headquarters, hoping that someone will pick it up and take it to India before I leave. Everyone but headquarters' doctor and myself have gone. We will set the houses afire with all the diaries, documents and anything of value as soon as it gets dark, and leave early tomorrow to try to catch Stilwell. We shall travel through what, to us, is uncharted area. I cannot reveal even a general route for fear the enemy might get on the trail.

We poured gasoline on a scout car and a couple of sedans, and shot tommy-gun bullets into them only a few hours ago. We still have a couple of cars to destroy but are waiting to see if someone trying to get out can't use them. I've just come from the Tank Corps with 1,000 rounds of machine-gun ammunition and we hope this is enough to last out our small unit on what promises to be a long journey. The Doctor and I had a box of food and killed a sheep which we put in a burlap bag, for emergency, but someone has stolen these already and we will have to manage to get along on a can of cheese we discovered in the litter of this abandoned headquarters. Our supply of boiled water is very low and unless we soon find Stilwell, I am afraid we must drink whatever we can find in dirty ditches along the way. Everything is happening so quickly that I cannot write a coordinated story.

(MORE)

Third Add, EVACUATION—Briefly, here are the last days of Burma. For the last two months the result of the campaign has been almost a foregone conclusion. In the first place, we lacked the sound political theory that we had no war aim in Burma. The people advocating independence were unfriendly from the beginning and when the Japanese began to gain in their successes, this unfriendliness ripened into open hostility. Not only the puppet army was formed, officered by Japs and fighting fanatically, but a vast behind-the-lines process of sabotage, fifth-columning, burning, looting, and semi-guer-rilla warfare was begun with devastating, demoralizing effects. Without air support, the open hostility caused us to fight blindly. We scarcely ever knew exactly where the enemy was, where he would appear, or in how much strength.

Intelligence broke down almost completely, but the Japs were led by Burmese through jungle thickets into the rear of our positions time and again, causing road blocks, clogging supply lines, disrupting communications and causing an adverse psychological effect on men and officers. As the Japanese advanced, lawlessness behind the lines increased. Railroads were wrecked, cars were fired upon in the dark, and even in the daylight several Chinese were murdered on the road. Gangs of *dacoits*, as many as 500, armed with butcher-knife-like *dahs* and with torches in hand, often went through towns completing the work of destruction begun by Jap incendiary bombs. The Japanese, and the small but active group of Burmese, literally and devastatingly burned their way through Burma. In the Sittang River Valley from Toungoo to Mandalay, a distance of over 2,000 miles, and in the Irrawaddy Valley between Prome and Mandalay, every town, to my personal knowledge and observation, was burned to the ground. Pyimana, Yenangyaung, Meiktila and others—these are only names now. Nothing remains of the wooden-housed marts which once stood on the road to Mandalay.

(MORE)

Fourth Add, EVACUATION—We also lacked (1) air support. The Japs continually knew our movements and picked holes in our lines, through which they pushed troops. We scarcely ever were able to reconnoiter the enemy's positions. We were constantly strafed on roads lined with wrecked cars, dead donkeys and human corpses.

(2) Our lines of communications were uncertain. The railroads often did not run because the railway personnel ran away or was intimidated by Burmese. Our radio communication between echelons was poor.

(3) Water was insufficient in the hot wastelands north of Prome and Toungoo, and with the Japs constantly cutting our rear, we often were cut off from watering holes and small rivers.

(4) We never received any reinforcements. British troops had to stay in line and slug it out for three months. Not only were the ranks woefully depleted, but the men were tired beyond telling.

Again I must close and try to rush this off. All about me there is nothing but utmost misery. Roads are lined with belongings abandoned by refugees, 20,000 of whom crossed the Irrawaddy only yesterday hoping to get to India, but their chance is very slight. Evacuation to Bhamo via the river route is practically useless with the Jap capture of Lashio.

Must go. Goodbye.

Battle of the Coral Sea: Stanley Johnston Describes the Sinking of U.S. Aircraft Carrier *Lexington*

[May 8, 1942]

"I would suggest, sir, that if you have to take any more torpedoes you take 'em on the starboard side."

By the spring of 1942 the Japanese had reached the limits of their "defensive" perimeter in the Pacific. In May they launched the first stage of an operation designed this time to extend the line to enclose northern and eastern Australia. The Americans, fortified with growing naval strength, decided to put a halt to further Japanese expansion.

A major sea battle took place on May 7-8, 1942, in the Coral Sea touching New Guinea and the Solomons. The opposing forces were approximately equal in strength. This was the first naval action in history in which surface ships did not exchange a single shot. The battle was fought entirely in the air. Two Japanese carriers and several cruisers and destroyers were badly damaged. The U.S. aircraft carrier Lexington *was sunk. Tokyo claimed a victory.*

Actually, neither side had scored a clear-cut triumph. Significantly, the Japanese called off their convoy slated for Port Moresby. Japanese expansion was checked. Within a month came the great American victory at Midway.

Stanley Johnston, correspondent for the Chicago Tribune, *the only newsman present throughout the engagement, was aboard the* Lexington *almost to the moment she was sunk. Here is his exciting story.*

(Chicago Tribune, *June 17, 1942. By permission of the Chicago* Tribune.)

This is the story of the aircraft carrier *Lexington*'s last hours.

The great old ship was hard hit in the Japanese attack that began at 11:16 A.M., May 8, and continued for seventeen minutes. Five torpedoes had torn huge holes, 20 to 30 feet in diameter, in her port side along the water line and below it. In addition to the direct hits by torpedoes and bombs, the *Lexington* also had been damaged to some extent by scores of misses.

Also a heavy bomb that struck the rail of the forward flight deck had penetrated into the living quarters below. There a quantity of 5-inch shells, which were stacked so as to be close at hand for rapid firing, had been set off. The combination of explosions had started a fire and had been responsible for heavy casualties among the Marines who formed the gun crews.

These quarters also happened to be those of Rear Admiral Aubrey W. Fitch, whose guest I was.

Three fire rooms of the *Lexington*'s engine system had been damaged. The damage, however, was not sufficient to stop her. Her speed never dropped below twenty-five knots until hours after the attack. She stayed with the other carrier, and with the cruisers and destroyers. We were all bound for the Japanese, the intention of Admiral Fitch and Rear Admiral Frank J. Fletcher being to close in and finish them off.

Commander H. R. Healy had telephoned to the bridge to tell Captain Frederick C. Sherman, the *Lexington*'s skipper (since promoted to Rear Admiral): "We've got the torpedo damage temporarily shored up, the fires are out and soon we'll have the ship back on an even keel. But I would suggest, sir, that if you have to take any more torpedoes you take 'em on the starboard side."

At 14:45 in the afternoon there was a heavy, dull explosion inside the hull. I was standing on the flight deck and my knees buckled as the ship shook. Going below with damage parties, I found that the blast had come from deep within, and had twisted heavy steel watertight doors from their hinges.

We discovered that the explosion had been caused by the ignition of volatile vapors from aviation gasoline that had seeped through fractured bulkheads from the huge storage tanks where fuel for the *Lexington*'s air fleet was stored. Fires at a number of points in the open holds were burning fiercely.

All the ship's chemical equipment was rushed to the job but it was not enough. The blast had smashed water mains and the auxiliary pumps, and had cut off light and power to the hold. The flames spread swiftly.

A destroyer was called alongside, and its hose lines were run aboard, but there were far too few auxiliary hose lines on the *Lexington* and the destroyer did not help because its pumps could not lift water high and far enough.

About 1 P.M. we found that the first blast had killed Commander

Healy, who had been working below. It had also thrown Commander Arthur J. White, the ship's surgeon, through one of the hospital doors, breaking his collar bone and one ankle.

Despite these injuries he dragged himself around for five hours, attending other casualties. He quit only after the order to abandon ship had been given and he had seen the last wounded man evacuated from the hospital and laid out on the flight deck.

The second explosion came about twenty-five minutes after the first. It was the beginning of a series that ultimately came at intervals of a few seconds. That, however, was hours later. After the third and fourth explosions the navigator reported that the steering apparatus, which had functioned perfectly in the battle and up to that time, had failed.

With the failure of the electrical power systems came an interruption of the great blowers—the ship's ventilating system. Heat quickly rose in the engine and fire rooms to between 145 and 162 degrees. Nevertheless the engineer's gang stayed at their posts and kept their equipment going to give the twenty-five knot speed demanded.

Commander Seligman was leading his fire-fighting squads. Smoke below became so dense that beams from electric flashlights would not penetrate it. Only the familiarity of the men with the internal plan of the ship enabled them to move around at all. Some of these fire-fighters were killed or burned by almost every explosion. Several times Commander Seligman was blown through open doors and out of scuttle holes.

It is not possible to estimate the number of men lost fighting the fire but medical records for the *Lexington* show that at least half of the casualties were those caused by explosions and burns.

Singed, his clothing half burned off, Commander Seligman reported to Captain Sherman the existing conditions below decks and the imminence of a devastating explosion of the ship's munitions. The time had arrived to make the momentous decision to abandon the famous old ship.

Admiral Fitch leaned over the high railing around his little bridge on "the island" and spoke to Captain Sherman, who was pacing the navigating bridge ten feet below him. The admiral pitched his voice in a conversational tone, saying:

"Well, Fred, I guess it's time to get the men off."

It was 5:15 P.M., the end of the battle for the *Lexington*.

Admiral Fletcher sent several destroyers alongside and we transferred our wounded, 160 men, to the vessels. Hundreds of other crew members also stepped aboard the destroyers. Still other hundreds let long hemp ropes down the sides of the *Lexington*, slid down them, and entered the waters of the Coral Sea. Many life rafts soon were floating around the *Lexington*'s stern. Big Navy whaleboats from cruisers and destroyers were plying back and forth. A few men struck out to swim the quarter mile to the nearest cruisers.

I joined a group of pilots who remembered that the ship's store of ice cream would melt soon with the refrigerator's electric current cut off. Rather than lose it they got several two-gallon cans and we sat around under the wings of the planes parked on the deck and ate ice cream from paper drinking cups.

This was typical of the way in which the ship was abandoned. There was no hurry, no scrambling. This discipline was part of the reason roll-calls later revealed that 92 per cent of her personnel were safely transferred from her.

I did a last turn on the deck with Lieut. Comdr. Edward H. Eldredge, an air officer, after most of the crew had left. We decided to take the next favorable chance ourselves. My preparations consisted of transferring all notes to a breast pocket of my shirt, where I hoped they would stay dry. Then I picked a rope with a big knot at its end, where I might sit until picked up, and cautiously slid down.

In two minutes I was picked up in a whaleboat with other men. We towed several life rafts as well, and got a number of men to a cruiser. I stayed aboard the cutter with the coxswain, and we began gathering in men who were swimming and showing signs of exhaustion.

While we were thus engaged there came a heavy explosion aboard the *Lexington* that sent the amidship portion of the flight deck hurtling into the air. Flames burst through. Immediately afterward came a blinding flash, a tremendous shock and a billowing cloud of black smoke soaring skyward as the 1,000-pound bombs exploded. Bits of the steel deck and side plates showered the sea for hundreds of yards around, endangering all in the water and in the boats.

I learned that Commander Seligman had just slid down a rope into the sea, and Captain Sherman was still on a rope when this explosion came. They had stayed to the last to see that every man got away.

Luckily they were not harmed by the debris that fell all around them and they were rescued.

It was almost dark when our boat reached the mother ship and unloaded. The whole length of the *Lexington* was ablaze as I climbed aboard the rescue cruiser. It was a fierce white fire, evidently consuming the 80,000 gallons of aviation fuel.

Blast after blast rent the ship but she floated high and upright. A few small vessels poking among the debris around her for possible swimmers were ordered to leave her side.

A destroyer stood by to administer the finishing coup. This consisted of a salvo of four more heavy torpedoes, delivered at close range. The *Lexington* slowly filled with water and gradually, still upright, slid with a prolonged hiss beneath the water.

"She was a lady to the end," one of her officers remarked.

Bombing of Cologne: Robert E. Bunnelle Gets the Story of the First Great Air Armada Over Germany's Big Industrial Center

[May 30, 1942]

"Cologne glowed like a big cigarette end in a blackout."

London, May 31, 1942
Communiqué from the Air Ministry

Last night a force of considerably over one thousand bombers attacked targets in the Ruhr and the Rhineland. Cologne was the main objective. Full reports are not yet available, but preliminary reports of crews indicate the attack was an outstanding success. By dawn fires and smoke were visible from the coastline of Holland and reconnaissance early this morning reported a pall of smoke was rising to a height of 15,000 feet over the target. During this operation other aircraft of the bomber command and aircraft of the fighter, coastal, and army co-operation command attacked enemy airdromes and enemy fighters which attempted to intercept. Forty-four of our aircraft are missing from all these operations.

Thus, with typical British understatement, the world was informed about the greatest mass air raid in history to that date. It was bad news for the German public. Word of this devastating air assault, far greater than any Hitler had loosed upon England, spread quickly through the Third Reich. The German people were learning the hard way about the luxury of infatuation with conquest.

The raid was planned with painstaking care. Some 6,000 British, Canadian and Australian airmen, assisted by another 100,000 men at scores of airdromes throughout the British Isles, were called to prepare for the raid. The target was bristling with defenses—a concentration of 500 large and small anti-aircraft guns, more than a hundred giant searchlights, and veteran Luftwaffe squadrons. But nothing could stay the operation.

On the night of May 30, 1942, 1,250 planes took off for the target. To each crew went a message from Air Marshal Arthur Harris:

Press home your attack on this night's objective with the utmost determination and resolution in the full knowledge that if you individually succeed,

174

the most shattering and devastating blow will have been delivered against the very vitals of the enemy.

The raid was a great success. The Royal Air Force lost forty-four bombers, but pulverized at least 300 acres in the middle of Cologne. German war production in the great city was set back effectively for many weeks.

No newsmen were permitted to accompany the bombers. But Robert E. Bunnelle, born in 1903 at Urbana, Ohio, got the story for the Associated Press when the last planes came home. The news sped to the corners of the earth.

(*Associated Press, May 30, 1942. By permission of Associated Press.*)

The grass grew neatly to the edge of England's flare-lighted runways with peaceful lushness of a country club lawn. But there peace ended, for it was 8:08 P.M.—and take-off time for the greatest raid in all aerial warfare.

In the soft dusk of England's spring, dozens of heavily loaded bombers squatted at the top of the line. Their propellers beat an impatient rattle awaiting the green light from the control tower. And the same thing was happening at hundreds of hidden bomber bases over England. Already the sky was filled with roar of planes from the other fields, all getting ready for the 1,250-bomber party at Cologne—the world's first four-figure air raid.

The best way to describe the unprecedented battle perhaps will be to describe what happened aboard one of those planes. It was a feat that was being duplicated by all the others.

The captain of a four-motored Stirling in one group of waiting ships suddenly heard an anxious voice on the intercommunicating telephone.

"Captain," the voice said, "if we have to wait much longer, we'd better switch off. Engine three's getting hot."

But before the captain could reply, the green light flashed from the control tower. The big plane began to move. The raid was on.

The crew in the Stirling looked to the left. In the flickering light of flare-path number two, they saw the others taking off—plane after plane like streetcars leaving a terminal. The Stirling moved faster. As it began to lift, a voice on the interplane phone sang: "We're off to see the Wizard, the wonderful Wizard of Oz." The field dropped swiftly away and the Stirling circled to set its course. The crew suddenly felt a mighty bump—but it was only the slipstream from another Stirling that roared near by.

Before the planes reached the coast they were climbing through clouds. A dejected voice on the Stirling's phone complained: "Just our luck to find ten-tenths cloud (thick clouds) at Cologne." But the clouds began to break and soon dykes and towns in Holland loomed in the moonlight. The moon was to the starboard and straight ahead was a rose-colored glow in the sky.

"It's probably something to do with the German-Dutch frontier searchlight belt," somebody said. But just then the captain broke in on the plane's phone to warn the Stirling's three gunners: "We're in the danger zone now. Keep your eyes skinned for any aircraft of the enemy."

The front gunner spoke up quickly.

"Light ahead to port," he reported.

All eyes turned to the front, just in time to see a sudden shower of incendiaries, apparently jettisoned by a bomber under attack by a Nazi night fighter. Soon they saw the burning wreckage of a plane on the ground. Disaster had struck in the soft moonlight. By this time the Stirling was in the searchlight belt and in the blue streaks piercing the sky the crew saw other planes—some traveling their way and others headed back for England. The going was rougher now because the captain was dodging and weaving the ship to avoid lights and flak that sailed up from the ground like white mushrooms.

The front gunner broke the tenseness. "Keep weaving, captain," he shouted on the plane's phone. "The flak is getting so thick you could walk on it."

"There's a plane on our tail," cut in the rear gunner, then, half disappointedly, he added: "Hell, it's only one of ours."

The rose-colored glow was still ahead and the captain came on the phone again.

"How much longer before we're there, navigator?"

"About ten minutes," replied the navigator.

"Well, we don't need you any more. That light's Cologne. The fellows have built up quite a fire."

By this time the sky became so full of flak, tracers, shell bursts, and spotlight streaks that it was like the fireworks at the county fair. The Germans were throwing everything they had at the attackers. From the bomb aimer's hatch, Cologne glowed like a big cigarette end in a blackout. Then the plane was directly over the fires and the captain ordered: "Bomb doors open!"

"Bomb doors open," came the reply.

The captain spoke again. He said: "Hell, wait a minute. No use wasting stuff on burning buildings. Let's look for a black spot."

Block after block of the town was blazing under the craft, smoke drifting past the flame-outlined wings. In the blaze could be seen what appeared to be white-hot skeletons of steel framework.

There were Wellingtons, Halifaxes, Manchesters, more Stirlings—in fact, about everything but helicopters—flying above, below, and on either side of the Stirling. All were silhouetted against the towering flames of Cologne. And all were dropping their loads on Cologne. While the town blazed like a furnace, the blasts of high explosive bombs continued to hurl the walls of buildings across the flames. From time to time, in the outer dark spaces, showers of incendiaries poured down in platinum-colored flashes that turned slowly red.

One tiny dark spot showed on the Rhine river's flowing west bank.

"That might be Elektra Stahldraht Fabrik (a steel wire plant)," said the captain. "Let's try it."

There followed an anxious moment of leveling off and moving right and left to get on the target. Then the bomb aimer pressed the button and the plane gave a lift from the release of the heavy bomb cargo. A piece of flak tore through the ship six inches above the pilot's head and for a few minutes everybody was busy with the guns, rudders, and cameras as the Stirling wove its way out of a blazing curtain of anti-aircraft fire. The ship slipped through the flak and the rear gunner shouted: "We got it! I saw the white flash of debris flying, then red and yellow flames shooting up."

There were shouts of elation on the ship's phone. The job had been done. The Stirling's bombs had found their mark. The Stirling skirted the city, setting a homeward course. The burning area had increased tremendously in the eight minutes over the target. New fires were springing up everywhere. About ninety miles from Cologne, the captain turned in a complete circle to take another look. From this distance, the three major fires had merged into one immense volcano of flame.

The Stirling dodged and spiraled on to England, trying to confuse Nazi night fighters and ground observers.

"Can't anybody see our coast yet?" the captain asked.

"Not yet," the phone said. Then—with obvious relief—came: "Yes, there it is and you can still see Cologne."

"Well," said the captain, "throw the navigator overboard. We won't need him any more tonight!"

It was a breeze from there on to the home station. The Stirling radioed in and the flare-path control informed the pilot he was fourth in and gave him the height at which to circle for a landing.

As he rounded the field awaiting his turn to land, a Wellington fluttering from the opposite direction, nipped past one wing.

"What's wrong with that idiot!" growled the navigator. But he quickly added: "Sorry, looks like he had a rough trip."

It turned out later that the Wellington was short-cutting home with a badly wounded crew.

Three planes ahead of the Stirling were shepherded in quickly without incident—one every three minutes with timetable precision —and within a few moments after the Stirling touched ground she was in the hands of a ground crew hurrying to heal her battle wounds.

The bus that took the cheerful crew to quarters for interrogation by intelligence officers also carried others just back from Cologne. One lanky pilot with sun-reddened face and white eyebrows said with a laugh:

"Well, that was the only time I enjoyed being over Cologne—and this is my fifth trip. God, what a pretty fire!"

"Damned good show," another agreed.

Interrogation finished, the crews went off to eat bacon and eggs— a special treat.

Midway: Ensign G. H. Gay, Wounded and Afloat in the Sea, Watches the Battle as Japanese Ships Pass by in Flames

[June 3–7, 1942]

"For some reason I put the bullet into my mouth."

The Japanese public was understandably delighted by the steady stream of victories. In June 1942 Tokyo sent a great armada of 53 warships and a score of transport and supply ships to attack American-held Midway. The strategy was clear—Hawaii would be next.

The Japanese never landed on Midway. From June 3 to 7 there took place a sea battle fought entirely by planes and submarines. U.S. Army land-based bombers and Navy carrier planes went to work on the Japanese fleet. When the action was over, the Japanese had lost four carriers, two heavy cruisers, three destroyers, and transports. American plane losses were heavy. Moreover, the hard-fighting Japanese sank the carrier Yorktown.

Midway, a brilliant victory for the United States, was the turning point of the Pacific war. The Japanese tide of conquest receded from Midway on.

One of the combatants at Midway was Ensign G. H. Gay, a 25-year-old torpedo-plane pilot, son of a Texas oil operator. Crashing his plane into the sea in the midst of the battle, young Gay survived to give an amazing fish-eye view of the action. His story was reported by Walter B. Clausen, Associated Press correspondent.

(The New York Times, *June 9, 1942. By permission of Associated Press.*)

The first eyewitness account of the Battle of Midway Island, detailing its most violent stages, was related today by a wounded American naval aviator who told of floating in the sea and watching a line of burning Japanese ships pass by.

He told of a thunderous—and highly successful—attack by American dive bombers and torpedo planes on Japanese aircraft carriers. And from his "fish-eye" view he watched the desperate circlings of

179

Japanese naval planes, unable to settle on their blazing and battered mother ships. The story was told by Ensign G. H. Gay, twenty-five-year-old torpedo-plane pilot of Houston, Texas. His wounds were not serious.

For ten hours the pilot, careful to conceal himself from vengeful Japanese fliers by hiding his head under a cushion from his wrecked plane, drifted in the sea and obtained one of the most amazing stories of a major naval engagement.

Ensign Gay occupied what naval men called "a fish-eye view" of the attack on three Japanese carriers. His squadron met fierce enemy fighter-plane opposition while driving home a torpedo assault on one of the larger Jap carriers. It occurred early on June 4, opening day of the battle. He was the only one of the crew of three to survive the crash of his ship.

Taking off from his fleet carrier with his squadron, Gay approached the objective in midmorning. Visibility was unlimited. Below lay three Japanese carriers, less than ten miles extending between the first and last of the enemy ships that were screened by a considerable force of cruisers and destroyers. Gay took stock of the drama below him. Two *Kaga*-class carriers had been taking on their aircraft. Another smaller carrier lay between them, also receiving planes. One of the larger carriers already burned fiercely, while enemy cruisers and destroyers wheeled around it, waiting to rescue personnel.

Twenty minutes later the American dive bombers rocketed into view. In the face of terrific anti-aircraft fire and enemy fighter attack, they leveled for the assault. Gay heard his machine gunner say he had been hit. But the approach continued. Near the great Japanese carrier, Gay launched his projectile, then swung sharply over the target and sped astern as fast as his plane could carry him.

Suddenly an explosive shell from a Zero fighter ripped through his torpedo plane's rudder controls. The detonation seared Gay's left leg. Almost simultaneously, a small-caliber bullet struck his upper left arm. Coolly, he brought his heavy plane into a stall and pancaked into the sea several miles astern of the enemy carrier. His gunner was dead, and in the emergency landing his radioman was unable to pull free.

At 11 A.M. Gay, alone, watched the tail surfaces of his plane disappear. Then a bit of luck held with him. Out of the sinking wreckage floated the bag containing the deflated rubber life raft—and a black cushion on which the bombardier kneels while working. Gay figured his chances quickly and accurately. There had been reports of

Japanese strafing helpless pilots bailing out by parachute, and of machine-gunning of men in such life rafts as had floated clear of his own plane. He declined to offer himself as such a victim. He ducked under the cushion as enemy fighters swarmed overhead. Not knowing the extent of his wounds, he felt cautiously at his arm. The bullet, which apparently had struck him at the spent end of its trajectory, dropped out in his hand.

"For some reason," Gay recalled, "I put it in my mouth. Maybe I wanted a souvenir. Anyhow, I lost it before long."

He bandaged his injured leg under-water. Then from his fish-eye view, he saw two other Jap carriers hit squarely by U.S. bombers. Tremendous fires burst from these vessels. Great billows of smoke churned upward with the flames billowing from the apex in dark columns. Internal explosions sent new gushes of smoke and fire belching from the carriers. As the ferocious Pacific-fleet attack ended, the second *Kaga*-class carrier was on fire from bow to stern.

Surface craft gave Gay some narrow brushes. One enemy destroyer appeared to be driving straight at him as she sped to aid a stricken carrier. He thought she would run him down, but at the last instant she plowed past. A heavy Jap cruiser steamed by less than five hundred yards away. He saw her crew lining the rail, their white uniforms gleaming against the battle paint, grimly watching the destruction of their force.

As the afternoon waned, the Japanese made frantic efforts to stem the damage. An enemy cruiser sought to stand alongside a crippled cruiser, but seemed unable to approach close enough. Gay observed this vessel's big guns commence to rake the wounded carrier, presumably to scuttle her. Sometime later a destroyer managed to come alongside the still-floating carrier to remove survivors. Overhead, Japanese planes appeared to be circling in a vain attempt to land on the smashed carrier. They would pass above her, then soar out of sight and return.

Darkness fell, and Gay never learned what became of them. In the twilight, "maybe a little earlier than was wise," he inflated his life raft from his carbon-dioxide bottle. He said he had his fill of salt water. He had to make emergency patches on several bulletholes in the rubber boat before it would sustain him safely. He clambered in. The long night began.

Far to the north, great glowing patches appeared in the sky. Gay thought these might have been the searchlights of Japanese rescue vessels seeking to pick up carrier personnel. There didn't seem to be much else to do, so he "tried to catch a few winks of sleep." Toward morning, he was awakened by three explosions, which he believed may have been demolition charges. Several hours after sunup a Navy patrol plane, winging out on a search, spotted his rubber boat and picked him up. A Navy doctor asked him what treatment he had had for his burns and he replied: "Well, I soaked 'em in salt water for ten hours."

Fall of Sevastopol: Soviet War Correspondents Recall the Defense of the Mighty Crimean Naval Base

[July 21, 1942]

Hitler's drive in the south was more successful than the offensives against Leningrad and Moscow. Aided by Hungarian and Rumanian divisions, he took the rich Ukraine and then pushed on to the great Black Sea port of Odessa. Then his forces turned south to try to capture the strategically vital Crimea with its powerful naval base at Sevastopol.

It was not an easy task, for the Russians resisted stubbornly. Sevastopol is surrounded by a ring of hills in which the Germans found their tanks immobilized. In the first assault, commencing in December 1941, the Germans used their artillery and the Luftwaffe *to blast a large part of the city into ruins. For some six months the great Black Sea city remained under attack. Life in besieged Sevastopol was as grim as that in Leningrad.*

In June 1942 the Germans opened another furious assault on the city. The colossal battle raged for a full month. General Fritz Erich von Manstein described it:

On the morning of 7 June, as dawn turned the eastern sky to gold and swept the shadows from the valleys, our artillery opened up in its full fury by way of a prelude to the infantry assault. Simultaneously the squadrons of the *Luftwaffe* hurtled down to their allotted targets. . . .

The offensive . . . was marked on both fronts by a bitter struggle for every foot of ground, every pill-box and every trench. Time and time again the Russians tried to win back what they had lost by launching violent counter-attacks. In their big strong-points, and in the smaller pill-boxes too, they often fought till the last man and the last round.

The story of the defense of Sevastopol was recounted by Soviet war correspondents Ilya Ehrenburg and Alexei Tolstoy in these two vivid dispatches. Note that Ehrenburg ended his dispatch with these words: "Tolstoy immortalized the heroic defense of Sevastopol in the saddest days in the history of Russia. A time will come and a new Tolstoy will describe the heroism of Sevastopol in the Second Patriotic War."

183

That time came. The coincidence seems remarkable—Alexei Tolstoy wrote the story.

SEVASTOPOL

(Ilya Ehrenburg, "Sevastopol," in The Heroic Defense of Sevastopol [*Moscow,* 1942], pp. 15–18. Foreign Languages Publishing House, Moscow.)

"Death is the best medicine for the Russians."

"Sevastopol is still holding out"—these words which have flown round the world are being repeated with pride by all champions of liberty. When the Germans first began to storm the city, friend and foe and impartial observer alike weighed the chances of the contending sides. The forces were unequal, and military observers predicted: "It's a question of three days, a week at the outside. . . ." The Germans boasted at the time: "On the fifteenth of June we'll be drinking champagne on the Grafsky." They knew how many planes they had; they knew how difficult it was to defend the city, all the roads to which had been cut off. But they overlooked one thing: Sevastopol is no ordinary city. Sevastopol is the glory of Russia, the pride of the Soviet Union.

A heap of ruins. The statue of Lenin, which by some miracle escaped the holocaust, looks on the raging fires. There the statue stands—symbolic of the spirit of our country. Sevastopol is an island. On three sides Germans, on the fourth water—water teeming with German mines, seething with German shells, water, over which hover German planes. Krasnodar or Novorossiisk are now looked on as the mainland by the Sevastopolites. Two thousand plane flights a day—the Germans bomb and bomb. Twelve, fifteen enemy divisions. And still Sevastopol holds out.

Towns, famed fortresses, entire countries have capitulated to the enemy, but Sevastopol does not surrender. Soviet troops do not play at war—they fight as long as there is a spark of life in them. When the enemy has two and three times the number of figures on the chessboard of the battlefield they do not say: "I surrender." They fight.

At the beginning of June the Germans, basking in the sun, were in high spirits: they were told that within three days they would be in Sevastopol. Kurt Kunsewitz wrote from Braunschweig to his brother Otto, a corporal: "I hope to hear that you're in Sevastopol soon; once you're there don't hesitate. If you see anybody suspicious —stand him up against the wall! There's no need to show them mercy. And kick them out of their houses without ceremony. Take whatever you want—bread, eggs, and if they dare to grumble, shoot them and have done with it. Death is the best medicine for the Russians." On June 11, Otto Kunsewitz gave up the ghost at the approaches to Sevastopol: instead of eggs he had received a hand grenade.

Death has proved an excellent sedative for the maniacal Germans. With horror the whole of Germany is repeating: "Sevastopol . . . Sevastopol. . . ." The wife of Oberfeldwebel Ludwig Reihert writes to her husband: "I dreamt I was looking for you near Sevastopol and couldn't find you—everywhere were graves, graves, graves. What a nightmare!"

Simferopol is crammed with crippled Germans. Yalta reeks of carbolic. Oberleutenant Oscar Greiser jotted down in his diary which our men found near Sevastopol: "Near Bakhchisarai is a valley which the local inhabitants call 'The Valley of Death.' Now it has justified its name. A considerable portion of the population of Erfurt, Jena and my own Eisenach lie buried there. . . ."

War prisoner Kneidler snivels: "We did not expect such resistance. Here, every rock shoots. How I managed to get through this inferno is simply a miracle. . . ." Another war prisoner by the name of Klein admits: "At first we felt pretty cocky. Now our men are terribly on edge. Many of them are doubtful whether we'll ever take the blasted city. . . ."

Yes, the Germans have been put on edge. They did not expect to meet with the Sevastopolites at Sevastopol. In superstitious terror the Germans call our Soviet sailors the "Black Death." The other day one sailor wiped out thirty Germans. He was brought into the hospital wounded. His jersey was red. From every side one could hear: "There's a splendid chap for you—one against thirty!" The sailor replied: "I don't know. I didn't count them—I simply pitched into them."

A battery was defending a hill. The supply of shells gave out. Meanwhile the German tanks were rumbling up the slope. The commander despatched the following message: "Request that you open fire on me."

One company repulsed three tank attacks. The Germans launched a fourth. The leading tank broke through to the Soviet trenches. Political Officer Tkachenko attached a bundle of hand grenades to his belt and threw himself under the treads of the oncoming tank.

The men intensified their fire and the remaining tanks turned back. The fourth attack was repulsed. That is how Tkachenko barred the road of the enemy to Sevastopol.

The Germans occupied a Soviet trench. The men began to fall back. Political Officer Gakokhidze, armed with a rifle and hand grenades, hurled himself at the Germans. Three men dashed after him. Gakokhidze burst into the trench, let fly two hand grenades, bayoneted a German officer and three soldiers, and then, seizing their submachine-gun, began to mow down the Germans at short range. The four heroes destroyed seventy Germans. The lost trench was recaptured.

"It's a miracle," the newspapers the world over say of the defence of Sevastopol. The military observers are looking for an explanation. They speak of the cliffs or of coast batteries. But there is only one explanation for the miracle at Sevastopol—valor. No matter how this unequal battle for the ruins of the city ends it will remain a victory for Soviet arms. The duel between the small garrison and fifteen enemy divisions will go down in history.

The heroism of the Sevastopol garrison serves to inspire the Red Army, which is now, on various sectors of the front, repulsing the attacks of the hated enemy, causing it enormous losses in men and materiel. And tomorrow it will inspire the soldiers of the second front, who will also say: "We'll fight like the champions of Sevastopol."

Tolstoy immortalized the heroic defence of Sevastopol in the saddest days in the history of Russia. A time will come and a new Tolstoy will describe the heroism of Sevastopol in the Second Patriotic War, an epic of wrath and glory. From now on two words will forevermore be interwoven in the minds of man: Sevastopol and valor.

THE FLAG OF SEVASTOPOL

(Alexei Tolstoy, "The Flag of Sevastopol," in The Heroic Defense of Sevastopol [Moscow, 1942], pp. 124–128. Foreign Languages Publishing House, Moscow.)

"The Germans surged forward only to be mowed down . . . ran, crawled, howling like mad dogs."

The flag over Sevastopol was lowered on the night of July 2. During the final days of the defense of the city—a city whose traditions reflected glory on Russia—the garrison, with wrath burning high and utter disregard for death, fought tooth and nail in the suburbs and streets of Sevastopol in order to gain a few more hours in which to evacuate the troops and civilian population and to make the Germans pay still more dearly for the beloved city they were surrendering.

The sailors of the Black Sea Fleet and the Red Armymen of the heroic garrison did all that was humanly possible, and even more, to convert the victory of the Germans into their defeat, to make not German but Russian glory resound throughout the whole world. It is not he who dashes headlong into the jaws of death who is brave, but he who looks death coolly in the face and says to it calmly: "Now then, my gaunt friend, step aside a bit, I'm too busy just yet. . . ." Such is the Russian soldier: to him duty comes first, and as for the rest, important or not important, he'll think about it when he has the leisure; down in the dumps he'll crack a joke, and going to meet death—don a clean shirt.

For seven months and twenty-five days the 11th German Army—a force of three hundred thousand men, nearly a thousand planes, a tank corps and powerful artillery, which included guns of a larger calibre than even the famous "Big Berthas"—tried to crack the Sevastopol nut and finally broke its teeth.

The Germans had all the advantages on their side: the Crimea as a springboard, and the aerodromes and railways to bring up their reserves and munitions. They had Hitler's latest order before them—to finish with Sevastopol in four or five days regardless of the losses incurred. The three hundred thousand Germans and Rumanians had no choice but to scramble over the mountains of their own dead and storm the city or to be mowed down by the machine-guns of the "SS" units trained on their backs.

And on they came, scrambling and crawling over the disintegrating mash of their own dead—a mash sprinkled from the air with formalin and carbolic, but constantly rising higher and higher. And still the city did not surrender. And still the machine-guns of the "SS" units trained on their backs impelled them to keep on.

Sevastopol was no more than a tiny dot on the map of the Crimea. Reserves, munitions and supplies could be brought up only by sea, with great difficulty and losses as a result of the constant attacks of enemy torpedo and dive bombers. The Sevastopol garrison had absolutely no possibility of maneuvering or, consequently, of taking the initiative. The men defending the naval base fought with an inferiority of at least one to five, and when this one sent these five to their forefathers fresh replacements of lanky Germans and swarthy Rumanians were brought up on trucks.

There, on that holy strip of Sevastopol soil the valor of Russia's sailors and soldiers, staunch in their ancient traditions and pride of country, burned with an unquenchable flame.

The task assigned to Sevastopol was to divert and hold as large as possible a force of the enemy, to maul them and exterminate them, and thus to upset Hitler's plans for a spring offensive. One of the reasons for the ultimate defeat of the Germans in 1918 was the monstrous and senseless way in which they sent their picked divisions to their slaughter at Verdun. Ludendorff never succeeded in stopping this hemorrhage in his army.

The German losses in and around Sevastopol for twenty-five days in June 1942 were: seven German and three Rumanian divisions wiped out to a man, more than half their tank corps, and a third of their aircraft. The total German losses for the eight months of the siege of Sevastopol were approximately three hundred thousand officers and men, of which at least one hundred thousand were killed. This was the blood money they paid for the ruins of Sevastopol, which will be retaken by us—this the defenders of Sevastopol have vowed to do; today the whole of the Soviet Union pledges itself: this city of glorious traditions will be Soviet again.

Last year the Germans stormed Sevastopol twice—in November and December. The third assault on the city, which was launched at the beginning of June, was ushered in by the fierce bombardment from land and air. The number of shells fired is absolutely unprecedented in the present war.

Sevastopol went underground. The workers, the majority of whom were women, never left their benches during these hours, turning out trench-mortars, bombs, shells and hand grenades, repairing tanks, guns and trucks. The casualties were very light: several men per regiment. The bombardment continued for five days—the clock round. The whole city was in flames.

Early on the morning of June 7, after a short artillery preparation, dive bombers swooped down on our companies and batteries, which theoretically should have been smashed to smithereens, and following on the dive bombers came German tanks and infantry units.

Our front, a wasteland of shell-holes and craters, came to life. Machine-guns, rifles and automatic-rifles bristled from crannies; the muzzles of cannon loomed up from their underground emplacements, some even being rolled out onto the field; anti-tank gun crews prepared for action; the naval vessels and forts trained their heavy guns on the enemy; correctors took up their posts at field telephones. Sevastopol sent its death-dealing salvos on the advancing German divisions.

With death in front of them and death behind them, the Germans surged forward only to be mowed down, replaced by others who pressed on, ran, crawled, howling like mad dogs. Some managed to reach the outer rim of our defenses—only to come up against the bayonets of the sailors of the Black Sea Fleet and the Red Armymen. The sailors had discarded their steel helmets and had gone over the top in their sailor hats with the ribbons fluttering behind them. The hat of our sailors will yet be famed in song and verse!

The first assault lasted fifteen hours. The Germans turned tail and ran, took cover, hid in shell-holes, crawled to safety, fled. Nor was there anyone to bring in their thousands of killed and wounded. And so it went on for twenty-five days.

With aching heart the whole country watched the deathless heroes who were defending the honor and glory of our native land. And with every new day that passed, hearing the news that Sevastopol was still holding out, though now but a smoking pile of ruins on the shores of the historic bay, pride and thankfulness, anguish and anxiety filled our hearts. Sevastopol lowered its flag, carried out the order that had been given, but only soon, soon to raise it high again at the very first call to battle stations. Its defenders did not surrender a whit of the honor and glory of their country; they added to this honor and glory for themselves and for their country. Sevastopol was and will be again the stronghold of the Black Sea Fleet.

Over the radio the Germans are loudly proclaiming their victory for all the world to hear. It cost them dearly this victory of theirs— a truly Pyrrhic victory.

Guadalcanal: American Newsmen Describe the First of a Long Series of Offensives That Finally Paralyzed Japanese Power in the Pacific

[August–November, 1942]

It was a bleak summer of 1942 for the Allies in Europe. The prognosis seemed to be much better in the Pacific. On three major fronts there the Allies, especially the United States, were on the offensive—in the Aleutians in the north, at Midway in the center, and at Guadalcanal in the Solomon Islands in the south.

In occupying the Solomons in the spring of 1942 the Japanese had laid a block on the Allied supply line to Australia. At Guadalcanal they had built an airfield from which they hoped to cut the American lifeline altogether. For the Americans that airstrip on Guadalcanal was vital. It was to be the target of an offensive move to protect supply lines and at the same time inaugurate a series of blows that would paralyze Japanese power in the South Pacific.

On August 7, 1942, U.S. Marines, the First Marine and elements of the Second Marine Divisions, protected by a naval task force, landed on Guadalcanal and the nearby islands of Tulagi and Florida. There was strong opposition, but the airstrip on Guadalcanal was taken. It was renamed Henderson Field.

The Japanese rallied. The next day they struck at the American fleet off Savo Island and sank four cruisers (three heavy American cruisers and one Australian). It was a vicious blow.

The land campaign on Guadalcanal was savage and long drawn out. The Americans clung desperately to a beachhold just seven miles long and four miles deep. Equally fierce was the naval fighting.

The struggle for Guadalcanal stimulated some of the finest reporting of the war. In the first selection, Ira Wolfert, correspondent for the North American Newspaper Alliance and winner of the Pulitzer prize for international reporting (1943), compared the fighting quality of Japanese and American troops. The second selection, written by a U.S. Marine combat reporter, gives a stirring picture of the naval action off Guadalcanal. While this is an outstanding piece of war reporting, it is at the same time

190

*a good reminder that reporters must be careful not to indulge in general-
ized judgments. Far from being "the greatest naval victory of the war,"
the battle off Savo Island was closer to the worst naval defeat of the war
for the United States.*

GUADALCANAL: THE LAND SIDE

(*Ira Wolfert, November, 1942. By permission of North American Newspaper
Alliance, Inc.*)

"Heroes don't win wars."

In the five battles of the Solomons, the least we have done is keep
the Japs from winning—which is victory, in a military sense when a
long, hard war is still in its preliminary stages—and in our biggest
successes, in the fourth and fifth battles, we not only have kept the
Japs from winning, but have made them pay heavily for trying to
win.

We've licked the Japs on land, on sea, and in the air. We've shown
that we have more military brains than they have, are better at war,
all kinds of war, from strangling and knife-fighting and head-tram-
pling on up into the complicated mechanized operations of modern
battle. The Solomons haven't shown yet that we can outproduce the
Japs, but we think that's true, that we can make as good material as
anybody and can make more of it than the Japs, and can replace it
faster than they can.

But there's one thing that nobody in the world can be better at
than the Japs and that's in the guts department. They have more
guts than the Germans have. At least, they have shown thus far in
the Solomons deal, which is the first deal where they've had to hold
their chins out and take it, that they have more guts. The Germans
have said "Kamerad" in the past and may be relied on to say it in
the future. But the Japs have never surrendered, never *en masse*, and
only rarely as individuals. We have not yet taken a single officer alive
on Guadalcanal, although we have tried in every way we know how.
And the great majority of the few soldier prisoners we have taken
have been wounded and in a condition where their minds have not
been up to par.

Every day I was there, the Jap gave new evidence of his intense
willingness to go to any lengths to win, or, if unable to win, to go on
fighting until his breath stopped.

Under the heading of going to any lengths to win, the following incident may be cited as an illustration. The Jap seems to think it useful in land fighting to put snipers in our rear to harass us. Once, early in November, our fellows, working their way west of the Matanikou River, were held up for a day and one-half along a narrow sector. They drove the Japs out of that sector about dawn of a Wednesday and held there all that day and the next day. Toward five o'clock Thursday afternoon, a Marine, deciding to dig in for the night, found some soft-looking dirt on the edge of a tree and with the first poke of his shovel hit a Jap body. The Jap was covered over very lightly with a sprinkle of dirt, but his uniform had made him look only like some leaves and rotting twigs lying amid the dirt. The Marine uncovered the Jap and through the whole brushing-off process the Jap did not move except as pushed and jostled. But nobody who knows anything takes chances with the Japs any more. So the Marine picked up this Jap's arm and let it drop. It dropped limply and the face remained motionless and emotionless as in death. The Marine did it again, half-heartedly this time, very sure that this was a dead Jap. But the Jap, who had performed the superhuman task of lying under our feet feigning death for a day and a half just in order to get behind our lines and snipe at us, proved to have a human touch around his eyes. This second time he couldn't stand it any more and one eyelid twitched nervously.

Under the heading of willingness to go on fighting, this story may be told. I haven't my notes with me, and I can't remember this Marine captain's name, but everybody called him Wimpy. Wimpy was out on patrol and ran into some Japs holed up in a native hut. Quite a hot little brush followed, and after about fifteen minutes our side got no more answering fire.

Wimpy crawled up close and saw that all the Japs were dead except one, who seemed badly wounded. This one was lying on the floor of the hut in a corner farthest from the door. He was bleeding from the mouth and stared solemnly at Wimpy, and Wimpy decided to try taking him prisoner.

For twenty minutes, Wimpy cajoled and begged and tried everything he knew, waving a handkerchief as a flag of truce, offering "pogie bait," as the Marines call candy, as a bribe. The Jap did not answer. The blood flowed steadily from his mouth and his face occasionally broke under pain, but he just stared solemnly at Wimpy.

So the Marine captain decided to go in after the man. He went in the door, holding his revolver in his hand, and stood there pointing the revolver. He stood as far away as he could because wounded

Japs, so hurt they could not throw a grenade, have been known to pull the pin as somebody comes near them and blow up the reckless one as well as themselves.

So Wimpy stayed as far away as possible and pointed his gun. The Jap lifted himself to his hands and knees and began to crawl toward a dead Jap officer who was wearing a sword. "Don't do that!" cried Wimpy, "I'll have to shoot you." Wimpy didn't dare go near the man. All he could do was point his gun and shout. The Jap kept crawling slowly for the sword and took out the sword and Wimpy stamped his foot and shouted, "You damn fool! Oh, you damn damn fool! I'll have to kill you." Then the Jap lifted himself to his feet and lifted the sword over his head and started for Wimpy, and Wimpy had to shoot him dead.

These are not exceptional cases. They are typical. So there can be no question of our being better fighters than the Japs. The best any-body can possibly do is be as good, and rely on our superiority in all other departments of war to give us the victory in the long run.

It's not easy to be as good. And it's important that we should be, because if we aren't we're going to lose this war, or, if not lose it, make a compromise peace which will turn over to the next genera-tion the job of winning it. Our fellows fighting have to be as tough and the people back home have to be able to stand the losses, stand all the terrible sorrow and misery that the dead leave in their wake, and have to be able to feel that the dead husband and dead lover and dead son have not died for something that we could do without, but have swapped their lives for something worth the price. And they have to be able to keep on feeling it steadily every day for all the time it will take to win.

Our losses have been very small thus far. That is because we have been on the defensive in the Solomons since the day we took the place. The Japs have had to come after us. Soon we'll have to start north and go in after them. Then our losses are very likely to in-crease. There are a lot of people better able than I am to guess how the people back home are going to stand up under that. What I can say is how our fighting fellows are going to stand up under it because I've seen them do it.

In every battle I've watched out here, our side turns up with quite a few heroes, fellows who do more than they are supposed to do.

But heroes don't win wars. They help, just as everything else that's good helps. But the heroes are the exception, and it's the ordinary, run-of-the-mill guy who doesn't feel tempted to do more than his share who has to be relied on to win for our side. This doesn't sound glamorous, but I think it's accurate. So all the words that follow will be devoted to the ordinary fighting man on our side and how he measures up to this most difficult job in our history—being as tough, man for man, as the Japs.

As I have noted previously, our fellows look very calm in battle. The look of them is very provocative because, as I know from personal experience, a part of the mind seems to run away during battle and keeps trying to make the rest of the mind run away with it. The conscious mind, which is the part of the mind that knows all the things it has been taught, wants to stay and do the job it's supposed to do, and this other part of the mind, the subconscious part, doesn't want to know from nothing and just wants to get the hell away from there. The subconscious mind can't go off all by itself. It has to take you along with it. And to a fellow in this position, particularly when the battle is long and the struggle in himself is prolonged, it actually feels as if the subconscious mind is laying rough hands on the rest of him and pulling, hauling, and screaming at him. And I know in my own case whenever I have been in an action there has always been this uproar in my head, this steady, wild-eyed, wild-haired screaming, making it very difficult to think about the work I had to do there.

But our fellows, filled inside with this demented uproar and hemmed in all around outside by the uproar of battle, just stay there and do the work they have to do. They don't look like actors being brave. They look mostly like fellows working.

Nobody looks young in a fight. I've seen lots of twenty-year-olds out there in the middle of all that stuff flying around and some eighteen-year-olds, but I never saw anybody who looked much under forty while the fight was going on. That's one way our fellows show what they're up against. The blood in their young faces gets watered with a kind of liquid of fear and takes on that blued-over color of watery milk. Their skin looks clothlike, with the texture of a rough, wrinkled cloth.

Then, when things get really thick, like when fellows start getting hit and dropping and crying out with pain all around you, and you can't pay any attention to that, but just have to keep on working your little gadget, pressing that little button or turning that little wheel or adding up that little set of figures, whatever it is—well, when it gets like that, still the faces of our fellows don't show what an actor's would.

Sometimes the flesh around their mouths starts to shake as if they were whimpering, and their eyes . . . you can see their eyes coated over with a hot shine as if they were crying. But they go right on doing what they have to do. The bombardiers keep right on figuring with their pencils on little white scratch-pads of paper, right in the middle of all that's going on, marking down figures and adding them up or subtracting or dividing and checking the answers, just like in school, looking—except maybe for the crying in their eyes and the whimpering around their mouths—all puckered up with thought, too, like earnest students in a school. And the gunners and radio operators, all the technicians and specialists, the plumbers, mechanics, cooks, the skilled laborers, doing the work of war—they're the same.

GUADALCANAL: THE FIFTH BATTLE OF THE SOLOMONS

(Tech. Sgt. Hurlburt, Marine Corps combat correspondent, quoted in The U.S. Marines in Action *by Keith Ayling [Boston, 1943], pp. 152–155. By permission of Houghton Mifflin Company.)*

"She's burning pretty good," the lookout reported.

From a cliff overlooking the ocean, I watched an American task force engage Japanese in one phase of what may be the greatest Allied naval victory of the war.

Early yesterday we heard that a sizable Jap force was heading our way—twenty-five war vessels and twelve transports. We were ready for them.

Throughout the afternoon, reports had been received of air contact with enemy ships. But the Japs kept on coming, in spite of damaging hits. At six o'clock they were reported to be only sixty miles away. Then a message came that five of the transports were stopped and four were on fire.

Until seven o'clock we had had no word of the location of our ships. Things were getting tight. Then we heard: "U. S. battleships are headed this way and will be in time to intercept the enemy."

I climbed to an outpost on top of Tulagi's cliff. Three hours went by without incident. Then one—two—three—four destroyers moved our way around the north end of Savo Island. After two minutes battleships appeared. A Navy signalman peered through binoculars. "They're ours, all right," he said. "The destroyers are in the moonlight now," he added after a pause. "They're going straight across toward Guadalcanal. There come the battle-wagons. The PT boats are going up to them." He continued: "They're all over by Guadalcanal now. They're lined up from Lunga Point along the coast to the west."

He shifted the glasses. "Wait a minute! Two more destroyers just came around Savo. A third one is coming down from the tip of Florida."

"Whose are they?"

"Well, they're not ours. They're long, lean, low jobs, with the superstructure way forward."

"Jap destroyers!"

"Looks like it. They're moving out into the channel. The first one is in the moonlight. Now they're all in line. Hey! They must have seen something. They've all turned around and are going like hell for the west side of Savo."

We peered at the black outline of Guadalcanal. Nothing but darkness. We felt a lash of anxiety that the Japs were going to get away.

"Look at that!" A tremendous burst of light had split the gloom near Lunga Point. "I think that was a salvo from a battle-wagon," the Navy signalman declared. "There it goes again."

This time the heavy turret fire was obvious. Then there was another blast, almost simultaneous with one a few hundred yards farther west.

Three or four minutes later sharp stabs of white light even farther west indicated action by our destroyers. So far there had been no return fire from the Japanese position.

Suddenly the sky lit up on the west side of Savo. "The Nips are opening up!" the signalman exclaimed. The whole sky was ablaze with mushrooms of flame from battleship turrets, incredibly rapid white flashes from our destroyers, dull yellow flashes from beyond Savo. The firing from the Guadalcanal side was four times as heavy as that from the north. A red glow suddenly stained the clouds above Savo.

"There's a hit!" the Navy signalman cried out suddenly. "Good one, too!"

More firing. The battleships were moving steadily north and west. The big flashes were coming from the tip of Cape Esperance. Lines of red tracers pierced the low-hanging clouds.

"Must be some cruiser planes in the air. Yeah, there's one. Looks like they got him. He's coming down."

The powerful binoculars brought the battle close to the lookout. We couldn't see the falling plane, but as we looked there was another eruption of red flame. This time it was right at the south edge of Savo and it didn't go out. A ship—apparently a Jap vessel—had been set afire.

"She's burning pretty good," the lookout reported.

The burning vessel moved slowly toward mid-channel and then crept back toward Savo.

On the horizon, right on the end of the moonlight path, a huge mountain of red flame rose slowly. Star shells flew out of the red mass at crazy angles. It seemed to hang there a full minute and then darkness began to envelop its bulk. The burning ship was in the area where the Japs were located. It must have been one of theirs.

As though the blast had been the signal for the end of the first act, the firing stopped. The only light on the horizon was the burning ship.

"It looks like a heavy cruiser," the lookout said. "Flames are spreading out on the water. Probably oil."

Ten minutes later two heavy flashes blazed from the southwest end of Savo. Almost immediately there were heavy yellow blasts from the north. It was not destroyer fire—much too heavy for that. Then the whole sky beyond the yellow flashes was lit up by scores of star shells. Twenty-five or thirty miles away, they were still bright enough to bathe our cliff in daylight.

"Those are our star shells. They're firing them beyond the Nips to silhouette 'em."

The fighting was terrific. Every minute or so, a red flash signaled a hit. The two forces stood toe to toe and slugged it out. There was hardly a pause between the second and third acts. Without any cessation in the fire from the ships on the south, the slugging match turned into a chase. And it was a chase to the northwest. Each bright, white flash was farther away.

"Well, the lookout announced cheerfully, "somebody's running— and it isn't us. I don't think our ships would be trying to get to Bougainville."

We watched the ship burning on the horizon for a few minutes and then trekked slowly down the hill to our bunks. It was 1:30 on Sunday morning. For the third straight night, we had watched naval action in the Guadalcanal-Tulagi channel.

We don't get the news very quickly, but the reports we have received seem to bear out our conviction that America has won the greatest naval victory of the war.

Dieppe Raid: A. B. Austin of the London *Daily Herald* Accompanies British Commandos on One of the Costliest and Most Tragic Exploits of the War

[August 21, 1942]

"That saucy sniper is too bloody cocky."

The night of August 18, 1942. Two hundred and fifty-two ships, with 6,086 officers and men, mostly British and Canadians but some Americans, moved out silently from the English south coast ports of Southampton, Portsmouth, Shoreham, and Newhaven. Destination—the coast of France. "Operation Jubilee" was designed to penetrate enemy mine fields and assault the heavily defended seaport of Dieppe and its flanking beaches.

For months Joseph Stalin, Russian generalissimo, with monotonous insistence, had demanded the opening of a "second front" to take the pressure off his hard-pressed troops in the East. The Allied High Command wanted to go along with Stalin, but first it decided on exploratory combined-operation raids on France as a kind of reconnaissance or dress rehearsal before the big invasion. Dieppe was chosen as one target for these preliminary feelers.

The Dieppe raiders were trapped on the beaches. From the Germans safely entrenched above them poured a blizzard of steel. There were 4,384 casualties—killed, wounded and missing. The Royal Navy lost a destroyer and thirty-three other small ships. Of the sixty-seven squadrons of Royal Air Force planes, 107 planes were lost, but thirty planes were saved.

A. B. Austin, who was later killed in the fighting in Italy, covered the show for the entire British press. His moving eyewitness report is reprinted here.

It is difficult to judge whether the Dieppe raid was a success or a failure. A British expert, R. W. Thompson, concluded: "As a naval operation it was a success. The air battle was a victory. The military operation was a disaster."

Winston Churchill believed that, even if immediate results were not favorable, they fully justified the heavy cost:

198

Looking back, the casualties of this memorable action may seem out of proportion to the results. It would be wrong to judge the episode solely by such a standard. Dieppe occupies a place of its own in the story of war, and the grim casualty figures must not class it as a failure. It was a costly but not unfruitful Reconnaissance in force. Tactically it was a mine of experience. It shed revealing light on many shortcomings in our outlook.

The German press termed the Dieppe raid a complete failure. The Deutsche Allgemeine Zeitung *put it this way: "As executed, the venture mocked all rules of military logic and strategy. The invasion recalls the fate of Dunkirk. It was forced by Stalin and as such was conceived under an unlucky star."*

Hitler's Völkischer Beobachter *deemed it a major victory. Under the caption HANDS OFF EUROPE! the paper warned: "The collapse of the attack should remind Prime Minister Winston Churchill that every similar attempt will swiftly founder on German defenses."*

Operation Overlord in June 1944 was the Allied response to that challenge.

(*London* Daily Herald, *August 21, 1942. By permission of the London* Daily Herald.)

We landed west of Dieppe at dawn.

The British Commando troops to whom I was attached, Lord Lovat's No. 4 Commando, were the first men of the Dieppe raid force to jump ashore.

They had been told a few hours earlier by Admiral Louis Mountbatten, Chief of Command Operations: "Your task is most vital. If you don't knock out the German howitzer battery, the whole operation will go wrong. You have got to do it, even at the greatest possible risk."

They had heard their colonel, Lord Lovat, say: "This is the toughest job we've had. Remember that you represent the flower of the British army."

And as we nosed in under the Dieppe cliffs, I heard a Commando trooper whisper to his mate: "Don't fergit the other bastards is twice as scared as you!"

They knew that if they failed there would be a great disaster. They did not fail. The German guns were shattered, their ammunition dump blown up, and the German gunners were wiped out at the bayonet's point in hand-to-hand fighting.

Because of that and with superb support from the RAF, our detachments were able to land on their five appointed beaches. No German has ever been able to do that in England.

One question worried all of us in those last silent twenty minutes after the long, cramped voyage in the starlight: "Would the Germans be ready for us?"

The thought of it made me hang on, in my rising bunk, to the thought that "the other 'bastards' were twice as scared as I."

A sergeant crouching up front of me kept a whispered running commentary:

"'Bout five hundred yards now . . . see the cliffs? . . . There's the crack we want. . . . Look at the Jerry tracer bullets. . . . Don't think they're firing at us, though! . . . A hundred yards now . . . Fifty . . . God, there's a bloke on the cliff!"

So our question was answered. I could just make out a figure, silhouetted for an instant in the half-light. The next moment we grounded on the shingle at full tide, a few yards from the foot of the cold-looking, unscalable, one-hundred-foot overhanging chalk-white cliffs.

That was the worst moment.

The assault craft grounded, hesitated, nosed a little to port, grounded again, and stayed put.

As we blundered, bending, across the shingle to the cliff foot, a German machine gun began to stutter from up above. The oerlikon guns from our support craft answered.

Red-hot tracer bullets flashed past each other between clifftop and sea.

At the same moment the other half of No. 4 Commando, led by Lord Lovat himself, had landed a little farther west. They were to try to take the battery in the rear while our force, covered by its mortar fire, made the frontal attack.

There were only two cracks in the cliffs up which we could pass, and we found in a few minutes that one of these was so crammed full of barbed wire that we could not take time to risk it.

The second crack, a little to the left, ended in an almost vertical beach staircase for holiday bathers and fishermen, about twenty feet wide, between walls of chalk.

Had the Germans prepared their defense properly, we would not have had a chance. One platoon with a machine gun would have held it against a fair-sized army.

But the Commando leaders knew that there was just a chance that the Germans would not believe anyone could be fool enough to try such a suicidal approach.

It came off. In a few minutes the two banks of the barbed wire at the top of the steps had been blasted with explosives, and the Commando spearhead, followed by the mortar platoon, were creeping cautiously up the gully.

At that moment the howitzers fired. The light had grown just enough for any observers to spot craft a fair way out to sea.

For a few minutes I watched the soaring fireworks across the Dieppe approaches.

The naval bombardment, timed for twenty minutes after our landing, had begun. The shore batteries, and all the light German guns, were replying.

The sky was spotted with the tracks of incendiary shells, and the Dieppe basin was beginning to rumble and thud like the explosive growling of a volcano crater.

A formation of four-cannon Hurricanes dived out of the sky on the cliffs above us, spitting fire at the machine-gun posts.

Commando troopers under the cliffs yelled: "Give them hell!"

I passed several times up and down the gully, carrying messages or mortar shells. Snipers seemed to be the Germans' favorite defense.

Where the gully ended there was scrub, and beyond that a narrow road into the woods. A cow was grazing by it. She gave an occasional worried moo, but never budged—in spite of all the bullet whine and mortar crash—from the corner of the field which was on her grazing schedule for that morning.

Just as I got back from the gully stairs a bullet or two began to whistle past.

"That saucy sniper," said a Navy signaler, "is too bloody cocky."

A chain of mortar-shell carriers were winding up the gully and through the woods. I caught up with a load of shells and went with them.

"Lord, I'm in a muck," said a man in front of me.

"Never mind the sweat, mon," said a Scot behind him. "It'll thin ye off, and think how much more beer ye'll be able tae soak in."

An explosion in front of us, louder and longer than any we had heard that morning, made us crouch suddenly.

Presently Major Mills Roberts, the leader of our part of the Commando force, came back from the trees, grinning with pleasure:

"We've got their ammunition dump," he said. "Mortar shell bang on top of it. Bloody fools, they'd got their ammunition all in one lot. Must have been drunk with power!"

A minute later I was running down the cliff gully again with another message to pass to England.

It read: "Flak gun demolished 0650."

Quickly after me came another message which said: "Assault has gone in."

This meant that Lord Lovat and his men had worked their way round and were swarming over the battery position from the rear.

In a pause of the firing I looked up to find Lord Lovat sitting against a rock beside me.

You could see that he was bubbling with happiness.

"By God, we did that job all right," he said. "Went in straight with the bayonet. Cut them in shreds. Not a man left in the battery. How glad I am I wasn't in the battery. But they fought hard."

He was easy to pick out anywhere in that day's battle. "Cool as a trout," as a trooper said.

The enemy mortars banged down a bit of cliff near us.

"Getting a bit hot," said Lord Lovat. "I'm going aboard," and he strolled into the sea up to his knees, following the long lines of men who were clambering into the assault landing craft.

"Hi," he yelled to the nearest craft some way out. "You come in here. Why should I get my knees wet?"

On the long, weary voyage back our men shared their cigarettes, water, food, and blankets with the prisoners.

So busy were the Messerschmitts and the Focke-Wulf 190's kept by our fighters that they had no time to strafe our craft.

All through the afternoon I watched German and British fighters scribbling their quarrels across the sky. Many planes fell, whether German or British I could not see.

Once an American pilot in a Spitfire whirled down, bailing out as he fell. One of our craft picked him up. Then we attacked a German pilot, who parachuted down, and we stopped to pick him up, too.

After many hours, even watching one of the most significant air battles of the war palled. We huddled slackly down in our boat, dead-tired, filthy-looking, ragged, lolling, happy men—happy because we knew that the Commandos had made the battle of Dieppe possible.

British Cruiser *Curacao* Lost: Crash with the Giant Liner *Queen Mary* Is Revealed by United Press Eyewitness

[October 2, 1942]

"The *Queen Mary*'s crash bow . . . was curled back like a torn tin can and open to the waves."

Censorship was an important weapon on both sides during the war. The belligerents were careful to censor any dispatches that might have given useful information to the enemy. The purpose was to keep losses in combat and in accidents unknown to the enemy.

On October 2, 1942, the 78,000-ton liner, Queen Mary, in use as a transport ship, rammed and sank the British light cruiser Curacao in a tragic accident. Not until May 15, 1945, did the Admiralty lift the war-long secrecy on the incident. Clinton B. Conger's eyewitness account of the sinking was then released by the United Press.

(*New York* Herald Tribune, *May 18, 1945. By permission of United Press International.*)

ABOARD THE TRANSPORT *Queen Mary*, Oct. 2, 1942 (Delayed by Censor)—The 78,000-ton *Queen Mary*, while transporting American troops to the European theater of operations, today rammed and sank the British light cruiser *Curacao* in one of the war's strangest and most tragic accidents.

As the transport approached the British Isles, the cruiser, acting as an escort, cut too sharply in front of the liner's massive crash bow. Slashed cleanly in two, the *Curacao* and most of its men went to the bottom in less than seven minutes.

I watched the shattered, smoking segments of the *Curacao* drift past the *Queen Mary*. Only a handful of her normal complement of about 400 men could be seen anywhere, and it seemed inevitable that they, too, must perish, either in the liner's thrashing propellers or in the final plunge of the cruiser remnants. It was learned later that fifty-eight men, including the *Curacao*'s captain, were saved.

203

There were no casualties aboard the transport. The *Queen Mary* had a miraculous escape, since the after end of the cruiser where the liner struck appeared to carry depth charges. If they had exploded they would have ripped the *Queen*'s bow wide open. Still well out from land, there might have been severe casualties among the thousands of troops aboard.

The *Queen Mary*'s crash bow—built to withstand just such a collision—was curled back like a torn tin can and open to the waves. The big ship limped into port at less than fourteen knots through submarine-infested waters and in danger of attack by long-range German bombers.

General Clark's Pre-Invasion Mission to North Africa: Godfrey B. Courtney Tells How a Daring American General Loses Pants But Saves Face

[October 22, 1942]

"This is going to be the craziest thing yet."

General Dwight D. Eisenhower wanted a bloodless invasion of North Africa. To achieve this military end, he sent a high-ranking officer from his own staff to contact anti-Nazi generals in enemy-held North Africa. The mission was to be made by plane and submarine. For this task he chose from among many volunteers his deputy, General Mark Wayne Clark. "He and I," said Eisenhower later, "worked together constantly in many phases of the field exercises we both so much enjoyed, and I gained a lasting respect for his planning, training, and organizing ability."

Eisenhower chose the right man. On General Clark and his nine-man Commando force depended in large part the success of the future Allied undertaking. His expedition gathered valuable information. Clark was an officer of high intelligence and great personal courage, who became a brilliant combat commander in later phases of the war.

The expedition, which started on the night of October 21–22, 1942, nearly ended in disaster. The Commandos had no idea that the enemy had learned of their mission. The dramatic story was told by an Englishman, Godfrey B. Courtney, who went along on the mission.

("Clark's Secret Mission," by Godfrey B. Courtney, from History in the Writing by the Correspondents of Time, Life and Fortune, ed. by Gordon Carroll; copyright Time Inc. 1945.)

In Mountbatten's Combined Operations Command, life is always a gamble. So I was ready for anything when I was told to select from my outfit a good navigator and an expert to handle small boats, and report aboard a British submarine. I picked Capt. R. P. Livingston who can shoot stars at any angle, and Lt. J. P. Foote, a baby-faced boy of 20 who can make small boats do inside loops. The three of us reported aboard the submarine wondering what it was all about.

We were sitting around speculating when we heard a noise forward. My eyes popped when I saw a U. S. officer with two stars on his shoulders. There were four other Americans, and after they had passed by Livingston whispered, "This is going to be the craziest thing yet." The tall chap with the general's insignia was not built for a submarine: he kept bumping his head against pipes and knobs.

The sub's skipper, whom I had met before, introduced us to our traveling companions. The tall fellow was Maj. Gen. Mark Clark, second in command to Eisenhower. The others were Brig. General Lemnitzer, Colonel Holmes, Colonel Hamblen, and Captain Wright of the Navy. We did not ask any questions then.

Clark and his party had the wardroom and the sub's officers doubled up with us. With eight passengers aboard, it was pretty crowded and a crowded sub is not very comfortable. The next day Submarine Commander Lieutenant Jewell said he did not know exactly what the expedition was all about so I interrupted Clark's bridge game to ask him to "brief me on plans," and he said he would after lunch.

I went back to my bunk to check rations, tommy guns and knives. Livingston, who is a scholar and architect as well as a navigator, had his head buried in a heavy tome. Foote seemed trying to doze. After lunch Clark told me his party wanted to land on the Algerian coast to meet some people and discuss certain things, then get away. That was where Livingston, Foote and I came in. He told me he wasn't even sure he wasn't walking into a trap. But he said he didn't want any shooting if it could be avoided. Then he said: "You know how to do these things and we're completely in your hands. It's your baby."

As I went back to my little hole in the corner to break the news to the others, I noticed the American officers resuming their bridge game. There were a lot of uncertain factors to be considered. First, we didn't know what was going to happen when we landed. Second, the shoreline was strange. Third, no one knew how long Clark and his men would stay ashore. All afternoon we mulled over arrangements. After supper we decided to give Clark and his men a little practice with boats. We made them get in and get out of them in the submarine, and then asked the skipper to heave to so we could practice in the water.

It was a beautiful Mediterranean night. The moon was nearly full and there was only a slight swell. As Clark and the others practiced with the boats, a lot of joking went on. Oddly enough, Colonel Holmes, civil affairs adviser of the party, was the only one who showed real boat sense. Wright, a naval captain, didn't show up much better than the rest, although before the trip ended he was the only one who never got wet.

Clark had told me that a light would be shown from the rendezvous for which we were making. Before dawn we saw it shining against a dark background of mountains. But it was nearly daybreak and the rendezvous wasn't until the next night, so we spent the day cruising submerged offshore. Livingston, his eye glued to the periscope, made some excellent sketches which proved useful later.

When that night we saw the light again, we prepared to go ashore. We got the boats ready and decided that Holmes, who knew some of the men ashore, should go first with Livingston. Lemnitzer and Foote went next, then Wright and Hamblen. The first three boats got off safely. Clark and I were going last but before he could get in, a wave came up and overturned me. That was the first time Clark showed any excitement. "I've got to get off," he shouted. "I've got to go now."

I recalled Wright's boat and Hamblen gave up his place to Clark. My boat was cracked in several places but Hamblen and I decided to take a chance and went on anyway. We caught up with the rest of the party and all landed more or less together.

I heard Holmes or somebody sloshing up the beach, talking with people he seemed glad to see. The rest of us carried our boats up a cliff to a white-walled house which turned out to be the place we had been making for. Inside, Clark and his men separated into groups, talking with men who had been awaiting them. Everybody was talking at once, gesticulating and toasting each other with highballs. We had a drink too, then went to our rooms. Clark had asked us to keep out of the way as much as possible; the less seen of British uniforms the better.

The next morning we oiled our weapons and Foote repaired the damage to my boat. My trousers were still not dry, so I wrapped a curtain around me and had lunch looking like that Hollywood sarong girl. After lunch there were a couple of false alarms and everyone rushed to hide. Livingston, Foote and I got our guns ready but every time Clark and his men saw us they said: "For God's sake, put those things away!"

In the late afternoon we saw a servant bring in 16 chickens. They were killed for our supper. But we never had a chance to eat them. Around 7 P.M. there was a commotion in the courtyard. One of Clark's party called: "Get your kit ready! There are two policemen on the way."

The turmoil downstairs increased. Some of the local party were leaping from ground-floor windows. Others were getting out of uniform. Then the order to get on the beaches was countermanded and we—that is, Clark's group and mine—shoved through a trap door into the dusty, dark cellar. Upstairs the local party walked about whistling nonchalantly until there came a loud knocking on the gate. A loud argument developed. Clark was trying to load his carbine in the dark but he wasn't getting on too well.

"How in the hell do you load this thing?" he whispered. We asked him please to put it away. Then my throat began to tickle from the dust. I began to choke and wanted to cough. I stuffed a handkerchief in my mouth and rolled over on my stomach but I couldn't suppress a wheeze. Clark finally found some chewing gum. This saved the day for me.

We were in the cellar for one hour and a half before we heard tin cans, which had been placed over the trap door to hide it, being removed. We held our breath. Our guns were ready to shoot. But it was one of our local friends. He had told the police a story about playing host at a wild party in the house which was supposed to have been deserted. The police weren't satisfied, however, and our local friends told us to get away as soon as possible.

Back on the beach we found a heavy ground swell had developed. We signaled the sub to come in close. Clark and Livingston were to make the first attempt. We helped them into the boat, then pushed it through the surf as far as we could. But a comber caught the boat and flipped it end over end. After that, Clark decided to put off the departure and we hid our boats in the bushes while two of our crowd stood guard.

Then began the swapping of trousers according to seniority.* Clark, who was soaking wet, borrowed Lemnitzer's. Lemnitzer, who is a general too, borrowed Foote's. Foote, who is only a lieutenant, couldn't borrow anyone's but he made the sacrifice gladly after seeing Lemnitzer in all his dignity doing sentry duty with a carbine over his knees and nothing else. I was sitting under a bush with my trousers on, counting the waves to see if the swell was decreasing. With a trained crew it might have been possible to get through the surf, but it seemed pretty hopeless with these men. I was beginning to feel discouraged when I noticed the surf less heavy at a certain

---

* General Clark's pants ultimately reached the Smithsonian Institution. The General's wife, who presented them, announced that they had been rescued from the African beach and ultimately returned to the General, who discovered they had shrunk and sent them home.

point on the beach. I decided that, by carrying the boats beyond the breakers, we might be able to get away. Clark asked me what I thought the chances were and I told him we could count on two of the four boats reaching the submarine safely.

"I've got to get them all back as long as there's a chance," Clark told me. He decided to wait a little longer. By 4 A.M. he came down to the beach, but when he saw that the surf was still high he told us we should prepare to wait another day rather than risk losing a man. As soon as they heard this, the local hosts got excited and said it would be suicide for us to stay. "All right," said Clark to me, "we'll try your scheme." We signaled the sub again to come in, warning the skipper we were in difficulties. I asked everybody to dump everything he had because I had to keep the boats light. Wright, the Navy man, said "You can lose anything but oars," which proved sound advice later.

Wright and Clark as representatives of the Navy and Army were to go first. Their return was imperative if the operations on the African front (whereof we were still ignorant, of course) were to succeed. Four of us carried their boat beyond the breakers and then heaved the captain and the general into it by the seat of their trousers. We gave the boat a shove and off it went, teetering but upright. We could see their oars churning the air and water when they disappeared in the darkness.

Disaster overtook the next pair—Lemnitzer and Foote. Their boat overturned. The next time they had better luck and so half our group was on its way. Holmes, whose French was fluent, decided to stay until the last with Livingston, so that if the police returned, he could reason with them.

I got my second ducking when Hamblen and I were leaving. A big wave spilled us into the water. I came up spluttering and all I could see of my companion was one arm holding up an oar as if it were Excalibur. He had taken Wright's advice to heart. On our next attempt we got away, Holmes and Livingston following without any mishaps. Jewell had done a wonderful job edging in close to shore and it wasn't long until we were all back on the submarine.

Putting out to sea we saw bright headlights come to a standstill by the house on the cliff. We learned a few days later that the police arrived in full force. We had escaped just in time.*

* The story of Clark's expedition was released at the same time as the announcement of his promotion to Lieutenant General. Later he was appointed commanding general of the U. S. Fifth Army. For his exploit in North Africa, Clark was awarded the Distinguished Service Medal.

Back in the wardroom everyone relaxed, Clark slapping us on the back and shouting to Lemnitzer, "Say, Lem, I lost my pants." We all had "to the Navy" rum but we were too excited to eat dinner. Back in our corner Livingston said to me, "Well, old chap, we've fulfilled our contract." And Jewell shouted to us, "Good show, you bums."

El Alamein: The Defeat of Marshal Rommel in One of the Decisive Battles of the War as Recorded by American and German Correspondents

[October 23, 1942]

On July 1, 1942, Field Marshal Erwin Rommel, the shrewd Desert Fox, stopped at El Alamein, a stony, waterless desert spot seventy miles east of Alexandria. Early the next month, Winston Churchill placed General Bernard Montgomery in command of the British Eighth Army. Throughout the summer, reinforcements were rushed to Montgomery from the United States and England—Sherman tanks, jeeps, trucks, planes, ammunition. Clever, hard-bitten, careful, Montgomery had no intention of striking until he had superiority in armor and in the air.

Montgomery's preparation was a thing of military beauty. He reorganized his army virtually overnight. Using deception on a vast scale, he convinced the Germans that we would strike in the south instead of the north. He spoke coldly and plainly to his troops: "Kill Germans, even the padres—one per weekday and two on Sundays!"

On October 23, 1942, Montgomery hurled the full strength of his forces at the enemy. What happened there was described by Richard D. Macmillan, United Press, in one of the most dramatic dispatches of the war. The second account tells the story from the German side.

El Alamein was a tremendous victory for the Allies. "It may almost be said," commented Churchill, " 'Before Alamein we never had a victory. After Alamein we never had a defeat.' "

PUSH BEGINS IN MIGHTY BARRAGE

(Richard D. Macmillan, The New York Times, *October 26, 1942. By permission of United Press International.*)

"The whole horizon burst open into dragon tongues of flame. . . ."

INSIDE THE GERMAN LINES, on the Egyptian Front, Oct. 24 (Delayed)— The biggest battle of Egypt is under way.

The British have attacked violently and have penetrated the enemy

211

positions at many points. Tanks are passing in strength through gaps in the minefields.

The heaviest fighting is inside the German lines, and I am with the Fifty-first Highland Division, which burst through the German outer defenses.

The British have already advanced well into the enemy sector at some points, although they were held up in others, and fighting of the heaviest kind, involving both infantry and tanks, is going on.

This offensive began with the speed of lightning.

A skirl of bagpipes resounded from the Highlanders' front positions last night and the sound of music in the chill, moonlit desert must have been clearly audible in the German front lines, a few hundred yards away.

Suddenly the music was drowned out by the greatest blast of guns ever heard in Egypt.

The Allied barrage had opened with a terrifying roar from hundreds of guns. The battle was on.

All that night I advanced with the Highlanders, under the full moon. The Highlanders, famous bayonet fighters, were having their first action against the Germans since their unit was re-formed after the battle of France.

The first burst of guns soon gave way to a deafening clamor from hundreds of tanks rumbling out of hiding places in dry water courses. The tanks churned up a sandstorm as they raced into battle on our right, left and center. They pushed up to the enemy lines under a monstrous flaring and blaring of artillery and rode roughshod over the startled German African Corps.

By dawn German and Italian prisoners were streaming back across the deep-rutted track of No Man's Land.

The British Eighth Army seemed to pack a knockout blow from the word go. In two years of campaigns in the Western Desert I have never seen the British go at it with such drive, such coordination of effort and such meticulous timing. It made one realize that this was an offensive inspired by a new spirit. The timing was so perfect that all divisions, brigades and battalions seemed like parts of one electric clock.

One instant all was silent in the desert, except for the bagpipes and the soft shuffle of marching feet, where dimly outlined troops moved in single file along the powdery, gleaming sand trails.

Then, as if some one had pushed a button, the whole horizon burst open into dragon tongues of flames, with a tempestuous noise.

The barrage from massed batteries of medium cannon continued incessantly for six hours—a new record for the North African campaign.

Only twenty minutes after the first big bang troops with fixed bayonets were crossing the starting line, filing through corridors in our minefields and mopping up the enemy's forward posts.

They continued on through the enemy minefields. The sky across No Man's Land became a fairyland of multicolored lights as silver and red tracer bullets streaked the velvet darkness. There were angry splurges of red and ocher where shells exploded in countless profusion and munitions dumps went up in cascades of flame.

New lights began winking and flickering inside gasoline tins, to mark passageways for our troops advancing through the minefields. We went ahead in fairly quick time, stormed the first two minefields and took our objectives at bayonet point.

As the Highlanders, led by kilted pipers, bayoneted and machine-gunned their way through the strong points, other British, Australian, New Zealand and South African troops swung forward in a general advance. Considerable headway was made before dawn.

Our tanks followed the infantry through the gaps and deployed to engage German tanks within the enemy's main lines. This marked a change in desert warfare, which previously had been based on preliminary attacks by tanks to clear the way for infantry.

Successes of the Russians in destroying German tank spearheads in the battle of Stalingrad were believed to have influenced the change in tactics. Another consideration is that, by sending infantry-men ahead under artillery barrages to hack out a path for tanks, our tanks can deploy in mass formation, after they have crossed the minefields, and meet the full weight of the enemy's armor in force, instead of being strung out to be picked off by enemy guns as they approach in single file.

In the sector where I marched we crossed a half-mile-wide No Man's Land that was dotted with patches of camel thorn. We threw ourselves on the earth and dug in from time to time as German artillery and machine guns replied to our barrage. The enemy guns were feeble in comparison with our massed fire.

A Highlander officer used a walking stick resembling a shepherd's crook to signal his men, mostly waving them forward. The Highlanders then pushed on to clean up a mixed force of Germans and Italians that was dug into holes at the fringe of the enemy's outer minefields.

The first wave of infantry was able to infiltrate the Axis mine-fields without much difficulty. It met a stronger defense line, which also broke under the Highlanders' bayonet charge. All was going according to plan along the line of advance, except that the right wing was held up by an exceptionally well-fortified strong point, where the Germans and Italians held on grimly.

By midnight our wave had swept through the first objective and had pushed on without a halt to the second, which was taken after stiff fighting.

The battlefield was shrouded in haze from dust and cordite flares, either sent up by our land forces or dropped from planes—mostly ours, which were constantly overhead, bombing and gunning the enemy emplacements, trenches and pillboxes.

We stumbled upon wounded. Stretcher bearers alternately crouched and ran through the barrages, picking up the wounded and moving them to ambulances—which tried to keep pace with the advance, but had considerable difficulty in weaving in and out among the slow columns of tanks, trucks, artillery and anti-tank guns, with their succeeding lines of support troops.

Our casualties at present do not seem high—not as high as had been expected. I saw many wounded during that first night, but never heard one of those gallant lads utter a murmur from pain.

The Scots had named the enemy strong points after their home towns. One Axis knoll was called Perth. Our fellows quickly headed for others, designated Stirling, Nairn and Killin. Stirling fell at 4 A.M.

When a slight breath of wind cleared up the foglike haze, we could see on every side British infantry extended in single file or clustered in small groups with bayonets gleaming in the moonlight. Then a curtain of dust and fumes obliterated the troops again.

The first of our tanks had poured through one gap by midnight. They were met by fierce fire from German 88s. That battle was still going on at dawn, and a bigger battle was looming.

In my advance with the Highlanders, I walked five and a half hours and covered nearly five miles, two of which were into the German lines. We went through two enemy minefields, but there were still more minefields and barbed wire protecting the main enemy positions ahead.

Throughout the night fresh Allied troops moved up, riding on tanks. Many of the men slept peacefully while the tanks lumbered into battle positions amid a welter of fury and carnage.

A major told me he was lucky to be able to fight in the desert, because he had been taken prisoner during his division's gallant stand at St. Valery on the Somme.

"I was held by the Germans in three prisons, then by the French," he said. "I was in and out of thirteen prisons, all told, but I managed to escape from each one and finally reached Oran, where I escaped from a stinking jail, where I was held with seventeen Arabs. I stole a small cutter and sailed to Gibraltar. The British Navy picked me up and I rejoined the regiment after a year's adventures in France, Algeria and Morocco."

He was moving up to the battle line when I saw him.

I met troops from all parts of the British Isles, many of them reinforcements that Prime Minister Winston Churchill had promised.

There was a Cockney who whistled "Tipperary" as he marched a group of German and Italian prisoners back along a gap.

"I'd be mighty glad to take these boys all the way home to Brixton prison," he said.

The Forty-fourth and Fiftieth British Divisions are among others now in the line.

END OF THE AFRIKA KORPS

(*"Defeat at El Alamein," from* With Rommel in the Desert *by Heinz Werner Schmidt [London, 1960], pp. 138–141. By permission of George G. Harrap & Company Limited.)*

"A retreat is out of the question. Victory or death! Heil Hitler!"

Montgomery's offensive at El Alamein began on the night of October 23.

The secret of this massed, planned assault had been extraordinarily well kept. It came as a complete surprise, even though indications of an almost immediate offensive had been gathered and assessed by the German Staff during the twenty-four hours before the initial barrage opened.

The Eighth Army had been built up for a "kill" since August 1; it had been reinforced by 41,000 troops, over 1000 tanks, and 9000 vehicles of various sorts.

The peaceful stars were shaken in their heavens when nearly a thousand guns flashed and roared simultaneously against us that night. Never had this age-old land known so shattering a drumfire. The earth from the Qattara Depression to the Mediterranean quaked. Far back from the front line, men were jarred to their teeth.

Fifteen minutes of it, and then the firing let up for five minutes.

That was just a lull before a renewed storm. Punctually at 10 P.M. the same vast number of guns, plus thousands of tank and infantry weapons, concentrated on our front lines. Australians principally, but also Englishmen, Scots, New Zealanders, and South Africans, attacked. Their main objective was the Miteiriyeh Ridge. It was occupied on the first night of the battle, but Montgomery did not consolidate his hold on it until after two days of desperate fighting.

The 15th Panzer Division in the north and the 21st in the south lay a short way behind the turmoil of the forward line. They had been split into battle groups in accordance with defensive plans that Rommel had drawn up before he left Africa for medical attention in Germany. In this we made a grave blunder. Rommel had intended that these battle groups should exist independently only during the period preceding an anticipated enemy offensive. They were to be concentrated immediately an offensive became definite and its direction was perceived, since only a consolidated force of Panzers would prevail against the great tank strength which Montgomery had now built up. Rommel had never dreamed of allowing his Panzers to meet the enemy and be defeated in detail—as the enemy had in the past been defeated in detail by him.

Bayerlein, the Chief of Staff, was on leave. Rommel had to return, unavailingly, to the rescue. On the first day of Montgomery's offensive General Stumme had a heart attack when the unit he was with was attacked by enemy aircraft. Stumme's driver did not even see him fall out of his car onto the desert. His corpse was found only later.

Central Intelligence in Berlin had told us that the British could not attack before the end of the month. . . .

Hitler telephoned Rommel in a hospital in Germany at noon on the second day of the battle and asked him at once to fly back to Africa. The situation was desperate. Rommel had been under treatment for only three weeks and was still ill, but he did not think of saying No. He was airborne before daybreak the following morning, only stopping in Italy to find out what was going on, and particularly to learn whether his forces were getting enough petrol, whether more Panzers were on their way, and whether Kesselring had sent the supplies of *Nebelwerfers*—multiple-barrelled mortars—which Hitler had promised. He was at Panzer Gruppe Headquarters again a couple of hours after sunset that same night.

I think he knew then that El Alamein was lost: he had found out how short of petrol the Afrika Korps was. He told Bayerlein that we could not win, but he made desperate attempts to retrieve the situation. He was up almost all night planning a counter-attack against

Kidney Ridge (Miteiriyeh) in the north. He strove desperately to assemble his Panzer forces in a cohesive whole, as they should have been earlier. The 15th Panzer Division had been practically destroyed, so he summoned the 21st and the Italian Ariete Divisions north, and moved the 90th Light and the Italian Trieste Divisions from their rear areas to protect the front near the sea.

The counter-attack, which Rommel directed in person, was smashed up by our old enemies, the medium bombers and the 25-pounders. He tried again next day, but was beaten off once more. He lost Panzers he could ill afford—Panzers that would not now be replaced. The 9th Australian Division hammered him farther back.

Montgomery paused to regroup after three days of fighting. (The South Africans, apart from their ubiquitous armoured-car men, had now incidentally completed their main task in the El Alamein battle, and we were not to meet them again until Italy.) At Tel el Aqqaqir the fiercest tank engagement of the battle developed. Both sides suffered heavy losses, but we were the harder hit. Our Panzers were almost annihilated: only a few groups survived.

Montgomery's "Operation Supercharge"—the new onslaught that followed "Torch"—was the end at-El Alamein. The 21st Panzers had put up their last effective struggle, and, although at one time they almost mastered their old enemies, the British 1st Armoured, they were beaten. Rommel decided to withdraw on the night of November 2–3.

He wirelessed his decision and his reasons to Hitler's headquarters that night. The report was passed to Hitler only the following day: the officer who was on duty when it came through had failed to wake him. (He was reduced in rank.) Hitler raved, and reviled Rommel.

Rommel's retreat was in progress when a wireless signal came from Hitler's H.Q.: "The situation demands that the positions at El Alamein be held to the last man. A retreat is out of the question. Victory or death! Heil Hitler!" The message bore Hitler's personal signature. For some reason or other, although we were already withdrawing, the signal was circulated to Afrika Korps units.

The ridiculous signal could not improve our morale at that time. Nevertheless, having received it and being obliged to acknowledge it, Rommel could not treat it as non-existent.

Thus, when von Thoma, in command of the Afrika Korps, asked Rommel at the Panzer Gruppe Afrika H.Q. south of El Daba for permission to withdraw to Fuka, Rommel would not endorse the plan but merely gave him authority to act on his own judgment.

Next morning von Thoma gathered information that Tommy had

already outflanked the southern wing of the Afrika Korps and he passed the information up to Rommel. Rommel discredited the information, and said that the formation reported in the south must be a retreating Italian division. Von Thoma went out in a Panzer to checked for himself. British tanks pounced upon him, set his Panzer alight, and captured him.

Bayerlein, the Chief of Staff, who went out in search of von Thoma, was also within an ace of capture when he approached to within a few hundred yards and, through his field-glasses, saw von Thoma being rounded up. He scurried back to safety, and succeeded to the command of what was left of the Afrika Korps.

Operation Torch: Leo Disher, United Press, Receives Twenty-six Assorted Wounds While Covering the Battle of Oran

[November 7, 1942]

"Another bullet later hit the wall and bounced into my temple."

In early November 1942 an Anglo-American armada set sail from Gibraltar for the North African coast. Operation Torch, under command of Lieutenant General Dwight D. Eisenhower, was designed to capture the whole of Northwest Africa from French Morocco to Tunisia, as a preliminary step to invasion of Europe from the south. Landings were made at many small beaches and ports near the three main objectives of Casablanca, Oran and Algiers. In some areas, especially Oran, the French armed forces obeyed Marshal Henri Pétain's orders to resist any invader.

A U.S. Coast Guard cutter, the Walney, *overloaded with troops and depth charges, headed for the harbor of Oran. Aboard was Leo Disher, a United Press correspondent. On the journey from England, Disher had slipped on the deck, breaking his ankle. The ship officers tried to put him off at Gibraltar, but he refused to disembark. As the* Walney *pushed in to Oran, Disher attached a life preserver to the cast on his leg in the event that he had to swim. The chances for disaster were good—for the* Walney *had been assigned the task of breaking the boom or chain that the Vichy French had built to keep enemy vessels out of Oran harbor.*

How Disher remained alive through the worst of the bloodshed was almost incredible. Certainly it was one of the great action stories of the war. Here is a condensed version of his own report. He was awarded the Purple Heart for his wounds received in the action.

(From Springboard to Berlin by John A. Paris and Ned Russell, in collaboration with Leo Disher and Phil Ault, 1943. Thomas Y. Crowell Company, New York, Publisher.)

I made my way from the stern toward the bridge. . . .

My crutches had begun to wedge painfully into my arm pits and my right leg was becoming exceedingly weary. To ease it, I braced the crutches across the passageway and leaning on them with my fore-arms, rested by pushing hard with my back against the bulkhead. From that position I could see, across the twenty feet of the bridge, the high bulk of cliffs, now very near. We were running parallel to them, heading westward. Ahead now I saw the gleam of scattered lights.

It was Oran.

We became silent on the bridge. There was no sound anywhere except the constant swish of the water against the ship's plates.

Then a searchlight blazed. . . .

And then came a stream of bullets.

Flaming tracer lead arched out lazily before the ship. And then the sound of stuttering machine guns. Heavy crashes came from the shore and the *Walney* shook. A moment later she shook again. We were being hit with cannon. . . .

[*Commander*] Meyrick passed an order to the men below:

"Lie flat for crash. We are approaching boom."

We braced ourselves against the devilish symphony of machine-gun and artillery fire. Our tommy guns began talking back.

Shells and bullets crashed into us, and almost as the *Walney* shud-dered with the impact, she snapped the boom. We were through. It had been as easy as that. . . .

Our chief of staff took his hands off the butts of his six-shooters, gripped the loudspeaker microphone and began talking to the French on shore in their own language. He even spoke French with an American accent. "Cease firing," he said. "We are your friends. We are Americans. Cease firing."

It seemed to me then that all hell broke loose around us. We were hit time and again. The chief of staff was a brave man. His voice went on amid the awful noise of battle until he fell against the microphone with his six-shooters still unfired in their holsters.

Everything was happening at once. The officer below decks began directing American assault troops to midships, where they were partially screened by the superstructure as they went over the side. A shell hit one of our fuel drums, spreading liquid fire along the deck. A destroyer loomed in front of us. We tried to ram but missed, and there was a savage burst of fire from its guns at almost muzzle-end range. The bridge was raked and raked again.

A French cruiser began firing, too, and then a submarine on our port side opened up. My crutches were knocked away in the first crush of falling men. I fell and crawled to the outside wing bridge in an attempt to see. Shell bursts wounded me in both legs. The *Walney* caught fire below deck. . . .

"Okay!" shouted Lieutenant Cole. "Everybody get off! Get ashore!" Somewhere below our depth charges began exploding. "Everybody ashore!" Our ammunition began blowing up. . . .

In the darkness bodies had fallen against me; and the bodies had risen and fallen again and again. I had somehow lived through it so far. . . .

My hand found a body that was soft and yielding. Then the night exploded again. It went apart in sheets of flame. It was splitting, blasting. Shells were hurling metal, tossing bodies. Bullets cut through the sides in red streams. All hell had engulfed the *Walney;* and what had gone before was as nothing. . . .

In the first deluge of fire I lived possibly because I was crawling. The first concussion of shells caught me and tossed me. The blasts were so loud they hurt and seemed solid.

I was tossed . . . and I crawled. I pulled up . . . . was hurled down. . . .

I dropped to my knees again and began crawling behind the bridge toward the port ladders. I reached them. They were swept by flame, but I went down. I went down one, then the other. I was on the main deck. Pushing my helmet from my head, I toppled through a shell-torn gap in the rail to the water.

I almost drowned.

The life-tube on my chest had been burst by shrapnel. The one John Cole had tied to my leg was still intact, and my leg floated, while my head stayed below water. Struggling and choking, I pulled at the tube, finally tearing it loose. I began swimming away from the ship while bullets and bits of metal rained down on the water.

Somehow I was not hit. Foot by foot, I swam on, conscious now of pain in my legs. . . .

With infinite weariness I swam into the blackness between a lurching merchant ship and the pier. My eyes closed. My fingers clawed water. I touched a rope and discovered I was again determined to live. I hauled myself up until I got my elbows over the pier rim. Then the full weight of the cast on my leg caught me and I knew I couldn't make it. Slowly and painfully I began losing my grip. Then a single hand groped down and braced me. I swung my good leg up and it caught. Then the hand from above began to pull, and I rolled over the edge with open, gasping mouth pressed against the stone surface of the pier. I could see the man who had pulled me up as a hazy, unreal figure swaying near me. But I saw enough. He had used only one hand because the other had been shot away. I never knew his name, never even knew his nationality, because just then a bullet struck my injured foot. Another bullet later hit the wall and bounced into my temple. I was crawling, sprawling into the dirt, crawling again. . . .

Finally, a French soldier took me over his back like a sack of meal and carried me into a hole in the cliffs. The hole led on, became a corridor, then a system of corridors. . . .

In the long hospital ward, a French nurse stuck a cigarette between my lips and a doctor found a total of twenty-six assorted holes in me. I tried to sleep but the hospital shuddered to the roar of big guns.

In the next bed the American soldier who had helped carry me woke up and grinned. "Ain't it," he asked, "a helluva day?"

Leningrad, 1943: Soviet Journalist Nikolai Tikhonov Reports the Breaking of the Blockade of Russia's Second City

[January 1, 1943]

"Shoulders were straightened, eyes shone."

When Hitler's armies crashed across the Soviet borders on June 22, 1941, they closed with the Russians on an extensive battle line of 1,800 miles. In the north the Germans dashed for Leningrad, the second city of the Soviet Union. "I do not know of any city so beautiful," wrote Ilya Ehrenburg. "Everything in it is unique—the stone and the water, the fogs and the blizzards, the poetry and the labor. Is there anyone in the world who has not heard of the Nevsky Prospekt?"

Leningrad was to be a vital cog in Hitler's machine of conquest. If he had Leningrad in the north and Sevastopol in the south, he could then close a giant pincers move on the Soviet capital and crush the Bolsheviks. He sent his best troops to the north—among them his own bodyguard, various other S.S. divisions, Alpine troops, Jaegers, even the Spanish Blue Division. Meanwhile, Goering's Luftwaffe pounced on the city.

But Leningrad did not fall. From September 1941, when the German attack began, to the spring of 1943, the great city remained under blockade and siege. Hitler tried to starve its people, who had no water, no light, no fuel, no bread. The civilian population worked day and night on the fortifications surrounding the city. Old men and women, even children, toiled away under the bombs and shells, turning out weapons. For two winters a life-line was kept open across the frozen waters of Lake Ladoga. A line of trucks crossed the ice to bring food to the beleaguered city—"the Road of Life" the Leningraders called it. In the spring the ice cracked into fissures and tore the life-line to shreds.

In January 1943 the blockade was broken, as reported by Nikolai Tikhonov, Soviet war correspondent. But Leningrad was not finally relieved until February 1944.

(*From* The Defense of Leningrad, Eyewitness Accounts of the Siege *by Nikolai Tikhonov* [*London, n.d.*], *pp. 112–113. By permission of Hutchinson and Company, Ltd.*)

Whereas in January last year the inhabitants of Leningrad lived like Arctic explorers, hibernating in darkness and cold, mustering all their will-power and firmly determined to put up with everything and survive till the spring brought warmth and light again, sometimes having to summon their last ounce of strength to carry on the daily work for the front and the city, it was a different people in quite a different mood who greeted January this year.

The city was living a rigorous, austere life in want and anxiety, but there was already a presentiment not of the calendar spring, still a long way off, but of a secret, deep-seated confidence that there would soon be a change, that the long, laborious succession of trials was coming to an end and that events were about to take a turn for the better. And this knowledge made the work go faster, made everything more cheerful, so that even the children's Christmas trees seemed to shine more brightly.

And suddenly, on the historic night of January 18th, the Leningraders heard news from the front which the wireless repeated three times, and then it became clear to everybody that the long-awaited thing had happened—the blockade had been broken! All night long in the city nobody slept, the radio broadcast the whole night through and songs and music filled the air.

It is difficult for anyone who did not live in Leningrad in the days of the blockade to understand the feelings which filled the hearts of the inhabitants. All through the night the telephones rang, people talked in flats and meetings were held in the workshops. New records were set up in the armament factories. All the people got out their flags and hung them out on their houses, so that in the morning the whole city might be ablaze with red bunting. Everybody's thoughts turned to the men at the front, and the city itself, its splendid buildings, sparkling with frost patterns, rose up in new beauty. Shoulders were straightened, eyes shone. Everyone wanted to know the details, everyone spoke at once.

In the dark, far-off days of the autumn of 1941 hundreds of thousands of Leningrad citizens joined the army to defend their city. And they defended it. To-day it is a question of liberating it, and again a great number of them are fighting to set their city entirely free. Everywhere you meet people you know.

Here is a commander who fought in the Shimsky forests, and you will find out from him who is alive and who has already died a hero's death. Here is a girl with an axe in her hand, her face smudged with tar. She had been working in the House of the Red Army. And now a typist calls you by your name as she taps out a communique while the gun-fire roars incessantly. She has altered so much that you fail to recognize her at first, and then you remember she used to work as a typist in the Writers' Union. Here is a commander whose poetry is published in the Leningrad newspapers. He has a Guardsman's badge and a dark-red ribbon on the left side of his tunic.

But the Leningrad citizens are not only fighting. They have already come here to put things in order again, to fix up all the municipal services and restore transport facilities. Seamen are already bustling about the Schlüsselburg wharf, railwaymen are inspecting the lines and specialists are examining what is left of the cotton-printing factory. They are already reckoning up how much peat they have regained from the enemy and how it will help the industries of the great city. Schlüsselburg is in ruins, but the builders are ready to begin restoring it.

On the opposite bank where it was impossible for anyone to show himself before, locomotives are openly puffing out smoke and steam, and trains are running across the Neva. Over the river crossings there are long columns of vehicles, infantry detachments are on the march and the wheels of guns and the caterpillars of tanks crunch in the snow.

January, 1943, came in full of good omens for Leningrad. In the middle of the month the blockade was broken. But the people realized that the battles on the Neva were only the beginning of a great, ferocious combat. The enemy will not retreat; he must be annihilated. He will go on bombing and shelling the city even more malevolently and stubbornly. He will fight for every strong point. He can't simply go away. It is the beginning of his end and he wants to put it off as long as possible.

The methods of fighting him here are not like the ordinary ones. All along the front there are fortified defence positions and innumerable obstacles.

It is a struggle in the ramifications of an enormous fortified *place d'armes*, which it is possible to gnaw through but impossible to take with a single blow. The battle of the Neva has shown that victory lies rather with the one who uses skill.

Epic of Stalingrad From Both Sides: Soviet Correspondent Roman Karmen Witnesses the Death Throes of Paulus's Sixth Army, and Heinz Schröter, War Correspondents' Staff of the Sixth Army, Sees Horror in the Cellars

[February 2, 1943]

February 2, 1943:
On your orders the forces operating on the Don front have on February 2, 1943, at 16 hours completed the defeat and destruction of the enemy surrounded at Stalingrad.

. . . As a result of the complete annihilation of the encircled enemy troops, active operations in the city and region of Stalingrad have now come to an end.

This was Report No. 0079 of the Don Command to Joseph Stalin, Supreme Commander-in-Chief of the armed forces of the Soviet Union. In these brief words was described the finale at Stalingrad, one of the decisive battles of history. It was the worst German defeat since Napoleon's triumph at Jena in 1806.

Stalingrad and the Caucasus were Hitler's prime objectives in his summer offensive of 1942. His aim was to cut Russia's main north-south line of communications by crossing the Volga in the Stalingrad area and at the same time seize the oil fields of the Caucasus. He was infuriated by the very name of the city—Stalingrad, "the City of Stalin."

The Nazi Fuehrer made a critical mistake when he tried to take both Stalingrad and the Caucasus in one blow. General Ewald von Kleist later told the ironic story: "The 4th Panzer Army, advancing on my left, could have taken Stalingrad without a fight at the end of July (1942), but was diverted south to help me in crossing the Don. I did not need its aid, and it merely congested the roads I was using. When it turned north again, a fortnight later, the Russians had gathered sufficient forces at Stalingrad to check it."

The struggle lasted for the rest of the year and into 1943. The Germans took most of the city as winter quarters for their troops. But the Russians refused to surrender. They fought in the shattered houses, in the alleys,

226

the streets, the courtyards, the shops. They erected great barricades of rubble from which they fought the enemy to a standstill. "Stalingrad," wrote one observer, "was a monstrous graveyard of shattered buildings, shaking walls, and rotting flesh."

Early in November Hitler made a strange speech:

I wished to reach the Volga at a certain point, near a certain city. That city happens to bear the name of Stalin himself. . . . I wished to take that city: we do not make exaggerated claims, and I can now tell you that we have captured it. Only a very few small parts of it are not yet in our hands. Now people may ask: 'Why does the army not advance faster?' But I do not wish to see a second Verdun. I prefer to reach my objectives by limited assaults. Time is of no importance.

Curious reasoning from the self-confessed "greatest German of all time." Here Paulus's Sixth Army was being ground to pieces despite its battering-ram tactics, but the more deeply it penetrated into Stalingrad the slower was its progress. And the gentle Fuehrer, his heart bleeding, "did not wish to see a second Verdun"!.

What it was like for the Germans in Stalingrad was described in this diary of a German soldier:*

Diary of a Private First Class, 10th Company, 578th Regiment, 305th Infantry Division (Stalingrad Front).

. . . 5/12. (December 5) Things are getting worse. Heavy snowfall. My toes are frost-bitten. Gnawing pain in my stomach.

Toward evening, after an exhausting march, we entered Stalingrad. We were welcomed by bursting shells but managed to reach a cellar. Thirty people are there already. We are indescribably filthy and unshaven. Can hardly move. There is very little food. Three or four fags to go round. A terrible, savage mob. I am very unhappy. All is lost. Constant bickering. Everybody's nerves are on edge. No mail gets here. Awful.

6/12. Same. We are lying here in the cellar with hardly a chance to go out as the Russians spot us at once. Now we get at least a quarter of a loaf a day, one tin for eight men and a pat of butter.

7/12. No change. Oh God, help me return home safe and sound! My poor wife, my dear father and mother! How hard it is for them now. God Almighty, put an end to all this torture! Give us peace again. If we could only go home soon, return to a human way of life!

9/12. At to-day's dinner the portions were a bit larger but each loaf and tin must be shared by twelve. Yesterday was my blonde wife's birthday. I have a hard cross to bear. Life has become absolutely useless. Here there is one row after another. All caused by hunger.

*(True to Type, *A Selection of Letters and Diaries of German Soldiers and Civilians on the Soviet-German Front* [London, n.d.], p. 77. By permission of Hutchinson and Co., Ltd.)

10/12. Have been fasting ever since yesterday. Only had some black coffee. I am in utter despair. Heavens, is this going to go on much longer? The wounded stay with us. We can't get them away. They've got us surrounded. Stalingrad is a hell on earth. We cook horse carcasses. There is no salt. Many are suffering from dysentery. It's a terrible life. What evil did I do to deserve such punishment? Here, in this cellar, thirty people live in awful congestion. At two in the afternoon it already gets dark. The nights are very long. Will it ever be day?

11/12. To-day we got one-seventh of a loaf, a bit of fat and a hot meal was promised us. But in the evening I just collapsed, I was so weak.

12/12. Still in Stalingrad. A new unit is issuing us our supplies. The food situation is still very bad. Yesterday I did get some horse meat but to-day there is nothing doing. Somehow I expect to pull through it all. Matters simply must improve. Lively doings last night: artillery fire and grenades. The earth fairly shook. Our corporal went into action. We shall follow soon. There are some dysentery cases among us. I am frightfully hungry. If things only eased up a bit. Only not get sick or be wounded. God in Heaven, protect me!

The two selections below describe the epic at Stalingrad from differing angles. In the first, Soviet correspondent Roman Karmen, one of the best-known Red reporters in World War II, narrated "the inglorious finale of the Nazi adventure." In the second, Heinz Schröter, attached to the War Correspondents' Staff of the German Sixth Army, gave an unforgettable picture of the disaster from the German point of view. Schröter's report was one of the most striking pieces of reporting to come out of the war.

Hitler ordered four days of public mourning for his legions lost at Stalingrad.

THE INGLORIOUS FINALE OF THE NAZI ADVENTURE

(*From* The Epic Story of Stalingrad *by Soviet Army correspondents. By permission of Hutchinson & Co., Ltd.*)

"Come on, mate! Let him have it!"

We flew to Stalingrad in a "U2" plane. The machine hedge-hopped over fields and shell-holes where the greatest battle in the history of war had raged so short a time ago. In the summer the reek of petrol and blood had mingled on these broad plains with the pungent scent of the artemisia of the steppes. On the boundless white steppe where the earth so recently boiled with raging metal, we flitted past thousands of vehicles, guns, tanks, hundreds of planes standing in orderly rows on the aerodromes. Long trains loaded with arms and supplies were to be seen on the railway tracks. As we landed and transferred from the plane to a motor-car this wealth of booty became even more evident. At every corner, in every village, on railway stations and roads we came upon German equipment taken by our forces.

We left Voroponovo and Sadovaya stations behind and entered the city from which the thunder of artillery and the unceasing chatter of machine-gun fire echoed in the frosty air.

The city was nearly cleared of the enemy. Only two nests remained where Germans were still offering futile resistance. Step by step, quarter by quarter, our troops were mopping up in Stalingrad, smoking the Germans out of the houses by artillery fire or digging them out at the point of the bayonet, and after each such drive hundreds and more hundreds of enemy soldiers would give themselves up.

The German prisoners were glad that in spite of the intentions of their commanders they were still alive. They were glad and they showed it. The liberated streets of the city were literally crowded with groups of German prisoners. They walked up to the Red Armymen and asked for food. They stepped over mounds of German bodies to join the great columns of prisoners who were being shepherded by special escort units.

A characteristic trifle: a field kitchen came up to the positions of one of the forward units with hot food. The Red Armymen began to eat. The Germans in their trenches got a whiff of cookhouse smell and scrambled out in a hurry. Within a few minutes, dozens of them surrendered here after shooting their officers who opposed their action.

The German officers had done their best to convince their men that surrender meant certain death, because the Russians killed all prisoners. The soldiers of the German armies surrounded in Stalingrad and now surrendering in their thousands, will have an opportunity of convincing themselves how grossly they have been deceived. Some prisoners begged our commanders to let them return and bring along their comrades. Such prisoners, who were allowed to go back, crawled through some crack in a wall, and in half an hour they returned beaming, and dragging behind them a tail of anything from thirty to fifty fellow-soldiers.

When a certain German infantry division surrendered, its officers stood in an isolated group apart from their soldiers. One of them, a tall *Ober-leutenant,* who managed even under the conditions existing in a surrounded army to preserve some remnants of aristocratic grooming, approached our major, saluted and asked his permission to ask a question.

"Herr Major," he said in broken Russian, "in the camp for prisoners of war will we be given blankets?"

The major clenched his fists. It cost him an effort to control himself.

"Yes, I think so," he said and turned away. The German saluted again and returned to his place.

Some days before this, that Red Army major and his unit had seized a German camp for Soviet prisoners of war. He had had to put his signature to a document describing the monstrous treatment, the inhuman torments to which our soldiers had been subjected in this camp. "Death Camp" was the name our men had given to this ghastly place. Here, in a large space hedged in with barbed wire, our prisoners had lived in the open, in burrows which they themselves had scooped out in the ground. Those of them who were found alive by our liberating troops looked hardly human. They were skeletons covered with skin. They were so feeble they could not even speak, much less move. Living men lay among those of their comrades who had perished as a result of such treatment. Our men captured a document which bears eloquent witness to the attitude of the Germans towards their prisoners of war. This document is the diary of the chief of the "sanitary services" of the camp. Daily entries show the number of men who perished from starvation, disease, ill-treatment or who had been simply shot. The first entries record a daily 20, 18, 22, 19 deaths; then the figures go up to 60, 58, 72 per day and finally to the terrible total of 120, 90, 118 deaths per day.

When they had recovered a bit, the surviving inmates of this camp described the conditions in it. All guards carried sticks. They beat the prisoners at the slightest provocation—for getting out of line in a queue at the distribution of the muddy water called "soup," for a loud word, for a slow movement. The beatings were merciless, bone-breaking. More often prisoners were just shot.

This was why it cost the major such an effort to control himself when he replied to the insolent German officer.

The city was reeling with the shock of artillery fire from guns of every calibre. A violent battle was developing in one quarter. Our troops had taken complete possession of two parks and the great square. Mopping-up operations were in progress in those streets in which small groups of Germans were offering a sporadic resistance.

In the liberated parts of the city the inhabitants immediately began to put in an appearance. I saw women digging in the ruins of their homes. I could hardly believe my eyes when in one of the streets piled with German dead I saw a child—a little girl about seven years old. She was helping her mother drag along their belongings on a little sled. The workers of the Stalingrad factories who in the darkest days took up arms as volunteers to defend their native city, will begin the reconstruction of their work-places in a few days' time.

While fighting is still continuing in the city, railway lines, junctions and stations are being repaired at a rapid rate. Soon, very soon, the military men will say farewell to Stalingrad. They are wanted on other fronts.

I saw a stirring sight: a group of air force men who had come to the end of their job here, were taking leave of the city. . . . They took off from their aerodromes on the outskirts, dozens of planes flying over the city towards the west. The last wave of dive-bombers formed a five-pointed star in the sky. The machines flew over the centre of the city, filling the air with the roar of their mighty engines.

The fighting in the streets was not ended even now. Street by street, quarter by quarter, our Stalingrad was cleared by the Red Army of the last Germans. . . .

In a sector occupied by troops under the command of General Tolbukhin, a group of German officers decided to surrender. In a uniform sparkling with the gold of decorations, a Hitlerite colonel walked slowly along the ruined street, stepping over the dead bodies of other Germans. After him came a few lieutenant-colonels, majors, captains, lieutenants and behind them a long column of soldiers, a straggling procession five hundred yards long, limping on frozen feet.

When one German colonel was told where the front line was at present, he opened his eyes wide. In their encirclement they had no idea of the situation at the front. Proof of this is that a small German detachment, pretending to be prisoners of war "escorted" by their own comrades dressed in Red Army uniforms, tried to leave the city in order to get through to their main forces at—Kalach!

Columns of our men go warily, in single file, to where they hear volleys of rifle fire or the chatter of tommy-guns, where the last nests of resistance of the surrounded German troops are being mopped up. "Get it over quickly" is the feeling which grows stronger in our men and commanders as the time goes by. Get it over with! Free the city!

The end is near. The last nests of stubborn resistance are weakening, the guns are breaking up the defences. Here and there the firing dies down; a pole with a dirty towel on it is poked through a hole in the wall and a crowd of Germans dribble out in the wake of the flag of surrender. Beyond the city the columns of prisoners stretch out for miles and miles; there are tens of thousands of them.

Our troops continue to draw the noose ever tighter round the encircled German forces. Soviet planes incessantly bomb the enemy still holding out in the centre of the city. This bombardment is even beginning to be dangerous. So small have the German islands of resistance become that the bombs may easily hit our own men.

The Fascists have taken up strong positions in a tall, many-storied building. They have even got a gun in there. From behind a corner we could observe the course of the battle. Two of our tanks drove up quite close to the house and opened fire on the spot from where the German tommy-gunners were firing. The gunners brought the gun to bear and, taking careful aim, began to batter at the loopholes. Now the barrel of a tommy-gun gleamed in one of them. Unhurriedly, the gun-layer began to direct his gun on to this loophole, while the Red Army men in cover behind the ruins egged him on: "Come on, mate! Let him have it!" The gun fired and the loophole was immediately transformed into a mass of fire and dense smoke. Done for. But almost instantly little flashes dart out from the next floor—the Germans have climbed up there. Firing shell after shell, as if he were hammering in a nail, our gunner chased the Germans higher and higher up. Already one tiny human figure could be seen on the roof. A shell bit a slice out of the edge of the roof and everything was wreathed in smoke. Our men jumped out from behind their cover and rushed the house. The gunner switched his fire to the next house. It was getting dark and tracers screamed through the air like fiery needles.

On January 29th one could already drive a car along many streets of central Stalingrad. Sometimes one had to get out and struggle through the ruins of houses where one was safe from the bursts of tommy-gun fire. As one walks along the streets and squares of this great and beautiful city destroyed by Hitler, which will now have to be entirely rebuilt, one feels one would like to bare one head's silently in front of these noble ruins, whose every stone, every fragment of it, is stained with the blood of our warriors and bears witness to the glory of the Soviet people. The accurate German strategists took everything into account. But in their variegated military terminology they forgot one word and its meaning: they forgot the word "Russia," and they met their death among the ruins of the city which has become the symbol of the stubborn strength of our country.

We will build you up again, you great city of Stalingrad! Inspired architects, painters and sculptors will create buildings of marble and granite and lay out green squares and parks. Our factories will be rebuilt. But mankind will never forget these ruins, nor the Soviet heroes who fought to the last throb of their hearts on staircases, behind smoking heaps of stones, in cellars and back alleys and held their city.

On the morning of January 30th, 1943, all forces advancing from every direction towards the centre of Stalingrad joined hands completely at last. The German troops were finally routed. Only small groups and single tommy-gun snipers were still shooting from among the ruins. Patrols were scouring the city to mop up the German cut-throats. Lieutenant-General Sanne, commanding the 100th Light Infantry Division, was surrounded and captured. The German soldiers who had surrendered were piling up their rifles, tommy-guns and machine-guns in heaps in the streets when suddenly several German transport planes appeared flying at a great height over the city. They dropped parachutes with loads of food. Our men undid the parcels and greatly enjoyed the sausage destined for Field-Marshal von Paulus.

Our patrols combed the city, and in little clashes finished the mopping-up of the last nests of German resistance. Machine-gun and rifle fire went on throughout the night, but by morning the firing died down. . . .

To-day, February 1st, firing in the central part of the city ceased completely. But at 9 A.M. the thunder of dozens of guns was heard from the direction of the northern outskirts. There the surrounded Germans are still resisting, but their hours are numbered.

Another day or so and this front-line city will suddenly find itself far to the rear. A staff officer, in his dug-out, wearied by many sleepless nights, raises his head from his maps, throws down his red pencil and says with a smile:

"Yes, we're rear-liners now! We must finish things up here and then we shall have to run after the front. And run pretty far and fast if we want to catch up . . . !"

THE MASS GRAVE AT DISTRICT COMMAND CENTRE

(*Heinz Schröter*, Stalingrad, *trans. by Constantine Fitzgibbon* [*New York, 1958*], *pp. 240–244. Copyright © 1958 by E. P. Dutton & Co., Inc. By permission of the publishers.*)

"Over all was the sickly smell of decaying bodies . . and filth."

"Care will be taken to ensure that all wounded arriving at Stalingrad are assembled at District Command Centre. Supply Sector Three will be responsible for food and supplies."

This order was issued by the Sixth Army on the 15th of January. All the divisions had been sent a copy and they, in turn, had passed it on to the field hospitals and dressing stations.

". . . assembled at District Command Centre."

Since the 15th of January thousands of wounded soldiers had converged on Stalingrad. The large building with its two wings seemed to exert a magnetic attraction.

The wounded stumbled along, great columns of men from Orlovka and Voroponovo, and from the west as well. Blood and the corpses of those who fell out marked their route. They were often marching for three days, and in many cases it took them two weeks. They were all young, yet their faces were those of old men. They stumbled through the hours of anguish, trying to keep to their feet, fighting against death. They were carried or pulled, they hobbled on sticks and boards. "To Stalingrad Centre," they muttered. "To the District Command."

They imagined a proper hospital, with a roof and a place where they could lie down, hot tea, and dressings for their suppurating wounds. District Command represented for them the island of salvation. It meant help and bandages and clean water and rest. In groups and columns they struggled towards their goal. Those coming from the west never saw the stone pillars that graced the front of the "City Centre" nor the inscription: *The Proletariat of the red Tsaritsyn to the freedom fighters who fell in 1919 in the struggle against Wrangel's hangmen.* While those coming from the south stared with unseeing eyes past the notice beside the Tsaritsa which said: *Keep out. Curiosity endangers your life and the lives of your comrades.*

Onwards, ever onwards, was their sole thought. Day and night the great crowds of wounded men shuffled along towards the apparent security which the large building represented in their eyes.

They reached Stalingrad's "City Centre" and the District Command.

The building of their dreams was filled to overflowing, and had been for many weeks past. It was filled with wounded and sick, shirkers and scroungers.

In the cellars were battle groups of the 29th and 3rd Motorised Infantry Divisions and what was left of the 376th Infantry Division, and the firing went on to right and left of them.

There were no beds and no bandages, no tea and no help. Sixteen doctors fought a hopeless fight, stretcher bearers and medical orderlies worked till they dropped, but the maelstrom of chaos was too much for them.

Newcomers were constantly arriving. They crawled over the heaps of men lying in the halls and corridors, and pushed down into the cellars or up the staircases. And there they stayed. Without a bed, or a word of encouragement, without any help or even the hope of help. They asked for water and food, but neither was given them; they called for a priest, a doctor, an orderly, for morphia, bandages and writing paper, for their friends, mother, wife or child, and some asked for a revolver.

Sometimes they were handed a revolver, and then their place was free for another to occupy.

"They have nowhere to lay their heads and their souls too are without shelter," said the padre of the 44th Infantry Division.

As the battle drew closer, District Command Centre came under fire from the enemy artillery. The building was soon well alight.

The first started in the west wing and the flames then spread to the attics of the main building.

Those who could move, and who were near the exits, were able to escape, but others blocked the corridors and stairways. Men scrambled over two layers of prostrate bodies. Panic broke out, and some flung themselves over the banisters and out of windows. The main entrance to the building collapsed when the upper floor fell in, thus blocking the way out. Men crowded back up the stairs in an attempt to reach the other part of the building through the upper corridors, but the dead and the dying were in the way, progress was impossible, and then they met another mass of panic-stricken soldiers who were struggling to reach the main entrance, unaware that it had already collapsed.

This desperate attempt to escape from the burning building lasted for three hours. Over three thousand men died there, trampled on, suffocated and burned to death, while others had been killed when they jumped from the windows or were buried under the ruins. Their cries drowned the crackle of the flames and the whine of the shells, and long re-echoed amongst the ruins.

Every house was by now a ruin or a heap of rubble, but most of the cellars were still in good condition. The walls of the houses had fallen across them, thus providing additional security. During the last days of the struggle these cellars acquired a tragic and horrible notoriety.

. . . Any man who entered one of them abandoned all hope of ever coming out alive. This was equally true of the tractor factory cellars, or the G.P.U. prison, the theatre vaults, the cellar of the Red Militia's house, of the library or of the leather exchange. The cellars of the District Command and of the Timoschenko bunker were no better than the vaults under the museum and the power station.

These places of refuge from bombs and mortar fire became collecting points for the dressing stations and field hospitals. They were hells in which men died, singly and *en masse*.

In the celler under Simonovich's warehouse eight hundred men lay pressed against the walls and all over the damp and dirty floor. Their bodies littered the stairs and blocked the passages. All men were equal here: rank and class had been shed as the dead leaves fall from the November trees. In the Simonovich cellars they had reached the end of life's journey, and if there were any distinctions to be drawn between them it was only in the severity of their wounds or in the number of the days that they still had to live. There was also one other difference, namely the way in which each man met his death.

A man lay on the steps dying of diphtheria, and beside him lay three others who had been dead for days, but no one had moved them because it was dark and they had not been noticed. Behind them a sergeant, whose tongue hung from his mouth like a piece of red hot iron, and whose feet had rotted off up to the ankles, screamed with thirst and pain.

On the wall in the middle of the cellar a foul-smelling wick burned in an old tin. It stank of paraffin, but also of fetid blood and gangrenous flesh and suppurating pus, and over all was the sickly smell of decaying bodies and iodine and sweat and excrement and filth.

The air was well nigh unbreathable, lungs and throat were parched, and eyes streamed tears.

The skin fell in strips from their bodies. They shook with tetanus, they screamed like animals and their bodies were covered with sores. Here a man choked to death, unable to get his breath, while another shivered with fever, calling for his wife and cursing the war or praising God. Spotted fever, typhus, pneumonia, gangrene, all claimed their victims. A lance-corporal was dying in one corner, his stomach and legs fearfully swollen; he neither spoke nor moved, nor asked for help, but just lay there with open eyes and folded hands. Across the passage and up the stairs a young man of twenty kicked and screamed, foaming at the mouth, his eyes rolling wildly, until death came and stilled his pain and stopped his convulsions.

They were given no food and a man who still had any kept it well hidden, for in the darkness a slice of bread was worth more than a man's life. This can only be understood by those who have themselves endured starvation and have known the value that a crumb of bread then has.

The lice were the worst. They bit through the men's skin, crawled into open wounds, and prevented the sleep so desperately needed. In their thousands they swarmed over the men's bodies and tattered underwear; only when death came, or high fever, did they depart, like rats leaving a sinking ship. A disgusting grey, swarming crowd would then move across to the next man and settle on him.

And there was no one there to help them. Whenever possible, the dead were taken out into the courtyard or stacked in bomb craters like logs. For a brief time there had been a doctor in the Simonovich cellar, but he had only taken refuge there during an air raid. His "own" cellar was elsewhere, and men were calling for him just as insistently there as they were here. Even he could only give the most superficial help. The mass of suffering was far too great.

Any man still capable of thinking could work out for himself when his end was due. And he would know that no purpose was served by screaming or complaining.

For to whom could he complain?

Many died, and it was often hours or even days before the next man noticed that they had gone. No one came to take away the dead, who were pushed and rolled from one man to the next, across the room and down the passage. Like logs or sacks, to a hole in the west wall and then out into the crater where the 500-pound bomb had exploded. Through the hole they were tossed, and into the crater. There were already a hundred bodies in it, many of them still warm; those were the men too weak to cry out.

Crowds of wounded waited outside the Simonovich cellar and

when there was room slowly made their way down into it. Nobody was surprised that although no one ever came up out of the cellar, there was always room for more to go in. The dead were not counted nor their identity discs removed, though frequently their pockets were searched for bread. The cause of death was of no interest. All that mattered was to die quickly and make room for the others, waiting outside in the icy wind.

Men died not only in the Simonovich cellar but in every cellar. A wave of misery and pain enveloped their weary, broken bodies. They were no longer afraid, there was no terror amongst them nor panic, nor any signs of the demoralisation which had set in amongst the Army staffs above ground. Down in the cellars their fingers were no longer closed about the triggers of their guns, nor did they sit sobbing in dug-outs, like some of those who were fighting to the last round.

". . . whatever sacrifice may be demanded of us as individuals is irrelevant. . . ." So Hitler had said.

Hell 26,000 Feet Up: Walter Cronkite, United Press, Representing "The Writing Sixty-ninth," Accompanies American Raid on Wilhelmshaven

[February 27, 1943]

"... Our bombs were on their way to Hitler."

By early 1943 Germany was beginning to feel the weight of Allied air power. On February 26, 1943, an American air armada, consisting of Flying Fortresses and Liberators, flew out on its third attack on Germany. The target this time was Wilhelmshaven, one of the most important German naval bases and an important submarine center. For the first time six correspondents were allowed to accompany an American air raid in the European theatre. Among them was Walter Cronkite, whose report of the raid, reproduced here, was called a "classic story" by Hugh Baillie, president of the United Press.

Twenty-five German fighter planes, including silver-nosed Focke-Wulf 190s and Messerschmitts 110s, and ten twin-engined Junkers 88s, looking for stragglers, rose to attack the formation. Anti-aircraft flak was heavy and accurate. The Reich base was seared, but Major General Ira C. Eaker's Eighth Air Force lost seven planes in the raid.

(The New York Times, *February 27, 1943. By permission of United Press International.*)

AT A UNITED STATES FLYING FORTRESS BASE in England, Saturday, Feb. 27 (U.P.)—American Flying Fortresses have just come back from an assignment to hell—a hell 26,000 feet above the earth, a hell of burning tracer bullets and bursting gunfire, of crippled Fortresses and burning German fighter planes, of parachuting men and others not so lucky. I have just returned with a Flying Fortress crew from Wilhelmshaven.

We fought off Hitler's fighters and dodged his guns. The Fortress I rode in came out without damage, but we had the element of luck on our side.

Other formations caught the blast of fighter blows and we watched

239

Fortresses and Liberators plucked out of the formations around us.

We gave the ship repair yards and other installations at the great German submarine and naval base of the North Sea a most severe pasting. As we swept beyond the target and back over the North Sea from which we came we saw great pillars of smoke over the target area.

Six of us represented the American news services, newspapers and radios—"The Writing Sixty-ninth"—after undergoing special high-altitude flight training. A seventh correspondent could not go because of illness and the plane taking another had to turn back because of technical difficulties.

Actually, the impressions of a first bombing mission are a hodge-podge of disconnected scenes like a poorly edited home movie—bombs falling past you from the formation above, a crippled bomber with smoke pouring from one motor limping along thousands of feet below, a tiny speck in the sky that grows closer and finally becomes an enemy fighter, a Focke-Wulf peeling off above you somewhere and plummeting down, shooting its way through the formation; your bombardier pushing a button as calmly as if he were turning on a hall light, to send our bombs on the way.

Our bombardier was First Lieutenant Albert W. Diefenbach, 26, of Washington, D.C. His job began at that thrilling moment when the bomb bay doors swing open on the lead ship on down the line to us.

That signaled that we were beginning the bomb run. Then we swept over Wilhelmshaven. There were broken clouds but through them there appeared a toy village below which was really a major seaport and I thought:

"Down there right now people are scurrying for shelters—which means interrupting work on vital submarines and ships and dock yards."

Lieutenant Diefenbach's left hand went out to the switch panel alongside him and almost imperceptibly he touched a button and said calmly over the communications system:

"Bombs away."

That was it. Our mission was accomplished—our bombs were on their way to Hitler.

Ghosts of War: Ernie Pyle Reports From the Battlefields of North Africa

[April 27, 1943]

"My mind seemed to lose all sense of proportion. . . ."

He was a slight, almost gnome-like little man with a camera-eye and a heart as large as humanity. One of the great correspondents of World War II, Ernie Pyle was a G.I. idol. He knew nothing about military strategy. He wrote little about the bigger issues of the conflict. Instead, he recorded the weariness, the dirt, the filth of war, about young men who did not want to die, about courage and anger and cussing and graves and more graves. He confessed that his was a "worm's eye view of the war."

To a public hungry for war news, Ernie Pyle's dispatches came as a blessing. His stories were filled with homely details—the name of a G.I., his home address, the members of his family. He wrote about little acts of consideration and kindness in the combat areas. He told of the loneliness of men behind the lines and of the courage of youngsters who in battle became men.

It was an extraordinary talent:

. . . Those hundreds of thousands of men were churning the highways for two thousand miles behind the lines with their endless supply trucks, they were unloading the ships, cooking the meals, pounding the typewriters, fixing the roads, making the maps, repairing the engines, decoding the messages, training the reserves, pondering the plans.

To get all that colossal writhing chaos shaped into something that intermeshed and moved forward with efficiency was a task closely akin to weaving a cloth out of a tubful of spaghetti.

Pyle followed the American troops across North Africa from the landings in Oran in November 1942 to the end of German resistance in Africa on May 15, 1943. On April 27, 1943, shortly before the Allied victory, he sent a dispatch to the New York World-Telegram, *reprinted below, which told of his experience with noisy battlefield ghosts.*

241

"Yes, I want the war to be over," he wrote at the end of the Tunisian campaign, "just as keenly as any soldier in North Africa wants it. This little interlude of passive contentment here on the Mediterranean shore is a mean temptation. It is a beckoning into somnolence. This is the kind of day I think I want my life to be composed of, endlessly. But pretty soon we shall strike our tents and traipse again after the clanking tanks, sleep again to the incessant lullaby of the big rolling guns. It has to be that way, and wishing doesn't change it."

The little reporter from Indiana hated the dirty business of war, but he had to go on. An unkind fate brought him to the island of Ie Shima during the closing months of the conflict. Here a Japanese bullet cut short his life. Grieving G.I.s placed this inscription at the spot where he was killed:

AT THIS SPOT

THE

77TH INFANTRY DIVISION

LOST A BUDDY

ERNIE PYLE

18 APRIL 1945

(*New York* World-Telegram, *April 27, 1943. By permission of Scripps-Howard Newspapers.*)

NORTHERN TUNISIA (By Wireless)—We moved one afternoon to a new position just a few miles behind the invisible line of armor that separates us from the Germans in Northern Tunisia. Nothing happened that first night that was spectacular, yet somehow the whole night became obsessed with a spookiness that leaves it standing like a landmark in my memory.

We had been at the new camp about an hour and were still setting up our tents when German planes appeared overhead. We stopped work to watch them. It was the usual display of darting planes, with the conglomerate sounds of ack-ack on the ground and in the sky.

Suddenly we realized that one plane was diving straight at us, and we made a mad scramble for foxholes. Two officer friends of mine had dug a three-foot hole and set their tent over it. So they made for their tent, and I was tramping on their heels. The tent flap wouldn't come open, and we wound up in a silly heap. Finally it did open, and we all dived through the narrow opening all at once.

We lay there in the hole, face down, as the plane came smack overhead with a terrible roar. We were all drawn up inside, waiting for the blow. Explosions around us were shatteringly loud, and yet when it was all over we couldn't find any bomb holes or anybody hurt.

But you could find a lot of nervous people.

Dusk came on, and with dusk began the steady boom of big guns in the mountains ahead of us. They weren't near enough for the sound to be crashing. Rather it was like the lonely roll of an approaching thunderstorm—a sound which since childhood has always made me sad with a kind of portent of inevitable doom.

We went to bed in our tents. A near-by farmyard was full of dogs, and they began a howling that lasted all night. The roll of artillery was constant. It never stopped in 24 hours. Once in a while there were nearer shots which might have been German patrols or might not.

We lay uneasily in our cots. Sleep wouldn't come. We turned and turned. I snapped on a flashlight.

"What time is it?" asked Chris Cunningham from the next cot.

"Quarter to one," I answered. "Haven't you been asleep?"

He hadn't.

A plane droned faintly in the distance and came nearer and nearer until it was overhead.

"Is that a Jerry or a Beaufighter?" Chris asked out of the darkness.

"It hasn't got that throb-throb to it," I said, "so it must be a Beaufighter. But, hell, I never can tell really. Don't know what it is."

The plane passed on, out of hearing. The artillery rolled and rolled. A nearer shot went off uncannily somewhere in the darkness. Some guinea hens set up a terrific cackling.

I remembered that just before dusk a soldier had shot at a snake in our new camp, and they thought it was a cobra. We'd just heard our first stories of scorpions, too. I began to feel creepy and wondered if our tent flaps were tight.

Another plane throbbed in the sky, and we lay listening with an awful anticipation. One of the dogs suddenly broke into a frenzied barking and went tearing through our little camp as though chasing a demon.

My mind seemed to lose all sense of proportion, and I was jumpy and mad at myself.

Concussion ghosts, traveling in waves, touched our tent walls and made them quiver. Ghosts were shaking the ground ever so lightly. Ghosts were stirring the dogs to hysteria. Ghosts were wandering in the sky peering for us in our cringing hideout. Ghosts were everywhere, and their hordes were multiplying as every hour added its production of new battlefield dead.

"What time is it?" comes out of the darkness from the next cot. I snap on the flashlight.

"Half-past 4, and for God's sake go to sleep!"

Finally just before dawn you do sleep, in spite of everything.

Next morning we spoke around among ourselves and found one by one that all of us had tossed away all night. It was an unexplainable thing. For all of us had been through dangers greater than this. On another night the roll of the guns would have lulled us to sleep.

It's just that on some nights the air becomes sick and there is an unspoken contagion of spiritual dread, and you are little boys again, lost in the dark.

Conquest of Tunisia: British and American War Correspondents Report a Brilliant Allied Victory in North Africa

[April 29–May 13, 1943]

Allied war planners agreed that a second front against Hitler was impossible until Tunisia was won and the Axis expelled from North Africa. In early 1943 the American army in North Africa, just a "test-tube baby," was welded into a tried and tested battle force. Meanwhile, the British were sending their tanks to tear holes in the Axis Mareth Line.

A giant pincers movement was started. While the British Eighth Army and French units pushed to Cape Bon in the southern sector of the front, the U.S. II Corps and the British First Army fought their way in the north from one mountain range to another toward Bizerte and Tunis. Both Americans and British faced exceedingly strong enemy positions.

The final phase of the battle for Tunisia came from April 29 to May 13, 1943. Tunis and Bizerte, the last main Axis strongholds in the area, were captured in a concerted Allied drive on May 7, 1943. Tens of thousands of Axis troops were caught in an iron trap from which all escape was blocked. The Axis lost 300,000 men in the debacle, of whom 266,000 were taken prisoners. The Allies suffered 70,000 casualties.

It was a tremendous victory. General Erwin Rommel, the Desert Fox, had been forced to flee before the final collapse. Egypt and Suez were now safe from Axis control. Hitler had lost his last remaining outpost in Africa. For him it was now the "beginning of the end."

General Eisenhower summed it up this way:

The Tunisian victory was hailed with delight throughout the Allied nations. It clearly signified to friend and foe alike that the Allies were at last upon the march. The Germans, who had during the previous winter suffered also the great defeat of Stalingrad and had been forced to abandon their other offensives on the Russian front in favor of a desperate defense, were compelled after Tunisia to think only of the protection of conquests rather than of their enlargement.

The Tunisian campaign stimulated some of the best reporting of the war. In the first selection below Christopher Buckley, of the London

Daily Telegraph, *described the storming of Longstop Hill, essential for the final drive. Frank L. Kluckhohn of* The New York Times *recounted the fall of the last two Axis strongholds. E. A. Montague, correspondent for the Manchester* Guardian, *told of the last two days. And Pierre J. Huss, of International News Service, showed how the Nazis cracked in ignominy without gallantry.*

THE STORMING OF LONGSTOP HILL

(*Christopher Buckley, London* Daily Telegraph, *April 29, 1943. By permission of the London* Daily Telegraph.)

"I have told the Corps commander we shall have Longstop by lunch. It may have to be late lunch, but I think we shall do it."

In all campaigns there are certain places which achieve a quite unpredictable degree of importance, which become focal points to which increasingly powerful forces on either side are drawn, points on which the whole fate of a campaign hinges. Ypres was just such a place on the Western Front in the last war. Tobruk enjoyed to a certain extent the same fate in the Western Desert in the last three years. . . .

On the First Army front I suppose there is no single point or feature that has acquired such significance for the British troops as Longstop Hill, 6 miles north-east of Medjez, which was mostly occupied by our troops in the early part of Good Friday afternoon— which also happened to be St. George's Day, April 23rd.

To the casual traveller, even one with an eye for military possibilities, Longstop Hill is not immediately and obviously a strong defensive position. View it with closer attention and with the aid of a large-scale map and the significance of Longstop becomes readily apparent; it dominates the good metalled highway from Medjez to Tebourba and thence to Tunis. . . .

Of fighting in this neighbourhood in the early part of the campaign I am not qualified to speak as a direct eye-witness. I was at that time following the long, long trail that leads from Benghazi to Tripoli. But, broadly speaking, what happened was that the British advanced troops pushed on through Medjez at the end of November and reached Tebourba, while their patrols even penetrated the outskirts of Djedeoda, only a dozen miles from Tunis.

But with the slender forces then at our disposal it was impossible to cover the flanks of the advance. Then came the enemy counter-stroke. We were driven back from Tebourba to Medjez, and the Germans established themselves on Longstop Hill.

The importance of Longstop was fully realised by our command, and just before Christmas a determined effort was made to take it. The Guards Brigade did in fact capture it, but it was handed over to an American combat team, lost by them, recaptured by the Guards and lost again.

Since that time the Germans had progressively fortified it with a network of trenches, dugouts and embrasures, had garrisoned it with picked troops, well supplied with mortars, anti-tank guns, light and heavy machine-guns, and had protected its lower slopes with mines.

That was the nut which the British troops had to crack when the barrage opened at eight o'clock on the evening of the 22nd; and within less than twenty hours they had cracked it.

The activity of the previous fortnight had enabled us to establish gun positions on the adjacent hills. Then, that Thursday night at eight o'clock, the artillery bombardment of 400 guns opened against Longstop.

It is not my purpose here to describe the spectacle of this bombardment, though it was on a scale that challenges comparison with Alamein. What is important is to see what was the aim of this gigantic expenditure of shell-fire. It had two purposes. The first was not so much to blot out the garrison of the hill as to compel them metaphorically and also literally to keep their heads down, to prevent them replying with effective counter-fire while our sappers picked up mines and our infantry went forward to fresh positions closer to the summit of the hill.

There exists also a secondary purpose for the bombardment. Get 400 guns laying down a barrage on an area not much more than 600 yards square, within which, however well dug in, is a force of, say, the best part of a battalion strong, a force of men with nerves and muscles; let this continue hour after hour through the night. Those defenders, however courageous and determined, will not be in the best condition to resist a series of vigorous attacks the following morning.

That, roughly, was what happened that Thursday night. No one will argue it as an ideal tactic. It is costly in shells. It does relatively little positive, immediate damage, and it somewhat resembles the employment of a sledge-hammer to crush a walnut. But assuming that the taking of Longstop was essential to our further advance, assuming that all methods of circumventing or turning this position were considered and found impracticable, it is not easy to think of a better tactic.

Under cover of the barrage the troops of an English South-Country regiment went forward to attack in the darkness very early in the morning of Good Friday, to assault this position, whose strength may not unjustly be compared with that of the Alcazar in the Spanish Civil War.

They were met with heavy machine-gun and mortar fire, and under a cloudy sky found difficulty in making their way through the enemy minefields, not all of which it had been possible for the sappers to clear, and which were thickly strewn with anti-personnel mines. The attack recoiled, but only temporarily, and at first light the same troops went forward a second time.

Again they made some progress; again they were repulsed.

Undaunted, the British commander laid on the third attack with fresh troops, employing double the strength of the previous two. He continued a brisk fire from the field guns, while at the same time, as a *tour de force*, a couple of tanks were sent to the rocky summit of a ridge overlooking Longstop, whence they proceeded to give covering fire when the infantry went in again.

All that morning of a Good Friday which was also St. George's Day I watched the struggle on Longstop from a spur of Heidous, intently following the white puffs as behind me came the crack of gun-fire and overhead the whining of shells. Far up in the blue one saw the neat, purposeful formations of our bombers—Bostons and Mitchells for the most part—one wave relentlessly succeeding another, while from time to time the enemy countered with spasmodic hit-and-run attacks by a couple or three Messerschmitts. And across the gaily-flowering fields, a vivid crimson with poppies, men went forward yet again to face death in the brilliant sunshine on this day which was Good Friday.

About half an hour before noon the third infantry attack went in with the support of tanks and still heavier covering fire. I had returned a few hundred yards, to the headquarters of the local British unit entrusted with the attack, to check up on the situation. The General greeted me breezily: "I have told the Corps commander we shall have Longstop by lunch," he said. "It may have to be late lunch," he added, chuckling, "but I think we shall do it. We've got men right round behind Longstop already."

I asked him about prisoners.

"We got about 200 on the lower slopes. They fought with tremendous toughness, but when one put up his hands you'd find that a good many others suddenly emerged from holes and put up their hands, too. After all, they've had a tremendous pasting. And they do now realise that their time in Tunisia is just about up. But I do not think that will affect their fighting capacity."

So the third and final attack of the day went in. Amid a crescendo of fire, a Scottish regiment, accompanied by the tanks, led the way up the hill. Having made half the distance in a series of short infantry rushes, they came to a halt in what natural cover they could find.

Then—and this was the decisive manoeuvre—an entirely fresh wave of English county troops moved up in support, and "leapfrogging" through the Scots, carried first the west and then the east of the twin crests which form Longstop Hill.

By 2:30 in the afternoon it was all over. The enemy had been ejected from all but a tiny north-eastern corner of the hill, well down below the summit. Most of Longstop had fallen, and all that remained was the nerve-racking process of going through the intricate network of dugouts with bayonet and hand grenades, mopping up small groups of prisoners whilst the shell-fire fell suddenly and almost eerily silent and the sun began to tilt slowly down westward.

The General had his lunch on Longstop—though a late one.

And that was how we passed this Good Friday that was also St. George's Day. Not without toil and sweat and blood.

CAPTURE OF TUNIS AND BIZERTE

(*Frank Kluckhohn*, The New York Times, *May 8, 1943. By permission of* The New York Times.)

"Now the fleeing, broken Axis remnants are being mercilessly strafed along roads jammed by their retreat."

ALLIED HEADQUARTERS IN NORTH AFRICA, May 7.—Tunis and Bizerte, last main Axis strongholds in Africa, were captured today by British and American forces just 181 days after the Allied landing in North Africa.

Amid the crash of artillery and the crackle of small arms, German and Italian forces—once within sixty miles of Alexandria—faced surrender or annihilation without a Dunkerque. And Southern Europe lies open to invasion by the Allies, who now control the southern shore of the Mediterranean.

·The Germans with their backs to the sea fought frantically to hold Tunis, but the avenging dust-streaked, bare-waisted Tommies of Britain's First Army, who were forced by the Germans to evacuate France in 1940, stormed into the city at 4:20 P.M. Five minutes earlier American armed reconnaissance units and light tanks had pushed into Bizerte, key naval base of this part of the Mediterranean.

The remnants of Field Marshal General Erwin Rommel's once victorious and highly touted Africa Corps, their leader apparently fled to Europe, and Col. Gen. Dietloff von Arnim's crack tank and infantry units, also perhaps without their leader, broke under the mighty force of Allied tanks, big guns, thousands of planes and divisions of veteran fighting men that General Sir Harold R. L. G. Alexander hurled against them yesterday morning.

Now the fleeing, broken Axis remnants are being mercilessly strafed along roads jammed by their retreat. The Allied air forces are lashing with machine gun and cannon at the fleeing men and vehicles that are madly racing toward the Cape Bon peninsula. Other enemy forces, cut off, are being mopped up. Only in the hills lying between the Enfidaville area and the plain of Tunis are Axis forces holding out strongly, and their future is regarded as hopeless.

Tonight, as word of the long-awaited triumph spread, there were demonstrations of joy all over North Africa. But up forward the Americans and the British were still grimly battling, determined to crush the enemy completely and to keep as many as possible from reaching Cape Bon. This hilly ground is the last place left for the Axis forces to make a stand, but they have lost guns, tanks and ammunition. They may not last long.

Today as yesterday, yellow clouds of dust, turned up by tanks and moving vehicles, as well as cordite smoke from explosives, hung over the battlefields along a sixty-mile area that could no longer be called a front.

Lumbering lethal American tanks ground into Ferryville in the Bizerte naval base ring at noon. Reconnaissance units including many New Yorkers were quickly thrust between Bizerte's twin lakes and were the first to reach the Bizerte outskirts. United States infantry on the north shore of Lake Achkel drove toward the red brick houses of the city that they saw yesterday from nine miles away.

From a point four miles beyond the village of Massicault, British armor followed by massed infantry thrust twelve miles to the white city of Tunis, whose many mosques had come into their view last night. It was bitter, bloody fighting all the way but early in the forenoon tanks captured suburban Le Bardo, center of much of the arterial system of Tunis, and placed the city under their guns.

Last night guns of American tanks cast shells into Ferryville, throwing plumes of fire into pitch black darkness. Simultaneously, British guns were flashing in the Tunis area.

The Germans, hard-pressed, their morale weakening, had no rest as the two-pronged American drive reached toward Bizerte and the British slashed toward Tunis.

In the far-reaching events of today sight had been lost of the exact position of American units, including New Yorkers, fighting their way toward Tebourba Junction northwest of Tunis, and of the British battling northward to join them. The Americans were known this morning to be not more than four miles west of Chouigui Pass. An Anglo-American junction would cut off and make easier the capture of many Axis troops between Tunis and Bizerte.

In late November, 1942, a light, combined Anglo-American striking force came to within twelve miles of Tunis near the village of Djedeida. It lost, however, what amounted to a race to get to Tunis before the Germans established themselves.

Today, as General Alexander noted in his order of the day, read to troops before the final victorious onslaught, the Allies struck with "two victorious armies"—armies that would not be denied.

The British drive to Tunis was begun at 3 A.M. yesterday morning on a ten-mile front from north of Medjez-el-Bab near Djebel-bou-Aoukaz, captured the previous day. It followed the lines of the shortest road to Tunis.

Infantry divisions took hill positions, thus eliminating danger to British armor from anti-tank artillery fire on the flanks.

Then the armored divisions were hurled forward as a spearhead.

The armored force on the right or southern flank of the drive toward Massicault, the pivot of the whole Axis Tunis position, encountered thirty-five enemy tanks at a point six miles south-southwest of Massicault.

The enemy tanks were being employed as a stationary strong point of defense. A number of them were destroyed by the British tanks and the others were forced to withdraw.

An infantry brigade equipped with large anti-tank guns was then placed in a position four miles south of Massicault to protect against a counterattack by German tanks.

Another strong British armored force on the left or north flank passed in the direction of St. Cyprien, seven miles beyond Massicault and just north of the Tunis road, by-passing Furna and forcing twenty-five enemy tanks to withdraw and cutting the road north of Massicault.

By 3 P.M. Massicault had been occupied, leading armored elements moving on the line running obliquely north and south four miles east from this town. The enemy suffered heavy losses despite his hasty withdrawal. By dusk Tunis, only twelve miles from St. Cyprien, was brought under artillery fire.

Second United States Corps forces yesterday ran into stubborn resistance all along their front from the sea to a point just north and west of the Tebourba.

In the north, near the seacoast, an American force advanced to within nine miles of Bizerte, an advance of three miles from their starting point. They took 250 prisoners, mostly Italians.

Other Americans, after bloody fighting, completely cleared Djebel Achkel, which previously had been mistakenly reported taken, and Djebel Zarour. Their tanks charged right into anti-tank guns, destroying six in one case by over-running their position. Three hundred prisoners were picked up by this unit.

Still another large American infantry force captured high ground between Chouigui Pass and Tebourba at a point only four miles from the latter. While the pass was not completely cleared at the time the last word was received, the Germans in the Tebourba area were in a precarious position, with the Americans coming from the northwest and the British from the south.

In the center of the line yesterday divisions of the Nineteenth French Corps made slow but steady progress toward Zaghouan, threading through extensive mine fields in stiff fighting. The Eighth Army advanced somewhat in an area nine miles northeast of Djebibina. It also went through bloody fighting and some of the worst mine fields yet encountered in Tunisia.

THE FINAL TWO-DAY ATTACK

(E. A. Montague, Manchester Guardian, May 11, 1943. By permission of the Manchester Guardian.)

"Tunis continues to be a city almost hysterical with happiness."

WITH THE BRITISH FIRST ARMY IN TUNISIA, May 11 (By Cable—Delayed)— . . . The final two-day attack resulting in the capture of Tunis was carried out by a force consisting of troops half from the

First Army and half from the Eighth. The two armies contributed exactly equal shares of infantry and armor.

Tunis was entered at the same moment, 3:40 on the afternoon of May 7, by armored cars of both armies, the Derbyshire Yeomanry of the First Army and the Eleventh Hussars of the Eighth entering at different points unknown to each other.

The air support which contributed immensely to the victory was shared almost equally by Britain and America and one French Spitfire squadron, the first of Giraud's air force to see action, played its part. The whole operation was a joint affair to which both British armies and all three Allies contributed.

It was learned that the Germans made an attempt at evacuation of the Bizerte area between Ras Zebib and Porto Farina, but it was quite abortive and was soon given up.

However much these conform to the known temperament of their race they are not, it should be emphasized, being taken here as an indication that if the Allied armies here are ever called upon to fight an enemy in Europe, they will find anything but the grimmest resistance.

It is recognized that the Germans here, if they did not fight to the bitter end, did not give in easily in spite of the discouraging failure of those in the north ever to hold the initiative and despite the gruelling trial of those in the south forced to retreat over 3,000 miles with diminishing hope of ever arresting our advance.

But the campaign was planned and conducted by General Anderson and the staff of the First Army, to whom a large part of the credit for the brilliant success is due.

Meanwhile, Tunis continues to be a city almost hysterical with happiness. Yesterday morning picked French contingents entered the city and were given a wonderful welcome. In spite of the early hour the streets were crowded and people in nightgowns, pajamas and dressing gowns appeared at every window and balcony. Spectators rushed into the roadway and broke into the column of marching troops to embrace sons and husbands not seen in many months.

Today a big procession of Jewish workers marched to the house of the resident general Admiral Estava, the craven Frenchman who admitted German troops to Tunisia as soon as the Allies landed in North Africa. Estava left Tunis by a German transport plane on the morning of the day we entered the city. Today the Jewish workers ended their march outside the residency and sang the "Marseillaise" while crowds of Gentiles applauded.

Other prominent French collaborationists had been leaving the city for ten days before our arrival. They would have had short shrift from their fellow-citizens had they been caught. Tunis is a strongly patriotic city with a big de Gaulle element.

On May 7, when it was realized that the Germans were trying to evacuate the city the citizens spontaneously slowed down the evacuation, thousands walking diagonally across the streets again and again so that the German transports had to go slowly.

A contributory cause to the strongly pro-Allied feeling in Tunis is fear and hatred of the Italian ambitions and the 80,000 Italian inhabitants of Tunis now are nervous. The French denounced those who helped the Germans but otherwise they have not been persecuted.

The Arabs on the whole are not enthusiastic about our arrival, partly because Tunis is a hotbed of Arab nationalism and partly because of fear that the presence of the Allies will bring German bombing. Many Arabs have been leaving the city, causing some dislocation of the food supply, particularly vegetables which are largely handled by the Arabs, but steps are being taken to remedy this.

THE END IN TUNISIA

(*Pierre J. Huss, "I Saw the Nazis Crack,"* Cosmopolitan Magazine, *August, 1943. By permission of Cosmopolitan Magazine.*)

"Jeeze, fellows, them Heinies have gone nuts. They're trying to scare us."

ALLIED HEADQUARTERS IN NORTH AFRICA, June, 1943—Tunisia was the proving ground which certified the Allied invasion of the Continent. In the acid test, our assault armies, air forces and generals emerged with flying colors. By the same token, the Axis—from Hitler's ablest generals and most elite troops down to the dispirited Italians—revealed inherent weak spots which are bound to become bleeding wounds, once the conflict for the "European Fortress" develops cyclonic violence.

Current events will record that the Axis signed its own death warrant at the historic moment when the German Commander in Chief in North Africa, General Jurgen von Arnim, raised the white flag in defeat south of Tunis. We know Hitler still has millions of battle-seasoned men behind formidable fortifications. In North

Africa we didn't wipe out his main armies or fortification systems—not even a fraction of them—but we did wipe out the flaming Nazi myth, upset traditional Prussian military creeds and demonstrated as a necessary prelude to the recapture of the Continent that the proud Wehrmacht can be pummeled into dust—can even be made to cry for mercy.

I saw it happen, step for step, from St. Patrick's Day to the spectacular collapse early in May. I covered decisive battles and examined at first hand the underlying causes of this turn in the tide. I know the Wehrmacht like my own pocket from long years in Berlin for International News Service and was thus able to evaluate straws in the wind. That's why I put so much stock in an incident experienced by the Americans in the latter part of March.

It was a spring night over El Guettar and the African sky was studded with diamond-bright stars and lighted by a Turkish moon. The highway to Gabès curved like a dark macadam carpet through a mile-wide valley which, drenched with the hot sun by day, cools to freezing after sunset. Across the valley thousands of American soldiers slept in uneasy silence under a couple of blankets, sometimes awakening to listen to Luftwaffers sneaking overhead.

Djebel Berda—that bullheaded sweeping ridge flanking the right edge of El Guettar Valley—sat in gloomy silence. A whole nest of stinging Nazi 88-mm. guns infested the tree-bearded slopes and ravines. On the left a pale dust road streaked off from the main highway into the jagged ridges of horseshoe-shaped Djebel Mcheltat.

During the day Gumtree Road was the favorite target of Nazi artillery and dive bombers; at night anything was apt to happen, especially while Rommel's hard-pressed Afrika Korps slowly passed northwards from Gabès to the sea. Djebel Berda and Djebel Mcheltat were Axis steel gates barring the United States Second Corps thrust to the Mediterranean; any break-through in that sector would have cut off the doomed retreating German troops. Djebel Mcheltat stretched deeper toward the sea and was more strongly held, for which reason Gumtree Road became an American lance prodding into Rommel's flank. In turn, he snapped back viciously and repeatedly feinted dangerously toward El Guettar.

Consequently, the Americans' ears stayed sharply alert on this starry night. Outposts on the far edge of Gumtree Road heard suspicious movements on the slopes held by Nazi grenadiers. A dark smoke cloud came drifting over the valley. Suddenly it lighted with blood-red flashes mixed with rocket bursts. Deafening explosions, machine gunning, hysterical howling, even demoniacal laughter turned the broken silence into a nightmare. Through the whole sector sleepy-eyed Yanks stumbled into slit trenches, grabbing for rifles and machine-gun belts. Seconds seemed hours; everything was in an uproar like a panic-stricken mob. Amid the eerie din came the roar of racing motors and gun flashes—presumably Nazi armored cars and Panzers under way in waves. Above all sounded the strange metallic shouting: "HITLER KOMMT! SURRENDER!"

Random shots rattled from the American side. Then from somewhere out of a foxhole came an angry Brooklyn voice:

"Jeeze, fellers, them Heinies have gone nuts. They're trying to scare us. Them bastards ain't got nothing back of 'em. Give 'em hell."

That broke the spell. Within seconds, hundreds of Yanks turned loose every gun and hand grenade they could lay their hands on and stopped the German panic tactics dead.

Three years ago I heard laughter in Berlin cafés when fighters on leave from the front recounted these tricks. I had seen those Nazi motor trucks equipped with loudspeakers with magnified phonograph voices. All of it was part of the German psychological warfare, but so far as I know the Yanks never fell for Hitler hokum.

Many times during those hot dusty days, I looked across valleys foaming with richly colored spring flowers and pictured Nazi gun crews loading and firing their guns with the practiced precision so familiar to me. I could hear the cryptic German commands, constant heiling and heel-snapping I had endured for many years when covering the Reich for INS. To all outward appearances, the Wehrmacht in Tunisia was as powerful as in the days when it swept over Poland and France. It required careful probing to ferret out the truth and reach the conclusion that Hitler's forces in North Africa were like a porcelain egg, with a hard exterior and a hollow inside, ready to collapse once the outside shell was crushed.

Looking back, I am convinced Allied leaders like Eisenhower and Alexander divined that truth and incorporated it in their final battle plans. The 2,000-mile trek across Egypt and Libya had taken the heart out of the Afrika Korps, a fact which the wily Rommel realized early enough to return to Berlin on sick leave and pass the buck to von Arnim.

On smoking firing fronts, I recognized forerunners of inevitable disaster. The failure of Nazi terror tactics against the Yanks on Gumtree Road was prophetic.

The German mentality simply couldn't or wouldn't grasp the fact that the Allied Armies had become full-grown under a unified command and were ready to assert their mastery of Tunisia. Nazi ground troops gained false courage from misleading Berlin propaganda in which the Yanks were depicted as easy marks. The Axis shock of surprise was all the more effective, therefore, when the Second Corps uncorked a stunning offensive and knocked the stuffing out of picked German troops.

In the same way, the Germans misjudged the stolid, pipe-sucking British soldier. Daily on British fronts, I heard glib-tongued Goebbels mouthpieces harp over Axis waves that aristocratic British officers, too indolent to fight the war, paused in the middle of the afternoon to enjoy a leisurely tea instead of attending to the battle. Perhaps so, but I saw those British officers get in their full day's fighting without missing tea. There's a knack to it as natural as the American's knack of chewing gum.

The stolid Tommy with his 1918 soup-plate helmet is never flustered, not even under the heaviest fire. That's what the Germans ran up against. I have General Eisenhower's word that General Alexander anticipated the German mind perfectly. He outsmarted them by planning with Montgomery to take over the rôle of "holding army" above Enfidaville while the task of capturing Bizerte and Tunis was assigned to the United States Second Corps and the British First Army respectively. The Germans fell for that ruse and concentrated their whole defense reserves down south against the Eighth Army. They realized their error too late.

To my mind, another weak link in the Axis armor was the monotony of the Berlin–Rome propaganda. It hasn't changed since I was in Berlin. Either Goebbels was stumped, or else he was kept in blissful ignorance of the African situation.

The Yanks and Tommies have it over the ironclad Nazi military mentality. Whenever the going gets tough they find refuge in an innate sense of humor, which serves to blow off steam.

The Luftwaffe was simply wiped out of the skies by improved Anglo-American planes and synchronized air–land operations. The Allied Air Forces did something else which left the Nazis gasping, when Allied technical laboratories converted fast Hurricane planes into flying artillery by attaching cannon firing armor-piercing shells beneath each wing. Panzers and field positions never knew what hit them. The deadly effect of this flying artillery contributed extensively to our African victory and is a tribute to Allied inventive genius.

The drain on Hitler's manpower in the Reich was increasingly evident in Tunisia, where for the first time I saw companies made up of political unreliables who had been given the choice of fighting or rotting in concentration camps.

Tunisia demonstrated that the Nazis, if arrogant in victory, are servile in defeat. Even the crack Hitler regiments couldn't take it. They cringed when shells from Allied tanks and planes swept over them like hail. They recoiled in terror before naked American, British and French bayonets. In capitulating, every Nazi from von Arnim down disobeyed Hitler's personal orders, "Stand and die."

From the military viewpoint, the Axis end in Tunisia was ignominy without gallantry. For Allied purposes, we proved to our own conclusive satisfaction that Hitler's Wehrmacht is vulnerable and can be defeated behind the strongest fortifications. That is a big fact. The Wehrmacht can be cracked rapidly under combined attacks planned and executed on mass-scale principles.

It was Hitler who used to shout, at officer assemblies in secret Berlin Chancellery meetings on the eve of an invasion, that victory in his eyes is incomplete unless the opposing armies are totally wiped out. In Tunisia, Allied arms applied that principle successfully against the Wehrmacht and gave Hitler a prophetic sample of the pattern and ability with which we are now ready to enact the Casablanca verdict that the Axis' unconditional surrender alone will terminate the war.

One-Man War Survey: Irwin Shaw Discovers That the Favorite Subject of G.I. Conversation Is Women, Women, Women

[June 19, 1943]

"Chicago. That's a hell of a place to leave a wife."

Irwin Shaw, born in 1913, American playwright and short-story writer, had written among other works a sensational anti-war play called Bury the Dead *(1936). But a few years later he found himself in the midst of a global war. Formerly a semiprofessional football player, Shaw now covered the war fronts for* Stars and Stripes *and* Yank. *While in the Mediterranean theatre of operations, he made the following one-man survey of favorite subjects of conversation among American servicemen. To no one's surprise few of them revealed any interest in Clausewitz on war but virtually all talked about one special item.*

(Stars and Stripes, *Africa edition, June 19, 1943. Courtesy of the U.S. Army.*)

The people back home are very interested in hearing what soldiers talk about, and when I came over here I resolved to send back accurate reports on what the army says in bivouac, on leave, and in the front lines. I'm not so sure that's entirely possible any more.

I've been at all the airfields between Miami and Cairo and I've talked to hundreds of soldiers on the long road between Egypt and Algiers. I don't think you'd want to print the ordinary conversations among GI's.

Aside from the richness of the language, army conversation has a beautiful simplicity and directness. It is all on one solid everlasting subject . . . Women. This makes it different from the talk about women and baseball.

Occasionally a soldier will deviate a little and his control will leave him, like a pitcher tiring in the late innings, and he will talk about frivolous things like what he did when his company was cut off by the Jerries and what he thinks ought to be done with Germany after the war. But very soon he will suddenly catch himself and start talking about the blonde girl he knew back at Purdue who measured thirty-seven and three-quarter inches around the chest, so help him God.

In Puerto Rico, where my plane stopped for a few hours, the first thing I was told was that the food was good and there was plenty of girls if you knew Spanish.

In Khartoum, where I slept on the same porch with a Liberator crew, the tail gunner was talking about his wife who was in Chicago.

"Chicago," the radio operator said. "That's a hell of a place to leave a wife."

"The Great Lakes Naval Training Station is in Chicago," the top turret gunner said dreamily. "There are 5,000,000 sailors in Chicago."

"That's all right," the tail gunner said grimly. "Every couple of weeks I send home a fifty calibre machine-gun bullet. My wife puts them on the mantelpiece to remind those sailors her husband's a gunner. She ain't had no trouble yet."

In Cairo a young British Hurricane pilot who had lived in America, talked for a whole night about how he was going to buy a house on the top of Lookout Mountain in Hollywood after the war, and live there with his wife and produce five children. After a long while I got him to admit that he had personally sunk a four thousand ton freighter in the English Channel.

A French private who travelled with me for a whole day, returning to his unit, which had granted him ten days' leave in which to get married in Constantine, merely said, "*Je suis très fatigué*," and nothing more.

In Algiers the conversation about fair sex has a severely practical turn. The men watch the pretty girls going by in their pretty dresses, and they sigh and turn to the newcomer and say, "It is necessary to know French."

I suppose there are a few fellows somewhere who spend all their spare time talking about Clausewitz's theories and the war aims of the Allies, but I haven't found them yet.

Does anybody want to hear about the Swedish girl I met in Madison, Wisconsin, in 1939 . . . ?

Death of a Pilot: Hugh Baillie, United Press, Reveals the Story of Pete Peterson, the Man Who Didn't Come Back

[July 6, 1943]

"Aw, he just floated along with his head under his arm and I shot him."

In the summer of 1943, Hugh Baillie, president of the United Press, went into the combat areas with the correspondents covering the war. From England and from Sicily he sent back a series of dispatches that matched the fine work of his own men in the field. This story of Pete Peterson, an American pilot who didn't come back, reflected in microcosm the heartbreak that went along with the glamour of war.

(*United Press, July 6, 1943. By permission of United Press International.*)

LONDON, July 6 (U.P.)—Last month I wrote a dispatch about the scene at a fighter base where we listened to the calm, whimsical voice of a commander over the wireless warning of "bandits at 2 o'clock." . . . saying he was going down to keep the bandits off some fellows bailing out of a Fortress . . . telling the crowd, "Keep your eyes open" . . . instructing the pilots to check gas gauges and head for home if their gas was low.

That commander was Col. Arman Peterson.

Pete came back from the fight that day but he hasn't come back from the last fight he and his boys had with the Germans over the occupied countries.

You folks back home might not get the full impact of what it meant when Pete didn't come back unless you knew him, and the way he ran his fighter squadron.

Pete was 28 years old. He came from Flagstaff, Arizona, and called his Thunderbolt fighter "Flagari."

"I don't want people to forget the old home town," he remarked with a grin, pointing out the name on the ship to visitors.

He always went out with his gang on sweeps after German fighters or protecting the Flying Fortresses on their massive raids. He presided at the head of the table in mess hall and talked about this and that with casual ease even with a "mission" scheduled to start within the next hour.

The atmosphere of his fighter base was one of comradeship and high élan. The boys at Pete's station grinned easily. They were streamlined and eager. When sorties were delayed by weather they sat around chafing, reading magazines, listening to the deafening blare of the radio.

There was something about Pete that eased down nervousness and tension. I met him after he had finished his fight the other day—wheeling slowly away from the place on a bike. Quite a comedown from 400 miles per hour at 25,000 feet. The young colonel rather shyly accepted congratulations on having shot down a German. Asked how he did it, he said something to the effect that "Aw, he just floated along with his head under his arm and I shot him." Pete had a cannon shell hole in his plane and, asked why he didn't say anything regarding it over the wireless, he replied, "I was doing all right. It cut down my speed a little, that's all."

The hole, incidentally, was from a Fortress gun but Pete did not resent being shot by his own team. Pete's idea of his job was to protect the Fortresses and see that they got through and delivered the bombs. If he got too close and accidentally took a slug from the Fortress, that was just part of his job.

When Pete failed to come back from the last scrap his gang sat around waiting. Plane after plane came in. But no Pete. The softball game fell apart. Minutes seemed like hours when you sit like that.

When was the last time anyone had seen him? Well, he spotted a bunch of bandits below and said, "There they are. Here we go." Pete's boys swooped in at 90 degrees. They think they saw Pete vanish into a cloud but nobody realized he was gone until they began counting noses at home. Finally, after hours of waiting as long as they thought they could, Pete's crowd fueled up their fighters. Nobody gave them orders for that—the boys just did it spontaneously.

They went back over the area where they had fought. Looking for Pete—also looking for the German or Germans, the more the better. The boys flew around hunting and looking, hunting and looking, until their gas ran low. Then without the whimsical, almost kidding voice of Pete to tell them to scram, they had to turn back for home base.

That night there was a vacancy at the head table in the mess—a vacancy but no mourning. Pilots aren't like that.

Of course, there is always the chance that Colonel Peterson parachuted down, that he fell into the "drink" and was picked up by rescue craft, or that he descended behind the German lines and was made a prisoner of war.

It is a cinch that all the fellows at Pete's fighter base will keep on hoping that some day Pete will show up again and his familiar drawl will be heard instructing his crowd to watch out for bandits. It is a long shot, but perhaps he may even read this story some day. I hope so.

Peterson led his group on every mission or sweep it ever made, regardless of its importance. He was accredited with 42 missions, almost a third again as many as the next busiest man on the field. He was credited with one German fighter destroyed and two damaged.

LONDON, *Sept. 26 (U.P.)—Colonel Arman Peterson, 28, of Flagstaff, Arizona, was shot down on July 1, leading a Thunderbolt Squadron in action over France and has been officially reported dead, the U.S. Army Air Corps announced today.*

Invasion of Sicily: John Mason Brown Narrates The Landings in the Next Step in Liberation of Europe

[July 10, 1943]

"The Fourth of July was never like this!"

Operation Husky was planned as the next step in the liberation of Europe. On July 10, 1943, just eight weeks after the last Axis troops had surrendered in Tunisia, a combined British and American army invaded Sicily by sea and by air. The enemy garrison on the island, already wearied by false alerts, relaxed its vigilance as a gale roared overhead. Surely no one would want to attack in this foul weather! But attack it was and it turned out to be an outstanding success for the invaders.

The seaborne invasion was witnessed by John Mason Brown, born in 1900, American drama critic serving with the U.S. Navy. Here is a part of his exciting dispatch.

(*With permission of McGraw-Hill Book Co., Inc. from* To All Hands: An Amphibious Adventure *by John Mason Brown* [*New York, 1942*], *p. 119 ff. Copyright © 1943 by the McGraw-Hill Book Company, Inc.*)

2:40 A.M., *July 10, 1943*

We are within five minutes of what should have been the time for "H" hour. But "H" hour has been delayed until 3:45 at the request of the Commander of Transports. Blame the choppy seas for this, and difficulties they have caused in getting the small boats out. So take time off to get your second wind.

Don't think that things have not been happening above, in spite of this delay. Do you remember those enemy searchlights which I have mentioned several times? Well, they have given us some uneasy moments. There's a hell of a lot of difference between our searchlights when they are looking for the enemy, and enemy searchlights when they are looking for us.

As far as I can make out, there have been three of these searchlights sweeping from the shore. When we were stealing in, and even

264

after we reached our anchorage, they swept only the sky. They kept raking it back and forth, back and forth, sticking up like nervous white fingers in the darkness. They were after our planes then, and didn't seem to know we were here.

Even when they followed the transport planes out, these searchlights swung far above us—which was precisely what we kept hoping they would do. One of these beacons, however, carried its search toward the horizon until its lowered light hovered over our ships to port. Then it blinked and went out, apparently not having spotted anything of interest.

This made us breathe the easier.

But only for a while. Because in a few minutes those searchlights were in motion again. The same one that had blinked before, woke up in alarm. When it came on, it was aiming straight above it at the sky, which was still all right with us. Then it began circling its light out to sea, lower and lower each time, until it started skimming the waves. In its sweep it landed on one of our ships lying at an angle. It paused there for an awful time before starting to move again. Then it swung slowly past the other vessels ahead, seeming to halt for the same awful time on each of them, icing them with light or showing them up as silhouettes, as neat and black as you will ever find on any Ship Identification cards.

The beacon finally reached us. Our turn came just the way it used to in school. Waiting for it wasn't pleasant. The light cut closer and closer until it was full upon us, blinding us when we looked straight at it. It wasn't hard, then, to make out the faces on the Admiral's Bridge. It would have been hard *not* to make them out. The faces of the men up there looked the way an actor's face does without make-up under a spotlight. You know that sallow look? Even the ship's gray was lighter than the sun at midday had ever made it.

I thought they had found us. I couldn't see how they had missed us.

"Can they see us?" I asked Captain Wellings, our Gunnery Officer.

"No. We can see them all right," he smiled, "but I don't think they can see us on a night like this. Anyway we are out of their range of vision."

This was good news. It still is.

4:15 A.M., *July 10*

The Fourth of July was never like this! These are the biggest fireworks I've ever seen. Our guns have really been speaking up, and it looks like they are much more than just big talkers. The sky is as bright as a summer parasol with the sunlight streaming throught it.

The darkness is fighting a losing battle. Light is everywhere. Never for long. Always changing. Always in the swiftest motion. Then the night seeps back, only to be driven away again. Overhead it's all dots and dashes that you can see, quivering as they race to rise and fall; dots and dashes, and streamers of heat, and rockets overtaking rockets.

Light and noise. The noises are as different as the lights. There's the froglike *glump* of flak as it thuds through the water after a brief splash. There's the staccato stitching of the 20- and 40-millimeters. There's a sigh, a whine, and a whistle coming from something—I don't know what.

There are big guns, little guns, medium-sized guns—all of them fluent, and all of them demanding to be heard from, whether they are on the ships around us, in the Task Force ahead, with the enemy on shore, or the British to the east. The big guns bellow in a full, damp, dull tone. They sound the way a goldfish bowl might sound if—water and all—it exploded in your tummy.

Under this flaming cover the small landing boats have been pushing into shore. Bright as the sky is, the sea is still so dark that I have been able to see the Viking outlines of only a few of our little boats. But once in a while, in the din, the sputter of their motors has been heard.

Our big guns appear to have got two of those prying searchlights. They have been snuffed out for quite a while. It was a cruiser, I think, that scored a bull's-eye on one of them. The beacon scarcely had time to wink. Then it was done for.

7:15 A.M., *July 10*

We are weighing anchor now to move closer in to shore.

The Spitfires have been patrolling once more. They have come back again and again, in spite of their warm welcome.

Everyone topside has been nibbling on or at "K" rations and feels the better for coffee, with its illusion of breakfast.

Most of the shore batteries are silenced by now, due to the spectacular accuracy of Naval gunnery. One by one they have been snuffed out like candles.

Some jeeps have been lowered into the landing boats panting alongside of us. And the LCT's are now going in, rolling quite a bit and crowded with boys in khaki, only a few of whom look seasick and are holding their heads. These LCT's have been escorted and given fire cover by our destroyers. The Army is leaving us in large numbers. As it does so, one of our cruisers is thundering away at an inland target, and a big fire is burning on the beach to port. . . .

July 11

The city of Ragusa has fallen to us, and at 6:30 this afternoon Comiso airfield was captured. The leading elements of our invading forces from the 45th Division are from twelve to fifteen miles inland by now. Some of our other troops, notably the 1st Division, are progressing in spite of stiff opposition. By last night some 5,500 German and Italian prisoners had been taken. This we know definitely. From Scoglitti comes a rumor, unverified though perhaps symptomatic, which says that when we took the town we did so with the loss of only one American while 300 Italians were killed. Up until 10 this morning less than 250 injured were reported in this particular Task Force. Near us during the day a British monitor has been pounding away with ominous regularity, her big guns trained on an enemy tank concentration inland.

Of immediate concern to us all is the progress of the unloading of the transports and supply ships. The reports continue to be excellent. One transport is 100 per cent cleared. Most of the other ships are getting through a difficult job rapidly. Our air attacks on Sicilian airfields continue like an unbroken serial. A flight of eighteen B-17's passed this area, headed inland to drop their loads on enemy air centers. AA gunners with itchy fingers appear to have controlled their desire to shoot at the first plane in sight. Our air cover of Spitfires now patrols without every ship in the harbor sending up clouds of flak in appreciation. One of these patrolling Spits at about 11 A.M. this morning scored a kill on a low-flying Messerschmitt that had dodged his way in to drop bombs on the beach near Scoglitti. Earlier this morning two German bombers—JU-88's—were hit and believed to have been shot down. We had some bad moments this afternoon when several German planes swept toward the convoy and were successfully engaged by three Spitfires. Another uncomfortable few minutes came for the *Spelvin* when a JU-88 was spotted directly above us, at an altitude of 25,000 feet. Some say bombs were dropped; all agree that Spitfires drove off the JU-88.

Yesterday the Italians gave us the bird. And a very nice bird. At 9:47 P.M. a tired enemy carrier pigeon flew down to rest on one of our mine sweepers. It proved to be a comforting bird-in-the-hand. The pigeon was carrying a message from the Italian Army's 206th

Division to the Italian 12th Army Corps. When translated, the message read:

"Situation 3:00 P.M.—12 o'clock Croce Camerina about to fall. . . . Col. Bartimo resisting. . . . After fifteen hours of struggle, infantrymen and artillerymen are resolutely doing their duty against overwhelming forces and means. Hundreds of anchored ships unloading material undisturbed. Our aviation absent. I have ordered shot two soldiers of the fixed defense of Pachino for being out of presence of the enemy and in civilian clothes. Please send requested pigeons."

July 12

On Invasion Night the enemy did not know exactly where we were. They may even have been surprised by our coming. Last night the coin was to a certain extent flipped the other way. The Germans and the Italians knew exactly where we were. It was hard, if not impossible, for us to locate their airmen in the low-hung gray clouds. From time to time only the mad hornet's buzz of their machines could be heard as they zoomed uncomfortably near. Or their many flares could be seen lanterning the sky with terror. Or their bombs could be watched as they splashed close by in the Mediterranean or exploded on the beach.

Just after dinner—at 7:50—the Task Force to the west underwent a heavy bombardment. This bombardment rumbled ahead of us like a storm sweeping down a valley. No enemy planes could be seen from our bridge, but our ears ached from the thunder of antiaircraft guns. Tracer bullets raced across the heaven, pursuing one another as if discharged from a giant's Roman candle.

By 8:10 P.M. some Messerschmitts roared shoreward to bomb the beaches. They were followed by Spitfires. Then the shore batteries began to erupt. When they were in full eruption the *Spelvin* shook for the first of many times last night; shook as if it were a muffled gong struck once but accurately. The mystery of those disquieting single quavers remains unexplained.

July 13

After all these months of preparation, these weeks of mounting suspense, and these three brief but long, crowded, and unforgettable days and nights off Scoglitti, we left Sicily that night. For us, as front-line participants, the Sicilian invasion was over. Some of us came away with a few poor trophies. All of us took away our memories; memories that will grow into tales; tales that will grow faster than poplars and taller than the tallest redwoods. . . .

Some of us felt guilty about leaving. We knew how the Army men on these contested beaches must feel as they saw us, their one connection with home, pull out. Our ships, as ships, were conscienceless. As they swung into the single line we joined, they seemed almost as glad to be going home as horses heading for their stables. . . .

Why did we leave Italy so abruptly? Because our business was done; because our troops were landed; because the ships with us in this convoy were unloaded; because these ships were too valuable to be left around, needlessly exposed to enemy bombers and subs in perilous waters. Our immediate usefulness was over.

Rescue Off Kolombangara: John F. Kennedy, Harvard '40, Is Hero in the Pacific as Destroyer Splits His PT Boat

[August 2, 1943]

"I looked up and I saw a red glow and streamlined stacks."

On August 20, 1943, The New York Times *ran this story:*

KENNEDY'S PARENTS OVERJOYED

HYANNIS, MASS., Aug. 19 (A.P.)—Former Ambassador and Mrs. Kennedy shouted for joy when informed of the exploit of their son.

Mrs. Kennedy, first to hear the news by telephone at their summer home, expressed "deep sorrow" for the two crewmen who had lost their lives.

"That's wonderful!" Mrs. Kennedy said when told that her son was safe.

The former Ambassador then exclaimed: "Phew, I think Mrs. Kennedy has said enough for both of us."

This was only part of the story. The young naval officer, his back injured, swam more than three miles to shore, towing an injured ship-mate by a life-jacket held between his teeth. Later he swam out into enemy controlled waters to seek help.

The Times gave front-page attention to the news from New Georgia. There was no by-line on the Associated Press dispatch reprinted here. The story first revealed young Kennedy's nickname, "Shafty," given him by his crewmen because of his fondness for the naval slang phrase "I was shafted!" (equivalent to "What dismal luck!" or "That's a raw deal!" or "We wuz robbed.") Apparently, his experience on Harvard's swimming team served him well in the Pacific. In 1961, in response to the will of the American people, Kennedy moved his residence to the White House in Washington.

(The New York Times, *August 20, 1943. By permission of Associated Press.*)

A UNITED STATES TORPEDO BOAT BASE, NEW GEORGIA, Aug. 8 (Delayed) —Out of the darkness, a Japanese destroyer appeared suddenly. It sliced diagonally in two the PT boat skippered by Lieut. (j.g.) John

270

F. Kennedy, son of the former American Ambassador in London, Joseph P. Kennedy.

Crews of the other PT boats, patrolling close by, saw flaming high octane gasoline spread over the water. They gave up "Skipper" Kennedy and all his crew as lost that morning of August 2.

But Lieut. Kennedy, 26, and ten of his men were rescued from a small coral island deep inside Japanese-controlled Solomon Islands territory, and within range of enemy shore guns.

The PT boat making the rescue performed a daring and skillful bit of navigation through reef-choked waters off Ferguson Passage (Ferguson Passage is between Gizo and Wanawawa Islands in the New Georgia group).

Two men of Lieut. Kennedy's crew were lost when the enemy destroyer rammed the boat, at a speed estimated by the skipper at forty knots.

Those who were rescued with Lieut. Kennedy were:

Ensign Leonard Thom of Sandusky, Ohio, executive officer and former Ohio State tackle; Ensign George Henry Robertson (Barney) Ross of Highland Park, Ill.; Machinist's Mate Patrick H. McMahon, 39, of Los Angeles; Machinist's Mate Gerald E. Zinser of Belleville. Ill.; Gunner's Mate Charles Harris of Boston; Radioman John Maguire of Hastings-on-Hudson, N.Y.; Machinist's Mate William Johnston of Dorchester, Mass.; Ordnanceman Edmond Mowrer of St. Louis; Torpedoman Roy L. Starkey of Garden Grove, Calif.; and Seaman 1st Class Raymond Albert of Cleveland.

McMahon was burned badly on his face, hands and arms. Although the burns were infected by salt water and exposure, he did not once utter a word of complaint.

"McMahon's a terrific guy," Lieut. Kennedy said. "It was something which got you, seeing old Mac lie there."

"You could see he was suffering such pain that his lips twitched," Ensign Thom added. "You'd watch him and think if you were in his place you'd probably be yelling, 'Why doesn't somebody do something?' But every time you asked Mac how he was doing, he'd wrinkle his face and give you a grin."

Zinser suffered burns on both arms. Johnston, a tough little fellow called "Jockey," was sickened by fumes he had inhaled. Ensign Ross was unhurt, but suffered an arm infection from coral cuts. All the others came through their experience without injury.

On three nights, Lieut. Kennedy, once a backstroke man on the Harvard swimming team, swam out into Ferguson Passage hoping to flag down PT boats going through on patrol. Ensign Ross did the same one other night. But they made no contacts.

On the afternoon of the fourth day two natives found the survivors and carried to the PT boat base a message Lieut. Kennedy crudely cut on a green coconut husk.

Chronologically, Lieut. Kennedy, Ensign Thom and the crewmen told the story this way.

Four Japanese destroyers came down Blackett Sound around the south coast of Kolombangara Island about 2:30 A.M. on August 2. In two phases of a confused engagement the PT's claimed three hits and three probable hits on one of the enemy ships.

It was while the destroyers were returning, probably after delivering supplies and reinforcements near Japan's base at Vila, on Kolombangara, that the ship rammed the Kennedy boat. Ross and Kennedy saw the destroyer coming.

"At first I thought that it was a PT," Kennedy said. "I think it was going at least forty knots. As soon as I decided it was a destroyer, I turned to make a torpedo run."

But Kennedy, nicknamed "Shafty" by his mates, quickly realized the range was too short for the torpedo to charge and explode.

"The destroyer then turned straight on us," he said.

"It all happened so fast there wasn't a chance to do a thing. The destroyer hit our starboard forward gun station and sliced right through. I was in the cockpit. I looked up and I saw a red glow and streamlined stacks. Our tanks were ripped open and gas was flowing in the water about twenty yards away."

Kennedy went out to get McMahon, who had been at the engine station and was knocked into the water in the midst of flaming gasoline.

"McMahon and I were about an hour getting back," Kennedy said. Watertight bulkheads had kept the bow afloat, the skipper explained. "There was a very strong current."

After getting McMahon aboard, Kennedy set out again to get Harris.

The skipper and his men shouted and called for the two missing men but could get no response.

"We seemed to be drifting toward Kolombangara," Kennedy said. "We figured the Japs would be sure to get us in the morning, but everybody was tired and we slept."

Just before dawn the current changed to carry the survivors away from the Japanese-held coast. About 2 P.M. Kennedy decided to abandon the bow section and try to reach a small island.

Kennedy swam to the island, towing McMahon. The others clung to a plank and swam in a group. It took about three hours to make it. The men stayed on this island until Wednesday, when all coconuts on the island's two trees had been eaten.

Late that afternoon they swam to a larger island, where there were plenty of coconuts.

At night Kennedy put on a lifebelt and swam into Ferguson Passage to try to signal an expected PT boat.

The two natives found the survivors Thursday afternoon. On Saturday morning a large canoe loaded with natives brought food and a small kerosene stove and gave the men a real feed and hot coffee. That night, a little after midnight, a PT rescue boat, guided by a native pilot, went in the twisting passages to make contact with Kennedy on an outer island.

The Patton Slapping Affair: American and British Versions of an Incident in the Sicilian Campaign

[August 3, 1943]

"Spit-and-Polish Patton." "Cowboy Patton." "Blood-and-Guts Patton." These were some of the more innocuous terms used by G.I.'s to describe Lieutenant General George S. Patton, Jr., commander of the Seventh Army. The fiery general had a reputation as a rare combination of tank warfare expert and perennial teen-ager. A flamboyant warrior, he ranged the battlefields wearing pearl-handled revolvers in a 'holster, cowboy fashion. A gifted military leader, he imagined that he was an expert in all related and some unrelated fields. It was said that whenever he opened his mouth he made certain to put his foot into it.

In the midst of the campaign in Italy General Patton found himself in unexpected trouble. His bizarre behavior nearly promoted him out of the Army. Some say that the matter was unimportant and inconsequential, others point to its seriousness because it involved a matter of morale.

Nothing would have come of it had not an American columnist with a nose for news published the story. General Patton had entered a military evacuation tent to visit the wounded. When he came across a G.I. whom he suspected of feigning illness, he lost his temper and before the astonished, outraged doctors and nurses excoriated and slapped one of the men. Five days later Patton repeated the slapping, this time on another G.I.

The sensational news traveled like darts of fire through the entire American Army and into the homes of parents, wives and sweethearts of men serving at the fronts. The Supreme Commander, General Eisenhower, hated to lose the services of a highly competent but bull-headed general, but at the same time he had to maintain the morale of his troops.

Eisenhower told about it in his Crusade in Europe *(1949):*

Because of the time and place of his action Patton's offense was a serious one, more so because of his rank and standing. Thus to assault and abuse an enlisted man in a hospital was nothing less than brutal, except as it was

274

explained by the highly emotional state in which Patton himself then existed. . . .

I felt that Patton should be saved for service in the great battles still facing us in Europe, yet I had to devise ways and means to minimize the harm that would certainly come from his impulsive action and to assure myself that it would not be repeated. . . .

I first wrote him a sharp letter of reprimand in which I informed him that repetition of such an offense would be cause for his instant relief. I informed him, also, that his retention as a commander in my theater would be contingent upon his offering an apology to the two men whom he had insulted. I demanded also that he apologize to all the personnel at the hospital present at the time of the incident. Finally, I required that he appear before the officers and representative groups of enlisted men of each of his divisions to assure them that he had given way to impulse and respected their positions as fighting soldiers of a democratic nation.

Several weeks after the incident, Patton wrote to Eisenhower:

Replying to your letter of August 17, 1943, I want to commence by thanking you for this additional illustration of your fairness and generous consideration in making the communication personal.

I am at a loss to find words with which to express my chagrin and grief at having given you, a man to whom I owe everything and for whom I would gladly lay down my life, cause for displeasure with me.

I assure you that I had no intention of being either harsh or cruel in my treatment of the two soldiers in question. My sole purpose was to try and restore in them a just appreciation of their obligation as men and soldiers.

In World War I, I had a dear friend and former schoolmate who lost his nerve in an exactly analogous manner, and who, after years of mental anguish, committed suicide.

Both my friend and the medical man with whom I discussed his case assured me that had he been roundly checked at the time of his first misbehavior, he would have been restored to a normal state.

Naturally, this memory actuated me when I inaptly tried to apply the remedies suggested. After each incident I stated to officers with me that I felt I had probably saved an immortal soul. . . .

Patton later added to this explanation. He said that he originally went into the tent with the commanding officer and other medical officers. "I spoke to the various patients, especially commending the wounded men. I just get sick inside myself when I see a fellow torn apart, and some of the wounded were in terrible, ghastly shape. Then I came to this man and asked him what was the matter. When he replied, 'I guess I can't take it,' I simply flew off the handle."

In the second case Patton lost control of himself completely. He shouted at the soldier: "Your nerves, hell! You are just a ———— coward, you yellow b————." He slapped the soldier hard across the face and cried: "Shut up that ———— crying. I won't have these brave men here who have been shot seeing a yellow ———— sitting here crying." And then Patton himself began to sob.

The Patton incident received considerable attention in the American press, as indicated by the following story reported by Edward Kennedy for the Associated Press. For days American newspapers were filled with news stories and editorial comment on the affair. Kennedy's report should be compared with the brief treatment accorded the story in The Times, London. *Note that the "special correspondent" added an editorial comment in the last sentence of his news story.*

THE PATTON SLAPPING CASE

(Edward Kennedy, St. Louis Post-Dispatch, *November 23, 1943. By permission of Associated Press.)*

"Don't tell my wife! Don't tell my wife!"

ALLIED HEADQUARTERS, ALGIERS, Nov. 23 (AP)—It was disclosed officially today that Lt. Gen. George S. Patton, Jr. had apologized to all officers and men of the Seventh Army for striking a soldier during the Sicilian campaign.

While Patton was not relieved of his command and was not given a formal reprimand, he received a castigation from General Dwight D. Eisenhower such as has seldom been administered to a commander of an army.

Permission to write the story, which had been known to thousands of soldiers since last August, was given correspondents following a broadcast by Drew Pearson from Washington Sunday night. Pearson in his broadcast said that Patton had been "severely reprimanded" by Eisenhower and gave as his opinion that Patton would not "be used in combat any more."

Pearson's broadcast resulted in the formal statement from Allied headquarters last night, saying Patton was still in command of the Seventh Army and that he had been reprimanded.

This statement was technically correct, though it does not give the full picture. There was no formal reprimand, as the term is known in the army. Correspondence on the subject is in Eisenhower's personal files, and known to the War Department. But it is not in Patton's record.

The story is a strange one—the story of a General, whose excellence is admitted by all, who in the heat of battle lost his temper and later admitted he was wrong and made amends.

The incident consisted of this, according to eyewitnesses:

Gen. Patton slapped a shell-shocked soldier in a hospital tent because he thought that the soldier was shirking his duty. The incident occurred early in August when the Sicilian campaign was in one of its most critical periods.

Patton visited the evacuation hospital and went among the wounded, trying to cheer them. He patted some on the back, sympathizing with them. He then came upon a 24-year-old soldier sitting on a cot with his head buried in his hands, weeping.

"What's the matter with you?" Patton asked, according to persons who were in the hospital at the time.

The soldier mumbled a reply which was inaudible to the General. Patton repeated the question.

"It's my nerves, I guess I can't stand shelling," the soldier was quoted as replying.

Patton thereon burst into a rage. Employing much profanity, he called the soldier a "coward," "yellow belly," and numerous other epithets according to those present. He ordered the soldier back to the front.

The scene attracted several persons including the commanding officer of the hospital, the doctor who had admitted the soldier and a nurse.

In a fit of fury in which he expressed sympathy for men really wounded but made it plain that he did not believe that the soldier before him was in that class, the General struck the youth in the rear of the head with the back of his hand.*

A nurse intent on protecting the patient made a dive toward Patton but was pulled back by a doctor. The commander of the hospital then intervened.

Patton then went before other patients, still in high temper, expressing his views. He returned to the shell-shocked soldier and berated him again. The soldier appeared dazed as the incident progressed but offered to return to the front and tried to rise from his cot.

Patton left the hospital without further investigation of the case.

The facts concerning the soldier were later ascertained: He was a regular Army man who had enlisted before the war from his home town in the South. He had fought throughout the Tunisian and

---

* The soldier fell over slightly and the liner of his helmet which he was wearing fell off and rolled over the floor of the tent.

Sicilian campaigns and his record was excellent. He had been diagnosed as a medical case the week previous, but had refused to leave the front and continued on through the strain of battle. He finally was ordered to the hospital by his unit doctor.

After Patton left, the soldier demanded to be returned to the front. This request was refused at the time, but after a week of rest, he was in good shape and returned to his unit at the front.

Immediately after the incident the soldier was reported in a miserable state. As a regular Army man with pride in his record, he felt his whole world dashed to pieces.

"Don't tell my wife! Don't tell my wife!" he was quoted as saying by persons who had talked with him later. The chaplain at the hospital, however, pointed out that the incident was the result of an outburst of temper due to the strain of battle and after several conversations with the soldier, persuaded him to accept it in that light.

The incident was reported to Eisenhower. The Commander-in-Chief wrote Patton a letter in which he denounced his conduct and ordered him to make amends or be removed from his command.

"The Old Man certainly took the hide off him," an Allied headquarters spokesman said.

Patton's conduct then became as generous as it had been furious. He apologized to the soldier whom he had struck, to the commander of the hospital and to all those present at the time. He then went before as many officers and men as could be assembled from each division under his command and repeated his apology.

At the close of the campaign in talking to correspondents, Patton, after recounting the history of the Sicilian drive, said:

"When these things are happening a commanding general is under great nervous tension. He may do things he may afterwards regret. I know a great many people regard me as a————.

"But I have patted five soldiers on the back for every one I have spoken a harsh word to. I dealt harshly with a couple of soldiers and was wrong. I am going to apologize to them."

Soon after the hospital incident, this correspondent told General Eisenhower that since it was known to thousands of persons, many of them returning to the United States, it was almost certain that it would eventually find its way into print. I expressed the view that it might be preferable for correspondents here to write the story.

Eisenhower agreed in principle and said he might arrange a press conference at which Patton himself would bring the matter up.

Eisenhower described Patton's conduct as "despicable" and said Patton himself had admitted the incident and realized he was in error and willing to apologize fully. The Commander-in-Chief, at the same time, expressed the greatest confidence in Patton as a general and said no one else could have achieved such results in Sicily.

Eisenhower indicated that after Patton's apology was accepted, his only other course would be to investigate and see whether there was animosity on the part of the troops and toward Patton which would impair his value as a commander. Presumably, the investigation disclosed no such animosity because Patton was retained as Seventh Army commander.

Eisenhower imposed no censorship on correspondents in connection with the matter. He said they were free to write the story if they chose, but made it clear that he believed its publication would be of value to the enemy as propaganda and might embarrass the command in this theatre.

This placed correspondents in a difficult position. Because of the possibility the publication of the story might help the enemy, no correspondent in this theatre sent the story.

Then followed the period in which the incident was known to thousands of soldiers here and continued to be a widespread subject of discussion and debate among them. This, however, was not publicized at home.

After the Pearson broadcast, censorship in the matter was applied temporarily and when the headquarters statement was issued last night, correspondents were told they might not send any information on the incident other than what was in the statement. This morning, however, a high officer at headquarters appeared before the correspondents telling them they might now send anything on the matter which they knew to be facts. This officer again stressed what all correspondents knew to be true—that Patton would make amends for his conduct.

This incident reflected the character of Patton—a general who drives both himself and his men to the very limit in battles, who is highly emotional at times and is given to outbursts when under strain. But he is regarded by many officers as the best field general in the American Army.

While many soldiers under Patton's command may not have much affection for him, they all respect him as a great general and have confidence in him as a commander. Patton himself doesn't care whether they like him or not—he regards his job as winning battles.

AN UNFORTUNATE EPISODE

(The Times, London, November 24, 1943. By permission of the London Times.)

"... this unpleasant business."

From Our Special Correspondent

ALGIERS, Nov. 23—An unfortunate episode centering on General Patton, Commander of the U.S. Seventh Army, might have faded quietly as a footnote to military history but for a garbled version of the affair given last Sunday in an American broadcast. An officer of General Eisenhower's staff today gave a clear and straightforward account of this unpleasant business which should at least put the matter in its proper perspective.

It appears that General Patton, when visiting an American field hospital in Sicily, lost his temper while speaking to a soldier who he reckoned as a malingerer. The soldier was in fact suffering from shell shock, but General Patton, apparently irked by his demeanour, accused him of cowardice and actually struck him in the presence of medical officers, and a nurse. The incident was reported to General Eisenhower, who made it clear to General Patton that such conduct would not be tolerated.

General Patton thereafter took the simple and soldierly course of apologizing to the soldier and to each assembled division of the Seventh Army. In American phraseology General Patton was "castigated" personally by General Eisenhower; he was neither reprimanded or admonished, both of which are technical punishments. Still less was he removed of his command. General Patton—known as "Blood and Guts" throughout the U.S.A.—is too great a commander to be anywhere but in the field of active service.

Chungking: Brooks Atkinson Finds That After Six Years of War Free China Is Still Undefeated

[August 16, 1943]

"People precariously clinging to the steep bank and life itself."

Japan began large-scale military operations in China in the summer of 1937. Most people believed that the ragged, backward country could not last more than a few months against Japanese power. But the Chinese held on. "If we can keep this up," said one Chinese general, "China can exterminate the male population of Japan while losing 105 million men. And we still have 300 million left."

Japan had joined Germany and Italy in the Tripartite Pact of September 1940, just a year after the outbreak of World War II. Thereby the European and Far Eastern issues were merged. After Pearl Harbor, Washington regarded China as a wartime base for action against Japan. Starting in 1942, the United States gave heavy financial and economic aid to China in military lend-lease, bank credits, and relief funds.

Refusing to admit defeat, the Chinese stubbornly fought on against the Japanese. The Nationalist Government, as well as Chinese industry, took a long march from the coast into the interior. How the mood of Chungking, capital of Free China, kindled new hope was described by Justin Brooks Atkinson, drama critic of The New York Times *in a series of reports of which that reprinted here was one of the best. "The* Times *man who looked least like a potential war correspondent," wrote Meyer Berger (1951), "was Justin Brooks Atkinson. He never weighed more than 130 pounds, even in a rainstorm, and was more apt to tip the scales at 115. He was—and still is—the tweedy, spectacled, pipe-smoking scholarly type."*

From the China-Burma-India theatre Atkinson reported the real face of war quite as well as he did the make-believe world of the stage. Illness overtook him as everyone predicted it would. His weight fell below 114 pounds under a jaundice assault and a hernia attack. But out of his next assignment, which resulted in a famed series on Russia, came a Pulitzer prize for distinguished reporting (1947).

281

(The New York Times, *August 21, 1943. By permission of* The New York Times.)

CHUNGKING, CHINA, Aug. 16 (Delayed)—Even after six years of war people must go on living. Homely as it is there is a kind of gallantry in it. And as I was sitting on the ancient city wall last evening surrounded by the dusty chaos of old bombings that had never been cleared away, the ordinary life of this unlovely Chinese city seemed to me the one thing of transcendent importance.

Perhaps it was because I was low in mind and had spent most of the afternoon with a thoughtful government Minister examining the endless military, economic and social problems of this long blockaded nation. There seemed to be no rift in the mass of dark barriers that surround China. The enemy seemed to have all the dynamic advantages, but the swarming Chinese vitality that rose from the Chialing River a couple hundred feet below me was overwhelming, and perhaps had not changed basically in a thousand years.

In the west which was full of golden fleece, the setting sun was burning a fiery streak across the brown river—the last tongue of flame that licked us all day. In the blue haze that hung in the river gorge floated sun-streamed smoke from charcoal fires in the shacks where people were precariously clinging to the steep bank and life itself.

Twelve dingy river steamers were anchored in the swift stream, retaining there a lonely individual dignity amid the frantic skitter of moving junks and sampans. One of the steamers just up the river from the combat areas was camouflaged with some crazy structure around her funnel.

It was typical of the carelessness of China that the rim of the city wall was unprotected. There was no fence or railing to prevent a man from stumbling straight down to the dirty-tiered roofs far below. But if he had pitched over, it is unlikely that he would have been missed. For the narrow shelf of the river bank was wiggling with humanity. Little figures in white shorts and blue gowns were scurrying through the pinched streets. In the cloying heat a thousand straw fans all busily waving looked like a thousand tiny yellow flickers. In the mass the street gave the impression of nervous energy. There was not room enough for all the life that had to be packed into the area.

Two steamers were moored abreast to a floating steel pier discharging a running throng of passengers and a third steamer was whistling for a chance to put her passengers ashore, lunging wildly in the current while she waited.

Out of the gorge rose the cry of many voices. Occasionally an individual voice cut patiently through the babble like a threat or warning. In general, the sound was like an overwrought song expressing excitement and persistence—never happy or sad, but anxious, as if a thousand people were trying to escape simultaneously from something that was not what they wanted to something they could not imagine. There was a note of irrational expectancy in it. The brass clangor of a ceremonial gong, perhaps honoring a man who had just died, periodically split the air in a splintering crescendo.

The vividness of the cry in many voices in China may be because there are no other sounds like those of street cars, trucks and machinery to dominate the free air. Chinese are naturally noisy, speaking a language based on tone, they give out with passionate volume. But the vividness of the cry of many voices is also because the Chinese have a kind of taut energy that can be temporarily diverted but not permanently dammed.

Sitting on the rim of the crumbling city wall, I felt unaccountably reassured by what I was seeing and hearing. For nothing in China is so violently triumphant as a people who go on living year after year in the face of tragic odds.

Saved by Jungle Headhunters: Eric Sevareid, CBS Correspondent, Parachutes into Mountains of Burma From Crippled Transport Plane

[September 11, 1943]

"In four days we hope to reach civilization."

Newsmen roamed far and wide to combat fronts over the world with one aim in view—to get the white-hot reports of war as it was fought. Some were wounded on assignment. Other perished in the tragedies they witnessed. Some gave their health, others their lives, in the task of getting the story.

Eric Sevareid, Columbia Broadcasting System and United Press correspondent, fortunately survived what might have been a tragic experience. When the engines of an American transport plane flying over the India–Burma jungle in mid-September 1943 failed, twenty men parachuted into the Burmese mountains. Natives in this area had a reputation as killers.

Sevareid lived to tell the thrilling story.

It was all a part of the imponderables of war. The story of Ensign Denby (Time, *January 29, 1945*) *shows that a kind destiny refused to let some men die:*

Ensign George Denby of Van Nuys, Calif., on air patrol off Luzon, was jumped by Zeroes. A shell fragment wounded him in the right leg. His Hellcat's tail was shot off. Denby was thrown from the spinning plane, pinned against the outside of the cockpit; he pushed himself free, pulled his rip cord and blacked out. When he came to, he was hanging in a half-broken parachute harness. Three Zeroes missed him with strafing passes. His life jacket was punctured. Denby plopped into the sea, swam with one hand, used the other to keep his dye marker dry lest it reveal his position to the Japs. Four sharks appeared; one gashed his leg, another rubbed against him like a cat. A U. S. destroyer steamed up, missed running him down by six feet. He was sucked under, passed by the churning propellers, bobbed up in the ship's wake.

That was all. The destroyer turned around and rescued him.

(CBS broadcast September 15, 1943. By permission of Eric Sevareid.)

THE INDIA-BURMA JUNGLE—Burmese jungle headhunters, every one of them a primitive killer, saved our lives when twenty of us leaped by parachute from a crippled U. S. Transport plane into the mountains of northern Burma three weeks ago today.

I am grinding this out on a hand-crank wireless set dropped to us by one of the rescue planes of the Air Transport Command. We are in the middle of a village of aborigines perched atop one of the 6,000-foot mountains. In four days we hope to reach civilization.

Ahead of us, however, lie more mountain peaks and tortuous valley trails; but our party is in good shape.

Our party—twenty-one passengers and members of the crew of a four-engine transport plane—was enroute from India to China when engine trouble developed. Below were ragged mountain peaks and steaming jungle growth somewhere in northern Burma.

Those aboard the plane, besides myself, were John Davies, Jr., second secretary of the American embassy in Chungking; William L. Stanton of the U. S. Office of Economic Warfare; two Chinese officers and the plane's crew.

When we ran into trouble we dumped our baggage, hoping to gain altitude. But the pilot told us to jump, because the plane refused to climb on the one motor still functioning.

When my chute opened I saw the plane strike the ground and explode in a geyser of angry orange flame below me and I was drifting rapidly toward it.

Suddenly a gust of wind blew me into a hillside where I landed, rolling over through dense undergrowth.

I scrambled around and a short distance away I found our radio operator, Sergeant Walter Oswald of Ansonia, Ohio. His leg was broken. I tried as best I could to make a splint and bandage his leg with the silk parachute. He was able to hobble with me to the wreckage of the plane where we collapsed.

Until the very last moment in those sickening minutes before the plane crashed, Sergeant Oswald had stuck to his radio.

His appeals had been heard, for within an hour a plane appeared.

Slowly the members of our party collected on a trail near an aborigine village.

It was wild, savage country. We didn't know what kind of a reception we would get. Some of the world's most primitive killers live in these mountains.

But the natives came bearing food and drink. They helped us and led us through the maze of undergrowth to their village, where they killed goats and pigs for us.

These aborigines became our devoted friends.

Toward sundown of that first day one of our Air Transport Command planes came over and spotted our signals asking for medical aid.

It was a cheering sight when parachutes blossomed from the plane and three rescuers joined us with medical and other supplies. The nearest outpost, we learned, was only about 100 miles away; but so difficult is the country that it might take weeks—possibly months—for us to reach it afoot.

Later planes of the Air Transport Command came over daily, dropping tents, food, clothing.

We have come out of our ordeal without any sufferings that a few days rest won't cure—all except our sorrow at the loss of our co-pilot, Lieutenant Charles William Felix, 21, of Compton, Cal.

Natives found his body under the wreckage of the plane when the flames had died away.

Naples: Herbert L. Matthews Observes How the Germans Left the University in Smoldering Ruins

[October 12, 1943]

"There was something apt about it, something symbolic of the whole German attitude."

It had happened before. Richard Harding Davis, first of the dashing war correspondents in World War I, told the story of how, on August 20, 1914, the Germans had put the Belgian University of Louvain to the torch and left it an empty blackened shell. The destruction was methodical. "In each building," Davis wrote, "they began at the first floor, and when that was burning steadily passed to the next." The hardened reporter was appalled:

> At Louvain that night the Germans were like men after an orgy. . . . It was like a scene upon the stage, so unreal, so inhuman, you felt that it could not be true, that the curtain of fire, purring and crackling and sending up hot sparks to meet the kind, calm stars, was only a painted backdrop; that the reports of rifles from the dark rooms came from blank cartridges. . . . You felt it was only a nightmare, cruel and uncivilized. And then you remembered that the German Emperor has told us what it is. It is his Holy War.

Allied propagandists seized on the Louvain incident to castigate Wilhelmian Germany. "There shall be no peace," they cried, "till the crime of Louvain is compensated to the full in money, in blood, and in kind."

In the light of this experience it would have seemed the better part of discretion for future German military leaders to keep their troops away from universities of any kind. But the same thing happened in World War II. When the Allied Fifth Army pushed the retreating Germans out of Naples and entered the city on October 7, 1943, it found that the Germans had left the harbor facilities in ruins, the water supply destroyed and the major buildings alive with booby traps. But perhaps the most senseless crime was the destruction of the University of Naples. This time there could be no angry denunciations from Berlin of "fanciful Allied propaganda." Herbert L. Matthews, correspondent of The New York Times, *was there to record the atrocity for the history books.*

(The New York Times, *October 12, 1943. By permission of* The New York Times.)

On Sunday the Germans broke into the university after having carefully organized their procedure—squads of men, trucks with dozens and dozens of five-gallon gasoline tins and supplies of hand-grenades. Their objective was deliberate and their work was as methodical and thorough as German work always is. The university was founded in 1224 by Emperor Frederick II. The soldiers went from room to room, thoroughly soaking floors, walls and furniture, including archives that went back for centuries. The part of the university chosen was that where the rector, the dean and wholly administrative personnel worked. That it happened to contain archives and valuable documents on law and letters was beside the point.

When everything was ready, the second stage began. The soldiers went from room to room, throwing in hand-grenades. At the same time, in an adjoining building a few hundred yards up the street, an even greater act of vandalism was being perpetrated. There was something apt about it, something symbolic of the whole German attitude. It did not matter to the Germans that they were destroying the accumulated wealth of centuries of scientific and philosophical thinking.

The rooms of the Royal Society contained some 200,000 books and manuscripts, from not only Italy but every country in the world. These books were stacked neatly and soberly on shelves along the walls; in the middle of the rooms were plain wooden tables with chairs. In several rooms there were paintings—some of them by Francesco Solimene of Nocera, the great baroque architect of the seventeenth century. These had been lent by the National Museum, but they will never be returned.

Like everything else they are now heaps of ashes that I plowed through today like so much sand on a beach. Here too the Germans used the same efficient technique—gallons and gallons of gasoline and then hand-grenades. . . .

Every one knows how difficult it is to burn one solid unopened book thoroughly until nothing remains but a heap of fine ashes. The Germans burned some 200,000 books in that way. Of course, the fire had to rage a long time and—also of course—the German thoroughness was going to see to it that nothing interfered with the fire.

They set it at 6 P.M. Sunday. At 9 P.M. Italian fire-fighting squads came up to extinguish the flames. German guards prevented them from entering the Via Mezzocannone. For three days those fires continued burning and for three days German guards kept Italians away.

Role Reversal: James Reston, of *The New York Times*, Reports How British and Germans Change Positions in the War

[October 22, 1943]

"Adolf Hitler made possible his own downfall. . . ."

In October 1943, just a year after the Battle of El Alamein, there was a major reversal in the war position of the British and German people. In 1940 England had been reeling under the blows of the Luftwaffe. *Now Germany was feeling the weight of bombs dropped by the Royal Air Force. The sharp contrast was reported by James Reston for* The New York Times *in this perceptive dispatch. "Scotty" Reston later emerged as a most brilliant political analyst on the staff of the great New York newspaper.*

(The New York Times, *October 22, 1943. By permission of* The New York Times.)

LONDON, Oct. 22, 1943—A few German planes raided London tonight for the seventh consecutive night; but all these attacks do now is to bring back memories.

Maybe the start of these raids is the same as in 1940. They begin at twilight with the same eerie sound of sirens rising and falling over the million smoky London rooftops. But there similarity ends.

On the eve of this first anniversary of the Battle of El Alamein, great changes have come over this capital. Everything goes up now in the direction of the attacking planes and very little comes down except showers of shrapnel from the anti-aircraft guns.

The theory is that these raids—they hardly come within the scope of "attack"—have a propaganda value for the Germans. The fact is they merely serve to remind the people of the island of their almost miraculous deliverance.

It is true, of course, that before these few Nazis get away they drop some bombs and kill a few persons. But on the whole they perform an important service for the Churchill government, which has been having a little trouble lately in keeping its vast home defense personnel on the alert.

After long months, in which men and women waited at listening posts and lonely anti-aircraft batteries for an enemy that never came and after four winters of unrelieved blackout, the British Government had been faced with repeated demands in the last few weeks to relax the blackout and cut down the civilian defense organization —actions it hesitated very much to take. These seven nights, just before winter comes, have done Prime Minister Winston Churchill a service.

Not all the changes in London since the 1940–41 Blitz are for the better. That remarkable kindness and considerateness among the people, the thankfulness merely to be alive that inspired London and lifted the spirits of every man who lived in the valley of the Thames through those days, are gone.

People have slipped back to the normality of hard work and petty preoccupations. It is only when they get seven straight raids that they think of those terrible ninety nights when 22,837 persons were killed and 28,435 others injured.

But the sharpest contrast with those days lies in the way in which British and Germans have changed positions in the war.

Three years ago the British were yelling about Germany's violating the rights of neutrals. Now one finds the German papers speaking about the Allies' violating the rights of neutrals, and in almost the same phrases.

Indeed, by reading from German papers on the Allied air attacks on Germany it is possible to recapture the feeling one had in 1940 about the destruction in Britain.

Here, for example, are excerpts from German newspapers reaching this office tonight regarding the recent Royal Air Force bombings of Hanover:

"Hanover suffered the heaviest terror raid yet on the night of October 8–9. Considerable damage was caused in residential quarters by innumerable explosives and incendiary bombs, mines and phosphorus cannisters. Large fires inflicted deep wounds on the town. The losses suffered by the population in killed, injured and homeless were very great."

Another German newspaper said of same RAF blow:

"The Anglo-American air pirates struck Hanover with extraordinary force and hardness. Many fires were started and a wave of annihilation and destruction swept through the town.

"Glowing skeletons of houses sheathed in smoke and fire crashed and occasionally threatened to block the exits from burning streets. Thanks to the infinite bravery of the people and the work of all available forces there was no panic."

These confessions of the power of the Allied air offensive illustrate one of the most striking facts of the war, which is that Adolf Hitler made possible his own downfall by resorting to the use of bombing planes against civilian population in the early days.

Nobody who knows the puritanical British would believe they would sanction the kind of bombing the Allies are now visiting upon Germany unless Hitler had first burned and blasted the cities and villages of Britain.

Patriot at War: Arthur Krock Reports on the Role of Bernard Baruch, the Nation's Elder Statesman, on the Home Front

[October 31, 1943]

"Don't waste one young life."

The American people responded with tremendous energy and enthusiasm to President Roosevelt's call to make the United States the arsenal of democracy. A miracle of production was accomplished by a determined people under great leadership. Once again an American President was fortunate to have the loyal assistance of distinguished citizens, notably Bernard Mannes Baruch (born 1870), famous economist and financier. In 1918 President Wilson made Baruch chairman of the War Industries Board, a body invested with vast power to coordinate American industries. During World War II, from 1943 on, this personal adviser of Presidents and lifelong friend of Winston Churchill dedicated his energy to the Office of War Mobilization.

The genius of Bernard Baruch was a vital factor in the defeat of the Axis and the preservation of the United States in a global conflict. Among the seemingly impossible jobs accomplished by Baruch and his committee was the creation almost overnight of a new multi-million dollar industry which in a short time was producing 800,000 tons of synthetic rubber annually.

The story of the man who held no titles, yet served the President as counselor and philosopher, was told by Arthur Krock in The New York Times.

(The New York Times, *October 31, 1943. By permission of* The New York Times.)

WASHINGTON—He is everywhere in Washington—ubiquitous by unanimous consent—a very tall, lean, eagle-nosed old man, stooping a little now and growing increasingly hard of hearing. The blue eyes, gentler than in the days when he pitted his wits against the keenest of those concentrated in the market place, flash with their old fire

292

when the steel of his viewpoint strikes the flint of another. And those who steadily meet him in high council, or seek his advice, testify that his mind is as penetrating as it was when he read the economic and financial auguries as well as any man.

He is sought as counselor of every important administration of the war program from the President down, and he is willing to give council to the humblest. His suggestions and his guidance have often been disregarded, along with his presence and his vast experience, and time after time, when the event has proved him right, he has been sought out again by those that thrust him aside.

Sometimes when his counsel is not asked, and the issue seems to him sufficiently momentous, he barges in anyhow, and none has the self-confidence to deem it an intrusion. For always his thought has been of his country and its interests, of the lives of young men on the battlefronts he saved, of the international structure to end war, or make it rare and brief, which he sought to erect 25 years ago under the leadership of Woodrow Wilson.

The others have titles, he has none. Yet he is the President's counselor, philosophic guide, and he serves in the same capacities for innumerable officials, including those military and naval men who are impatient of the views of any other civilian. He is an honored visitor in the Pentagon and Navy Department, the Department of State, the War Manpower Commission and the Office of the Director of War Mobilization, to which technically he is attached. His rooms at the Carlton and the Shoreham, or the bench in Lafayette Square where he likes to warm his old bones in the sunshine, are the gathering places for all those with problems growing out of the State's business which call for solutions they cannot furnish themselves.

He is the nation's elder statesman. He is Bernard Mannes Baruch.

Much about Mr. Baruch is known: his birth, his breeding, his career in Wall Street and in the chancelleries and conference rooms of the world, his love of and proficiency in riding and shooting, his sociability, his classic good looks, his humor and his odd mixture of hard caution and lavish kindness. It has been much circulated that he is the son of a Confederate surgeon (later a benefactor of the poor as a doctor in New York City) and a lady of pre-Revolutionary stock in South Carolina. The story has been told how President Wilson, finding the supply front of World War I was not going well, wrote him a letter which gave him full authority over everyone else to make things right, so that, with General Pershing, he was estimated by many as one of the two most responsible for successful American action in the field. Clemenceau once said as much.

The files of the newspapers bear unswerving testimony to these things also: that, like President Roosevelt, he foresaw the coming war, but that Mr. Baruch pressed specific preparations for it that were not made; that, one by one, as the shadow of crises impeded, he pointed them out and offered provision to dispel them; that when his counsel was ignored and the crises came, he was called in to solve them and then only was his counsel adopted; that years before the war came, and again in time to anticipate it, he offered an organizational blueprint to the Administration against inflation and commodity shortages, and in direction of close, non-duplicating cohesion and control of the war program, a blueprint which was accepted only bit by bit and lost vital efficiency in the process.

This is an old story, enough to discourage any man. But Mr. Baruch has never become discouraged, though at times he has felt and said that everything for which he has labored was in vain. He has carried his standard unflinchingly and never taken his eyes off what is written there:

"Win the war. Don't lose the peace again. Don't lose our democracy in any victory. Don't waste one young life."

This burning goal for all his gentle manner, his overpowering reputation, his handsome presence and his unassailable and impersonal patriotism, has at times made a nuisance of Mr. Baruch. He has not minded at all when men one-tenth his stature have smiled with vexation and spoken of him behind his back as "Old Bernie." He has gone ahead with his errand as steadily when out of White House favor as when in it. Though no man in the United States could say "I told you so" as often as Mr. Baruch could, and to persons of equal authority, he avoids the phrase.

Yet he cannot avoid the fact that his very footsteps in Washington echo these words—in the White House, in the Pentagon, in the Navy Department, in the offices of the independent agencies, in Lafayette Park where once he said to a squirrel who sat up before him expectantly:

"I have nothing to give you that you want—today!"

Women at War: Margaret Bourke-White, *Life* Photographer, Survives Sinking of Transport Off West Coast of Africa

[November 1943]

"Keep away from us. We're dropping depth charges!"

Because of the inferiority of their war fleet, the Germans struck at the Allies from below the surface of the seas. In the very first week of the war German U-boats sent eleven British merchantmen to the bottom. In the first two months the British lost fifty-four ships representing a total of 236,532 tons. The number of sinkings decreased sharply when the British organized the convoy system that had been so effective in World War I.

The deadly Battle of the Atlantic cost the lives of some 35,000 British and American seamen. The Germans, too, suffering heavy casualties, lost at least twenty of their original U-boats during the first two months of the war. Some 30,000 U-boat personnel lost their lives—only one in four survived.

The sinkings continued as the war went on. By fall 1943, freighters and tankers were still being sunk in the North and South Atlantic. Sometimes transports, carrying personnel as well as supplies, were torpedoed. Here is an exciting report of one such sinking as described by Margaret Bourke-White, famed staff photographer for Life. *It reveals how courageous women endured the vicissitudes of war.*

("*Women in Lifeboats*" *by Margaret Bourke-White, from* History in the Writing *by the Correspondents of* Time, Life *and* Fortune; *copyright Time Inc. 1945.*)

The torpedo did not make as loud a crash as I had expected, nor did the ship list as much as it does in the movies. But somehow everyone on the sleeping transport knew almost instantly that this was the end of her.

Tossed out of my upper bunk, I snapped on the light switch. The power had gone. I managed to find my flashlight and began a race into my clothes. I remember deciding whether I should take time to put on a belt and tie. I decided in favor of the belt and against the tie. Should I wear my greatcoat or trenchcoat? The trenchcoat was waterproof but the greatcoat was warmer. I decided on the greatcoat.

My two Scottish roommates were nursing sisters, so-called not from any religious convictions but because they belonged to Queen Alexandria's Military Nursing Reserve Service. Sister Ismay Cooper scrabbled through the bureau for her money and Sister Violet Mac-Millan pulled on her trousers. Even in the faint flashlight beam I was impressed by the trousers. We had joked about them during the convoy voyage because the nursing sisters, operating under "Old Battle-Axe," their strict Scottish matron, had been forbidden to wear slacks except for a torpedoing.

When it came to choosing which of my six cameras I should save I didn't hesitate a second, for I had worked that out in advance. Instead of packing my musette with extra clothing, I had stored in it my Rolleiflex and an emergency film supply, together with one other camera, my favorite Linhof, and the five most valuable of its 22 lenses. I put on my greatcoat, crammed my field cap into my pocket, slipped my lifebelt over my shoulders, my helmet on my head, and started up the companionway.

Although it was less than three minutes before we were out of our cabin, everything seemed to be happening in slow motion. Up from the holds came two orderly lines of troops, one filing toward the starboard side, the other toward port. Instead of going to my boat station, No. 12 on B deck, I raced up to a spot under the bridge. In case of enemy action I had arranged with the commanding officer to stay on deck and take pictures. As I reached the top flight of steps I was hoping that dawn had come so I would be able to use a camera, but I came out under a night sky gleaming with moon and stars. One of the ship's crew came running over to send me down to my boat station. But when I explained, "I am the LIFE photographer and I have permission to be here," he went on.

The ship's deck tilted like a silver tea tray to port side. The gun stations on their pedestals looked like giant mushrooms silhouetted against the sky. As long as there had been a possibility of working I had felt no great need for haste, but now that I had decided there was not enough light for pictures my boat station suddenly became the most desirable place in the world. I was sure that No. 12 must have pulled out and it was with grateful surprise that I found my group of American nurses and British sisters climbing over the rail into the boat under the calm direction of "Old Battle-Axe."

In the lifeboat I was astonished to find myself in water up to my hips. The torpedo splash had flooded the boats on the port side aft. I hugged my cameras to keep them dry but as we made our quivering descent, columns of water began pouring down on us from lifeboat No. 11, swinging over our heads. Its crew was pulling out plugs to empty the hull before lowering away. On our interminable descent I looked up to see the ship's hulk rising against cloud banks of pure silver. "If that were the sun instead of the moonlight on those clouds," I thought, "this would be a perfect K2 sky!" Just then the attention of all of us was caught by a heavy, dangling chain which swung cruelly back and forth while we twisted our heads out of the way.

We were in the water at last. The sea, which from above had looked so calm, began beating us back against the ship. Our crew strained at the oars. There was so little space left in our crowded boat that we started singing, bending our bodies in rhythm to give the rowers room to move their arms. Just as we had created a small margin between ourselves and the big ship, down came lifeboat No. 11 with its load of British sisters. Its crew had been unable to replace the plugs properly and it filled to the gunwales. A couple of dozen sisters were washed over the side. Some of them were carried immediately back into their flooded boat on the next wave. Others started swimming toward rafts.

We tried to force our way toward the swimmers but our rudder broke and we found ourselves being drawn magnetically toward lifeboat No. 14. Getting clear of No. 14 was as long a job as I have ever known. Our ten oarsmen were Goanese from the Portuguese colony of Goa, India. They had made excellent dining-room stewards on the troopship, but this was a different kind of job. We were not swaying our bodies now just to give them elbow room. All of us who were close enough to reach them were helping with the oars.

"Start bailing!" shouted our skipper, and those of us who were wearing helmets took them off and began to dip and pour. I emptied the batteries out of my synchronizing guns and took the cuplike case off my telephoto lens. They made two more small vessels for bailing.

Two nurses opposite me began trembling in a peculiar way. At first I thought it was fright. In less than five minutes 40 nurses in that boat were as seasick as only human beings in a tossing lifeboat can be. I admired the two American nurses opposite me who kept on bailing between spasms of seasickness.

Toward the stern of the big ship a lifeboat was still trying to free itself. Its crew pushed and struggled until one of the Tommies dived under the lifeboat to disengage its ropes from the propeller. The big ship settled down a little lower now, its great bulk listing more sharply to port. In the moonlight I could see that her side was a network of rope ladders, and clinging to the one nearest us was a cluster of nursing sisters. The nurse on the lowest rung was being dipped into and raised out of the sea and the end of the ladder was whirling her about dizzily. A raft drifted close enough so that we could pull a girl into our boat. She had a broken leg and the sisters sitting behind me held her tight to keep her from bouncing back and forth with each swell.

We were bobbing farther away from the big ship but were still too close to lifeboat No. 14, which was also maneuvering a rescue from a raft. Just as a soldier let go of the raft to reach for a rope from the lifeboat, a wave flung the raft against him and cracked his skull. The skipper of No. 14 dived overboard, caught hold of the soldier and the two were dragged back into the lifeboat. Before the night was over the soldier had died. During all this we heard a voice from a distant raft shriek out, "I am all alone! I am all alone!" Over and over. We tried to steer our rudderless craft toward the cry but it drifted farther and farther away until it was lost in distant silence. Now the swell was carrying us toward one of two destroyers which stayed behind as the convoy plowed on without us. "Keep away from us. We're dropping depth charges!" There was little we could do to guide our crippled boat but the deep roar of those depth charges was music to us.

Late the afternoon before, we had scored a "probable" on a submarine. I knew that we had been pursued for three days, and the talk among the few passengers in the know had been that a pack of subs was after us. The chase followed the most savage and relentless storm that the troopship's captain had experienced in 45 years at sea. For five days we had battled our way through waves sometimes 60 feet high. The furniture was roped back in the lounge after several passengers had been injured by flying sofas. One afternoon the piano broke loose and rushed back and forth like a great mad beast until it crashed against the wall.

That all seemed like ancient history now. Three whole hours ago we had left the big boat for the little one. Our steering problems were under better control. The Indian rowers in their white turbans had succumbed to dizziness and a few of us who seemed seasick-proof were dragging at the oars under the direction of the little quartermaster who was acting as skipper. A splendid big Scottish girl, Elspeth Duncan, one of General Eisenhower's clerical staff, made the best rower of all. Rafts with soldiers clinging to them were still drifting by and we managed to intercept three, picking up a total of nine soldiers. Some joked as we dragged them over the gunwales but some had a glazed look in their eyes from shock and exposure which I have never seen before and hope never to see again. We peeled off our sweaters for them and our diminutive skipper wrapped them in yellow-hooded oilskins. "You're all right now, mate," he would say as he tied the cape around each one. "You look just like the donkey in the Christmas play."

We had the boat pretty well bailed out by now. The nurses made the girl with the broken leg as comfortable as they could on the floor boards. I saw that she had no socks and, remembering that I had wrapped one of my lenses in a spare pair, I dug them out of my camera case. The nurses drew them on her feet as gently as they could.

Near us a lifeboat was towing three heavily loaded rafts. The sisters in the boat were passing lighted cigarettes back to the men on them. From the rafts came snatches of a song: "You are my sunshine, my only sunshine." Sunshine, I thought. That was all I needed to record this drama in pictures instead of words. I felt in my pocket for my notebook and discovered with joy my fountain pen was still stuck in the cover, so I started jotting down notes in the moonlight.

People began joking now. The irrepressible Kay Summersby, Eisenhower's pretty Irish driver, announced her breakfast order. She wanted her eggs sunny-side up and no yolks broken. One soldier said he'd take his brandy with a dash of hot milk in it. Alfred Yorke, our little skipper, confided to me the story of his life—how he had been a baby photographer before he went to sea.

The moon was sinking, incredibly large and golden. As it lost itself in the sea, the night seemed to darken and the stars blazed brighter than ever. We had drifted away from our little community of boats but could still see dimly the shapes of the mother ship and a destroyer. From the destroyer we could just barely hear a voice through the megaphone say something about towing the ship away, then something we couldn't quite catch about "survivors." A new loneliness came upon us while we watched the fading outline of our mother ship.

"Survivors," I thought. This was the first time I had thought of myself as a survivor. I made a resolution not to allow myself to become impatient until the end of the sixth day. We had each been given a can labeled "emergency ration," about the size of a tin of sardines. It was stamped: "Purpose of contents: to be consumed only when no other rations of any kind are procurable." I resolved not to let myself think again about that can until the morning of the 14th day.

It was growing light now. "Let's tidy up the ship," Skipper Yorke said, and began throwing odd lengths of rope and bits of planks overboard. "Toss out those helmets to save weight," he ordered. But no one would part with a helmet because too many nurses were still getting seasick into them. Around the complete circumference of the horizon, bands of tumbled clouds were picking up the light of dawn—a photographer's dawn.

The skipper, an enthusiast about photography as any baby photographer would be, helped me up on the gunwales to get as favorable a viewpoint as possible for snapping my fellow passengers. One of the American nurses had unaccountably saved an orange which she passed out generously, section by section, as far as it would go. Then there was a hum in the sky and a British flying boat dipped over us while we waved back wildly.

After a few more hours we could make out our destroyer appearing over the horizon and by her interrupted course we guessed that she was picking up other survivors. She reached us after we had been eight hours in our lifeboat and as soon as we were dragged aboard her we were given cups of steaming Ovaltine. I climbed up to the gun station and photographed the last of our family of lifeboats as their occupants were helped to the deck. The man who had died from a cracked skull was handed up strapped to a pair of oars. Another boat yielded a soldier who had died from shock and exposure. Several nurses were brought up, suffering from sprained ankles, twisted arms and broken legs, and one Scottish sister was moaning about her back, crushed when she had to jump from the ship's ladder into a lifeboat. But the soldier who took all our hearts was sitting alone in the middle of his raft and when we drew close he raised his thumb toward our destroyer and shouted, "Hi, taxi!"

When the last survivor had been transferred, the destroyer pulled away, leaving behind us the deserted lifeboats which swept down our wake like empty walnut shells. I came back to the teeming deck where friends were greeting each other with cries of joy. I was delighted to find my two roommates: Sister Violet still had a few curlers stuck in her hair. I was happy too to find our ship's charming young radio officer, Lord David Herbert III, son of the Earl of Pembrook. He was groping through his pockets for a little box which luckily he had not left behind. In it was a pair of red-enameled cuff links set with gold crowns which had belonged to his great friend, the Duke of Kent, and had been given to him as a keepsake by the Princess Marina.

Then everyone began fishing in his pockets. The beauteous Kay still had two precious possessions, her lipstick and her French-English "soldier's speak-easy." Lieut. Ethel Westermann of Englewood, N. J., on her way to be chief nurse of the General Dispensary Headquarters, still had her rosary, and blonde, petite Jeanne Dixon of Washington, D. C., secretary to Eisenhower, had saved her prayer book.

The nursing sisters were comparing experiences and white-haired Helen Freckleman from Edinburgh turned out to be the sister I had seen clinging to the ladder with the waves over her. "How long were you on that ladder?" I asked. "Half an hour," she replied. "I kept telling myself: 'I must concentrate on holding on with both hands.'"

I glanced at those hands which had nursed the wounded of two wars. They were not young enough for such a stern assignment. But they had held.

I hunted up the girls who had managed to stay in flooded lifeboat No. 11. It had stopped sinking just as its gunwales were even with the water. Its buoyancy chambers had held it up, but until the girls were picked up seven hours later they had been in water up to their chests.

Two other boatloads of British nurses had been so far away from the destroyer and so tired from rowing that they dubbed themselves Oxford and Cambridge to keep up their spirits. Cambridge reached the destroyer half a length ahead of Oxford.

I climbed again to the gun station. Far over the horizon our mother ship was still afloat. She was listing much lower to port now and destroyers were taking off all the troops that were left. The hundreds of survivors on our destroyer watched the mother ship disappear in the distance. She had meant something very special to all of us. She had stood by us through 60-foot waves and 70-mile-an-hour gales. When wounded she had held up until the last living man was removed from her decks. Our destroyer picked up speed now and before the day was over we sighted the purple hills of Africa.

Tribute to Shorty: Pvt. William Saroyan on the Sweetheart of Company D—a Pooch of Undetermined Origin

[1943]

"I am convinced he does not know that the men of Company D are soldiers. I believe he has some vague notion we are orphans."

The face of war is not always dramatic—battles and heroics and surrenders. Much of it was composed of large doses of boredom, ennui, loneliness. Swept from their homes and after a few weeks of basic training plunged into barracks life on posts and in camps or into the combat areas, millions of men fought highly personalized battles against tedium.

Among the men-at-war was William Saroyan, short-story writer, novelist and playwright. Born in 1908 of Armenian parentage, Saroyan already had a wide reputation for whimsical and sentimental writings. Americans loved his impressionistic stories and sketches in which his deep emotions burst from the printed page. In 1943 Saroyan found himself lifted bodily from a peaceful career of creative writing into the army at a stateside post near New York. He managed to do some writing for Yank, The Army Weekly.

The Saroyan story reproduced here is a tribute to a wonderful canine personality "who did not know that there was a war going on." G.I.'s everywhere loved the story. There were thousands of "Shortys" doing the same work as the chaplains were doing and "sending in no reports to anybody."

Saroyan himself lived to become a middle-aged man on the flying trapeze.

("The Sweetheart of Company D," in Yank, The Army Weekly. *Quoted in* The Best From Yank [New York, 1945], pp. 136–137. *Courtesy of the U.S. Department of Defense.*)

There is something in the heart of street dogs which draws them close to men, and there is probably no camp or post of the Army which does not have at least one dog, whether the post is in a Far

Western desolation or in a suburb of New York, as my post is.

Our Company D has one of these dogs. He is called Shorty by some of the men, Short End by others and Short Arm by still others. Shorty is small, lazy and given to a bitter attitude toward civilians, including children. Somewhere in Shorty's family is a dachshund, as Shorty has the lines of such a dog, but not the hair.

The theory of the men of Company D is that Shorty spends the greater part of his time dreaming of women—or at any rate women dogs. He doesn't come across such creatures very often; he doesn't come across any kind of dog very often. Whenever he does, male or female, Shorty goes to work and gives the matter a stab, so to speak. It is a half-hearted stab, with Shorty more bored than fascinated and not the least bit sure of what he is trying to do, or whether or not he isn't making a fool of himself.

Now and then Shorty will be discovered in the middle of the street, dreaming of love or whatever it is, while two or three trucks stand by discreetly waiting for him to make up his mind. Shorty may have come into the world thoughtlessly, but it is not likely that he will leave any children standing around. He is either too tired, too troubled or too old, even though he is probably not more than 2.

I have observed that Shorty makes himself available to any man in uniform, bar none, and while our post is made up mostly of men of talent, Shorty is not above giving himself over to the affections of a man of practically no talent at all, such as our top sergeant, who was not in civilian life the famous man he is now. Our top sergeant may be a genius, the same as all the rest of us: Two-Teeth Gonzalez, Bicycle Wilkinson, Henry the One Hundred and Fifty-first Million and all the others. He probably deserves a story all to himself, but somebody else will have to write that story, as I want to write sonnets. (That is, if I ever learn to spell.)

My hero is Shorty, not our first sergeant. The sergeant is his mother's hero, I suppose, and I wish to God she'd never let him out of the house. If he thinks getting me to do KP is the way we are going to bring the war to a satisfactory conclusion, I believe his education has been neglected. That is not the way to do it. Give me a map of the world, a pointer and a good-sized audience and I believe I can figure the whole thing out in not more than an afternoon. The idea that generals are the only kind of Army personnel capable of figuring out ways and means and all that stuff is unsound. For every general there ought to be one private on the ground floor. As it is, half the time I don't know what is being done, what the idea is, or anything else. The result is that I must go out into the yard and whistle for Shorty, who instead of leaping to his feet and running to me opens his eyes and waits for me to run to him.

Shorty knows me all right, but what kind of planning can you do with a dog, and a sleepy one at that—a day-dreamer, an escapist, a lover of peace, an enemy of children in sailor suits? I don't know who the chaplain of Company D is, but for my money he can pack up and go to some other post, because Shorty is doing the same work and sending in no reports to anybody. He is a quiet creature, he is patient, he will listen to reason or anything else, and he will get up after a half hour of heart-to-heart talk and slowly wag his tail. He will wag thoughtfully, with effort, and unless you are blind, you will know what advice he is giving you after carefully considering your case.

Now, there was the celebrated case of Warty Walter, the Genius from Jersey, who had a secret weapon all worked out in his head which he believed could finish the war in two weeks. Warty mentioned this weapon to our top sergeant only to hear the man say, "You do what I say, Warty, or you're going to hear otherwise."

Warty went out into the yard to Shorty and unburdened his heart, whereupon Shorty got to his feet, stretched his body until it hurt, wagged his tail three times, kissed Warty on the hand, turned and began wending his way across the street where a girl of 6 in a sailor suit was looking at a movie billboard. That was the end of Warty's secret weapon. The following day he got his orders to go to Louisiana, took Shorty in his arms to say good-bye, and the war is still going on—a good three months after Warty got his idea for the secret weapon. Our top sergeant said, "If it's a secret, what the hell are you coming to me about it for? Keep it a secret."

Not every man at our post is as brilliant or as sincere as Warty, but I can think of no man who is not as devoted to Shorty. No girl of the USO has done Army morale as much good as Shorty. He may not be a dancing dog, but he's got eyes and many a man's seen a lot of understanding in those brooding eyes—many and many a man.

As for the little girl in the sailor suit, she turned and ran, so that Shorty, not knowing what else to do, went up to a second lieutenant and bit him. The following day there was a notice on the bulletin board saying: "Yesterday an enlisted man was bitten by a dog who might or might not have had rabies. Therefore, in the future, any man caught without his dog tags will be given extra duty." This of course was a subtle way of saying that Shorty had rabies, a lie if I ever heard one.

The basic failing of Shorty, if he must be given a failing, is his love of comfort, his passion for food and his devotion to sleep or The Dream. Shorty probably does not known this is 1943. I doubt very much if he knows there is a war going on, and I am convinced he does not know that the men of Company D are soldiers. I believe he has some vague notion we are orphans.

Shorty eats too much and never does calisthenics. He has seen a lot of men come and go. He has loved them all, and they have all loved him. I have seen big men with barracks bags over their shoulders bend down to whisper good-bye to the sweetheart of Company D, get up with misty eyes, swing up into the truck and wave to the little fellow standing there in a stupor. And I have heard them, as the truck has bounced out of the yard on its way to the war, holler out—not to me or to our top sergeant, but to Shorty: "So long, pal! See you after the war!"

I don't think they will see Shorty after the war. I think he will lie down and die of a broken heart once the boys take off their uniforms. Shorty lives to watch them stand reveille and retreat. All that stuff will stop after the war and Shorty will be out in the cold, just another dog of the streets, without honor, without importance— lonely, unfed, despised and unwanted.

That is why I have written this tribute to him.

Square-Cut Diamond: Allen Churchill, a Navy Reporter, Tells the Story of a Raucous Marine

[November 1943]

"He was twice as strong and three times as nasty as the youngest boot in the Corps."

Every army has its share of heroes and heels, of eager beavers and expert gold brickers. It is part of the mystifying aura of war that men quickly forget the horror and filth of combat and even enjoy the rough camaraderie existing among fellow male sufferers. Perhaps this is nature's way of protecting the mind in troublous times. Soldiers quickly snatch heroes from oblivion and place them on little pedestals while at the same time avoiding unsympathetic characters as if they had the plague.

Such a hero was Master Gunnery Sergeant Leland Diamond, the most famous Marine of World War II. Allen Churchill, Navy yeoman third class, reporter for Yank, The Army Weekly, *gave "Square-Cut Diamond" a measure of immortality in this word-picture. Churchill's story carried the Diamond legend to all corners of the globe.*

(Yank, The Army Weekly, *November 7, 1943. Courtesy of the U.S. Department of Defense.*)

The United States Marine Corps is celebrating its 168th anniversary this month, so that makes Lou Diamond, the most famous marine in this or any other war, 200 years old.

Any leatherneck will tell you that Lou has been the best mortarman in the Corps since it was founded by the Continental Congress, Nov. 10, 1775. They claim he was rather old when he enlisted—32; so by now he must be rounding out his second century.

Nobody is exactly sure about this, however, because Master Gunnery Sgt. Leland Diamond is not a man who likes publicity and he flatly refuses to divulge his correct age to anybody. It is on his service record, of course, but Lou takes great care to make sure this record is kept secret. According to strict Marine standards, Lou was even rather old for combat service in the last war, but his boundless energy and tremendous vocal powers were well known all over France.

Last year, just before his outfit was to embark for Guadalcanal, there was scuttlebutt that the tough old sarge might be left behind because the South Pacific was no place for such a venerable and ancient man, even though he was twice as strong and three times as nasty as the youngest boot in the Corps.

When Diamond heard these rumors, as he hears everything, he acted upon them as he always acts—energetically and in full voice. All the ground he had to cover he covered at a fast trot. All the orders he had to give—and he gives more orders than five generals—he gave in a raucous bellow. The trotting and bellowing began every morning at 5 A.M. and in three days Lou had everybody in the camp worn to a frazzle. But when the transport moved away from the dock, Lou was aboard.

The Diamond legend grew considerably in the South Pacific where Lou roared his way through the battles of Guadalcanal and Tulagi and did much to back up the Marine Corps contention that he is far and away the most expert mortar sergeant in any branch of the service.

At Tulagi he demolished 14 Jap buildings with his trusty 81-mm. Then he turned to the colonel and bet him $50 that he could put a shot down the chimney of the 15th. He won.

The story was a bit different one morning when a Jap destroyer tried to creep around the island. Diamond's first shell fell in the water a few feet behind the tin can.

The sergeant's bull voice arose in anguished thunder that shook the tropical foliage. From the deluge of profanity, only the last sentence was distinguishable:

"Forgot to allow for the —— forward movement!"

John Hersey, the war correspondent, saw Diamond in action at Guadalcanal and described him as "a giant with a full gray beard, an admirable paunch and the bearing of a man daring you to insult him. As we went by, he was, as usual, out of patience. He wanted to keep on firing and he had been told to hold back. 'Wait and wait and wait!' he roared. 'God, some people around here'll fall on their a—— from waiting!'"

Writing in the Marine magazine, *The Leatherneck*, Frank X. Talbot describes Diamond as an inch or so under 6 feet, pushing the scales to the vicinity of 200 pounds. Most of the time he is talking or roaring, and when he isn't roaring, his tongue hangs out of the corner of his mouth, relaxed and ready for the next outburst. When he can get it, he drinks beer by the case. He always drinks standing at the bar, with his hat on.

In mid-November last year the tension of the Guadalcanal campaign showed signs of wearing on Lou. He was ordered to New Zealand for hospital care. Protesting with wolf-like howls, he was dragged into a plane and later deposited in a clean hospital bed where he immediately got into trouble because he refused to permit his beard to be shaved off and because he patted a pretty nurse in the right place. Lou had been there only two days when the hospital superintendent said: "I thought I was head of this hospital until Diamond got here. Now I'm not so sure."

When the sergeant was released from the hospital he promptly made tracks for Guadalcanal. When he got there he found the Army in charge, his unit gone and himself farther than ever from joining them. His curses of rage and frustration tore the air and made the soldiers cringe. Anger spent, Lou then efficiently began thumbing a ride across the Coral Sea to Australia.

Some weeks later his burly figure appeared on the remote Australian field where his company was drilling. It was 50 miles from the nearest port to that field. It was hot and there were no transportation facilities, but Lou had covered the distance on foot. Walking smartly up to the major, he snapped to attention, saluted and said: "Sir, I'm here."

Diamond gives his mortars more affection than anything in this world. At the Marine base in New River, N. C., he spent many nights sleeping with a ring of 81-mm mortars around his bunk. He called them his sweethearts, and nobody dared approach them.

The only other things for which the sergeant shows affection are his pets, of which there has been an endless chain. They include Bozo, the ugly bulldog described by Master Gunnery Sgt. Mickey Finn as much prettier than Lou, and a disagreeable goat named Rufus and a couple of trained chickens whose names are unprintable. This select menagerie is now waiting patiently at New River for the momentous day when the rough Diamond returns from the wars.

Lou rules his men with an iron hand. They fear him at first, get to like him when they know him and end by loving him as much as a marine can love anything. Lou treats anyone who has less than 10 years of service like the meanest boot. This gripes some of the men who serve with him, but they end by taking it philosophically. "After all," one of them said, "if you can get used to that old bastard's voice, you can get used to anything."

DEAR YANK:

In reference to an article in your YANK magazine [in a November issue], I wish to state that I have been insulted by the article on "Square-Cut Diamond," written by Allen Churchill Y3c, and I have written to my lawyer in Toledo, Ohio, to take action on the article. 1) I am not an old bastard. 2) I am not 200 years old. 3) My tongue does not hang out and I did not hike 50 miles to get back to my outfit. 4) And those chickens I had was named "Bud." 5) I had orders to report to the 1st Marine Division on Guadalcanal, which was on the same place and I did leave with a part of the 1st Marine Division. 6) Who gave your outfit permission to use my name? 7) Also I am figuring on a nuisance charge against you. I served in the last war and am trying to do my bit in this one, and I do not like the way your outfit is trying to do it.

—MASTER GUNNERY SGT. LOU DIAMOND

Parris Island, S. C.

DEAR YANK:

The article on Lou Diamond was splendid and everyone in our office enjoyed reading it. It was called to the commandant's attention. We thought it an especial tribute, on our anniversary, to have a meeting of the services in your article: a Marine subject in an Army publication, written by a Navy man. Let those who are captious on the cooperation of the services be silent.

Hq. USMC,
Washington, D. C.

—BRIG. GEN. ROBERT L. DENIG
Director, Division of Public Relations

Tarawa: Richard W. Johnston on the Toughest
60 Hours in Marine Corps History
[November 23, 1943]

"Dead Japanese are everywhere. . . ."

Tarawa atoll in the Gilbert Islands lay 2,500 miles southwest of Hawaii and 1,200 miles northeast of Guadalcanal. This keystone of the Gilberts was composed of twenty-six islands grouped around a lagoon and linked by channels of wading depth. The islands were only a few feet above sea level.

The main island, Betio, a tiny speck in the vast Pacific, was considered valuable property by Tokyo. Here the Japanese stationed a garrison of 3,000 Imperial Marines and set up an elaborate system of defenses. They lined the beaches and the reef with obstacles and constructed emplacements covered with seven feet of concrete and reinforced by steel, coral sand and coconut logs. They believed the island to be impregnable.

Most important of all, the Japanese constructed on Betio a three-strip landing field, critically important for both sides. For the Japanese it was the nearest point to the Allied travel routes from San Francisco to Hawaii to Australia. For the Allies its capture would be the first step to the powerful enemy naval base at Truk in the Carolines. Once this bastion fell, the Allies would be on the way to Tokyo.

Three days of naval and air bombardment began on November 17, 1943. Hour after hour the great battlewagons lobbed shells onto the tiny island. At the same time planes dropped thousands of bombs on the constricted target. Could anything possibly survive that assault?

The Marines who got ashore from the landing barges soon learned that the defending garrison was far from dead. This was the first time American troops were attacking a strongly defended enemy atoll. After a day of fighting the Marines held only a few yards of narrow beachhead. On the second day they assaulted the pillboxes. On the third day the Japanese fell apart.

It was the toughest fight in the history of the Marine Corps. Lieutenant

Colonel Evans F. Carlson, leader of Marine raiders on Guadalcanal and Makin Island in August 1942, and accompanying this assault as an observer, described it as "really a blood-and-guts battle—just blood and guts. This was not only worse than Guadalcanal. It was the damnedest fight I have seen in thirty years of this business."

Robert Sherrod described it: "Thirty-one Marines are now laid out in a line beyond the command post. Some are bloated, some have already turned a sickly green. Some have no faces, one's guts are hanging out of his body. The eyeballs of another have turned to a jellied mass, after so long a time in the water."

Richard W. Johnston, Associated Press correspondent, went along with the attacking forces. Here is his story from the desolate tropical island.

(Associated Press, November 23, 1943. By permission of Associated Press.)

WITH THE UNITED STATES MARINE FORCES AT TARAWA, Nov. 23. (A.P.) —Bloody, bandaged heroes of the United States Marines have broken the back of this lizard-shaped Japanese Gibraltar of the Gilbert Islands today after sixty hours of the toughest fighting in the century-and-a-half history of the corps.

In a four-hour push supported by naval gunfire, strafing and dive-bombing, the Marines cleared the vital airstrip and confined the Japanese defenders—Tojo's corps, the Imperial Marines—to the island's tapering tail and to a small blockhouse pocket on the north coast.

The Japanese soldiers are not surrendering, but are beginning to commit hara-kiri. There is every indication, however, they will fight to the end from strong positions and that many more American boys will die before the last Japanese are driven from Tarawa.

No victory in American military history was ever attained at a higher price. . . .

The sweet, sickening smell of death literally permeates the blasted, shell-torn beaches, scarred blockhouses and riddled plateau topped by splintered, topless coconut trees on this tiny island—only two and one half miles long and 800 yards wide.

Until late this afternoon there was no time to bury the bodies of either the Marine or Japanese dead—many of them killed in the first fierce hours of the assault landing. . . .

Dead Japanese are everywhere, in blockhouses, in the surf and scattered among tattered palm fronds which they have used incessantly as cover for sniping.

The assault was made against three designated beaches by three battalion landing teams going shoreward through a lagoon on the north coast of the fortified air base island of the Tarawa atoll.

These battalions and others supporting the three landing teams went shoreward in Higgins boats and other landing craft under cover of naval and air attacks, but they encountered ferocious fire from Japanese shore batteries and emplacements, of which few were affected by the bombing and shelling.

A shelving reef hung up most of the Higgins boats and wave after wave of infantry had to struggle 500 yards through water neck deep under a murderous Japanese barrage. At low tide many of their bodies dot the reef.

Maj. Gen. Julian C. Smith and most of his staff were blown out of a boat when they attempted to circle the west tip of the island and land at regimental headquarters. The general was rescued by an amphibious tractor obtained by Major R. M. C. Thompkins, who waded half a mile through water chest deep under enemy sniping to hail a rescue boat.

The Japanese continued to fire at General Smith's boat during a two-hour wait, but only the coxswain was wounded. . . .

In the initial landings at 8:30 A.M., November 21, one of the three landing teams was so powerfully opposed that only two companies were able to land. They held a beachhead seventy yards wide for more than twenty-four hours.

I landed at the center beach under Major Henry Pierson Crowe, 44, and like the Marines, I had to walk 500 yards shoreward through a machine-gun crossfire.

Because of the low altitude of the island, which is under ten feet above sea level at all points, it was impossible to secure any point against enemy fire. Throughout the last sixty hours, and probably through the next sixty, Japanese snipers have been taking, and will take, a heavy toll.

From the outset the Japanese fought with amazing fury and even now with occasional surrenders and hara-kiris there is no indication of mass surrenders or evacuation. Instead the indication is the Japanese will fight to the death, which means they will make a vicious defense of an area more than a mile long and subject only to frontal assault and naval and aerial bombardment.

The Japanese defenses in this area like those throughout the island include heavy concrete emplacements, pillboxes with tank-proof walls three feet thick and blockhouses made from coconut logs lashed together and filled in with coral sand. These make four-foot barriers which can withstand much punishment.

Today's victory push began at 1 P.M. after the arrival of Colonel Merrit A. Edson [chief of staff to General Smith] and additional light and medium tanks. Reinforcing Marine battalions landed in the relatively lightly defended west end of the island late yesterday and pushed east down an airstrip which forms a diagonal line across the island where the powerful Japanese concrete and log emplacements held up Major Crowe's battalion. This battalion might have been outflanked but for the excellent supporting naval gunfire.

At the zero hour Navy Hellcats strafed the Japanese-held area in successive waves. Infantry and tanks advanced only fifteen yards behind the strafing planes while battleships and cruisers bombarded the Japanese-held area behind the lines.

Despite the intensity of our attacks the Japanese fought back with undiminished ardor. This was testified by the constant arrival of stretcher-bearers with wounded and dead Marines. But when the east end of the airstrip finally was reached the Japanese doom was sealed and victory—slow and painful no doubt, but victory—became certain.

In these hellish sixty hours the heroism of the Marine officers and enlisted men alike was almost beyond belief. Time after time they unflinchingly charged Japanese positions, ignoring deadly fire and refusing to halt until wounded beyond the ability to carry on.

Men with gaping stomach and back wounds almost certainly fatal begged doctors to fix them up so they could return to their outfits, and one captain who was shot through one arm and both legs sent a message to Crowe apologizing for "letting him down."

Characteristically, the officers throughout the division led the men into battle and as a consequence officer casualties in the battalions ran high. The commanding officer of one landing team was shot through the throat and killed instantly as he waded into the initial assault. . . .

The exact strength of the defenders is unknown, but it is believed to number at least 3,000 Imperial Japanese Marines.

An educated Gilbertese native said the Japanese had moved in 4,000 soldiers and 4,000 coolie-class laborers when they first occupied the island, but it is believed many of the latter were shipped home.

Significantly, most surrenders, which probably total not more than 200, were by laborers. The soldiers prefer hara-kiri. . . .

Poker for Keeps: John Steinbeck Tells How a Yank Paratrooper Talks Eighty-seven Germans into Surrender

[December 10, 1943]

"The lieutenant knew that . . . if he were hit in the head he wouldn't hear or feel anything."

"They're a curious, crazy, yet responsible crew." This was novelist John Steinbeck's tribute to his colleagues when he became a war reporter for the New York Herald Tribune *in June 1943. "To this hard-bitten bunch of professionals," he wrote later, "I arrived as a Johnny-come-lately, a sacred cow, a kind of tourist. I think they felt I was muscling in on their hard-gained territory. When, however, they found that I was not duplicating their work, was not reporting straight news, they were very kind to me and went out of their way to help me and to instruct me in the things I didn't know."*

Steinbeck was modest and he was also one of the best reporters of World War II. His descriptive powers and eye for detail served him well. Written under pressure, in haste and in high tension, his dispatches telephoned across the sea were as immediate, as packed with punch as bursts from a tommy gun.

On December 1, 1943, the Americans decided to capture a German radar station on the Italian island of Ventotene in the Tyrrhenian Sea. The radar installation, which scanned the whole area north and south of Naples, was a key objective. Forty American paratroopers and three officers were transferred from somewhere in North Africa to do the job. They had no idea that the radar crew numbered eighty-seven heavily armed men. One of the American officers, a lieutenant, asked his captain's permission to try and talk the Germans into surrender instead of battling it out with heavy casualties.

What happened on Ventotene was described by Steinbeck in a series of dispatches to the New York Herald Tribune, *of which the two following told the climax of the story.*

314

(From Once There Was a War *by John Steinbeck [New York, 1960], pp. 168–173. Copyright 1943 by John Steinbeck. Reprinted by permission of The Viking Press, Inc.)*

December 10, 1943—The lieutenant walked slowly up the hill toward the German positions. He carried his white flag over his head, and his white flag was a bath towel. As he walked he thought what a fool he was. He had really stuck his neck out. Last night when he had argued for the privilege of going up and trying to kid the Jerry into surrender he hadn't known it would be like this. He hadn't known how lonely and exposed he would be.

Forty paratroopers against eighty-seven Jerrys, but Jerry didn't know that. The lieutenant also hoped Jerry wouldn't know his guts were turned to water. His feet sounded loud on the path. It was early in the morning and the sun was not up yet. He hoped they could see his white flag. Maybe it would be invisible in this light. He kept in the open as much as possible as he climbed the hill.

He knew that the forty paratroopers were crawling and squirming behind him, keeping cover, getting into position so that if anything should go wrong they might attack and stand some chance of surprising the Jerry. He knew the fieldglasses of the captain would be on the German position, waiting for something to happen.

"If they shoot at you, flop and lie still," the captain had said. "We'll try to cover you and get you out."

The lieutenant knew that if he were hit and not killed he would hear the shot after he was hit, but if he were hit in the head he wouldn't hear or feel anything. He hoped, if it happened, it would happen that way. His feet seemed very heavy and clumsy. He looked down and saw the little stones on the path, and he wished he could get down on his knees to see what kind of stones they were. He had a positive hunger to get down out of line. His chest tingled almost as if he were preparing to receive the bullet. And his throat was as tight as it had been once when he tried to make a speech in college.

Step by step he drew nearer, and there was no sign from Jerry. The lieutenant wanted to look back to see whether any of the paratroopers were in sight, but he knew the Germans would have their fieldglasses on him, and they were close enough so that they could even see his expression.

It happened finally, quickly and naturally. He was passing a pile of rocks, when a deep voice shouted an order to him. There were three Germans, young-looking men, and they had their rifles trained on his stomach. He stopped and stared at them as they stared back. He wondered whether his eyes were as wide as theirs. They paused, and then a hoarse voice called from up ahead. The Jerries stood up and they glanced quickly down the hill before they came out to him. And then the four marched on. It seemed a little silly to the lieutenant, like little boys marching up an alley to attack Connor's woodshed. And his bath towel on a stick seemed silly, too. He thought, Well, anyway, if they bump me our boys will get these three. In his mind's eye he could see helmeted Americans watching the little procession through their rifle sights.

Ahead was a small white stone building, but Jerry was too smart to be in the building. A trench started behind the building and led down to a hole almost like a shell hole.

Three officers faced him in the hole. They were dressed in dusty blue and they wore the beautiful high caps of the Luftwaffe, with silver eagles and swastikas. They were electronics engineers, a ground service for the German Air Force. The faced him without speaking, and his throat was so tight that for a moment he could not begin. All he could think of was a green table; Jerry had three deuces showing and the lieutenant a pair of treys. He knew they had no more, but they didn't know what his hole card was. He only hoped they wouldn't know, because all he had was that pair of treys.

The Oberleutnant regarded him closely and said nothing.

"Do you speak English?" the lieutenant asked.

"Yes."

The lieutenant took a deep breath and spoke the piece he had memorized. "The colonel's compliments, sir. I am ordered to demand your surrender. At the end of twenty minutes the cruisers will move up and open fire unless ordered otherwise following your surrender." He noticed the Oberleutnant's eyes involuntarily move toward the sea. The lieutenant lapsed out of his formality, as he had planned. "What's the good?" he said. "We'll just kill you all. We've got six hundred men ashore and the cruisers are aching to take a shot at you. What's the good of it? You'd kill some of us and we'd kill all of you. Why don't you just stack up your arms and come in?"

The Oberleutnant stared into his eyes. That what's-in-the-hole look. The look balanced: call or toss in, call or toss in. The pause was centuries long, and then at last, "What treatment will we receive," the Oberleutnant asked.

"Prisoners of war under Convention of The Hague." The lieutenant was trying desperately to show nothing in his face. There was another long pause. The German breathed in deeply and his breath whistled in his nose.

"It is no dishonor to surrender to superior forces," he said.

December 13, 1943—When the lieutenant went up to the Germans with his bath towel for a white flag, the captain of paratroopers, peering through a crack between two buildings, watched him go. The men hidden below saw the lieutenant challenged, and then they saw him behind the white stone building. The watching men hardly breathed then. They were waiting for the crack of a rifle shot that would mean the plan for kidding the Germans into surrender had failed. The time went slowly. Actually, it was only about fifteen minutes. Then the lieutenant appeared again, and this time he was accompanied by three German officers.

The watchers saw him walk down to a clear place in the path and there pause and point to the ground. Then two of the officers retired behind the white building again. But in a moment they reappeared, and behind them came the German soldiers. They straggled down the path and, at the place that had been indicated, they piled their arms, their rifles and machine guns, and even their pistols. The captain, lying behind his stones, watched and counted. He tallied the whole eighty-seven men who were supposed to be there. He said to his lieutenant, "By God, he pulled it off!"

And now a little pageant developed. As the Germans marched down the path, American paratroopers materialized out of the ground beside them, until they were closely surrounded by an honor guard of about thirty men. The whole group swung down the path and into the little white town that stood so high above the harbor of Ventotene.

Since Ventotene had been for hundreds of years an Italian prison island, there was no lack of place to put the prisoners. The top floor of what we would call a city hall was a big roomy jail, with four or five big cells. The column marched up the steps of the city hall and on up to the third floor, and then the Germans were split into three groups and one group was put into each of three cells, while the fourth cell was reserved for the officers. Then guards with tommy guns were posted at the doors of the cells, and the conquest was over.

The lieutenant who had carried the white flag sat down on the steps of the city hall a little shakily. The captain sat down beside him. "Any trouble?" the captain asked.

"No. It was too easy. I don't believe it yet." He lighted a cigarette, and his shaking hand nearly put out the match.

"Wonderful job," the captain said. "But what are we going to do with them?"

"Won't the ships be back tonight?"

"I hope so, but suppose they don't get back. We can't let anybody get any sleep until we get rid of these babies."

A trooper lounged near. "Those Jerry officers are raising hell," he said. "They want to see the commanding officer, sir."

The captain stood up. "Better come with me," he told the lieutenant. "How many men did you tell them we had?"

"Six hundred," the lieutenant said, "and I forgot how many cruisers offshore."

The captain laughed. "One time I heard about an officer who marched fifteen men around a house until they looked like an army. Maybe we better do that with our forty."

At the door of the officers' cell the captain took out his pistol and handed it to one of the guards. "Leave the door open and keep your eye on us all the time. If they make a suspicious move, shoot them."

"Yes, sir," said the guard, and he unlocked and opened the heavy door.

The German officers were at the barred window, looking down on the deserted streets of the little town. They could see two lonely sentries in front of the building. The German Oberleutnant turned as the captain entered. "I demand to see the colonel," he said.

The captain swallowed. "Er—the colonel? Well, he is engaged."

For a long moment the German stared into the captain's eyes. Finally he said, "You are the commanding officer, aren't you?"

"Yes, I am," the captain said.

"How many men have you?"

"We do not answer questions," the captain said stiffly.

The German's face was hard and disappointed. He said, "I don't think you have six hundred men. I think you have only a few more than thirty men."

The captain nodded solemnly. He said, "We've mined the building. If there is any trouble—any trouble at all—we'll blow the whole mess of you to hell." He turned to leave the cell. "You'll be taken aboard ship soon now," he said over his shoulder.

Going down the stairs, the lieutenant said, "Have you really mined the building?"

The captain grinned at him. "Have we really got six hundred men?" he asked. And then he said, "Lord, I hope the destroyer gets in tonight to take these babies out. None of us is going to get any sleep until then."

Bombing of Monte Cassino: German and Italian Reports on the Destruction of Benedictine Monastery

[February 15, 1944]

After the American landing behind German lines and the assault on Anzio in late January 1944, Field Marshal Albert Kesselring ordered counterattacks in the vicinity of Cassino, seventy miles to the southeast. This was the key point of the German Gustav Line guarding the approaches to Rome. Cassino became the immediate goal of the Allied Fifth Army in Italy.

Cassino itself, with a normal population of 19,000, was on flat land along the lower slopes of Monte Cassino. At the pinnacle (Hill 516 on Allied war maps) was the famed old monastery, parent house of the Benedictine Order. Originally, there had been a Roman temple on this site. In the sixth century St. Benedict established a hermitage there, and in the eighth century the monastery was constructed. In its tiny cells the black-clad followers of St. Benedict copied and illuminated Greek and Roman manuscripts.

The Allied High Command was faced with a grave problem. Marshal Kesselring had constructed elaborate fortifications in and around Cassino. From the vicinity of the monastery the German defenders could pour a withering fire on the Allied troops on the flat ground below. What to do? Should an attack on the sacred Catholic shrine be ordered or not? After some grim soul-searching the decision was finally made. On February 15, 1944, 1,500 tons of bombs were dropped to pulverize the old monastery in a record-breaking air assault.

There were immediate repercussions. The Allied press justified the bombing as a "necessary act of war." It was said that only volunteer bombardiers of the Catholic faith were permitted on the all-out raid. The monastery would be rebuilt after the war (as, indeed, it was). But to the Germans and Italians this was a "barbaric crime."

MONKS OF THE CASSINO CLOISTER
DESCRIBE THE ATTACK

(Deutsche Allgemeine Zeitung, *Berlin, February 19, 1944. Translated by the editor.*)

"At the end of the attack there was nothing left."

By Our Correspondent

ROME, February 18—In Rome there is the greatest indignation because the time-honored old Benedictine Monastery of Monte Cassino has been almost wholly destroyed. It was a devilish work of destruction without any military justification whatever. A 1,400-year-old cultural monument of the Occident has fallen sacrifice to the terror of American fliers.

A special correspondent of the *Corriere della Sera* describes an interview he has had with three monks of the Benedictine Monastery of Monte Cassino who fled to a cave at the foot of the hill. They are Father Don Salconio, Nicola Clementi, and Brother Zaccaria Diraimo.

Don Salconio is the bishopric delegate of the diocese of Monte Cassino, Nicola Clementi the administrator of the monastery.

At 9:45 on February 15, so they said, just after the reading of canonical prayers, they heard the steady drone of aircraft directly above the monastery. Many artillery shells had already fallen since February 8 near the cloisters and had wrought much damage on the outer walls and the roof.

"However, what happened on February 15 I can never forget, even though I was once a soldier. We were all with our bishop and Abbot Gregorio Diamare in the back of our air-raid shelter. And then came the first bombs. The walls shook and we could hear the noise of their cracking. The treasury of the church, in the middle of the cloisters, was the initial target of the American fliers. At the end of the attack there was nothing left. Out of the smoke and the thick dust of the fallen ruins came the cries of the wounded and the whimpering of the children."

As he spoke, Father Salconio wept over the destruction of his monastery, where he had spent most of his life. For three months, as if by a miracle, it had escaped the general blood bath. That night they managed to stay alive in the air-raid shelter. Then they saved themselves by walking along the steep cliffs and hiding in a cave. They were rescued by German soldiers.

To the question whether German troops or German combat positions were in the monastery, Father Salconio and the others responded with an emphatic "No!" He insisted that never were German soldiers quartered inside the cloister walls. He is now going to Rome to report to higher authorities about the situation.

THE FINAL HOURS OF MONTE CASSINO

(La Nazione, *Florence, Italy, February 20–21, 1944. Translated by Alba Rosa Bettazzi.*)

"A crime of unbelievable ferocity."

ROME, January 19—Christianity, and with it the civilized world, will be grievously appalled by the destruction of the old monastery of Monte Cassino, which represents, with its fourteen centuries of glorious life, pages of holiness, of civilization, of learning. This inestimable treasure, one of the most picturesque monuments of the Church, has been destroyed in a fury of vandalism by Anglo-American bombardiers who could never really justify their work of destruction as a necessary act of war.

The venerable abbot, Father Diamare, almost 80 years old, together with a small number of colleagues endured the tragic last hours of the monastery. With excruciating sadness of heart at the destruction of the holy walls they finally left the smoking ruins because of the fires caused by the bombs. They left only when there was nothing more to take care of or to save, when death and desolation had come to the holy spot, when there was no more life in it.

On the morning of the 17th everyone left the place where peace had reigned. The old abbot was first. In his trembling hands, due not to old age but to the sorrow that afflicted him, he had a crucifix. Father Martino, Father Agostino, and the lay brothers Pietro, Giacomo, and Rocco followed him, all terribly sad. Following them were about 600 civil evacuees, who had come to the holy mountain in the belief that war would certainly not touch St. Benedict's house. The laity supported the more dangerously wounded. Father Diamare began to say the rosary as the sorrowful procession began the sad emigration.

They descended the mountain by the side called San Rachisio just opposite the national road and which through great spirals reaches Cassino. The singing procession headed for Villa St. Lucia some five kilometers from Cassino. The passage was without any important incidents, although the gunfire continued. The abbot and the monks took shelter in a little country house transformed into a first-aid station by the Red Cross.

Yesterday morning all of them were taken by German trucks to Rome where they arrived at 5 o'clock at the International College of St. Anselmo. Father Stotzingen, head Benedictine abbot, warmly welcomed Father Diamare and the other brothers. The meeting was very touching. In the convent there were other monks who had been present at the destruction of the monastery. The corridors and the halls were crowded with people from Cassino who came for news about their relatives and friends.

The Benedictine, Father Odorigo Graziosi, secretary of the diocesan office of Catholic Action of Monte Cassino, wrote a brief report on the dramatic days of Monte Cassino, based on information given by a German official passing through Florence. The latter told a Stefani Agency reporter what had happened to the monastery during the last few months from the first shell until the day of final destruction.

"After the order for evaculation of people and objects of art was given on October 14," he said, "Abbot Diamare, with five brothers, a priest, and five laity remained in the monastery. With them there were about 150 people—farmers' families who lived in the neighborhood of the monastery. The number of these people increased more and more in recent months with the arrival of evacuees from Cassino and its environs. They settled in a spot near the monastery which they regarded as a neutral zone.

"At the doors of the monastery three German policemen (instead of Italian *carabinieri*) stood guard. Several monks remained inside the monastery to take care of it and the grave of its founder, St. Benedict. After the monks were gone, it was decided to protect the treasures of the monastery, such as the archives, the library, some relics, and paintings of great value. As we recall, the German authorities saved them by bringing them to Rome and placing them for safekeeping in the hands of the Vatican.

"Considering the heavy fighting around the monastery, it was feared that the famous edifice could not be saved from enemy destruction. The first shells were dropped on Monte Cassino in the early days of January. The monastery was damaged, but, fortunately, not seriously. A shell reached the little courtyard, hitting an ancient large marble pillar belonging to the Apollo Temple. The second one went into the Priests' Cloister, but it dug into the ground without causing any damage with the exception of breaking the cloister windows. The third shell went into the church through a window, hitting an oil painting by Luca Giordano, representing the consecration of the church in the eleventh century at the time of Father Desiderio who became Pope Victor III. The splinters also slightly damaged the frescoes of the wonderful ceiling. As the battle became more and more violent, shells began to fall more frequently on the monastery. The high point of intensity was reached on February 5 and subsequent days.

"It must be repeated that in Monte Cassino monastery there were no German soldiers and absolutely no defensive or offensive posts. It was never occupied by German troops. There was only one German guard instead of three as there had been earlier and that was in the last part of January. The only German guard was removed so that there remained in the monastery only eleven monks and three families (sixteen people in all), who worked in the monastery and who had not been able to leave because they were ill.

"The shelling of February 5, 8, 10, and 11 damaged the top floor of the monastery, the chapter of the church, the choir in the arcade called 'Paradise' and that called 'Purgatory,' and also the very old bronze doors of the church constructed in Constantinople in the 11th century, as well as other places. Shells killed ten civilian evacuees who had taken refuge there since February 5.

"The first Anglo-American bombing came on February 15. From 9:30 A.M. to 2 P.M. they came in several waves. The monks remained near the abbot as they resignedly prayed for death. Bombs of every size exploded with tremendous crashes. The monks could hear the buildings fall.

"Soon wicked flashes of fire appeared in different part of the monastery. Flames destroyed the diocesan pharmacy, some parts of the college, and the electric works in the old part of the monastery. Big bombs split open the bottom of the water tank in the cloister as well as the one in front of the church. Strange to say, the water ran red as if it were life blood.

"The monks were miraculously saved. The ceiling over them was very strong. Surrounded by ruins, the monks were able to dig a passage to safety only after the hardest kind of work. Unfortunately, that portion of the ceiling under which some 200 evacuees had taken refuge, crashed down. None of these evacuees was saved. Others were more fortunate because the ceilings over them held fast.

"Once having grasped the meaning of the disaster, the monks sought refuge elsewhere. They helped the evacuees. It was suggested that they leave the smoking ruins of the monastery. As soon as they were out there was another big bombing. Some monks left that same night. There remained the abbot, two monks, four lay clergy, and the wounded or dead civilians.

"The shelling went on during the night. In the afternoon of the next day some Anglo-American bombers dropped more bombs and fired machine-gun bullets at the convent. This time a part of the monastery called St. Benedict's rooms, arranged as chapels, with frescoes and richly ornamented, was ruined.

"Concluding that life was impossible at Monte Cassino, the abbot and the other monks finally decided to leave the ruins. But the wounds, as those of every member of St. Benedict's family and of every believer, are still there, in that place sanctified by martyrdom, where the holy corpse of the great saint lies.

"The monastery will be built again, more splendid and more glorious than ever. Bombs and shells destroyed the stones, but not the faith which has always overcome barbarism."

Anzio: Homer Bigart Reports How U.S. Observer, Circled by Nazis, Orders Barrage on His Own Post

[February 20, 1944]

"What difference does it make? Go ahead and shoot."

Many people have been disappointed with the progress there [*in Italy*] since the capture of Naples in October. This has been due to extremely bad weather which marks the winter in a supposedly sunshiny land and which this year has been worse than usual. Secondly, it is because the Germans bit by bit have been drawn into Italy and have decided to make exertions for the retention of the city of Rome.

Thus spoke Prime Minister Winston Churchill to the House of Commons in early 1944. The Allies in Italy faced not only problems of rough terrain and atrocious weather but also the determination of the Germans to hold fast. About sixty miles south of Rome the Germans set up a powerful defensive line along a favorable natural barrier. Here they stationed nearly 100,000 men.

Allied strategists reasoned that, if the German Gustav Line could not be breached, why not outflank it? Accordingly, on January 21, 1944, the American Fifth Army under the brilliant General Mark Clark, together with British units, made a spectacular leap-frog jump to the beaches near Anzio, thirty miles south of Rome. Protected by a great umbrella of planes, the invaders quickly carved out a beachhead about ten miles wide and six miles long.

The Germans reacted as if by Pavlovian reflex. Instead of retreating, they stayed on the high ground of the hinterland and poured a murderous fire down on the closely packed Allies on the low and marshy beachhead. Within a couple of weeks the prospects for a quick breakthrough disappeared. It seemed to be Dunkirk all over again.

It was a unique beachhead. Bill Mauldin, the American war artist, described it as the only place in Europe which held an entire corps of infantry, a British division, all kinds of artillery and special units, with an immense supply and administration setup, but without a rear echelon.

325

There was no rear. There was no spot on the beachhead which could not be covered by enemy shells. Mauldin described it:

> You couldn't stand up in the swamps without being cut down, and you couldn't sleep if you sat down. Guys stayed in those swamps for days and weeks. Every hole had to be covered, because the 'popcorn man' came over every night and shovelled hundreds of little butterfly bombs down on your head by the light of flares and exploding ack-ack. You'd wake up in the morning and find your sandbags torn open and spilled on the ground.

The Americans and British caught on Anzio lived close to death but they managed to survive. They set up signs all over the beachhead— "42nd & BROADWAY," "BEACHHEAD HOTEL: SPECIAL RATES TO NEW ARRIVALS." Since there was no place to go when off duty, the troops made the best of an unhappy situation by indulging in beetle racing, which became extremely popular. There were plenty of beetles swarming out of the slit trenches. Various colors were painted on the backs of the insects. The entries were placed in a glass jar in the center of a ring six feet in diameter. Then the jar was lifted. The first beetle out of the circle was the winner.

For five months these beleaguered troops were little more than beetles themselves. Eventually, they, too, broke out toward Rome.

There were tales of heroism from both sides. One of the best was this story by Homer Bigart, veteran correspondent of the New York Herald Tribune.

(New York Herald Tribune, *February 20, 1944. By permission of the New* York Herald Tribune.)

WITH THE 5TH ARMY ON ANZIO BEACH HEAD, Italy (Delayed)—A young American artillery observer, finding himself surrounded by German infantry in today's fluid fighting southeast of Carroceto (Aprilla), performed the highest act of heroism possible for a field artilleryman. He ordered a barrage put down on his own position—a farmhouse which was being overrun by enemy troops.

In a steady, quiet voice, this twenty-four-year-old lieutenant, a former Mid-West school teacher, gave by telephone the co-ordinates of the yellow concrete farmhouse from which he had observed and reported a German advance. At the other end of the wire Captain Harry C. Lane, of Tulsa, Oklahoma, protested, but the voice said firmly: "What difference does it make? Go ahead and shoot."

A moment later shells from twenty howitzers crashed down upon the farmhouse and surrounding area. The telephone went dead.

It was assumed that the lieutenant either was killed by the barrage or was taken prisoner by the Germans, who, despite heavy losses, remained in control of the area. He had been warned at dawn by Major Franklin T. Gardner, of Tulsa, that the Allied outpost line probably could not withstand another attack. He was told that when the infantry retired to new defensive positions he should fall back with them.

But the lieutenant had won the Silver Star in December by staying after infantry had fled. In that action near Venafro, he called for fire on his own position. The barrage killed scores of Germans and broke up their counter-attacks. The lieutenant came out uninjured, and possibly he figured today that he could do it again.

So, when the Germans began their infiltration tactics the lieutenant kept lowering the range of Allied guns until the heavy howitzer shells were bursting a few hundred yards in front of the farmhouse. His protecting screen of infantry began to retreat and the lieutenant sent his own men back with them. They took the radio, leaving him alone with a telephone.

For thiry minutes the lieutenant continued to adjust two fire missions—on the Germans approaching the farmhouse and on another enemy group just beyond. Then the Germans closed in. The lieutenant adjusted the fire first to the right of the farmhouse, then to the left. He told Captain Lane that he was burning his codes. Then he said: "All right, pour it on."

A Dog's Life: Love at First Sight Wins a Battle
on the Italian Front for a Shrewd Canadian
[February 24,1944]

"... thoughtless of anything but love."

In February 1944 William H. Stoneman sent one dispatch after another to the Chicago Daily News *describing the melancholy situation of Allied troops trapped on the exposed Anzio beachhead. On February 24, as a welcome relief, he reported by special radio a minor incident from Naples.*

(*Chicago* Daily News, *February 24, 1944. By permission of the Chicago* Daily News.)

NAPLES, February 24—The fatherland was betrayed in unseemly fashion a few nights ago by its most faithful servants—an odd collection of Dobermans and police dogs which had been set to guard a stretch of German lines against Allied night patrols.

The Canadian troops facing this section of the German front had been having trouble with the German hounds, all of which were trained to bark like mad the minute they heard or smelled our troops moving around in the dark. One patrol after another had been found to retire before accomplishing its mission.

Then a Canadian soldier, who knew something about dogs, had a happy thought.

The next night the Canadians took their own kennel out into no-man's-land—a lady dog.

There was no barking that night, and when the patrol returned to the Canadian lines its kennel had increased. A small flock of enemy dogs brought up the van, thoughtless of anything but love. Frantic attempts were made to catch the pack, but most of the dogs had to be shot.

This is one not so secret weapon about which even the Germans, obviously, just cannot do anything.

328

Cassino: Christopher Buckley, London *Daily Telegraph*, Watches an Operation in Destruction

[March 16, 1944]

"I scarcely remember since Alamein such a pandemonium."

All through February 1944 the Allies hammered away at Cassino in Italy. They managed to take one-third of the city. On the night of March 16 there was a terrific aerial bombardment, described by Christopher Buckley in the dispatch printed here.

The raid virtually leveled Cassino. Yet, when the Allied troops sought to extend their hold on the city, they found the streets so choked with rubble that they could not use their tanks. Ordered by Hitler to hold or die, the Germans fought desperately in the cratered streets. Once again they had stopped the Allies.

Cassino finally fell on May 18 after a week of bloody fighting by General Mark Clark and his Fifth Army. In the meantime the Poles entered the monastery on the hill above the town.

(*London* Daily Telegraph, *March 16, 1944. By permission of the London* Daily Telegraph.)

Between breakfast and lunch to-day, in brilliant weather, I saw Cassino flattened from the air by persistent, almost ceaseless, bombing over the space of nearly four hours.

General Alexander, C.-in-C. in Italy; Lt.-General Devers, Deputy Supreme Commander; Lt.-General Eaker, commanding Mediterranean Allied Air Forces; and General Mark Clark, commanding the Fifth Army, watched the operation, which is officially described as "unsurpassed in the history of warfare."

Picture to yourself this fantastic backcloth of hills, rising sheer above the plain, with the town of Cassino and the thin silver stream of the Rapido River at its foot dominated by the shattered and whitened ruins of the monastery. Beyond in a majestic semi-circle are the snow-capped peaks of the Apennines. That was the spectacle

329

at which American and British troops in turn have gazed fruitlessly during the past two months. For more than three weeks a profound calm had settled on this front. To-day there was a change, abrupt and dramatic.

Punctually at 8:30 A.M. it started. The first wave of medium bombers, silver-grey against the serene dispassionate blue of the sky, hummed overhead, perhaps 8,000, perhaps 10,000 feet up. In the calm spring sunshine they passed on their majestic way towards the town. One saw them dip, saw the bombs, tiny black specks, released one after another.

Then below, spout after spout of thick black smoke leaped from the earth, from the town itself, joined and coiled slowly upwards like some gigantic monstrous dark forest of fantasy until three-quarters of the town was completely obscured in a widening and deepening dark smudge.

I counted some 18 separate waves, averaging from 18 to 36 bombers in each, between 8.30 A.M. and noon. The mediums started the ball, then the heavies. Fortresses and Liberators, took up the running. Finally, the mediums came in once more with some extremely accurate bombing slap on the town itself. It was during that last hour, I should judge, that the major part of the damage was done.

There is a quality of lordly, even arrogant, impersonality about a bombing attack on this scale, particularly when, as was the case to-day, there was an almost total absence of opposition.

Standing on the hillside, in perfect safety in the pleasant spring sunshine, it was easy, perhaps too easy, to feel compunction; but I was in Warsaw on September 1st, 1939, and I remember from the evidence of my own eyes who was responsible for letting loose this terrible weapon.

The attack had a clear-cut and definite object—to destroy every building in Cassino and reduce to rubble the ancient stone houses concealing the countless guns which have so stubbornly blocked the Fifth Army's advance in Italy. Every unit of the Mediterranean Allied Air Forces was in action. Fortresses, Liberators, Marauders, Mitchells and Bostons were supported by Lightnings, Thunderbolts and Spitfires as escorts. It is believed that the total number of sorties to-day is likely to have exceeded 3,000.

At noon the operation passed into a fresh phase when the British artillery opened up in immense strength against the entire German front line on the Rapido sector at and on either side of Cassino. I scarcely remember since Alamein such a pandemonium—I use the word advisedly. The shell-bursts of our 25-pounders looked pigmy beside the immense explosions caused by the bombing, but they were wonderfully accurate and one could see that the entire enemy line was being plastered preparatory to our next move. The noise was greater than ever and far more constant. It seemed impossible that anything could live in the tortured, pounded rectangle which formed the enemy's forward line.

The mass air attack on Cassino had long been expected after the failure of the earlier infantry assaults in January and February, but its delivery was delayed for about three weeks by a serious break in the weather.

There is no doubt that the Germans have organised their defence in depth and have left the smallest possible number of troops in the more vulnerable forward positions. Even here they will be dug in deeply, with concrete and steel emplacements and other devices. To-day's massive assault will at least provide a test case of the possibilities of this method of attack. Our air forces dropped 1,400 tons of bombs on an area of less than one square mile. The town is now absolutely unrecognisable.

"Lili Marlene": Edgar Clark on the Bitter-Sweet Song That Became Top Favorite of Both Axis and Allied Troops

[March 31, 1944]

"It manages to do something all Tin Pan Alley has failed to do."

World War I produced a fair quota of great songs, including "Keep the Home Fires Burning," "There's a Long, Long Trail A-Winding," "Tipperary" and "Over There." Early in World War II a sad, bitter-sweet German song, "Lili Marlene," rose to the top in the song hit sweepstakes and stayed there. Its haunting melody became familiar all across North Africa, in Sicily, in Italy, as well as in Germany.

When the Americans got to Europe, they were supplied by Tin Pan Alley with such dubious classics as "Shoo-Shoo Baby," "Boogie Woogie," and "Take It Easy." No wonder, then, that G.I.'s, too, fell for the charms of "Lili Marlene." "Our musical geniuses at home," said Bill Mauldin, the famed cartoonist, "never did get around to a good, honest, acceptable war song, and so they forced us to share 'Lili Marlene' with the enemy. Even if we did get it from the krauts it's a beautiful song, and the only redeeming thing is the rumor kicking around that 'Lili' is an ancient French song, stolen by the Germans. It may not be true, but we like to believe it."

Here is a story written by Edgar Clark for the G.I. newspaper, Stars and Stripes, *about "Lili Marlene."*

(Stars and Stripes, *Sicily edition, March 31, 1944. Courtesy of the U.S. Army.*)

WITH THE 5TH ARMY—When German composer Norbert Schultze penned the bitter-sweet song, "Lili Marlene," he may have had some hopes that it would become a favorite of Nazi marching men. But he couldn't possibly have foreseen that the haunting and wistful "Lili" would also become a favorite in the Allied camp.

The story of "Lili Marlene" dates to the early days of the war. The song gained immortal fame during the years of war in the Western

Desert. Germany's famed *Afrika Korps* sang it during the long desert marches, sang it until the Korps itself disappeared in the debacle of Cape Bon.

"Lili Marlene," by all the rules of war, fell captive at Cape Bon. Britain's 8th Army picked it out of captivity, put English words to it and once more the tune went on the march, this time through Sicily, across the Straits of Messina and up the boot of Italy.

But "Lili Marlene" was no stranger in Italy. The Italians, lovers of music as they are, had long before fallen victim to its haunting strains. Many an Italian "juke box" told the story of "Lili Marlene" and when the juke boxes quit, the signorine carried on.

Here, too, the Americans are learning "Lili Marlene" from the Tommies and the signorine, but mostly the signorine. If the American doesn't know a girl who speaks English, he learns it in Italian.

"Lili Marlene" is a simple song—as all great songs are. It is the story of a girl and a soldier and the usual hopes of the two put down to music that is good for marching, cafe singing and humming to one's self on lonely outposts. But it manages to do something all Tin Pan Alley has failed to do.

War being what it is, the privileges of copyright ownership have little value, particularly to the enemy. But perhaps Author Schultze will draw some comfort from having written a universal hit and the copyright owners, Apollo-Verlag, Paul Lincke, Berlin, will have the pleasure of hearing the Allies sing it as they march into the German capital.

Here's a copy of the verse as translated from German to Italian by N. Rostelli and from Italian to English by Capt. Vincent A. Cato-zella. There are as many variations in the choice of words as there are translations but the ideas of all are essentially the same.

Lili Marlene

Outside the barracks, by the corner light,
I'll always stand and wait for you at night.
We will create a world for two,
I'd wait for you, the whole night through
For you, Lili Marlene, for you, Lili Marlene.

Bugler, tonight don't play the call to arms,
I want another evening with her charms.
Then we must say goodbye and part.
I'll always keep you in my heart
With me, Lili Marlene, with me, Lili Marlene.

Give me a rose to show how much you care,
Tie to the stem a lock of golden hair.
Surely tomorrow you'll feel blue,
But then will come a love that's new
For you, Lili Marlene, for you, Lili Marlene.

When we are marching in the mud and cold,
And when my pack seems more than I can hold,
My love for you renews my might,
I'm warm again, my pack is light.
It's you, Lili Marlene, it's you, Lili Marlene.

Sevastopol: Harrison Salisbury Relates How Death, Not Ships, Arrived for 25,000 Germans Trapped on Russian Shelf

[May 19, 1944]

"The whole Sevastopol area looked like a military junk yard."

Red correspondent Alexei Tolstoy had this to say on July 2, 1942, when the Russians abandoned Sevastopol: "Sevastopol will be again ours." He was right.

In a series of crushing blows the Red Army struck at the Germans in the north, in the center and in the south. In April and May it surged on Sevastopol and threw the Germans into the Black Sea. This was but one of the blows that cleared the invaders from Russian soil.

In the dispatch reprinted here, Harrison Salisbury, writing for United Press, tells about the death of the German 17th Army. There were 25,000 Germans trapped on the one-mile wide Sevastopol shelf. They waited in vain for evacuation ships.

(*Newark* Evening News, *May 19, 1944. By permission of United Press International.*)

SEVASTOPOL (U.P.)—This is the story of the death of an Army—the German 17th Army—which was literally blasted to bits on a gaunt, three-mile stretch of the Khersones Peninsula waiting for evacuation ships that never came.

Correspondents flew here from Moscow to view the scene of the 17th's death under blows so terrible, according to our Red Army guides, that during the last days the Germans assigned a guard over Maj. Gen. Gruner, one of two surviving generals, to prevent him from committing suicide.

From the red sandstone shores of Khersones Peninsula, I saw hundreds of German bodies littering a 15-foot ledge along the narrow, rocky beach. These were the bodies of Germans drowned attempting to reach boats or killed in the final Russian charge.

That shelf was all of Russia that remained for them to cling to. Behind them was only the sea and their sunken ships.

Other dead carpeted the three-mile stretch. Into this peninsula, for 60 hours after the final capitulation of Sevastopol, were jammed 60,000 Germans. The slaughter in that area, roughly three miles long and one mile wide, was epic.

When the battle was over, shortly after 10 A.M. on May 12, some 25,000 were prisoners. The others were dead.

You couldn't walk more than a yard or two in any direction without stepping on a body.

Lt. Gen. Sergei Birjuzov, chief of staff of the Fourth Ukraine front and newly promoted and decorated for this campaign, told correspondents that between April 6 and May 12 the Germans had evacuated 25,000 men from the Crimea—little more than 10 per cent of the forces left to defend it.

The battle cost the Germans four generals—Lt. Gen. Boehme, commander of the Fifth Army Corps; Maj. Gen. Gruner, commander of the 111th Infantry Division; S. S. Lt. Gen. Kurt and Maj. Gen. Reinhardt, commanders of the 98th Infantry. Boehme and Gruner were taken prisoners. Kurt and Reinhardt were found dead on the battlefield.

The whole Sevastopol area looked like a military junk yard. The Khersones promontory was covered with wrecked tanks, field and siege guns. Along the shore were remnants of small rafts the Germans had attempted to use for escape.

Thousands of papers swirled in the dust—passports, military documents, letters, playing cards. Interspersed were other relics—German song books, prayer books, postage stamp albums, bullet-punctured blouses, broken helmets, heaps of ammunition.

Russian salvage crews swarmed over the battlefield like ants, sorting usable parts from wrecked ME-109 and FW-190 planes, trucks and tanks.

The City of Sevastopol itself is rubble. In a 90-minute drive through the streets I saw only five buildings which appeared habitable. Mayor Vassely Yetrimov estimated that 10,000 civilians remain from the prewar population of 100,000. I saw only 30 civilians.

He told us that only 15 per cent of the city was still standing when the Russians abandoned it in 1942. He now estimated about only 3 per cent still stood. About 500 houses are habitable, he said, and a bakery and bath house have been set up. The military has established a 150-bed hospital and two clinics.

The harbor is a mass of wrecked hulks and mines which must be removed before ships can enter.

D-Day: Five Combat Reporters Describe the Greatest Invasion in History as Hitler's Fortress Europa Is Smashed From Air, Sea and Ground

[June 6, 1944]

UNDER THE COMMAND OF GENERAL EISENHOWER, ALLIED NAVAL FORCES, SUPPORTED BY STRONG AIR FORCES, BEGAN LANDING ALLIED ARMIES THIS MORNING ON THE NORTHERN COAST OF FRANCE.

This was communiqué No. 1 from Supreme Headquarters, Allied Expeditionary Force, issued at 9:00 on the morning of June 6, 1944. This, at long last, was it! This was the day for which the Allied world had waited patiently. An enslaved continent was on the verge of liberation. Hope was born again in the hearts of millions.

To the troops under his command General Eisenhower issued an order of the day:

Soldiers, sailors and airmen of the Allied Expeditionary Force: You are about to embark on a great crusade, toward which we have striven these many months. The hopes and prayers of liberty-loving people everywhere go with you. In company with our brave Allies and brothers in arms on other fronts you will bring about the destruction of the German war machine, elimination of Nazi tyranny over the oppressed peoples of Europe, and security for ourselves in a free world. . . .

The tide has turned. The free men of the world are marching together to victory. I have full confidence in your courage, devotion to duty and skill in battle. We will accept nothing less than full victory.

Good luck and let us beseech the blessing of Almighty God upon this great and noble undertaking. . . .

President Roosevelt was moved to broadcast a prayer for the Allied troops in France:

Almighty God: Our sons, pride of our nation, this day have set upon a mighty endeavor, a struggle to preserve our Republic, our religion and our civilization, and to set free a suffering humanity.

Lead them straight and true; give strength to their arms, stoutness to their hearts, steadfastness in their faith. . . .

With Thy blessing, we shall prevail over the unholy forces of our enemy. . . .

There was a dramatic story behind the great invasion. For two years Joseph Stalin, dictator of Russia, had clamored for a second front. But Roosevelt and Churchill would not be stampeded by propaganda or tantrums into a premature assault that might be thrown back into the sea. The preparation was slow, careful and effective.

After two years of invasion planning, a giant host of nearly two million American, British and Empire troops was massed in the British Isles. It was a striking force of tremendous power. After months of painstaking maneuvers and false "wet runs," this vast power was unleashed on Hitler's Fortress Europa. Operation Overlord, planned to the minutest detail, was the greatest amphibious invasion of all time.

On June 6, 1944, a great armada of 4,000 ships, guarded by 702 warships, set off from southern England to invade the Normandy coastline. A flotilla of mine sweepers cleared the way. The big guns of Allied battlewagons smashed the German coastal batteries, while sleek destroyers dashed in to rake the shores with shellfire. Overhead the skies were alive with some 11,000 Allied warplanes of all types and descriptions, unloading tons of bombs on the enemy below. In the interior, paratroopers floated to earth to take key points, while gliders brought in more and more assault troops. And a maze of landing craft pushed ashore to unload their human cargoes.

By the end of that day more than a quarter of a million Allied troops, mostly Americans and British, were ashore at four beaches on the soil of France. It was a military achievement such as the world had never before seen. The "decadent democracies" had opened the eyes of an astonished Fuehrer.

Hundreds of first-rate battle reports came from the battle areas on D-Day. Following are five of the best, chosen to illustrate the great day from the air, the sea and the land. This was reporting in depth, the finest type of combat journalism.

D-DAY FROM THE AIR

(Roelif Loveland, Cleveland Plain Dealer, June 7, 1944. By permission of the Cleveland Plain Dealer.)

"I'd sure hate to do this for a living," said the sergeant.

A NINTH AIR FORCE MAURAUDER BASE IN ENGLAND, June 6—We saw the curtain go up this morning on the greatest drama in the history of the world, the invasion of Hitler's Europe.

We saw it from a balcony seat high up in God's heaven, in a combat Marauder piloted by a Cleveland boy, First Lieutenant Howard C. Quiggle, 17118 Lipton Ave., S.E. Flak flew about us and tracer bullets missed us by uncomfortable margins, but our bombardier dropped sixteen 250-pound bombs on military installations near the area in which our troops later were to come ashore for the invasion.

Being only one of thousands riding the tail of a comet to see history in the making leaves a witness drained of all emotion and too numb to be very articulate.

With a chance to write something immortal, such a witness realizes that words sometimes are weak.

How can words describe properly the deathless bravery that the world saw on the shores of France? How can words describe properly a sky filled with planes, fighters, bombers, risking life itself to give the infantry the best possible chance to succeed? What magnificent teamwork!

The fliers did not wear shiny armor when they went out to their planes, the sleek, fast, deadly Marauders. They looked bulgy, and no man can look otherwise who is wearing a Mae West life preserver, a parachute, a flak suit, earphones, and a flak helmet: Before we got into the plane we had to remove all personal letters and such. I was assigned to Lieutenant Quiggle's plane, the *Dottie Dee*, named after his wife. When you start out on a strange adventure at that time in the morning you sort of like to be with a hometown boy. It's kind of scary, no fooling.

The moon was in the sky when we started, and it followed us all along, and presently we were riding over clouds which looked like cotton wool of a lavender color. I can't imagine that heaven could be more beautiful. But angels would probably ride the clouds better than we could have done it if the *Dottie Dee* had not been purring along sweetly.

Purring is a bad word. The *Dottie Dee* roars, but your earphones sort of dim the noise. When you are in a fighting plane advancing toward the enemy the plane becomes your one little world and none of the sweet things of life exist any more. And your fellows become the most important people in the world, even more important to you than Mr. Churchill or Mr. Roosevelt.

I stood up front behind the pilots and watched England fade from view. And not long afterward, so perfectly had the job been synchronized, we saw the invasion ships.

The sea—the Channel, if you prefer—was thick with them, as thick with ships as the sky was thick with clouds. In addition to the big landing craft were large naval vessels, and fighters were hovering over the ships guarding them.

Nothing which could have been thought of to save life was spared. The lads had everything which it was humanly possible to give them.

We saw our own naval vessels shelling the daylights out of German installations on the French coast. We could see the red flames as the shells struck home. They were big shells.

Flak began to come pretty soon, and tracer bullets shot in front of us like red-hot rivets, but the expression on the face of the kid from Cleveland who was piloting the plane did not change in the slightest degree. He followed the course to the target, and then the bombardier did his stuff, and the plane fairly leaped up in the air and down before flames shot up.

Then we started back. We had taken off at 4:45 A.M., but by now it was light. Guns shot at us again, but missed badly. The Allied battle wagon was continuing to pour in shells.

In a few minutes all danger seemed to be past. Later, when all danger was past, the sergeant with twenty missions to his credit remarked: "I'd sure hate to do this for a living."

Daylight showed strained faces, and we got back at breakfast time.

One will never forget the sight of the ships and the landing craft heading for France any more than a knight would have forgotten the appearance of the Holy Grail.

WITH THE SKY TROOPS

(Leonard Mosley, London Daily Telegraph, *June 9, 1944. By permission of the London* Daily Telegraph.)

"Thank God you've come now, monsieur."

June 6—At two minutes past one this morning I parachuted into Europe—six-and-a-half hours before our seaborne forces began the full-scale invasion. I was near the shore, hiding from Nazi patrols as I watched our first forces go ashore from the sea at 7:15 A.M. These paratroops and glider-borne troops I consider the bravest, most tenacious men, I have ever known. They held the bridgehead against Hitler's armies for over sixteen hours, despite overwhelming odds. I believe that the things they have done are almost solely responsible for the great success of the invasion so far in this sector.

Our prime job as an airborne force was to silence a coastal battery, which might otherwise have blown our ships to bits as they came to the shore. We silenced it.

Our other job was to secure two important bridges over the canal and river north of Caen and to hold them against all comers until the main armies arrived. We are still holding them. They are still intact.

I emplaned in "C. for Charlie," a great black bomber, at 11:20 last night, and we took our place in the taxi-ing line of planes that stretched from one end to the other of one of the biggest airfields in Britain. There were Lancashire men, Yorkshiremen and Northumbrians.

Half an hour before us went the gliders and paratroopers who were going to try to take the vital bridges before they could be blown up. It was our job to bring them aid within thirty minutes of their surprise attack, and to prevent the Nazis from counter-attacking.

As our plane, the third in the formation, took the air and pointed for France, little Robson, next to me, was singing softly.

It was five minutes to one when the light snapped off and a door in the plane was opened. Under it we could see the coast of France. Flak from the coast defences was spouting flame everywhere.

The red light flashed and swiftly changed to green, and we were all shuffling down the hole and jumping into space. We knew we were going down to enemy territory covered with poles and holes, and thick with Nazis waiting for us.

I looked, as I twisted down, for the church I had been told to use as a landmark, but the wind caught me and was whisking me east. I came down in an orchard outside a farmhouse.

As I stood up with my harness off and wiped the sweat of my brown-painted face I knew I was hopelessly lost. Dare I go to the farmhouse and ask for directions? Suddenly there was a rip and tear in my flapping jumping-smock, and I flung myself to the ground as machine-guns rattled. There were two smashing explosions—hand-grenades. I could now see figures manoeuvring in the moonlight. I dived through a tangle of barbed wire into the next field, and began to run at the crouch.

Then, suddenly, at the farther edge there were two more figures, and they were coming towards me, carrying guns. There was a crash of Sten-gun fire, and both men crumpled up not 15 yards from me. Into the field stealthily came five men to challenge me—and I was with our own paratroopers again.

For two long weary hours we wandered the country. We hid from

German patrols in French barns. We shot up a Nazi car speeding down a lane. A youth appeared with a German flask full of Normandy wine, and after we had drunk it he led us away from the enemy. Just after 3 A.M. we made our rendezvous.

I dropped my heavier equipment and made my way to the bridges, where the battle had ceased. Over both the river and the canal, spans were in our hands and firmly held by paratroop machine-gunners. Only beyond, in the west country, could the noise of battle be heard as we beat back a German counter-attack. The situation was grim. We had taken the Nazis by surprise, but they knew what was happening now and we could expect their tanks at any moment.

At 3:20 A.M. every Allied paratrooper breathed a sight of relief as he heard the roar of bombers towing gliders towards the dropping ground. We watched the gliders unhooking and then diving steeply for earth. One, hit by A.A., caught fire and flew around like a ball of flame. We heard the crunch of breaking matchwood as gliders bounced on rocks and careened into still-undestroyed poles. But out of every glider men were pouring, and jeeps and anti-tank guns and field guns—and we knew that even if Nazi tanks did come now we could hold them.

And now, as a faint glow began to appear in the sky, there was a roaring that rapidly grew to a thunderous roll. The climax of Phase One of the invasion was approaching. Bombers were swarming in like bees to give the coastal defences their last softening-up before our seaborne forces landed.

We were about two miles away, but the shudder of explosions lifted us off the ground. Soon the sky was lit with a green and purple glow from the burning German dumps, and still more bombers came in and more bombs thudded to earth.

As dawn came I moved across country through Nazi patrols to get nearer to the coast. Everywhere there were traces of our airborne invasion—empty containers still burning their signal lights, wrecked gliders, and parachutes. It was hazardous going; one Nazi patrol was within a few yards of us, but we hid in a quarry and dodged them. Eventually we reached high ground overlooking the coast and waited until our watches showed 7:15.

A few minutes before it there was an earth-shaking holocaust of noise. Approaching the coast under cover of naval ships, the invasion barges were coming in, and firing as they came. It was a terrific barrage that must have paralysed the defences.

Then ships began nudging towards the beaches, and we shook hands in the knowledge that the invasion had at last begun.

By 10 A.M. the area of ground where we had established head-quarters was getting a roasting from shells and mortar bombs. Prisoners were coming in now. I went into the village to drink a glass of cider with the Mayor. "Thank God you've come now, monsieur," he said. "Next week all the men in the area were to be conscripted to drape barbed wire across the poles in the area where you dropped." He arranged to give us a regular supply of milk and eggs from the farm. "I've three sons in Nazi prison camps, and I hate Boches," he said. "We have waited a long time for the hour of liberation."

There were children playing in the streets unmindful of the war only a few yards away.

Just outside the town, along the road to Caen, one paratroop unit was fighting a grim battle against the Nazi panzers, including two Panther tanks. One of the posts had been over-run and their anti-tank guns destroyed, but everywhere men were fighting desperately yet confidently.

I made my way back to the bridges to contact one of our units holding the bridgehead on the other side. The road was impassable, and one walked at a crouch through a ditch. Every few hundred yards one "ran for it," with snipers' bullets smacking the mud around. Nazi counter-attacks were coming every few minutes. But these Lancashire lads were holding on, though their numbers were growing hourly smaller. The unit fought on until all opposition from the north-west ceased, and to their delight and relief a long line of green bereted men came into view. They were men of a noted commando unit.

More panzer grenadiers and self-propelled guns were massing on our southern flank. Around 6 P.M. a counter-attack was reaching full strength. We were all asking ourselves: Will relief come—relief from the sky?

They did not let us down. It was just on 9 P.M. when the sky was suddenly filled with twisting and turning fighter planes, and under them a great fleet of bombers and gliders. As the gliders unhooked they wheeled through clots of ack-ack fire and dived steeply for earth. They were bigger gliders this time. Smoothly, with only a low whine of wind, down they came. It was a glorious sight. It lasted half an hour and became a maelstrom of noise as the Nazis tried vainly to hold them back. But I saw only one glider and one tug-plane hit. Then they were all down on the dropping ground and more men and more guns were pouring out. A general said to me, "Well, it's very satisfactory. It is still all going according to plan." We are confident it will continue to go according to plan.

FROM AN AMERICAN NAVAL FLAGSHIP
IN THE ENGLISH CHANNEL

(CBS broadcast by George Hicks, June 6, 1944. By permission of George Hicks.)

"If you'll excuse me, I'll just take a deep breath for a moment and stop speaking . . ."

This is George Hicks speaking. I am speaking now from a tower above the signal bridge of an American naval flagship and we're lying some few miles off the coast of France where the invasion of Europe has begun. It's now twenty minutes to six and the landing craft have been disembarked from their motor ships and are moving in in long irregular lines towards the horizon of France which is very plain to the naked eye.

Our own bombardment fleet lying out beyond us has begun to blast the shoreline and we can see the vivid yellow burst of flame quite clearly although the sound is too far away to be heard, and at the same time from the shore are answering yellow flames as the Nazi batteries are replying.

Overhead planes are high up in the thin cloud which is a gray screen over the sky but which is not thick nor heavy, and is not low enough to be an inconvenience to bombing.

The LCT's and LCI's have begun to pass along the side of us. Those are the amphibious beach-landing craft that carry the tanks, trucks, the bulldozers, and finally the men ashore. They have been churning along and are bouncing along in the choppy channel sea now, and all around us on either side are stretched the vast transports at anchor, which have disembarked the small craft. All over the surface of the sea here they can be seen cutting and zigzagging and then falling into those somewhat irregular lines that make a black pencil-point across the sea itself, heading towards the ribbon of land that's France and the coast of Normandy. . . .

It's now becoming quite near daylight as six A.M. approaches on June 6th, 1944. . . . We can hear the thud of shells or bombs landing on the French coastline, perhaps eight or ten miles before us, and the steel bridge on which we stand vibrates from the concussion of the heavy guns that are firing on the American and British battleships and heavy cruisers on the long line right behind us. I can count twenty-two of the squat square-nosed landing craft, carrying vehicles ...as they turn and bounce in the chopping sea awaiting the exact timing to form their lines and start in toward the beach.

On our first (*static*) ... it was the shore batteries of the Nazis that had spotted us here at sea (*static*) ... and our naval bombardment squad has replied to them.

One battleship is in as close as three miles, and one of the famous American battleships, the *Texas* was ... (*static*) ... finally in her firing position. (*Static*) ... battleships lying just a couple of miles off the French shore and firing broadsides into the land. The Germans are replying from the land with flashes and then the battleship lets go with its entire broadside again. The whole side of the battle-wagon lights up in a yellow flare as a broadside goes off, and now we can see brown and gray smoke drifting up from her, from her gun-barrels ... and now batteries are firing from the beach ... the broadsides of the battleship are pouring it back at them. Overhead, high, planes are roaring ... they just came in and dropped a salvo of bombs. ...

The, (*static*) ... One of America's famous cruisers, is in off the shore near (*static*) ... as well as the *Texas*, the *Nevada*, and the *Arkansas;* old battleships ... They're just anchored off shore and blowing into the Nazi batteries on shore ... The first Allied forces are reaching the beaches in France. ...

That baby was plenty low!

I think I just made the statement that no German planes had been seen and I think there was the first one we've seen so far ... just cleared our stack ... let go a stream of tracers that did no harm ...

(*Sound of ship's whistle*)

Our own ship has just given its warning whistle and now the flak is coming up in the sky. ...

It's planes you hear overhead now ... they are the motors of Nazis coming and going. ... The reverberation of bombs. ...

(*Sound of crash*)

That was a bomb hit, another one. That was a tracer line, shaped arching up into the darkness.

Very heavy firing now off our stern. ... Fiery bursts and the flak and streamers going out (several words drowned out by voice in background and static) in the flak.

(*Sound of explosions*)

Now, it's died down. ... We can't see the plane. ... Here comes a plane. ... More anti-aircraft fire ... in more toward the shore ...

the Germans must be attacking low with their planes off our stern because the streamer fire of the tracers is almost parallel with the water. (*Noises in background*) . . . Flares are coming down now. You can hear the machinegunning. The whole seaside is covered with tracer fire . . . going up . . . bombs . . . machinegunning. The planes come over closer (*sound of plane*), firing low . . . smoke . . . brilliant fire down low toward the French coast a couple of miles. I don't know whether it's on the shore or is a ship on fire.

Here's very heavy ack-ack now—(*heavy ack-ack*)—right . . . the plane seems to be coming directly overhead . . . (*sound of plane and machinegun fire and ack-ack*)

Well, that's the first time we've shot our guns . . . directly right over our head . . . as we pick up the German bombers overhead.

VOICE: What was that—a bomb?

VOICE: Cruiser firing over there.

HICKS: Heavy fire from the naval warships . . . twenty mm. and forty mm. tracer . . . was the sound you just heard. . . .

Well, it's quiet for a moment now. . . .

If you'll excuse me, I'll just take a deep breath for a moment and stop speaking. . . .

Now the air attack has seemed to have died down. . . . See nothing in the night. . . .

Here we go again! (*Noise*) Another plane has come over . . . right over our port side . . . tracers are making an arc right over the bow now . . . disappearing into the clouds before they burst. . . .

Looks like we're going to have a night tonight. Give it to her, boys . . . another one coming over . . . a cruiser on . . . pouring it out . . . something burning is falling down through the sky and hurtling down . . . it may be a hit plane. (*Terrific noises in background*) . . . Here he goes . . . they got one! (*Voices cheering*) They got one! (*Voice:* Did we?) Yeah . . . . Great splotches of fire came down and are smoldering now just off our port side in the sea . . . smoke and flame there. (*Various sounds and voices in background*) . . . The lights of that burning Nazi plane are just twinkling now in the sea and going out. . . .

To recapitulate, the first plane that was over . . . was a low-flying German JU-88 that was leading the flight and came on the convoy in surprise, we believe, because he drew up and only fired as he passed by, and perhaps he was as surprised as we were to see each other. . . . One bomb fell astern of this warship, a hundred and fifty yards away as the string of rockets were fired at a cruiser beside us on the port side. No damage was done and gun number forty-two at our port, just beside the microphone, shot down the plane that fell into the sea off to the port side. . . . Scheiner (?) of Houston, Texas, who is the gunnery control officer, and seaman Thomas Snyder (?) of Baltimore, Maryland, handled the direction finder. It was their first kill for this gun and the boys are all pretty excited about it. A twin-barrel forty mm. anti-aircraft piece.

They are already thinking of painting a big star on their chart and will be at that first thing tomorrow morning. . . . It's daylight. . . .

REUTER CORRESPONDENT FOR THE COMBINED ALLIED PRESS ABOARD A BRITISH DESTROYER

(*Desmond Tighe,* The New York Times, *June 7, 1944. By permission of* The New York Times.)

"By now everything is an inferno."

ABOARD A BRITISH DESTROYER, OFF BERNIÈRE-SUR-MER, June 6—Guns are belching flame from more than 600 Allied warships. Thousands of bombers are roaring overhead and fighters are weaving in and out of the clouds as the invasion of Western Europe begins.

Rolling clouds of dense black and gray smoke cover the beaches southeast of Havre as the full fury of the invasion force is unleashed on the German defenses. We are standing some 8,000 yards off the beaches of Bernière-sur-Mer and from the bridge of this little destroyer I can see vast numbers of naval craft of all types.

The air is filled with the continuous thunder of broadsides and the crash of bombs. Great spurts of flame come up from the beaches in long snake-like ripples as shells ranging from four to sixteen inches find their marks. In the past ten minutes more than 2,000 tons of high-explosive shells have gone down on the beachhead.

At 7:25 A.M., through glasses, I could see the first wave of assault troops touching down on the water's edge and fanning up the beach. Battleships and cruisers were steaming up and down drenching the beaches ahead of the troops with withering broadsides. The guns flashed and great coils of yellow cordite smoke curled into the air. Great assault vessels were standing out to sea in their hundreds and invasion craft were being lowered like beetles from the davits and heading toward the shore in long lines. They were crammed with troops, tanks, guns and armored fighting vehicles of all types.

The British and Canadian forces in this sector were cheerful and smiling as they went in. A tank-landing craft passed with the crew of one tank, sitting on top of the open hatch. They gave the thumbs-up sign and grinned as they passed.

Bombers passing over by thousands could not be seen, as they were well above cloud level, but the air reverberated with the thunder of Flying Fortress engines. We could see the bombs crashing down on the German gun positions and defenses just inland of the first assault troops.

Fighters kept up a constant patrol protecting this great invasion fleet. Spitfires and Airacobras streamed overhead below cloud level. So far there has been no enemy air opposition at all.

The invasion fleet came over to the shores of northwestern France unmolested. Just ahead of us lay the little town of Bernière-sur-Mer; we could see the spire of the belfry rising out of the swirling smoke.

Some German shore batteries opened up on us, but their fire was ineffective and ragged. Away on our port beam, a destroyer had a ding-dong duel with one battery, and great coils of water plunged up around her as the German gunners tried to find their mark.

Other destroyers were streaking up and down close in-shore protecting the landing troops and plugging shore batteries with shells. The gunfire was so terrific that we were deafened.

The plans for the invasion allowed for four separate phases: landings by air-borne troops and paratroopers in the rear; a tremendous full-scale night bombing by the Royal Air Force on the landing beaches; a sea bombardment by more than 600 battleships, cruisers, monitors and destroyers, and finally a daybreak bombing attack by the full strength of the United States Army Air Forces just after dawn and before the initial landings went in.

From the bridge of this destroyer I have had a grandstand view of every phase.

As we plunged through the Channel on the last stages of our trip late last night, we heard the roar of plane engines as wave after wave of air-borne troops passed overhead. It was just after 4 A.M. when we reached a position some eighteen miles off France. The night bombing was in full swing, and from the distance we could see enormous blood-red explosions and heard the rumble of bursting bombs.

What followed is described by the diary kept on the bridge. It was cold and, wrapped in duffle coats and thick mufflers, we watched the dawn come in and the invasion start in all its intensity. The times are British Double Summer Times.

5:07 A.M.—Lying eight miles from the lowering position for invasion.

5:20—In the grey dawn the great shapes of innumerable assault ships appear smudgily on our starboard beam. A little MTB follows in our wake, obviously off course. A young signalman stands on the bridge and flashes: "We are lost. Please direct us to such and such a beach." We put him on his way.

5:37—The night bombing has ceased and the great naval bombardment begins. The wind is high and from our position we can hear little sound.

5:33—We move in slowly and the coastline becomes a thin smudge of gray.

5:36—Cruisers open fire on our starboard bow. We can now recognize the *Belfast* and the *Mauritius*. They are firing tracers and we see the shells curving in a high trajectory toward the shore.

5:45—The big assault ships start lowering their boats, crowded with troops. There are at least 1,000 ships of all sizes in our sector. The naval bombardment intensifies.

The big battleships join. On our port bow we see H.M.S. *Warspite*, the old lady of Salerno fame, belching fire from her 14-inch guns. The *Orion*, the *Mauritius* and the *Black Prince* are belting away with all they have. Fleet destroyers are darting around us.

5:50—I saw the first flash from a German shore battery. Above us we hear the sweet drone of our fighter cover. The sky is cloudy but has a fairly high ceiling. Four Spitfires pass overhead. So far not one German plane has put in an appearance, but it is yet early. It appears that we have taken the Germans by surprise.

5:55—On our port beam I can see a thin line of stout tank landing craft heading toward the shore. Gray mine-sweepers that have been close in shore sweeping are returning.

6:00—The coast is clearly visible. German batteries are opening fire spasmodically. The cruisers continue to belt away, taking on shore targets. One of Britain's brand-new Captain class frigates passes. The bombardment continues and by now big fires are burning ashore. Clouds of black smoke rise hundreds of feet into the air.

6:30—The whole invasion fleet is now waiting just seven miles off shore.

6:30—The destroyers now close in on the shore, bombarding any target that they can see. A string of tank landing craft passes us. The troops wave. Weather is growing worse, the sky is turning gray and big clouds are coming up. Spitfires and Airacobras roar over.

The first wave of Fortresses—their wings gleam through small patches of clouds. Mostly they are invisible. The roar of the Fortress engines, coupled with the shriek of bombs and crashing of shells is terrific. The coastline is by now covered with palls of smoke. One pattern of bombs flattens out the beach section opposite our destroyer. An inferno of battleships, cruisers, monitors and destroyers are giving the Germans all they've got. It is by now quite light. I can see the spire of the Bernière's belfry. We are 900 yards from the shore and still closing. The town is covered with smoke. Buildings appear to be smashed and crumpled. Now 800 yards off shore.

The first wave of landing craft has reached the shore. I see them touch down. Red tracers from close-range enemy weapons are searing across the beach. Men leap out of the craft and move forward. Tanks follow them. By now everything is an inferno.

ACTION ON THE AMERICAN BEACHHEAD

(Don Whitehead, Associated Press, June 6, 1944. By permission of Associated Press.)

"Hundreds of troops . . . burrowed shallow trenches in the loose gravel."

As our boat was lowered from the transport it heaved and pitched, but it swung clear and we joined the other small craft bobbing about among the big transports stretching as far as I could see. . . . We could see the warships' guns flash and the explosions ashore. Gradually we moved toward shore. Some men leaned over the sides and vomited, seasick after only a few minutes in the boats. . . . A plane exploded in the air with a shower of sparks. Behind us came ducks wallowing through the swells. I didn't see how they could make it in such rough water, but I did not see a single one in trouble. Behind them followed the whole amphibious family of strange looking craft, loaded with troops and equipment. We patrolled offshore for a while, then headed for the beach. . . .

The enemy on the right flank was pouring direct fire on the beach. Hundreds of troops, pinned to the cover of the embankment, burrowed shallow trenches in the loose gravel. No one was moving forward. The congestion was growing dangerous as more troops piled in. Snipers and machine gunners were picking off our troops as they came ashore. . . .

Then the brigadier began working to get troops off the beach. It was jammed with men and vehicles. He sent a group to the right flank to help clean out the enemy firing directly on the beach. Quietly he talked to the men, suggesting next moves. He never raised his voice and he showed not the least excitement. Gradually the troops on the beach thinned out and we could see them moving over the ridge.

Courage Under Fire: Richard D. Macmillan Reports No Purple Heart for Tilly

[June 27, 1944]

". . . She was the first dog to enter the war-ravaged citadel."

Richard D. Macmillan, United Press correspondent, found the homeless pooch, named her for the town in which he picked her up, and then made her known to the entire world in this dispatch describing her courage under fire.

Wounded by shrapnel, the correspondent was sent back to London for treatment. Here he learned the sequel to his own story, related to him by Captain Philip Dunn:

She died in action. We were under heavy mortar fire during the battle for Caen. Tilly tried to cross the road under a barrage of shells to join us. Suddenly a group of British tanks crashed down the road. For once Tilly lost her nerve, hesitated, and was crushed to death under the treads.

In a subsequent dispatch McMillan wrote that Tilly was buried beside the road. "Her marker reads merely, 'Tilly,' but scores of American and British soldiers will remember her as the dog who shared field rations with privates and generals alike, who was the first French dog to welcome General Charles de Gaulle when he landed and who stood at attention when King George VI arrived on the Normandy beach."

(*United Press, June 27, 1944. By permission of United Press International.*)

WITH AMERICAN FORCES IN CHERBOURG, June 27 (U.P.)—We found her amidst the powder and rubble of the shellswept little township of Tilly-sur-Seulles when the British battered their way through after nearly two weeks of bitter fighting. That is why we christened her Tilly right away.

She was shell and bomb happy and she shivered nervously and whined and whimpered. She was an ersatz fox-terrier puppy of about five months. Just another battlefield stray. She joined our party.

Today she is a veteran of both British and American fronts—a heroine of the capture of Cherbourg, and if she were able to write front-line dispatches, she could begin by saying she was the first dog to enter the war-ravaged citadel. That's true, and she would have a story to tell, too.

The French are not travelers. I think she must be of English ancestry. Her taste for travel suggests it. She goes into the front lines every day. When we start off, she comes to the jeep and puts her forepaws up and gets lifted in, since she is too small to jump.

Then she stands with her feet planted on someone's stomach as we whizz through the countryside.

It's true she does not like gunfire. It sends the tiny stump of her tail drooping. But she never shows signs of deserting. She has suffered the thunder of Monty's famous barrages and has been strafed by machine guns time and again.

But her worst taste of fire happened with the Americans during the siege of Cherbourg.

We went forward toward the rip-snorting, crackling bonfire of the battlefield. Below us the port spouted smoke and sparks like a mighty railroad engine at full belch.

Flames seethed and swayed over the arsenal's rooftops around Fort du Roule.

Some tanks came over the brow of the hill to the east of Octeville.

"Let's go down that way," someone suggested.

Our jeep bumped over the shell craters past dead Germans and Americans, freshly killed and awaiting burial, through narrow lanes past the grinning skulls of ruined houses. We edged through the tanks and came to a field.

It began to look hot as the enemy barrage came closer. Up the hill toward us we could hear the thunderous whoof of each burst, and deadly black smoke poured up through the trees ahead.

Tilly's tail went down. She looked at us with appealing eyes and seemed to say: "Boys, shouldn't we be getting out of this?" We ignored her.

We did not hear her whine, or the shell or the explosion in the continuous din about us. I got it in the back—a piece of shrapnel just below my spine. A young sergeant next to me was killed outright.

A few others, mainly officers, were badly wounded, their noses, mouths, and ears trickling blood. One captain crawled feebly towards me, a hole in his back the size of a pudding basin.

They took me to the dressing station where they patched me up.

The doctor told me to get an X-ray since the splinter might still be beneath the skin.

In the meanwhile, we had forgotten about Tilly—that is we forgot about her until we saw her shivering. For she had been hit too. A splinter had struck her square between the eyes and blood oozed down the soft velvet star over her nose. After we had bathed her wound, she thanked us with her customary lick behind the ear.

The American doctor told me, "You can get a Purple Heart for this if you wish."

I told him that I didn't deserve it, that the Purple Heart should be only for soldiers who were doing the real fighting. Besides, I said to myself, if I deserved a Purple Heart, what about Tilly?

Liberation of Russia: Vassili Grossman with the Red Army in Poland and Byelorussia

[June–July, 1944]

"From east to west, from the Volga and the Caucasian mountains, flows the river of blood and tears."

During the year 1944 the soil of Russia was finally cleared of the German invaders. From January to June a series of sledge-hammer blows descended upon the once arrogant but now hapless Germans. Slowly but inevitably Hitler's armies were pushed from Russia. In June and July, while the Allies stormed the beachheads of Normandy in the west, the Red Army moved against the Germans in Vitebsk, Bobruisk and Mogilev and encircled entire divisions in the Minsk area. The whole Byelorussian Soviet Republic was liberated as Red troops reached the Vistula and occupied a considerable part of Poland.

The Russian propaganda machine hummed with activity. "In these days and hours," was the word, "every Soviet man and woman must remember that each kilometer nearer to the frontier calls for us to exert every effort, and to be prepared for every conceivable trick on the part of the Fascist gangsters." And again: "We shall expel the Germans from our soil like a swarm of scorpions, vipers and locusts."

One of the leading Soviet war correspondents, Vassili Grossman, wrote the following story. With the Red Army in Poland and Byelorussia. It is powerful writing but with no understanding of the difference between straight reporting and editorializing. So great was Russian hatred for the German invader that virtually all Soviet war correspondents, from the famous to the obscure, wrote their dispatches as if they were in a propaganda mill. This was their way of fighting the enemy.

(*From* With the Red Army in Poland and Byelorussia, June–July, 1944 *by Vassili Grossman [London, n.d.], pp. 38–43. By permission of Hutchinson & Co., Ltd.*)

We have covered over hundred kilometres with our advancing troops in the past three weeks. The division with which I set out on my travels is now far beyond the Niemen. From the upper reaches of the Dnieper to the upper reaches of the Niemen our way lay through dense forests of leaf and cone, through fields of rye, wheat and barley, across sandy soil and yellow wastes of clay, over leafy hills and through shady valleys, along rivers, brooks, and rills that glistened in the light of sun and moon; and through the streets of burning towns and cities.

Never, in all the three years of war, have troops had to deal with such dust on the roads. The dust was not so thick, so penetrating, in the Ukraine in 1941, or even on the steppes of the Don and Stalingrad regions in the summer of 1942. There are moments when the cars slow down and stop, for the bright sunlight is suddenly obscured by a yellow fog that hides everything from view a few centimetres from one's eyes. Dust runs down the windshield like water. It coats the armour of the tanks, the muzzles of the guns, the faces and clothing of the men. The green woods are milky white with the myriads of dust particles that have settled on the foliage. The dust swirls up in clouds like the smoke of a tremendous con-flagration, as though the earth were ablaze. And truly the earth is burning.

Dry forests, set on fire by the shells, burn with a heavy red flame, and acrid blue-and-white smoke merges with the yellow dust of the forest roads. It is often hard to breathe, and people's eyes grow blood-shot and inflamed because of the dust and smoke. And up above shines the white-hot sun of July. There has not been a cloud in the sky for several days.

After the mud of the winter offensive many longed for that scourge of warfare—dust. But now their song is: Oh, for some rain and some mud! Anything rather than dust!

When the offensive began, when the first shells went over, the grain was still green in the fields. Today the ears are full, and the stalks have grown yellow, streaked with copper and gold. People look about in glad surprise. Such a short time ago, only a month, the grain was still young and green. A month ago our troops were on the Dnieper and the Drut. . . . It is hard to fight under the merciless sun, in the smoke of burning forests and villages, in the dust of sixteen-hour marches. But the spirits of our warriors are high. One can often hear singing through the dust, and the strains of accordions resound from passing cars and from the jolting wagons of the regi-mental baggage trains. It is only on the road that one really comes to understand why the accordion is the true instrument for the soldier at war. There is not another instrument in the world that a person could play in a truck speeding down bumpy roads, or in a cart rumbling over cobblestones. The *balalaika* would perforce remain silent, and so would the horn. But your accordion-player is never bothered by bumps. Down goes the truck into a rut, and everything in it flies up in the air—fuel tanks, and boxes of hardtack, and the packs of the men sitting on top of the load. And just at that instant the accordion, tossed skyward together with its player, emits such a jolly, rousing strain that everyone on the road smiles involuntarily, and looks to see from whence it comes. And how well a witty, acid sally is appreciated: what full-throated laughter greets a clever jest.

During a brief halt the men lie down to rest in the shade of a tree. A liaison man named Skvortsov comes riding up—a short, pock-marked fellow, one of the veterans of the division and a participant in the most ferocious and bloody battles of this war. He sits astride a big German horse and carries a German tommy-gun slung across his chest. He is just itching for a laugh. Like most really humorous people, Skvortsov maintains the utmost gravity in telling his funniest stories. This peasant knows the true roots of laughter as well as do the world's famous humorists. Now he explains that he has formed a pen friendship with three women in the rear. One of them, he says, has bought a cow for him; the second a gold watch; and the third a new suit, only it's the wrong size. And he meditates aloud as to which of the three he ought to marry. In a few minutes his audience, including the author of these lines, is prostrated with laughter, so amusing are the arguments he adduces for and against each candidate. Yet he speaks of these friendly women with genuine respect, and with gratitude for their letters.

Finally he remarks to a girl in Red Army uniform:

"Well, Raya, that's how it is. We're all booked up in the rear, and you poor girls'll get left when the war's over. Chasing after pips on your shoulder-straps! I'm sorry for you—honest to God, I am!"

And the girls smile in enjoyment.

Skvortsov whips up his horse, but it refuses to budge.

"Get a move on, Frau!" he shouts. "Get a move on! I'll teach you to fight for liberty . . . !"

And he disappears into the dust. The men look after him, exclaiming:

"What a fellow! Good boy, Skvortsov!"

Their dust-inflamed eyes have been cleared by their laughter, as though rinsed with fresh, cold water.

An hour later the men move on. Their eyes are heavy, their faces grim and stern, as they watch the flaming villages. Such is the soul of our people, in whom inexorable resolution goes hand in hand with a ready smile.

In these past weeks I have visited many towns in liberated Byelorussia, visited them on the day of their liberation, or on the day after. Bobruisk, Minsk, Stolbtsy, Novogrudok, Baranovichi. . . .

Last year, during our offensive in the Ukraine, I saw Glukhov, Bakhmach, Nezhin, Kozelets, Chernigov, Yagotin, Korostyshev, Zhitomir, immediately after their liberation. I saw Odessa, Orel, Elista in the smoke and flame of the first day of freedom.

I have visited other towns at periods several weeks after their liberation: Voroshilovgrad, Kiev, Kharkov, Novograd-Volhynsk, Rovno, Lutsk, Krivoi Rog. . . .

And everywhere, everywhere, in the smoke and flame of Orel and Minsk, in the chilly ruins and grass-grown streets of Gomel, amidst the cold ashes of Voronezh, I read the frightful tale of the crimes of German Fascism. As we get nearer and nearer to the border it unfolds before us in ever-widening vistas, this scroll indited in the blood of millions of children and old folk—indited by the light of conflagrations, to the accompaniment of the groans and shrieks of the executed and the choked breathing of victims buried alive. For three years on Byelorussian soil the Hitlerites indulged in such brutality and foulness as has never before been encountered in history.

Minsk was an appalling sight, visible from afar as a cloud of smoke and flame. It was a city of prisons and concentration camps, bristling with barbed wire; a city fettered by Fascists; a city of torture chambers; a city half-dead, half-demolished, sodden with blood.

In the appalling winter nights the Germans shot down many thousands of unarmed prisoners of war in the streets of Minsk. Thousands of partisans were tortured to death in prison cells by the Gestapo, the police, the commandant's troops, the gendarmerie. Over a hundred thousand Jews were killed in Minsk in the course of two years—women, children and old folk; workers, engineers, doctors, office-workers. The executioners had mercy for none, neither for feeble old ladies, nor women in childbirth, nor new-born babes. They massacred their victims block by block. Or they murdered them trade by trade. They killed them all. Every kilometre of our march to the border adds new pages to this awful record.

There is not a village nor a town that has not victims to mourn.

During the fight for one village a seventy-five-year-old Byelorussian pleaded with our colonel to take him into his regiment.

"They killed all my folks," he repeated, over and over again. "They killed 'em all. Give me a rifle!"

A few days later, on the fringe of a wood that was still in the hands of the Germans, I met another old man. His beard was bristly and untrimmed, his eyes faded with age. He carried a rifle.

"Grandfather," I said, "it's time you rested. Don't you think you're too old for the partisans?"

"I've got to keep on," he said sadly. "The Germans killed my folks. They killed my old woman and my daughter and my grandchildren. And they burnt down my house."

He rose and strode towards a thicket crackling with tommy-gun and machine-gun fire.

From east to west, from the Volga and the Caucasian mountains, flows the river of blood and tears. From every village, forest hamlet or settlement, from towns and cities come the streams and rivulets to join the great torrent of the people's suffering and wrath. The sky is dark above, for ashes and smoke have blotted out the sun and stars. Only the smoky flames of the buildings the enemy fired on the banks of the Volga light the path of the river across the steppes of the Don, through the fields around Voronezh and Kursk, through the Orel woods and the valleys by Kiev and across the spaces of Volhynia.

And now there remains but a score or two of versts to the border. The river grows ever broader; its waters rush on with mounting speed. A deep, everlasting furrow marks the brow of the Soviet earth where this river has cut its bed. A people, grim and mighty, has been wrought upon the anvil of anguish and conflict.

The men of evil can already hear the murmur of pursuing vengeance. The cries of the innocent, the blood of the murdered, the tears of the mourners, have merged with the roar of our cannon, with the swift flow of steel that speeds on in conflict to the borders of the enemy's land. The night is coming to its end.

The day will be ours, on from the break of dawn. Let the guilty tremble!

Second Battle of Britain: Ernest Hemingway Tells How London Fought Hitler's Vengeance Weapon #1

[August 19, 1944]

"There isn't any woman and there isn't any horse . . . that is as lovely as a great airplane. . . ."

On D-Day plus six Hitler released his secret "Vengeance Weapon No. 1" on Britain. The pilotless plane, a bomb with wings and an engine to propel it, was destroyed when it exploded. Sent into the air by catapult from mystery installations on the northern coasts of France, ninety miles from London, the robot bombs, began to rain down from the skies. The British called them "bumble bombs" or "buzz bombs."

In three months some 8,000 of these bombs, at the rate of about 100 a day, were launched against England. British official sources revealed that out of every 100 flying bombs sent over by the Germans in the eighty days of the second Battle of Britain, 46 were destroyed by defense measures, 25 were inaccurate and plunged into the sea, or exploded in France, doing considerable damage to the Germans, and 29 got through to the London region. More than 1,104,000 houses were destroyed or damaged, as well as 149 schools, 111 churches, and 98 hospitals. Hampton Court Palace, St. Thomas's Hospital, the Royal Lodge, Windsor, and the Guards' Chapel were hit by V-1's.

Soon the German press was boasting that "half of England lies in ruins under the rain of flying bombs." German soldiers reported that they went "almost crazy with joy" when they heard of the secret weapon. "There was panic in London," wrote one storm-trooper, "the town was in flames, and we saw again how the Fuehrer had kept his word. It is now only a matter of his wonderful intuition when the final onslaught is going to take place to force the proud British on to their knees and make a vast desert of their country."

An accurate picture of how London fought the robot bomb was given by Ernest Hemingway, the American novelist turned reporter. Fascinated with bravery and death, a war buff all his life, Hemingway went to

360

Europe on behalf of Collier's *to describe the Battle for Paris, the Second Battle of Britain, and war in the Siegfried Line. Big, burly, bearded and brash, Papa Hemingway was a unique war correspondent. The day of the swashbuckling journalist was long past, but Hemingway neither knew it nor cared about it. He was never satisfied to be just an observer. It was said that he carried hand grenades and, on occasion, used them, set up his own headquarters, and dispatched his irregulars on reconnaissance missions.*

Hemingway's life ended on a note of mystery. It is believed that on a Sunday morning in early July 1961, he, clad in pajamas, went to the gun rack in his house at Ketchum, Idaho, took out his favorite twelve-gauge, double-barreled shotgun inlaid with silver, put the barrel in his mouth and pulled the trigger. The blast blew away the top of his head except for his mouth, chin and part of his cheeks. Thus death came to the master of lean, muscular prose whose credo had been: "There is no remedy for anything in life."

("London Fights the Robots," Collier's, *August 19, 1944. Copyright 1944 Estate of Ernest Hemingway.)*

The Tempest is a great, gaunt airplane. It is the fastest pursuit job in the world and it is as tough as a mule. It has been reported with a speed of 400 and should dive 'way ahead of its own noise. Where we were living, its job was to intercept the pilotless planes and shoot them down over the sea or in open country as they came in on their sputtering roar toward London.

The squadron flew from four o'clock in the morning until midnight. There were always pilots sitting ready in the cockpits to take off when the Very pistol signaled, and there were always a number of planes on permanent patrol in the air. The fastest time I clocked a plane as airborne, from the sound of the pop of the flare pistol that would arc a twin flare over toward the dispersal area from the door of the Intelligence hut, was fifty-seven seconds.

As the flare popped, you would hear the dry bark of the starting cartridge and the rising scream of the motor, and these hungry, big, long-legged birds would lurch, bounce, and scream off with the noise of two hundred circular saws hitting a mahogany log dead on the nose. They took off downwind, crosswind, any way the weather lay, and grabbed a piece of the sky and lurched up into it with the long, high legs folding up under them.

You love a lot of things if you live around them, but there isn't any woman and there isn't any horse, nor any before nor any after, that is as lovely as a great airplane, and men who love them are faithful to them even though they leave them for others. A man has only one virginity to lose in fighters, and if it is a lovely plane he loses it to, there his heart will ever be.

Mustang is a tough, good name for a bad, tough, husky, angry plane that could have been friends with Harry Greb if Greb had had an engine instead of a heart. Tempest is a sissy name out of Shakespeare, who is a great man anywhere, but they have put it onto an airplane that is sort of like a cross between Man o' War and Tallulah Bankhead in the best years either of them ever had. They were good years, too, and many a man has been taken by the bookies because he looked at a colt that had the swelling Big Red's neck had and not any of the rest of it. And there have been many husky voices since, but none that carried good across the Western ocean.

So now we have this squadron of Tempests. They were running out of terms for meteorological disturbances when they named that one. And all day long they shoot down this nameless weapon, day in and day out. The squadron leader is a fine man, tall, small-spoken the way a leopard is, with the light brown circles under his eyes and the odd purple complexion of a man whose face has been burned away, and he told the story of his exploit to me very quietly and truthfully, standing by the wooden table in the pilots' mess.

He knew it was true and I knew it was true and he was very precise in remembering exactly how it had been, because it was one of the first pilotless aircraft he had shot down, and he was very exact in details. He did not like to say anything personal but it was evidently all right to speak well of the plane. Then he told me about the other sort of shooting down. If you do not explode them in the air, you crash them.

"It is a sort of giant bubble of blast that rises from them," he said. "Bubble" has been quite a venturesome word to use, and he took confidence from it and tried a further word. "It is rather like a huge *blossoming* of air rising."

We were both embarrassed by this articulateness, and as my mind watched the giant bubble blossoming, all tension was taken away by an American flying in the same squadron, who said, "I dropped one on a greenhouse, and the glass rose straight up a million feet. What am I going to say to the guy who owns that greenhouse when we go into the pub tonight?"

"You can't just say exactly where you'll shoot them down," the squadron leader said, standing there, speaking shyly, patiently and with strange eagerness, from behind the purple mask he would always wear now for a face. "They go very fast you know."

The wing commander came in, angry, happy. He was short, with a lot of style and a tough, bad tongue. He was twenty-six, I found out later. I had seen him get out of an airplane before I knew he was the wing commander. It did not show then, nor did it show now when he talked. The only way you knew he was the wing commander was the way the other pilots said "Sir." They said "Sir" to the two squadron leaders, one of whom was a tough Belgian like a six-day bicycle rider, and the other was the shy, fine man who lived behind the destroyed face. But they gave a slightly different "Sir" to the wing commander, and the wing commander returned no change from it at all. Nor did he notice it when he pocketed it.

Censorship, in war, is a very necessary thing. It is especially necessary about aircraft because, until a new aircraft has fallen into enemy hands, no information as to the exact speeds, dimensions, characteristics or armament should be written, since all of that furnishes information the enemy wants and needs.

It is appearance, characteristics and performance that make a man love an airplane, and they, truly told, are what put the emotion into an article about one. They are all out of this article now. I hope the enemy never shoots down a Tempest, that the Tempest will never be released from the secret list, and that all I know and care about them can never be published until after the war.

All information about tactics employed in the shooting down of pilotless aircraft is out, too, along with all the conversation that would let you know how the types feel that do the shooting down. Because you cannot have the conversation without conveying the tactics. So there isn't much in this article now, except a guy loving an airplane. It is written in tough language because this was, in the main, a tough-speaking outfit. The only exception was the squadron leader, fragments of whose conversation are given. Some outfits in the R.A.F. are pretty rough spoken, and some speak as gently and correctly as in the film, Target for Tonight. I like ("like" is a very mild term to employ for the emotion felt) both kinds, and sometime, if it is ever possible to write anything interesting that the censor can conscientiously pass, I would like to try to show both kinds. In the meantime you get this.

Writing under censorship is necessary and proper in time of war, and we all censor out ourselves everything we think might be of any possible interest to the enemy. But in writing about the air on the basis of trying to include color, detail and emotion, there is a certain analogy to sports writing.

It is sort of as though in the old days you had found Harry Greb having a breakfast of double orders of ham and eggs and hashed brown potatoes in bed at nine o'clock in the morning on the day he was to fight Mickey Walker. Greb, placed on the scales, weighed exactly 12 pounds over the 162 he was to make at two o'clock that afternoon. Now suppose you had seen the weight rubbed and pounded off of him and got rid of by several other means, and him carried on the scales too weak to walk and almost too weak to curse you.

Then suppose you had seen the meal he ate and seen him enter the ring weighing exactly the same weight he had left bed with that morning. Then suppose you had seen the great, crowding, smashing, take it, come in again, thumbing, butting, mean, nasty, bloody, lovely fight he made, and you had to sum up the whole business in these terms: One of our fighters named Greb whose characteristics have not been revealed was reported to have encountered an M. Walker last night. Further details will be released in due course.

If this ever seems a screwy story, remember that through the sky at all times are passing pilotless aircraft which look, in flight, rather like an ugly metal dart with a white-hot bunghole, travel at speed up to 400 miles an hour, carry, as of this writing, 2,200 pounds of explosive in their noses, make a noise like a glorified motorcycle and, at the moment, are passing overhead the place where this is written.

One of my most esteemed colleagues told me in New York that he was not returning to the European theater because anything he might write would merely be a repetition of what he had already written. At this point I am authorized to state to my esteemed colleague that the danger of repetition in a story is one of the more negligible hazards that his old co-workers are at present confronted with.

Now if you are following this piece closely—which I am not, due to a certain amount of windowpane trouble—we should be somewhere in southern England where a group of Tempest pilots have in seven days shot down their share of pilotless aircraft. Lots of people call this weapon the doodlebug, the robot bomb, the buzz bomb and other names hatched in the brains of the keener Fleet Street types, but so far nobody I have ever known who has fought him has referred to Joe Louis as Toots. So we will continue to refer to this weapon as the pilotless aircraft in this release from your pilotless-aircraft editor, and you can call it any of those quaint or coy names you wish, but only when you are alone.

The day before your pilotless-aircraft editor started studying the interception angle, he or I (I guess it is I, although sometimes it doesn't seem the right man in the right place and I have thought some of leaving the whole thing and going back to writing books in stiff covers), went out in one of forty-eight Mitchell bombers— that is, eight boxes of six bombers each—to bomb one of the sites from which the pilotless aircraft are launched.

These sites can be readily identified by the merest tyro by the quantity of old Mitchell bombers which are strewed around them and by the fact that, when you get close to them, large, black circular rings of smoke appear alongside of the vehicle you are riding in. These circular black rings of smoke are called flak, and this flak is the author of that old piece of understatement about two of our aircraft failed to return.

Well, we (that is Wing Commander Lynn, who is nice company in an airplane and who has exactly the same voice on the intercom when Kees, the bombardier, has her held in on the run and is saying, "Bombing—Bombing—Bombing—Bombing—" as though you were not on the last mile) bombed this site with proverbial pin-point accuracy. I had a nice look at the site which appeared to be a gigantic concrete construction lying on its side or its belly (depending on whether you saw it just before the run or just after it) in a woods completely surrounded by bomb craters. There were two small clouds that didn't look lonely the way the clouds were in "I wandered lonely as a cloud."

There were many rings of black smoke in a line coming right straight alongside of us inside the box between us and where the other Mitchell on our right was going along in the air, looking just like a picture of a Mitchell in an advertisement by the manufacturers. Then, with the smoke rings forming along her side, the belly of this kite—looking just like in moving pictures—opened, pushed out against the air, and the bombs all dropped out sideways as if she were having eight long metal kittens in a hurry.

We all were doing this, although you could not see what anybody did except this one. Then we all went home just as fast as we could go home, and that is bombing. Unlike a lot of other things, the best part is afterward. I suppose it is something like going to college. It isn't so much how much you learn. It is the wonderful people you meet.

Your pilotless-aircraft editor never went to college (here we call it a university), so now he is going to R.A.F. instead, and the main subject he is studying is trying to understand English on the radio telephone. Face to face with an Englishman, I can understand almost everything he says. I can speak, read and write Canadian clearly and have a smattering of Scottish and a few words of New Zealand. I can understand enough Australian to draw cards and order drinks and to shove my way into a bar if it is crowded. South African I can dominate as a spoken tongue almost as well as I do Basque. But English over the RT is just a glorious mystery.

Close up, over the intercom in a bomber, I get most of it. When you press the button on the stick, that isolates conversation to what is said in the cockpit, so you have those long, intimate chats that go, "Wonder who that b—— is that's talking," and you answer, "Don't know. Must be the same Jerry that on the night of D-Day kept saying "Turn back. Turn back. The operation has been canceled!"

"Wonder how he gets on our wave length?"

You shrug your shoulders and take your thumb off the button. That close conversation I get all right, but when real Englishmen speaking English start talking to one another between one kite and another kite and back and forth from control, I just study it hard like homework, as if you had brought home somebody's calculus book and were still on the plane geometry.

Actually, I cannot understand English very well yet on the ordinary telephone, so, having been indoctrinated in the Good Neighbor policy, I always say, "Yes," and just make them repeat the time the car will be around in the morning to take us to whatever field we will be starting from.

This accounts for many of the curious sorties your pilotless-aircraft correspondent goes on. He is not a man who has a perpetual urge to seek peril in the sky or to defy the laws of gravity; he is simply a man who, not understanding very well the nature of the propositions offered over the telephone due to faulty earwork, constantly finds himself involved in the destruction of these monsters in their hellish lairs or in attempts at interception in that fine, 400-mile-an-hour airplane, the Mosquito.

At present, your pilotless-aircraft editor has stopped all telephone calls of any description in order to attempt to bring the story up to date before someone proposes something so startling and so generous to your editor in the nature of an operation that he would fail in his duties to this great book to have recorded what has happened up to this time. However, before all calls were stopped, two or three rather lovely propositions were received, and I understand that there is a feeling freely expressed in some quarters that, "Ernie is yellow. With a chance to go on absolutely wizard ops, he is up in his room at that pub, doing what do you think?"

"What?" in a horrified tone.

"Writing."

"My God! The old boy's had it!"

"To Be Forgiving": Virgil Pinkley, Reporting German Robot Attack on London, Contrasts a Dead Child and a Sermon

[August 21, 1944]

"The sobbing father said: 'Those dirty bastards. Those dirty bastards.' "

The recipients of Hitler's robot bombs often found it difficult to be forgiving of their enemies. Virgil Pinkley, United Press correspondent in London during the era of the flying bomb, gave this first-hand version of a latter-day conflict between faith and the trials of war.

(United Press, August 21, 1944. By permission of United Press International.)

LONDON, Aug. 21 (U.P.)—The radio church service was concluding as the pastor intoned: "Lord, teach us to be forgiving of our enemies."

Then, wham, and I "had it."

I was blown from one end of the room over a settee and against the wall at the other. My head roared. Gongs rang in my ears.

The radio had gone dead. I lay there against the wall, feeling my eyes. I heard glass falling. From outside came screams, moans and sobs. I got to my feet, swaying, smelling smoke. Through the broken windows, I saw a great funnel of debris 50 yards away.

The apartment was a mess and a robot bomb had hit only in the vicinity. One door was knocked off its hinges and another had had its lock ripped out.

Waiting for an elevator that did not come, I recalled that I had not heard that flying bomb roar in, nor the motor cut off. Usually just before they hit and loose their ton of explosive, the robots sputter and cough once or twice like a cold outboard motor before they cut off, glide briefly and explode. This one hadn't.

When I reached the lower floor the shattered glass of doors was littered half-way up the staircases. Reaching the street level reception hall, I walked over a crust of glass. At the doorway desk, the woman attendant was bleeding severely. A moment later an ARP first aid worker rushed up and applied a bandage.

"What a lovely Sunday morning packet!" she said.

I hurried several doors down the street to a large apartment house into which the flying bomb had ploughed near the top. Already ARP workers, bobbies, American GI's, sailors and Red Cross workers were arriving.

Stumbling through the doorway came a father carrying his four- or five-year-old daughter in his arms. The entire right side of her face had been sheared off. She was mercifully asleep forever. "Lord, teach us to be forgiving of our enemies." The radio preacher's edict rang through my brain.

The sobbing father said: "Those dirty bastards. Those dirty bastards." The American corporals said over and over as they backed their jeeps off piles of bricks: "Those . . . . Those . . . ." "Lord, teach us to be forgiving of our enemies."

Then came a steady stream of Sunday morning recipients of Germany's terror weapon, applied blindly to women, children and old people.

One young woman stumbled out on the arm of a policeman, her nightgown tied around her badly cut arm.

Two American MP's carried out an elderly man, still in pajamas, his injured head wrapped in a shirt.

I left the scene and walked past two beaten, broken churches, blasted in the big blitz of former years, and they reminded me of that dead child and the sermon.

I will never forget that child and—"Lord, teach us to be forgiving of our enemies."

Sensation at Notre Dame: Robert Reid, BBC Correspondent, Makes a Remarkable Running Commentary
[August 27, 1944]

"It was the most extraordinary example of courage I've ever seen."

General Charles de Gaulle had refused to submit to the Germans. On August 27, 1944, this tall, intense Gallic chieftain who had led his countrymen in the struggle against Hitler, arrived at the Cathedral of Nôtre Dame in Paris to join in celebrating a solemn Te Deum *to give thanks for the liberation. Some 40,000 people gathered around the mother cathedral of France to greet the French leader.*

Inside the church Robert Reid, a BBC correspondent, was stationed to record the ceremony. Little did he suspect that he was soon to witness a sensational scene. Nor did he know that his remarks turned out to be one of the most extraordinary running commentaries of the war.

(BBC broadcast on August 27, 1944. By permission of The British Broadcasting Corporation.)

Immediately behind me through the great doors of this thirteenth-century cathedral I can see, in this dim half-light, a mass of faces turned towards the door, waiting for the arrival of General de Gaulle, and when the general arrives, this huge concourse of people both inside and outside the cathedral, they'll be joining in a celebration of the solemn *Te Deum* in the mother church of France.

You may be able to hear that I'm talking amid the noise of tanks; now those are the tanks from General Leclerc's Division, the boys who were instrumental in punching a hole right through the German defences outside Paris and into the heart of the capital. I believe the original intention was that these tanks were going to be used as a guard of honour, but thousands of Parisians have now climbed on to the top of those tanks and I believe I can only see one track of the end tank. The police are having rather a bad time trying to keep the crowds back—they're all trying to press right through to the cathedral.

Immediately in front of me are lined up the men and women of the French Resistance Movement; they're a variegated set of boys and girls—some of the men are dressed in dungarees, overalls, some look rather smart, the bank-clerk type, some are in very shabby suits but they've all got their red, white and blue armlets with the blue Cross of Lorraine, and they're all armed, they've got their rifles slung over their shoulders and their bandoliers strapped round their waist. And now here comes General de Gaulle. The general's now turned to face the square, and this huge crowd of Parisians (*machine-gun fire*). He's being presented to people (*machine-gun fire*). He's being received (*shouts of crowd—shots*) even while the general is marching (*sudden sharp outburst of continued fire*)—even while the general is marching into the cathedral . . . (*Break on record*)

Well, that was one of the most dramatic scenes I've ever seen. Just as General de Gaulle was about to enter the Cathedral of Nôtre Dame, firing started all over the place. I'm afraid we couldn't get you the noise of that firing because I was overwhelmed by a rush of people who were trying to seek shelter, and my cable parted from my microphone. But I fell just near General de Gaulle and I managed to pick myself up. General de Gaulle was trying to control the crowds rushing into the cathedral. He walked straight ahead in what appeared to me to be a hail of fire from somewhere inside the cathedral —somewhere from the galleries up near the vaulted roof. But he went ahead without hesitation, his shoulders flung back, and walked right down the central aisle, even while the bullets were pouring around him. It was the most extraordinary example of courage that I've ever seen. But what was to follow was horrible, because it happened inside Nôtre Dame Cathedral. While the congregation were trying to take shelter lying flat on the ground under the chairs and behind the pillars, the firing continued at intervals; the police, the military, and the Resistance Movement—all these people, they came in and were trying to pick off the snipers. Some of the snipers had actually got on to the roof of the cathedral.

There was an awful din going on the whole time. Just by me one man was hit in the neck, but I will say this for this Parisian crowd, there was no real panic inside the cathedral at all; they simply took reasonable precautions. Round every pillar you'd see people shelter-ing, women with little children cuddled in their arms. I saw one child being carried to safety in the arms of a young priest who sheltered the youngster to his breast and carried it to the shelter of one of the pillars.

It was—as I say—it was a most extraordinary scene, as the snipers were spotted around the gallery by the police and by the soldiers, and there was a smell of cordite right throughout the cathedral. But Paris had come to celebrate the solemn *Te Deum* and it did; even while the firing was going on the people rose to their feet and stood there and sang the *Te Deum* with General de Gaulle at the head of them. And then, when it was all over, the general marched right down the aisle; heaven knows how they missed him, for they were firing the whole time; there were blinding flashes inside the cathedral, there were pieces of stone ricocheting around the place.

I saw him marching down the aisle, this very tall upright figure, with his chin well up in the air, his shoulders flung right back; and his exit was the scene of another attempt. There were battles—there were bangs, flashes all around him, and yet he seemed to have an absolutely charmed life as he walked down the aisle towards the door, because nothing touched him, and he never hesitated for one moment. And when he got to the door it was a signal for another burst of firing outside. But I don't know how many people have been hit; I doubt possibly whether very many have. As I say, I only saw one casualty myself.

But even now the firing's going on there are people still about the square, so I think the firing which is apparently coming from surrounding roofs must be rather erratic, because I can't see anybody being carted away. But a lot of people are taking shelter, and I don't mind saying that at the moment I'm just squatting cross-legged on the floor by the side of the cathedral making this recording; I thought it was rather a wise precaution to take. I didn't want to be too conspicuous standing up with the microphone in my hand.

That shouting and cheering you can hear is four prisoners just being taken away. These are four of the snipers who have been caught inside the church. They were all in civilian clothing—grey flannel trousers, and simple white singlets; they've got their hands above their heads, and they look very obviously Germans. They're being brought out by the gendarmes, and are now being taken through the square with crowds running after them hooting them. And even now firing is still going on here. (*Shot*) That was one that just came over us.

Return of the Native-by-Adoption: Gertrude Stein Describes Her Return Describes Her Return to the City to the City of Light

[August–September, 1944]

"Then there were such funny things, the Germans are funny."

Among the happy refugees who delightedly returned to Paris was the noted poet and novelist, Gertrude Stein. An American expatriate, Miss Stein had come to Paris in 1902 and, except for a lecture tour in America in 1935, had remained there until the defeat of France in 1940. She could not suppress her joy on returning to Paris, nor could she suppress her unique style with its emphasis upon simple diction, the monosyllabic, and patterns of sound.

(*From "We Are Back in Paris,"* Transformation Three.)

We in Culoz, Ain, along with most of France were liberated in August and September of 1944. It was wonderful to be liberated.

For several months, we were so busy just being excited and being liberated that we did not think of Paris. Yes in the darkest days of the occupation I was very homesick for Paris, I used to say that I was homesick for the quays of Paris and for a roast chicken, a roast chicken and the quays of Paris. Now every day I walk up and down the quays of Paris and the other day a friend took us to a restaurant and there we ate, perhaps we should not have, but we did eat—we ate a whole roast chicken. Basket the white poodle got the bones. So the liberation for us was complete and we are in Paris.

As I say for two months in Culoz and almost three we were so busy just feeling free and talking to everybody who was feeling free too that we almost forgot about going back to Paris and then we began to think about coming back, and we began to write to everybody to ask whether we could exist if we did come back. Some said we could and some said we could not. Some said that there was no light no food and no gas and that it was all dark and dreary

373

and some said it was very pleasant but no food but plenty of gas and light and others said plenty of food and plenty of everything and finally they wrote to us that the Gestapo in the month of August of '44 had been in the apartment and what was the state of the apartment, nobody seemed to want to say, and we were nervous. It was easy to be nervous.

All through the war I had been superstitious, I had not wanted anyone to mention the apartment to mention anything in it, it would be kind of safer that way, and then finally someone wrote that it was alright but frightfully dirty—and then finally some one found the nice Russian exile who had always cleaned our house when we came back and closed it up when we left and he apparently had weathered the storm and he had started to work and in three weeks our apartment would be as lovely as ever and so we made up our minds to come, and to come back the middle of December. It was cold and there were floods, and we had to have a camion and a taxi a wood burning one and we had to pack and we did not know whether to bring up everything we had accumulated in those five years or to give them away and finally we decided to bring up almost everything and we did, luckily we did.

We in the taxi were to start earlier that is to say at midnight and the camion later that is to say at day-break and we started.

It was midnight and we left the country and for us the war was over, we were taking the road to Paris, would we remember it, what it was like.

There was no more war there in the middle of December but there were floods, and the first thing we could not do was to take the regular road to Bourg so the driver decided to go by Hauteville and climb through the pass and then go merrily on to Bourg. It was midnight and we climbed and climbed and then there was snow on the ground and the driver jumped out and the car went on and he pushed it on with a sort of dancing run, it was strange and we felt strange, and then the car stopped, pushing was no more use, so he said he would back down the hill, that scared me so I got out and walked but the others not being used to driving were not scared so he backed down that hill in the snow in the midnight dark. It was strange, peace was being stranger than ever. Since I have been back in Paris I have asked a lot of American drivers if they could back down a twisting road at night in the snow for three kilometers and they said they would not like to. At least we were back to where we started from and decided to go by Lyon, that road was foggy and strange too everything was strange not being either awake or asleep it was all strange. I cheered myself up with American K rations. They are sustaining, crackers, sugar, candy and a touch of lemon, very comforting.

Every now and then the tyres they were ersatz tyres and that backing in the snow was not good for them, and so every hour or two they burst and the driver only had an ersatz jack so it got longer and longer being on the road and it was night again before we got to Fontainebleau.

It was very mysterious going over all those roads over which I had driven so often, they looked quite natural, they were surprising all there, all the pieces of road that I remembered so well, only now I was being driven in a charcoal burning taxi and being sustained by K rations that was all the difference.

It was getting later and later and nearer and nearer and we were all pretty well asleep when some one stopped the car. They were three F.F.I. men and one woman and the woman had a gun on her back not the men. That was quite different to what we were accustomed. They asked the driver for his papers and they were satisfied and then they asked me. I said I was American, well said they there are Germans, not we, said I indignantly giving him my papers. Alright he said and looking into the back where were Alice Toklas and the little servant we were bringing up from the country, Miss Toklas said with dignity she was an American, and she, pointing to the maid, she out of her sleep woke up and said sir I am a Savoyarde. Oh yes he said, and all these bundles said he. Oh those I said are meat and butter and eggs now don't touch them they are all carefully packed and enough to keep us a week in Paris. Ah yes he said and this big thing, that said Miss Toklas with decision is a Picasso painting don't touch it. I congratulate you said the F.F.I. and waved us on.

So then soon it was the gates of Paris and was it real yes there it was the same as always and I got quite excited and told the driver where to go and sent him wrong naturally but we backed in and we backed out and finally I saw the Lion of Belfort and the Boulevard Raspail and we could not go wrong then it must be Paris and it was dark but we did find our way and there at last was the rue Christine, and out we got and in we came. Yes it was the same so much more beautiful but it was the same.

All the pictures were there the apartment was all there and it was all clean and beautiful. We just looked and then everybody running in, the concierge, the husband of the laundress downstairs, the secretary of our landlord and bookbinder they all came rushing in to say how do you do and to tell us about the visit of the Gestapo, their stamp was still on the door.

I did not want to know because knowing is frightening but I had to know and it is interesting. One way and another, the apartment had not been troubled, it being in a part of town and with an entrance that does not look like a good apartment and also it was not on the rue de Fleurus mentioned in the Autobiography of Alice Toklas, but somehow some Gestapo in August, 1944, heard of it. They broke in. The secretary of the proprietor who has a book-binding establishment below us heard them walking about in the apartment, she suspected that it was the Gestapo but she did not come up to see, she telephoned to the French police and said robbers had broken into the house. The French police came twenty strong and everybody came up to see. It was the Gestapo, the French police asked for their papers and they were not in order, they had no authority to enter this apartment, so the police feeling strong in August, 1944, told them to get out and they went after flourishing a photograph of me in the air and saying they would find me. They also went off with the keys which was not noticed, and the next day at noon they came in while everybody was away and they stole linen and dresses and shoes and kitchen utensils and dishes and bed covers and pillows, but no pictures and no furniture and they broke nothing strange to say, whereupon the secretary had the locksmith change the locks and that was that.

It was all over it was very frightening, the apartment was very lovely the treasures were all there and we went to sleep, quite a little frightened but still asleep, not warm not cold, a little tepid, and on the whole very happy.

And the next day was the next day and I began to say, how many days are there in a week, so nice.

I walked and I walked and Basket my dog and I are still walking, my dog and I. The first thing that struck me in Paris after the miracle that it was Paris and was all there was that there were so many dogs in Paris and lots of them such big dogs too and not so very young. I began to ask everybody about it, I talk to everybody in Paris just as I do in the country that is one of the nice things about Paris. Well we talked dogs and they explained, well one way and another way you did keep your dog, sometimes the restaurants gave you left overs, or the butcher, or if your dog was a great favourite in the street you put out a basket and people put in scraps, one way and another you did go on keeping your dog. I walked and I walked and I am still walking, Paris is so lovely. Twice now I have come back to it saved and beautifully lovely. In the last war after being in London at the outbreak we came back to Paris 1914 came back on a moonlight night and there it was all lovely and saved, and this time even though the Germans had been there it was all lovely and saved.

Picasso had been impatient waiting our return, he came in the next morning and we were very moved when we embraced, and we kept saying it is a miracle, all the treasures which made our youth the pictures the drawings the objects all there.

I began to think that the whole thing was a nightmare it wasn't true, we had just been away for a summer vacation and had come back. Every little shop was there with its same proprietor, the shops that had been dirty were still dirty the shops that had been clean before the war were still clean, all the little antiquity shops were there, each with the same kind of things in it that there used to be, because each little antiquity shop runs to its own kind of antiquities, there they all were with I almost thought the same stock of antiquities. It was a miracle, it was a miracle.

And then I walked and I walked, and the architecture began to impress me so much more than it ever had, it was no longer a background but a reality. I realised that architecture was made for people who go about on their feet, that that is what architecture is made for. How lovely it all was and the quays of the Seine.

Then there were such funny things, the Germans are funny. They took down some statues and not others, they left strangely enough a bronze Lafayette given by the school children of America, and they left an enormous large statue of King Albert with all its inscription about the last war and strangest of all they did not touch the inscription upon the arch in the Tuileries with the horses on top of it and on which is carved, when the voice of the conqueror of Austerlitz was heard the German empire was dead. They certainly are funny people the Germans.

And then there are the soldiers who wander eternally wander about the streets, they do funny things. The other day I was watching one look at the reflection of the Louvre in a glass show-window, he said he seemed to get it better that way. I talk to them all, they seem to like it and I certainly do, at first I hesitated a bit it's all right, everybody seems to have plenty of fun, of course when you have to walk so much you must have plenty of time and so we are back in Paris, yes back in Paris, how often has Paris been saved, how often, yes I walk round Paris, we all walk around Paris all day long and night too, everybody is walking around Paris, it is very nice, how many days are there in a week so nice, very many, happily very many.

Florence: Bernard Berenson Narrates Sadistic Destruction by Retreating Germans

[September 3, 1944]

"I doubt whether deliberate havoc like this had been perpetrated before in the course of history."

Bernard Berenson (1865–1959), a frail, spirited, little man with a magnificent brain, had a deep, long-lasting love for Italy, the Italians and Renaissance art. Born in Lithuania, he was brought to the United States at the age of ten. A brilliant student, he was graduated from Harvard in 1887, after which he became one of the world's outstanding art critics.

From 1900 on Berenson made his permanent home at I Tatti, an eighteenth-century villa at Settignano near the sun-drenched city of Florence, a home which he had been able to purchase with his handsome income as adviser to wealthy art collectors. With its forty acres of fir, cypress, and formal gardens, I Tatti was a perfect setting for this distinguished scholar and man-of-the-world.

During World War II, Berenson took refuge in a diplomat's villa near his home. The punctilious little graybeard developed contempt and hatred for the Germans in Italy, whom he accused of being "pilferers, petty thieves, marauders and assassins." The Germans, he said, believed themselves to be the Chosen People, the Herrenvolk, with one law for themselves and another for the rest of mankind. "It takes the dense conceit of the Germans to blind them to the fact that from the beginning of their occupation they treated people and things in a way to confirm the stories of massacres, devastations and terrorism rumored but scarcely believed."

In the summer of 1944, at the cost of much blood, the Allies slowly pushed the Germans up the Italian peninsula. On September 3, after the expulsion of the Germans from the incomparably graceful city of Florence, Berenson was able finally to return to his villa I Tatti. Like millions of others, he had hoped that the city would be spared the demolition and destruction of war. Here was his disappointed report.

(From Rumor and Reflection *by Bernard Berenson. Copyright 1952 by Bernard Berenson.)*

Yesterday afternoon a car sent by Major Sampson came to take me for a visit to my house.

An errand obliged us first to go to the Piazza dei Giudicci on the Arno, close behind the Uffizi. Driving there, I could get an impression of what had happened. On both sides of the Mugnone nearly all the houses were empty shells, like buildings I remember seeing at Rheims after the first German retreat during the last war. Driving by the outer avenues toward the Arno, the destruction showed up less and less until we came to our destination. There I got out of the car and walked to the Ponte Vecchio. In the course of these few steps I saw nothing but piles of ruins heaped high as in 18th-century drawings of the Roman campagna. Only the early medieval towers remained erect. Of the S. Trinita bridge no more than points of the pillars remained standing. Between the two bridges the so picturesque and continuous façade of houses was pounded to dust. I doubt whether deliberate havoc like this had been perpetrated before in the course of history. Attila the Hun and Genseric the Vandal may have had the will but lacked the machinery. It has taken science, at the service of the dehumanized spirit of militarism, to bring about what my eyes have seen.

What I heard was worse still. I cannot begin to recount it, but one fine Nazi act I must note. I am assured, before leaving, that Germans put mines in the rubbish coating of the ruins so to blow up the first who rummaged in them.

These monstrosities were ordered by a commander who is a fervent Roman Catholic. But of what avail is Roman Catholicism pitted against Potsdam militarism?

If they had been fighting hard to take a town, there might be some faint excuse. The sadistic destruction of one of the most beautiful, as well as most historic, spots on earth, for no more useful purpose than to hold up the enemy's advance for a couple of days at most.

They continued to bomb Florence. Already they have killed some three hundred and fifty, mostly civilians, for there are few Allied soldiers as yet in the town. So, at least, I am told. If I was to judge by the numberless tanks, armored cars, caterpillars, etc., we saw lining the roads as we dashed along, I should say there were never a great many. All the way to my house, the drive, the farm, and the orchard grounds opposite were crowded with vehicles and swarming with troops. These looked anything but military and like nothing else than factory hands in their overalls, like laborers in steel and other heavy industries. We have touched the fundamental fact, at last. War, no matter what its origin and our attitude towards it, turns out to be an outlet for overproduction and unemployment; or, if you like to mythicize it, war now unites in one person Mime the forger of the sword and Siegfried who wields it.

I found my wife no better for the year, less one week, that has separated us. She was suffering spasms of acute pain and her speech was clogged. I carried away a sad and painful impression.

Nicky's sister, brother-in-law, and nephew, the Anreps, I saw next. They cared for my house and my wife while I was away. Thanks to their devotion and their tact, the Germans who in successive hundreds occupied the place did not sack or destroy it. The only mischief these did was to soak in full bathtubs, carelessly letting the taps open so that both our copious reservoirs have been emptied and are now without water. I may add that in times of drought all the houses surrounding us profited from our supply, and are now suffering from a water famine.

It is not the only calamity that afflicts the peasants and small people in our neighborhood. They are starving. Even the Anreps are living chiefly on rationed bread and tomatoes. The German soldiery here flushed every tree bare, have left no vegetable on the ground, have even picked the olives, although they do not begin to be ripe before January. They have seized what wheat they could lay hands on and dragged the cattle with them when they left. Needless to add that they left no fowl or rabbit alive. . . .

My house has had the honor of a visit from Marshal Kesselring, the so pious and so humane commander-in-chief of the Nazi forces in Italy. Perhaps it was at his orders that artillery was placed in the garden not a hundred feet from my wife's bedroom. It is a miracle that the place has not been more damaged. Most of the glass has gone—a serious matter, as it cannot easily be replaced and rain followed by cold will soon be here. Part of the *fattore*'s house was smashed with all his furniture. The garage bore marks of shelling. The garden looked unkempt and shaggy, not so much through damage as through lack of care. With the approach of the Allies, and the consequent intensification of bombardment, two of the gardeners deserted, as did half of the domestics. When I proposed that the cook should be ordered to return, I was answered that there was no need to hurry for there was nothing to cook.

The disastrous impression I carried away was due most of all to the squalor, the filth, the disorder conspicuous in the farmland and in the orchard opposite—a combination of city refuse heaps, automobile cemetery and gypsy camp. Unfortunately, narrow and winding as the road is, which, after passing through my estate, climbs up the hill, it happens at the moment to be the only one available for our armies to reach the Via Bolognese in pursuit of the Boches. Every kind of mastodonic ponderous vehicle goes up and down all the time, raising clouds of dust unbreathable, bumping into and smashing park wall and gates.

I went away discouraged. I could not face returning home until at least this traffic stopped and the fields were cleared of squalor. Indoors we can manage—somehow. The problem is how to feed the household and how to light it now that days are getting short and then, in the near future, how to heat the few rooms into which we must huddle.

International Crash Force: Martha Gellhorn Watches the Eighth Army Smash into Powerful Gothic Line Before Onset of Winter

[September 1944]

". . . Terrified civilians, noise, smells, jokes, pain, fear, unfinished conversations and high explosives."

September 1944. A year ago the Allies had stormed ashore on the beaches of Salerno. For twelve months they had moved slowly up the Italian boot, expending blood and sweat to take city after city. But the Germans were not finished yet. Across Italy north of Pisa and Florence, now in Allied hands, they set up a new Gothic Line.

German resistance was still furious. Fighting for time, the Germans stripped the industrial north of Italy of every piece of equipment that could be moved back to the Third Reich. They would do everything possible to prevent the Allies from taking Bologna and entering the rich industrial valley.

The Allied High Command had already withdrawn some of its best troops to be used for the invasion of France. The veteran Eighth Army, with its battlewise Britons, Canadians, Poles and East Indians, punched headlong into the Gothic Line to get as far as it could before winter set in to make the front inactive. But still another winter of hard fighting was necessary to gain control of the rich Po Valley.

The drive against the Gothic Line by the Eighth Army was witnessed by Martha Gellhorn, who sent this dispatch to Collier's.

(From "Cracking the Gothic Line," Colliers, October 28, 1944. By permission of Martha Gellhorn.)

The great Gothic Line, which the Germans have used as a threat ever since the Hitler Line was broken, would, under normal circumstances, be a lovely range of the Apennines. In this clear and dreaming weather that is the end of summer, the hills curve up into a water-blue sky: in the hot windless night you see the very hills as a soft, rounded darkness under the moon. Along the Via Emilia, the road that borders the base of these hills, the Germans dynamited every village into shapeless brick rubble so that they could have a clear line of fire. In front of the flattened villages they dug their long canal to trap tanks. In front of the tank trap they cut all the trees. Among the felled trees and in the gravel bed and the low water of the Foglia River, they laid down barbed wire and they sowed their never-ending mines, the crude little wooden boxes, the small rusty tin cans, the flat metal pancakes which are the simplest and deadliest weapons in Italy.

On the range of hills that is the actual Gothic Line, the Germans built concrete machine-gun pillboxes which encircle the hills and dominate all approaches. They sank the turrets of tanks, with their long, thin snout-ended 88-mm. guns, in camouflaged pits so that nothing on wheels or tracks could pass their way. They mined some more. They turned the beautiful hills into a mountain trap four miles deep where every foot of our advance could be met with concentrated fire. . . .

It was the Canadians who broke into this line on the Adriatic side by finding a soft place and going through. It makes me ashamed to write that sentence because there is no soft place where there are mines and no soft place where there are Spandaus and no soft place where there are 88-mm. guns, and if you have seen one tank burn on a hillside you will never believe that anything is soft again. But, relatively speaking, this spot was soft, or at any rate the Canadians made it soft and they got across the mined river and past the dynamited villages and over the asphalt road and up into the hills and from then on they poured men and tanks into the gap and they gouged the German positions with artillery fire and they called in the Desert Air Force to bomb it and in two days they had come out on the other side of the Gothic Line at the coast of the Adriatic. But before that, many things had happened.

First of all, the main body of the Eighth Army moved from the center of Italy to the Adriatic coast in three days' time, and the Germans did not know it. That sounds very easy, too, written like that. What it meant was that for three days and three nights the weaving lateral roads across the Apennines and the great highways that make a deep V south from Florence and back up to Ancona were crowded with such traffic as most of us have never seen before.

Trucks and armored cars and tanks and weapon carriers and guns and jeeps and motorcycles and ambulances packed the roads, and it was not at all unusual to spend four hours going twenty miles. The roads were ground to powder by this traffic, and the dust lay in drifts a foot thick and whenever you could get up a little speed the dust boiled like water under the wheels. . . .

So this enormous army ground its way across Italy and took up positions on a front thirteen miles long. The Eighth Army, which was now ready to attack the last German fortified line outside the Siegfried Line, had fought its way to these mountains from the Egyptian border. In two years since El Alamein, the Eighth Army had advanced across Africa through Sicily and up the peninsula of Italy. And all these men of how many races and nationalities felt that this was the last push and after this they would go home.

We watched the battle for the Gothic Line from a hill opposite, sitting in a batch of thistles and staring through binoculars. Our tanks looked like brown beetles; they scurried up a hill, streamed across the horizon and dipped out of sight. Suddenly a tank flamed four times in great flames, and other tanks rolled down from the sky-line seeking cover in the folds of the hill. The Desert Air Force planes, which cavort around the sky like a school of minnows, were signaled to bomb a loaf-shaped hill called Monte Lura. Monte Lura went up in towering waves of brownish smoke and dirt. Our artillery dug into the Gothic Line so that everywhere cotton bolls of smoke flowered on the slopes. . . .

Later—but I don't remember when, because time got very confused—we crossed the Foglia River and drove up the road our tanks had taken. . . . An American Sherman, once manned by an English crew, lay near a farmhouse: across the road a German Tiger tank was burned and its entire rear end had been blown off. The Sherman had received an 88 shell through its turret. Inside the turret were plastered pieces of flesh and much blood. Outside the Tiger, the body of a German lay with straw covering everything except the two black clawlike hands, the swollen blood-caked head and the twisted feet. . . . A battle is a jigsaw puzzle of fighting men, bewildered, terrified civilians, noise, smells, jokes, pain, fear, unfinished conversations and high explosive. . . .

Historians will think about this campaign far better than we can who have seen it. The historians will note that in the first year of the Italian campaign, in 365 days of steady fighting, the Allied armies advanced 315 miles. They will note this with admiration because it is the first time in history that any armies have invaded Italy from the south and fought up the endless mountain ranges toward the Alps. Historians will be able to explain with authority what it meant to break three fortified lines attacking up mountains, and the historians will also describe how Italy became a giant mine field and that no weapon is uglier, for it waits in silence, and it can kill any day, not only on the day of battle.

But all we know who are here is that the Gothic Line is cracked and that it is the last line. Soon our armored divisions will break into the Lombardy plain and then at last the end of this long Italian campaign will become a fact, not a dream. . . . No one wants to think of what men must still die and what men must still be wounded in the fighting before peace comes.

V-2 Rocket Attack: Henry B. Jameson on Bombardment of England by Hitler's New Vengeance-Weapon

[November 11, 1944]

"The first one I saw reminded me of the moon exploding."

In late October 1944 a desperate Hitler unveiled his second Vergeltungswaffe *(vengeance weapon), a long-range flying bomb. Containing approximately the same quantity of high explosives as the V-1 flying bomb, the V-2 rockets were designed to penetrate deeply into the ground before exploding. They flew through the atmosphere going up to sixty or seventy miles and outstripped the sound of their own propelling blast. By a phenomenon of physics, people in the vicinity could hear the rockets strike and explode before they could hear the noise heralding the approach. No warning, therefore, was possible against this weapon. The sort of defensive measures used against the V-1 were useless now.*

Hitler was making a last attempt to destroy the morale of the British people. Dr. Joseph Goebbels, his Propaganda Minister, was sure that this was the ultimate weapon. The V-2's were, indeed, dangerous, but they could not win the war for Germany. As Allied armies overran the launching sites, they brought about a diminution of the barrage. But the Germans continued using V-2's to the end of the war.

How London reacted to the V-2's was described by Henry B. Jameson, an A.P. newsman, in the following story.

(*Associated Press, November 11, 1944. By permission of Associated Press.*)

LONDON, Nov. 10 (A.P.)—The new V-2 rockets fall like shooting stars and although they are nothing compared to the buzz bombs as a terror weapon, they make a whale of a bang that can be heard for ten miles.

One man who lived through such an explosion less than 50 yards away said, "I didn't hear any noise whatever before the explosion— then I thought it was the end of the world."

Another man, describing the same incident, said a "terrific explosion" was preceded by a noise like thunder. Others say the rockets looked like great balls of fire, and a few even claim to have been close enough to call them "great black arrows."

The first one I saw at night in the country reminded me of the moon exploding. There was a brilliant flash, followed by a jolting bang.

Many persons have reported hearing double explosions, one at the time of the flash in the sky and a second presumably when the rocket landed.

While censorship regulations still prevent publication of detailed damage reports, the "flying telegraph poles" so far have been too inaccurate to be of much military value.

Many narrow escapes have been disclosed, however, since the secret of "*Vergeltungswaffe*" No. 2 was launched.

In one incident a Mrs. French, an employe of a bakery which was demolished, was having tea with the proprietor and his wife after the shop had closed. "Something seemed to fall on top of us," said the proprietor. "Mrs. French was killed instantly, but my wife and I, sitting on the other side of the table, were only badly cut."

An elderly woman walking along a sidewalk when a rocket fell near by saw "a vivid flash"—and the next moment found herself sitting in the middle of the street—hardly scratched.

Houses, schools, hospitals, churches, public houses and other buildings have been among those destroyed or damaged in rocket attacks.

Eyewitnesses who have seen them fall estimate their length from 30 to 50 feet and from two to four feet in diameter, with a warhead about the same size as the flying bomb.

"I saw a black cloud of smoke and then what appeared to be a very bright star traveling fast," said George Matthews, who saw his neighbor's house demolished. "Then later there was an orange-and-red explosion which appeared to have two distinct reports."

Frank Turner said it was almost a minute from the time he saw "something in the sky that looked like a red football" until he was rocked on his heels by an explosion.

Many pieces of exploded rockets have been recovered in scattered sections of the country.

Some parts of mechanism, from which experts may be able to piece together a composite picture of the rocket, also have been found.

Twisted-off-looking pieces of machinery littered the ground near the scene of several explosions. Tough white metal, some in rolls and some in flat sheets a yard square, have been picked up. There were also numerous lengths of metal chain like those on the wheels of oversized bicycles; curiously shaped blocks of wood and bright red iron piping apparently from the tail section resembling gutters with many slotted holes.

Hurtgen Forest: Henry T. Gorrell, United Press, Tells How a War Correspondent Covers the Start of a Major Offensive in Germany

[November 21–22, 1944]

"I can't believe anything, myself included, can survive."

Henry T. Gorrell, United Press correspondent, had covered the war with the British and American forces in Italy, Africa and the Middle East. From a base in Egypt he rode with a U.S. bomber force raiding the Greek coast. His plane—the last over the target—was badly crippled, and, on the run back, he saved the life of a crew member by applying first aid. For this, in March 1943, he was awarded the Air Medal for extreme gallantry under fire.

Gorrell accompanied the Allied drive into and across France and into Germany. With the advanced units in Germany, near the Hurtgen Forest, he sent in this play-by-play description of how a front-line reporter covered the beginning of an American drive.

(United Press, November 21–22, 1944. By permission of United Press International.)

I had the feeling the end of the world was coming. As the Americans blasted out a forward path near Hurtgen Forest, man and beast shuddered in their tracks, whole towns were disintegrating, life seemed to disappear from the scene.

The animals, too, had the feeling that the world's end was near. After the smoke had cleared I could see a red fox madly chasing its tail in no man's land, a mute cow that had dropped a calf from the shock, and plow horses that emerged from shattered stables charging about in a race to escape from their own torment.

In the center of that frightful scene, the Germans were entrenched as a human wall. They were dug in fox-holes and inside houses of fortified towns. Many died without knowing what hit them.

389

Yet, when our tanks and doughboys went over the top after the barrage, there were Germans still alive, and they fought with violence. Straight into this valley of death they charged; straight into the place where a minefield had been; straight into the heart of what had been one of the toughest sectors in Adolf Hitler's defense line.

Here is a play-by-play description of how a reporter covers the start of a major offensive:

7 A.M.: The telephone rings in United Press Headquarters in a requisitioned house in an occupied German town. I am told that my six days' wait for the offensive to start is over. The preliminary bombing attack is to begin at 11:15 A.M.; H-hour is 12:45 P.M.

7 A.M. to 11 A.M.: I breakfast with novelist Ernest Hemingway on powdered eggs and coffee, and then make the rounds of the various commands for the final briefing. We shove off in a jeep for the advance command post, slithering and bumping along a muddy, deep-rutted track through a dense, snow-covered fir forest.

11 A.M. to 11:15 A.M.: Six Piper Cubs are soaring, hawk-like, overhead. The Germans are punking over an occasional shell and our batteries respond lackadaisically. In the far distance, comes the drone of our heavy bombers and someone says, "Here they come!" Our leading fighters scamper in, dropping smoke flares to mark the bombing line. Our ack-ack is helping them mark the line by firing tracers that arc over.

11:15 A.M.: The bombing starts. It is like an earthquake—a tremendous roar, numbing the senses. I forget instantly my feet are cold. I can't believe anything, myself included, can survive. The artillery also is firing. It is one of the heaviest barrages yet, but compared to the roar of the bombs, the shells sound like firecrackers.

12 Noon: I realize the earth has been trembling for three quarters of an hour. I lift my glasses and see that some cows are still out in the fields, standing statue-like, apparently paralyzed.

12:15 to 12:45 P.M.: The artillery is really letting them have it—one round per gun from hundreds of guns every 15 seconds. Our tanks are closing up in the rear, are soon in position around our house, firing their 75's and 50's as cover for the infantry about to go over the top on the right flank and seize the first town. The din is terrific.

12:45 P.M. to 1:30 P.M.: H-hour. Tanks and infantry are going forward. There is nothing but German mortar fire, but it is thick. Our infantry is approaching the first of the towns it is to occupy, and it is in flames. Then our tanks advance through the lane cleared by the artillery fire. Through glasses I see the following half-tracks loaded with infantry. The tanks draw no fire.

1:30 P.M.: I'm on my way back to the press camp to file this dispatch and, not far away, I see two German kids playing tag. From a doorway their mother watches. Her face is mask-like and white. She has seen the bombers go over, the infantry and tanks pass. She knew, even if her kids didn't, what was happening inside her Fatherland.

Cossack Exploits: Maurice Hindus Interviews Soviet Leader General Nikolai Kirichenko

[November 14, 1944]

"The Cossack does not know the meaning of the word 'no.'"

Maurice Gerschon Hindus, born in 1891, a Russian–American writer, author of The Russian Peasant and the Revolution (*1920*) *and* Humanity Uprooted (*1929*), *obtained an interview with General Nikolai Kirichenko, Russia's best-known Cossack general, on November 14, 1944. Here is Hindus's report on his interview. It explains in part the German soldier's dread of his Russian enemy.*

(*New York* Herald Tribune, *November 17, 1944. By permission of Maurice Hindus.*)

MOSCOW, Nov. 14.—I have had an interview with Nikolai Kirichenko, Russia's most distinguished Cossack general and one of the most spectacular figures of the Red Army. On Aug. 22, 1942, "Red Star," organ of the Red Army, wrote of General Kirichenko and his Cossacks: "They are setting an example of how to fight the Germans. . . . That is the way all parts of the Red Army should fight." Russia has many brilliant generals. Yet Kirichenko is the only one "Red Star" has singled out for such high praise.

The occasion for "Red Star's" praise was the general's dashing exploits at the village of Kushtshevskaya. The time was August, 1942, one of the most dismal months of all Russian history. The Germans had swept over the Cossack territory and were plunging toward Stalingrad, the oil fields of Grozny and Maikop and the entire Caucasus. The Red Army could only delay but could not halt the many-pronged German advance. Russia needed an incident, an adventure, a figure or symbol to demonstrate to the civilian population and to all the men in uniform that Russian force, traditionally and historically Russian, could have a frightful reckoning with the enemy.

392

General Kirichenko and his Cossacks provided the symbol. They broke through the German lines, swept unexpectedly into Kushtshevskaya, and with their narrow, curved razor-sharp sabers slashed away at the Germans for three hours and forty minutes. It took the Germans eight days to bury their dead as a result of this sensational raid in their rear. Speaking of this incident, the general said: "I undertook the attack at an enormous risk, but in war risk is a noble principle." The incident thrilled Russia. The Cossacks, age-old warriors and conquerors, were showing their mettle again, this time against the most heavily armored and most highly mechanized army the world has ever known. Kirichenko and his Cossacks became a symbol of Russia's invincibility.

There were two special reasons why I sought an interview with Kirichenko. First, despite the prophecies of the Germans and other high military authorities that in this day of mechanized warfare the Cossacks would only make a superb target for tanks, planes and machine guns, Russia's Cossacks have played an eminent and some times a decisive role in many a battle.

The other reason was that this year, according to "Red Star," marks the five-hundredth anniversary appearance of the Cossacks on the Russian scene.

"You must remember," said Kirichenko, "that the Cossack is a special type of warrior. His father fought, his grandfather and all his ancestors fought. His sons and grandsons will fight. It is a family tradition.

"The father teaches the son the art of Cossack warfare. You've seen our Kuban villages, with their broad streets and immense squares. In these streets and squares on Sundays and holidays, double rows of saplings are set out and the father teaches his son how to gallop through these rows and cut the saplings without cutting off the tops."

Interrupting, I said, "Don't heads roll when the Cossacks fight?"

"Only when the Cossack is a bad fighter," replied Kirichenko. "A skilled Cossack slashes deep into the side of the throat, so that the head settles down but does not roll off the body. That is only one of the strokes we use."

"There are others?" I asked.

"There are many. It all depends on the size and personality of the enemy in Cossack fighting. If he is a little fellow the Cossack will cleave his skull. If he is large he will use the stroke I just described or across the spine from the shoulder to the hip. It takes a lot of practice to develop skill in the use of the saber. A man attains perfection when, leaping over a stream, he can cleave the water without stirring any spray. Anyway, the father teaches the son the art of Cossack warfare.

"The result is that the boy grows up with pride in his father and his ancestor warriors. Then we Cossacks always fight with people from our own village. Each village forms its own companies and regiments and divisions. The Cossack fights not only for his fatherland but for his family and his village. This multiple loyalty intensifies his fighting spirit.

"Besides, his training makes the Cossack utterly fearless. He does not know the meaning of the word 'no.' He only knows the meaning of the word 'yes.' He gets up, say at 5 A.M. in the morning, pulls his cap over his ears and gallops away without looking back. The Cossack always looks forward, and whatever obstacle he meets he must overcome it. If he wavers his horse will pull him along. If his horse wavers, he will bend down and pep up the horse with a few strokes of the lash over the feet.

"The Cossack needs such fearlessness to take advantage of the extraordinary mobility the horse gives him. There are nights when we cover a distance of 120 kilometers (seventy-five miles). Where the tank cannot pass and the human foot cannot tread the horse can make his way. Weather means nothing to the Cossack. To the contrary, bad weather, like darkness, is one of his best friends, and makes it easy to achieve the element of surprise.

"In our operations in the enemy's rear we isolate and disorganize the enemy's armies. Then our artillery, our tanks, our infantry and our aviation proceed to capture or annihilate the enemy troops. We always co-ordinate our actions with our fighting forces."

"In the reconquest of Taganrog," I said, "your Cossacks were credited with playing a decisive role, weren't they?"

"Yes. The Germans were nearly two years fortifying the city. In the south they were protected by the sea and to the east by Rostov. The land around bristled with firing points. A frontal attack was useless. So, during one night we penetrated the German rear for a distance of sixty-five kilometers (forty miles). We destroyed fuel and operation reserves. The next night we plunged still deeper. We cut more communications and destroyed more fuel. We were in his rear, actually pulling his army back toward us. Then we helped surround and annihilate this army.

"Take our campaign at Rostov. The enemy crossed the Don River and blew up the bridge. Mechanized forces were unable to get across, so we plunged forward. The river was frozen ice and gleaming like a mirror. Horses slid, slipped and fell. So we took off our burkas, our long, black sleeveless woolen coats, and laid them out on the ice. Five Cossack divisions made their way across on the burkas. During the night we penetrated into the enemy rear. We tore up rails, burned fuel, seized eighteen carloads of munitions and disorganized and scared the Germans. It was a beautiful campaign. That is the way we always try to act on our missions. It would have taken the infantry and mechanized forces five days to get across the Don. By that time the Germans could have so reinforced themselves that it would have cost us very many lives to drive them out."

Battle of the Bulge: John Wilhelm and James Cannon Tell How Yanks Fought Their Way Out of German Trap

[December 20-26, 1944]

Soldiers of the West Front! Your great hour has struck. Everything is at stake.

This order of the day, December 15, 1944, by Field Marshal Gerd von Rundstedt, set into motion the last great German offensive of the war. It achieved complete surprise. The Germans drove wedge-like prongs into the American lines, after which massive formations of armored and infantry divisions poured through under fog and cloud. There was still life in the German army.

The Battle of the Bulge was a serious, if temporary, setback for the Allies. The reaction was instantaneous. General Eisenhower immediately sent strong forces to contain the enemy's thrust. Yet, for many Americans trapped in the center of the counteroffensive it was a story of death and misery. Men who had thought the war was in its last days were suddenly called upon to fight for their lives. John Wilhelm and James Cannon recorded the story in these two dispatches.

AMERICANS CAUGHT IN DEVILISH TRAP

(*John Wilhelm, Baltimore* Evening Sun, *December 21, 1944. By permission of Reuters.*)

"There is no conversation—only silence."

WITH THE AMERICAN 1ST ARMY NEAR STAVELOT, BELGIUM, Dec. 20 (Reuter—Delayed)—Standing in this wintry mist-filled forest outside Stavelot, we can begin to piece together a tragic story—the story of American soldiers fighting huge German Royal Tiger tanks with only rifles and bazookas, fighting with tears in their eyes, realizing

396

the extent of the German drive, fighting even when surrounded beyond hope.

Gray hordes of the *Wehrmacht*, with masses of 70 and 80 ton tanks, were thrown against this area by the German high command, seeking to ride over the American infantry with brute force.

The Boche has gained much ground, but he hasn't overrun these soldiers at Stavelot.

Beyond Stavelot, in the Monschau Forest, another story is told—a chaotic story of wrecked American equipment, similar to the casual eye (if not in its over-all total) to the devastation of Dunkerque.

It is a story of bumper-to-bumper American vehicles frantically trying to pull back before the German colossus. It is also a story of some American troops overrun and surrounded and pounded by the German guns until a dull glaze formed over their eyes, and many surrendered.

German camermen for the first time in this campaign were able to photograph long lines of American prisoners. Where there were dribbles before, now there were hosts.

I saw some of these photographs of the area beyond Stavelot and through the Monschau Forest, identifiable by road signs and background.

There were pictures of vehicles lurching crazily off the road in a frantic attempt to avoid the *Luftwaffe* and of blackened, burnt-out, jammed columns of American lorries and halftracks and ambulances with American bodies—sprawled around them. These were non-combatant units of the 1st Army who attempted to break away as ground units fought to stem the gray Nazi tide.

Only the pictures can tell whether enemy artillery or air power poured leaden destruction into these columns, but I surmise from last week-end's air activity that a strafing, bombing *Luftwaffe* was mainly responsible.

To realize what a devilish trap caught these American forces you must understand the Monschau Forest, with its thickness and few small trails over which to evacuate men and equipment.

Then you must visualize huge dumps of supplies and equipment and large rolling convoys which make up an army. Then slowly you will begin to see a partial picture of what occurred when the German offensive overran this area and forced a retreat under bursting shells and bombs.

But not too far in the future these same forces, with different faces for the most part, will fight back along these same trails, into this same area, and a big part of the cleaning-up job to do will be the establishing of many small, forest-enclosed American cemeteries.

This black tragedy of devastation, of miles of American troops and columns of armor trapped by a burning, overwhelming, bullet-ridden wave of death and destruction has unbelievably altered the outlook of those troops of the 1st Army still fighting.

There is hatred and madness in their eyes, and bitterness in their hearts; in the eyes and hearts of the once youthful American G.I.'s, who only a day or so ago willingly, inconceivably, extended food and shelter and, yes, even kindness, to captured enemy soldiers and civilians.

The picture as a whole is still jumbled, but reports filter back from the more forward lines—reports of American soldiers so filled with remorse and vindictive revenge that they fall upon the enemy with only knives in their hands and with tears streaming from their eyes.

There is no conversation—only silence. The sting and frustration of defeat is too salty. Only a conclusive rout of this gray-clad horde engulfing us can relax the livid faces of these men around me.

Defeat has changed both the hearts and faces of American youths and former business men. Only yesterday they moved as a smooth-working, clear-thinking army. Today they are a savage bitter mélange, refusing to acknowledge seemingly insurmountable odds —soldiers from the heart out.

ONE SOLDIER'S RECOLLECTION OF THE BATTLE OF THE BULGE

(James Cannon, Stars and Stripes, *Paris edition, December 29, 1944. Courtesy of the U.S. Army.)*

"On the 24th they really made our noses bleed."

WITH 101ST AIRBORNE DIV. IN BASTOGNE, Dec. 28 (delayed)—History is what man remembers and records. It is the custom of historians to interpret wars through the records and the memories of big and powerful men. But this is the history of one soldier's recollection of what happened during the eight days that this division was cut off in and around Bastogne.

The soldier is Sgt. Vernon M. Christopherson, 26, who comes from

Beldenville, Wis., but migrated to Burbank, Calif., to work in a Lockheed aircraft plant.

"I'll start at the beginning," said Christopherson, who is a platoon sergeant operating a light machine-gun. "We were cut off Dec. 19 but we didn't know it. We went into Noville, three miles northeast of Bastogne, that day and it started to get rugged.

"It was a lousy day, with the clouds hitting your helmet. There weren't many Jerries in town. They were waiting for us on the high ground outside the town with tanks and artillery. We just dug in and took it all that day. Those Jerries can really use those 88s! Just like they were big rifles. That night the fire was so thick you could get it made into a suit.

"On the 20th we fell back inside Noville and those Heinies came right in after us.

"On the 21st we started south into Foy. This is a kind of mystery, but for some reason those Heinies didn't fight so hard and we got past. Maybe they were saving us to get later. I don't know.

"On the 23rd we got our first support from the air. Boy, those planes looked beautiful. They were still giving us plenty of artillery but it felt good to know they were getting it worse than we were.

"On the 24th they really made our noses bleed. That night their planes came over and let go with everything they had. It was a hell of a night, Jack.

"Christmas Day was a pig. They really tried to get us and we had to fight like hell to keep them off but we killed a lot of them and our artillery got four tanks.

"On the 26th a guy busted through the door in the house where we were and he told us that 15 American Shermans and five light tanks just busted through into the town. We looked at one another but no one said anything wise or good that you would want to put down in the paper. But we all knew how the other guy felt. That's about all I can remember."

Battle for Budapest: S.S. Combat Reporter Kalweit Describes the German Defense of the Hungarian Capital

[January 2, 1945]

"Every defender of Budapest knows the necessity of this battle."

In two years the Russians pushed 1,170 miles from Stalingrad westward. At the beginning of 1945 three great Red armies stood poised on German and German-controlled soil. One of the great military offensives of history was under way. One newspaperman confessed that he looked at it with something like paralysis of expression.

At the beginning of the new year, Red army units overran three hundred blocks of houses and buildings in Buda, the western half of the Hungarian capital, and drove three miles into Pest, the eastern part. The city was jammed with two million civilians without food and water. The Nazi garrison was doomed but it tried to hold out until it could be relieved by comrades attacking northwest of the Hungarian capital.

The battle lasted for two more weeks, but the outcome was never in doubt. It was clear that the Russians were winning the tank, artillery and air battles fought in and around the city. Russian reports told of 16,000 Germans killed and 650 German tanks destroyed in two weeks.

The following dispatch was written by German combat reporter W. Kalweit for the Völkischer Beobachter, *the official Nazi party newspaper. Note the emphasis on the bravery of S.S. (Schutz Staffeln, or élite) units, Hitler's personal troops.*

(Völkischer Beobachter, *January 2, 1945.*)

(SS-PK.) The sky gleams in red and violet colors over the Hungarian capital. The thud of shots and the clatter of machine guns mingle with the muffled rumbling of the aircraft circling over Budapest. Bitter street fighting rages in the extreme western sectors of the city.

Cowering behind quickly erected barricades, moving with exemplary tenacity from cellar to cellar, SS-men, tank grenadiers of the army, Hungarian parachutists, supported by German tanks,

400

encounter the attacking Soviet storm troops again and again. Every defender of Budapest knows the necessity of this battle. Therefore the defiant perseverance, the repeated thrusts into the masses of the enemy. Counterattacks by SS-men and grenadiers close the breaches again and again. German tankmen and storm troops clash repeatedly with the enemy.

There are many reports indicating that the defenders of Budapest have taken a heavy toll of Soviet tanks. When a SS cavalry regiment or a grenadier division ran out of munitions, it carried on with sidearms.

Budapest, for weeks on the front line, was assaulted in mid-December by the Soviets by way of Hatvan at the northern knee of the Danube. The Russian command, believing that it had breached the German defenses, made a massive attack in both north and south. But excellent German leadership built up strong defenses in the north and east. The enemy struck with the mass of his tank troops in the northern suburb of the Hungarian capital against the battalions of the Panzer-Grenadier division "Feldherrnhalle." But under the bold leadership of First Lieutenant Borf some 60 Soviet tanks were disabled in just a few days. Moreover, the enemy could not displace the SS cavalry divisions from their positions in the south of Budapest.

Then the Soviet High Command tried it from the west. Soviet forces crossed the Csepel line to the west shore of the Danube, and joined by a Soviet division coming from the direction of Stuhlweissenburg, pushed north and west in order to complete the encirclement of Budapest during the Christmas holidays. A part of the enemy turned west to win the area of Komorn, while strong forces pushed against the western edges of Budapest. These enemy moves were frustrated. Quickly assembled combat units turned to the western sectors of the city and stopped the Soviets. Moreover, through counterattacks by German Panzer troops the enemy assault in the direction of Komorn was brought to a halt.

In the heart of Budapest the German garrison defends itself with fanatical bravery. Daily it inflicts tremendous losses on the Soviets. Its obstinate perseverance is not in vain. It is giving the German command precious time to take extensive countermeasures in the Hungarian theatre of war.

Iwo Jima: William F. Tyree, United Press, Sees U.S. Marines Storm Ashore on a Tiny Island 600 Miles From Tokyo

[February 19, 1945]

"Iwo itself looked like a fat pork chop sizzling in the skillet."

Iwo Jima, about 600 miles from Tokyo and 700 from Saipan, was a tiny island, eight miles square, in the Volcano group. Bare of vegetation, it was covered with soft, volcanic ash. At its southern end was Mount Suribachi, an extinct volcano.

On this soft, sulphurous island the Japanese had stationed more than 23,000 troops to defend three vital airfields. To the Allies this miserable piece of volcanic rock was priceless because of its strategic position. From these precious airstrips could be mounted the final assault on the Japanese homeland.

The 5th Marine Corps went ashore on Iwo Jima on February 19, 1945. It was, said Major General Harry M. Smith, "the toughest fight we've run across in 168 years." This first invasion of Japan's doorstep was launched after naval gunfire and rocket air bombardment unprecedented in the Pacific war. The Marines hit the beaches under cover of fire from warships standing so close inshore that from the assault craft the superstructure of the ships seemed as high as Mount Suribachi.

Despite the intensive bombardment, stunned but courageous Japanese defenders emerged from caves to send mortar fire down on the beaches. American flame-throwing teams then went in to attack the maze of defensive casements. "There is no room for maneuver in Iwo Jima," reported one correspondent, "no place for forward passes and flanker plays. It has got to be done right through the middle of the line."

Correspondent Morrie Landberg, in a radio dispatch to the Associated Press, reported:

There is no front on bloody Iwo. The whole of the small, gourd-shaped island is a battle zone, in the gray mist of day and through the chill blackness of the night. The front line may be the northern edge of the southern airfield captured by the marines. It may be at the foot of Suribachi Yama under assault by other leathernecks. Or it may be just anywhere on the bomb- and shell-torn beachhead.

It took twenty-six days of bloody battle before Iwo Jima was captured. The Japanese fought and died practically to the last man—at least 21,000 were killed. There were few prisoners. The three Marine divisions suffered 19,938 casualties, including 4,189 dead.

To wrest possession of this tiny island, the Americans put ashore one of the largest forces to take part in a single Marine action. What it was like on that first day—February 19, 1943—was described by William F. Tyree for the combined Allied press from the vantage point of a Navy Liberator over the island.

(*United Press, in the Chicago* Daily News, *February 19, 1945 By permission of United Press International.*)

ABOARD A NAVY LIBERATOR BOMBER OVER IWO JIMA (U.P.)—Tiny, tough Iwo Jima was ablaze from end to end today as our bomber dropped down into its battle smoke to watch wave after wave of Marines plow ashore from an 800-ship invasion armada for a showdown fight in the enemy's front yard.

From 1,000 feet over the beachhead, it was obvious the Marines had a terrific battle on their hands.

Even as the mighty battleships, cruisers and destroyers circled endlessly, sending crushing salvos into the volcanic slopes of the island, I could see Marines dashing for cover on the rocky southeast beach. Some were far inland toward the airstrip.

However, the Japs certainly were fighting back from their underground defenses. Twice as we swung over Mount Suribachi's crater at the south end of the island and around the northern wooded section the Japs gave us bursts of anti-aircraft fire.

While their defenses were being riddled with offshore bombardments, some fire twinkled at us from the ground.

As we approached the island hundreds of small craft moved towards the beach, unleashing a fierce barrage of thousands of rockets.

Waves of Marines followed within 45 minutes.

Smoke and dust covered the entire island. Iwo itself looked like a fat pork chop sizzling in the skillet as carrier planes swept in under us, strafing and bombing every installation they could find.

One fighter crashed in flames just inland from where the Marines struggled to consolidate their beachhead. In the calm waters off the island, hundreds of ships maneuvered endlessly while old prewar battleships—*New York, Texas, Nevada, Arkansas, Idaho,* and *Tennessee*—belched shells from their squat platforms.

There wasn't a single Jap plane in the skies.

Iwo Island appropriately was named "Hot Rock" for the occasion of this attack. Our aircraft personnel chattered furiously over the command's frequency as they took stations for anticipating the fight.

Two Navy photographic planes with Webley Edwards of CBS, representing the combined networks, and myself, representing the combined American press, took off from the Marianas early this morning, but Edwards' plane was "Lucky Louie." It got there first and mine, "The Lemon," lived up to its name and sprung a disastrous gas leak three hours out.

After a disheartening return to base, Lt.-Cmdr. L. R. Gehlback, the pilot, of Beason, Ill., grabbed us another bomber and we reached the target about 10 A.M. just as the fight began to get rough.

Co-pilot En. John Q. Schell, Jr., Asheville, N.C., gave me headphones and we heard the Marines calling for fire support from the fleet. Bursts of orange flame sprang from the muzzles of the battleships' and cruisers' big guns and huge columns of smoke and fire rose skyward from the island seconds later.

It was a systematic murder and destruction. Suribachi's crater steamed from successive hits along its ridges overlooking the beach. I could see many formidable pillboxes along the beaches as well as a few rusty ship hulls, already put out of action.

None of our surface forces had been disturbed by enemy counteraction by mid-afternoon, although the water literally was alive with Yanks going ashore or carrying supplies to the beach.

The invasion armada had spread out for scores of miles around the island. There was no mistaking the fact that the Americans arrived to stay on Tokyo's doorstep, but the fight looked like it will require a week or more before the finish and as if an awful lot of blood would be spilled before it was over.

Remagen Bridge: Americans Seize a Vital Link Across the Rhine with Ten Minutes to Spare

[March 9, 1945]

The ten minutes between 3:50 and 4:00 P.M. on the afternoon of March 9, 1945, were among the most momentous in combat history. During this time a handful of American G.I.'s seized a bridge across the Rhine and changed the entire course of the war.

No one expected it, neither the German nor the Allied High Command. The Ludendorff Bridge, thirty miles below Cologne, stretched 1,200 feet across the Rhine between Remagen and Erfel. No military commander in his right mind would have chosen this spot for a river crossing. On the east bank were steep mountains permitting the defenders excellent observation. "The crossing," said one American officer, "could have been one of the dumbest moves in military history. It developed on the spur of the moment, caught the Germans off balance, and it worked. And that's how wars are really won."

It was one of the great stories of the war. What happened at Remagen was reported by Gladwin Hill for The New York Times *and Howard Cowan for the Associated Press. Both Hill and Cowan missed one fact—the first man to cross the bridge was a thirty-four-year-old butcher from Holland, Ohio, a sergeant who led the third platoon of a rifle company across the bridge. Sergeant Alexander A. Drabik later said: "We ran down the middle of the bridge shouting as we went. I didn't stop because I knew if I kept moving they couldn't hit me. My men were in squad column and not one of them was hit. We took cover in some bomb craters. Then we just sat and waited for the others to come in. That's the way it was."*

In the stories reprinted here the first platoon across the bridge was led by Lieutenant Emmett J. Burrows. According to a Times *reporter, Mrs. Burrows, who lived in the Bronx, New York, was amazed when she was told that her husband had found the bridge. Whenever she sent him to the drug store, she said, or to the grocers, she had to write out directions.*

Hermann Goering, dumbfounded by the disaster, complained: "It

*made a long Rhine defense impossible, and upset our entire defense
scheme along the river. The Rhine was badly protected between Mainz
and Mannheim as a result of bringing reserves to the Remagen bridgehead. All this was very hard on Hitler."*

THE REMAGEN BRIDGE

(Gladwin Hill, The New York Times, *March 9, 1945. By permission of* The
New York Times.)

AT THE RHINE BRIDGEHEAD, March 9—Details of the American capture
of the Ludendorff railroad bridge over the Rhine at Remagen revealed today that the Americans had seized the bridge just before
the Germans had planned to blow it up. [The Associated Press said
they had just ten minutes to spare.]

As the Americans reached Remagen Wednesday afternoon German
prisoners told them that Germans had ordered the bridge destroyed
at 4 P.M. They raced for the structure.

As the Americans approached, a German demolition worker at the
west end of the bridge pulled a switch and ran across the east bank.
Some damage was caused, but before the remainder of the charges
could be set off the Americans ripped out all the wires and the
bridge was saved.

Censorship permitted these details of the great coup to be released:

Forces of the Ninth Armored Division commanded by Maj. Gen.
John W. Leonard of San Antonio, Texas, operating in the area of
Euskirchen, 25 miles northwest of Remagen and pushing south, encountered yielding resistance to the east. They kept pushing on,
captured a German ammunition dump in the Rheinbach forest and
captured the towns of Rheinbach and Stadt-Meckenheim.

From Stadt-Meckenheim elements of the division's Combat Com-
mand B, commanded by Brig. Gen. William M. Hoge of Lexington,
Missouri, and spearheaded by the Twenty-seventh Armored Infantry
Battalion of Maj. Murray Deevers of Hayville, Arkansas, shoved off
Wednesday morning.

They swept down through the steep-sloped vineyard valleys, en-
countering such lessening resistance that by the time they approached
the Rhine they were taking towns unscratched with improvised
American flags hanging from the windows.

They were moving so fast that Major Deever's command post,

which ordinarily is advanced from one community to another in stages, remained in a moving half track.

Major Deevers said he had orders from General Hoge, the engineer who directed the building of the Alcan Highway, that he wanted a bridge, "and when he says he wants something he wants it and has a good reason for wanting it."

German prisoners in Remagen said that the Germans were going to blow up the bridge at 4 P.M., so Major Deevers sent in Company A, headed by Lieut. Carl Zimmerman of West Point, Nebraska. The first platoon across was led by Lieut. Emmett J. Burrows of 2917 Grand Concourse, the Bronx.

When the German watchman set off the demolition charge, Major Deevers sent Company B onto the bridge to clear it of demolition charges. The first vehicle across was a Medical Corps car driven by Protestant Chaplain William T. Gibble of Arkansas.

The wind was so taken out of the German sails that some ferried across the river from the east to the west to surrender.

Forces on the west side of the Rhine quickly shifted southward, pushing plans to exploit the gain. By last night, despite almost mountainous country, poor narrow roads, lashing rain and thick mud that engulfed new vehicles almost to their roofs, the roads to the bridge were jammed for many miles with trucks, men and equipment pouring in.

Tonight the Germans were rushing forces far across the country in an effort to contain the bridgehead. Last night two big German columns were seen driving west with full lights towards the breach. Today American planes through the clouds essayed bombing attacks on three railroad yards 15 miles north of the bridgehead at Siegburg, Oberlar-Troisdorf and Hennef to disrupt the flow of German reinforcements.

Although the bridgehead is not an ideal door into the interior of Germany because of an expanse of wild, rugged country to the east, it offers considerable opportunities for expansion north and south along the Rhine, facilitating more crossings.

There is a north-south superhighway 6 miles east of the river that our forces may reach soon, if they have not already.

Hampered by bad flying weather, with a ceiling only 200 feet, the Germans had made only four small aerial attacks on the bridge up to this afternoon. They dusted off three old Junkers 87 dive bombers to make, with a single-engined Messerschmitt, several bombing passes over a period of an hour late yesterday afternoon and all four planes were shot down by crack American anti-aircraft crews. A lone single-engined Focke Wulf tried to ski-bomb it at 8 o'clock this morning, three more planes came an hour later, and two of them were shot down, and four more took individual passes at noon. The Germans did some shelling of the west end of the bridgehead today with little effect.

AMERICANS RISK LIVES

(Howard Cowan, The New York Times, *March 9, 1945. By permission of Associated Press.)*

ON THE RHINE BRIDGEHEAD, March 9—One of the great dramatic moments of the war occurred late Wednesday when a nerveless band of Americans jerked loose the wires attached to tons of German-set explosives. Lieut. John Mitchell of Pittsburgh, Pa., found the cache of explosives and directed the disconnection of the wires.

Only one-way traffic was possible over the bridge for several hours, but engineers, working under fire, then repaired the slight damage to its surface and released the full torrent of men and machines.

Some tank crews, too impatient to wait, trained their guns across the river and blasted the Germans on the east bank from the streets of Remagen. Field guns hastily wheeled to the west bank also joined in throwing a sheet of fire across to protect the bridge, and the terror-stricken residents of Remagen fled to the fields behind the town.

So stunned were the Germans by the act of the Americans in dashing onto the explosive-laden structure that two prisoners actually were taken on the bridge itself. Within two hours hundreds of other prisoners were laying down their arms and confusing the situation on the east bank.

The inhabitants of Erfel on the east bank, believing they were secure behind the great Rhine moat, had made no move to evacuate, but they quickly produced white flags and set them flapping from the buildings.

A German medical officer surrendered to Chaplain William Gibble and asked him to take over the town. He led Capt. Gibble to the Erfel hospital, where there were 600 German wounded and a few Americans.

Jump into Germany: Richard C. Hottelet Obtains
One of the Last Big Stories of the European War
[March 24, 1945]

"It sounded like a riveting machine, a heavy one.
For a split second I didn't catch on."

*Richard C. Hottelet, war correspondent for the Columbia Broadcasting
System, had taken a ride in the first wave of Marauders over the French
coast on D-Day, June 6, 1944. At that time he reported:*

We saw medium bombers and fighters crossing on the way to the target,
without a sign of a German plane. We turned in over the coast about ten
minutes before H-Hour. We saw a fast assault boat race along parallel to the
beach laying a smoke screen. We opened our bomb bay doors. The flight
ahead of us dropped their bombs, the guns on the ships off shore resumed
fire. The bombs and the shells burst together. Four and a half thousand feet
up our plane was rocked by the concussion and we got the stench from the
explosives. . . . One thing we can say already, and that is that our supremacy
over the invasion zone today is not seriously challenged.

*Hottelet apparently enjoyed his sky view of the fighting so much that
again, on March 24, 1945, he begged his way on to a Flying Fortress
scheduled to bring photographers and radio reporters to witness a great
airborne offensive on Hitler's Germany. The dying Third Reich was
being covered with a vast armada of planes. Hottelet had no intention of
joining the cascading paratroopers. But through accident he learned at
first-hand the fear and thrill of jumping to earth, as described in this
report for* Collier's.

(Collier's Magazine, *May 5, 1945. By permission of Richard C. Hottelet.*)

D-Day was set for March 24th, and two divisions, the British Sixth
Airborne and the US Seventeenth Airborne, were to be flown low
across the Rhine inland five miles to the high ground northwest of
Wesel and dropped there. Simultaneously, the engineers were to
blanket 30 miles of the area with smoke, and General Miles C. Dempsey's British 2nd was to effect a Rhine crossing six hours before the
air drops, push inland and join the paratroopers.

409

The great airborne offensive March 24th was probably one of the last big stories of the European war, and from a news as well as from a technical reporting angle, the Army wanted complete coverage. So the US Troop Carrier Forces put aside a beautiful silver Flying Fortress, loaded it with their cameramen and observers, let me go on board with my sound recording equipment and sent us out to cover the operation.

The plan was to take a small, but very important, bite out of the German east bank of the Rhine. To the South other Armies were poised and ready to jump the river but, up in the north near the Dutch border, the British Second was held up by heavy opposition coming from around Wesel. Days before the operation, the four areas selected for landing of paratroopers and gliders were given a careful going over by tactical aircraft, which stitched up and down the roads around the areas and smashed the antiaircraft gun positions and spotted German reinforcement columns miles east of Wesel and left them wrecked and blazing.

Meanwhile, the US Seventeenth Airborne, which had not had combat jump experience, practised drops in northern France. It had only reached Europe in December. The British Sixth Airborne, a combat wise group, was in England practising drops.

At 8:30 A.M. on the 24th, a great parade of English planes and another great column of American planes met over Brussels, Belgium. There were five thousand ships in all, counting fighter escort, and then swung northeastward to the Rhine. As they crossed the river, the quiet paratroopers were hooking up to the guide lines and could see great globs of black smoke arising from the drop zones; the heavy bombers were just finishing the softening up.

The weather was on our side. For eleven days the sun had crossed the sky, brilliant from the moment it rose to its last setting red. It helped the men patrolling the sky, and the bomber fleets that went out day after day and night after night. It helped the men on the ground by drying out the soil over which they would have to move.

The sky above was pale blue. Below us, golden soil and bright green meadows were cut by long morning shadows.

Flying at a few hundred feet, banking steeply to let the cameramen get their shots, we saw the solid phalanxes of olive-green troop carriers and tow planes and gliders nose to tail on the perimeter tracks of the ground bases.

On my right was Colonel Joel O'Neal, the Deputy Chief of Staff of the US Carrier Forces, come to see the execution of what he had helped to plan.

It was warm despite of the fact that we had taken the windows out of the waist, and the wind was rushing through. Outside the sun was climbing, and you just about absorbed the roaring of the four engines and the screaming of the slip-stream into the open fuselage as a thoroughly acceptable part of a perfect day, when some one nudged you and pointed out of the side.

You got up and looked, and there they were—hundreds of C-47s flying along in tight formation. This was the realisation of months of training and planning. It was an olive-green river that surged steadily and inevitably over Germany, and over the Germans crouched behind their last great defense line below.

Colonel O'Neal put his flak suit on over his parachute harness and strapped the steel flaps of his flak helmet down over his ears. We all did the same. The three photographers, their cameras clicking away, jostled one another at the waist windows as we swooped around the drop ships.

P-hour, the drop hour for the paratroopers, was 10 A.M. Just after 9:45 we passed our last check point. It was called the IP, or initial point, the same as a bombing run. Its code name was Yalta. All of a sudden the ground below us, which had been golden in the morning sunlight, turned gray. For a moment I thought that we had run into clouds. It seemed impossible. Then we caught a whiff. It was chemical smoke. Below us and around us was a bank of misty smoke that ran for miles up and down the west bank of the Rhine, across the river and over the east bank.

Below us there was no sign of life. We looked for troops going across, for the familiar invasion LCVP's and LCM's of our Rhine navy. We saw none. The river below us was a slate gray ribbon winding through a dull gray land; on our left the troop carriers, pregnant dolphins in an eerie sea; and down to our right, straight into the sun, the dark mass of the city of Duisburg. From its broad, regular inland harbor the sun reflected panels of light into the battle area.

Over the roar of the engines and the screaming of air in the waist windows we heard a faint thumping. Colonel O'Neal grabbed me by the shoulder and pointed. The intercom crackled and a dry voice said, "Flak at twelve o'clock and nine o'clock. But they're off the beam." Outside, coming from Duisburg, were the shells from Nazi 88s. Black puffs of smoke feathered pretty far off to our right.

And just at that moment we were over the first drop zone. It was 9:50, ten minutes early. On our left, paratroopers were tumbling out of the C-47s, their green camouflage chutes blending with the dark gray around. The troop carrier serial seemed like a snail; leaving a green trail as it moved along.

We were watching the bright blue and red and yellow supply parachutes mix with the falling troopers, admiring the concentration of that first jump, when we first got it.

It sounded like a riveting machine, a heavy one. For a split second I didn't catch on. Then I smelled the explosive. There was a sharp rap on the ship somewhere. We had been hit.

We turned and circled for a minute or two, and then joined another serial going into its drop zone. On the ground we could see occasional gun flashes, but no sign of life apart from them. No flak was coming near, so again a gradual relaxation made me see how tense I had become in every muscle. We watched the serial, with its fifteen tight little three ship V-formations, drop its load.

This bunch finished its job and turned for home. We turned off and joined a third formation, flying level with them at their speed and altitude. One of the photographers, crowded away from the window, was probably thinking along identical lines with me. There were a couple of extra flak suits back with us, and he stretched the double aprons flat out on the wooden floor.

And then we hit trouble. In the waist we heard the riveter again. A short burst, then a longer one. The heavy steel-scaled flak suit and the heavy helmet, which had been weighing me down, now felt light and comforting. Then we got hit in a ripple. The ship shuddered.

Over the intercom, Snow was telling our pilot, Lieutenant Colonel Benton Baldwin, that the left wing had been hit, and that fire was breaking out between the engines. The flak stopped. Baldwin was gaining altitude in a climbing turn. Smoke began to pour down through the plane, and in the left waist window. A tongue of flame licked back as far as the window, and the silver inner skin of the ship reflected its orange glow. The crew chief told Lieutenant Albert Richey that gasoline was sloshing around in the bomb bay.

Up in the cockpit, Colonel Baldwin was keeping the ship under control, watching the fire eat a larger and larger hole in the left wing like a smouldering cigarette in a table cloth. Looking down on the wing from above, he could not see a large fire. The flame was mainly below the wing.

Suddenly we went into a sharp dip. Back aft we did not know what was happening. All we had was the smoke and the deafening noise and the tiny fragments of molten metal which the wind was throwing back and which twinkled in the sun as they raced past the waist window.

We pull off our flak suits and helmets. I reached down and buckled my chest chute. It was obvious we would have to jump. But down below was still the cold, smoky country east of the Rhine. Impossible to tell what was happening down there. If it was not in enemy hands, it was a battlefield.

As we went into the dip, I thought the pilot had been hit and I put my hands on the edge of the window to vault out. But the Colonel brought her back into control, and we hung on. There was no movement among the men in the waist. We stood and waited—for flak, or more flames or explosion or for the Rhine to slide by below. There was nothing else to do. After what seemed hours the Rhine was below us at last. The left wing was blazing, but three motors were still running.

We were hardly across the river when Roy Snow came back and told us that the pilot wanted us to jump. That and the Rhine river were all we had been waiting for.

The Colonel got the door open and crouched in it for a moment I shouted, "Okay, Colonel, get going." He didn't hear but tumbled out. I got into the doorway. Down below, the ground was green and golden and friendly again. We had left the smoke zone, the sun was bright and the air was warm. So I let myself tumble forward on my face.

We were jumping at about six hundred feet, so I pulled the rip cord almost immediately. I pulled it so hard I almost jerked my shoulder out. There was more confusion. I felt as if I had come to a dead stop. The harness straps were digging into my flesh. My main thought was to save the ring, and I put it in my pocket. My next thought was gentle surprise that I should have been successful in parachuting the first time I tried.

I landed in a pasture. Trying to gauge my height to brace myself for the fall, I kept opening and closing my eyes, but was barely able to keep pace. I remembered to flex my knees. The next second I hit with a grunt. I snapped off my parachute and got to my feet.

It was the British Second Army area, and—true to the old Battle of Britain tradition—the parachuting visitor was promptly filled with tea and whisky.

By that time there was good news from the front. Some 6,400 Nazis had been taken prisoners in the drop zone; the whole operation was a great success, and the British Second Army was slashing across the top of Germany—east of the Rhine.

Road to Berlin: Hal Boyle Rides Along at Full Speed with Rampaging American Military Machine

[March 27, 1945]

"This is the greatest armored joyride in history."

Germany was in ruins. The people were bewildered and shocked in defeat. Conditioned by the Nazi press to rejoice in the glory of Hitler's unbeatable Blitzkrieg, they now saw lightning war such as the Fuehrer himself had never dreamed possible. Valhalla had crashed.

Hal Boyle described the great push on German soil.

(*Associated Press, March 27, 1945. By permission of Associated Press.*)

This is the greatest armored joyride in history—and Adolf Hitler literally paved the way for his own downfall. The great single- and double-lane highways he built in peace to shuttle his armies out from the heart of Germany to attack neighboring countries are proving his undoing.

They are smooth concrete avenues to Berlin and other great German cities over which the mightiest masses of armor ever assembled in the west are now rolling at true blitzkrieg pace in a dozen columns, coming from so many directions the Germans are powerless to scrape together enough troops to halt them all.

The Nazi military machine has gone to pieces on its own home grounds. It is in chaos in many sectors. Tanks of Lt. Gen. Hodges's United States First Army and Lt. Gen. Patton's Third Army have yet to crack up against a really strong line—and there is none yet in sight.

Hodges has thrown into the grinding combat the largest tank task forces ever used by any American army on one battlefront—forces which make El Alamein look like a sandlot maneuver. And other attacking Allied armies have armored strength almost as powerful. . . .

Minefields, road blocks and antitank guns slow these giant columns

414

only momentarily. Doughboys leap from the iron tanks and sweep in from the flanks to drive away or kill the enemy antitank gunners with rifle fire. Bulldozers move up in front of the column under cover of protecting tank guns and shove aside road-blocking debris from blown bridges and overhead spans as combat engineers sweep a path through the minefields. Then the column smashes forward again at full speed.

Whenever the columns run into a strong enemy position, one section coils off to deal with it as the rest of the tanks wheel onward. In this leapfrog fashion doughboy and tank teams have kept up the impetus of the advance.

They have swept through some towns so fast the householders hadn't time to put up white flags of surrender and the surprised Nazi garrisons were caught outside their positions, their guns unmanned. After a few minutes shelling they give up readily and infantry units then move in to clean out the snipers.

No attempt is being made to save Nazi real estate. Whenever the tankmen suspect a building or home may house a German strongpoint, they blow it apart and race by.

"When in doubt—fire first," is their motto.

Armored vehicles escort ammunition and food trains trailing behind the far-ranging columns and guard them from ambush. Despite advances of twenty to thirty-five miles a day, no tank has run out of shells and no man has gone without food.

In Desert Germany: British Journalist V. S. Pritchett Surveys the Scene Gone Beyond Argument

[April 7, 1945]

"I remember the sweet stench of the destroyed villages."

Nearly all Germany was a grotesque heap of rubble. A shattered, miserable people were paying a hundred times over for the luxury and bestiality of Nazism. The Fuehrer had started it with his bombing of Warsaw and Rotterdam. Now the angered Allies were repaying in kind—with interest.

"You can call me Meyer if a single bomb drops on Berlin," boasted arrogant, obese Hermann Goering at the beginning of the war. The Nazi air marshal had overwhelming confidence in his Luftwaffe. Now with Allied bombers cascading blockbusters by the hundreds on Germany's capital city and on other cities throughout the doomed Reich, the embittered Germans cursed their "Meyer" roundly.

The Allied air offensive was designed to reduce every major German city to ruins. In early 1944 the pace was stepped up. In round-the-clock bombing, British Lancasters at night and American Flying Fortresses and Liberators by day plastered German targets with a seemingly endless supply of bombs. In a single week in February 1944 at least 17,000 tons of bombs were dropped on Germany—more than twice the amount hurled by Goering's Luftwaffe on England during the entire Battle of Britain.

Large areas in the center of Germany's greatest cities—Berlin, Hamburg, Frankfurt-am-Main, Dresden, Munich—lay in ruins. The streets were cut up by bomb and shell holes. Communications were shot to pieces, water supplies destroyed. There were dead people everywhere. The smell of the corpses became unbearable. Entire areas of large cities were abandoned to the rats. Germans by the tens of thousands were dying because they had made the mistake of allowing Adolf Hitler and his barbarians to act in their name.

Victor Sawdon Pritchett, a highly talented British journalist, went into

416

*Germany in April 1945. He reported that a whole nation, which, for a
brief hour, had ruled the entire continent, was wrecked by war.*

("In Desert Germany," New Statesman and Nation, *April 7, 1945. By permission of V. S. Pritchett.*)

It was a grey morning with intervals of weak rain and we drove
towards Germany like ghosts, enclosed in the cab of a three-ton truck.
We were doing 60 most of the time, whining round bends, jumping
corners, hitting our heads when the road was rough. No one spoke,
for no one could be heard unless he shouted, and it was too early in
the morning to shout. Between Winchester and Wantage one had
seen this kind of country, but here it was on a larger scale, and not
so green, a hedgeless, rolling, park-like region with square camps of
woodland set off military fashion from the road. There were beech
woods with their red floors and the long, bearded parade of the victorious pine. And then we saw the first wounds: a branch stripped
off an apple tree, the grass roughed up by mortar fire, the fantastic
scroll of tank tracks like the ritual images made by primitive man.
The litter of fighting began; torn paper in the turf and the ration
tins thrown down. The war looked like Box Hill after a Bank Holiday, a picnic or paper chase that ended in a village with its roofs
blown off and its rafters sticking up like fish bones.

After this, we followed a rearguard action. Strips of war were
followed by strips of peace and by strips of war again. The wrecked
car, the trackless tank lay where they had been annulled. We came
to the small towns of the frontier where windows exist no more. For
a few seconds it was pleasant to cross a wide blameless river and,
beyond the sunken tugs and barges, to see it turn like a face going
out of sight into the hills.

And then we were in Germany. There had been a first-across race
here. A score of wrecked tanks pointed in random directions in the
ditches and the woods. The summer villa and the rich man's country
house were pocked by shell fire or split clean open. The white tapes
of the engineers were fixed along the roadside and made sudden
detours into field and coppice, as if some estate were for sale in lots.
Little Keep-off-the-grass notices were posted. "Mines Cleared to
Ditch," they said. What happened where the tapes ended? A countryside which hitherto seemed to be the victim, now becomes hostile
and without innocence. "Stay in the truck," it said. "Do not get out
on the road. It will burn you. Do not touch anything." The traveller's
eye wanders naturally forward; in imagination one is already living

miles ahead. But here the wandering instinct was checked and reversed: "Do not touch" seemed to be posted on notice boards all over that country.

The phrase sung all day in my ears. With its double echo a carpet-beating noise began over the hill tops and one had a first false impression that the rain clouds were dirtier in that direction because of the inconsequent guns. They were hammering up the "Do not touch" notice in the sky itself. Spotters flew up from the green flying strip, to drive the words home. We crawled into a slow convoy on a broken road, and were wedged in with another from the opposite direction. We crawled. We oozed like worms in the mud. We stopped. Heads stuck out of trucks and tanks, stupefied by the silence and no one said a word to break it. Two columns of men, their faces filmed with dry mud and dust, stared at one another from their vehicles like so many dust-choked ants. The movement of a pair of eyes was startling. That I chiefly remember and the deep cut lines bracketing the lips of the men in the tanks. They were coming back to rest. Then the gears of two convoys went in and we were jerked away.

I remember the sweet stench of the destroyed villages, pale German children jeering, cattle loose among the ruins, the peasants with pick and shovel digging a wide deep grave. There was a soldier cleaning his trousers on a box, too, oblivious of the uproar around him; and by his anti-aircraft gun sat another soldier wearing an opera hat and with bottles of wine standing beside his shell cases. We passed the batteries under their nets—a park-like scene—and we could hear the other guns punching ahead of us and—not so pleasant—punching behind us, too. Pom-Pom-Pom is an exact definition of the sound. It is like a boxer's chest-blow that makes the lungs ring, a deliberate sound, but unreasonable in its intervals which cannot be guessed; and after air raids one does not care for guns which do not aim at the sky. After one long bout our driver took my tin hat. "I've always wanted to touch a British piss pot," he said. "Just to feel it." He put it on his knee and stroked it and went into helpless laughter as if it were tickling him. "Jesus," he said, handing it back, "isn't it wonderful!" I cannot explain this, except to say that he had the collector's instinct and from now on laughed out loud when he caught my eye.

We had seen signposts to Saarbrücken, signposts to Bonn, Mannheim and even Mainz, and chalked up on the walls the German words, "Better death than slavery." The prisoners began to trickle back, happy, I think, because their helmets had been taken from them and they wore only the light forage caps which gave these thin, fair men a clownish and addle-headed air. But now we came to the town which was our destination.

It was a place about the size of Reading. Three days before, though it was nearly surrounded, the Germans had occupied the town. They had been told to surrender or the town would be destroyed. They did not give in until it was too late. The white flags sagged vainly on their poles from the attic windows of the few surviving houses. We have become connoisseurs of ruin in this war. We have learned to distinguish between the bombed, the shelled, the burned, the blasted. But in England we have never seen a town that has been killed, completely written off and abandoned, a place as empty as Pompeii, that has the sour stench of a rubbish heap from one end to the other, and where the only sound is the drip of water from the broken roofs. Large areas of the town were waves of chocolate rubble and in the streets that remained the walls had bulged and the roofs capsized. There can have been few habitable houses left; no doors or windows remained; inside the houses one climbed—one did not step—from room to room. Outside, where it had been cleared for traffic, the rubble was shovelled into embankments. From what was left of one street, one looked into the ruins of the next, and to streets beyond framed in the fretwork of destruction. From the wreckage of one building one listened to the drip of water in the next. And this drip of water was startling, piercing, and idiotic in its monotony. A vacant field, an empty moorland, a desert, hum with sounds, but a dead town is like the grave.

For a long time one stands unable to move. Disgust furs the tongue and sours the stomach. One does not pity the people of the town, nor does one hate them. One says, "They did it to us," but one is left just staring.

The scene has gone beyond argument. The terrible thing is that one has no feeling at all. One is faced by the boredom of destruction; one is stripped of every feeling, the humane and the inhumane, and curiosity grows feeble. This is negation. The mind and heart have got to begin at the beginning again and learn all they knew once more. You peep over a window-sill, and the disgusted body refuses to follow the eye into the affairs of its enemy. You are careful not to let your coat touch the sill as you look inside. If a soldier passes the end of the street you step back. Then again you look. And then, it occurs to you, the street is yours. Any street. Any house. You can have the lot. Climb over the wreckage, dig out a motor bicycle, "Help me with this goddam door, I've seen a box of tools I want. Boys! wine glasses! What have you got? Anything in there? Books? Wine?

Cameras? Some son of a bitch has been here before." You go in, your boots crunching the glass; you climb gingerly into a bedroom. The wardrobe has fallen on to the bed. What awful hats the woman wore. Why only one evening shoe? There's her sewing. She left her hairpins. She read *Tristan and Isolde*. She hoarded face powder. Her child had a red engine. She did not finish knitting the jumper. Climb out into the next door house. The fat is still in the frying-pan. She hadn't washed the dishes. Photographs and letters are thrown over the floor. Here are three S.S. men with fat girls on their knees, each one holding a wine glass and the sun shines on them. They were well fed, fatter people than we are. And here is the priest's study. Christ points to his heart in dreadful chromo-lithograph and on the bookshelf beneath it are all the anti-Jewish books and the Party literature, an air-raid warden's helmet, the man's scattered correspondence, his stomach pills, his letter scales and—poor wretch—his contraceptives. Open the trunk by his bed and there is his store of forbidden literature: the Zweigs, Mann and Alain Fournier. Really, these things tell you nothing about people. They parody their owners. Do not touch: the words come back. You feel that you must not put a finger on these things or that you must not displace them. It would be fatal to put the cotton reel back in the wrong drawer or move the child's train. Fear and conscience do not restrain you; it is that hesitation we at first feel in touching the property of the dead. Or perhaps you fear the contagion of calamity and think every object leprous and unlucky and that even the dust is tainted. You have returned to the forgotten habits of primitive magic and you seek to avert the evil eye of that cheap Art Nouveau furniture which stares at the intruder and seems to offer itself. Or can it be that even in catastrophe, one wishes to save something, if only the position of a cotton reel, for civilisation?

But against this, there is the fever. The Germans themselves felt it before we did, for there are Nazi warnings against looting on the walls. Someone shouts: "Say, hold this goddam gun while I give this guy a hand." And the reply, "Aw, hell, what you going to do with that, anyways?" And then a car crawls by with a trailer stacked with wine and its seats padded with bedding. Our lieutenant says thoughtfully, "I have a kinda dim suspicion that some unkind people at a court-martial would say those guys were liable for 25 years." "Aw, hell," says a G.I., "the Krauts stripped my whore's house in France before they left." And some said it was a lousy principle and others that maybe she was a lousy whore. But the M.P. controlling the traffic among the ruins of the main boulevard later on called out,

"Hiya fellers. How are you doing? I've got mine." He had four bottles of champagne by his motor bike. A couple of tanks going by with mattresses and quilts tied on to them rolled forward to the artillery duel outside the town.

For over the town's silence the guns went on deliberately. Ack-Ack opened up on a spotter. There was the feeble whimpering of shells. A G.I. tumbled off the bike he was learning to ride. "Feel kinda scared when I hear that," he said. "I hate the noise." We had two frights ourselves; the truck missed a pile of grenades by a few inches, and later in the afternoon there was a counter-attack. But most of all, the stench haunted us, that damp, sweet odour of rot. I remember the backs of two sullen German women, the ridiculous hand-flappings of a drunk German waiter in his apron, tottering into the ruins of his hotel with the cellar keys. And the one instance of fraternisation. There was a madman in this town, a man with a few teeth and a pasty, melancholy head that wagged on his neck as though it were on a spring. He wore a shabby suit; someone had put a top-hat on him. He was being driven round on the bonnet of a jeep and he sat there gazing at his knees and never looking up. They said there were two or three hundred Germans left somewhere; but those were the only ones I saw and the nodding madman was the last. It must have been the supreme hour of a manic-depressive's life.

Death of F.D.R.: Walter Lippmann and Tom Reedy Record a Nation's Tribute and Farewell to Its Commander-in-Chief

[April 12, 1945]

The entire nation was plunged into mourning by the news that at 5:50 P.M. on Thursday, April 12, 1945, President Franklin D. Roosevelt, at the age of 63, had died from a cerebral hemorrhage at Warm Springs, Georgia. From diplomats to carpenters, from surgeons to housewives, Americans received with shocked disbelief the word of the President's death. People everywhere gathered and repeated the words: "The President is dead."

The great war leader did not live to see the triumph of the United Nations, for which he had worked so long and so well.

"As for myself," said Winston Churchill, "I have lost a dear and cherished friendship which was forged in the fires of war." Stunned, Generalissimo Chiang Kai-shek could touch no food and lapsed into sorrowful meditation. Pope Pius XII was visibly distressed. Millions throughout Europe and the world mourned the President who had worked so unerringly to save the democratic way of life.

The next day the newspapers of America recorded the death of F.D.R. in a way that gallant American would have loved:

ARMY-NAVY CASUALTY LIST

WASHINGTON, April 13—Following are the latest casualties in the military services, including next-of-kin.

ARMY-NAVY DEAD

ROOSEVELT, Franklin D., Commander-in-Chief, wife, Mrs. Anna Eleanor Roosevelt, the White House.

Newspapermen throughout the country who had known and respected F.D.R. wrote some of their finest pieces on the occasion of his death. In the first selection below Walter Lippmann of the New York Herald Tribune, dean of American publicists, paid tribute to the President in three powerful paragraphs. In the second selection, Tom Reedy, of the Associated Press, told how America's capital said its farewell.

(*Walter Lippmann, New York* Herald Tribune, *April 13, 1945. By permission of the New York* Herald Tribune *Inc.*)

Roosevelt lived to see the nation make the crucial decisions upon which its future depends: to face evil and to rise up and destroy it, to know that America must find throughout the world allies who will be its friends, to understand that the nation is too strong, too rich in resources and in skill, ever to accept again as irremediable the wastage of men who cannot find work and of the means of wealth which lie idle and cannot be used. Under his leadership, the debate on these fundamental purposes has been concluded, and the decision has been rendered, and the argument is not over the ends to be sought but only over the ways and means by which they can be achieved.

Thus he led the nation not only out of mortal danger from abroad but out of the bewilderment over unsettled purposes which could have rent it apart from within. When he died, the issues which confront us are difficult. But they are not deep and they are not irreconcilable. Neither in our relations with other peoples nor among ourselves are there divisions within us that cannot be managed with common sense.

The genius of a good leader is to leave behind him a situation which common sense, without the grace of genius, can deal with successfully. Here lay the political genius of Franklin Roosevelt: that in his own time he knew what were the questions that had to be answered, even though he himself did not always find the full answer. It was to this that our people and the world responded, preferring him instinctively to those who did not know what the real questions were.

THE PRESIDENT COMES HOME

(*Tom Reedy, Associated Press, April 15, 1945. By permission of Associated Press.*)

President Roosevelt came home to the White House for the last time today over a sorrow-laden route he traveled in triumph so often before.

The body of the commander in chief arrived by train from Warm Springs, Ga., at 9:50 A.M. A black army caisson bore it past a vast silent multitude to the East Room of the Executive Mansion for this afternoon's funeral services. . . .

Police estimated the crowd was the biggest in Washington history —between 300,000 and 400,000.

Many wept, unashamed.

Overhead, big bombers and fighter planes roared back and forth, symbol of the armed might Mr. Roosevelt worked to develop to such great magnitude.

Men and women of the armed forces marched in slow, measured cadence ahead of the catafalque and service bands played the dirge of a commander in chief fallen in war.

Symbolic of the unfaltering stride of the nation at war the military escort marched straight ahead down historic Pennsylvania Avenue when the caisson turned aside into the White House grounds.

The family and old friends of "The Chief" rode in the cortege, in shocked sorrow. Their automobiles followed the caisson into the Executive Mansion grounds.

In the procession, too, was President Truman.

Soldiers with fixed bayonets lined the way, six feet apart. One of them fainted and gashed his chin.

Thousands across Pennsylvania Avenue from the grounds jammed Lafayette Park but they were so silent that the rustling of squirrels and the chirping of birds near the stately white-columned mansion could be heard distinctly.

The caisson halted before the main entrance and eight noncommissioned officers under Master Sergeant James Bowder removed the flag-draped casket and bore it indoors.

At 4 P.M. President Truman joined the widow and close relatives, associates of many years and representatives of many foreign governments in the rites of the Episcopal Church.

The Right Rev. Angus Dun, Bishop of Washington, officiated at the simple . . . ceremony of the faith in which Mr. Roosevelt was a lifelong communicant.

On one side stood a vacant wheelchair, mute symbol of the malady which struck the president down in his prime but couldn't keep him down.

Mrs. Roosevelt was stoically dry-eyed through the prayers and hymns her husband liked so much but there was many a damp cheek through the room. There, too, sat Mrs. Woodrow Wilson who endured the same grief a score of years ago.

President Roosevelt's expression of faith—"The only thing we have to fear is fear itself"—was made a part of the funeral services at the request of Mrs. Roosevelt.

At the close of the funeral prayer in the White House and just before the benediction, Bishop Dun paused and said:

"In his first inaugural the President bore this testimony to his own deep faith: 'So first of all let me assert my firm belief that the only thing we have to fear is fear itself—nameless, unreasoning, unjustified terror which paralyzes needed efforts to convert retreat into advance.'

"As that was his first word to us," Bishop Dun continued, "I am sure he would wish it to be his last; that as we go forward to the tasks in which he has led us, we shall go forward without fear, without fear of the future, without fear of our allies or of our friends, and without fear of our own insufficiency."

Mrs. Roosevelt was first to leave the room when the service ended at 4:23 P.M., and the others filed out slowly.

Throughout the nation, 4 P.M. was the signal for silent prayer. The army and navy set aside five minutes of meditation, here and abroad where war conditions permitted.

Hitler's Inferno: Eyewitnesses Edward R. Murrow, Gene Currivan and Robert Reid Describe Nazi Death Factory at Buchenwald

[April 15-18, 1945]

As the Allied armies surged into the interior of Germany they came across one horror camp after another. Men toughened by combat were sickened by the sights and smells they encountered, cruelties almost incomprehensible to the human mind.

General Eisenhower saw his first horror camp near the town of Gotha. He described his reactions in Crusade in Europe *(1948):*

I have never felt able to describe my emotional reactions when I first came face to face with indisputable evidence of Nazi brutality and ruthless disregard of every shred of decency. Up to that time I had known about it only generally or through secondary sources. I am certain, however, that I have never at any other time experienced an equal sense of shock.

I visited every nook and cranny of the camp because I felt it my duty to be in a position to testify at first hand about these things in case there ever grew up at home the belief or assumption that the stories of Nazi brutality were just propaganda. Some members of the visiting party were unable to go through the ordeal. I not only did so but as soon as I returned to Patton's headquarters that evening I sent communications to both Washington and London, urging the two governments to send instantly to Germany a random group of newspaper editors and representative groups from the national legislatures. I felt that the evidence should be immediately placed before the American and British publics in a fashion that would leave no room for cynical doubt.

Gradually the appalling truth dawned on the world that Hitler had inaugurated a plan to destroy his civilian enemies. It was necessary to coin a new word to describe this slaughter of the millions—"genocide" (from the Greek genòs *[people] and the Latin* cide *[kill]). The berserk Nazi would destroy all his enemies—Jews, Poles, Czechs, Frenchmen, Russians—all those "inferior races" who stood in the way of German–Aryan–Nordic domination of mankind.*

Dozens of concentration camps, veritable factories of death, were spread throughout Germany. In 1939, when war broke out, there were

*only six camps holding 20,000 prisoners. By the end of the war there were
dozens. Sir Hartley Shawcross, chief prosecutor for the United Kingdom
at the Nuremberg trials, said in his closing speech:*

> Twelve million murders! Two-thirds of the Jews in Europe exterminated,
> more than six million of them on the killers' own figures. Murder conducted
> like some mass production of industry in the gas chambers and the ovens
> of Auschwitz, Dachau, Treblinka, Buchenwald, Mauthausen, Maidanek, and
> Oranienburg.

*One of the worst camps was at Buchenwald, on a wooded hill six miles
from Weimar, one of the shrines of German culture and famous for
association with the names of Goethe, Schiller, Herder and Wieland. For
nearly eight years this camp was the scene of such barbarism as seldom, if
ever, recorded in history. According to the report of a Congressional
Committee sent to investigate Buchenwald:*

> It was an extermination factory and the means of extermination were
> starvation, beatings, tortures, incredibly crowded sleeping conditions, and
> sickness. The effectiveness of these measures was enhanced by the require-
> ments that the prisoners work in an adjacent armament factory for the manu-
> facture of machine guns, small arms, ammunition, and other matériel for the
> German Army. The factory operated 24 hours a day, using two 12-hour shifts
> of prisoners.

*Buchenwald was liberated by the U.S. Eightieth Division on April 10,
1945. Within a few days the entire world began to read terrible reports
from Buchenwald. Here are three eyewitness accounts on three successive
days by reputable journalists—the first by Edward R. Murrow for CBS,
the second by Gene Currivan for* The New York Times *and the third by
Robert Reid for BBC. These should set to rest forever the rumors that
Buchenwald was a figment of Allied propagandistic imagination.*

EDWARD R. MURROW AT BUCHENWALD

(CBS broadcast, April 15, 1945. By permission of Edward R. Murrow.)

"It sounded like the hand-clapping of babies."

During the last week, I have driven more than a few hundred miles
through Germany . . . most of it in the 3rd Army sector, Wiesbaden,
Frankfurt, Weimar, Jena and beyond. . . . The tanks on the concrete
road sound like a huge sausage machine, grinding up sheets of cor-

rugated iron. . . . The power moves forward, while the people, the slaves, walk back, pulling their small belongings on anything that has wheels.

The Germans are well-clothed, appear well-fed and healthy, in better condition than any other people I've seen in Europe.

In the large cities there are many young men of military age in civilian clothes, and in the fields there are a few horses; most of the ploughs are pulled by cows, for the ghosts of horses dead in Russia and in Normandy will not draw ploughs. Old men and women work in the fields. There are cities in Germany that make Coventry and Plymouth appear to be merely damage done by a petulant child. But bombed houses have a way of looking alike, wherever you see them.

But this is no time to talk of the surface of Germany. Permit me to tell you what you would have seen and heard, had you been with me on Thursday. It will not be pleasant listening. If you are at lunch, or if you have no appetite to hear what Germans have done, now is a good time to switch off the radio.

For I propose to tell you of Buchenwald. It's on a small hill, about four miles outside Weimar.

This was one of the largest concentration camps in Germany . . . and it was built to last. As we approached it, we saw about a hundred men in civilian clothes, with rifles, advancing in open order across the fields.

There were a few shots. We stopped to inquire. We were told that some of the prisoners had a couple of S.S. men cornered in there. We drove on, reached the main gate. The prisoners crowded up behind the wire. We entered. And now let me tell this in the first person, for I was the least important person there, as you can hear. There surged around me an evil-smelling crowd; men and boys reached out to touch me. They were in rags and the remnants of uniforms. Death had already marked many of them, but they were smiling with their eyes. I looked out over that mass of men to the green fields beyond, where well-fed Germans were ploughing.

A German, Fritz Kirchheimer, came up and said: "May I show you around the camp? I've been here ten years." An Englishman stood to attention, saying: "May I introduce myself? Delighted to see you. And can you tell me when some of our blokes will be along?" I told him "soon," and asked to see one of the barracks. It happened to be occupied by Czechoslovakians. When I entered, men crowded around, tried to lift me to their shoulders. They were too weak. Many of them could not get out of bed. I was told that this building had once stabled eighty horses. There were twelve hundred men in it, five to a bunk. The stink was beyond all description. When I reached the center of the barracks, a man came up and said: "You remember me, I'm Peter Zenkl, one-time Mayor of Prague." I remembered him, but did not recognize him. He asked about Benes and Jan Masaryk.

I asked how many men had died in that building during the last month. They called the doctor. We inspected his records. There were only names in the little black book . . . nothing more . . . nothing to show who had been where, what he had done or hoped. Behind the names of those who had died, there was a cross. I counted them. They totaled two hundred forty-two—two hundred forty-two out of twelve hundred, in one month.

As I walked down to the end of the barracks, there was applause from the men too weak to get out of bed. It sounded like the hand-clapping of babies. They were so weak. The Doctor's name was Paul Heller. He had been there since 'thirty-eight. As we walked out into the courtyard, a man fell dead. Two others, they must have been over sixty, were crawling towards the latrine. I saw it, but will not describe it. In another part of the camp they showed me the children, hundreds of them. Some were only six. One rolled up his sleeves, showed me his number. It was tattooed on his arm . . . B-6030, it was. The others showed me their numbers. They will carry them until they die. An elderly man standing beside me said: "The children . . . enemies of the State!" I could see their ribs through their thin shirts. The old man said, "I am Professor Charles Richer, of the Sorbonne." The children clung to my arms and stared. We crossed to the courtyard. Men kept coming up to speak to me and to touch me . . . professors from Poland, doctors from Vienna, men from all Europe, men from the countries that made America.

We went to the hospital. It was full. The doctor told me that two hundred had died the day before. I asked the cause of death. He shrugged and said: "Tuberculosis, starvation, fatigue, and there are many who have no desire to live. It is very difficult." Dr. Heller pulled back the blanket from a man's feet to show me how swollen they were. The man was dead.

Most of the patients could not move.

As we left the hospital, I drew out a leather billfold, hoping that I had some money that would help those who lived to get home. Professor Richer from the Sorbonne said: "I should be careful of my wallet, if I were you. You know there are criminals in this camp too." A small man tottered up, saying: "May I feel the leather, please.

You see, I used to make good things of leather in Vienna." Another man said: "My name is Walther Roede (?). For many years I lived in Joliet, came back to Germany for a visit and Hitler grabbed me."

I asked to see the kitchen. It was clean. The German in charge had been a Communist, had been at Buchenwald for nine years, had a picture of his daughter in Hamburg, hadn't seen her for almost twelve years . . . and if I got to Hamburg, would I look her up?

He showed me the daily ration: one piece of brown bread about as thick as your thumb, on top of it a piece of margarine as big as three sticks of chewing gum. That, and a little stew, was what they received every twenty-four hours.

He had a chart on the wall . . . very complicated it was. There were little red tabs scattered through it. He said that was to indicate each ten men who died. He had to account for the rations, and he added: "We're very efficient here."

We went again into the courtyard, and as we walked, we talked. The two doctors, the Frenchman and the Czech, agreed that about six thousand had died during March. Kirchenheimer, the German, added that back in the winter of 'thirty-nine, when the Poles began to arrive, without winter clothing, they died at the rate of approximately nine hundred a day. Five different men asserted that Buchenwald was the best concentration camp in Germany. They had had some experience in the others.

Dr. Heller, the Czech, asked if I would care to see the crematorium. He said it wouldn't be very interesting, because the Germans had run out of coke some days ago and had taken to dumping the bodies into a great hole nearby.

Professor Richer said perhaps I would care to see the small courtyard. I said yes. He turned and told the children to stay behind. As we walked across the square, I noticed that the Professor had a hole in his left shoe and a toe sticking out of the right one. He followed my eyes and said: "I regret that I am so little presentable, but what can one do?"

At that point, another Frenchman came to announce that three of his fellow-countrymen outside had killed three S.S. men and taken one prisoner.

We proceeded to the small courtyard. The wall was about eight feet high. It adjoined what had been a stable or garage. We entered. It was floored with concrete. There were two rows of bodies stacked up like cordwood. They were thin and very white. Some of the bodies were terribly bruised, though there seemed to be little flesh to bruise. Some had been shot through the head, but they bled but little. Only two were naked. I tried to count them as best I could, and arrived at the conclusion that all that was mortal of more than five hundred men and boys lay there in two neat piles. There was a German trailer, which must have contained another fifty, but it wasn't possible to count them. The clothing was piled in a heap against the wall. It appeared that most of the men and boys had died of starvation; they had not been executed.

But the manner of death seemed unimportant. Murder had been done at Buchenwald. God knows how many men and boys have died there during the last twelve years. Thursday, I was told that there were more than twenty thousand in the camp. There had been as many as sixty thousand. Where are they now?

As I left that camp, a Frenchman who used to work for Havas in Paris came up to me and said: "You will write something about this perhaps." And he added: "To write about this, you must have been here at least two years, and after that . . . you don't want to write any more."

I pray you to believe what I have said about Buchenwald. I reported what I saw and heard, but only part of it. For most of it, I have no words.

Dead men are plentiful in war, but the living dead—more than twenty thousand of them in one camp . . . and the country round that was pleasing to the eye, and the Germans were well-fed and well-dressed; American trucks were rolling towards the rear filled with prisoners. Soon they would be eating American rations, as much for a meal as the men at Buchenwald received in four days.

If I have offended you by this rather mild account of Buchenwald, I'm not in the least sorry. I was there on Thursday . . . and many men and many tongues blessed the name of Roosevelt. For long years, his name had meant the full measure of their hope. These men who had kept close company with death for many years did not know that Mr. Roosevelt would, within hours, join their comrades who had laid their lives on the scales of freedom.

Back in 'forty-one, Mr. Churchill said to me, with tears in his eyes: "One day the world and history will recognize and acknowledge what it owes to your President." I saw and heard the first installment of that at Buchenwald on Thursday. It came from men all over Europe.

Their faces, with more flesh on them, might have been found anywhere at home. To them the name Roosevelt was a symbol, a code-word for a lot of guys named Joe, who were somewhere out in the blue with the armor, heading east. At Buchenwald they spoke of the President just before he died. If there be a better epitaph, history does not record it.

GENE CURRIVAN REPORTS THE TRAGEDY

(The New York Times, *April 18, 1945. By permission of* The New York Times.)

"Those who didn't weep were ashamed."

BUCHENWALD, April 16, 1945—German civilians—1200 of them—were brought from the neighboring city of Weimar today to see for themselves the horror, brutality, and human indecency perpetrated against their "neighbors" at the infamous Buchenwald concentration camp. They saw sights that brought tears to their eyes, and scores of them, including German nurses, just fainted away.

They saw more than 20,000 nondescript prisoners, many of them barely living, who were all that remained of the normal complement of 80,000. The Germans were able to evacuate the others before we overran the place on April 10.

There were 32,705 that the "visiting" Germans didn't see, although they saw some of their bodies. It was this number that had been murdered since the camp was established in July, 1937. There was a time when the population reached more than 110,000, but the average was always below that. It included doctors, professors, scientists, statesmen, army officers, diplomats, and an assortment of peasants and merchants from all over Europe and Asia.

There was a group of British officers among those left behind and one of seven French generals, but this was obviously an oversight in the great confusion that followed the news of our approach.

Five generals died and one escaped. This government-controlled camp was considered second only to that at Dachau, near Munich, as the world's worst atrocity center.

It had its gallows, torture rooms, dissection rooms, modern crematoria, laboratories where fiendish experiments were made on living human beings, and its sections where people were systematically starved to death.

This correspondent made a tour of the camp today and saw everything herein described. The statistics and an account of the events that happened before our troops liberated the camp were obtained from a special committee of prisoners, some of whom had been in the camp since its inception and others who had been German prisoners for twelve years. Their information was documented and in most cases confirmed by the records.

This story has already been told in part, but not until today has the full import of the atrocities been completely felt.

One of the first things that the German civilian visitors saw as they passed through the gates and into the interior of the camp was a display of "parchment." This consisted of large pieces of human flesh on which were elaborate tattooed markings. These strips had been collected by a German doctor who was writing a treatise on tattoos, and also by the twenty-eight-year-old wife of the *Standartenführer*, or commanding officer. This woman, according to prisoners, was an energetic sportswoman who, back in Brandenburg, used to ride to hounds. She had a mania for unusual tattoos, and whenever a prisoner arrived who had a rare marking on his body, she would indicate that that trophy would make a valuable addition to her collection.

In addition to the "parchments" were two large table lamps, with parchment shades also made of human flesh.

The German people saw all this today, and they wept. Those who didn't weep were ashamed. They said they didn't know about it, and maybe they didn't, because the camp was restricted to Army personnel, but there it was right at their back doors for eight years.

The visitors stood in lines, one group at a time passing by the table on which the exhibits were displayed. A German-speaking American sergeant explained from an adjacent jeep what they were witnessing, while all around them were thousands of liberated "slaves" just looking on. Even the barracks roof was crowded with them. They watched silently. Some of them looked as if they were about to die, but this assemblage of "slaves" constituted the more healthy elements of the camp.

In barracks farther down the line were 3000 sick who could not move and 4800 aged who were unable to leave their squalid quarters. In addition, there were untold hundreds just roaming around, not knowing where they were or what was going on.

There were human skeletons who had lost all likeness to anything human. Most of them had become idiots, but they still had the power of locomotion. Those in the sick bay were beyond all help. They were packed into three-tier bunks, which ran to the roof of the barn-like barracks. They were dying there, and no one could do anything about it.

The German visitors were to see them, too—and much more—but at the moment they were merely seeing "Exhibit A" and fainting.

Some Germans were skeptical at first, as if this show had been staged for their benefit, but they were soon convinced. Even as they had milled along from one place to another, their own countrymen, who had been prisoners there, told them the story. Men went white and women turned away. It was too much for them.

These persons, who had been fed on Nazi propaganda since 1933, were beginning to see the light. They were seeing with their own eyes what no quantity of American propaganda could convince them of. Here was what their own government had perpetrated.

ROBERT REID'S IMPRESSIONS OF BUCHENWALD

(BBC broadcast, April 17, 1945. By permission of The British Broadcasting Corporation.)

"Every bit of it is German."

The twenty-one thousand inmates of the Buchenwald concentration camp near Weimar had something new and interesting to see to-day. It was ten or a dozen processions of German men and women, and youths and girls, being herded willynilly around the camp compound, through those stinking, infamous huts where forty men died every day, past the mound of the dead and through the camp crematorium.

These sightseers, escorted by American Military Police and block leaders from some of the huts, were civilians from Weimar who'd been rounded up by the Americans and marched out to the camp just to let them see things for themselves so that there'll be no arguing in the months and years to come.

It was a hot April afternoon, and the dusty compound of Buchenwald stank. Some of the more stolid Germans just looked at those bodies and said nothing. Some of the women wept. Others fainted. Some wrung their hands and said they had no idea that all this had happened near their home.

While those Germans were trudging around, American doctors and nurses and Army officers and G.I.s were grappling with the problem of rescuing the living. One of the first steps taken by the American Third Army was to move hospital facilities into the camp. It is estimated that there are at least five thousand sick. Forty of them are typhus cases. The remainder are suffering from starvation, tuberculosis, and dysentery. Approximately twenty-five hundred are desperately ill. The doctors say that for many of them nothing more can be done than to alleviate the pain and suffering of their last days.

The first thing has been to evacuate the sick from the huts where they had been left to die. The big S.S. Hospital outside the compound has been taken over and cleaned out. Ambulances were rushed into the camp from every army unit in the entire district to help clear the hutments as quickly as possible. Equally energetic steps have been taken to combat the spread of disease, to feed and clothe the inmates of the camp, and to administer the place generally. Every one of the twenty-one thousand folk in the camp is being dusted with delousing powder. All foul clothing is also being gathered and burned.

The main hutments where the prisoners lived without proper beds or bedding will be abandoned. Eighteen German army barracks are providing alternative accommodation. And, if that is not enough, any other likely German building will be taken over.

Feeding is another great problem—not the lack of food, but the necessity of providing a suitable diet for men who have been systematically starved for years. The main food provided by the Germans for the prisoners had been a thin soup. The Americans have started out to build up from this point with a soup containing meat and vegetables. Also a ration of three hundred grammes of bread per day has been increased to seven hundred and fifty grammes. In this way the diet will gradually be enriched until the prisoners can really face a square meal without disastrous consequences. All this food, by the way, is German—all captured stocks, with the bread supplied by German bakeries in the district. So is the clothing which is now being issued to the prisoners. Every bit of it is German.

One of the greatest tragedies in the camp was the plight of nine hundred fatherless children—all boys, whose ages range from two and a half years to fourteen—boys whose fathers were once prisoners in Buchenwald, but are long since dead. These pathetic, ragged waifs, looking like little old men with yellow faces and shrunken cheeks, had been living in one hut, cared for by some of the older prisoners. A special child-welfare unit has been sent for to look after these children. And one of the first things done for them was to bring in supplies of fresh milk from local farms. Another thing was to make sure that the soldiers don't give them too much candy and make them ill. Another thing was to remove them at once to better quarters. The camp is being administered by the military government authorities with the aid of an international committee composed of twenty-one inmates—one representative for each thousand of the different national groups. The American Camp Commandant and his staff deal with this committee, whose members pass on the camp orders to their nationals, who provide the working parties for cleaning, maintenance, and policing.

Fall of Leipzig: Edward R. Murrow Broadcasts an Eyewitness Story on the Taking of a City

[April 22, 1945]

"My, my, somebody done broke a window! Things are sure gettin' tough around here. Folks are DESTROYIN' things."

April 22, 1945. Soviet tanks are three miles inside Berlin. Stuttgart is encircled. Bremen is all but cut off. Allied troops are entering the suburbs of Hamburg. The floodgates are open as German armies everywhere crumble apart. The end is near.

On that same day Leipzig, a city of 700,000, fell to the Allies. Edward R. Murrow, CBS director of European news, made a memorable sortie into the city. Here is his eyewitness report.

(CBS broadcast, April 22, 1945. By permission of Edward R. Murrow.)

"Tell them resistance was slight"—that's what a GI shouted to us as we entered Leipzig. There were two tankers dead at the corner. Somebody had covered them with a blanket. There was a sniper working somewhere in the next block. Four boys went out to deal with him; then there was silence. The Gestapo Headquarters had been evacuated in a great hurry, but they had taken all their files with them. Down in the air raid shelter, the floor was covered with money; Belgian, Polish, Hungarian, wherever the Germans had been. The money was ankle deep and it was dirty, and it had no meaning. The Germans were fighting for a bridge. They were doing what they had done for many days, firing off a few bazookas, killing a few boys, and then surrendering. There is not much German desperation about this German defense. They shoot until they are about to be killed and then they give up. I have seen them do it at Leipzig and in Nurnberg.

But let me tell you about the taking of Leipzig, the Town Hall. At 16:45 on Wednesday they lined up the tanks. The boys draped themselves around them. They were part of the Sixty-Ninth Division. It was about a thousand yards to the City Hall. There were one hundred eighty-five men on the outside of the tanks. They started down the street. There were thirteen tanks and five tank destroyers. They were in a column, moving down a single street. When they began to roll they were hit with bazookas and machine guns. When they turned a corner the wounded slipped off. The medium tanks were traveling almost thirty miles an hour and no man turned back. Lt. Ken Wilder started with a total of thirty-nine men and when they reached the City Hall he had eight. They had a company of Infantry riding on the tank, a hundred eighty-five men—sixty-eight reached the City Hall. The tanks were marked with machine gun fire and they were splattered with blood. An hour after reaching the City Hall, those boys were driving German cars and motorcycles about the streets. We were sitting outside.

A sniper's bullet broke a pane of glass in a window and a dough-boy said: "My, my, somebody done broke a window! Things are sure gettin' rough around here. Folks are *destroyin'* things." The Germans had given up, a few had shot themselves. One said he *couldn't* be taken prisoner by the Americans—the disgrace was too much. He *must* commit suicide. A young Lieutenant said: "Here's a gun!" And he slipped a clip out of a forty-five. The German took it and shot himself, just under the right ear. In the basement of the City Hall, German civilians were looting. The underground rooms were filled with rifles, grenades, bazookas, food, and wine. The day we took Leipzig there was a fairly stiff wind blowing and the air was filled with dust; heavy, red brick dust that filled the eyes and nostrils. The shelling had caused no fire. There was nothing left to burn. The city had been killed by bombing. It was merely a dusty, uneven desert.

Not far away, at Leuna, there was another kind of desert. Acres and acres of twisted, rusted pipe, huge tanks ripped open, steel girders pointing to the sky. Leuna was the greatest petroleum products plant in Germany. It produced more than a quarter-million gallons of gasoline every day. The Eighth Air Force hit it with ten tons of bombs and the RAF put down five thousand tons. There were more flak guns around Leuna than there were defending Berlin. Altogether, some fifty thousand American boys flew over Leuna and the losses were not light—thirty-five shot down in a single mission, but they did the job.

When we arrived a couple of officers had the plant managers in the board room. They were checking production figures. The officers had their charts made up from aerial photographs. They would ask the managers, "What was your production on this date?" and the Germans would look at their records and the answers were consistently within one or two per cent of the estimates that had been made in London. The Germans had brought in a force of four thousand men, just to carry out repairs, and they would get the plant producing forty or fifty per cent of capacity and then would come another bombing and production would cease altogether. The German official said that it had all been very discouraging. Leuna is an ugly monument to airpower. It doesn't prove that bombers can win wars, but it does demonstrate that bombers can make it impossible for armies to move or for planes to fly. . . .

After a couple of weeks traveling in Germany, one gets the feeling that for the Germans this is a kind of delayed-action war. Their cities have been ruined and in many cases the destruction is complete. They have lost many dead and wounded. Most of their men will be in Allied prison cages when the war is over and it will be some time before they are home again. But in addition to all this the Germans will have no transport left. They have wrecked their bridges. The war has swallowed up their horses and their hopes. Their factories are in ruins.

For the rest of Europe, the end of the war will mean some improvement in living conditions. For the Germans, things will get worse and worse. There won't be any bombers next winter, but there will be less food, fewer workers. The Germans will gradually realize that they have only started to pay the price. For Germany the end of the war will be the beginning of great suffering and shortages of all kinds. One gets the feeling that here is a nation committing suicide. A city is completely surrounded and is asked to surrender. The local authority refuses and our troops start in. There is resistance from a couple of houses. Tanks move up and cut the houses down. The Germans pull back, nearer to the center of the city, but they keep shooting. They did that for three days at Nurnberg and that city may be said to be dead. There are a few walls still standing and the cathedral spires are still there, but Nurnberg has been wiped out. Most of Bayreuth is gone, too. Wagner's piano is still there, but part of the house has been knocked down. Rare books and fine manuscripts are trampled under foot. There is an empty champagne bottle on top of the piano. The young Lieutenant in charge of Military Government has written a letter to Army, asking for permission to put a guard on the place. There is no lack of looting in

Germany. The foreign workers are interested in food and clothing and they will go after it right under the machine-gun fire.

The other day a Pole found a suit of clothes in a boxcar. As he carried it away he said: "This, my pay, five years' work." In Nurnberg a Russian walked down a street that was under small-arm fire. He carried a huge cheese. It must have weighed seventy pounds. He was interested in that cheese, not in the firing. As a new burp gun opened around the corner, an American Corporal said: "Hey, Mac, do you know any place around here where I can get some films developed?" There wasn't a building standing in a radius of a mile, but he was entirely serious.

There are places near the Czechoslovakian border where you can drive for sixty miles on a superhighway and meet no traffic. You are never sure of where our forward elements are and when you find an outfit they're never sure just where they are in relation to other units. The tired driver of an armored car said he remembered a town but that was about three days ago and he couldn't recall its name but he'd had a glass of beer there and it was a dusty little place.

In the larger cities there's occasional firing at night but not very much. The werewolves aren't very active, at least not in the areas behind the First and Third Armies. The other night we were caught in a traffic jam leaving a pontoon bridge. There was a half-moon and the night was mild. A Strauss waltz came from the radio in a command car. The two lines of traffic did not move. A western voice said: "What's the trouble down there?" and a voice from the deep south answered: "There's a one-way bridge and the traffic is moving in three directions." We crawled forward a few yards. There was a jet plane somewhere high overhead. A Negro truck driver said: "He's acomin' over!" but he didn't come. The apple blossoms on the right were golden in the moonlight. There were apple blossoms when some of those boys landed in Normandy. Someone began to sing, "She'll Be Comin' Round the Mountain." We made another fifty yards and then paused again. The sound of the motors died away. There was a cow bell down near the river. I heard one soldier say to another: "Did you hear about Ernie Pyle?" and the reply was: "Yeah, that's rugged! He was a good guy." I think Ernie would have settled for that.

I've just been looking at some dusty notes made in Leipzig. The names of some of the boys who were in that thousand-yard dash down the streets that they named "Suicide Alley"—Lt. Arch Ferrar, of Somerville, Georgia, was in the lead tank. He had twenty-five men left out of thirty and he thought himself lucky. Staff Sergeant John

James Fitzgerald from Chicago said he wished his wife knew he was OK. He hadn't much time to write what with all this fighting and moving.

The Germans at Leipzig were beaten, but their bullets killed men just as though they were not beaten. As this war rolls forward it would be well to remember that.

Torgau: U.S. Newsmen Witness the Meeting of American and Russian Troops at the Elbe River

[April 26, 1945]

April 20, 1945, was Adolf Hitler's birthday. It was by no means a happy one. The Third Reich was cracking. The death rattle was approaching. Six days later American and Russian forces met at Torgau on the Elbe River in the heart of Germany. Soon the two great armies were linked up along two hundred miles of the Elbe.

G.I. Joe and Ivan Ivanovitch drowned their joy in cascades of wine. Americans and Russians sat on both sides of the Elbe, drinking champagne and beer, singing and dancing far into the night. An eyewitness reported: "They tried to make the first meeting of Russian and American divisional commanders on the German front a grand opera event but it ended like the finale of a circus performance."

Don Whitehead and Hal Boyle, veteran newsmen, shared the joy with the triumphant troops. They saw military formalities give way to good will, but guessed incorrectly "and that probably was the best thing possible for future international relations." The first selection below was their combined dispatch, which succeeded in catching the emotional impact of the day. The second story, describing the celebration at Torgau, was written by Andy Rooney, Stars and Stripes staff writer, for the Paris edition of April 28, 1945.

THE MEETING AT TORGAU

(Don Whitehead and Hal Boyle, Associated Press, April 26, 1945. By permission of Associated Press.)

"Today is the happiest day in all our lives!"

It was a celebration unlike anything seen before in this war. One great party, with doughboys and Russians singing, laughing and

442

dancing and trying to talk to each other in sign language. A few Americans who spoke Russian interpreted for their friends.

A Russian sat on a stone wall playing an accordion while an American sergeant joined in the Red Army song—"If war should come tomorrow we will be prepared on land, at sea and in the air." A Russian woman in uniform sang in a sweet, throaty voice. It was pleasant on the waterfront in the warm sun.

Whenever an American approached a group of Russians they smiled broadly, saluted and shook hands. Some of the more enthusiastic ones who had "liberated" stores of German champagne and cognac, elaborated on this greeting with a great hug that cracked the ribs.

At the command post there was a milling throng of Americans and Russians about tables loaded with fried eggs, bread, sardines, salmon and spaghetti.

Maj. Mitri Livitch of Marshal Konev's 58th Division welcomed the Americans by saying:

"Today is the happiest day in all our lives. The most difficult for us were those days when the Germans were at Stalingrad. Now we meet one another and this is the end of our enemy. Long live your great leader! Long live our great leader!"

The entire day was a fantastic, memorable one, crammed with emotional outbursts from the time a column of the 69th Infantry set out for Torgau on the Elbe, where contact had been made with the Russians the previous day.

As the doughboys marched along the road from the Mulde River to the Elbe they met thousands of German civilians fleeing before the Russians, hoping vainly to find safety within American lines. The pain and misery of defeated Germany were etched in their faces.

On the east bank of the Mulde thousands of civilians were gathered, their belongs stacked into little carts. Bedding, food, clothing, pots, pans and huge bundles burdened the carts. Women stumbled along with huge bundles on their backs in the choking dust, just as the frightened people of Belgium and France fled before the Nazis five years ago. Fear and fatigue lined their faces and there was frantic urgency in their attitudes.

There were incongruous lines of wagons with their tops covered by rich Oriental rugs, and wagons pulled by tractors or automobiles or anything that would make them mobile. There were old and young, ill and crippled, with personal belongings hurriedly packed as the Russians drew near. The roadside was littered with the debris of this army of misery.

Columns of German soldiers marched along the road to the west without anyone to guard them. They had had enough and were quitting the fight. Many still carried their sidearms. Liberated British prisoners of war walked in long columns alongside the German soldiers and Hitler youths. It was a league of nations on the march.

And there was no chance for the Germans to pass through the American lines. Orders had been issued that all Germans in the path of the Russian advance must stay east of the Mulde.

THE MAD SCENE OF CELEBRATION AT TORGAU

(*Andy Rooney,* Stars and Stripes, *Paris edition, April 28, 1945. Courtesy of the U.S. Army*).

"They sing and laugh and cut patterns with their tommy-guns up against brick walls."

WITH KONEV'S UKRAINIAN ARMY, April 26 (Delayed)—There was a mad scene of jubilant celebration on the east and west banks of the Elbe at Torgau today, as infantrymen of Lt. Gen. Courtney H. Hodges' First U.S. Army swapped K rations for vodka with soldiers of Marshal Konev's First Ukrainian Army and congratulated each other, despite the language barrier, on the linkup, which means the defeat of the German Army as a fighting unit.

Men of the 69th Inf. Div. sat on the banks of the Elbe in warm sunshine today, with no enemy in front of them or behind them, and drank wine, cognac and vodka while they watched their new Russian friends and listened to them as they played accordions and sang Russian songs.

Russian soldiers, strong and young looking, built a little heavier and shorter than most Americans, inspected American equipment and Americans took the chance to fire the Russian automatic rifle. When the day was over many a U.S. soldier walked back to his jeep in Russian boots while the Russian soldier he traded with fought with the straps of his newly acquired GI shoes.

The Russian uniform consists of high, fitted leather boots, not unlike the German officer's. His pants are built like riding breeches of a light cotton material. His blouse is a tunic that buttons to the neck and his cap resembles an overseas cap spread farther apart at the top than the American one. Many Russians soldiers wear medals of various descriptions.

If today was not an extraordinary day in the lives of most Russians along the Elbe at Torgau, then Russian soldiers are the most carefree bunch of screwballs that ever came together in an army. They would be best described as exactly like Americans only twice as much.

If you know what a German soldier is like, the Russian soldier seems to be the exact opposite. It is impossible to imagine a regimented, goose-stepping Russian. They sing and laugh and cut patterns with their tommy-guns up against brick walls.

The road into Torgau was a strange scene. Russian laborers who had been working German farms were streaming down the highway into Torgau to contact their army which at last had come to liberate them. Across the road, going in the other direction, there was a column of sullen, tired, frightened people—Germans fleeing from the Russian army.

German soldiers made their way toward American lines along with civilians, and while some of them still carried guns, none of them attempted to shoot, giving strength to rumors that Germans in the area had been ordered not to fire another shot to the west, whence the Americans were coming.

When the caravans reached the river edge where Russian troops were mingling with Americans the Russian soldiers went to talk and sing and make love with young Russian girls that had come in on wagons. They formed in groups of twenty around accordions and sang Russian songs, all of which sounded like the Volga Boat song to most Americans.

Mussolini Killed! American and Italian Reports on the Ignominious End of Italy's Sawdust Caesar

[April 29, 1945]

Twenty-three years of Fascism demonstrated effectively that Benito Mussolini was operating in the wrong century. Italy's geographic position, the hard core of the old Roman Empire, was outdated in the twentieth century, when it became merely a peninsula locked in the Mediterranean. Mussolini sought to mold an entire people in his own image. He denounced democracy as a "putrescent corpse," insisted that the masses were incapable of governing themselves, demanded a new élite, and glorified war. The Italian people eventually learned about the cost for all this. Instead of glory and prosperity, they got defeat and misery.

Mussolini was the first of the twentieth-century dictators to rise to power and the first to drop into oblivion—ousted when the Allies invaded Sicily in July 1943. Forced to convene the Fascist Grand Council, which had not met since 1939, he demanded support, but got only denunciation. He resigned on July 24, 1943. Arrested by the carabinieri, *he was held until September 12, when the Germans rescued him. Thereafter, he was never again an important figure. He tried to form a new Government of "Fascist Republican Italy," aimed at overthrowing the King and returning himself to power. But the old days of gigantic bluff were over. Italian Partisans caught him and put an end to his life.*

Milton Bracker, foreign correspondent for The New York Times, *was in Milan when Mussolini's corpse was maltreated and reviled in a macabre public display. His story of the scene at the Piazza Loretto and the background of the execution was one of the most vivid dispatches to come out of the war. The second report is a version of the execution appearing in an Italian newspaper.*

The New York Times itself marked the end of the Italian dictator with this editorial (April 30, 1945), which accurately reflected public opinion in the Allied nations:

The wretched death of Mussolini marks a fitting end to a wretched life. Shot in the back by a firing squad, together with his mistress and a handful

446

of former Fascist leaders, the first of the Fascist dictators, the man who once boasted that he was going to restore the glories of ancient Rome, is now a corpse in a public square in Milan, with a howling mob cursing and kicking and spitting on his remains.

If his "trial" seems a bit rapid, his guilt was a thousand times beyond dispute. He himself rose to power over the corpses of Matteotti and others to whom he gave even less chance than the Italian Partisans gave him. Those who dealt with him so quickly must have had in mind, also, his previous "rescue" by the Germans in 1943; they had no wish to take another such risk. He died at last without a vestige of honor or even the palliative of a misguided "patriotism." He might have used the last as an excuse when he decided to play the jackal role and pounce upon a grievously wounded France or ravage his little neighbor Greece. But in his last two years, when nothing further could be accomplished by collaborating with Germany save to increase the misery and ruin of Italy that he had already brought about, he became the wretched puppet of Hitler and turned on his countrymen in the hope of saving himself.

By the final manner in which those countrymen have dealt with their former dictator, they have spared the Allies a problem.

THE DEATH OF MUSSOLINI

(*Milton Bracker,* The New York Times, *April 30, 1945. By permission of* The New York Times.)

" . . . a hideous crunch that wholly disfigured the once-proud face."

MILAN, April 29—Benito Mussolini came back last night to the city where his fascism was born. He came back on the floor of a closed moving van, his dead body flung on the bodies of his mistress and twelve men shot with him. All were executed yesterday by Italian Partisans. The story of his final downfall, his flight, his capture and his execution is not pretty, and its epilogue in the Piazza Loretto here this morning was its ugliest part. It will go down in history as a finish to tyranny as horrible as any ever visited on a tyrant.

At 9:30 A.M. Mussolini's body lay on the rim of the mass of corpses, while all around surged a growing mob wild with the desire to have a last look at the man who once was a Socialist editor in this same city. The throng pushed and yelled. Partisans strove to keep them back but largely in vain. Even a series of shots in the air did not dissuade them.

Mussolini had changed in death, but not enough to be any one else. His closely shaved head and his bull neck were unmistakable.

His body seemed small and a little shrunken, but he was never a tall man. At least one bullet had passed through his head. It had emerged some three inches behind his right ear. There was another small hole nearer his forehead where another bullet seemed to have gone in.

As if he were not dead or dishonored enough, at least two young men in the crowd broke through and aimed kicks at his skull. One glanced off. But the other landed full on his right jaw and there was a hideous crunch that wholly disfigured the once-proud face.

Mussolini wore the uniform of a squadrist militiaman. It comprised a gray-brown jacket and gray trousers with red and black stripes down the sides. He wore black boots, badly soiled, and the left one hung half off as if his foot were broken. His small eyes were open and it was perhaps a final irony that this man who had thrust his chin forward for so many official photographs had to have his yellowing face propped up with a rifle-butt to turn it into the sun for the only two Allied cameramen on the scene.

When the butt was removed the face flounced back over to the left. Meanwhile I crouched over the body to the left in order not to cut off the sun from his turned face. A group of us had been thrust by the enthusiastic Milanese, who had not yet seen any Americans, right into the circle of death. It was naturally one of the grimmest moments of our lives, but it will at least serve to give absolutely authentic eyewitness accounts.

Mussolini lay with his head on the breast of his mistress, Clara Petacci, who had sought to rise to movie fame through him. Younger even than his daughter, she had been executed with him in a suburb of the village of Como on the shore of Lake Como, and now she lay in a ruffled white blouse, her dark hair curly and her relative youth apparent even now.

The other bodies lying in a semicircle, only a few kilometers from the Piazza San Sepolcro, where fascism actually began, included those of Allessandro Pavolini, Mussolini's Secretary of State; Francesco Barracu, vice chairman of the Cabinet; Paolo Zerbini, Minister of the Interior, and Goffredo Coppola, rector of the University of Bologna, who had fled ten days before the Allies' entry. Some counts placed the total number of bodies at eighteen but that left four unidentified, and even from my vantage-point it was impossible to count accurately so tangled a mass of flesh.

The last chapter in the life of the man who led a phony March on Rome in October, 1922, began last Wednesday, when, after a transport workers' strike on the previous Sunday, a general strike of all Milanese workers tied up the whole city of more than 1,000,000 people. Mussolini was still chief of the puppet Fascist Republican Government. He appealed to Ildefonso Cardinal Schuster to act as intermediary at a meeting with the leaders of the Committee of National Liberation. This took place at the archiepiscopal residence just off the Piazza Fontana.

At this meeting Mussolini appeared more tractable than Marshal Rodolfo Graziani. Told that the Germans in Milan had already indicated a desire to surrender to the Allies, however, Mussolini turned on his Axis partners and declared that they had "betrayed" him.

According to the Popolo of Milan, he said: "They have treated us as servants, and harshly—for many, far too many years. Now we have had enough."

Returning to his quarters after having asked an hour's leave to discuss the terms, Mussolini then sent word that the terms were not acceptable and he would leave. We arrived in Como at 10 P.M. on Wednesday and made efforts throughout the night to arrange passage across the Swiss frontier. The first reports said that his wife, Rachele, was with him but it would appear now that it was not she but Signorina Petacci.

Some time on Thursday morning in a caravan of some thirty cars, Mussolini headed north up the west shore of Lake Como. He was wearing a black coat over his uniform. Near Dongo, a sheltered village about three-quarters of the way up the shore, a Partisan named Urbano Lazari spotted him. Like the fleeing Marie Antoinette, he was made to alight and temporarily sheltered in a cottage in the tiny hamlet of Giulino de Mezzegre, near Dongo. Signorina Petacci was with him but the others in the caravan were held separately. After a brief trial they were sentenced and executed.

[Mussolini died shouting: "No! No!" to the firing squad, the United Press reported.]

The others, except Signorina Petacci, were shot elsewhere. Pavolini was said to have died bravely, proclaiming: "Viva l'Italia." Barracu wore a high military decoration; he died saying: "Do not hit the medal."

Signorina Petacci's brother, Marcello, tried to flee but was shot. Possibly his was one of the otherwise unidentified "extra bodies" in the Piazza this morning.

All the corpses were loaded into the moving van, which started down twenty-five miles of the superb autostrada after dark. The bodies were dumped in the Piazza Loretto because recently fifteen patriots were executed there. In fact, the name of the piazza has been changed to Piazza Quindici Martirs. The bodies arrived much later than scheduled because the van was repeatedly stopped enroute by heavily armed Partisans who wanted to make sure that the driver was not a Fascist trying to take the bodies to honorable burial. This doubt grew so serious at one point that the driver and the men with him were actually lined up for execution and it took an hour's argument to persuade the Partisans to let the truck proceed. The bodies were dumped without ceremony and the truck rolled away. Word that they were there did not get around generally until this morning, when the papers carried last-minute make-over stories. The effect on the city was obvious.

The first American soldier to see the bodies was Pfc. Kenneth Koplin of Huron, S.D., who drove the correspondents' jeep. Hailed by a hysterical crowd as an "American Colonel on an official mission to see the bodies," Private Koplin was pushed into the dreadful circle just as we were. "All I know is that I wanted to get out of there," he said.

Others whose bodies are on exhibit were Fernando Mezzasoma, Minister of Propaganda; Ruggero Romano, Minister of Public Works; Augusto Liverani, Minister of Communications; Paolo Porta, a party inspector; Luigi Gatti, a Prefect; Ernesto Daquanno, editor of Stefani; Mario Nudi, president of the Fascist Agricultural Association, and Nicola Bombacci, a former Communist. There is no way of telling how long the gruesome show will go on.

But if many more misguided young men leap through the circle aiming their boots at what is left of Mussolini there will be hardly enough left for burial.

AN ITALIAN REPORT OF THE EXECUTION

(L'Unita, *Milan, April 30, 1945.*)

"Mussolini was terror-stricken."

The command of the 52nd Brigade, aware of the importance of the prisoners, divided them into three groups. Mussolini and Petacci were placed in a peasants' cottage, guarded by two partisans.

"I entered," the executioner said, "with my sub-machine gun at the ready. Mussolini asked, 'What's the matter?'

"I had planned to carry out the execution not far from the house. To get him there I had to resort to a stratagem. I said, 'I have come to liberate you. Hurry.'

"Mussolini pointed to Petacci. 'She must go first,' he said. She seemed unable to understand, and, losing patience, he left the hut before her.

"Once in the open we walked down a mule track to a road where a car was parked.

"At this point I whispered to him, 'I have also liberated your son Vittorio,' as I wanted him to think we were taking him to Vittorio.

"Mussolini answered, 'I thank you from the bottom of my heart. And where are Zebino and Mezzasoma?' [two of the group of Fascists who were executed.]

"I answered, 'We are liberating them, too.'

"When we reached the car, Mussolini motioned to Petacci to precede him, but I said, 'You go first. You are better concealed.'

"Then we set off for the place I had chosen, a small square formed by fences.

"I stopped the car, and we walked to the end of the wall. 'Get over in that corner,' I said.

"Even though Mussolini obeyed promptly, he no longer appeared to be convinced. Petacci was on his right. There was silence.

"Suddenly I pronounced sentence: 'By order of the General Committee of the Liberty Volunteer Corps I am entrusted with rendering justice to the Italian people.'

"Mussolini was terror-stricken. Petacci threw her arms around him and screamed, 'He must not die.'

"From a distance of about three paces I shot five bursts into Mussolini, who slumped to his knees.

"Then it was Petacci's turn. Justice had been done."

End in Italy: Hubert D. Harrison Reports the Italian Surrender for the Combined British Press

[April 29, 1945]

"It was a sullen, beaten enemy, coldly admitting defeat to an implacable adversary."

By the third week of April 1945 General Mark Clark's spring offensive was rolling and his troops were pursuing the Germans across the Po Valley. For months the lines in northern Italy had remained frozen, but now the Allies were moving almost at will.

The end came on Sunday, April 29, 1945, when the German forces in Italy surrendered unconditionally to the Supreme Allied Commander. The document of surrender was signed in a small chamber at Allied Headquarters in the great Royal Palace of Caserta north of Naples. For nearly a year the palace had been headquarters of the Supreme Allied Commander in the Mediterranean theatre, Field Marshal Sir Harold Alexander, Supreme Allied Commander in the Mediterranean theatre.

The negotiations, short and swift, lasting only seventeen minutes, were described in this report for the Combined British Press by Hubert D. Harrison. The surrender automatically carried the Allies across the Alps. It meant that the whole route to the Brenner Pass was cleared in a single swoop and the Allies would soon be in Berchtesgaden.

(*The London* Daily Telegraph, *May 3, 1945. By permission of the London* Daily Telegraph.)

CASERTA PALACE NEAR NAPLES, Sunday (Delayed)—If the unconditional surrender document is carried out it means the end of the war in Italy and a penetration deep into the heart of what was to have been Hitler's last stronghold.

I watched the signing of this historic document. Representatives of all branches of the armed forces of Britain and the United States gathered at one end of a long, narrow, highly polished table, Lt.-Gen. Morgan, Chief of the General Staff to the Supreme Commander, entered, took a seat at the table, and called for the German delegates to be admitted.

The ceremony took place in a small room on the second floor of the Caserta Palace.

As the German delegates entered hesitatingly, Gen. Morgan stood grimly at the end of the table, surrounded by other Allied representatives.

The tall German lieut. col., representing Vietinghoff, squinted his bloodshot pale blue eyes in the glare of camera floodlights. A little behind him stood the stocky major, representing Karl Wolff. Both looked glum and nervous.

The Germans were dressed in civilian clothes—smart-cut checks, sports coat, grey flannels and lightweight brown shoes. Civilian clothes were worn because there were reasons for secrecy.

Gen. Morgan addressed the Germans sternly, asking if they were prepared to sign terms in behalf of their respective generals. When they assented, he said, "I am empowered by Field-Marshal Alexander to sign on his behalf.

"The terms are effective from noon, May 2. I will now ask you to sign the document."

The German lieut-col. rather truculently asked permission to make a statement. When permission was given he declared that he had received a limited command to negotiate and had exceeded these limits on his own initiative and was therefore unable to guarantee that the terms would be accepted.

Gen. Morgan accepted this condition. The Germans signed the document, which was then signed by Gen. Morgan.

The Germans were given three copies of the document, one of which was in German. The others were kept by the Allied Supreme Command.

After he had signed and given their copies to the Germans, Gen. Morgan, in the stern tone he had used all along, said: "Thank you. I ask you to withdraw now." The German officers bowed politely and withdrew with the escorting officers.

The whole ceremony had taken just over 17 minutes, though the negotiations preceding it had taken over a month. There was no hint of friendliness throughout the ceremony.

It was a sullen, beaten enemy, coldly admitting defeat to an implacable adversary.

Explaining to the Press representatives what the surrender meant, Gen. Morgan said: "If the terms just signed are obeyed, we are practically in Berchtesgaden."

As we were leaving the room we caught a glimpse of Field-Marshal Alexander, spick and span as usual, chatting gaily in Russian with two of the Russian representatives.

The room where the document was signed was probably a bed or dressing-room. It had the traditional Italian marble-flagged floor and a few rather worn carpets.

On its walls were huge maps, with curtains, which could be drawn over them. One map was of the Italian front, another a large-scale map of the city of Vienna. A microphone was hung over the long, narrow table.

Besides sound-recording, the room was floodlit to allow cinematic records to be made. The ceiling of the room bore the coat-of-arms of the Italian Royal families. In the center was the motto: *Incipit novus ordo*—"Here the new order begins."

Götterdämmerung: Pierre J. Huss, International News Service, on the Last Days of Adolf Hitler

[April 30, 1945]

"I don't care what happened. I shall stay here and die."

Berlin was a dying city. Great clouds of smoke hovered in the mid-day sky. Russian artillery shells exploded incessantly. Gunfire thundered through the canyons of rubble.

The Fuehrer *decided to remain in the Reich capital to the last. In his fortified bunker beneath the Chancellery, surrounded by his most fanatical cronies, he gave way to despair. "Meine Herren," he said, "I see that all is lost. I will remain in Berlin. I shall fall here in the Reich Chancellery—I can serve the German people best in that way. There is no sense in continuing any longer." "The greatest German who ever lived," according to his own confession, was finished.*

Hitler married his mistress, Eva Braun, in a gruesome, underground ceremony. He dictated his last will and testament. In the quiet of his bunker room he then shot a bullet into his mouth. His body was drenched in gasoline and burned.

What it was like in that "cloud-cuckoo land of the bunker" was described by Gerhardt Herrgesell, Hitler's principal secretary for the last two years of the war, in this interview with Pierre J. Huss, correspondent for International News Service.

(International News Service, May 15, 1945. By permission of United Press International.)

Herrgesell is thirty-five. He was a member of the SS and he served briefly on the Russian front. He was a champion short-hand writer who had studied law, and in September 1944, he was assigned to be one of two stenographers always at Hitler's elbow even in most secret and limited conferences.

He and the other stenographer were flown out of Berlin from the Gatow Airfield late on the evening of April 22, 1945, under orders from Hitler to proceed to Berchtesgaden and transcribe their notes for posterity. Herrgesell said the Condor plane in which he left Berlin was the last transport to leave the capital. It carried the wives and children of some Nazi officials. Herrgesell heard that Hitler's adjutant, Julius Schaub, got out some time later aboard a fighter plane. [Hence it would have been possible for Hitler to leave also.]

Just before he left, Herrgesell said, Eva Braun gave him a tiny package, apparently containing a ring, and wrote a long farewell letter to be handed over to a Herr Mueller, at Obersalzberg, for an unidentified person.

Hitler's headquarters had been at the Berlin Chancellery since January 16, Herrgesell said. By April 1, all meetings had been shifted down below into the bunkers, where some ten to fifteen high officers took part in conferences with Hitler at a map table.

The living quarters of Hitler and Eva Braun were a couple of small adjoining rooms. The electrically-lighted bunker, just behind the old part of the Chancellery, was two stories deep, sixteen feet square with an upholstered bench along the wall. It had all the comforts that could be provided and was well stocked with food and luxuries from all over plundered Europe.

Early in the afternoon of April 21, a heavy-calibre Russian shell rocked the bunker in the middle of a conference.

But until the next afternoon, April 22, Hitler's order forbidding all talk of a lost war remained in effect. Herrgesell quoted Hitler as having said in March or early April:

"We shall fight until the last scrap of German ground is gone."

This motto stood while the entire reduced Chancellery quarters staff awaited a decision as to when to leave for the so-called national redoubt in South Germany. Until the last everything continued to pivot around Hitler, everyone hoped he would give the word to go south although it was clearly and silently understood that as soon as Hitler abandoned the capital the war would degenerate into a last stand in Bavaria. Nevertheless, most of them wanted this chance to save their skins.

Absent from Berlin was Heinrich Himmler, who commanded the army of the Upper Rhine and later the Vistula group.

At noon on April 20, Chief of Staff Krebs, who had succeeded Gen. Heinz Guderian, characterized the situation in Berlin as being critical. Whereupon Hitler ordered the bulk of Fuehrer headquarters transferred to Berchtesgaden, retaining only a skeleton staff representing the army, navy and air force.

There were no Wehrmacht troops left in the capital except for stray units of volksgrenadiers, volksturmers, non-combat soldiers and herds of picked-up and mobilized clerks, dishwashers and waiters, Herrgesell said. The only regular troops at Berlin's disposal were those of the Twelfth Army facing the American Ninth Army along the Elbe to defend Berlin.

It was fairly quiet the 20th but the next day about 10:20 A.M. Russian shells started falling in the government area. During the day they came in every few seconds in a shifting radius interspersed with strafing raids.

"It seemed that every few minutes somebody ran into the bunker excitedly to warn the Fuehrer that the Russians were closing in," said Herrgesell. "One of the busiest back and forth was Goebbels, who was defense boss of Berlin. We two stenographers had a hard time keeping tab on the goings and comings. Nobody even seemed to notice we were there. Jodl, Keitel, Bormann, Hitler's SS Adjutant Fuensche and Himmler's liaison SS officer Fegelein with a handful of Wehrmacht representatives, hung within beck and call. Goering had left. I never saw Doenitz and von Ribbentrop in those days but heard Hitler talking to them on the phone occasionally."

In the forenoon of Sunday, April 22, five hundred Chancellery clerks, guards, cooks and minor officials were mobilized into Hitler's special escort body and sent to the Alexanderplatz to try and block any Russian breakthrough in that direction. For the first time during the afternoon Hergesell heard Hitler make a vague remark suggesting the war was lost.

" 'It doesn't make any sense to continue any longer,' he said. 'I shall remain here.' "

"Since he didn't elaborate, the entourage let it pass as a tired man's offhand remark.

"By 5 P.M. shells were pretty audible through the open bunker door. It was obviously our last chance to get away unless Hitler had some secret escape prepared. Then at 5:30 P.M., Hitler told Jodl, Keitel and Bormann he wished to see them alone and in his usual gruff way told Fegelein and a handful of others to get out.

"He told Bormann to shut and lock the steel door. We two stenographers sat in dead silence, scarcely daring to breathe and we knew that the fatal moment was at hand."

Hitler wore dark trousers, a field-gray tunic, a white collar with a black tie. An Iron Cross was his only decoration. His grey-flecked moustache was unchanged but his famous forelock was less conspicuous. His face, formerly tanned by the sun, was puffy and florid.

His eyes were sleep-weary. He talked in front of a small map table while the others stood informally around.

The shorthand notes of that dramatic fifteen to twenty minutes were only ten pages. Most was ranting by all present, with Hitler blaming everyone except himself for Germany's downfall and finally yelling: "Get out, get out! Go to South Germany. I'll stay here. I'll stay here. It's all over anyhow."

Keitel's bull-voice cut in: "We won't leave you. I'd be ashamed to face my wife and children if I deserted you."

Hitler waved that aside and again demanded that they go south. Bormann said: "This would be the first time I ever disobeyed you. I won't go."

Jodl, who had been quietly standing aside and was known to be a rare man who would occasionally tell Hitler the straight truth, spoke up calmly as the others momentarily stopped arguing. "I shall not stay in this mouse-hole. Here one cannot establish headquarters and direct a battle or do anything. We are soldiers, *mein Fuehrer.* Give us an army group and orders to fight wherever possible. But I won't stay in this mouse-hole."

In other days Hitler undoubtedly would have exploded and ordered Jodl shot. But this time he snorted and shrugged saying: "Do what you wish—it doesn't mean anything to me any more. I don't care what happens. I shall stay here and die."

Keitel broke in boldly, stating that what sufficient armies remained would continue to fight and could "turn the tide."

"No, it's all over," Hitler said. He told Bormann to start packing.

Then Jodl said: *"Mein Fuehrer,* do you yield herewith complete leadership for continuation of the war?"

Hitler, intentionally or otherwise, evaded a direct answer and turned wearily to Keitel and Bormann: "Go to South Germany," he said, and then he added somewhat incoherently: "Goering will build a government. Goering is my successor anyhow—*ja,* Goering will negotiate everything."

The last obviously was sarcastic, for Hitler now regarded Goering as a traitor to the Nazi cause.

Jodl then repeated his previous question but again was side-tracked when Hitler just said "You must all go south right away." He rose to indicate the conference had ended and declined to listen further.

"Outside I heard Keitel telling the others they must take Hitler by force to Berchtesgaden," Herrgesell said, "but apparently no one knew just what to do except to rush about and telephone. As it turned out they got several like Doenitz to phone Hitler in an effort to persuade him to leave."

Krebs, Guensche and Fegelein all tried to argue Hitler out of his decision. He didn't even shout back, merely motioning everyone aside with repetition of the words: "It's all over. I stay here."

Von Ribbentrop telephoned and strove to convince Hitler he at last had authentic information indicating tension among the Allies and said something about direct word from the British cabinet that a split between the Western Allies and Russia was assured. Hitler formerly had staked much hope on this. But now he showed no interest and said: "Ach, that's what you say. Thanks. *Heil,*" and hung up the phone.

Preliminary Surrender: Chester Wilmot, Speaking for BBC, Records the Ceremony of Surrender to Montgomery at Lüneburg Heath

[May 4, 1945]

"The day's work is done. The triumph of the British armies in Europe is complete."

On May 3, 1945, as tens of thousands of dejected German troops were entering the Allied lines to surrender, Admiral Hans Georg von Friedeburg, Commander-in-Chief of the German Navy, together with several other officers, came to Montgomery's headquarters at Lüneberg Heath to open negotiations for surrender.

The German party was brought to General Montgomery's caravan site. The British general later described it:

> They . . . were drawn up under the Union Jack, which was flying proudly in the breeze. I kept them waiting for a few minutes and then came out of my caravan and walked towards them. They all saluted, under the Union Jack. It was a great moment; I knew the Germans had come to surrender and that the war was over.
>
> I said to my interpreter, "Who are these men?" He told me. I then said, "What do they want?"

Admiral von Friedeburg read a letter from Field Marshal Wilhelm Keitel offering to surrender three German armies withdrawing in front of the Russians between Berlin and Rostock. The Russians, said von Friedeburg, were savages, and it was unthinkable to surrender to them. Montgomery replied that the Germans should have thought of this before they went to war. He sent the emissaries back to Marshal Keitel with a demand for unconditional surrender of the forces in his area.

In his Memoirs *(1958) Montgomery said that "I then decided to spring something on them quickly. I said to Friedeburg: 'Will you surrender to me all German forces on my western and northern flanks, including all forces in Holland, Friesland, with the Frisian Islands and Heligoland, Schleswig-Holstein, and Denmark? If you will do this, I will accept it as a tactical battlefield surrender of the enemy forces immediately opposing me, and those in support of Denmark."*

Montgomery recorded this as an idea of his own. But Eisenhower put it a bit differently in his Crusade in Europe *(1948):*

> I had already told Montgomery to accept the military surrender of all forces in his alloted zone of operations. Such a capitulation would be a tactical affair and the responsibility of the commander on the spot. Consequently, when Admiral Friedeburg returned to Montgomery's headquarters on May 4 with a proposal to surrender all German forces in northwest Germany, including those in Holland and Denmark, Montgomery immediately accepted.

This, then, was a purely military capitulation which ended the war for the British armies in Europe. The main instrument of surrender was signed at Reims on May 7.

Following is an eyewitness account of the surrender on Lüneburg Heath on May 4, 1945, by Chester Wilmot of the British Broadcasting Corporation.

(BBC broadcast, May 4, 1945. By permission of The British Broadcasting Corporation.)

Hallo BBC, hallo BBC, this is Chester Wilmot speaking from the Second Army front in Germany. This is not so much a description of what happened this afternoon, but the actual thing—recorded at Field-Marshal Montgomery's headquarters this afternoon—the full ceremony which took place when the German plenipotentiaries came to sign the instrument of surrender. I've just got to the transmitter and so I haven't had time to edit these recordings and will play them to you as we recorded them on the hill of the Lüneburg Heath this afternoon at Field-Marshal Montgomery's headquarters. There is an opening description of the arrival of the plenipotentiaries, and then you hear Field-Marshal Montgomery himself reading the terms of surrender. These are the recordings we made.

Hallo BBC, this is Chester Wilmot speaking from Field-Marshal Montgomery's tactical headquarters on a high wind-swept hill on the wild Lüneburg Heath near the River Elbe.

It's ten minutes past six on Friday May 4th: the hour and the day for which British fighting men and women and British peoples throughout the world have been fighting and working and waiting for five years and eight months. The commanders of the German forces opposing Field-Marshal Montgomery's Twenty-first Army Group have come to this headquarters to-day to surrender. To make unconditional surrender. The plenipotentiaries are General Admiral von Friedeburg, Commander-in-Chief of the German Navy, who succeeded Admiral Doenitz in that post when Doenitz became the new Fuehrer. With him are General Kinzel, Chief of Staff to Field-Marshal Busch; Rear-Admiral Wagner who is Chief of Staff to von Friedeburg, and another staff officer.

They came here yesterday hoping to parley—to talk terms. But they were told to go back and return to-day with power to make unconditional surrender. They have come back through the lines again to-day, to make that surrender. And now we're waiting for them to come through the trees that surround Field-Marshal Montgomery's headquarters. And here they are now. General Admiral von Friedeburg is leading with Colonel Ewart, of Field-Marshal Montgomery's Staff; with him is the General of Infantry Kinzel . . . Rear-Admiral Wagner, and they're now walking up to the caravan which the Field-Marshal uses for his headquarters in the field. And now von Friedeburg is entering the caravan. He's gone inside, he stood for a moment at the door, saluted. He walked in.

The four other Germans also saluted and they're now standing outside at the bottom step. They're standing underneath the camouflage netting screen, and ten yards away to their right is a Union Jack flying in the breeze, and they're just saluting Field-Marshal Montgomery under the shadow of that flag which is honoured by the troops to whom they're surrendering to-day.

The caravan in which this final conference is being held is the caravan which the British troops captured from General Bergonzoli when they first destroyed an enemy army in this war, the army of Graziani in Cyrenaica in February 1941. In that caravan, souvenir of the first victory in this war, the discussions leading to our final victory are now taking place, and in a few moments Field-Marshal Montgomery and the German plenipotentiaries will move to a tent where the final ceremony of signing will take place.

It's now twenty minutes past six, the discussions have been short and to the point. Admiral von Friedeburg has stepped down from Field-Marshal Montgomery's caravan; he is now walking over to the tent where the signing ceremony will take place with the other German plenipotentiaries, and Field-Marshal Montgomery is following behind carrying the instrument of surrender which they have agreed to sign. Now inside the tent, which is an ordinary camouflaged army tent, the five German plenipotentiaries are standing round the table, an ordinary army table covered with rough army blankets. Field-Marshal Montgomery enters, they salute, and he sits down.

FIELD-MARSHAL MONTGOMERY: Now we've assembled here to-day to accept the surrender terms which have been made with the delegation from the German Army. I will now read out the terms of that instrument of surrender. "The German Command agrees to the surrender of all German armed forces in Holland, in north-west Germany, including the Frisian Islands and Heligoland and all other islands, in Schleswig-Holstein, and in Denmark to the Commander-in-Chief 21st Army Group. This to include all naval ships in these areas. These forces to lay down their arms and to surrender unconditionally. All hostilities on land, on sea, or in the air by German forces in the above areas to cease at 0800 hours British Double Summer Time on Saturday the 5th May, 1945. The German Command to carry out at once and without argument or comment all further orders that will be issued by the Allied Powers on any subject. Disobedience of orders or failure to comply with them will be regarded as a breach of these surrender terms, and will be dealt with by the Allied Powers in accordance with the accepted laws and usages of War. This instrument of surrender is independent of, without prejudice to, and will be superseded by, any general instrument of surrender imposed by or on behalf of the Allied Powers and applicable to Germany and the German Armed Forces as a whole. This instrument of surrender is written in English, and in German. The English version is the authentic text. The decision of the Allied Powers will be final, if any doubt or dispute arises as to the meaning or interpretation of the surrender terms." That is the text of the instrument of surrender and the German delegation will now sign this paper, and they will sign in order of seniority and General Admiral von Friedeburg will sign first. . . . Now General Kinzel will sign next. . . . Rear-Admiral Wagner will sign next. . . . Colonel Pollek will sign next. . . . And Major Freidel will sign now.

Now I will sign the instrument on behalf of the Supreme Allied Commander, General Eisenhower. Now that concludes the formal surrender and there are various matters now, or details to be discussed, which we will do in closed session.

WILMOT: And now the discussions, of which Field-Marshal Montgomery spoke, are completed. The German generals have left the tent. They're moving through the trees to the visitors' camp where they will spend the night, as visitors in Field-Marshal Montgomery's headquarters. And the Field-Marshal himself has walked briskly across the grass square in front of his caravan, entered and closed the door behind him. The day's work is done. The triumph of the British armies in Europe is complete. To-morrow morning at eight o'clock the war will be over for the British and Canadian troops, and for the airmen of Britain and the Commonwealth who came to liberate the occupied countries and to conquer Germany.

To-morrow morning their victory will be complete.

Berlin Falls: American Newsmen Describe the Devastated Capital of the Third Reich

[May 5–9, 1945]

May 2, 1945. After two weeks of desperate street fighting, the remaining German troops in Berlin, their ammunition gone, surrendered.

It was an incredible spectacle. The largest city on the European continent and the capital of the Nazi Third Reich was almost as dead as Pompeii or Carthage. American and British bombardment from the air and Russian artillery had smashed the giant metropolis beyond recognition. Scarred skeletons of buildings teetered precariously on their foundations. The streets were filled with rubble, the air with dust. Bodies were left where they had fallen.

The people of Berlin were shattered by panic and fear. Those still alive moved in the subways, in the tunnels, or burrowed into the ruins to share quarters with the rats. There was no water, no electricity, no telephone. Shops were bare. It was a fitting memorial to the madman of Berchtesgaden.

Several American reporters reached the German capital in time to record a story of terrible retribution. Here are two of the most memorable reports on the grievously wounded city.

BERLIN—BROKEN SKELETON OF A CITY

(*Ernest Leiser*, Stars and Stripes, *Paris Edition, May 10, 1945. Courtesy of the U.S. Army.*)

"Berlin is one great tombstone."

BERLIN, May 5 (Delayed)—Berlin, the capital of defeat, today is a charred, stinking, broken skeleton of a city.

It is impossible to imagine what it looked like before. It is impossible to believe that the miles of disembowelled buildings, of cratered streets, of shattered masonry once could have been the capital of Greater Germany and the home of 4,000,000 people.

Only a handful of those 4,000,000 still remain as the last clatter of machine-gun fire echoes through the hollow city. There are no factories left for them to work in, no shops, no theatres, no office buildings.

But the handful are busy today: They are shovelling the rubble from the streets, sweeping the dead out of the way—working while the Russian conquerors still walk the streets with straggling columns of prisoners or wander around staring at the shells of once-great buildings of state. They are working, oblivious of the light, chill rain that is the only mourning for the death of their homes.

The Russians are everywhere—their tanks rumble down the Charlottenburger Chaussee which slices through the great Tiergarten Park; a pert girl MP smartly directs traffic at the west end of Unter den Linden; an infantry battalion forms up in front of the shrapnel-scarred statue of Wilhelm the Great; single armed soldiers wander in and out of cellars; cavalrymen wash their horses at the edge of the River Spree in shambles that was the city's center.

A Cossack rides down the Wilhelmstrasse raising a cloud of dust from the powdered stone and concrete that, despite the rain, coats everything. Horse and wagon convoys creak down Leipziger Strasse, pass the bodies of two German soldiers, with mouths open, in a grin of death.

In front of the bomb-hollowed Reichtag's hole-filled dome, a torn Red flag flies. In the circle that is the center of the Tiergarten, a group of Soviet soldiers pose for a picture in front of a statue of the haughty Moltke.

At the eastern end of Unter den Linden, a band plays and Russian soldiers dance to native songs in the great place before the Opera. A few blocks away, a Russian machine gun fires, and from the northwestern edge of the city, near the Beusselstrasse railroad station comes the sound of Russian artillery.

Unter den Linden, which a 1929 guide book proudly calls the "most beautiful avenue in all the city," is gray with the universal powder of death and broken as all the rest. We stopped to pick up a grim souvenir—a street sign with the enamel partly chipped off and a bullet hole through it. Beside the sign were a German man and woman, dead among the debris.

The street is still the "gathering place best known to foreigners." Today, the foreigners are multi-uniformed, battle-dirty Russians, walking slowly with slung tommy-guns, or pushing down the streets in convoys of U.S.-made jeeps and trucks honking constantly. No one is buying anything from the "smart shops, catering to the most elegant tastes." The shops are closed for good.

The trees in the Tiergarten—Berlin's once-beautiful zoological park—looked as though a hurricane had ripped through the city. Shell-shredded, half leafless, they are as broken as the buildings. A red parachute dangled from a smashed branch. The hull of a burnt-out Panther tank lies beneath a fallen trunk.

On the avenues, beside the long columns of red-flagged Russian tanks, are smashed six-barrelled, self-propelled mortars, trucks, sedans. Branches, dirty leaves, broken glass and the ever-present stone dust surface the road.

Nearly intact is the great Brandenburger Tor—the Brandenburg Gate—Berlin's triumphal arch and symbol of its military glory. Its columns still stand, their bases partly covered with debris. On top, one bronze horse pulls the chariot of Victory, but the chariot is smashed and Victory is only mangled metal. One of the horses has fallen to the ground.

In the center of the seven-pointed Grosser Stern—Great Star— where wide avenues sweep together in the Tiergarten, a statue of the Victory Amazon, in smoke-streaked gold atop a stone column, is untouched. High above the park, at the base of the statue, Russian soldier-sightseers look down on the city they have taken. Another soldier plays an accordion at the foot of the column.

On the Wilhelmstrasse, the Reichschancellery is gutted, as are all the buildings where the Nazi great made their plans to make this street the nerve center of the world. No one seems to know if Hitler's body is inside the Chancellery. No one seems to care.

On Wallstrasse, the entrances to the Berlin subway are choked with broken concrete and timbers. Smoke rises from a new fire in one of the already-burned buildings down the street.

On Lindenstrasse, a horse picks his way among the debris. At the Belle Alliance Platz, the graceful statue dedicated to the "beautiful alliance" stands high on its slender column in the midst of ruin.

It is difficult to go to many parts of Berlin. Streets everywhere are blocked. It is the same in all of the districts, residential, industrial, business. Only some of the suburbs, like Mariendorf, are still alive, and they are scarred and damaged.

Thus it is with the German capital today, two days after its official capture by the Russians. Street fights are just coming to an end, and the smell of sewage and death is everywhere. It is one great tomb-stone.

As you ride out of Berlin, on the single wall that remains in a whole block, near the city's southern limits, you see a sign, white-washed into the crumbling bricks. It says: *"Mit Unser Fuehrer, Zum Zieg."* Translated, that means: "With our *Fuehrer*, to Victory."

BERLIN—A MODERN CARTHAGE

(Harold King for the Combined Allied Press, May 9, 1945. By permission of Associated Press.)

"The Blitz on London was a bank holiday compared with this one."

BERLIN, May 9 (A.P.)—This town is a city of the dead. As a metropolis it has simply ceased to exist. Every house within miles of the center seems to have had its own bomb.

I toured the Nazi capital from the east to the center and back to the south this morning in company with Air Chief Marshal Sir Arthur Tedder and the Russian military commander of Berlin, General Berzarin.

The scene beggars description. I have seen Stalingrad; I have lived through the entire London *Blitz;* I have seen a dozen badly damaged Russian towns, but the scene of utter destruction, desolation and death which meets the eye in Berlin as far as the eye can rove in all directions is something that almost baffles description.

"The *Blitz* of London was a bank holiday compared with this," one of my colleagues remarked.

Dozens of well-known thoroughfares, including the entire Unter den Linden from one end to the other, are wrecked beyond repair. The town is literally unrecognizable.

The Alexander Platz, in the east end, where the Gestapo head-quarters was, is a weird desert of rubble and gaping, smoke-blackened walls. From the Brandenburg Gate, everything within a radius of from 2 to 5 miles is destroyed. There does not appear to be one house in a hundred which is even useful as shelter.

Among hundreds of well-known landmarks which have disappeared or been irreparably damaged are the former Kaiser's palace, the opera house, the French, British, American and Japanese embassies, Goering's Air Ministry, Goebbels' Propaganda Ministry, the Bristol and Adlon Hotels.

Hitler's Chancellery in the Wilhelmstrasse is like some vast abandoned ancient tomb of the dead. It has had several direct hits, and it is impossible yet to tell who lies buried beneath the rubble, perhaps Hitler himself.

The only people who look like human beings in the streets of what was Berlin are the Russian soldiers. There are 2,000,000 inhabitants in the town, the Russian authorities told me, but they are mostly in the remoter suburbs. In the central part of the town you only see a few ghostlike figures of women and children—few men—queueing up to pump water.

If Stalingrad, London, Guernica, Rotterdam, Coventry wanted avenging, they have had it, and no mistake about it.

The Red flag, or rather several Red flags, fly on top of the Reichstag which is burned hollow. The Tiergarten opposite the Reichstag looks like a forest after a big fire. There was heavy street fighting here.

I motored from the Tempelhof airport in a fast car and during 30 minutes' unhampered driving, I spotted only six houses which you were not able to see straight through and in which there were signs of habitation.

The population and Red Army soldiers are attempting to clear some of the main streets.

The Russian command has already erected at all main squares and crossings huge sketch maps, without which it would be impossible to find one's way about.

Except for an occasional Russian army car or horses drawing Russian army carts, there is complete silence over the city, and the air is filled with rubble dust.

One sign of life, however, are the interminable columns of displaced persons of all European nationalities who seem to be marching through Berlin in various directions, carried forward by a homing instinct more than by any clear idea of where they are going. These columns of freed slaves are sometimes a mile long.

They trudge along slowly, one or two abreast, drawing tiny carts, or six or eight of them at a time dragging with ropes wagons which need a lusty horse. In these columns there are many little groups, carrying the flag of their nationality—Italians, French, Belgians, mostly. Many are in soldier's uniform and appear to be escaped or freed prisoners of war.

The Russian military command of this modern Carthage is already feeding hundreds of thousands of Berliners. The Red Army has seized what food stocks the town had, and has added from its own supplies.

Berliners get 500 grams of bread a day (more than many got in Moscow in the winter of 1942), a little meat, sugar, coffee, potatoes. Attempts are being made to get the water supply working. The Russians are obviously not wreaking any vengeance on the population.

I asked one well-known Russian writer, who was attending the surrender ceremonial, why the Russians bothered about the population.

"We must look after the people," he said with a note of surprise at the question. "We cannot let 2,000,000 people die."

Many wounded German soldiers lying in underground hospitals have been sent to Russian-organized hospitals, and are looked after by German doctors and German nurses.

End of the War in Europe: Edward Kennedy of the Associated Press Beats the World Press on German Surrender and Is Promptly Accused of Unethical Journalistic Double Cross

[May 7, 1945]

"Germany surrendered unconditionally. . . ."

Sixteen reporters, including Edward Kennedy of the Associated Press, were flown by SHAEF from Paris on May 7, 1945 to witness the unconditional surrender of Germany at Reims in France. The newsmen were told that the story was entirely off the record until the heads of the governments concerned had announced it. The news release was to be synchronized in Washington, London and Moscow.

As soon as the reporters arrived back in Paris after the surrender ceremony, Kennedy went to an Army telephone and reported the following story to London. The next day fifty-four correspondents accredited to SHAEF sent an outraged letter to General Eisenhower: "We have respected the confidence placed in us by SHAEF and as a result have suffered the most disgraceful, deliberate and unethical double cross in the history of journalism."

The correspondents who had been scooped by Kennedy subjected him to a merciless tongue-lashing. SHAEF immediately suspended Associated Press's filing facilities in Europe, but withdrew this action just six hours and twenty minutes after it was taken. Kennedy himself lost his job and was discredited as a war correspondent.

Defenders of Kennedy pointed out that he had made a historic news beat and how he did it was his own business. Editor and Publisher *commented: "Had we been in Kennedy's position we are inclined to believe that we would have attempted to do just as he did. . . . We believe that his story will go down in the books as one of the greatest journalistic beats in history." Others said that the reporters who had been scooped had forgotten about the telephone line that Kennedy used.*

Kennedy himself later claimed that he had never given a promise to keep his mouth shut until it was opened officially. "The request for a delay was made by the Russians, who wanted to hold a surrender cere-

471

mony of their own in Berlin. The second surrender was meaningless, since Russia had already accepted the German surrender. . . . Shortly after noon on May 7 the German government . . . publicly announced the unconditional surrender over the radio at Flensburg, Denmark. I then immediately informed the censorship that since the Supreme Command had itself released the news, I felt no longer obligated to accept the gag imposed on the correspondents. . . . I sent the story."

Historic news beat or unethical double cross, it made little difference at the time. The flash, speeding throughout the Allied world, set off thunderous celebrations everywhere.

(The New York Times, *May 8, 1945. By permission of Associated Press.*)

THE WAR IN EUROPE IS ENDED! SURRENDER IS UNCONDITIONAL; V-E WILL BE PROCLAIMED TODAY

By Edward Kennedy

REIMS, FRANCE, May 7—Germany surrendered unconditionally to the Western Allies and the Soviet Union at 2:41 A.M. French time today. [This was at 8:41 P.M. Eastern war time, Sunday, May 6, 1945.]

The surrender took place at a little red schoolhouse that is the headquarters of General Dwight D. Eisenhower.

The surrender was signed for the Supreme Allied Command by Lieutenant General Walter Bedell Smith, chief of staff for General Eisenhower.

It was also signed by General Ivan Susloparov of the Soviet Union and by General François Sevez for France.

General Eisenhower was not present at the signing, but immediately afterward General Jodl and his fellow delegate, General Admiral Hans Georg Friedeburg, were received by the Supreme Commander.

They were asked sternly if they understood the surrender terms imposed upon Germany and if they would be carried out by Germany.

They answered yes.

Germany, which began the war with a ruthless attack upon Poland, followed by successive aggressions and brutality in concentration camps, surrendered with an appeal to the victors for mercy toward the German people and armed forces.

After having signed the full surrender, General Jodl said he wanted to speak and received leave to do so.

"With this signature," he said in soft-spoken German, "the German people and armed forces are for better or worse delivered into the victor's hands.

"In this war, which has lasted more than five years, both have achieved and suffered more than perhaps any other people in the world."

Final German Capitulation at Reims: Charles Collingwood of CBS Broadcasts "Perhaps the Best News the World Has Ever Had"

[May 7, 1945]

"The mad dog of Europe was put out of the way, the strange, insane monstrosity that was Nazi Germany had been beaten into submission."

Germany had collapsed. Many thousands of prisoners had been taken by the Allies. Other thousands were trying desperately to surrender either to the Americans or to the British rather than to the dreaded Russians. The German Government ordered all U-boats to return to home port.

On May 5, 1945, Admiral Hans Georg von Friedeburg, as representative of Admiral Karl Doenitz, the new head of the German Government, arrived at Eisenhower's headquarters. Friedeburg said he wanted to "negotiate," but he was told quickly that there was no point in discussing anything. There would be unconditional, total surrender of all German forces everywhere. Eisenhower made it plain, through Lieutenant General Walter Bedell Smith, that unless the Germans ceased all pretense and delay, he would close the entire Allied front in the west to German refugees.

The end came on May 7, 1945, when representatives of Germany signed the instrument of surrender in a red schoolhouse at Reims, France. Charles Collingwood, of the Columbia Broadcasting System, who was present with sixteen other correspondents, broadcast this eyewitness report several hours later from SHAEF, Supreme Headquarters Allied Expeditionary Force. Collingwood's account included a description of the last-minute negotiations preceding the ceremony.

(CBS broadcast, May 8, 1945. By permission of Charles Collingwood.)

Germany surrendered at 2:45 on the morning of May 7, 1945. At that moment, General Jodl, Chief of Staff of the German Army, signed the last document. He sat there very straight, with his head bent over the papers, and when he had signed the last one, he put the cap back on the pen and looked up at the men sitting across the plain wooden table. Opposite him sat General Bedell Smith, Eisenhower's Chief of Staff. General Smith looked tired. He'd been negotiating for thirty-three hours, but his mouth was hard and so were his eyes.

As he looked to his right, General Jodl could see a big, powerful man in the uniform of a Russian General, sitting next to General Smith. He was General Susloparov, the Russian delegate. Over his shoulder peered the extraordinary head of another Russian. The head was bald as a gourd, with fierce, unwavering eyes, whose bright and sinister gaze did not for an instant leave the drawn face of General Jodl. Jodl did not meet his eyes for long but looked around the table at Admiral Sir Harold Burrough, the Allied Naval Commander, at General Spaatz, the Air Commander, at General Sevez, the French representative.

Then General Jodl looked again at General Smith. "I would like to say something," he said.

Smith nodded.

Jodl rose stiffly to his feet: "Herr General," he said in a voice that choked and almost broke, "with this signature the German people and the German armed forces are, for better or worse, delivered into the victor's hands. In this war, which has lasted more than five years, both have achieved and suffered more than perhaps any other people in the world. In this hour, I can only express the hope that the victor will treat them with generosity." Then, General Jodl sat down quickly.

No one else said anything. The Germans looked around as though wondering what to do next and at another nod from General Smith they got up—General Jodl, his aide, and Admiral Friedeburg, who commands the German Navy. With Jodl in the lead they walked quickly out of the room.

With sixteen other correspondents I witnessed this scene, which formalized the complete and resounding defeat in the history of the world, which meant relief and hope to millions of sorely tried people. It was the end of the war, the climax of a series of piecemeal surrenders. The final surrender took place at a quarter to three on Monday morning.

The negotiations began late Saturday afternoon. Admiral Friedeburg, who had earlier surrendered northern Germany, Denmark and Holland to the British, arrived at General Eisenhower's Headquarters at Reims, France, just after five P.M. on Saturday. He wanted to talk about complete surrender.

He tried to pull once more the old dodge about surrendering to the western Allies and not to the Russians. He was, of course, flatly refused.

Since Friedeburg was not empowered to sign a final surrender, he was told to get someone who was. He sent a message to Doenitz, asking for someone who could sign. The next day, Sunday, at 5:08 P.M., Jodl landed at Reims. The expectation was then that the surrender would be signed almost immediately, but Jodl turned out to be a tough customer.

Colonel General Gustav Jodl, the German plenipotentiary, is a typical, stiff-necked, Prussian professional soldier. He is ugly, and his face is ravaged by what appears to be some kind of skin disease, but he is as straight as a gun barrel and the embodiment of what we think of as Prussian arrogance.

Admiral von Friedeburg was relatively easy to negotiate with. He seemed rather a pleasant old fellow, but there was nothing pleasant about Jodl.

The conference dragged on. Finally Jodl dispatched another message to Admiral Doenitz. Everyone sat down to wait. The Russians had a cocktail party. The French general went back to his quarters. Some of the British and American negotiators took a quick nap. The Germans sat morosely in the house that had been set aside for them.

Just before two o'clock in the morning when it looked as though everything was over for the night, the negotiators began to drift back to the Supreme Headquarters at the College Moderne et Technicale in Reims. General Spaatz came in first. He looked quietly content. Then General Bedell Smith drove up. He is not given to visible emotion, but as he walked up to his office he looked almost jubilant. Then the Russians came in grinning from ear to ear and after them the rest trickled in.

About two-thirty they began to go into the war room where the instruments of surrender were to be signed. Let me try to picture for you this scene as I saw it when I was there early Monday morning.

Here's this room—not a very big room as rooms go. The walls are covered with maps in bright reds and greens almost up to the ceiling. On these maps is all the information General Jodl would have traded an army group to have a week ago. Our battle order, our communications system, our supply network, our casualties, and perhaps most important of all, the Germans' own hopeless position clearly marked out. This room, General Eisenhower's war room, is bathed in the hot glow from the blinding lights the photographers have set up. At one end is a long table. A very plain, very old, rather rickety wooden table the top side of which is painted black. Around this table are fourteen chairs. Twelve of them are arranged around one side and the other two with their backs to us, occupy one whole side of the table. This is where General Jodl and Admiral Friedeburg had to sit.

The only people in the room now besides us correspondents are a milling mass of photographers in constant movement climbing up and down ladders, aiming cameras, and around the walls there is a battery of recording apparatus set up to catch every word by our friends the radio engineers of SHAEF, the people who get our broadcasts through.

The whole place is brilliantly lit. It looks like a movie set. About two-thirty in the morning General Tooey Spaatz walks in. He is followed in quick succession by the Russians. Then Air Marshal Robb comes in; Admiral Burrough. Pretty soon Bedell Smith himself enters, the man who bore the brunt of the long hours of negotiations. He looks tired, but there's a look of grim satisfaction about his tight mouth. The other generals come in. The last is the little French general, Sevez. He looks out of breath as though he'd run up the stairs. Everyone stands about by their chairs, waiting for the Germans. Spaatz makes a soldierly pleasantry to the Russians and they grin broadly. Everyone tries to appear completely at ease, but the air is tense, tense, tense.

Then the Germans come in. Jodl's face is like a death mask; drawn, unnatural-looking, and with every muscle in it clenched. Admiral Friedeburg is more relaxed, but he, too, is not enjoying himself. Jodl's aide bobs about like a head waiter in a restaurant. Their uniforms are immaculate and rather spectacular in the German fashion. Both Jodl and his aide have the double red stripe of the German General Staff on the sides of their cavalry breeches. They reach the table, bow in unison, and wait. General Smith motions them to sit down. Everyone sits down.

Then the cameramen start bounding about after the fashion of cameramen, like so many monkeys in the zoo. They run at top speed all around the room, up and down ladders, flash-bulbs going all the time. It's an incredible scene. The generals are clearly annoyed, but still the photographers untiringly dash about, getting in the way of General Strong, Eisenhower's G-2, who is by this time handing around the documents to be signed.

Jodl signs the surrender, at 2:41, and then General Smith who hands it to the Russian General Susloparov—and finally the French General Sevez signs it. This happens four times . . . a copy for each nation. Meanwhile, Admiral Burrough and General Smith sign a paper relating to the conditions for disarming the German Navy. And Smith and Spaatz sign one for the ground and air forces.

By 2:45 the last signature has been affixed. The photographers are still in full cry, leaping over one another to get their pictures. It has become completely ridiculous, but still they go on. They're fascinated by the face of General Susloparov's interpreter. He's a Russian with a head completely bald, not a hair, and a glittering eye which he fixed on the Germans like the very eye of doom. To get a good shot at him, a photographer leans over the Germans, elbowing Jodl out of the way, and flashes his bulb at the Russian.

The Germans sit there, through it all, stiff, unblinking, tasting to the bitter dregs their cup of humiliation.

Then came the most dramatic moment of all. Everything had been signed. There was no longer any possibility of quibbling or evasion. The German Third Reich, which had once made the world tremble, had collapsed in blood-stained fragments. Colonel General Jodl, Chief of Staff of the German Army, asked General Bedell Smith's permission to speak. He stood up stiffly, like a man holding himself in against some unbearable pain.

In a strangled voice, like a sob, he said: "With this signature the German people and the German armed forces are, for better or worse, delivered into the victor's hands. In this hour, I can only express the hope that the victor will treat them with generosity."

I will let you hear now how it sounded. Here is a recording made at the table of his actual words as General Jodl spoke in that moment filled with such tremendous meaning.

(*Collingwood plays the recording.*)

When General Jodl sat down after that, it was all over. At a sign from General Smith, the Germans stood up, bowed again, and quickly left the room.

Up to this time they had not yet seen General Eisenhower or Air Chief Marshal Tedder, his deputy. All the negotiations were undertaken by General Smith and General Strong, but after the surrender, Jodl and Friedeburg were taken to the Supreme Commander. Eisenhower and his deputy, Air Chief Marshal Tedder, stood side-by-side behind Eisenhower's desk, unsmiling.

The Germans bowed and stood there. Eisenhower asked them curtly whether they had understood the terms of surrender and whether they agreed to carry them out. The Germans said "Yes," and then they were taken away.

It was all over—the Germans had surrendered—and later General Eisenhower said a few words. This is what he said:

"In January, 1943, the late President Roosevelt and Premier Churchill met in Casablanca. There they pronounced the formula of unconditional surrender for the Axis powers. In Europe, that formula has now been fulfilled. The Allied force, which invaded Europe on June 6, 1944, has, with its great Russian ally, and forces advancing in the south, utterly defeated the Germans by land, sea and air. Thus, unconditional surrender has been achieved by teamwork, teamwork not only among all the Allies participating but amongst all the services—land, sea and air. To every subordinate that has been in this command, of almost five million Allies, I owe a debt of gratitude that can never be repaid. The only repayment that can be made to them is the deep appreciation and lasting gratitude of all free citizens of all the United Nations."

With these words General Eisenhower finished the evening's ceremonies. It was all over. Eisenhower relaxed, everyone relaxd. One almost forgave the photographers. The most terrible war in human history had finally come to an end. The mad dog of Europe was put out of the way, the strange, insane monstrosity that was Nazi Germany had been beaten into submission. To millions of people this was the end of suffering. It was perhaps the best news the world had ever had—the surrender of Reims had been signed.

V-E Day: In the Midst of Global Celebration Gordon Cobbledick of the Cleveland *Plain Dealer* Points to Japanese Steel on Okinawa

[May 8, 1945]

"I know where the bastard is and I'm going to get him."

The news came with the impact of a hurricane. Londoners happily streamed toward Buckingham Palace. British pubs were filled with joyous customers and there was much singing. Moscow buzzed with excitement. Times Square in New York burst into an all-out hi-de-ho celebration. Everywhere there was the roar of victory. There was also the lamentation of defeat: in Berlin crowds of weeping women shouted: "The war is kaput. Das ist gut!"

At the doorstep of Japan, on the other side of the world, there was no celebration. The enemy was still fighting and Americans were dying even as crowds shouted their joy in the streets of Chicago and Los Angeles. Winston Churchill gave this analysis:

> Japan, with all her treachery and greed, remains unsubdued. The injuries she has inflicted upon Great Britain, the United States and other countries, and her detestable cruelties call for justice and retribution. We must now devote all our strength and resources to the completion of our task.

How the news of V-E Day was received on Okinawa was described in this dispatch by Gordon Cobbledick. It was a sobering reminder that the slaughter was not yet over.

(*Cleveland* Plain Dealer, *May 9, 1945. By permission of the Cleveland* Plain Dealer.)

OKINAWA, May 8 (Via Navy Radio)—We stood in the rain this morning and heard the voice from San Francisco, only half believing. There had been so many false reports. But this seemed to be the McCoy.

"Confirmed by Gen. Eisenhower's headquarters," the voice was saying. "Prime Minister Churchill proclaimed May 8 as V-E Day."

480

Artillery thundered and the planes roared low overhead and we couldn't hear all that the voice was saying.

"President Truman . . . Marshal Stalin announced . . . the Canadian government at Ottawa . . . unauthorized announcement . . . American news agency . . ."

So this was V-E Day. It was V-E Day in the United States and Great Britain and Russia, but on Okinawa the ambulances skidded through the sticky red mud and bounced over rutted, rocky coral roads. Some of the men who rode them gritted their teeth behind bloodless lips and let no cry escape them. Some stared skyward through eyes that were dull with the look of men to whom nothing mattered greatly. Some screamed with pain that the morphine couldn't still. And some lay very quiet under ponchos that covered their faces.

It was V-E Day all over the world, but on Okinawa two doughboys lay flat behind a jagged rock and one said, "I know where the bastard is and I'm going to get him."

He raised his head and looked and then he stood, half crouched, and brought his Garand into position.

When he tumbled backward the rifle clattered on the rocks. The boy looked up and smiled sheepishly and said, "I hurt my arm when I fell," and the blood gushed from his mouth and ran in a quick torrent over the stubble of beard on his young face, and he was dead.

It was V-E Day at home, but on Okinawa men shivered in fox holes half filled with water and waited for the command to move forward across the little green valley that was raked from both ends by machine-gun fire.

It was V-E Day, but on Okinawa a staff officer sat looking dully at the damp earthen floor of his tent. A young lieutenant, his green field uniform plastered with mud, stood awkwardly beside him.

"I was with him, sir," the lieutenant said. "It was a machine-gun bullet, sir. He never knew what hit him." He paused. "He was a good marine, sir."

The staff officer said, "He was the only son we had."

On Okinawa a flame-throwing tank lumbered across a narrow plain toward an enemy pillbox. From a cave a gun spat viciously and the tank stopped and burst into fire. When the crewmen clambered out machine guns chattered and they fell face forward in the mud and were still.

It was V-E Day everywhere, but on Okinawa the forests of white crosses grew and boys who had hardly begun to live died miserably in the red clay of this hostile land.

It was a day of celebration, but on Okinawa the war moved on. Not swiftly, for swift war cannot be waged against an enemy who burrows underground where bombs and shells and all the instruments of quick destruction can't touch him. Not gloriously, for there is little glory in any war and none at all in cold and mud. But the enemy wouldn't wait and the war moved on.

It was V-E Day, and on Okinawa a soldier asked, "What are they going to do back in the States—get drunk and forget about us out here?"

Another said, "So they'll open the race tracks and turn on the lights and give people all the gas they want and the hell with us."

Another said, "They'll think the war is over and they'll quit their jobs and leave us to fight these bastards with pocket knives."

You told them it wasn't so. You said the people would have their day of celebration and then would go grimly back to the job of producing what is needed so desperately out here.

And you hoped to God that what you were saying was the truth.

Aftermath: CBS Correspondents Describe the Last Few Days Following Germany's Surrender

[May 9-24, 1945]

"Himmler was caught like a tramp and he died like one."

Hitler's mighty machine of conquest was ready for the scrap heap. Germany was beaten, completely and utterly. Still the American public was hungry for more news. It continued to come—sensation after sensation—during the days following the unconditional surrender.

The Russians had their own separate surrender. Field Marshal Herman Goering was captured. Hitler's successor, Admiral Karl Doenitz, was taken into custody. Heinrich Himmler ended it all with a capsule of poison. These stirring events were described over the air by correspondents of the Columbia Broadcasting System. The newsmen referred to in the following broadcasts were Howard K. Smith, Charles Collingwood, Larry Leseuer and Richard C. Hottelet. These, with other CBS stalwarts such as Edward R. Murrow, Eric Sevareid, Maj. George Fielding Eliot, William L. Shirer, Quincy Howe and others, had done consistently fine work through the entire course of the war. These were truly the great voices of journalism in stirring days.

(CBS broadcasts. By permission of Howard K. Smith, Charles Collingwood, Larry Lesueur, Richard Hottelet.)

May 9

9:15 A.M.

HOWARD K. SMITH (*from Paris*):

. . . It was half an hour before midnight over here when the Union of Soviet Socialist Republics officially accepted the unconditional surrender of Nazi Germany. . . . It was accepted and signed by Field Marshal Wilhelm Keitel for the German Army, by General Admiral Hans Georg von Friedeburg for the German Navy and by Colonel General Stumpf for the Luftwaffe. . . .

I was there in Zhukov's headquarters in the east Berlin suburb

483

of Karlshorst. The ceremony took place in the dining-hall of a former German Army engineering school. . . . Zhukov's jaw was calm with the calmness of a commander who can and did fight his way from the inferno of Stalingrad to a thousand miles across Europe, to triumph in Berlin. Keitel was nervous, irritated, arrogant at being reduced to the most humiliating gesture a Prussian martinet can know—having to face and beg surrender from a "prolet" of Red Russia. . . . He was presented with the articles of surrender. Hardly reading them he shrugged his shoulders and placed his hands on his hip in a blunt expression of disgust. No pen to sign with had been placed before him. Zhukov said nothing and did nothing, nor did anyone else. Finally, Keitel pulled out his own fountain pen and signed with it. . . .

Then he began really to play showman. He suddenly discovered that he had not read the document until after he had signed it. . . . He insisted that he must have an additional twenty-four hours to inform his troops that they had not only to surrender but to give up their guns. The brow of Zhukov, about ten yards away, looked like a gathering storm. The American interpreter told Keitel to explain his case to the Russian interpreter. Keitel did. He also asked the Russian to request of Zhukov the twenty-four hours reprieve. The interpreter went to Zhukov. Zhukov gave no answer. He didn't alter his expression. He acted as though he hadn't heard a thing. Keitel, then, let the world hope, with the last gesture of Prussianism, slammed his portfolio shut on the already signed documents, arose, saluted stiffly, and marched out of the room.

6:45 P.M.
COLLINGWOOD (*from SHAEF*):

Field Marshal Goering, the fat one, the one with all the medals, has given himself up. By his own story he has been hiding from Hitler's SS troops; he had telephoned Hitler on April 24 as the Russian and American forces were about to meet in the center of Germany.

He had reminded Hitler that he, Goering, was next in line and due to take over power in case anything happened. Goering suggested that it had happened. Hitler was furious and had Goering arrested by the SS and condemned him to death. Goering's own Luftwaffe troops are then said to have shot their way through his SS guards and rescued him.

Goering is supposed to be a drug addict, but men who saw him said he didn't appear to be hopped up. He complained that the bombing of Berchtesgaden had destroyed half his medals, but he still insisted on dressing up for dinner in a fancy gold-braided uniform hung with decorations like a Christmas tree. He was ridiculous to the last.

May 16
5.50 P.M.
LESUEUR (*from Paris*):

. . . Clear-eyed and firm-jawed Lieut. General Lucius Clay, who'll be Deputy Military Governor of the American occupation of Germany under Eisenhower, told us flatly today that the government the Americans will set up in Germany will be *military* government and the Germans will know that it's military government. And anyone who's ever been in the Army knows what General Clay means. . . .

May 23
4:30 P.M.
LESUEUR (*from Paris*):

The Third Reich is dead! It came to an end at ten o'clock this morning in a setting similar to that in which it was spawned . . . a bar. The beer parlor of a captured German Hamburg-American liner anchored in the docks of the little German Baltic seaport of Flensburg. At 9:45 this morning, Grand Admiral Doenitz and Colonel General Jodl were ordered to appear on board. . . . As they mounted the gangplank, Admiral Doenitz turned to Colonel General Jodl and said: "It's clear what this is all about.". . .

There was no saluting or handshaking. . . . Rooks sat opposite Doenitz and a Russian, Major General Nicolai Trusof, member of Marshal Zhukov's staff, sat opposite Vice Admiral Friedeburg. The British Brigadier General, Edward Ford, sat opposite General Jodl. . . . General Rooks began simply by saying in a cool voice, "Gentlemen, I am in receipt of instructions from the Supreme Command of the Allied Expeditionary Forces, from General Eisenhower, to call you before me this morning to tell you that he has decided, in concert with the Soviet High Command, that today the acting German Government and a German High Command shall be taken into custody, with several of its members, both military and civilian, as prisoners of war. . . .

"When you leave this room, an Allied officer will attach himself to you and escort you to your quarters. There you'll pack, eat your lunch, and complete your affairs. You may take what baggage you require and you'll be escorted to an airfield for emplaning at 1:30. That is all I have to say.". . .

Finally, Admiral Doenitz gathered himself together and said, in a voice that began weakly but ended more firmly: "Any words would be superfluous." General Rooks nodded his head, as if to say "you're right.". . .

Doenitz, leading the German party, slumped and shuffled out of the room. Hitler's ill-fated successor did not straighten up until he got out of the door and passed some enlisted men. He then made a last effort to draw himself up and he strolled down to the gangplank. Followed by six armed Allied officers and clasping his powerless baton in his hand, Hitler's successor . . . walked down the dockside, as hundreds of scowling soldiers and sailors watched. . . .

May 24
6:51 P.M.
HOTTELET (*from Paris*):

Heinrich Himmler is dead: The head of the Nazi terror machine escaped human justice by swallowing poison last night. He had been taken prisoner by the British 2nd Army. He had been caught like a tramp and he died like one. Sometime on Tuesday, **Himmler** and two aides tried to walk across a bridge . . . they wore shabby civilian clothes. Himmler's little spectacles were gone and one of his watery blue eyes was covered with a black patch. His moustache was shaved off but his weak chin was covered with stubble. He produced an army discharge in the name of Hitzsinger, but, stupidly enough, it was not a regular army discharge but one from the military Gestapo, the field security police. It was suspicious in itself.

. . . They were sent to British Army Headquarters for interrogation. There, the little man, who had spent the last twelve years barking orders that sent thousands to their death, spent the last twelve hours of his life wheedling and pleading. . . . His story rang false. . . . Finally, he . . . admitted who he was. He had been carefully searched and given new clothes, but neither coat nor trousers. Wrapped in a blanket he was driven away . . . searched again from head to foot. But somehow he had concealed a phial of poison in his mouth and, while a doctor was looking into his mouth, Himmler jerked his head back, crunched the phial and swallowed cyanide of potassium. Only a few hours before, up in Flensburg, the Commander of the German Navy, Admiral Friedeburg, had done the same thing.

Kamikazes: Phelps Adams's Eyewitness Account of Attack on Admiral Mitscher's Flagship by Japanese Suicide Pilots Off Okinawa

[May 11, 1945]

"The next minute the *Bunker Hill* was a pillar of flame. It was as quick as that—like summer lightning."

It started at the sea battle of Leyte on October 29, 1944. Japanese planes were seen to dive on American warships with the purpose of crash-landing on top them. At first this was attributed to mere accident. However, soon it became clear that a new weapon had been born of desperation.

In a last attempt to halt the Americans before they reached the sacred home islands, the Japanese organized "special attack" units called Kamikazes. *These groups were named after the "divine wind," or typhoon, which, according to Japanese legend, had swamped Kublai Khan's invasion fleet in 1281. The Japanese Naval Air Force was the first to organize suicide squadrons, but the Army soon followed. This was to be Tokyo's secret weapon to snatch victory from the jaws of defeat.*

There were several kinds of Kamikazes. *One was the* Baka *bomb (from the Japanese word meaning "stupid" and named by Americans), a two-ton plane with no landing gear and carrying a ton of TNT in its nose. The pilot could not possible escape once he had begun his dive. Another type of* Kamikaze *plane was any aircraft holding a large explosive charge set to go off on contact.*

The Kamikaze *pilots knew well that they would die. Most aimed for capital ships on the understandable assumption that the smaller ships were not worth the sacrifice of their lives.*

The orders to the Kamikaze *pilots were explicit:*

It is absolutely out of the question for you to return alive. Your mission involves certain death. Your bodies will be dead but not your spirits. The death of a single one of you will be the birth of a million others. . . . Do not be in a hurry to die. If you cannot find your target turn back. Next time you may find a better opportunity. Choose a death that brings maximum results.

In their ready rooms the Kamikaze *pilots drank a final farewell toast. They were proud of their insignia—a cherry blossom, with three petals, indicating the tenuous nature of life. There were even songs to enliven the last moments on earth, such as this "Kamikaze Song of the Warrior":*

> In serving on the seas, be a corpse saturated with water.
> In serving on land, be a corpse covered with weeds.
> In serving the sky, be a corpse that challenges the clouds.
> Let us all die close by the side of our sovereign.

The last letters, already sent home, contained such expressions as these:

> Please do not weep because I am about to die. If I were to live and one of my dear ones to die, I would do all in my power to cheer those who remain behind. . . . I bid you farewell. . . . Excuse this illegible letter and the jerky sentences. Keep in good health. . . . I will show you that I know how to die bravely.

The zenith of the suicide attacks came during the Okinawa landings. The New York Times *reported: "During the Okinawa campaign, when our ship damages were at their peak, West Coast shipyards were glutted with ship repairs and some of the worst-damaged vessels were sent to East Coast yards." In all, nearly a hundred ships were either lost or damaged off Okinawa with heavy personnel loss to the American Navy. The* Kamikazes *were in truth a grisly danger. But in the long run they had no effect on the course of the war. Nippon was doomed.*

For some reason, explainable only by the fates, Japanese Kamikaze *pilots were attracted to the person of Vice Admiral Marc A. Mitscher who had come to Okinawa with several task forces. The Divine Wind blew hot and often wherever the admiral appeared. It started on May 11, 1945. Mitscher was on his flagship, the aircraft carrier* Bunker Hill, *when it was attacked by* Kamikaze *planes. He was unhurt, but his losses were heavy— 373 dead, 19 missing, and 264 wounded.*

Following is an eyewitness account of the disaster by war correspondent Phelps Adams, who was on another carrier only two hundred yards away at the time of the attack. The Bunker Hill *came home under her own power and was brought to the Puget Sound Navy Yard for repairs.*

Three days later, on May 14, Admiral Mitscher was on the carrier Enterprise *when it was attacked in force by* Kamikazes *in a dawn strike. The embattled admiral, wearing his famed baseball cap, was probably the most exposed man on board as he stood on the flag-bridge. Once again he came through the violent attack unscathed.*

(*Baltimore* Sun, *May 28, 1945. By permission of North American Newspaper Alliance.*)

ABOARD A FAST CARRIER IN THE FORWARD PACIFIC AREA, May 11 (Special—Delayed)—Two Japanese suicide planes carrying 1,100 pounds of bombs plunged into the flight deck of Vice Admiral Marc A. Mitscher's own flagship early today, killing several hundred officers and men and transforming one of our biggest flat-tops into a floating torch, with flames soaring nearly 1,000 feet into the sky.

For eight seemingly interminable hours that followed the ship and her crew fought as tense and terrifying a battle for survival as had ever been witnessed in the Pacific, but when dusk closed in, the U.S.S. *Bunker Hill*—horribly crippled and still filmed by wisps of smoke and steam from her smoldering embers—was plowing along under her own power on the distant horizon, safe. Tomorrow she will spend another eight terrible hours burying at sea the men who died to save her.

From the deck of a neighboring carrier a few hundred yards distant I watched the *Bunker Hill* burn. It is hard to believe that men could survive those flames or that metal could withstand such heat.

One minute our task force was cruising in lazy circles about 60 miles off Okinawa without a care in the world and apparently without a thought of an enemy plane. The next the *Bunker Hill* was a pillar of flame. It was as quick as that—like summer lightning.

The oriental equivalent of Lady Luck was certainly riding with Japan's suicide corps today. Fleecy-white, low-hanging clouds studded a bright sky to conceal the intruders from lookouts manning all the stations on the ships of Task Force 58. Not until the Japs began their final plunge from the cover of these clouds did the *kamikazes* become visible.

And it was sheer luck, of course, that they happened to strike on the particular day and at the exact hour when their target was most vulnerable. Since there was no sign of the enemy and because the *Bunker Hill* and her men were weary after 58 consecutive days in the battle zone off Iwo Jima, Tokyo, the Inland Sea and Okinawa, her crew was not at general quarters when she was hit.

For the first time in a week, our own ship had secured from general quarters an hour or two before. Some of the water-tight doors that imprisoned men in small, stifling compartments were thrown open. The ventilators were unsealed and turned on, and those men not standing the regular watch were permitted to relax from the deadly sixteen-hour vigil they had put in at battle stations every day since we had entered the danger area.

So it was on the *Bunker Hill*. Exhausted men not on watch were catching a catnap. Aft, on the flight deck, 34 planes were waiting to take off. Their tanks were filled to the last drop with highly volatile aviation gasoline. Their guns were loaded to the last possible round of ammunition.

Young pilots, mentally reviewing the briefing they had just received, were sitting in the cockpits warming up the motors. On the hangar deck below, more planes—also crammed with gasoline and ammunition—were all set to be spotted on the flight deck, and in the pilots' ready rooms, other young aviators were kidding around, waiting their turn aloft.

Just appearing over the horizon were the planes returning from an early mission. They jockeyed into the landing circle and waited until the *Bunker Hill* could launch her readied craft and clear the deck for landing.

Then it was that a man aboard our ship caught the first glimpse of three enemy planes and cried a warning. But before general quarters could be sounded on this ship, and before half a dozen shots could be fired by the *Bunker Hill,* the first *kamikaze* had dropped his 550-pound bomb on the ship and plunged his plane squarely into her 34 waiting planes in a shower of burning gasoline.

The delayed-action bomb pierced the flight deck at a sharp angle, passed through the side of the hull and exploded in mid-air before striking the water. The plane, a single-engined Jap fighter, knocked the parked aircraft about like ten-pins, sent a huge column of flame and smoke belching upward, and then skidded crazily over the side.

Some of the pilots were blown overboard by the explosion. Many managed to scramble to safety. But before a move could be made to fight the flames, another *kamikaze* came whining out of the clouds, straight into the deadly anti-aircraft guns of the ship. This plane was a Jap dive bomber, a Judy.

A five-inch shell that should have blown him out of the sky set him afire and riddled his plane with metal. But still he came. Passing over the stern of the ship he dropped his bomb right in the middle of the blazing planes. Then he flipped over and torched through the flight deck at the base of the "island."

The superstructure, which contains many of the delicate nerve centers from which the vessel is commanded and controlled, was enveloped in flames and smoke which were caught in turn by the maws of the ventilating system and sucked down into the inner compartments of the ship. Scores of men were suffocated in these below-deck chambers.

Minutes later a third Jap suicider zoomed down to finish the job. Ignoring the flames and the smoke that swept around them, the men in the *Bunker Hill's* gun galleries stuck to their posts, pumping ammunition into their weapons and filling the sky with a curtain of lead. It was a neighboring destroyer, however, which finally scored a direct hit on the Jap and sent him splashing harmlessly into the sea.

That was the end of the attack and beginning of the fight for survival. The entire rear end of the ship by this time was burning with uncontrollable fury. It looked much like the newsreel shots of a blazing oil well only worse, for this fire was feeding on highly refined gasoline and live ammunition. Smoke rose in a huge column from the stern of the ship, shot through with angry tongues of flame.

Blinding white flashes appeared continuously as ready ammunition in the burning planes or in the gun galleries was touched off. Every few minutes the whole column of smoke would be swallowed in a great burst of flame as another belly tank exploded or as the blaze reached another pool of gasoline flowing from· the broken aviation fuel lines on the hangar deck below.

For more than an hour there was no visible abatement in the fury of the flames. They would seem to die down slightly as hundreds of thousands of gallons of water and chemicals were poured on them only to burst forth more hungrily than ever as some new explosion occurred within the stricken ship.

The carrier itself was listing and as each new stream of water was poured into her, the angle increased more dangerously. Crippled as she was she plowed ahead at top speed, and the wind that swept her decks blew the flames and smoke astern over the fantail, prevented the blaze from spreading forward on the flight deck and through the island structure. Trapped on the fantail itself, men faced the flames and fought grimly on; with only the ocean behind them, and no way of knowing how much of the ship remained on the other side of that fiery wall.

Then, somehow, other men managed to break out the huge openings in the side of the hangar deck, and I saw the interior of the ship. That, I think, was the most horrible sight of all. The hangar deck was a raging blast furnace. Even from where I stood the glow of molten metal was unmistakable.

By this time the explosions had ceased and a cruiser and three destroyers were able to venture alongside with hoses fixed in their rigging. Like fire boats in harbor they pumped great streams of water into the ship, and the smoke at last began to take on that grayish tinge which showed that somewhere a flame was dying.

Up on the bridge, meanwhile Capt. George A. Seitz, the skipper was concerned about the list his ship had developed. He resolved to take a gambling chance. Throwing the *Bunker Hill* into a 70-degree turn, he heeled her cautiously over onto the opposite beam so that the tons of water which had accumulated on one side were suddenly swept across the decks and overboard on the other. This wall of water carried the heart of the hangar deck fire with it.

That was the turning point in this battle. After nearly three hours of almost hopeless fighting, she had brought her fires under control, and though it was many more hours before they were completely extinguished, the battle was won and the ship had been saved.

A goodly thick book could not record all the acts of heroism that were performed aboard that valiant ship today.

There was the executive officer, Commander H. J. Dyson, who was standing within 50 feet of the second bomb when it exploded and who was badly injured, yet refused medical aid and continued to fight the blaze until it was safely under control.

There was the squad of Marines who braved the white heat of the hangar deck to throw every bomb and rocket out of a near-by storage room.

But the most fruitful work of all, perhaps, was performed by the pilots of the almost fuelless planes that had been circling overhead for a landing when the ship was struck. In the hours that followed, nearly 300 men went overboard, and the fact that 269 of these were picked up by other ships in the fleet was due, in no small measure, to the work of these sharp-eyed airmen.

Although our own flight deck had been cleared for their use and they had been instructed to land on it, these pilots kept combing every inch of the surface of the sea, tearing packets of dye marker from their own life jackets and dropping them to guide destroyers and other rescue vessels to the little clusters of men they saw clinging to bits of wreckage below them.

Calculating their fuel supply to a hair's breadth, some of them came aboard us with such a close margin that a single wave-off would have sent them and their planes into the sea before they could make another swing about the landing circle and return.

In all, I am told, 170 men will be recommended for awards as a result of this day's work.

Late today, Admiral Mitscher and 60 or more members of his staff came aboard us to make this carrier his new flagship. He was unhurt—not even singed by the flames that swept the *Bunker Hill*

—but he had lost three officers and six men of his own staff and a number of close friends in the ship's company. It was the first time in his long years of service that he had personally undergone such an experience.

As he was hauled aboard in a breeches buoy across the churning water that separated us from the speedy destroyer that had brought him alongside, he looked tired and old and plain, downright mad. His deeply lined face was more than weather-beaten—it looked like a badly eroded hill. But his eyes flashed fire and vengeance.

He was a man who had a score to settle with the Japs and who would waste no time going about it. He had plans that the Japs will not like, not at all.

But the enemy is already on the losing end of the *Bunker Hill* box-score. Since she arrived in the Pacific in the Fall of 1943, the *Bunker Hill* had participated in every major strike. She was initiated at Rabaul, took part in the invasions of the Gilberts and the Marshalls, pounding at Kwajalein and Eniwetok. With Task Force 58 she had struck twice at Tokyo and also at Truk, the China coast, the Ryukyus, Formosa, the Bonins, Iwo Jima and Okinawa.

During this time the pilots of her air groups have sunk or damaged nearly a million tons of Jap shipping. They have shot 475 enemy planes out of the air, 169 of them during the last two months. In two days here off Okinawa, they splashed 67 Nipponese aircraft and the ship herself has brought down 14 more by anti-aircraft fire.

On a raid last March at Kure Harbor, when the Japanese fleet was hiding out in the Inland Sea, *Bunker Hill* planes scored direct bomb hits on three carriers and one heavy cruiser, and then sent nine torpedoes flashing into the side of the enemy's beautiful new battleship, *Yamoto*, sinking her.

In the Jap column stands the fact that at the cost of three pilots and three planes today the enemy killed a probable total of 392 of our men, wounded 264 others, destroyed about 70 planes and wrecked a fine and famous ship. The flight deck of that ship tonight looks like the crater of a volcano. One of the great 50-ton elevators has been melted almost in half. Gun galleries have been destroyed and the pilots' ready rooms demolished. Virtually the entire island structure with its catwalks . . . is a twisted mass of steel, and below decks tonight hospital corpsmen are preparing 352 bodies for burial at sea, starting at noon tomorrow.

But the ship has not been sunk. Had it been, it would have taken years to build another. As it is the *Bunker Hill* will steam back to

Bremerton Navy Yard under her own power and there will be repaired. While she remains there, one American carrier with a hundred or so planes and a crew of 3,000 men will be out of action. But within a few weeks she will be back again, sinking more ships, downing more planes, and bombing out more Japanese airfields.

Perhaps her next task will be to cover the invasion of Tokyo itself.

Hara-Kiri: Alva N. Dopking Tells How Two Okinawa Generals Died Under the Nipponese Samurai Code

[June 27, 1945]

"Without regret, fear, shame, or obligation. . . . Age of departure 51 years."

American G.I.'s who fought the Japanese during the closing days of the Pacific war were bewildered by the way Japanese troops took their own lives. Sometimes the defeated enemy deliberately sought death in wild banzai *charges. On occasion, groups would run screaming to their death by jumping over cliffs. Others would stab themselves or pull the pins from grenades held against their bodies. American doughboys had never seen anything like this orgy of self-immolation.*

Alva N. Dopking, correspondent for the Associated Press, described in this dispatch the suicide and burial of two Japanese generals who had commanded the Japanese forces on Okinawa. This was the ritual of hara-kiri *performed according to the* samurai *code, a medieval rite in a modern setting. It was regarded as atonement for defeat on Okinawa.*

(Baltimore Sun, *June 28, 1945. By permission of Associated Press.)*

OKINAWA, June 27 (A.P.)—The bodies of Lieut. Gen. Mitsuru Ushijima, commander of the Japanese Army destroyed in Okinawa, and his chief of staff, Lieut. Gen. Isamu Cho, were buried under United States military auspices today near the cave where they died a hara-kiri death in the last hours of fighting on the island.

The graves were twenty yards from the pole where the United States flag later was raised on Hill 89 in services honoring 7th Infantry Division doughboys, who wrested this last ridge defense from the Nipponese last week.

Gen. Joseph W. Stilwell, new commander of the United States 10th Army which conquered the island, attended the flag ceremony. Present also were corps commanders, 7th Division general officers and 500 infantrymen who helped take the hill.

495

The bodies of the two Japanese generals were lowered into graves almost above their cave headquarters, which was sealed during the American flag service.

When I visited the cave today it presented a horrible scene of death, self-inflicted in accordance with the Nipponese samurai code. The headless bodies of Ushijima and Cho were first found by 32d Regiment infantrymen in shallow graves outside the cave, which overlooks the Pacific from the south shore of Okinawa.

They had died Friday as prescribed by the face-saving precepts of the samurai code, while American doughboys in foxholes 100 yards away were mopping up the last Nipponese holdouts.

The story of the officers' deaths was told by a captured Japanese, who said he cooked the last meal for Ushijima and his staff.

On the night of June 21 the cook was ordered to prepare an extra large dinner for Ushijima and his staff. The menu included rice, canned meats, potatoes, fried fish cakes, salmon, bean soup, fried cabbage, pineapple tea, with saki rice wine as an appetizer.

The meal was served at 10 o'clock, the cook said, and at 11:30 the sentry guarding the last remaining entrance to the cave was dismissed and ordered to join the fight against the near-by Americans.

At 3 o'clock in the morning the cook was preparing breakfast when Ushijima's orderly came to him and whispered that the commanding general and Cho were about to commit seppuku, honorable suicide.

Forty minutes later both generals accompanied by their aides and staff members came out onto a narrow ledge before the cave. While the aides placed a heavy comforter on the rough shelf and laid a white sheet over it as a symbol of death, the two generals conversed in monotones.

Ushijima knelt on the sheet, his head bent forward. Cho knelt on his commander's left. They faced west toward the Pacific because the narrowness of the ledge prevented them looking north toward the Japanese imperial palace, as is customary in hara-kiri.

A lieutenant held two knives, each with its blade wrapped in a white cloth. Ushijima's adjutant stood on the general's right with the samurai sword in his hand.

Ushijima received the knife and, holding it with both hands, plunged it into his abdomen. The adjutant with a skillful stroke of the sword beheaded the general.

The ceremony was the same for Cho, and when it was completed the staff officers reentered the cave and three orderlies took the bodies to the base of the cliff for burial.

Cho had written his own epitaph on a white silk mattress cover found near his body. It read: "Without regret, fear, shame or obligation. Army chief of staff Cho Isamu. Age of departure 51 years. At this time and place I hereby certify the foregoing."

General Ushijima's body lay on a khaki wool army blanket. The head was missing and a stab mark on the abdomen showed he had begun the traditional incision with the ceremonial knife when his adjutant clipped off his head with a long samurai sword.

Cho's head lay beside his body and there also was a stab mark on his abdomen. Both officers had worn white gloves and highly polished boots.

Ushijima and Cho wore full uniforms, with decorations and medals pinned to their blouses, for the final death ceremony in the early morning of June 22, one day after the Yanks crushed Japanese organized resistance.

In the cave tunnel Americans found the bodies of a lieutenant colonel, a captain and a lieutenant, Ushijima's adjutant, aide and assistant aide, respectively. All had been shot through the throat.

Hiroshima: American and Japanese Accounts of the First Atomic Bomb Dropped on Japan

[August 6, 1945]

Sixteen hours ago an American airplane dropped one bomb on Hiroshima, an important Japanese Army base. That bomb had more power than 20,000 tons of T.N.T. It had more than 2,000 times the blast power of the British "Grand Slam," which is the largest bomb ever yet used in the history of warfare. . . .

It is an atomic bomb. It is a harnessing of the basic power of the universe. The force from which the sun draws its power has been loosed against those who have brought war to the Far East.

Thus President Harry S. Truman announced one of the great events of history. A lone Superfortress, the Enola Gay, *had carried the atomic bomb to Japan. It would have taken 2,000 bombers to carry 20,000 tons of T.N.T. In an incredible instant—majestic, horrible, terrifying—all concepts of war and peace were changed. Science had at last achieved the incredible—it had extracted from Nature the secret of dynamic energy.*

Most of Hiroshima was blown from the face of the earth. An Allied report later noted that 78,150 people had been killed by this most terrible weapon ever devised by man.

From the stunned Japanese came a stream of adjectives—"bestial," "barbaric," "inhuman," "diabolical." President Truman replied: "The Japanese began the war from the air at Pearl Harbor. They have been repaid manyfold." He urged the world to note that the first atomic bomb had been dropped on a military base. The bomb had been used "in order to shorten the agony of war, in order to save the lives of thousands and thousands of young Americans. . . . That attack," he said, "is only a warning of things to come. If Japan does not surrender, bombs will have to be dropped on war industries and, unfortunately, thousands of civilian lives will be lost. I urge Japanese civilians to leave industrial cities immediately, and save themselves from destruction."

The atomic bomb dropped on Hiroshima created an entirely new body of literature. Millions of words went into news reports, books and maga-

498

zines. The shock was so great that even the end of the war became secondary news. People were fascinated by news of this "cosmic hot potato" and eagerly devoured the millions of words.

Here are four reports on the tragedy of Hiroshima. In the first, Kenneth McCaleb of International News Service tells the story from the viewpoint of the crew of the Enola Gay. *The second brief report from Radio Tokyo is notable for its curious air of wonderment and bewilderment, as if the speaker could scarcely believe what he was saying. The third report was written by a Japanese journalist, Leslie Nakashima, three weeks after the bomb was dropped. Nakashima, employed by the United Press in Tokyo, expected to be interned, but he was set free. In the fourth dispatch James F. McGlincy, United Press, found continuing shock and hatred on the streets of Hiroshima.*

HIROSHIMA

(*Kenneth McCaleb, International News Service, August 7, 1945. By permission of United Press International.*)

"The crewmen said, 'My God!' "

Little is left where Hiroshima was.

Brick, wood, concrete, steel and flesh—a city of 340,000 hardly exists any more.

The crewmen said, "My God!" This is their story.

The first atomic bomb dropped on Japan "dissolved" Hiroshima in a cloud of dust.

Said one observer:

"The only way we could tell it was a city was because we had seen it a moment before."

This was the work of a single bomb. Only one was dropped.

The closest anyone could seem to come to describing what happened at Hiroshima—where man first released the manifestations of atomic force—was contained in the word "dissolved," or "dissolution."

Four and one-tenth square miles, or 60 percent, of the city was destroyed and additional damage was shown outside that area. The reconnaissance photographs revealed five major industrial targets wiped out.

AAF Col. Paul Tibbets of Miami, commander of the B-29 *Enola Gay*, which dropped the capsule of scientific devastation said:

"We selected Hiroshima as the target when we made the landfall. There was no opposition, conditions were clear and we dropped the bomb visually at 9:15 A.M.

"We knew immediately that we had to get the hell out of there and made a sharp turn in less than 30 seconds to get broadside to the target.

"Then—it was hard to believe what we saw.

"Below us, rising rapidly, was a tremendous black cloud. Nothing was visible where seconds before the outline of the city with its streets and buildings and waterfront piers were clearly apparent."

Navy Captain William S. Parsons [who assembled the bomb enflight] was the least surprised man aboard at the effect of the bomb. He had witnessed the test in New Mexico. There, he said, the facsimile bomb fused the sand in a large radius because it generated heat like something in the stellar regions.

"I knew what the Japs were in for, but I felt no particular emotion about it."

He described others aboard the *Enola Gay* as "amazed and speechless" in the wake of the explosion. "They said, 'My God!' and couldn't believe what happened.

"We made a tight turn away from the target in order to get a maximum distance between us and the explosion.

"It was a little more than a minute after we dropped the bomb that we felt the impact.

"We were at least ten miles away. There was a visual impact— even though every man wore colored glasses for protection.

"What had been Hiroshima was going up in a mushroom with the stem coming down. At the top was white smoke, but up to 1,000 feet from the ground there was swirling dust. Soon small fires sprang up on the edge of the town but the town was entirely obscured. We stayed a few minutes and by that time the smoke had risen to 40,000 feet.

"The top of the white cloud broke off and another soon formed."

Only three men of the 11-men crew knew the B-29 was carrying an atomic bomb—a container of energy the secret of which many sober-thinking scientists had hoped would never be revealed to mankind.

[The flight started from Tinian.]

In addition to Tibbets and Parsons, only the bombardier, Maj. Thomas Ferebee of Mocksville, N. C., knew that this mission was to be a bookmark in military history alongside of Lepanto, Agincourt, Crecy, Ypres, Pantelleria—but so much more than these.

For here man would demonstrate his control of a force that can only be comparable to his discovery of the properties of fire—which banished his fear of the dark and lifted him above the beasts.

(Up to this time who could say that this was not the most significant physical miracle since the control of fire and the mastery of the principles of the wheel and the lever?)

To the eight other crew members the mission was for a time a "milk run." They were:

Co-Pilot Capt. Robert A. Lewis, Ridgefield Park, N. J.; electronics officer, 2d Lt. Maurice Jeppson; flight engineer, Wyatt E. Duzenbury, Lansing, Mich.; radar operator, Sgt. Joe A. Steiborik, Taylor, Tex.; radio operator, Pfc. Richard H. Helson, Los Angeles; gunner, Staff Sgt. George R. Ceron, Lynbrook, N. Y.; gunner's assistant and flight engineer, Sgt. Robert R. Shumard, Detroit, and navigator, Capt. Theodore Z. Van Kirk, Northumberland, Pa.

Up to the bomb run Capt. Lewis was writing a letter to his mother, Mrs. George Lewis, 28 Hazelton St., Ridgefield Park, N. J. Casually breaking off, Lewis told his "Mom" he would resume the letter as soon as the bombs were away.

Lewis found it difficult to describe the thunderous blast and blinding flash that he witnessed. They came as a shock and surprise. Finishing his letter to his mother was no easy task after that.

Gen. Carl Spaatz, commander of the U. S. Army Strategic Air Forces, said that the crew which had been hand-picked took out the B-29 named in honor of Col. Tibbets' mother sometime after midnight on Sunday, Guam time. By early Monday the "Enola Gay" was soaring close to the Japanese coast.

At 9:15 A.M., the bomb explosion told the crew men for the first time what they had been chosen to do.

Their briefings had been meager. Their knowledge of the lethal, destructive atomic bomb was limited. Their expectations had been roused only by the fact that they had been given dark glasses as protection against a blinding flash, and told to "get the hell out of there."

Maj. Gen. Curtis E. LeMay, chief of staff of the Army Strategic Air Force, was at the side of Gen. Spaatz during the interview. A newsman asked LeMay if there was any danger in carrying the atomic bomb. LeMay quipped:

"What do you think?"

Spaatz then said, impressively:

"I pinned the Distinguished Service Cross on Colonel Tibbets immediately after he returned from the mission."

Spaatz was obviously elated. He said that if he had had the bomb in Europe "it would have shortened the war six to eight months." LeMay said that if this bomb had been available there would have been "no need to have had D-Day in Europe."

RADIO TOKYO

(Radio Tokyo broadcast beamed to American listeners, as recorded by the Associated Press, August 8, 1945. By permission of Associated Press.)

"Those indoors were killed by the indescribable pressure and heat."

With the gradual restoration of order following the disastrous ruin that struck the city of Hiroshima in the wake of the enemy's new-type bomb on Monday morning, the authorities are still unable to obtain a definite checkup on the extent of the casualties sustained by the civilian population.

Medical relief agencies that were rushed from neighboring districts were unable to distinguish, much less identify, the dead from the injured.

The impact of the bomb was so terrific that practically all living things, human and animal, were literally seared to death by the tremendous heat and pressure engendered by the blast. All the dead and injured were burned beyond recognition.

With houses and buildings crushed, including the emergency medical facilities, the authorities are having their hands full in giving every available relief under the circumstances.

The effect of the bomb was widespread. Those outdoors burned to death while those indoors were killed by the indescribable pressure and heat.

The methods the United States has employed in the war against Japan have exceeded in horrible cruelty the atrocities perpetrated by Genghis Khan in India and Afghanistan.

HAVOC AT HIROSHIMA

(*Leslie Nakashima, for the United Press, August 27, 1945. By permission of United Press International.*)

"What had been a city of 300,000 had vanished."

TOKYO, Aug. 27 (U.P.)—Hiroshima was destroyed by the atomic bomb dropped by a Superfort on the morning of Aug. 6. There is not a building standing intact in the city, which had a population of 300,000. The death toll is expected to reach 100,000, and people continue to die daily from burns suffered from the bomb's ultra-violet rays.

I arrived at Hiroshima at 5 A.M. Aug. 22 to find out about my mother, who lived in the outskirts.

Alighting from the train, I found that Hiroshima Station—once one of the largest in western Japan—no longer existed. The only thing left was a concrete platform.

Getting out into the open, I was dumbfounded at the destruction before me.

The center of the city immediately south and west of the station was razed, and there was a sweeping view to the foot of the mountains to the east, south, and north of the city. What had been a city of 300,000 had vanished

As far as the eye could see there were skeletons of only three concrete buildings standing in the chief business center. They were a seven-story former department store, a five-story newspaper building and a two-story bank.

Except for parts of brick gates and burned-out underground air-raid shelters, there was no trace of private dwellings.

I also found very little corrugated iron left. This was significant, inasmuch as every other Japanese city hit by fire bombs was found after the fires to be littered with corrugated iron.

The sight before me as I headed for the outskirts where my mother lived was unbelievable. It was unbelievable because only a fortnight before the bombing I had seen the city intact when I evacuated my wife and two daughters to central Japan.

Two miles from the center of the city I found dwellings heavily damaged. Many of them were crushed, as if from heavily descending pressure. Another half-mile farther I found walls of dwellings smashed in and the roofs shattered, attesting to the air pressure the bomb created. Such was my mother's dwelling.

But I found my mother safe. She had been weeding grass in a relative's vegetable field about two miles southeast of the city when she saw the flash.

She immediately threw herself face down on the ground. The next moment she heard a terrific explosion. Rising, she saw columns of white smoke rising from all parts of the city, high into the sky.

She said she started running away to her home as fast as she could, because she did not know what would happen next.

A school in the suburbs near mother's home had been converted into a field hospital to care for people who suffered burns. A majority of the cases are believed hopeless. Many of the victims are unidentifiable.

Even now, two or three patients are dying daily at this one hospital.

Even at that locality, some three miles from the city, leaves of vegetable plants are scorched, and it is feared the plants eventually will die.

The death toll was particularly heavy, I was told, because the governor of the Hiroshima prefecture had issued a call for people on labor service to come to the city that day and haul away lumber from a number of buildings which had been torn down to create fire-breaks in the event of raids. Thousands of school boys and girls, accordingly, were victims, and the number of those missing is astounding.

Japanese officials at first tried to minimize the effect of the atomic bomb, but since Japan's unconditional surrender they have been releasing the full details.

A MONTH LATER

(James McGlincy, for the United Press, September 5, 1945. By permission of United Press International.)

"It is all the ruined cities in the world put together and spread out."

It is all the ruined cities in the world put together and spread out.

The suburbs are no great shock. They are like many bombed-out districts I have passed through in Europe. But the center of what only a month before was a prosperous, living city is almost beyond description.

For two miles in every direction we found nothing but complete and utter ruin. The center literally had been bombed flat. Only a few concrete buildings appear upright, and they are little more than optical illusions.

Everywhere is the heavy inescapable smell of death. And roosting in the scorched branches of the few remaining trees are the buzzards the stench attracts.

The scattering of living beings I came upon poked through the piles of stone and wood that once were their homes. They knew they had little chance of finding anything salvagable, but somehow those piles of rubble represented a link with the past, and with sanity.

As I and other correspondents passed these people, in their eyes was hate, all the hate it is possible for a human to muster.

Nagasaki: William L. Laurence of *The New York Times* Sees the Dropping of Second Atomic Bomb

[August 9, 1945]

"A thousand Old Faithful geysers rolled into one."

The obliteration of Hiroshima left the Japanese stunned and bewildered. Yet, when President Harry S. Truman issued a new surrender ultimatum, he was ignored.

At noon on August 9, 1945, Japanese time, a second atomic bomb—one that made the first one dropped on Hiroshima obsolete—was released over the western Kyushu seaport and railway terminal of Nagasaki. This city with its quarter of a million population was a more critical military target than Hiroshima, since its port was used to forward troops and supplies to the whole Pacific area. In Nagasaki there were great steel mills, torpedo factories, shipbuilding plants. The blast virtually wiped the city from the map. Associated Press's Vern Haugland described it:

Nothing remains of the municipal area three miles long and two miles wide save debris. Eighteen thousand buildings have vanished from the earth and every one of the 32,000 that remain has been damaged. Not even the protecting canyons and hills, offering far more shelter than Hiroshima's plain, could save the buildings and the people from the desolating blast of atomic energy. . . .

Modern structural steel buildings sheathed with steel plate, 2,000 feet from the center of the blast, became a single mass of twisted girders and were completely burned out, while the buildings of the torpedo plant, some 4,000 feet from the center, were completely wrecked by the force of the blast.

William L. Laurence, science reporter for The New York Times, *had followed the story of atomic energy from January 31, 1939, when he had reported the splitting of a uranium atom into two parts by Columbia University's Department of Physics. On August 9, 1945, he had a front seat in the Superfort* The Great Artiste, *which left Tinian, and twelve hours later, just past noon, released the second atomic bomb on Nagasaki. Laurence saw its smoke curl up to 17,000 feet. His great report of the shattering event is reprinted below.*

Journalistic tradition has it that any second report, even a world-shaking event such as the atomic bomb, has less impact than one that comes earlier in the day. Hence, Laurence's dispatch was subordinated in this Times' *headline:*

SOVIET DECLARES WAR ON JAPAN; ATTACKS MANCHURIA, TOKYO SAYS: ATOM BOMB LOOSED ON NAGASAKI

Laurence saw the crushing of Nagasaki while flying with the instrument of destruction. Fujie Urata Matsumoto, a 35-year-old Japanese farm woman, was working in a millet patch at nearby Koba. She endured the tragedy:

Suddenly I heard a loud roar overhead. It sounded as though a plane had just dropped its bombs and was flying away.

Here it comes, I thought.

There was a sudden flash of red light.

Then a flash of blue.

The red was bright enough to stun a person, but the blue!—it was so bright that not even the worst liar could find the words to describe it.

That was all. There was a wind which blew away the weeds.

I scanned the sky. Rising high a puffy black smoke began boiling up and up, filling that whole part of the sky. [Mount] Kawabira seemed to divide the world in two, one part looking normal as ever and the other strange and terrible.

(The New York Times, *September 9, 1945. By permission of* The New York Times.)

WITH THE ATOMIC-BOMB MISSION TO JAPAN, August 9 (Delayed)—We are on our way to bomb the mainland of Japan. Our flying contingent consists of three specially designed B-29 Superforts, and two of these carry no bombs. But our lead plane is on its way with another atomic bomb, the second in three days, concentrating in its active substance an explosive energy equivalent to twenty thousand and, under favorable conditions, forty thousand tons of TNT.

We have several chosen targets. One of these is the great industrial and shipping center of Nagasaki, on the western shore of Kyushu, one of the main islands of the Japanese homeland.

I watched the assembly of this man-made meteor during the past two days and was among the small group of scientists and Army and Navy representatives privileged to be present at the ritual of its loading in the Superfort last night, against a background of threatening black skies torn open at intervals by great lightning flashes.

It is a thing of beauty to behold, this "gadget." Into its design went millions of man-hours of what is without doubt the most concentrated intellectual effort in history. Never before had so much brain power been focused on a single problem.

This atomic bomb is different from the bomb used three days ago with such devastating results on Hiroshima.

I saw the atomic substance before it was placed inside the bomb. By itself it is not at all dangerous to handle. It is only under certain conditions, produced in the bomb assembly, that it can be made to yield up its energy, and even then it gives only a small fraction of its total contents—a fraction, however, large enough to produce the greatest explosion on earth.

The briefing at midnight revealed the extreme care and the tremendous amount of preparation that had been made to take care of every detail of the mission, to make certain that the atomic bomb fully served the purpose for which it was intended. Each target in turn was shown in detailed maps and in aerial photographs. Every detail of the course was rehearsed—navigation, altitude, weather, where to land in emergencies. It came out that the Navy had submarines and rescue craft, known as Dumbos and Superdumbos, stationed at various strategic points in the vicinity of the targets, ready to rescue the fliers in case they were forced to bail out.

The briefing period ended with a moving prayer by the chaplain. We then proceeded to the mess hall for the traditional early-morning breakfast before departure on a bombing mission.

A convoy of trucks took us to the supply building for the special equipment carried on combat missions. This included the Mae West, a parachute, a lifeboat, an oxygen mask, a flak suit, and a survival vest. We still had a few hours before take-off time, but we all went to the flying field and stood around in little groups or sat in jeeps talking rather casually about our mission to the Empire, as the Japanese home islands are known hereabouts.

In command of our mission is Major Charles W. Sweeney, twenty-five, of 124 Hamilton Avenue, North Quincy, Massachusetts. His flagship, carrying the atomic bomb, is named *The Great Artiste*, but the name does not appear on the body of the great silver ship, with its unusually long, four-bladed, orange-tipped propellers. Instead, it carries the number 77, and someone remarks that it was "Red" Grange's winning number on the gridiron.

We took off at 3:50 this morning and headed northwest on a straight line for the Empire. The night was cloudy and threatening, with only a few stars here and there breaking through the overcast.

The weather report had predicted storms ahead part of the way but clear sailing for the final and climactic stages of our odyssey.

We were about an hour away from our base when the storm broke. Our great ship took some heavy dips through the abysmal darkness around us, but it took these dips much more gracefully than a large commercial air liner, producing a sensation more in the nature of a glide than a "bump," like a great ocean liner riding the waves except that in this case the air waves were much higher and the rhythmic tempo of the glide was much faster.

I noticed a strange eerie light coming through the window high above the navigator's cabin, and as I peered through the dark all around us I saw a startling phenomenon. The whirling giant propellers had somehow become great luminous disks of blue flame. The same luminous blue flame appeared on the plexiglas windows in the nose of the ship, and on the tips of the giant wings. It looked as though we were riding the whirlwind through space on a chariot of blue fire.

It was, I surmised, a surcharge of static electricity that had accumulated on the tips of the propellers and on the di-electric material of the plastic windows. One's thoughts dwelt anxiously on the precious cargo in the invisible ship ahead of us. Was there any likelihood of danger that this heavy electric tension in the atmosphere all about us might set it off?

I expressed my fears to Captain Bock, who seems nonchalant and unperturbed at the controls. He quickly reassured me.

"It is a familiar phenomenon seen often on ships. I have seen it many times on bombing missions. It is known as St. Elmo's fire."

On we went through the night. We soon rode out the storm and our ship was once again sailing on a smooth course straight ahead, on a direct line to the Empire.

Our altimeter showed that we were traveling through space at a height of seventeen thousand feet. The thermometer registered an outside temperature of thirty-three degrees below zero Centigrade, about thirty below Fahrenheit. Inside our pressurized cabin the temperature was that of a comfortable air-conditioned room and a pressure corresponding to an altitude of eight thousand feet. Captain Bock cautioned me, however, to keep my oxygen mask handy in case of emergency. This, he explained, might mean either something going wrong with the pressure equipment inside the ship or a hole through the cabin by flak.

The first signs of dawn came shortly after five o'clock. Sergeant Curry, of Hoopeston, Illinois, who had been listening steadily on his earphones for radio reports, while maintaining a strict radio silence himself, greeted it by rising to his feet and gazing out the window.

"It's good to see the day," he told me. "I get a feeling of claustrophobia hemmed in in this cabin at night."

He is a typical American youth, looking even younger than his twenty years. It takes no mind reader to read his thoughts.

"It's a long way from Hoopeston," I find myself remarking.

"Yep," he replies, as he busies himself decoding a message from outer space.

"Think this atomic bomb will end the war?" he asks hopefully.

"There is a very good chance that this one may do the trick," I assured him, "but if not, then the next one of two surely will. Its power is such that no nation can stand up against it very long." This was not my own view. I had heard it expressed all around a few hours earlier, before we took off. To anyone who had seen this man-made fireball in action, as I had less than a month ago in the desert of New Mexico, this view did not sound overoptimistic.

By 5:50 it was really light outside. We had lost our lead ship, but Lieutenant Godfrey, our navigator, informs me that we had arranged for that contingency. We have an assembly point in the sky above the little island of Yakushima, southeast-of Kyushu, at 9:10. We are to circle there and wait for the rest of our formation.

Our genial bombardier, Lieutenant Levy, comes over to invite me to take his front-row seat in the transparent nose of the ship, and I accept eagerly. From that vantage point in space, seventeen thousand feet above the Pacific, one gets a view of hundreds of miles on all sides, horizontally and vertically. At that height the vast ocean below and the sky above seem to merge into one great sphere.

I was on the inside of that firmament, riding above the giant mountains of white cumulus clouds, letting myself be suspended in infinite space. One hears the whirl of the motors behind one, but it soon becomes insignificant against the immensity all around and is before long swallowed by it. There comes a point where space also swallows time and one lives through eternal moments filled with an oppressive loneliness, as though all life had suddenly vanished from the earth and you are the only one left, a lone survivor traveling endlessly through interplanetary space.

My mind soon returns to the mission I am on. Somewhere beyond these vast mountains of white clouds ahead of me there lies Japan, the land of our enemy. In about four hours from now one of its cities, making weapons of war for use against us, will be wiped off the map by the greatest weapon ever made by man: In one tenth of a millionth of a second, a fraction of time immeasurable by any clock, a whirlwind from the skies will pulverize thousands of its buildings and tens of thousands of its inhabitants.

But at this moment no one yet knows which one of the several cities chosen as targets is to be annihilated. The final choice lies with destiny. The winds over Japan will make the decision. If they carry heavy clouds over our primary target, that city will be saved, at least for the time being. None of its inhabitants will ever know that the wind of a benevolent destiny had passed over their heads. But that same wind will doom another city.

Our weather planes ahead of us are on their way to find out where the wind blows. Half an hour before target time we will know what the winds have decided.

Does one feel any pity or compassion for the poor devils about to die? Not when one thinks of Pearl Harbor and of the Death March on Bataan.

Captain Bock informs me that we are about to start our climb to bombing altitude.

He manipulates a few knobs on his control panel to the right of him, and I alternately watch the white clouds and ocean below me and the altimeter on the bombardier's panel. We reached our altitude at nine o'clock. We were then over Japanese waters, close to their mainland. Lieutenant Godfrey motioned to me to look through his radar scope. Before me was the outline of our assembly point. We shall soon meet our lead ship and proceed to the final stage of our journey.

We reached Yakushima at 9:12 and there, about four thousand feet ahead of us, was *The Great Artiste* with its precious load. I saw Lieutenant Godfrey and Sergeant Curry strap on their parachutes and I decided to do likewise.

We started circling. We saw little towns on the coastline, heedless of our presence. We kept on circling, waiting for the third ship in our formation.

It was 9:56 when we began heading for the coastline. Our weather scouts had sent us code messages, deciphered by Sergeant Curry, informing us that both the primary target as well as the secondary were clearly visible.

The winds of destiny seemed to favor certain Japanese cities that must remain nameless. We circled about them again and again and found no opening in the thick umbrella of clouds that covered them. Destiny chose Nagasaki as the ultimate target.

We had been circling for some time when we noticed black puffs of smoke coming through the white clouds directly at us. There were fifteen bursts of flak in rapid succession, all too low. Captain Bock changed his course. There soon followed eight more bursts of flak, right up to our altitude, but by this time were too far to the left.

We flew southward down the channel and at 11:33 crossed the coastline and headed straight for Nagasaki, about one hundred miles to the west. Here again we circled until we found an opening in the clouds. It was 12:01 and the goal of our mission had arrived.

We heard the prearranged signal on our radio, put on our arc welder's glasses, and watched tensely the maneuverings of the strike ship about half a mile in front of us.

"There she goes!" someone said.

Out of the belly of *The Great Artiste* what looked like a black object went downward.

Captain Bock swung around to get out of range; but even though we were turning away in the opposite direction, and despite the fact that it was broad daylight in our cabin, all of us became aware of a giant flash that broke through the dark barrier of our arc welder's lenses and flooded our cabin with intense light.

We removed our glasses after the first flash, but the light still lingered on, a bluish-green light that illuminated the entire sky all around. A tremendous blast wave struck our ship and made it tremble from nose to tail. This was followed by four more blasts in rapid succession, each resounding like the boom of cannon fire hitting our plane from all directions.

Observers in the tail of our ship saw a giant ball of fire rise as though from the bowels of the earth, belching forth enormous white smoke rings. Next they saw a giant pillar of purple fire, ten thousand feet high, shooting skyward with enormous speed.

By the time our ship had made another turn in the direction of the atomic explosion the pillar of purple fire had reached the level of our altitude. Only about forty-five seconds had passed. Awe-struck, we watched it shoot upward like a meteor coming from the earth instead of from outer space, becoming ever more alive as it climbed skyward through the white clouds. It was no longer smoke, or dust, or even a cloud of fire. It was a living thing, a new species of being, born right before our incredulous eyes.

At one stage of its evolution, covering millions of years in terms of seconds, the entity assumed the form of a giant square totem pole, with its base about three miles long, tapering off to about a mile at the top. Its bottom was brown, its center was amber, its top white.

But it was a living totem pole, carved with many grotesque masks grimacing at the earth.

Then, just when it appeared as though the thing had settled down into a state of permanence, there came shooting out of the top a giant mushroom that increased the height of the pillar to a total of forty-five thousand feet. The mushrom top was even more alive than the pillar, seething and boiling in a white fury of creamy foam, sizzling upward and then descending earthward, a thousand Old Faithful geysers rolled into one.

It kept struggling in an elemental fury, like a creature in the act of breaking the bonds that held it down. In a few seconds it had freed itself from its gigantic stem and floated upward with tremendous speed, its momentum carrying it into the stratosphere to a height of about sixty thousand feet.

But no sooner did this happen when another mushroom, smaller in size than the first one, began emerging out of the pillar. It was as though the decapitated monster was growing a new head.

As the first mushroom floated off into the blue it changed its shape into a flowerlike form, its giant petals curving downward, creamy white outside, rose-colored inside. It still retained that shape when we last gazed at it from a distance of about two hundred miles. The boiling pillar of many colors could also be seen at that distance, a giant mountain of jumbled rainbows, in travail. Much living substance had gone into those rainbows. The quivering top of the pillar was protruding to a great height through the white clouds, giving the appearance of a monstrous prehistoric creature with a ruff around its neck, a fleecy ruff extending in all directions, as far as the eye could see.

Victory: *Yank* Reporters Record the Pattern of Celebration as World War II Comes to an End

[August 14, 1945]

"The good news was almost too much. . . ."

The New York Times *reported it in four blazing headlines:*

JAPAN SURRENDERS, END OF WAR!
EMPEROR ACCEPTS ALLIED RULE:
M'ARTHUR SUPREME COMMANDER
OUR MANPOWER CURBS VOIDED

It was August 14, 1945, three years, eight months, and seven days after Pearl Harbor. The last Axis enemy had gone down to total defeat. In America there was an outpouring of emotion such as had never taken place in our history, not on VE-Day nor on Armistice Day, 1918. A roar of victory cannonaded throughout the Allied world. There was frenzied rejoicing and there were prayers. In Rome there was quiet, in Berlin the stillness of the tomb. Following is a selection of reports by correspondents for Yank, The Army Weekly *on reactions to the news of Japan's capitulation.*

(Yank, The Army Weekly, *September 9, 1945. Courtesy of the U.S. Department of Defense.*)

NEW YORK CITY—Tokyo jumped the gun and at 1:49 Tuesday morning broadcast a statement that Japan would accept the Allied surrender terms. Throughout the city late stay-uppers hopped on the phone to rouse their friends and tell them the good news. Some made immediately for Times Square, setting off a celebration that was to last well over 48 hours. It was still going strong at dawn and carried on right through the day and the next day as more and more yelling, laughing, horn-tooting thousands poured into the area.

514

By Tuesday noon there was still nothing official, but from the way the crowds carried on you would never have suspected that peace wasn't yet definitely in the bag. Frenzied babes rushed through the crowds kissing servicemen, and wolves, in uniform and out, prowled about mousing any and every likely-looking number while the cops looked on, grinning indulgently. At 3:17 in the afternoon a sailor and his honey were to be seen lying flat on the pavement necking furiously as the throngs shuffled about them. Traffic was barred from the Times Square area all day so that the mob, which ultimately numbered 2,000,000, could run loose.

All the way from Staten Island to Van Cortlandt Park, from the Hudson River to the remotest outposts of Queens, the streets were littered with tons of paper torn up and scattered about by New York City's seven and a half million elated citizens. In Chinatown, where the residents have relatives in the land the Japs first tried to overrun, they put on the sacred dragon dance ordinarily staged only on the Chinese New Year. Up in Harlem there was jive and jitterbugging in the streets. Flatbush Avenue and Fulton Streets, two of Brooklyn's main drags, were jammed.

Frantic and madcap as the shindy was by day, however, it was nothing compared to what it became at night after President Truman made his 7 o'clock announcement that the war was over. This, at last, was the official end, and at once the whole city, already a seething turmoil, seemed to explode. To the blasts of automobile horns and the shrilling of whistles the *Queen Elizabeth*, docked in the Hudson, added the deep, throaty boom of her horn. Some of the bars around Times Square closed down, unable to cope with the crush, but it was a cinch to get a drink since scores of people were wandering around carrying quart bottles of the stuff and all were in a generous mood.

On, on, on it went into the night and the next night as the biggest city in the world went its way toward picking up the biggest hangover in its history. It was a hangover few would ever regret.

—Sgt. Sanderson Vanderbilt

SAN FRANCISCO—Peace brought something akin to a state of chaos to the Pacific's largest port of embarkation. The good news was almost too much for San Francisco. Hundreds were injured and a number killed in a celebration that lasted two nights and that at no time had any element of the peaceful about it.

Some of the highlights: Firecrackers, hoarded in Chinatown for eight years, rattled like machine guns. . . . Servicemen and civilians played tug-of-war with fire hose. . . . Market Street, the wide, bar-lined thoroughfare that has long been the center of interest for visiting GIs and sailors, was littered with the wreckage of smashed War Bond booths and broken bottles. . . . A plump redhead danced naked on the base of the city's Native Sons monument after servicemen had torn her clothes off. A sailor lent the woman a coat, and the pair disappeared.

Marine Pfc. James Prim, 34, had as much to celebrate as anybody in San Francisco. He had come safely through bitter South Pacific campaigns. In the early hours of August 15, when the mass hilarity was at its height, Prim fell down a flight of stairs. He died of a fractured skull.

There were thousands of San Franciscans who marked the day soberly and with prayer, but the end of the second World War seems likely to be remembered here as a celebration that got way out of bounds.

BOSTON—Boston's peace celebration exploded suddenly after the official news of Japanese surrender poured out of countless radios. All morning and afternoon, while many other cities were already wildly celebrating, the Hub, with true New England caution, waited soberly for confirmation.

But this staid attitude was swept away in a surging tide of mass enthusiasm a few minutes after the news came. In a celebration that topped Boston's two-day madness following the collapse of Germany in 1918, over three-quarters of a million people crammed narrow, twisting downtown streets and the famous Common in the wildest riot of noise in the city's long history. It was like 50 New Year's Eves rolled into one.

The most general impulse seemed to be to shout, sing and hug passers-by. For men in uniform the celebration seemed to be more of a kissing fest than anything else. They were seized by girls and women of all ages, and their faces soon burst out in what the movie ads would have called "flaming Technicolor," because of the varied hues of lipstick prints.

Doors of hundreds of churches were opened, and many thousands entered them briefly, if only to pause in silence for a few moments in gratitude in the midst of an evening in which many ordinarily powerful Boston inhibitions were swept aside.

Though nearly 200 persons required treatment for minor hurts, as they were squeezed and pushed around in the throngs, there were no serious accidents.

The next day, happily, was a holiday, so Boston's celebrators enjoyed a late morning's sleep. They needed it.

LONDON—Two Canadian soldiers walked into a restaurant talking quietly about the Japanese surrender offer. A GI sitting in one of the American-style booths caught their words and let out a whoop. "We're going to tear this place apart!" he announced.

Then he lapsed into silence. Other Americans in the restaurant reacted pretty much the same way. As one soldier remarked, "We're still in Europe, bud."

There was a little more excitement as the evening wore on and there were crowds in Piccadilly Circus and Leicester and Trafalgar Squares. Quite a few people got rid of their waste paper by throwing it out of windows, a sign that the need for saving such things for the war effort was just about over.

Five hundred GIs who arrived that evening on furlough from the continent weren't exactly on fire about the news, either. Duffel bags and toilet kits on their shoulders, they queued up to register for rooms at the Red Cross Club as quietly as they have been queuing up for everything else during their army careers. A lot of the furloughing troops said they didn't believe the war was over and even if it was they'd still have to sweat out transportation home for a long time yet.

Quite a few GIs were more interested in talking about the atomic bomb than about Japan. They were afraid of the new weapon and its potential force for evil. Cpl. Paul Martin of Vauxhall, N. J., an anti-tank gunner with the 9th Division in France, Belgium and Germany and now with the army of occupation in Germany, was a little dazed.

"The news that Japan gave up seems impossible to me," he said. "Especially since the Russians have only been in the thing for one day. This atom bomb is sure a lotta hell; it had a lot to do with the surrender. I have to go back to Germany, but I'm glad for the guys who're sweating it out in the Pacific now. I'll get home eventually and it might be a little quicker than I thought this time last year. How long will we have to stay in Germany? Depends on how long we take to get those *buergermeisters* working right."

"Yeah, I know the atom bomb helped a lot. But it wasn't the only factor in the surrender. Right now I want to go home; I've got 134 points, and I've got a son two years old I never saw and a girl that I only saw once. Who doesn't want to go home, brother?"

Sgt. Bernard Katz of Pittsburgh, Pa., now with the 36th Bombardment Squadron, Eighth Air Force, has been in the Army for five years and had special reactions.

"I'm one guy who ought to be glad, because I saw my first action on Dec. 7, 1941. I was at Wheeler Field on Oahu, the first island the Japs attacked.

"We thought it was an earthquake until we found out that it was war, and war was worse. I jumped under a theater for shelter and found myself lying beside a two-star general. He didn't say anything about saluting, and neither did I.

"Now it's all over. For good, I hope. I think a combination of the Russians and the atom bomb did the trick in about equal proportions. I think the atom bomb is the best weapon to prevent future wars, and I also think it should be given to the whole world so it can be developed to its fullest extent. Even the Japs and Germans should be given it when they're domesticated enough."

—Sgt. Francis Burke

PARIS—The GIs had managed to keep their VJ spirit bottled up through most of the phony rumors, but when the real thing was announced the cork popped with a vengeance. A spontaneous parade, including jeeps and trucks and Wacs and GIs and officers and nurses and enlisted men, snaked from the Red Cross Club at Rainbow Corner down to the *Place de l'Opera* and back.

Jeeps crawled along in the victory celebration so loaded down with cheering GIs that the shape of the vehicles could hardly be discerned. Some GIs showed up with flags to add both color and an official note to the procession. By the time the demonstration hit its full stride trucks and cars were moving five abreast with pedestrian celebrants marching before and behind and between.

The most unusual note of the day was the spontaneous contribution campaign for the Red Cross which started up out of nothing at all except good humor when a GI at the Rainbow Corner pinned a couple of franc notes to a tree, announcing: "This is for the Red Cross."

His idea caught on and soon other GIs were unloading their spare currency. The sport was enlivened considerably by kissing French girls at the tree, whether as a bonus for contributions or just for the hell of it. At any rate, a late afternon check showed some $14,000 raised for the ARC by what had begun purely as a half-gag gesture of good will.

The whole show was a soldier—especially an American soldier—performance. French civilians were happy and pleased, and they showed it, but they still went about their work as much as usual as was possible. They had been drained of celebration first when their city had been freed and later when the European war had ended.

ROME—The people of Rome—Italian civilians and U.S. GIs—took the news of the Japanese surrender in their strides. There weren't any parades, bells didn't ring and there were few drunken soldiers. People went about their business as usual, including the girls on the *Via del Tritone.* . . .

It was a little after midnight and St. Peter's looked very solemn and impressive against the stars. The church was shut. GIs kept coming up and then standing and looking at the church as if they didn't know what to do. One soldier said, "I thought it would be open tonight."

An elderly Italian said that in Italy all churches close at dark.

"I know, but tonight . . ." the soldier said.

At the entrance to the Swiss Guard barracks a heavy-set guard in the ancient uniform of this small army was standing at the gate. His face was expressionless—his army life not dependent on the war's ending or beginning.

On the day when the greatest and most terrible war in world history came to an end, on the day when fascism was finally broken in the world, Rome—where fascism was born—was quiet and orderly. Rome has seen its share of this war. Maybe there should have been a lot of noise and great rejoicing. Here, where people know war, there wasn't shouting, ticker tape showers or hysterical parades, but the people were happy. In Rome most people were merely smiling quietly.

—Cpl. Len Zinberg

BERLIN—The city that had seen its own brand of fascism and international banditry tumble only a few months before had little energy left for reaction to the fall of Japan. The American Forces network broadcast the first authentic VJ news at 0210, and most of Berlin's polyglot occupation population, as well as most native Berliners, were asleep.

The U.S. Army newspaper *Allgemeine Zeitung* was the only Berlin paper which carried the news the next day. But the four days of false alarms made even the real thing seem unexciting.

Russian GIs interviewed had the same responses as their American counterparts. Said one of them, typically, "Now maybe I can get home to see my wife and children."

Tokyo Bay: Robert B. Cochrane, Baltimore Sunpapers War Correspondent, Covers the Surrender Ceremony Aboard the Battleship *Missouri*

[September 2, 1945]

"... as stately regal as a religious procession."

The Japanese loved their war jingles. Children sang this one on the streets:

> *Come out,*
> *Nimitz and MacArthur!*
> *Then we will send you*
> *Tumbling down to hell!*

This song was a morale booster:

> *Why should we be afraid of air raids?*
> *The big sky is protected with iron defenses.*
> *For young and old it is time to stand up;*
> *We are loaded with the honor of defending the homeland.*
> *Come on, enemy planes! Come on many times!*

By September 2, 1945 both these songs had joined the limbo of forgotten tunes. Japan lay prostrate at the feet of her conquerors. Allied airpower had reduced her tinderbox cities to a heap of ruins. Of 206 cities in Japan, 81 were destroyed or badly damaged. More than half the homes in Tokyo, Kobe and Yokohama were destroyed. Some 9,500,000 persons were homeless. The atomic explosions on Hiroshima (August 6) and Nagasaki (August 9) brought a sudden end to the war. On August 10 the Tokyo radio broadcast an acceptance of the Potsdam ultimatum, with the provision that Emperor Hirohito must retain his sovereignty.

Four days later, on August 14, the Emperor spoke to his people. "A continuation of the war," he said, "will result in ultimate collapse and obliteration of the Japanese nation."

The ceremony of unconditional surrender took place on board the battleship Missouri *in Tokyo harbor. Robert B. Cochrane, war correspondent for the Baltimore* Sunpapers, *sent in this report of the proceedings. Note the rigid attention to detail—mark of the able reporter.*

Masuo Kato, reporter for Domei, *who had been in Washington on the day of Pearl Harbor, was one of four Japanese newspapermen among those present. His recital of the facts was straightforward, but he could not resist adding a few editorial comments. "Somehow," he wrote, "I could not now regret Japan's defeat so much as the fact that she had resorted to a war that had resulted in much misery, not only for herself but for the rest of the world." He ended his report with this sentence: "Japan awaits the will of her new masters."*

(Baltimore Sun, *September 3, 1945. By permission of the Baltimore* Sun.)

ABOARD THE U.S.S. MISSOURI IN TOKYO BAY, Sept. 2 (By Radio)—World War II ended officially at 9:18 o'clock, Tokyo time, this morning.

It ended with the words of Gen. Douglas MacArthur: "These proceedings are closed."

Japan's dream of conquest died under the frowning guns of the mighty battleship *Missouri* when Foreign Minister Mamoru Shigemitsu and Gen. Yoshijiro Umezu, chief of staff of the Imperial Headquarters, affixed their names to the instrument of surrender which placed Japan unconditionally in the hands of the Allies.

It was a ceremony that followed a fixed military procedure, but was as stately regal as a religious procession.

MacArthur, conducting the ceremony in plain uniform but wearing his famous cap, spoke in firm full tones through a battery of five microphones and loudspeakers which carried the emphatic conviction in his voice echoing along the decks and across the waters to where the battleships *Iowa* and *South Dakota* were anchored.

The ceremony was watched by an attentive throng of 50 army generals, 50 senior naval officers, 36 foreign signers and delegates and 11 Japanese, all of whom were drawn up on the admiral's promenade deck amidships facing a ten-foot table covered with gold-trimmed green cloth, on which the instrument of surrender lay open.

Ranged around these were more than 200 correspondents, photographers and radiomen. The entire ship's complement of white-clad sailors and Marines were standing in formation on the fore and after decks during the ceremony.

Tht first signature, that of Shigemitsu, was affixed at 9:03 o'clock and the last, that of Air Marshal Isitt, of New Zealand, at 9:17.

Then MacArthur said:

"Let us pray that peace be now restored to the world and that God will preserve it always. These proceedings are closed."

That ended the war, but not the discussion over the instrument of surrender. Japan's emissaries objected that their copy was incorrectly signed, and Lieut. Gen. Richard K. Sutherland, MacArthur's chief of staff, found that Col. Moore Cosgrove, signer for Canada, had signed the wrong line on Japan's copy, and General Sutherland had to mark it correctly with his own pen before the Japs were satisfied.

The ceremony was scheduled early and completed early. With the exception of the Canadian's confusion, it went like clockwork from 7:45 A.M. when the ship's chaplain prayed for eternal peace, not forgetting those whose lives were the price of today's victory.

The day was heavily overcast, but two minutes after the close of the proceedings the sun broke through hot and brilliant like an omen of future peace for mankind.

The *Missouri* was anchored in the narrows of Tokyo Bay, off the Yokosuka naval base. To the starboard was the *Iowa* and astern the *South Dakota*.

Scattered as far as the eye could see were destroyers, troopships and escorts and overhead, before and after the signing, buzzed planes of the fleet and the strategic air force.

Observers and officers boarded the *Missouri* shortly after dawn after a trip down the bay by destroyer. Visitors were all assigned stations on the gun turret, main deck, bridge deck and superdeck. At stations up the mast were bluejackets. Every possible vantage point was crowded. Never before had the *Missouri* carried such a load of passengers.

There was a tremendous craning, twisting and maneuvering for position by reporters and photographers, professional and amateur. The entire starboard side of the ship was a facade of faces and uniforms.

A galaxy of officers arrived in a constant stream from 7:30 A.M.

The correspondents' destroyer tied up to the *Missouri*'s port side, but others arrived by small boats and were piped over the side by bosun's whistle and crowded onto the deck to chat and wait until time for the ceremonies.

"The Star-Spangled Banner" and "God Save the King" brought everyone to attention at 7:59 A.M., facing the flag and saluting.

The flag Admiral Perry carried ashore in Japan 92 years ago was placed, in its glass case, over the entrance of the captain's cabin overlooking the scene of the signing.

All guns were raised to their maximum elevation, lending an impression of strength and power.

Before the ceremony began carrier planes and seaplanes patrolled the bay. A few minutes after the last signature had been affixed, more than 300 fighters and 46 Superfortresses roared overhead in an impressive display.

The side of the bridge deck showed the *Missouri's* triumphs—eleven Rising Sun flags for planes shot down, four signs signifying bombardment actions.

Over the stern rail the Yokosuka naval base showed dimly through the mist. Over the port quarter, Tokyo lay invisible behind the grayness.

It was a gray day for Japan, and the squat little men who boarded the ship to make peace seemed grotesquely puny to have caused so much sorrow and worry in a nation which could produce weapons like this floating fortress. . . .

The signers came aboard via the starboard gangway at intervals, the French arriving at 8:15, the British at 8:20, and Russians, Chinese, Australians and on down the line.

The entire foreign delegation was standing behind the table when MacArthur arrived with General Sutherland and Col. Roger Egbert at 8:43 A.M.

Admiral Nimitz met MacArthur at the gangway and accompanied him as he walked swiftly, straight past the signing tables on which then lay only a plain white pad of paper, two pens in holders and a round glass paperweight.

Past the assembled delegations MacArthur strode to the admiral's cabin, one deck above, to wait the moment of surrender.

At 8:51 a small boat containing the Japanese circled in to the landing on the starboard gangway. Seated in the rear could be seen top-hatted Japanese and one uniformed officer. Others were inside.

The boat was lost to sight under the ship's side as it came in close and it seemed an interminable time before the Japanese arrived, led by Shigemitsu, whose artificial right leg hindered his progress.

Shigemitsu was followed by General Umezu, a short, typical Japanese figure in dull khaki and peaked cap, wearing yellow braid around his right shoulder. Then came two more top-hatted Japanese dressed, like Shigemitsu, in frock coat and morning trousers, with yellow gloves. Only Shigemitsu carried a cane.

The remainder of the party included one Japanese in white civilian clothes. The rest were uniformed like Umezu.

Proceeding slowly because of Shigemitsu's bad leg, the party halted across the table from the Allied delegations, with the two signers, the general and the minister, in the front line, five in the second line and four in the third.

The Japanese and Allies stared at each other in stony silence.

The Allied delegation itself was colorful. At the end of the line, next to the starboard rail, stood Admiral Nimitz in plain khaki and behind him stood three officers from the United States fleet.

General Hsu Yung-chang stood next, in tight-fitting dark-colored uniform with a Sam Brown belt and high-collared tunic with rows of ribbons on his chest.

Next stood Admiral Sir Bruce Fraser, trim in white shirt, shorts, socks and shoes, relieved only by gold shoulder bars.

To his left stood the powerful stocky figure of Lieut. Gen. Kuzma Nikolaevich-Derevyanko, in front of his top-ranking officers. Derevyanko wore a high-collared field green tunic, red-banded uniform cap and brilliant golden shoulder bars.

To the Russians' left stood General Sir Thomas Blamey, heavy, rotund commander in chief of the Australian forces, dressed in suntan khaki with four rows of ribbons, a Sam Brown belt and red-banded hat almost identical with Derevyanko's.

To Blamey's left was Colonel Cosgrove, of Canada, much slimmer and dressed like Blamey without the Sam Brown.

Next was Gen. Jacques Leclerc, French hero of the march from Lake Chad, carrying a cane and dressed in khaki tunic with three rows of ribbons, and four stars set in diamond fashion on his cap.

The Dutch representative, Admiral Helfrich, wore a khaki uniform with a white naval cap and no ribbons.

Air Vice Marshal Isitt, of New Zealand, wore a gold braided naval cap, plain khaki uniform with wings over the left breast and blue stripes of rank on his shoulders.

Next to them stood Generals Wainwright and Percival, honor guests at this historic climax.

All the American officials wore plain uniforms without ribbons or decorations or neckties. This is the official American uniform in this theater, and ribbons and medals are worn only on tunics.

None wore sidearms, and the Japanese did not even wear swords or belts.

It was 8:58 when MacArthur appeared from the admiral's cabin, walked swiftly down the ladder and strode to the microphone battery.

His remarks on the surrender were in his hands as he took his place, and he began reading in the firm, clear voice of the accomplished speaker. . . .

He pleaded for world peace and a new era of faith and understanding dedicated to the dignity of man. The two thin sheets of paper which contained his remarks trembled in his hands, but his voice did not quaver.

As supreme commander for the Allies, he said:

"I announce it as my firm purpose, in the tradition of the countries I represent, to proceed in the discharge of my responsibilities with justice and tolerance (his voice rising slightly in volume) while taking all necessary dispositions to insure that the terms of surrender are fully, promptly and faithfully complied with."

At this point he became the complete military commander, his voice cracking like a lash as he said:

"I now invite the representatives of the Emperor of Japan and the Japanese Government and Japanese imperial headquarters to sign the surrender at the places indicated."

There was no mistaking the stern command of that tone, and the Japs fidgeted under its impact.

A silk-hatted Japanese stepped to the table, laid aside his topper and spread out Japanese copies of the instrument. A second aide stepped from the left as Shigemitsu limped stiffly to the table, sat down, doffed his hat and slowly affixed his signature where an aide indicated.

The first signature was completed at 45 seconds after 9:03 A.M. Shigemitsu wrote the second signature with the same deliberate care as the first.

Just behind him General Umezu stepped up and replaced the minister as the latter withdrew. The general stood to sign both copies.

The Japanese all returned to their former places by 9:06 plus 30 seconds, and MacArthur announced he would sign for all the Allied powers. He walked four steps to the table, and before signing, turned and said:

"Will General Wainwright and General Percival step forward and accompany me while I sign?"

The two generals walked forward and stood behind and slightly to MacArthur's left. The general signed part of his name with one of a pile of fountain pens on the table, then turned and handed it to Wainwright.

He wrote again, then handed that pen to Percival.

He used six pens altogether, including the old-style red one he carried in the left breast pocket of his shirt.

His signing completed, he called the representatives of the United States, and Nimitz stepped forward to sign, calling Admirals Halsey and Sherman to accompany him.

This set the pattern that was followed all down the line.

Execution of Laval: Leon Pearson Reports the Death of a Hated Vichyite

[October 15, 1945]

<u>"I do not hold you responsible for this crime."</u>

The renegades who served Hitler as collaborators were meted swift punishment. The eighty-nine-year-old Marshal Henri Pétain, hero of World War I and Chief of State in the pro-Nazi Vichy government, was found guilty of collaboration, but his life was spared.

Pierre Laval was not so fortunate. The pro-Hitler French leader fled straight into the arms of American soldiers in Austria, who turned him over to the de Gaulle government. His trial was hurried and in the opinion of some observers a travesty on justice. The accused Laval was greeted by jeers and catcalls, in which the presiding judge, the prosecutor and jurors joined. The lawyers assigned to the defense suddenly resigned and returned only when they were threatened with disbarment. Twice during the three-day trial Laval was ejected from the courtroom.

In his defense Laval claimed that he was obliged to coöperate with the Germans in order to protect France from future harm:

If the Germans had been the first to invent the atomic bomb, and if they had won the war instead of losing it, what then would be the reproach against me?

Then perhaps I would be congraulated for having held out to the end in the interests of France. No one could worry about the heavy burden I bore and the moral suffering I had to undergo.

There are striking examples of Stalin and Molotov having pronounced certain words or done certain acts which may have appeared surprising later on but which were then useful to their country and army.

They had to gain time in order better to prepare for war. I also had to reduce risks and attempt to diminish the suffering imposed on us by the occupying forces.

My words have to be seen against the background of time in order to be understood and approved.

It was an ingenious defense but a lost cause. Pierre Laval represented treason to the humiliated, angered French people. Here is the report of

527

his execution written by Leon Pearson, International News Service correspondent in Paris.

(*International News Service, October 15, 1945. By permission of United Press International.*)

Saved from a last-minute attempt at suicide, Pierre Laval was executed for treason at 12:32 P.M. today tied to a stake in Fresnes Prison.

He died wearing the white tie which was his trademark. Just before the execution he asked that he be buried in it.

The former chief of the Vichy government, four times Premier of France in the course of his checkered political career, swallowed a dose of poison when he learned the execution by firing squad would soon take place. He went into a coma, but was revived and walked, eyes unbandaged to the execution post.

Laval faced the dozen soldiers assigned to dispatch him with his eyes unbandaged and said:

"I do not hold you responsible for this crime.

"Long live France!"

As the men took aim to end the career of the butcher's son who rose to rule France, Laval said:

"Fire at my heart."

Out of the twelve guns which faced him in the last minutes of his life, eleven bore lethal bullets. The last contained a blank cartridge. In keeping with French tradition, an officer stepped forward as the Vichyite slumped to his knees, placed a revolver behind Laval's right ear, and fired the *coup de grâce*.

Laval was to have been executed at the Fort de Chatillon, some 20 miles outside of Paris. But in death, as in life, Laval dictated events and circumstances. Because of his suicide attempt, the firing squad was brought to his prison.

He was buried in Thaïs cemetery. Next to Laval's plot was a grave marked: "Here lies an unknown collaborator."

Nuremberg: Kingsbury Smith, International News Service, Sees Ten Nazi Leaders Pay on the End of a Rope for Their Crimes

[October 16, 1946]

"Now it goes to God!"

On October 1, 1946, judgment was passed on twenty-two of Hitler's lieutenants by the International Military Tribunal which had conducted the Nuremberg trials for ten months. Twelve were condemned to death, seven sentenced to prison, and three others—Hans Fritsche, Franz von Papen and Hjalmar H. G. Schacht—freed. Pro and con arguments began almost immediately after the verdicts. One point of view hailed the verdicts as "the proper judgment of an outraged humanity." Another denounced the entire trial as unprecedented, unfair because it resulted in an ex post facto *decision.*

Those condemned to death, with the exception of Ernst Kaltenbrunner, applied to the Allied Control Council at Berlin for mercy. Their appeals were rejected. Nor were the appeals of Goering, Jodl and Keitel granted, to be executed by firing squad instead of hanging.

Master Sgt. John C. Woods, United States Army, wanted the job of executing the Nazi war criminals—and he got it. Eight newspaper correspondents, two each from the United States, Britain, France and Russia, the countries represented in the tribunal, were selected by lot to cover the hangings. Kingsbury Smith, European general manager of the International News Service, was one of the Americans chosen to represent the combined American press at the proceedings. His story of how the ten Nazis were executed at Nuremberg is reprinted below.

The dispatch was horrible enough, but one especially gruesome detail was missing from Smith's report—it concerned the death of Julius Streicher, the notorious Jew-baiter. Later Smith told that while Streicher was audibly strangling, the hangman disappeared into the dark interior of the scaffold. Streicher's groans stopped almost at once. What must have happened was that the hangman helped along the process of death in his own fashion. "After it was over," Smith wrote, "I was not in a mood to ask what he did, but I assume that he grabbed the swinging

529

*body and pulled down on it. We were all of the opinion that Streicher
had strangled."*

*President Harry S. Truman on the day after the executions said that
the Nuremberg verdicts "will stand in history as a beacon to warn international brigands of the fate that awaits them." He added: "This prece-
dent becomes basic in the international law of the future. The principles
established and the results achieved place international law on the side
of peace as against aggressive warfare."*

*That same day The New York Times editorialized that the men of
Nuremberg performed in death at least one service—their hanging was
"a grim warning to all who would emulate them in the future that mankind has entered a new world of international morality and that in the
end the angered forces of humanity must triumph over those who would
outrage it."*

(*New York* Journal-American, *October 16, 1946. By permission of United
Press International.*)

NUREMBERG, October 16—Ex-Reichsmarschall Hermann Wilhelm
Göring succeeded in cheating the gallows of Allied justice by committing suicide in his prison cell a short time before the ten other
condemned remnants of the Nazi hierarchy were hanged today.

Despite the fact that an American security guard was supposed to
be watching his every movement, the crown prince of Nazidom managed to hide in his mouth, chew, and swallow a vial containing
cyanide of potassium.

Göring swallowed the poison while Colonel Burton C. Andrus,
American security commandant, was walking across the prison yard
to the death-row block to read to him and the ten other condemned
Nazi leaders the International Military Tribunal's sentence of death.

Within little more than an hour after the reading of this sentence
to the condemned men in their cells, Göring was scheduled to be led
out to a near-by small gymnasium building in the jailyard to lead
the parade of death of the Nazi political and military chieftains to
the scaffold.

Göring had not previously been told that he was going to die this
morning, nor had any of the other condemned men.

How he guessed this was to be his day of doom and how he managed to conceal the poison on his person is a mystery that has con-
founded the security forces.

With former Foreign Minister Joachim von Ribbentrop taking
the place of Göring as the first to mount the scaffold, the ten other

condemned princes of Nazidom were hanged one by one in the bright, electrically lighted barnlike interior of the small gymnasium inside one of the prison yards of the Nuremberg city jail.

The execution of von Ribbentrop and the others took approximately one hour and a half. The once-arrogant diplomatic double-crosser of Nazidom entered the execution hall at 1:11 this morning. The trap was sprung at 1:16 and he was pronounced dead at 1:30.

The last to walk up the thirteen forbidding wooden steps to one of the two gallows used for the execution was Artur Seyss-Inquart, Austrian traitor and Nazi *Gauleiter* for Holland. He dropped to his death at 2:45 A.M. and was pronounced dead at 2:57.

All ten of the Nazis attempted to show bravery as they went to their deaths. Most of them were bitterly defiant, some grimly resigned, and others asked the Almighty for mercy.

All but Alfred Rosenberg, the pagan party theorist, made brief, last-minute statements on the scaffold, nearly all of which were nationalistic expressions for the future welfare and greatness of Germany.

The only one, however, to make any reference to Nazi ideology was Julius Streicher, the arch Jew-baiter. Displaying the most bitter and enraged defiance of any of the condemned, he screamed "Heil Hitler" at the top of his voice as he was about to mount the steps leading to the gallows.

Streicher appeared in the execution hall, which had been used only last Saturday night for a basketball game by American security guards, at twelve and a half minutes after two o'clock.

As in the case of all the condemned, a warning knock by a guard outside preceded Streicher's entry through a door in the middle of the hall.

An American lieutenant colonel sent to fetch the condemned from the death-row of the cell block to the near-by prison wing entered first. He was followed by Streicher, who was stopped immediately inside the door by two American sergeants. They closed in on each side of him and held his arms while another sergeant removed the manacles from his hands and replaced them with a leather cord.

The first person whom Streicher and the others saw upon entering the gruesome hall was an American lieutenant colonel who stood directly in front of him while his hands were being tied behind his back as they had been manacled upon his entrance.

This ugly, dwarfish little man, wearing a threadbare suit and a well-worn bluish shirt buttoned to the neck but without a tie, glanced at the three wooden scaffolds rising up menacingly in front of him.

Two of these were used alternately to execute the condemned men while the third was kept in reserve.

After a quick glance at the gallows, Streicher glared around the room, his eyes resting momentarily upon the small group of American, British, French, and Russian officers on hand to witness the executions.

By this time Streicher's hands were tied securely behind his back. Two guards, one to each arm, directed him to No. 1 gallows on the left entrance. He walked steadily the six feet to the first wooden step, but his face was twitching nervously. As the guards stopped him at the bottom of the steps for official identification requests, he uttered his piercing scream:

"Heil Hitler!"

His shriek sent a shiver down the back of this International News Service correspondent, who is witnessing the executions as sole representative of the American press.

As its echo died away, another American colonel standing by the steps said sharply:

"Ask the man his name."

In response to the interpreter's query Streicher shouted:

"You know my name well."

The interpreter repeated his request, and the condemned man yelled:

"Julius Streicher."

As he mounted the platform Streicher cried out:

"Now it goes to God!"

After getting up the thirteen steps to the eight-foot-high and eight-foot-square black-painted wooden platform, Streicher was pushed two steps to the mortal spot beneath the hangman's rope.

This was suspended from an iron ring attached to a crossbeam which rested on two posts. The rope was being held back against a wooden rail by the American Army sergeant hangman.

Streicher was swung around to face toward the front.

He glanced again at the Allied officers and the eight Allied correspondents representing the world's press who were lined up against a wall behind small tables directly facing the gallows.

With burning hatred in his eyes, Streicher looked down upon the witness and then screamed:

*"Purim Fest 1946!"**

---

* Purim is a Jewish holiday celebrated in the spring and commemorating the hanging of Haman, Biblical oppressor of the Jews.

The American officer standing at the scaffold said:

"Ask the man if he has any last words."

When the interpreter had translated, Streicher shouted:

"The Bolsheviks will hang you one day."

As the black hood was being adjusted about his head, Streicher was heard saying:

"Adele, my dear wife."

At that moment the trap was sprung with a loud bang. With the rope snapped taut and the body swinging wildly, a groan could be heard distinctly within the dark interior of the scaffold.

It was originally intended to permit the condemned to walk the seventy-odd yards from the cells to the execution chamber with their hands free, but they were all manacled in the cells immediately following the discovery of Göring's suicide.

The weasel-faced Ribbentrop in his last appearance before mankind uttered his final words while waiting for the black hood to be placed over his head. Loudly, in firm tones, he said:

"God save Germany!"

He then asked:

"May I say something else?"

The interpreter nodded. The former diplomatic wizard of Nazidom who negotiated the secret German non-aggression pact with Soviet Russia on the eve of Germany's invasion of Poland, and who approved orders to execute Allied airmen, then added:

"My last wish is that Germany realize its entity and that an understanding be reached between East and West. I wish peace to the world."

The ex-diplomat looked straight ahead as the hood was adjusted before the trap was sprung. His lips were set tight.

Next in line to follow Ribbentrop to the gallows was Field Marshal Wilhelm Keitel, symbol of Prussian militarism and aristocracy.

Here came the first military leader to be executed under the new concept of Allied international law—the principle that professional soldiers cannot escape justice for waging aggressive wars against humanity by claiming they were merely carrying out orders of their superiors.

Keitel entered the death arena at 1:18, only two minutes after the trap was dropped beneath Ribbentrop and while the latter was still hanging at the end of his rope.

The Field Marshal could not, of course, see the ex-Foreign Minister, whose body was concealed within the first scaffold and whose rope still hung taut.

Keitel did not appear as tense as Ribbentrop. He held his head high while his hands were being tied, and walked erect with military bearing to the foot of the second scaffold, although a guard on each side held his arms.

When asked his name he answered in a loud sharp tone, "Wilhelm Keitel!" He mounted the gallows steps as he might have climbed to a reviewing stand to take the salute of the German Army. He certainly did not appear in need of the guards' help.

When turned around at the top of the platform, Keitel looked over the crowd with the traditional iron-jawed haughtiness of the proud Prussian officer. When asked if he had anything to say he looked straight ahead and speaking in a loud voice said:

"I call on Almighty God to have mercy on the German people. More than two million German soldiers went to their deaths for the Fatherland. I follow now my sons."

Then, while raising his voice to shout, "All for Germany," Keitel's black-booted, uniformed body plunged down with a bang. Observers agreed he had shown more courage on the scaffold than he had in the courtroom, where he tried to hide his guilt behind Hitler's ghost.

Then he claimed that it was all the Fuehrer's fault, that he merely carried out orders and had no responsibility.

This despite the fact that documentary evidence presented during the trial showed he "approved and backed" measures for branding Russian prisoners, directed "Draconian measures" to terrorize the Russian people into submission, and issued secret orders for invasion of Poland three months before the attack took place.

With both Ribbentrop and Keitel hanging at the end of their ropes, there was a pause in the grim proceedings.

The American colonel directing the executions asked the American general representing the Allied Control Commission if those present could smoke. An affirmative answer brought cigarettes into the hands of almost every one of the thirty-odd persons present.

These included two official representatives of the German government in the American zone—Dr. Wilhelm Hoegner, Minister-President of Bavaria, and Dr. Jacob Leisner, Chief Prosecutor of Nuremberg.

Officers and GI's walked around nervously or spoke a few words to one another in hushed voices while Allied correspondents scribbled furiously their notes of the historic, though ghastly event.

In a few minutes an American Army doctor accompanied by a Russian Army doctor and both carrying stethoscopes walked to the first scaffold, lifted the curtain, and disappeared within.

They emerged at 1:30 A.M. and spoke to a short, heavy-set American colonel wearing combat boots. The colonel swung around and, facing official witnesses, snapped to attention to say:

"The man is dead."

Two GI's quickly appeared with a stretcher, which was carried up and lifted into the interior of the scaffold. The hangman, a sergeant, mounted the gallows steps, took a large commando-type knife out of a sheath strapped to his side, and cut the rope.

Ribbentrop's limp body with the black hood still over his head was speedily removed from the far end of the room and placed behind a black canvas curtain. This all had taken less than ten minutes.

The directing colonel turned to the witnesses and said: "Lights out, please, gentlemen," and then, addressing another colonel he called "Norman," said, "O.K." The latter went out the door and over to the condemned block to fetch the next man.

This creature was Ernst Kaltenbrunner, Gestapo chief and director of the greatest mass murder Europe has seen since the Dark Ages.

Kaltenbrunner, master killer of Nazidom, entered the execution chamber at 1:36 A.M. wearing a sweater beneath his double-breasted coat. With his lean, haggard face furrowed by old dueling scars, the terrible successor of Reinhard Heydrich had a frightening look as he glanced around the room.

He was nervous and he wet his lips as he turned to mount the gallows, but he walked steadily. He answered his name in a calm, low voice. When he turned around on the gallows platform he first faced a U. S. Catholic Army chaplain attired in a Franciscan habit.

Kaltenbrunner was asked for his last words and answered quietly:

"I would like to say a word.

"I have loved my German people and my Fatherland with a warm heart.

"I have done my duty by the laws of my people and I am sorry my people were led this time by men who were not soldiers and that crimes were committed of which I have no knowledge."

This sounded like strange talk from a man, one of whose agents— a man named Rudolf Hoess—confessed at a previous trial that under Kaltenbrunner's orders he gassed three million human beings at the Auschwitz concentration camp.

As the black hood was about to be placed over his head Kaltenbrunner, still speaking in a low, calm voice, used a German phrase which translated means:

"Germany good luck!"

His trap was sprung at 1:39 A.M.

Field Marshal Keitel had been pronounced dead at 1:44 A.M., and three minutes later guards had removed his body. The scaffold was made ready for Alfred Rosenberg, master mind behind the Nazi race theories, who sought to establish Nazism as a pagan religion.

Rosenberg was dull and sunken-cheeked as he looked around the court. His complexion was pasty brown. But he did not appear nervous and walked with a steady step to and up the gallows.

Apart from giving his name and replying "No" to a question as to whether he had anything to say, this atheist did not utter a word. Despite his disbelief in God he was accompanied by a Protestant chaplain, who followed him to the gallows and stood beside him praying.

Rosenberg looked at the chaplain once, but said nothing. Ninety seconds after he entered the execution hall he was swinging from the end of a hangman's rope. His was the swiftest execution of any of those condemned.

Then there was a brief lull in the morbid proceedings until Kaltenbrunner was pronounced dead at 1:52 A.M. Hans Frank, the *Gauleiter* of Poland and former SS general, was next in the parade of death. He was the only one of the condemned to enter the chamber with a smile on his lips.

Although nervous and swallowing frequently, this man, who was converted to Catholicism after his arrest, gave the appearance of being relieved at the prospect of atoning for his evil deeds.

He answered to his name quietly and when asked on the platform if he had any last statement replied in a low voice that was almost a whisper:

"I am thankful for the kind treatment during my captivity and I ask God to accept me with mercy."

Frank then closed his eyes and swallowed again as the black hood went over his head.

The sixth man to leave his prison cell and walk with handcuffed wrists across the corner of the small yard separating the condemned block from the death house was sixty-nine-year-old Wilhelm Frick, former Nazi Minister of the Interior.

He entered the execution chamber at five and a half minutes after two, six and a half minutes after Rosenberg had been pronounced dead. He seemed to be the least steady of any so far and stumbled on the thirteenth step of the gallows. His only words were "Long live eternal Germany" before he was hooded and dropped through the trap.

Following Streicher's melodramatic exit and removal of Frick's corpse after he was pronounced dead at 2:20 A.M., Fritz Sauckel, the slave-labor director and one of the worst of the blood-stained men of Nazidom, was brought to face his doom.

Wearing a sweater with no coat and looking wild-eyed, Sauckel proved to be the most defiant of any except Streicher.

Here was the man who drove millions into a land of bondage on a scale unknown since the pre-Christian era. Gazing around the room from the gallow's platform, he suddenly screamed:

"I am dying innocent. The sentence is wrong. God protect Germany and make Germany great again. God protect my family."

The trap was sprung at 2:26 A.M., and, like Streicher, this hatred-filled man groaned loudly as the fatal noose snapped tightly under the weight of his body.

Ninth to come was Colonel General Alfred Jodl, Hitler's strategic adviser and close friend. With the black coat collar of his Wehrmacht uniform turned up at the back as though hurriedly put on, Jodl entered the death house with obvious signs of nervousness.

He wet his lips constantly and his features were drawn and haggard as he walked forward, not nearly so steady as Keitel in mounting the gallows steps. Yet his voice was calm when he uttered his last six words on earth:

"My greetings to you, my Germany."

At 2:34 Jodl plunged into the black hole of the scaffold's death. Both he and Sauckel hung together in that execution chamber until the latter was pronounced dead six minutes later and removed.

The Czechoslovakian-born Seyss-Inquart was the last actor to make his appearance in the ghastly scene of Allied justice. He entered the death chamber at 2:38½ A.M., wearing the glasses which made his face a familiar and despised figure in all the years he ruled Holland with an iron hand and sent thousands of Dutchmen to Germany for forced labor.

Seyss-Inquart looked around with noticeable signs of unsteadiness and limped on his left clubfoot as he walked to the gallows. He mounted the steps slowly, with guards helping him on his way.

When Seyss-Inquart spoke his last words his voice was very low but intense. He said:

"I hope that this execution is the last act of the tragedy of the Second World War and that the lesson taken from this World War will be that peace and understanding should be between peoples.

"I believe in Germany."

INDEX

Abbéville, 57
Achilles, 30, 32, 33
Achkel, Lake, 250
Adams, Phelps, on kamikazes, 487-494
Admiral Graf Spee, scuttling of, 30-34
Admiral Scheer vs. *Jervis Bay,* 91-93
Africa
  Bourke-White in, 295-301
  Clark, Mark, mission to, 205-210
  El Alamein battle in, 211-218
  Oran battle in, 219-222
  Pyle, Ernie, in, 241-244
  Tunisian conquest in, 245-248
Agostino, Father, 321
Ajax, 30, 32, 33
Albert, Raymond, 271
Albert Canal, 45, 46, 47, 54
Alexander, Gen. Harold R. L. G., 165, 250,
  251, 257, 329, 452
Alexandria, 109
Algiers, 219, 276, 280
All Out on the Road to Smolensk, 115-118
Allen, Larry, on sinking of *Barham,* 119-
  122
Allgemeine Zeitung, 519
Allied Control Council, 529
Ancona, 383
Anderson, Gen., 253
Andrus, Col. Burton C., 530
Antwerp, 54, 55
Anzio, 319
  battle of, 325-327
Aprilla, 326
Ardennes Forest, 53
Ariete Division (Italian), 217

Arkansas, 345, 404
Arnim, Col. Gen. Dietloff von, 250, 254,
  256, 258
Assam, 164
Associated Press, 7-8, 11-12, 67, 82-83, 96-
  97, 107-108, 119-122, 149, 150-152, 152-
  155, 172-178, 179-182, 270-273, 311-
  313, 350-351, 386-388, 414-415, 442-
  444, 468-470, 472-473, 495-497, 506
Athenia, torpedoing of, 5-13
Atkinson, Brooks, on Chungking, 281-283
Atomic bombing
  of Hiroshima, 498-505
  of Nagasaki, 506-513
Ault, Phil, 219
Austin, A. B., on Dieppe raid, 198-202
Australia, MacArthur escape to, 156-159
Australians
  9th Division, 217
  at Tobruk, 104-105
Ava Bridge, 165
Ayling, Keith, 195

Baillie, Hugh, 239
  on death of a pilot, 261-263
  on war correspondents, xv
Baka bomb, 487
Bakhchisarai, 185
Bakhmach, 358
Baldwin, Lt. Col. Benton, 412, 413
Baltimore *Evening Sun,* 36-44, 396-398
Baltimore *Sun,* 495-497, 521-526
Bangka, 153
Baranovichi, 358
Barham, sinking of, 119-122

Barracu, Francesco, 448, 449
Barrie, Claud, 9-10
Barrington, Roy, 7
Barry, Capt. C. B., 121
Bartimo, Col., 268
Baruch, Bernard, Arthur Krock on, 292-294
Bastogne, 398-399
Bataan, 137, 139, 140, 156, 157, 158, 511
  prisoners' treatment on, 160-163
Batavia, 152
Battle of France, The, 63-65
Bayerlein, Gen., 216, 218
Bayreuth, 439
BBC. *See* British Broadcasting Company.
Belden, Jack, on Stilwell retreat in Burma, 164-168
Belfast, 349
Belgium, conquest of, 53-56
Benedictine Order at Monte Cassino, 319-324
Bennett, Maj. Gen. Henry Gordon, 159
Berchtesgaden, 456, 458
Berenson, Bernard, on destruction in Florence, 378-381
Bergen, 37
Berger, Meyer, 281
Bergeret, Gen., 79
Bergonzoli, Gen., 462
Berlin, 437, 460, 480, 514
  Allied move toward, 414-416
  fall of, 465-470
  Hitler's last days in, 455-459
  V-J Day in, 519
Bernièr-Sur-Mer, 347-350
Berzarin, Gen., 468
Best from Yank, The, 302-305
Betio, 310
Bettazzi, Alba Rosa, 321
Bewley, Mrs. Luther B., 141
Bewley, Virginia, 141, 142
Bhamo, 168
Bigart, Homer, on battle of Anzio, 325-327
Birjuzov, Lt. Gen. Sergei, 336
Bizerte, capture of, 245, 249-258
Black Prince, 349
Black Sea, 183
Blakang Mati, 151, 152
Blitzkrieg
  in Belgium, 53

Blitzkrieg (cont.)
  of London, 81-90
  in Poland, 19-22
Blücher, 39
Blücher, Field Marshal, 65
Bobruisk, 355
Bock, Capt., 509, 511, 512
Boehme, Lt. Gen., 336
Bombacci, Nicola, 450
Bonins, 493
Bordeaux, 62
Borf, 1st Lt., 401
Bormann, Martin, 457-458
Boston, V-J Day in, 516-517
Bougainville, 197
Bourg, 374
Bourke-White, Margaret, in a lifeboat, 295-301
Bowder, Master Sgt. James, 424
Boyle, Hal
  on Berlin road, 414-415
  on Torgau meeting with Russians, 442-444
Boynton, Damon, 8
Bracker, Milton, 446
  on death of Mussolini, 447-450
Brandenburg Gate, 467, 468
Brauchitsch, Col. Gen. von, 77, 78, 79
Braun, Eva, 455, 456
Braunschweig, 184
Bremen, 437
Bremerton Navy Yard, 494
Brenner Pass, 452
Briesen, Gen. Kurt von, 69, 70
Britain, battle of, 81-90, 360-367
British Broadcasting Company, 370-372, 434, 461-464
Britt, Maj. George, 140
Brown, Cecil, on *Repulse* sinking, 127-132
Brown, Elizabeth, 12
Brown, John Mason, on invasion of Sicily, 264
Brussels, 54, 56
Buchenwald, 1945 descriptions of, 426-436
Buckingham Palace, 480
  bombing of, 85
Buckley, Christopher, 245
  on battle of Cassino, 329-331
  on defeat of Tunisia, 246-249
Budapest, battle for, 400-401

Buduick, Ray, 125
Bukit Timah, 152
Bulge, battle of the, 396-399
Bunker Hill, kamikaze attack on, 488-494
Bunnelle, Robert E., on bombing of Cologne, 174-178
Burke, Sgt. Francis, on V-J Day in London, 517-518
Burma
    Sevareid, Eric, in, 284-286
    Stilwell retreat in, 164-168
Burrough, Adm. Sir Harold, 475, 477, 478
Burrows, Lt. Emmett J., 405, 407
Bury the Dead, 259
Busch, Field Marshal, 462
Buzz bombs, 360-367
Byelorussia, liberation of, 355-359

Caen, 341, 343
Cairo, 260
Caldwell, Erskine Preston, on bombing of Moscow, 115-118
Camling, 38
Candia, 109, 111
Canea, 110
Canne, 46
Cannon, James, on battle of the Bulge, 398-399
Cape Bon, 245, 250, 333
Cape Esperance, 196
Capiz Tarlac, 163
Carlson, Col. Evans F., 311
Carolines, 310
Carroceto, 326
Carroll, Gordon, 165, 205
Casablanca, 219, 258, 479
Caserta Palace, 452-454
Casey, Robert J., on London bombing, 88-90
Cassino
    battle of, 329-331
    bombing of Monte, 319-324
Catozella, Capt. Vincent A., 333
Caucasus, 226
Cavite, 137, 392
CBS. *See* Columbia Broadcasting System.
Ceron, Sgt. George R., 501
Chad, Lake, 524
Chamberlain, Neville, 14, 15, 53

Chancellery, Reichs, Hitler's death in, 455-459
Changi forts, 152
Château-Thierry, 62
Cherbourg, 352-354
Chernaya Gryaz, 147
Chernigov, 358
Chialing River, 282
Chiang Kai-shek, 123, 422
Chicago *Daily News*, 36, 54-56, 88-90, 328, 403-404
Chicago *Sun*, 156-159
Chicago *Tribune*, 75, 169-173
China, 123
    Brooks Atkinson on, 281-283
Cho, Lt. Gen. Isamu, hara-kiri of, 495-497
Chouigui Pass, 251, 252
Christian Science Monitor, 36
Christopherson, Vernon M., 398-399
Chungking, 150
    Brooks Atkinson on, 281-283
Churchill, Allen, on Sgt. Diamond, 306-309
Churchill, Winston, 5, 6, 12-13, 53, 62, 81, 106, 113, 149, 198-199, 211, 325, 422, 431, 479
City of Flint, 11
Clark, Edgar, on "Lili Marlene," 332-334
Clark, Gen. Mark W., 325, 329, 452
    mission to North Africa, 205-210
Clausen, Walter B., on battle of Midway, 179-182
Clay, Lt. Gen. Lucius, 485
Clementi, Nicola, 320
Cleveland *Plain Dealer*, 338-340, 480-482
Cnossus, 109-112
Cobbledick, Gordon, on V-E Day, 480-482
Cochrane, Robert B., on Japanese surrender, 520-526
Cole, John, 221
Collier's Magazine, 361-367, 382-384, 409-413
Collingwood, Charles, 483
    on German surrender, 474-479
    on Goering's surrender, 484-485
Cologne, bombing of, 174-178
Columbia Broadcasting System, 75-80, 85-87, 127-132, 284-286, 344-347, 404, 409, 427-432, 437-441, 474-479, 483-486
Combined Allied Press, 468-470

Comiso Airfield, 267

Commando
Africa mission with Clark, 205-210
Dieppe raid, 198-202

Como, Lake, 448, 449

Compiègne, 65
Hitler at, 75-80

Conger, Clinton B., on sinking of *Curacao*, 203-204

Cook, Capt. James, 6, 9

Cooper, Sister Ismay, 296

Coppola, Goffredo, 448

Coral Sea, battle of, 169-173

Cornish City, 92

Corregidor, 157, 158
MacArthur's retreat from, 137-142

Corriere della Sera, 320

Cosgrove, Col. Moore, 522

Cosmopolitan Magazine, 254-258

Cossacks, 466
exploits of, 392-395

Courtney, Godfrey B., on Clark's mission to Africa, 205-210

Coventry, 469
bombing of, 94-97

Cowan, Howard, 405
on capture of Remagen Bridge, 408

Cox, Raymond, 40

Cox, W. H., 8

Crépy-en-Valois, 65

Crete, conquest of, 109-112

Crimea, 183, 336

Croce Camerina, 268

Cronkite, Walter, on Wilhelmshaven raid, 239-240

Crowe, Maj. Henry Pierson, 312, 313

Crusade in Europe, 274-275, 426, 461

Csepel line, 401

Culoz, 373

Cumberland, 32, 33, 34

Cunningham, Chris, 243

Curacao, sinking of, 203-204

Currivan, Gene, report on Buchenwald, 432-434

Curry, Sgt., 509-510, 511

Cyrenaica, 462

Czenstochkowa, 2

Dachau, 432

Dacoits, 166, 167

Daniell, Raymond, on London bombing, 83-85

Dammartin, 65

Daquanno, Ernesto, 450

Davies, John, Jr., 285

Davis, Richard Harding, 19-20, 287

D-Day, 337-351, 409

Death March on Bataan, 160-162, 511

Dedovsk, 147

Deevers, Maj. Murray, 406-407

Defense of Leningrad, Eyewitness Accounts of the Siege, The, 224-225

de Gaulle, 527
at Te Deum in Nôtre Dame, 370-372

Dempsey, Sen. Miles C., 409

Denby, George, 284

Denig, Brig. Gen. Robert L., 309

Dentz, Gen., 66

Der Sieg in Polen, herausgegeben vom Oberkommando der Wehrmacht, 23-25

Derbyshire Yeomanry, 253

Derevyanko-Nikolaevich, Lt. Gen. Kuzma, 524

Desiderio, Father, 323

Deutsche Allgemeine Zeitung, 199, 320-321

Deutschland, 92

Devers, Lt. Gen., 329

Dexter, Franklin, 11

Diamare, Abbot Gregorio, 320, 321, 322

Diamond, Sgt. Leland, 306-309

Diefenback, 1st Lt. Albert W., 240

Dieppe raid, 198-202

Diller, Col., 140

Diraimo, Brother Zaccaria, 320

Disher, Leo, on battle of Oran, 219-222

Dixon, Jeanne, 301

Djebel Achkel, 252

Djebel Berda, 255

Djebel-bou-Aoukaz, 251

Djebel Mcheltat, 255

Djebel Zarour, 252

Djedeoda, 246, 251

DMHM Newspapers, 137

Dnieper, 356

Doenitz, Adm. Karl, 26, 457, 459, 462, 474, 476, 483
surrender of, 485-486

Dogs in the war, 302-305, 328, 352-354, 376

Domei, 521
Don River, 226-238, 394-395
Dongo, 449
Dopking, Alva N., on hara-kiri, 495-497
Dottie Dee, 339
Dow, G. W., 12
Drabnik, Sgt. Alexander A., 405
Dresden, 416
Drobak, 37, 38
Duffus, Robert L., on Dunkirk, 58
Duisburg, 411
Dun, Rt. Rev. Angus, 424, 425
Duncan, Elspeth, 298
Dunkerque, 33
Dunkirk, evacuation from, 57-61
Dunn, Capt. Philip, 352
Duzenbury, Wyatt E., 501
Dyess, William E., 161-163
Dyson, Cmdr. H. J., 492

Eaker, Gen. Ira C., 239, 329
Eben-Emael, German capture of, 45-48
Editor and Publisher, xv
Edson, Col. Merrit A., 313
Edwards, Webley, 404
Egbert, Col. Roger, 523
Ehrenburg, Ilya, 143, 223
  on Mozhaisk liberation, 144-145
  on Sevastopol, fall of, 184-186
18th Infantry Regiment (German), 135
Eighth Air Force (U. S.), 239, 438, 518
Eighth Army (Allied), 211, 215, 252, 253,
    333, 382-385
Eightieth Division (U. S.), 427
Eisenach, 185
Eisenhower, Gen. Dwight D., 205, 206, 245,
    256, 257, 396, 463, 471, 472, 485
  description of Buchenwald by, 426
  D-Day order by, 337
  on German surrender, 461, 478-479
  and Patton slapping affair, 274-280
El Alamein, battle of, 211-218
El Daba, 217
El Guettar, 255
El Pueblo, 34
Elbe, 461
  U. S. meets Russia at, 442-445
Eldredge, Lt. Cmdr. Edward H., 172
11th Army (German), 187
Eleventh Hussars, 253

Eliot, Maj. George Fielding, 483
Elista, 358
Emden, 39
Emsmann, Lt., 26, 27
Enfidaville, 250
Eniwetok, 493
Enola Gay, 498, 499-500, 501
Enterprise, 488
Epic Story of Stalingrad, The, 228-233
Erakleion, 109
Erfel, 405, 408
Erfurt, 185
Estava, Adm., 253
Evans, Jock, 88-90
Ewart, Col., 462
Exeter, 30, 32

*Fahrten und Fluge gegen England,
    Berichte und Bilder, herausgegeben
    vom Oberkommando der Wehrmacht,*
    27-29, 94-96
Falkenhorst, Gen. Nikolaus von, 42
Fascist Grand Council, 446
Fegelein, SS officer, 457
Felix, Charles William, 286
Ferebee, Maj. Thomas, 500
Fergen, Capt. Fogarty, 91
Ferguson Passage, 271, 273
Ferrar, Lt. Arch, 440
Ferryville, 250, 251
F. F. I., 375
15th Panzer Division (German), 216, 217
Fifth Army (Allied), 209, 287, 319, 325,
    329-331, 332
Fifth Army Corps (German), 336
Fifth Marine Corps (U. S.), 402
Fiftieth Division (British), 215
58th Division (Russian), 443
51st Highland Division, 212
52nd Brigade (Italian), 450
Finn, Master Sgt. Mickey, 308
First Army (British), 252-254
First Army (U. S.), 396-398, 414, 440, 444
First Army (Ukrainian), 444
First Marine Division (U. S.), 190, 309
Fitch, Rear Adm. Aubrey W., 170, 171
Fitzgerald, Sgt. J. J., 441
Fleming, Arthur Henry, 78
Flensburg, 472, 485, 486
Fletcher, Rear Adm. Frank J., 170

Florence, 383
destruction in, 378-281
Florida Island,. 190
Foch, Field Marshal, 75, 76, 78
Fodor, M. W., on conquest of Belgium, 53-56
Foglia River, 383, 384
Foote, Lt. J. P., 205, 206, 207, 208, 209
Ford, Brig. Gen. Edward, 485
Formosa, 493
Fornebo, 38, 40
Fort de Chatillon, 528
Fort de Russy, 124
Fort du Roule, 353
Forty-fourth Division (British), 215
Forty-fourth Infantry Division (German), 235
Fourth Panzer Division (German), 226
Fourth Ukraine front, 336
Foy, 399
Frank, Hans, 536
Frankfurt-am-Main, 416
Frankfurter Zeitung, 109-112, 113-114
Fraser, Adm. Sir Bruce, 524
Freckleman, Helen, 301
Freidel, Maj., 463
Frick, Wilhelm, 536
Friedeburg, Adm. Hans Georg von, 460-464, 472, 474-479, 483, 486
Friesland, 460
Frisian Islands, 460, 463
Fritsche, Hans, 529
Fuensche, SS Adjutant, 457
Fuka, 217

Gabès, 255
Gakokhidze, Political Officer, 186
Galatea, 119
Gamelin, Gen. Maurice, 62
Gardner, Maj. Franklin T., 327
Garnsee, 3
Gatow Airfield, 455
Gatti, Luigi, 450
Gay, Ensign G. H., on battle of Midway, 179-182
Gehlback, Lt. Cmdr. L. R., 404
Gellhorn, Martha, on the Allied 8th Army, 382-385
Gennep, 51, 52
Genocide, 426

Giacomo, Brother, 321
Gibble, Chaplain William T., 407, 408
Gilbert Islands, battle in, 310-313, 493
Giordano, Luca, 323
Giulino de Mezzegre, 449
Givet, 54
Gizo Island, 271
Glasgow, 6, 7, 9-11
Gleiwitz, 3
Glukhov, 358
Goans, 297
Godfrey, Lt., 510, 511
Goebbels, Dr. Joseph, 5, 386, 457, 468
Goering, Field Marshal Hermann, 35, 76, 77, 78, 79, 405-406, 416, 457, 458, 468, 483, 529, 530, 533
surrender of, 484-485
Golitsyno, 144
Gomel, 358
Gorski, 136
Gorrell, Henry T., on Hurtgen Forest, 389-391
Govorov, Lt. Gen., 144-145
Graf Spee, Admiral, scuttling of, 30-34
Graziani, Marshal Rodolfo, 449, 462
Graziosi, Father Odorigo, 322
Great Artiste, The, 506-513
Greb, Harry, 362, 364
Greenock, Scotland, 7-8
Greenwood, Arthur, 14
Greiser, Oscar, 185
Grochow, 24
Grosser Kurfuerst, 32
Grossman, Vassili, on liberation of Russia, 355-359
Grozny, 392
Gruner, Maj. Gen., 336
Guadalcanal, 307, 308
battle of, 190-197
Guam, 149
Guderian, Gen. Heinz, 456
Guernica, 469
Gumtree Road, 255
Gustav Line, 319, 325

Haape, Dr. Heinrich, on attack of Russia, 133-136
Halifax, 11-12
Halsey, Adm., 526
Hamblen, Col., 206, 207, 209

Hamburg, 437
Hamburger Anzeiger, 5, 12-13, 18
Hanover, 290
Hara-kiri, 495-497
Harris, Air Marshal Arthur, 174-175
Harris, Charles, 271, 272
Harrison, Hubert D., on end in Italy, 452-454
Hatvan, 401
Haugland, Vern, on Nagasaki bombing, 506
Hauteville, 374
Hawaii, bombing of, 123-126
Healy, Cmdr. H. R., 170, 171
Helfrich, Adm., 524
Heligoland, 460, 463
Heller, Paul, 429, 430
Helson, Pfc. Richard H., 501
Hemingway, Ernest, 390
  on battle of Britain, 360-367
Henderson Field, 190
Hennef, 407
Henshaw, Dennis, 133
Herbert, Lord David, III, 300
Heroic Defense of Sevastopol, The, 184-189
Herrera, Ricardo Diaz, on scuttling of *Graf Spee*, 31-34
Herrgesell, Gerhardt, 455-459
Hersey, John, 307
Hess, Ilse, 107
Hess, Rudolph, 78, 79
  parachuting in Scotland, 106-108
Hesse, Dr. Kurt, 45, 65
Heydrich, Reinhard, 535
Hickam Field, 125, 126
Hicks, George, on D-Day, 344-347
Highlanders at El Alamein, 211-215
Hill, Gladwin, 405
  on capture of Remagen Bridge, 406-408
Himmler, Heinrich, 456, 457, 483
  death of, 486
Hindus, Maurice, on Cossack exploits, 392-395
Hirohito, Emperor, 520
Hiroshima, 520
  bombing of, 498-505
History in the Writing, 165-168, 205-210, 295-301

Hitler, Adolf, 1, 2, 5, 18, 35, 94, 109, 143, 217, 226, 227, 386, 442, 484
  at Compiègne, 75-80
  last days of, 455-459
Hitzsinger, 486
Hodges, Lt. Gen. Courtney H., 414, 444
Hoegner, Dr. Wilhelm, 534
Hoess, Rudolf, 535
Hoge, Brig. Gen. William M., 406, 407
Holland, 49-52, 460, 461, 463, 475, 531
Holmes, Col., 206, 207, 209
Homma, Gen. Masaharu, 158
Honolulu, attack on, 123-126
Horten, 37, 38, 39, 40
Hottelet, Richard C., 483
  on Himmler's death, 486
  parachuting into Germany, 409
Howe, Quincy, 483
Humanity Uprooted, 392
Humlong, Mary Lee, 11
Hungary, battle for Budapest in, 400-401
Huntziger, Gen., 79
Huracan, 34
Hurlburt, Tech Sgt., on battle of Guadalcanal, 195-197
Hurtgen Forest, battle in, 389-391
Huss, Pierre J., 246
  on Hitler's last days, 455-459
  on Tunisian victory, 254-258

I Saw the Fall of the Philippines, 138-142
Idaho, 404
Ie Shima, 242
Indo-China, 123
Inishtrahull Island, 6
Inland Sea, 489, 493
International Military Tribunal, 529-537
International News Service, 455-459, 499-502, 528
Iowa, 521, 522
Irrawaddy River, 164, 165, 167, 168
Irvin, Warren, 36, 41
Isitt, Air Marshal, 521, 524
Italy
  end in, 452-454
  Mussolini's death in, 446-451
  V-J Day in, 519
Iwo Jima, 489, 493
  battle of, 402-404

Jackson, Henry, 83
Jaguari, 34
Jameson, Henry B., on V-2 attack in England, 386-388
Jane's Fighting Ships, 124
Jena, 185
Jeppson, Lt. Maurice, 501
Jervis Bay vs. *Admiral Scheer*, 91-93
Jewell, Lt., 206, 209, 210
Jodl, Col. Gen., 457, 458, 472, 473, 485
  death of, 529, 537
  at German surrender, 474-479
Johnston, Richard W., on Tarawa, 310-313
Johnston, Stanley, on battle of Coral Sea, 169-173
Johnston, William, 271

Kalach, 231
Kalang River, 152
Kalinin, 133, 135, 136
Kaltenbrunner, Ernst, death of, 529, 535, 536
Kalweit, W., S. S. reporter, on Budapest battle, 400-401
Kamikazes, 487-494
Kampferlebnisse aus dem Feldzuge in Polen, 1939, herausgegeben von Generalstab des Heeres, 3
Kapinsky, H., 82
Karlshorst, 484
Karmen, Roman, 227
  on battle of Stalingrad, 228-233
Kashira, 147
Kato, Masuo, 521
Katowice, 1, 2
Katz, Sgt. Bernard, 517-518
Kawabira, Mt., 507
Keitel, Col. Gen. Wilhelm, 76, 77, 78, 79-80, (Field Marshal) 457, 458, 460, 483
  death of, 529, 533-534, 536
  surrender to Zhukov, 484-485
Kennedy, Edward
  on German surrender, 471-473
  on Patton slapping case, 276-279
Kennedy, J. F., rescue off Kolombangara, 270-273
Kennedy, Joseph, 270, 271
Kesselring, Field Marshal Albert, 216, 319, 380

Kharkov, 358
Khartoum, 260
Khersones Peninsula, 335-336
Khimki, 143
Kiekheben-Schmidt, Leutnant, 63
  on fall of Paris, 65-67
Kiev, 358, 359
King, Harold, on fall of Berlin, 468-470
King, James F., on sinking of *Athenia*, 11-12
Kinzel, Gen., 462, 463
Kirchheimer, Fritz, 428, 429
Kirichenko, Gen. Nikolai, 392-395
Kleist, Gen. Ewald von, 226
Kluckhohn, Frank L., 246
  on capture of Tunis, 249-252
Knickerbocker, H. R., on MacArthur's escape from Philippines, 156-159
Koba, 507
Kobe, 520
Koch, Captain, 46
Koht, Halvdan, 38, 39
Kolombangara Island, 272
  J. F. Kennedy rescue off, 270-273
Komorn, 401
Konev, Marshal, 443, 444
Konoye, Prince, 123
Koplin, Pfc. Kenneth, 450
Korostyshev, 358
Kozelets, 358
Kra, Isthmus of, 164
Krakow, 2
Krasnodar, 184
Krasnova, 136
Krebs, Chief of Staff, 456, 459
Kremlin, bombing of, 115-118
Krivoi Rog, 358
Krock, Arthur, on Bernard Baruch, 292-294
Kunsewitz, Kurt, 184
Kunsewitz, Otto, 184, 185
Kure Harbor, 493
Kursk, 359
Kurt, Lt. Gen., 336
Kurusu, Saburo, 123
Kushtshevskaya, Cossacks in, 392-395
Kutno, 70
Kwajalein, 493
Kyushu, 506, 507, 510

La Nazione, 321-324
La Valleja, 34
Ladoga, Lake, 223
Landberg, Morrie, on Iwo Jima, 402-403
Lane, Capt. Harry C., 326, 327
Langamann, Otto, 32
Langsdorff, Capt. Hans, 30, 31, 32, 34
Lashio, 164, 168
Laurence, William L., on bombing of Nagasaki, 506-513
Laval, Pierre, execution of, 527-528
Lazari, Urbano, 449
Leatherneck, The, 307
Le Bardo, 251
Leclerc, Gen. Jacques, 370, 524
Leech, Capt., 131, 132
Leipzig, fall of, 437-441
Leiser, Ernest, on fall of Berlin, 465-468
Leisner, Dr. Jacob, 534
Le Luc, Vice-Adm., 79
LeMay, Maj. Gen. Curtis E., 501-502
Lemnitzer, Brig. Gen., 206, 207, 208, 209, 210
Leningrad, 143
blockade of, 223-225
Leonard, Maj. Gen. John W., 406
Leseuer, Larry, 483
on German surrender, 485
Leuna, 438-439
Levy, Lt., 510
Lewis, Mrs. George, 501
Lewis, John, 100, 102, 103
Lewis, Capt. Robert A., 501
Lexington at battle of Coral Sea, sinking of, 169-173
Leyte, 487
Liege, 54, 55
Life magazine, 67-70, 295
"Lili Marlene," 332-334
Lippmann, Walter, on death of Roosevelt, 423
Liverani, Augusto, 450
Liverpool, 6
Livingston, Capt. R. P., 205, 206, 207, 209, 210
Livitch, Maj. Mitri, 443
Llewellyn, Richard, 86
Lochner, Louis P., 63
on fall of Paris, 67-70

Lodz, 21
London, 468, 469
bombing of, 81-90, 98-103, 289-291
in opening days of war, 14-17
V-J Day in, 517-518
V-1 attacks on, 360-367, 368-369
V-2 attacks on, 386-388
London *Daily Herald*, 9-11, 58-61, 198, 199-202, 246-249, 329-331, 340-343, 452-454
London *Times, The*, 1-3, 15, 280
Long, Tania, on the *Jervis Bay*, 91-93
Longstop Hill, storming of, 246-249
Louis, Joe, 364
Louvain, 54, 55, 56, 287
Lovat, Lord, 199, 202
Loveland, Roelif, on D-Day, 338-340
Lubitsch, Ernst, 12
Lubitsch, Nicola, 12
Ludendorff, 188
Ludendorff Bridge, 405, 406
Luftwaffe, 257, 416, 484
at the Bulge, 397
Coventry bombing by, 94-97
Crete attack by, 109-112
London bombing by, 81-90, 289-291
Moscow bombing by, 115-118
Rotterdam bombing by, 49-52
Ventotene surrender by engineers of, 315-318
Luke Field, 125
Lüneburg Heath, German surrender at, 460-464
Lunga Point, 196
L'Unita Milan, 450-451
Lusitania, 5, 13
Luttich, 45, 46
Lützow, 92
Luzon, 160

Maastricht, 46
Macmillan, Richard D.
on battle of El Alamein, 211-215
on a puppy in France, 352-354
MacMillan, Sister Violet, 296
MacRitchie reservoir, 151
MacArthur, Gen. Douglas, 160
Corregidor retreat by, 137-142
at Japanese surrender, 521-526
Philippine escape by, 156-159

Maginot Line, 53
Maguire, John, 271
Maikop, 392
Makin Island, 311
Malacanan Palace, 141
Malaya, 149, 150, 164
Maleme, 109, 110, 111, 112
Manchester Guardian, 252
Mandalay, 165-166, 167
Manila, 149, 158, 160
Mannerheim Line, 144
Mansfield, Dr., on capture on Eben-Emael, 45-48
Manstein, Gen. Fritz Erich von, 183
Marine Corps (U. S.)
    Sgt. Diamond of, 306-309
    at Guadalcanal, 190-197
    at Iwo Jima, 402-404
    at Tarawa, 310-313
Mariveles airfield, 161
Marki, 23
Marshall, Gen., 142
Marshalls, 493
Martin, Cpl. Paul, 517
Martino, Father, 321
Masefield, John, 57
Massicault, 250, 251
Matanikou River, 192
Matsumoto, Fujie Urata, 507
Matteotti, 447
Matthews, George, 387
Matthews, Herbert L., on destruction of Naples, 287-288
Mauldin, Bill, at Anzio, 325-326
Mauritius, 349
Maurois, André, 62-63
    on fall of Paris, 63-65
McCaleb, Kenneth, on Hiroshima bombing, 499-502
McDaniel, C. Yates, 149
    on fall of Singapore, 152-155
McEwan, John, 7, 8, 9
McGlincy, James F., 499
    on Hiroshima bombing, 504-505
McMahon, Patrick H., 271, 272, 273
Medjez, 246, 247, 251
Meiktila, 167
Meuse River, 45, 46, 53
Meaux, 65
Meyrick, Cmdr., 220

Mezzasoma, Fernando, 450, 451
Midway, 149
    battle of, 179-182
Mikosch, 1st Lt., 46
Milan, 446, 447-450
Minsk, 358
Missouri, Japanese surrender on, 520-526
Mitchell, Lt. John, 408
Miteiriyeh Ridge, 216, 217
Mitscher, Vice Adm. Marc A., in kamikaze attack, 488-494
Mogilev, 355
Molotov, 527
Monschau Forest, 397
Montague, E. A., 246
    on Tunisian victory, 252-254
Monte Cassino, bombing of, 319-324
Monte Lura, 384
Montevideo, 31-34
    scuttling of *Graf Spee* in, 30-34
Montgomery, Field Marshal Bernard
    at El Alamein, 211-218
    German surrender to, 460-464
Morgan, Lt. Gen., 452-453
Morrison, Herbert, 97
Moscow, 145-148
Moscow, 470, 480
    battle of, 143-148
    bombing of, 115-118
Moscow Tram Stop, 133-136
Mosley, Leonard, on D-Day, 340-343
Moulmein, 164
Mountbatten, Adm. Louis, 199, 205
Mowrer, Edmond, 271
Mozhaisk, 143
    liberation of, 144-145
Mulde River, 443, 444
Munich, 146
Murrow, Edward R., 483
    on Buchenwald, 427-432
    on fall of Leipzig, 437-441
    on London bombing, 85-87
Mussolini, Benito, death of, 446-451
Mussolini, Rachele, 449
Mussolini, Vittorio, 451
Myitkyina, 165

Nagasaki, 520
    bombing of, 506-513

Nakashima, Leslie, 499
on Hiroshima bombing, 503-504
Namur, 54
Naples, 452-454
destruction of, 287-288
Narvik, 37
Nation, The, 14-17
National Broadcasting Company, 36
Neuhoff, 133, 134, 136
Neva, 225
Nevada, 345, 404
New Georgia, 270
New Guinea, 169
New River, N. C., 308
New Statesman and Nation, 417-421
New York, 404
New York City, V-J Day in, 515
New York *Evening Post,* 156
New York *Herald Tribune,* 35, 91, 92-93,
203-204, 314, 326-327, 392-395, 423
New York *Journal-American,* 530-537
New York Times, The, 20-22, 50-52, 58,
83-85, 179-182, 211-215, 249-252, 270-
273, 281-283, 287-288, 289-291, 292-
294, 347-350, 405-408, 432-434, 446-
450, 472-473, 488, 506-513, 514, 530
New York *World-Telegram,* 104-105, 241,
242-244
New Yorker, 98-103
Newark *Evening News,* 335-336
Nezhin, 358
Nikolaevich-Derevyanko, Lt. Gen. Kuzma,
524
Nimitz, Adm., 523, 524, 526
19th French Corps, 252
90th Light Infantry Division (Italian), 217
98th Infantry (German), 336
Ninth Air Force (U. S.), 338
Ninth Armored Division (U. S.), 406
Ninth Army (German), 135, 136
Ninth Army (U. S.), 457
9th Division (Australian), 217
9th Division (U. S.), 517
Noël, French Ambassador, 79
Normandy, D-Day invasion of, 337-351
Norway, German invasion of, 35-44
Nôtre Dame, shooting in, 370-372
Noville, 399
Novograd-Volhynsk, 358
Novogrudok, 358

Novorossiisk, 184
Nudi, Mario, 450
Nuremberg, trials at, 529-537
Nurnberg, 437, 439, 440

Oahu, 124, 125, 518
Oberlar-Troisdorf, 407
Octeville, 353
Odessa, 183, 358
Odintsovo, 144
O'Donnell, Camp, 163
Ohira, Col. Hideo, 150
Okinawa
hara-kiri at, 495-497
kamikazes at, 487-494
on V-E Day, 480-482
Olaf Trygvason, 38, 39
Oliver, Vic, 82
Once There Was a War, 315-318
111th Infantry Division (German), 336
101st Airborne (U. S.), 398-399
100th Light Infantry Division (German),
233
O'Neal, Col. Joel, 410, 411
Operation Dynamo, 57-61
Operation Overlord, 337-351
Oran, battle of, 219-222
Orel, 358, 359
Orion, 349
Orlovka, 234
Oskarsborg, 39
Oslo, occupation of, 36-44
Osmena, Sergio, 142
Oswald, Walter, 285
Otwock, 2

Pampanga province, 161, 163
Papen, Franz von, 529
Paris, 471
exodus of refugees from, 71-74
fall of, 62-70
Nôtre Dame shooting in, 370-372
Stein, Gertrude, return to, 373-377
V-J Day in, 518-519
Paris, John A., 219
Parsons, Capt. William S., 500
Patton, Lt. Gen. George S., 414
slapping affair, 274-280
Paulus, Field Marshal von, 227, 233
Pavolini, Allessandro, 448, 449

Pearl Harbor, 511
Japanese attack on, 123-126
Pearson, Drew, 276
Pearson, Leon, on execution of Laval, 527-528
Peel Line, 51
Pegasus, 26
Peirce reservoir, 151
Percival, Lt. Gen. A. E., 150, 524, 525
Pest, battle for, 400-401
Petacci, Clara, death of, 448-449, 451
Petacci, Marcello, 449
Pétain, Marshal Henri, 219, 527
Peters, C. Brooks, on bombing of Rotterdam, 49-52
Peterson, Arman (Pete), 261-263
Philadelphia *Public Ledger*, 156
Philippines, 160
MacArthur's escape from, 156-159
Phillips, Adm. Tom, 127, 131, 132
Picasso, 377
Pietro, Brother, 321
Pinkley, Virgil, on robot attack on London, 368-369
Pitkin, Dwight L., on London bombing, 82-83
Pius XII, Pope, 422
Plata River, 33, 34
Poindexter, Governor, 125
Poland, 23-25, 472, 536
Blitzkrieg in, 19-22
German invasion of, 1-4
Pollek, Col., 463
Pontoise, 65
Popolo of Milan, 449
Port Moresby, 169
Porta, Paolo, 450
Porto Farina, 253
Portsteffen, Sgt. Major, 47
Prien, Lt. Günther, 26-29
Prim, Pfc. James, 516
Prince of Wales, sinking of, 127-132
Pritchett, V. S., 1945 survey on Germany, 416-421
Prome, 167
Pya Lebar radio, 151
Pyimana, 167
Pyle, Ernie, 440
on North Africa, 241-244

Queen Elizabeth, 119-122, 515
Queen Mary crash with *Curacao*, 203-204
Quezon, President Manuel L., 139, 141, 142
Quiggle, 1st Lt. Howard C., 339
Quisling, Major Vidkun, 38, 41, 44

Rabaul, 493
Raeder, Adm., 77
RAF. *See* Royal Air Force.
Ragusa, 267
Rangitiki, 92, 93
Rangoon, 164
Rapido River, 329, 330
Ras Zebib, 253
Rawalpindi, 92
Red Star, 392
Reedy, Tom, on death of Roosevelt, 423-425
Reichstag, 469
Reid, Robert
Buchenwald report by, 434-436
Nôtre Dame broadcast by, 370-372
Reihert, Oberfeldwebel Ludwig, 185
Reims, 461
German surrender at, 471-473, 474-479
Reinhardt, Maj. Gen., 336
Remagen Bridge, capture of, 405-408
Repulse, 26, 27
sinking of, 127-132
Reston, James, on British-German role reversal, 289-291
Rethymno, 109, 111
Reuter, Admiral von, 27
Reuter's, 347-350, 396-398
Reynolds, Quentin, on exodus from Paris, 71-74
Rheinbach, 406
Rhine, 456
paratroop jump on, 409-412
Remagen Bridge capture on, 405-408
Rhineland, bombing of, 174-178
Ribbentrop, Joachim von, 78, 79, 457, 459
death of, 530, 531, 533, 534, 535
Richer, Charles, 429, 430
Riscoe, Arthur, 82
Robb, Air Marshal, 477
Roberts, Maj. Mills, 201
Rocco, Brother, 321
Roede(?), Walther, 430
Romano, Ruggero, 450

Rome, 514
V-J Day in, 519
Rommel, Field Marshal Erwin, 104
defeat of, at El Alamein, 211-218
defeat of forces of, in Tunisia, 245-258
Romulo, Carlos, on retreat from Corregidor, 137-142
Rooks, Gen., 485, 486
Rooney, Andy, 442
on celebration at Torgau, 444-445
Roosevelt, Franklin D., 62, 156, 431, 479
Baruch aid to, 292-294
death of, 422-425
prayer on D-Day, 337
Rosenberg, Alfred, 531, 536
Ross, George Henry Robertson, 271, 272
Rostelli, N., 333
Rostock, 460
Rostov, 143, 394-395
Rotterdam, 469
bombing of, 49-52
Rovno, 358
Royal Air Force
Cologne bombing by, 174-178
Dieppe attack by, 198
Dunkirk attack by, 59
Germany bombing by, 290
Hemingway on, 361-367
Royal Oak, sinking of, 26-29
Ruhr, bombing of, 174-178
Rumor and Reflection, 379-381
Rundstedt, Field Marshal Gerd von, 396
Russell, Ned, 219
Russia
Budapest conquest by, 400-401
Cossack exploits in, 392-395
Leningrad blockade in, 223-225
liberation of, 355-359
Moscow battle in, 143-148
Moscow bombing in, 115-118
Sevastopol battles in, 183-189, 335-336
Stalingrad battle in, 226-238
troops of, meeting U. S. troops, 442-445
Wehrmacht attack on, 113-114, 133-136
Russian Peasant and the Revolution, The, 392
Ryukyus, 493

Sachsenwinkel, 24
Sadovaya, 229

St. Brice, 66
St. Cyprien, 251, 252
St. Louis *Post-Dispatch*, 276-279
Salconio, Father Don, 320, 321
Salisbury, Harrison, on German defeat at Sevastopol, 335-336
Salween, 164
San Fernando (Bataan), 161, 163
San Francisco, V-J Day in, 515-516
Sanne, Gen., 233
Santos, José Abad, 142
Saroyan, William, on Co. D's pooch, 302-305
Sauckel, Fritz, 537
Sauer, Maj. Kenneth F., 140
Savage, Col., 140
Savo Island, 190, 191, 195, 196, 197
Sayre, Commissioner, 139, 141
Scapa Flow, 32
attack in, 26-29
Schacht, Hjalmar H. E., 529
Schaub, Julius, 456
Schell, En. John Q., 404
Schleswig-Holstein, 460, 463
Schmeling, Max, 109
Schmidt, Heinz Werner, at El Alamein, 215-218
Schoedt, Reichsamtsleiter, 44
Schroter, Heinz, 228
on battle of Stalingrad, 234-238
Schuster, Ildefonso Cardinal, 449
Scoglitti, 267, 268
Scripps-Howard, 242-244
Seals, Adj. Gen. Carl D., 140
Second Army (Allied), 461
Second Army (British), 409, 413, 486
Second Marine Division (U. S.) 190
Seiss, Karl Heinz, on attack of Russia, 113-114
Seitz, Capt. George A., 492
Seletar, 152
Seligman, Cmdr., 171, 172
Sembawang, 152
Sevareid, Eric, 483
in Burma, 284-286
Sevastopol, 143, 223
fall of, 183-189
German defeat at, 335-336
Seventeenth Airborne (U. S.), 409, 410
Seventeenth Army (German), 335-336

Seventh Army (U. S.), 274, 276, 280
7th Infantry Division (U. S.), 495
Sevez, Gen. François, 472, 477
Seyss-Inquart, Artur, 531, 537
"Shafty," 270
Shan States, 165
Shaw, Irwin, on GI conversation, 259-260
Shawcross, Sir Hartley, 427
Sherman, Adm. Frederick C., 170, 171, 172, 526
Sherrod, Robert, 311
Shigemitsu, Mamoru, at Japanese surrender, 521-526
Shirer, William L., 483
  on Hitler at Compiègne, 75-80
"Shorty," 302-305
Shumard, Sgt. Robert R., 501
Sicily, invasion of, 264-269
Sieburg, 407
Siegfried Line, 384
Simferopol, 185
Simonov, Konstantin, 143
  on battle for Moscow, 145-148
Sinclair, Archibald, 14
Singapore, 164
  fall of, 149-155
Sittang River, 167
Sixth Airborne Division (British), 409, 410
Sixth Army (German), 227, 234
Sixty-Ninth Division (U. S.), 438, 443, 444
"Sixty-Ninth, Writing," 239, 240
Skhodnya, 147
Smith, Maj. Gen. Harry M., 402
Smith, Howard K., on German surrender, 483-484
Smith, Maj. Gen. Julian C., 312
Smith, Kingsbury, on Nuremberg trials, 529-537
Smith, Gen. Walter Bedell, 472
  at German surrender, 474-479
Smolensk, 144
Snow, Roy, 412, 413
Snyder(?), Thomas, 347
Solomons, 169, 190, 191, 193, 195-197
South Dakota, 521, 522
Soviet War News Weekly, 144-145
Spaatz, Gen. Carl, 475, 501-502
  at German surrender, 475-478
Spelvin, 267, 268
Spree, River, 466

Springboard to Berlin, 219-222
S.S. units in Budapest, 400-401
Stadt-Meckenheim, 406
Stalin, 123, 145, 198, 226, 338, 527
Stalingrad, 234-238
Stalingrad, 392, 443, 468, 469, 484
  battle of, 226-238
Stanton, William L., 285
Staritsa, 135, 136
Starkey, Roy L., 271
Stars and Stripes, 259-260, 332-334, 398-399, 442, 444-445, 465-468
Stavelot, 396-398
Steele, Capt. Henry, 153, 154
Stefani, 450
Steiborik, Sgt. Joe A., 501
Stein, Gertrude, on returning to Paris, 373-377
Steinbeck, John, on a paratrooper capturing 87 Germans, 314-318
Stevens, Edmund, 36, 40, 41
Stilwell, Gen. Joseph W., 495
  retreat in Burma, 164-168
Stockholm, 36
Stolbtsy, 358
Stoneham, William H., on troops on Anzio, 328
Stotzingen, Father, 322
Stowe, Leland, on conquest of Norway, 35-44
Streicher, Julius, death of, 529-530, 531-533
Strong, Gen., 477, 478
Stuart, Caroline, 12
Stumme, Gen., 216
Stuttgart, 437
Suda Harbor, 109
Suicide pilots (kamikaze), 487-494
Sumatra, 154, 155
Summersby, Kay, 299, 301
Surabachi, 402, 403, 404
Susloparov, Gen. Ivan, 472, 475, 477, 478
Sutherland, Gen., 139, 522, 523
Sweeney, Maj. Charles W., 508

Tacoma, 33, 34
Taganrog, 394
Talbot, Frank X., 307
Tarawa, battle of, 310-313
Tczew, 2

Tebourba, 246, 247, 251, 252

Tedder, Air Chief Marshal Sir Arthur, 468, 478

Tel el Aqqaqir, 217

Tempelhof Airport, 469

Tengah, 152

Tennant, Capt. William, 128, 129

Tennessee, 404

10th Army (U. S.), 495

Texas, 345, 404

Thelle, 65

Third Army (U. S.), 414, 440

3rd Battalion (German), 133, 135

3rd Motorised Infantry Division (German), 235

31st Pursuit Squadron (U. S.), 161

36th Bombardment Squadron (U. S.), 517

Thom, Ensign Leonard, 271, 272

Thoma, Gen. von, 217, 218

Thomas, Col., 79

Thompkins, Maj. R. M. C., 312

Thompson, R. W., 198

305th Infantry Division (German), 227

376th Infantry Division (German), 235

Tibbets, Col. Paul, 499-500, 501

Tiergarten, 466, 467, 469

Tighe, Desmond, on D-Day, 347-350

Tikhonov, Nikolai, on blockade of Leningrad, 223-225

Tilly-sur-Suelles, 352

Time magazine, 124-126, 165-168

Tinian, 500, 506

Tippelskirch, Lt. Col., 79

Tkachenko, Political Officer, 185, 186

To All Hands: An Amphibious Adventure, 264-269

Tobruk, 104-105, 246

Tojo, Gen. Hideki, 123

Toklas, Alice, 375, 376

Tokyo, 489, 493, 514

 radio, 149, 150-152, 499

 on Hiroshima bombing, 502

 surrender at, 520-526

Tolbukhin, Gen., 231

Tolischus, Otto, on *Blitzkrieg* in Poland, 19-22

Tolstoy, Alexei, 183, 184, 335

 on fall of Sevastopol, 186-189

Torgau, U. S. troops meet Russians at, 442-445

Toungoo, 167

Tours, 62, 71, 74

Transformation Three, 373-377

Trieste Division (Italian), 217

Tripartite Pact, 123, 281

True to Type, 227-228

Truk, 310, 493

Truman, Harry S.

 announcement of Hiroshima, 498

 on Nuremberg trials, 530

Trusof, Maj. Gen., Nicolai, 485

Tula, 147

Tulagi, 190, 195, 197, 307

Tunel, 2

Tunis, 245

 battle for, 245-258

Tunisia

 conquest of, 245-258

 Ernie Pyle in, 242-244

Turner, Frank, 387

Twelfth Army (German), 457

12th Army Corps (Italian), 268

Twenty-first Army Group (British), 461, 463

21st Panzer Division (German), 216, 217

29th Infantry Division (German), 235

Twenty-seventh Armored Infantry Battalion (U. S.), 406

206th Division (Italian), 267-268

Tyce, Robert, 125

Tyree, William F., on battle of Iwo Jima, 402-404

Tyrrhenian Sea, 314

Ueber Schlachtfelde Vorwaerts, 45-48, 65-67

Ukraine, 183, 356, 358

Umezu, Gen. Yoshijiro, at Japanese surrender, 521-526

Underwood, Mary Katherine, 11-12

United Press, 6-7, 31-34, 104-105, 203-204, 211-215, 239-240, 261-263, 335-336, 352-354, 368-369, 389-391, 403-404, 499, 503-505

Unter den Linden, 466

Uruguay, 34

U. S. Marines in Action, The, 195-197

Ushijima, Lt. Gen. Mitsuru, hara-kiri of, 495-497

Valiant, 120, 121

Van Kirk, Capt. Theodore Z., 501

Vanderbilt, Sgt. Sanderson, on V-J Day in N.Y.C., 514-515

V-E Day, 480-482

Venafro, 327

Vengeance weapon 1, 360-367, 368-369

Vengeance weapon 2, 386-388

Ventotene, German surrender at, 314-318

Victor III, Pope, 323

Vietinghoff, 453

Vila, 272

Villard, Oswald Garrison, in London, on opening of war, 14-17

"Vinegar Joe," 164

Vistula, 2, 24, 355, 456

Vitebsk, 355

V-J Day, 514-519

Volga, 226, 359
death at, 133-136

Volhynia, 359

Volkischer Beobachter, 199, 400-401

von Arnim, Col. Gen. Dietloff, 250, 254, 256, 258

von Brauchitsch, Col. Gen., 77, 78, 79

von Briesen, Gen. Kurt, 69, 70

von Falkenhorst, Gen. Nikolaus, 42

von Friedeburg, Adm. Hans Georg, 472, 474-479, 483, 486
surrender of, 460-464

von Keitel, Col. Gen. Wilhelm, 76, 77, 78, 79-80, (Field Marshal) 457, 458, 460, 483
death of, 529, 533-534, 536
surrender to Zhukov, 484-485

von Kleist, Gen. E., 226

von Manstein, Gen. Fritz Erich, 183

von Papen, Franz, 529

von Paulus, Field Marshal, 227, 233

von Reuter, Admiral, 27

von Ribbentrop, Joachim, 78, 79, 457, 459
death of, 530, 531, 533, 534, 535

von Rundstedt, Field Marshal Gerd, 396

von Thoma, Gen., 217, 218

V-1 rocket, 360-367, 368-369

Voronezh, 358, 359

Voroponovo, 229, 234

Voroshilovgrad, 358

V-2 rocket, 386-388

Vyazma, 144

Wagner, Rear Adm., 462, 463

Wahiawa, 125

Waikiki, 124

Wainwright, Gen. Jonathan, 156, 524, 525

Wake, 149

Walker, Mickey, 364

Wall, Alfred, 94
on Coventry bombing, 96-97

Wallace, Mrs. McMillan, 12

Walney, 219-222

Wanawawa Island, 271

Warsaw, 1-3
surrender of, 23-25

Warspite, 349

Wehrmacht, 456, 457
attack on Russia, 113-114, 133-136

Weimar, 428, 432, 434

Wellings, Capt., 265

Wesel, 409

Wesola, 23

West, Rebecca, on bombing of London, 98-103

Westermann, Ethel, 301

Weygand, Gen. Maxime, 62

White, Cmdr. Arthur J., 171

White, Paul, 127

Whitehead, Don
on D-Day, 350-351
on meeting at Torgau, 442-444

Wheeler, Burton, 124

Wheeler Field, 518

Wilder, Lt. Ken, 438

Wilhelm, John, on the battle of the Bulge, 396-398

Wilhelmshaven bombing, 239-240

Williams, Douglas, on evacuation of Dunkirk, 57-61

Wilmot, Chester, on surrender at Lüneburg Heath, 460-464

Wilson, Mrs. Woodrow, 424

Wippell, Vice-Adm. Pridham, 121

With Rommel in the Desert, 215-218

With the Red Army in Poland and Byelorussia, 355-359

Witzig, 1st Lt., 46

Wolfert, Ira, 190
on battle of Guadalcanal, 191-195

Wolff, Karl, 453

Woods, Master Sgt. John C., 529
Wounded Don't Cry, The, 71-74
Wright, Capt., 206, 207, 209

Yagotin, 358
Yakushima, 510, 511
Yalta, 185
Yamashita, Lt. Gen. Tomoyuki, 150, 151
Yamoto, 493
Yank, The Army Weekly, 259, 302-305, 306-309, 514-519
Yetrimov, Maj. Vassely, 336
Yindrich, Jan H., on battle of Tobruk, 104-105
Yokohama, 520
Yokosuka, 523
Yorke, Skipper, 300

Yorktown, 179
Ypres, 246
Yung-chang, Gen. Hsu, 524

Zaghouan, 252
Zebino, 451
Zenkl, Peter, 429
Zerbini, Paolo, 448
Zhitomir, 358
Zhukov, 485
    Keitel surrender to, 483-484
Zimmerman, Lt. Carl, 407
Zinberg, Cpl. Len, on V-J Day in Rome, 519
Zinser, Gerald E., 271
Zrkopane, 2
Zvenigorod, 147